T0235098

Lecture Notes in Computer Science 10515

Commenced Publication in 1973
Founding and Former Series Editors:
Gerhard Goos, Juris Hartmanis, and Jan van Leeuwen

Editorial Board

David Hutchison
  Lancaster University, Lancaster, UK
Takeo Kanade
  Carnegie Mellon University, Pittsburgh, PA, USA
Josef Kittler
  University of Surrey, Guildford, UK
Jon M. Kleinberg
  Cornell University, Ithaca, NY, USA
Friedemann Mattern
  ETH Zurich, Zurich, Switzerland
John C. Mitchell
  Stanford University, Stanford, CA, USA
Moni Naor
  Weizmann Institute of Science, Rehovot, Israel
C. Pandu Rangan
  Indian Institute of Technology, Madras, India
Bernhard Steffen
  TU Dortmund University, Dortmund, Germany
Demetri Terzopoulos
  University of California, Los Angeles, CA, USA
Doug Tygar
  University of California, Berkeley, CA, USA
Gerhard Weikum
  Max Planck Institute for Informatics, Saarbrücken, Germany

More information about this series at http://www.springer.com/series/7409

Regina Bernhaupt · Girish Dalvi
Anirudha Joshi · Devanuj K. Balkrishan
Jacki O'Neill · Marco Winckler (Eds.)

Human-Computer Interaction – INTERACT 2017

16th IFIP TC 13 International Conference
Mumbai, India, September 25–29, 2017
Proceedings, Part III

Springer

Editors

Regina Bernhaupt
Ruwido Austria GmbH
Neumarkt am Wallersee
Austria

Girish Dalvi
Indian Institute of Technology Bombay
Mumbai
India

Anirudha Joshi
Indian Institute of Technology Bombay
Mumbai
India

Devanuj K. Balkrishan
Indian Institute of Technology Bombay
Mumbai
India

Jacki O'Neill
Microsoft Research Centre India
Bangalore
India

Marco Winckler ⓘD
Université Paul Sabatier
Toulouse
France

ISSN 0302-9743   ISSN 1611-3349 (electronic)
Lecture Notes in Computer Science
ISBN 978-3-319-67686-9   ISBN 978-3-319-67687-6 (eBook)
DOI 10.1007/978-3-319-67687-6

Library of Congress Control Number: 2017953425

LNCS Sublibrary: SL3 – Information Systems and Applications, incl. Internet/Web, and HCI

© IFIP International Federation for Information Processing 2017
This work is subject to copyright. All rights are reserved by the Publisher, whether the whole or part of the material is concerned, specifically the rights of translation, reprinting, reuse of illustrations, recitation, broadcasting, reproduction on microfilms or in any other physical way, and transmission or information storage and retrieval, electronic adaptation, computer software, or by similar or dissimilar methodology now known or hereafter developed.
The use of general descriptive names, registered names, trademarks, service marks, etc. in this publication does not imply, even in the absence of a specific statement, that such names are exempt from the relevant protective laws and regulations and therefore free for general use.
The publisher, the authors and the editors are safe to assume that the advice and information in this book are believed to be true and accurate at the date of publication. Neither the publisher nor the authors or the editors give a warranty, express or implied, with respect to the material contained herein or for any errors or omissions that may have been made. The publisher remains neutral with regard to jurisdictional claims in published maps and institutional affiliations.

Printed on acid-free paper

This Springer imprint is published by Springer Nature
The registered company is Springer International Publishing AG
The registered company address is: Gewerbestrasse 11, 6330 Cham, Switzerland

Foreword

The 16th IFIP TC13 International Conference on Human–Computer Interaction, INTERACT 2017, took place during September 25–29, 2017, in Mumbai, India. This conference was held on the beautiful campus of the Indian Institute of Technology, Bombay (IIT Bombay) and the Industrial Design Centre (IDC) was the principal host. The conference was co-sponsored by the HCI Professionals Association of India and the Computer Society of India, in cooperation with ACM and ACM SIGCHI. The financial responsibility of INTERACT 2017 was taken up by the HCI Professionals Association of India.

The International Federation for Information Processing (IFIP) was created in 1960 under the auspices of UNESCO. The Technical Committee 13 (TC13) of the IFIP aims at developing the science and technology of human–computer interaction (HCI). TC13 has representatives from 36 countries, apart from 16 expert members and observers. TC13 started the series of INTERACT conferences in 1984. These conferences have been an important showcase for researchers and practitioners in the field of HCI. Situated under the open, inclusive umbrella of the IFIP, INTERACT has been truly international in its spirit and has attracted researchers from several countries and cultures. The venues of the INTERACT conferences over the years bear a testimony to this inclusiveness.

In 2017, the venue was Mumbai. Located in western India, the city of Mumbai is the capital of the state of Maharashtra. It is the financial, entertainment, and commercial capital of the country and is the most populous city in India. *Mumbaikars* might add that it is also the most hardworking.

The theme of INTERACT 2017 was "Global Thoughts, Local Designs." The theme was designed to let HCI researchers respond to challenges emerging in the new age of global connectivity where they often design products for users who are beyond their borders belonging to distinctly different cultures. As organizers of the conference, we focused our attention on four areas: *India, developing countries, students,* and *research.*

As the first INTERACT in the subcontinent, the conference offered a distinctly Indian experience to its participants. The span of known history of India covers more than 5,000 years. Today, India is the world's largest democracy and a land of diversity. Modern technology co-exists with ancient traditions within the same city, often within the same family. Indians speak 22 official languages and hundreds of dialects. India is also a hub of the information technology industry and a living laboratory of experiments with technology for developing countries.

INTERACT 2017 made a conscious effort to lower barriers that prevent people from developing countries from participating in conferences. Thinkers and optimists believe that all regions of the world can achieve human development goals. Information and communication technologies (ICTs) can support this process and empower people to achieve their full potential. Today ICT products have many new users and many new uses, but also present new challenges and provide new opportunities. It is no surprise that HCI researchers are showing great interest in these emergent users. INTERACT 2017 provided a platform to explore these challenges and opportunities but also made it easier for people from developing countries to participate. We also introduced a new track called Field Trips, which allowed participants to directly engage with stake-holders within the context of a developing country.

Students represent the future of our community. They bring in new energy, enthusiasm, and fresh ideas. But it is often hard for students to participate in international conferences. INTERACT 2017 made special efforts to bring students to the conference. The conference had low registration costs and several volunteering opportunities. Thanks to our sponsors, we could provide several travel grants. Most importantly, INTERACT 2017 had special tracks such as Installations, a Student Design Consortium, and a Student Research Consortium that gave students the opportunity to showcase their work.

Finally, great research is the heart of a good conference. Like its predecessors, INTERACT 2017 aimed to bring together high-quality research. As a multidisciplinary field, HCI requires interaction and discussion among diverse people with different interest and background. The beginners and the experienced, theoreticians and practitioners, and people from diverse disciplines and different countries gathered together in Mumbai to learn from each other and to contribute to each other's growth. We thank all the authors who chose INTERACT 2017 as the venue to publish their research.

We received a total of 571 submissions distributed in two peer-reviewed tracks, five curated tracks, and seven juried tracks. Of these, the following contributions were accepted:

- 68 Full Papers (peer reviewed)
- 51 Short Papers (peer reviewed)
- 13 Case Studies (curated)
- 20 Industry Presentations (curated)
- 7 Courses (curated)
- 5 Demonstrations (curated)
- 3 Panels (curated)
- 9 Workshops (juried)
- 7 Field Trips (juried)
- 11 Interactive Posters (juried)
- 9 Installations (juried)
- 6 Doctoral Consortium (juried)
- 15 Student Research Consortium (juried)
- 6 Student Design Consortium (juried)

The acceptance rate for contributions received in the peer-reviewed tracks was 30.7% for full papers and 29.1% for short papers. In addition to full papers and short papers, the present proceedings feature contributions accepted in the form of case studies, courses, demonstrations, interactive posters, field trips, and workshops.

The final decision on acceptance or rejection of full papers was taken in a Program Committee meeting held in Paris, France, in March 2017. The full-paper chairs, the associate chairs, and the TC13 members participated in this meeting. The meeting discussed a consistent set of criteria to deal with inevitable differences among the large number of reviewers. The final decisions on other tracks were made by the corresponding track chairs and reviewers, often after additional electronic meetings and discussions.

INTERACT 2017 was made possible by the persistent efforts over several months by 49 chairs, 39 associate chairs, 55 student volunteers, and 499 reviewers. We thank them all. Finally, we wish to express a special thank you to the proceedings publication co-chairs, Marco Winckler and Devanuj Balkrishan, who did extraordinary work to put together four volumes of the main proceedings and one volume of adjunct proceedings.

September 2017   Anirudha Joshi
                                                                      Girish Dalvi
                                                                    Marco Winckler

IFIP TC13 (http://ifip-tc13.org/)

Established in 1989, the International Federation for Information Processing Technical Committee on Human–Computer Interaction (IFIP TC 13) is an international committee of 37 member national societies and 10 Working Groups, representing specialists of the various disciplines contributing to the field of human–computer interaction (HCI). This includes (among others) human factors, ergonomics, cognitive science, computer science, and design. INTERACT is its flagship conference of IFIP TC 13, staged biennially in different countries in the world. The first INTERACT conference was held in 1984 running triennially and became a biennial event in 1993.

IFIP TC 13 aims to develop the science, technology, and societal aspects of HCI by: encouraging empirical research; promoting the use of knowledge and methods from the human sciences in design and evaluation of computer systems; promoting better understanding of the relation between formal design methods and system usability and acceptability; developing guidelines, models, and methods by which designers may provide better human-oriented computer systems; and, cooperating with other groups, inside and outside IFIP, to promote user-orientation and humanization in system design. Thus, TC 13 seeks to improve interactions between people and computers, to encourage the growth of HCI research and its practice in industry and to disseminate these benefits worldwide.

The main focus is to place the users at the center of the development process. Areas of study include: the problems people face when interacting with computers; the impact of technology deployment on people in individual and organizational contexts; the determinants of utility, usability, acceptability, and user experience; the appropriate allocation of tasks between computers and users especially in the case of automation; modeling the user, their tasks, and the interactive system to aid better system design; and harmonizing the computer to user characteristics and needs.

While the scope is thus set wide, with a tendency toward general principles rather than particular systems, it is recognized that progress will only be achieved through both general studies to advance theoretical understanding and specific studies on practical issues (e.g., interface design standards, software system resilience, documentation, training material, appropriateness of alternative interaction technologies, guidelines, the problems of integrating multimedia systems to match system needs, and organizational practices, etc.).

In 2015, TC 13 approved the creation of a Steering Committee (SC) for the INTERACT conference. The SC is now in place, chaired by Jan Gulliksen and is responsible for:

- Promoting and maintaining the INTERACT conference as the premiere venue for researchers and practitioners interested in the topics of the conference (this requires a refinement of the aforementioned topics)
- Ensuring the highest quality for the contents of the event

- Setting up the bidding process to handle the future INTERACT conferences; decision is made up at TC 13 level
- Providing advice to the current and future chairs and organizers of the INTERACT conference
- Providing data, tools and documents about previous conferences to the future conference organizers
- Selecting the reviewing system to be used throughout the conference (as this impacts the entire set of reviewers)
- Resolving general issues involved with the INTERACT conference
- Capitalizing history (good and bad practices)

In 1999, TC 13 initiated a special IFIP Award, the Brian Shackel Award, for the most outstanding contribution in the form of a refereed paper submitted to and delivered at each INTERACT. The award draws attention to the need for a comprehensive human-centered approach in the design and use of information technology in which the human and social implications have been taken into account. In 2007, IFIP TC 13 also launched an Accessibility Award to recognize an outstanding contribution in HCI with international impact dedicated to the field of accessibility for disabled users. In 2013 IFIP TC 13 launched the Interaction Design for International Development (IDID) Award that recognizes the most outstanding contribution to the application of inter-active systems for social and economic development of people in developing countries. Since the process to decide the award takes place after papers are sent to the publisher for publication, the awards are not identified in the proceedings.

IFIP TC 13 also recognizes pioneers in the area of HCI. An IFIP TC 13 pioneer is one who, through active participation in IFIP Technical Committees or related IFIP groups, has made outstanding contributions to the educational, theoretical, technical, commercial, or professional aspects of analysis, design, construction, evaluation, and use of interactive systems. IFIP TC 13 pioneers are appointed annually and awards are handed over at the INTERACT conference.

IFIP TC 13 stimulates working events and activities through its Working Groups (WGs). Working Groups consist of HCI experts from many countries, who seek to expand knowledge and find solutions to HCI issues and concerns within their domains. The list of Working Groups and their area of interest is given here.

WG13.1 (Education in HCI and HCI Curricula) aims to improve HCI education at all levels of higher education, coordinate and unite efforts to develop HCI curricula and promote HCI teaching.

WG13.2 (Methodology for User-Centered System Design) aims to foster research, dissemination of information and good practice in the methodical application of HCI to software engineering.

WG13.3 (HCI and Disability) aims to make HCI designers aware of the needs of people with disabilities and encourage the development of information systems and tools permitting adaptation of interfaces to specific users.

WG13.4 (also WG2.7) (User Interface Engineering) investigates the nature, concepts, and construction of user interfaces for software systems, using a framework for reasoning about interactive systems and an engineering model for developing user interfaces.

WG 13.5 (Resilience, Reliability, Safety and Human Error in System Development) seeks a frame-work for studying human factors relating to systems failure, develops leading-edge techniques in hazard analysis and safety engineering of computer-based systems, and guides international accreditation activities for safety-critical systems.

WG13.6 (Human-Work Interaction Design) aims at establishing relationships between extensive empirical work-domain studies and HCI design. It promotes the use of knowledge, concepts, methods, and techniques that enable user studies to procure a better apprehension of the complex interplay between individual, social, and organizational contexts and thereby a better understanding of how and why people work in the ways that they do.

WG13.7 (Human–Computer Interaction and Visualization) aims to establish a study and research program that will combine both scientific work and practical applications in the fields of HCI and visualization. It integrates several additional aspects of further research areas, such as scientific visualization, data mining, information design, computer graphics, cognition sciences, perception theory, or psychology, into this approach.

WG13.8 (Interaction Design and International Development) is currently working to reformulate its aims and scope.

WG13.9 (Interaction Design and Children) aims to support practitioners, regulators, and researchers to develop the study of interaction design and children across international contexts.

WG13.10 (Human-Centered Technology for Sustainability) aims to promote research, design, development, evaluation, and deployment of human-centered technology to encourage sustainable use of resources in various domains.

New Working Groups are formed as areas of significance in HCI arise. Further information is available on the IFIP TC13 website at: http://ifip-tc13.org/

IFIP TC13 Members

Officers

Chair

Philippe Palanque, France

Vice-chair for Growth and Reach Out INTERACT Steering Committee Chair

Jan Gulliksen, Sweden

Vice-chair for Working Groups

Simone D.J. Barbosa, Brazil

Vice-chair for Awards

Paula Kotze, South Africa

Treasurer

Virpi Roto, Finland

Secretary

Marco Winckler, France

Webmaster

Helen Petrie, UK

Country Representatives

Australia
Henry B.L. Duh
Australian Computer Society

Austria
Geraldine Fitzpatrick
Austrian Computer Society

Brazil
Raquel Oliveira Prates
Brazilian Computer Society (SBC)

Bulgaria
Kamelia Stefanova
Bulgarian Academy of Sciences

Canada
Lu Xiao
Canadian Information Processing Society

Chile
Jaime Sánchez
Chilean Society of Computer Science

Croatia
Andrina Granic
Croatian Information Technology
  Association (CITA)

Cyprus
Panayiotis Zaphiris
Cyprus Computer Society

Czech Republic
Zdeněk Míkovec
Czech Society for Cybernetics
  and Informatics

Denmark
Torkil Clemmensen
Danish Federation for Information
   Processing

Finland
Virpi Roto
Finnish Information Processing
   Association

France
Philippe Palanque
Société informatique de France (SIF)

Germany
Tom Gross
Gesellschaft für Informatik e.V.

Hungary
Cecilia Sik Lanyi
John V. Neumann Computer Society

India
Anirudha Joshi
Computer Society of India (CSI)

Ireland
Liam J. Bannon
Irish Computer Society

Italy
Fabio Paternò
Italian Computer Society

Japan
Yoshifumi Kitamura
Information Processing Society of Japan

Korea
Gerry Kim
KIISE

The Netherlands
Vanessa Evers
Nederlands Genootschap voor
   Informatica

New Zealand
Mark Apperley
New Zealand Computer Society

Nigeria
Chris C. Nwannenna
Nigeria Computer Society

Norway
Dag Svanes
Norwegian Computer Society

Poland
Marcin Sikorski
Poland Academy of Sciences

Portugal
Pedro Campos
Associacão Portuguesa para o Desen-
volvimento da Sociedade da Informação
   (APDSI)

Singapore
Shengdong Zhao
Singapore Computer Society

Slovakia
Wanda Benešová
The Slovak Society for Computer
   Science

Slovenia
Matjaž Debevc
The Slovenian Computer Society
   INFORMATIKA

South Africa
Janet L. Wesson
The Computer Society of South Africa

Spain
Julio Abascal
Asociación de Técnicos de Informática
   (ATI)

Sweden
Jan Gulliksen
Swedish Interdisciplinary Society
  for Human–Computer Interaction
Swedish Computer Society

Switzerland
Denis Lalanne
Swiss Federation for Information
  Processing

Tunisia
Mona Laroussi
Ecole Supérieure des Communications
  De Tunis (SUP'COM)

UK
José Abdelnour Nocera
British Computer Society (BCS)

United Arab Emirates
Ghassan Al-Qaimari
UAE Computer Society

USA
Gerrit van der Veer
Association for Computing Machinery
  (ACM)

Expert Members

Dan Orwa	University of Nairobi, Kenya
David Lamas	Tallinn University, Estonia
Dorian Gorgan	Technical University of Cluj-Napoca, Romania
Eunice Sari	University of Western Australia, Australia and UX Indonesia, Indonesia
Fernando Loizides	Cardiff University, UK and Cyprus University of Technology, Cyprus
Frank Vetere	University of Melbourne, Australia
Ivan Burmistrov	Moscow State University, Russia
Joaquim Jorge	INESC-ID, Portugal
Marta Kristin Larusdottir	Reykjavik University, Iceland
Nikolaos Avouris	University of Patras, Greece
Paula Kotze	CSIR Meraka Institute, South Africa
Peter Forbrig	University of Rostock, Germany
Simone D.J. Barbosa	PUC-Rio, Brazil
Vu Nguyen	Vietnam
Zhengjie Liu	Dalian Maritime University, China

Observer

Masaaki Kurosu, Japan

Working Group Chairs

**WG 13.1 (Education in HCI
and HCI Curricula)**

Konrad Baumann, Austria

**WG 13.2 (Methodologies
for User-Centered System Design)**

Marco Winckler, France

WG 13.3 (HCI and Disability)

Helen Petrie, UK

WG 13.4/2.7 (User Interface Engineering)

José Creissac Campos, Portugal

WG 13.5 (Resilience, Reliability, Safety, and Human Error in System Development)

Chris Johnson, UK

WG 13.6 (Human-Work Interaction Design)

Pedro Campos, Portugal

WG 13.7 (HCI and Visualization)

Peter Dannenmann, Germany

WG 13.8 (Interaction Design and International Development)

José Adbelnour Nocera, UK

WG 13.9 (Interaction Design and Children)

Janet Read, UK

WG 13.10 (Human-Centered Technology for Sustainability)

Masood Masoodian, Finland

Conference Organizing Committee

General Conference Chairs

Anirudha Joshi, India
Girish Dalvi, India

Technical Program Chair

Marco Winckler, France

Full-Paper Chairs

Regina Bernhaupt, France
Jacki O'Neill, India

Short-Paper Chairs

Peter Forbrig, Germany
Sriganesh Madhvanath, USA

Case Studies Chairs

Ravi Poovaiah, India
Elizabeth Churchill, USA

Courses Chairs

Gerrit van der Veer, The Netherlands
Dhaval Vyas, Australia

Demonstrations Chairs

Takahiro Miura, Japan
Shengdong Zhao, Singapore
Manjiri Joshi, India

Doctoral Consortium Chairs

Paula Kotze, South Africa
Pedro Campos, Portugal

Field Trips Chairs

Nimmi Rangaswamy, India
José Abdelnour Nocera, UK
Debjani Roy, India

Industry Presentations Chairs

Suresh Chande, Finland
Fernando Loizides, UK

Installations Chairs

Ishneet Grover, India
Jayesh Pillai, India
Nagraj Emmadi, India

Keynotes and Invited Talks Chair

Philippe Palanque, France

Panels Chairs

Antonella De Angeli, Italy
Rosa Arriaga, USA

Posters Chairs

Girish Prabhu, India
Zhengjie Liu, China

Student Research Consortium Chairs

Indrani Medhi, India
Naveen Bagalkot, India
Janet Wesson, South Africa

Student Design Consortium Chairs

Abhishek Shrivastava, India
Prashant Sachan, India
Arnab Chakravarty, India

Workshops Chairs

Torkil Clemmensen, Denmark
Venkatesh Rajamanickam, India

Accessibility Chairs

Prachi Sakhardande, India
Sonali Joshi, India

Childcare Club Chairs

Atish Patel, India
Susmita Sharma, India

Food and Social Events Chair

Rucha Tulaskar, India

Local Organizing Chairs

Manjiri Joshi, India
Nagraj Emmadi, India

Proceedings Chairs

Marco Winckler, France
Devanuj Balkrishan, India

Sponsorship Chair

Atul Manohar, India

Student Volunteers Chairs

Rasagy Sharma, India
Jayati Bandyopadhyay, India

Venue Arrangements Chair

Sugandh Malhotra, India

Web and Social Media Chair

Naveed Ahmed, India

Program Committee

Associated Chairs

Simone Barbosa, Brazil
Nicola Bidwell, Namibia
Pernille Bjorn, Denmark
Birgit Bomsdorf, Germany
Torkil Clemmensen, Denmark
José Creissac Campos, Portugal
Peter Forbrig, Germany
Tom Gross, Germany
Jan Gulliksen, Sweden
Nathalie Henry Riche, USA
Abhijit Karnik, UK
Dave Kirk, UK
Denis Lalanne, Switzerland
Airi Lampinen, Sweden
Effie Law, UK
Eric Lecolinet, France
Zhengjie Liu, China
Fernando Loizides, UK
Célia Martinie, France
Laurence Nigay, France

Monique Noirhomme, Belgium
Philippe Palanque, France
Fabio Paterno, Italy
Helen Petrie, UK
Antonio Piccinno, Italy
Kari-Jouko Raiha, Finland
Dave Randall, Germany
Nimmi Rangaswamy, India
John Rooksby, UK
Virpi Roto, Finland
Jan Stage, Denmark
Frank Steinicke, Germany
Simone Stumpf, UK
Gerrit van der Veer, The Netherlands
Dhaval Vyas, India
Gerhard Weber, Germany
Janet Wesson, South Africa
Marco Winckler, France
Panayiotis Zaphiris, Cyprus

Reviewers

Julio Abascal, Spain
José Abdelnour Nocera, UK
Silvia Abrahão, Spain
Abiodun Afolayan Ogunyemi, Estonia
Ana Paula Afonso, Portugal
David Ahlström, Austria
Muneeb Ahmad, Australia
Deepak Akkil, Finland
Sarah Alaoui, France
Komathi Ale, Singapore
Jan Alexandersson, Germany
Dzmitry Aliakseyeu, The Netherlands
Hend S. Al-Khalifa, Saudi Arabia
Fereshteh Amini, Canada
Junia Anacleto, Brazil
Mads Schaarup Andersen, Denmark
Leonardo Angelini, Switzerland
Huckauf Anke, Germany
Craig Anslow, New Zealand
Nathalie Aquino, Paraguay
Oscar Javier Ariza Núñez, Germany
Parvin Asadzadeh, UK
Uday Athavankar, India
David Auber, France
Nikolaos Avouris, Greece
Sohaib Ayub, Pakistan
Chris Baber, UK
Cedric Bach, France
Naveen Bagalkot, India
Jan Balata, Czech Republic
Emilia Barakova, The Netherlands
Pippin Barr, Denmark
Oswald Barral, Finland
Barbara Rita Barricelli, Italy
Michel Beaudouin-Lafon, France
Astrid Beck, Germany
Jordan Beck, USA
Roman Bednarik, Finland
Ben Bedwell, UK
Marios Belk, Germany
Yacine Bellik, France
David Benyon, UK
François Bérard, France

Arne Berger, Germany
Nigel Bevan, UK
Anastasia Bezerianos, France
Sudhir Bhatia, India
Dorrit Billman, USA
Pradipta Biswas, India
Edwin Blake, South Africa
Renaud Blanch, France
Mads Bødker, Denmark
Cristian Bogdan, Sweden
Rodrigo Bonacin, Brazil
Claus Bossen, Denmark
Paolo Bottoni, Italy
Nadia Boukhelifa, France
Nina Boulus-Rødje, Denmark
Judy Bowen, New Zealand
Margot Brereton, Australia
Roberto Bresin, Sweden
Barry Brown, Sweden
Emeline Brulé, France
Nick Bryan-Kinns, UK
Sabin-Corneliu Buraga, Romania
Ineke Buskens, South Africa
Adrian Bussone, UK
Maria Claudia Buzzi, Italy
Marina Buzzi, Italy
Federico Cabitza, Italy
Diogo Cabral, Portugal
Åsa Cajander, Sweden
Eduardo Calvillo Gamez, Mexico
Erik Cambria, Singapore
Pedro Campos, Portugal
Tara Capel, Australia
Cinzia Cappiello, Italy
Stefan Carmien, Spain
Maria Beatriz Carmo, Portugal
Luis Carriço, Portugal
Stefano Carrino, Switzerland
Géry Casiez, France
Fabio Cassano, Italy
Thais Castro, Brazil
Vanessa Cesário, Portugal
Arnab Chakravarty, India

Matthew Chalmers, UK
Teresa Chambel, Portugal
Chunlei Chang, Australia
Olivier Chapuis, France
Weiqin Chen, Norway
Mauro Cherubini, Switzerland
Fanny Chevalier, France
Yoram Chisik, Portugal
Eun Kyoung Choe, USA
Mabrouka Chouchane, Tunisia
Elizabeth Churchill, USA
Gilbert Cockton, UK
Ashley Colley, Finland
Christopher Collins, Canada
Tayana Conte, Brazil
Nuno Correia, Portugal
Joelle Coutaz, France
Rui Couto, Portugal
Céline Coutrix, France
Nadine Couture, France
Lynne Coventry, UK
Benjamin Cowan, Ireland
Paul Curzon, UK
Edward Cutrell, India
Florian Daiber, Germany
Nick Dalton, UK
Girish Dalvi, India
Jose Danado, USA
Chi Tai Dang, Germany
Ticianne Darin, Brazil
Jenny Darzentas, Greece
Giorgio De Michelis, Italy
Clarisse de Souza, Brazil
Ralf de Wolf, Belgium
Andy Dearden, UK
Dmitry Dereshev, UK
Giuseppe Desolda, Italy
Heather Desurvire, USA
Amira Dhouib, Tunisia
Ines Di Loreto, Italy
Paulo Dias, Portugal
Shalaka Dighe, India
Tawanna Dillahunt, USA
Anke Dittmar, Germany
Andre Doucette, Canada
Pierre Dragicevic, France

Steven Drucker, USA
Carlos Duarte, Portugal
Julie Ducasse, France
Andreas Duenser, Australia
Bruno Dumas, Belgium
Paul Dunphy, UK
Sophie Dupuy-Chessa, France
Sourav Dutta, India
James Eagan, France
Grace Eden, Switzerland
Brian Ekdale, USA
Linda Elliott, USA
Chris Elsden, UK
Morten Esbensen, Denmark
Florian Evéquoz, Switzerland
Shamal Faily, UK
Carla Faria Leitao, Brazil
Ava Fatah gen. Schieck, UK
Camille Fayollas, France
Tom Feltwell, UK
Xavier Ferre, Spain
Pedro Ferreira, Denmark
Sebastian Feuerstack, Brazil
Patrick Tobias Fischer, Germany
Geraldine Fitzpatrick, Austria
Rowanne Fleck, UK
Daniela Fogli, Italy
Asbjørn Følstad, Norway
Manuel J. Fonseca, Portugal
Renata Fortes, Brazil
André Freire, UK
Parseihian Gaëtan, France
Radhika Gajalla, USA
Teresa Galvão, Portugal
Nestor Garay-Vitoria, Spain
Roberto García, Spain
Jose Luis Garrido, Spain
Franca Garzotto, Italy
Isabela Gasparini, Brazil
Cally Gatehouse, UK
Sven Gehring, Germany
Stuart Geiger, USA
Helene Gelderblom, South Africa
Cristina Gena, Ireland
Cristina Gena, Italy
Vivian Genaro Motti, USA

Rosella Gennari, Italy
Werner Geyer, USA
Giuseppe Ghiani, Italy
Anirban Ghosh, Canada
Sanjay Ghosh, India
Martin Gibbs, Australia
Patrick Girard, France
Victor Gonzalez, Mexico
Rohini Gosain, Ireland
Nicholas Graham, Canada
Tiago Guerreiro, Portugal
Yves Guiard, France
Nuno Guimaraes, Portugal
Tauseef Gulrez, Australia
Thilina Halloluwa, Sri Lanka
Martin Halvey, UK
Dave Harley, UK
Richard Harper, UK
Michael Harrison, UK
Heidi Hartikainen, Finland
Thomas Hartley, UK
Mariam Hassib, Germany
Ari Hautasaari, Japan
Elaine Hayashi, Brazil
Jonas Hedman, Denmark
Ruediger Heimgaertner, Germany
Tomi Heimonen, USA
Mattias Heinrich, Germany
Ingi Helgason, UK
Wilko Heuten, Germany
Uta Hinrichs, UK
Daniel Holliday, UK
Jonathan Hook, UK
Jettie Hoonhout, The Netherlands
Heiko Hornung, Brazil
Axel Hösl, Germany
Lara Houston, UK
Roberto Hoyle, USA
William Hudson, UK
Stéphane Huot, France
Christophe Hurter, France
Husniza Husni, Malaysia
Ebba Thora Hvannberg, Iceland
Aulikki Hyrskykari, Finland
Yavuz Inal, Turkey
Petra Isenberg, France

Poika Isokoski, Finland
Minna Isomursu, Denmark
Howell Istance, Finland
Kai-Mikael Jää-Aro, Sweden
Karim Jabbar, Denmark
Isa Jahnke, USA
Abhishek Jain, India
Mlynar Jakub, Switzerland
Yvonne Jansen, France
Camille Jeunet, France
Nan Jiang, UK
Radu Jianu, UK
Deepak John Mathew, India
Matt Jones, UK
Rui José, Portugal
Anirudha Joshi, India
Dhaval Joshi, China
Manjiri Joshi, India
Mike Just, UK
Eija Kaasinen, Finland
Hernisa Kacorri, USA
Sanjay Kairam, USA
Bridget Kane, Ireland
Shaun K. Kane, USA
Jari Kangas, Finland
Ann Marie Kanstrup, Denmark
Evangelos Karapanos, Cyprus
Turkka Keinonen, Finland
Pramod Khambete, India
Munwar Khan, India
NamWook Kim, USA
Yea-Seul Kim, USA
Jennifer King, USA
Reuben Kirkham, UK
Kathi Kitner, South Africa
Søren Knudsen, Denmark
Janin Koch, Finland
Lisa Koeman, The Netherlands
Uttam Kokil, USA
Christophe Kolski, France
Paula Kotze, South Africa
Dennis Krupke, Germany
Sari Kujala, Finland
David Lamas, Estonia
Eike Langbehn, Germany
Rosa Lanzilotti, Italy

Marta Larusdottir, Iceland
Yann Laurillau, France
Elise Lavoué, France
Bongshin Lee, USA
Matthew Lee, USA
Barbara Leporini, Italy
Agnes Lisowska Masson, Switzerland
Netta Livari, Finland
Kiel Long, UK
Víctor López-Jaquero, Spain
Yichen Lu, Finland
Stephanie Ludi, USA
Bernd Ludwig, Germany
Christopher Lueg, Australia
Ewa Luger, UK
Stephan Lukosch, The Netherlands
Jo Lumsden, UK
Christof Lutteroth, UK
Kris Luyten, Belgium
Miroslav Macik, Czech Republic
Scott Mackenzie, Canada
Allan MacLean, UK
Christian Maertin, Germany
Charlotte Magnusson, Sweden
Jyotirmaya Mahapatra, India
Ranjan Maity, India
Päivi Majaranta, Finland
Sylvain Malacria, France
Marco Manca, Italy
Kathia Marçal de Oliveira, France
Panos Markopolous, The Netherlands
Paolo Masci, Portugal
Dimitri Masson, France
Stina Matthiesen, Denmark
Claire McCallum, UK
Roisin McNaney, UK
Indrani Medhi-Thies, India
Gerrit Meixner, Germany
Johanna Meurer, Germany
Luana Micallef, Finland
Takahiro Miura, Japan
Judith Molka-Danielsen, Norway
Naja Holten Moller, Denmark
Giulio Mori, Italy
Alistair Morrison, UK
Aske Mottelson, Denmark

Omar Mubin, Australia
Michael Muller, USA
Lennart Nacke, Canada
Amit Nanavati, India
David Navarre, France
Carla Nave, Portugal
Luciana Nedel, Brazil
Matti Nelimarkka, Finland
Julien Nembrini, Switzerland
David Nemer, USA
Vania Neris, Brazil
Maish Nichani, Singapore
James Nicholson, UK
Diederick C. Niehorster, Sweden
Shuo Niu, USA
Manuel Noguera, Spain
Nicole Novielli, Italy
Diana Nowacka, UK
Marcus Nyström, Sweden
Marianna Obrist, UK
Lars Oestreicher, Sweden
Thomas Olsson, Finland
Juliet Ongwae, UK
Dympna O'Sullivan, UK
Antti Oulasvirta, Finland
Saila Ovaska, Finland
Xinru Page, USA
Ana Paiva, Portugal
Sabrina Panëels, France
Smitha Papolu, USA
Hugo Paredes, Portugal
Susan Park, Canada
Oscar Pastor, Spain
Jennifer Pearson, UK
Simon Perrault, Singapore
Mark Perry, UK
Anicia Peters, Namibia
Kevin Pfeil, USA
Jayesh Pillai, India
Marcelo Pimenta, Brazil
Aparecido Fabiano Pinatti de Carvalho,
  Germany
Claudio Pinhanez, Brazil
Stefania Pizza, Italy
Bernd Ploderer, Australia
Andreas Poller, Germany

Ravi Poovaiah, India
Christopher Power, UK
Girish Prabhu, India
Denise Prescher, Germany
Costin Pribeanu, Romania
Helen Purchase, UK
Xiangang Qin, Denmark
Venkatesh Rajamanickam, India
Dorina Rajanen, Finland
Rani Gadhe Rani Gadhe, India
Heli Rantavuo, Sweden
Noopur Raval, USA
Janet Read, UK
Sreedhar Reddy, India
Christian Remy, Switzerland
Karen Renaud, UK
António Nestor Ribeiro, Portugal
Michael Rietzler, Germany
Maurizio Rigamonti, Switzerland
Kerem Rızvanoğlu, Turkey
Teresa Romao, Portugal
Maki Rooksby, UK
Mark Rouncefield, UK
Gustavo Rovelo, Belgium
Debjani Roy, India
Hamed R-Tavakolli, Finland
Simon Ruffieux, Switzerland
Angel Ruiz-Zafra, UK
Katri Salminen, Finland
Antti Salovaara, Finland
Frode Eika Sandnes, Norway
Supraja Sankaran, Belgium
Vagner Santana, Brazil
Carmen Santoro, Italy
Vidya Sarangapani, UK
Sayan Sarcar, Japan
Somwrita Sarkar, Australia
Christine Satchell, Australia
Mithileysh Sathiyanarayanan, UK
Anthony Savidis, Greece
Susanne Schmidt, Germany
Kevin Schneider, Canada
Dirk Schnelle-Walka, Germany
Ronald Schroeter, Australia
Vinícius Segura, Brazil
Ajanta Sen, India

Audrey Serna, France
Marcos Serrano, France
Leslie Setlock, USA
Anshuman Sharma, India
Patrick C. Shih, USA
Shanu Shukla, India
Gulati Siddharth, Estonia
Bruno Silva, Brazil
Carlos C.L. Silva, Portugal
Milene Silveira, Brazil
Adalberto Simeone, UK
Jaana Simola, Finland
Carla Simone, Finland
Laurianne Sitbon, Australia
Ashok Sivaji, Malaysia
Keyur Sorathia, India
Alessandro Soro, Australia
Oleg Spakov, Finland
Lucio Davide Spano, Italy
Susan Squires, USA
Christian Stary, Austria
Katarzyna Stawarz, UK
Jürgen Steimle, Germany
Revi Sterling, USA
Agnis Stibe, USA
Markus Stolze, Switzerland
Selina Sutton, UK
David Swallow, UK
Aurélien Tabard, France
Marcel Taeumel, Germany
Chee-Wee Tan, Denmark
Jennyfer Taylor, Australia
Robyn Taylor, UK
Robert Teather, Canada
Luis Teixeira, Portugal
Paolo Tell, Denmark
Jakob Tholander, Sweden
Alice Thudt, Canada
Subrata Tikadar, India
Martin Tomitsch, Australia
Ilaria Torre, Italy
Noam Tractinsky, Israel
Hallvard Traetteberg, Norway
Giovanni Troiano, USA
Janice Tsai, USA
Robert Tscharn, Germany

Manfred Tscheligi, Austria
Truna Turner, Australia
Markku Turunen, Finland
Pankaj Upadhyay, India
Heli Väätäjä, Finland
Pedro Valderas, Spain
Stefano Valtolina, Italy
Jan van den Bergh, Belgium
Thea van der Geest, The Netherlands
Davy Vanacken, Belgium
Jean Vanderdonckt, Belgium
Christina Vasiliou, Cyprus
Radu-Daniel Vatavu, Romania
Shriram Venkatraman, India
Nervo Xavier Verdezoto, UK
Himanshu Verma, Switzerland
Arnold P.O.S. Vermeeren,
  The Netherlands
Jo Vermeulen, Belgium
Chi Thanh Vi, UK
Nadine Vigouroux, France
Jean-Luc Vinot, France
Dong Bach Vo, UK
Lin Wan, Germany

Xiying Wang, USA
Yi Wang, USA
Ingolf Waßmann, Germany
Jenny Waycott, Australia
Gerald Weber, New Zealand
Kurtis Weir, UK
Benjamin Weyers, Germany
Jerome White, USA
Graham Wilson, UK
Heike Winshiers-Theophilus, Namibia
Wolfgang Woerndl, Germany
Katrin Wolf, Germany
Andrea Wong, USA
Nelson Wong, Canada
Gavin Wood, UK
Adam Worrallo, UK
Volker Wulf, Germany
Naomi Yamashita, Japan
Pradeep Yammiyavar, India
Tariq Zaman, Malaysia
Massimo Zancanaro, Italy
Juergen Ziegler, Germany
Gottfried Zimmermann, Germany

Sponsors and Partners

Silver Sponsors

Adobe

LEAD PARTNERS

facebook

Gala Dinner Sponsor

Design Competition Sponsor

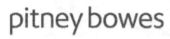

Pitney Bowes

Education Partners

Interaction Design Foundation (IDF)

Friends of INTERACT

Ruwido GmBH, Austria   Oxford University Press   Converge by CauseCode Technologies

Exhibitors

Partners

International Federation for Information Processing

In-cooperation with ACM   In-cooperation with SIGCHI

IDC
IIT Bombay   **HCI Professionals'**
                                  Association of India

Industrial Design Centre, IIT Bombay   HCI Professionals' Association of India

Computer Society of India   IIT Bombay

Contents

Multitouch Interaction

New Interaction Techniques

Personalisation and Visualisation

Persuasive Technology and Rehabilitation

Mediated Communication in eHealth

Co-designing a mHealth Application for Self-management of Cystic Fibrosis

Thomas Vilarinho(✉), Jacqueline Floch, and Erlend Stav

SINTEF Digital, Trondheim, Norway
{thomas.vilarinho,jacqueline.floch,erlend.stav}@sintef.no

Abstract. Self-management has the potential to improve patient care and decrease healthcare costs. It is especially beneficial for patients suffering from chronic diseases that require continuous therapy and follow-up such as cystic fibrosis (CF). Mobile phones have become pervasive and, therefore, are perfectly suited for self-management. However, due to the large amount of time CF patients spend in their treatment, usability and usefulness are critical factors for the adoption of an assistive mobile application (App).

In our work, we applied co-design in the development of high fidelity mockups for a CF Self-management App. The co-design was conducted as a series of workshops involving CF patients, theirs parents, as well as health professionals, from multiple countries in Europe. The results include design concepts and User Interface elements that conciliate the different perspectives between the stakeholders.

This paper describes the co-design process, the resulting design and further considerations which emerged along the process.

Keywords: Human factors · HCI · Self-management · m-health · User centered design · Mobile computing

1   Introduction

Chronic diseases are responsible for most deaths in the world [26] and they affect a large part of the population. It is estimated that about half of the American adult population has at least one chronic disease [23]. Chronic diseases require long term therapy which poses a challenge for patient adherence and for the sustainability of health care systems. Self-management programs are seen as a possible solution to that challenge due to theirs potential to improve care quality and reduce health care cost [20].

Self-management corresponds to the active involvement of the patients in tasks related to his health care. It includes the management of symptoms and treatment, and deals with the consequences of the disease in daily life. Self-management is not about delegating all care management to patients, but rather

© IFIP International Federation for Information Processing 2017
Published by Springer International Publishing AG 2017. All Rights Reserved
R. Bernhaupt et al. (Eds.): INTERACT 2017, Part III, LNCS 10515, pp. 3–22, 2017.
DOI: 10.1007/978-3-319-67687-6_1

about supporting a collaborative relationship where doctors empower patients in the day-to-day care as a complement to the traditional clinical treatment. Self-management strengthens the capabilities of the patients in terms of education, empowerment and confidence building [19].

ICT is a powerful tool to cost-effectively support self-management [8]. It can facilitate the communication between patients and carers and simplify the self-management tasks, leading to higher adherence. Indeed, different reviews [12,24] show that ICT can positively affect self-management.

This work investigates the User Interface (UI) elements and design concepts necessary for a mobile application (App) supporting the self-management of Cystic Fibrosis (CF). CF is a chronic disease that causes the body to release thicker and stickier mucus, affecting both the digestive system and the lungs. CF patients undergo an extensive therapy including nutrition management, medicine intake, airway clearance techniques and physical activity [1]. The extent of the therapy is such that the patient's adherence to the different parts of the treatment varies significantly [11]. The comprehensive treatment and the varying adherence make CF an interesting case in the study of self-management.

This paper is organized as follows: Sect. 2 presents the context of this research work and the relevant knowledge base for the App design; Sect. 3 introduces the research methodology; Sect. 4 describes the co-design process; Sect. 5 presents and discusses the co-design results related to the mockups and core design concepts while Sect. 6 presents transveral findings streching accross the whole App and self-management model; Sect. 7 concludes and presents future work.

2   Background

This section presents the context of this research work, and go through the current understanding of the stakeholders requirements for the self-management of CF. We present the requirements found in previous scientific works and contrast them with the existing CF self-management Apps available in the market. Due to a limitation of CF Apps in addressing those requirements, we stretch our investigations towards other Apps and works covering similar requirements.

2.1   Research Context

This work is rooted on a multidisciplinary project, MyCyFAPP [7], whose research aims at developing a mobile application ecosystem that addresses CF patients, parents of children with CF, as well as healthcare professionals involved in the treatment. The App described in this paper is the part of the system which will be used by patients who are about to start self-management of treatment routines, as well as by parents responsible for the management of the treatment of their children. A core research of MyCyFAPP is the development of an algorithm for the calculation of the enzyme dosage of enzyme. A well-adjusted enzyme intake during every meal is important for avoiding malnutrition and minimizing gastrointestinal complications [6]. The enzyme calculation algorithm will be implemented as part of the self-management App. In addition, the App will include features that support other aspects of the CF treatment. The App will be piloted in a six-month clinical trial in order to assess its impact in terms of quality of life, nutrition, CF care education and development of gastro-intestinal symptoms.

2.2 Requirements and Apps for CF Self-management

The first step for designing the App came with the understanding of the users needs leading to the identification of the potential features for the App and non-functional requirements. We both conducted interviews as described in [13] and took in consideration the single scientific work we found analyzing CF patients' preferences for self-management via mobile applications [16]. [16] surveyed and interviewed adult CF patients from a CF clinic in the United States while [13] did a similar study across 7 different countries in Europe, including a wider population: both young and adult patients; parents; CF patient associations and Health Professionals (HPs). In that work, a total of 466 requirements were identified across the different target groups interviwed. After analysis, we extracted a set of core features and non-functional requirements.

Our findings show that CF patients' main concern is of being able to live a normal life, i.e. maintaining a good health and having time for daily activities despite the time consuming treatment. Table 1 summarizes the core features and non-functional requirements.

Despite the fact that there are some CF specific Apps in App stores such as Google Play and Apple's App Store, we could not find any research work discussing the design concepts behind them. We found 24 Apps when searching for the string "Cystic Fibrosis" in both App stores in March 2014. Most of those Apps offer a time-consuming UI interaction and only cover a subset of the core features (maximum of five and often no more than two or three), while CF patients expressed the desire for an App to address them all.

The data registration they support is very simplistic and does not provide an overview allowing patients or doctors to follow-up the treatment. For example, My CF Free[1] nutrition management only supports patient's weight and height recording. It provides no support for food recording. Both My CF Free and CF Notebook[2] support the recording of symptoms and treatment as notes, but not the visualization of the health status over time. None of the identified CF Apps provides food registration at detail level allowing patients to follow-up nutrition. Just one App, CF Enzymen[3] supports enzyme calculation, though in a per dish basis instead of per meal, making it laborious for users. The calculation is not personalised as is the aim in MyCyFAPP.

---

[1] https://play.google.com/store/apps/details?id=com.mycffree.mycf.
[2] https://play.google.com/store/apps/details?id=com.OceanVector.CFnotebook.
[3] https://play.google.com/store/apps/details?id=com.ncfs.cfenzymen.

Table 1. Requirements for CF self-management App

Requirement	Description
Core features	
Enzyme management	Management of enzyme supplement intake: dosage calculation, recording and overview
Nutrition management	Due to the mal-absorption of fat, calories and proteins, CF patients need to closely manage their nutrition (especially children)
Recipes advice	Support to share recipes appropriate to the CF diet
Diary keeping	Support to record symptoms and health condition
Treatment follow-up	Support to CF patients and parents to visualize nutrition and health condition over time
Treatment organization	Reminders and follow-up of medicine intake, medical appointments and maintenance of treatment equipment
Education	Learning about the disease, its treatment and dealing with symptoms
Digital meeting place	Being able to communicate with other patients and or caregivers in order to: learn from each other, exchange tips and support each other
Communication with HPs	Facilitating sharing of treatment data, exchanging messages and advices between patients/parents and HPs
Non-functional requirements	
Time saving	Users want to be able to use the App features with few clicks, spend as little time as possible
Motivation	Patients expressed that they would sometimes experience a lack of motivation and that some support could be useful
Customization	Patients knowledge about health, nutrition and disease varies a lot requiring the App to be customizable
Privacy	Users were inclined towards controlling the sharing of health data rather than making it automatically accessible to HPs
One App	A mobile App is preferred over a web or desktop one. All features should be available in a single App rather than in multiple ones

2.3   Design Concepts from Other Self-management Apps

Due to the limited background available in terms of effective design concepts for CF self-management apps, we looked into design practices and features applied in other Apps related to the complex core features of Nutrition Management, Treatment Follow-up, Diary Keeping and Treatment Organization. Our search spanned the fitness, nutrition and health management Apps in the App

Stores and scientific literature covering design concepts applied on mobile self-management in chronic diseases. For food intake registration as part of nutrition management, we did not consider approaches that register only food pictures [14] or food groups [3] as such information is not detailed enough for the level of nutrition assessment expected by CF patients and HPs.

Table 2. Design concepts observed in relevant Apps

Design concept or sub-feature	Source
Nutrition management	
Determining portion sizes as handfuls	Was ich esse
Registering food item via bar code	FDDB Extender, Lifesum, Yazio, Nutrino, [10]
Visual representation of food attributes (e.g. gluten free, vegan, etc.)	FDDB Extender
Bookmarking meals or dishes	Yazio, Lifesum, Nutrino, [10,22]
Custom portions per product (i.e. slice for cake) with gram equivalency	Yazio, Lifesum
Tips	Yazio, Lifesum, Nutrino, [3]
Auto-complete search	Lifesum, Nutrino
Set meals as recurrent	Nutrino
Tracking nutritional goals and percentage of completion	FDDB Extender, Yazio, Lifesum, Nutrino, [3,22]
Physical activity logging as a complement to nutrition	FDDB Extender, Yazio, Lifesum, Nutrino, [22]
Diary keeping and education	
Help buttons attached to symptoms with theirs explanations	Fertility Friend
Treatment Follow-up	
Bar and line graphs for numerical data of small variation (nutrition, weight, etc.)	FDDB Extender, Yazio, Lifesum
Table chart for non-numerical symptoms	Fertility Friend
Graphs to highlight data which is missing, marked as uncertain or out of the norm	Fertility Friend
Pie charts to display nutritional proportions	FDDB Extender
Treatment organization	
Custom dosages per intakes, recurrence and end-period for medication	MyTherapy
Possibility to register med intake from within main screen notification	MyTherapy
Bar-code scanning of medication	MyTherapy

The following Apps were consulted: Was ich esse[4], FDDB Extender[5], Lifesum[6], Yazio[7], Nutrino[8], Fertility Friend[9] and MyTherapy Meds & Pill Reminder[10]. The design concepts inspired from them are presented in Table 2.

3   Research Approach

Our research in MyCyFAPP follows the design-science paradigm [18]. While behavioral-science approaches focus on the use and benefits of a system implemented in an organization, design-science approaches seek to create information systems to solve identified organizational problems. Design-science approaches follow a recursive process allowing a gradual understanding of the problem to be solved and the improvement of solutions. The creation and assessment of IT artifacts is central for understanding and improvement. The term IT artifact is used in a wide sense and denotes various items related to the creation of information systems, such as models, methods and software prototypes. The design-science paradigm does not impose any concrete research and evaluation method. The choice of a method depends on the nature of the problem to be solved and the type of IT-artifact being created. In MyCyFAPP, we plan to develop several IT-artifacts: mockups of the applications such as presented in this paper, intermediate versions of the apps to be assessed in a midterm evaluation, and final versions of the App ecosystem to be assessed in a clinical trial.

As the first step of our research, we aimed at understanding the user needs. The approach and results are presented in Sect. 2.2. In a second step, presented in this paper, we aimed at concretizing these needs and sketching useful and easy-to-use solutions to fulfill these needs. The research question we had is:

- How can we design a mobile self-management App for CF that fulfills the identified user needs, that is appealing for the users, and that does not introduce additional burden for the patients? What needs to be taken into account so it satisfies all stakeholders (parents, patients and HPs)?

To answer this question, we adopt co-design towards the creation of the UI for app. By co-design, we mean that potential end-users, i.e. CF patients and parents, as well as health professionals participated actively in the design as the domain experts in cooperation with the researchers [21]. Research shows that involving end-users in the design process improves the level of acceptance of the final design product and it is more likely to accurately match the users requirements [17]. As shown in [15], the success of the introduction of a technical

---

[4] https://play.google.com/store/apps/details?id=de.aid.android.ernaehrungspy ramide.

[5] http://fddbextender.de/.

[6] https://www.lifesum.com/.

[7] https://www.yazio.com/.

[8] https://nutrino.co/.

[9] https://www.fertilityfriend.com/.

[10] https://www.mytherapyapp.com/.

artefact into health care is more strongly connected with the understanding of the complex dynamics of care and how it affects the stakeholders than with the technology. Therefore, applying co-design with all stakeholders is suggested as a solution to avoid the development of systems that fail to be adopted in the care practice. [4] also illustrates several success stories of the application of co-design for healthcare and advocates its further usage in the design of healthcare services.

Co-design was conducted in an iterative manner allowing a gradual refinement of mockups of the UI. In addition to collecting feedback after each iteration, an evaluation of the mockups was performed at a final step of the research.

Stakeholders from different countries in the North and South of Europe were involved allowing to handle different needs due to variations in the provision of healthcare services and cultural diversity. Participants to co-design were recruited in cooperation with CF competence centres and CF patient organisations in the participating countries. Regarding ethics, MyCyFAPP follows the European legislation on privacy and the ethical principal for medical research according to Declaration of Helsinki. All participants voluntarily accepted to participate, and could retract at any time. They were informed about the research and the way collected data are managed, and they all signed a consent form. In the case of participants under 18 years old, their legal guardians also signed a consent form.

4   Design Process

The first step of the design process consisted in selecting the features which would be included in the application. Then, CF patients, parents of children with CF and HPs were involved in the co-design and evaluation of the UIs for the App.

4.1   Definition of the Scope of Features for the Co-design

The requirements presented in Sect. 2.2 were analysed and weighted in terms of how frequently they were mentioned during interviews. Then, they were discussed and prioritised with HPs with different background: dieticians, pulmonologists, nurses and paediatricians. The involvement of HPs is essential because they have the medical knowledge and can advice what is important for the treatment and how self-management interplays with the organization of the health services in their hospitals. From the initial core features (see Table 1), only the Digital meeting place and the messaging part of Communication with HPs were discarded. The first was left out because existing dedicated CF forums and closed groups on social networks fulfil this need, and the second because hospitals provide well-functioning channels for communication with patients. However, the sharing of data collected by patients and parents was kept as a relevant for the App.

4.2 Co-design Process

The co-design process was organized as an iterative process with data collection and prototyping refinement at each stage:

1. **Initial Workshops**: Workshops involving patients and parents were organized aiming at confirming the relevance of the selected core App features and sketching the UIs. These sketches served as input for the development of initial mockups using Balsamiq[11] (a computer-based prototyping tool).
2. **Refinement Workshops**: New workshops were carried out aiming at refining and validating the initial mockups.
3. **Validation by HPs**: HPs contributing to MyCyFAPP project gave their expert viewpoint on the refined mockups.
4. **Evaluation**: Videos (hosted on MyCyFAPP's youtube account[12]) presenting the final mockups were developed and distributed to patients and parents for evaluation and feedback.

Patients and parents involved in the research were recruited through HPs involved in the project and CF patient associations. Due to the risk of cross-infection between CF patients, the workshops involved a single CF patient, except for a few cases where patients with the same bacteria-flora could be recruited. Parents and HPs workshops were conducted as focus groups. Table 3 Summarizes the sample. The workshops lasted 2–3 h each.

Table 3. Distribution of participants on the workshops

Workshop set	Location	Participants				
		Patient 13–17 yo	Patient 17+ yo	Parent 0–12 yo	Parent 12+ yo	HP
Initial workshops	Netherlands			1		
	Norway	1	1		1	
	Valencia		4			
	Madrid		1	4	1	
Refinement workshops	Portugal	3	1	4	3	
HPs' validation	Portugal					7
	Netherlands & Belgium					5
Evaluation	Norway	1	2	1		

---

[11] www.balsamiq.com.
[12] https://www.youtube.com/channel/UCD63yFB92hwpnNJJmu5Dbgw.

The **Initial Workshops** were structured so that:

1. The concept and core features of the App were presented.
2. Participants were asked for feedback as to validate the relevance and applicability of the core features on the daily basis.
3. Moderators triggered the participants to imagine how the features could fit their daily life and to sketch interaction with the App.
4. The moderators suggested UI elements based in the background research, when participants were not able to sketch their ideas.

The mockups produced after the **Initial Workshops** implemented use cases derived from the selected core features, while the UI elements were designed taking in consideration the non-functional requirements (see Table 1). The App mockups included five different menu entry points: one for registering meals, one for managing food recipes, one for diary keeping, one for graphs and goals and finally one for managing reminders. The App features could then be triggered from subsequent screens started from those entry points. For instance, enzyme calculation was triggered when registering a meal, physical activity registration was prototyped as a part of the diary, and the educational content was implemented through help probes attached to App components.

The mockups were tested in the **Refinement Workshops** with patients or parents interacting with them in a think-aloud fashion [5]. Moderators asked the participants to think of a recent or hypothetical experience related to one of the use cases supported by the App, and to execute it using the mockup while describing the process. For example, we asked participants to register symptoms they had recently and to add their last meal. When several participants were involved in a session, all were asked to follow the steps of the active participant and give complementary feedback in the cases they would have interacted differently. Moderators asked questions at the end of each use case in order to ensure that all participants were able to voice their opinions.

The **validation by HPs** followed a different process. The moderators walked through the mockups to present the different features. The HPs were asked to comment underway. And, after each use case, moderators asked for additional feedback.

The mockups were refined and submitted to a final **Evaluation** by 5 patients and parents. Descriptive videos of the different features implemented in the mockup were distributed and participants were asked to answer a questionnaire including both qualitative and quantitative questions. The qualitative questions were open questions inquiring what they liked, disliked or missed. Meanwhile the quantitative questions asked them to rate the usefulness of the different UI elements using a five-level likert scale.

In general, the feedback given by participants from the workshops and evaluations was positive. They considered that all the features they need were covered by the mockups and they were very eager to try using the App.

5   Results

In this section, we present some of the mockups and the rationale behind the UI elements (for a complete coverage of the mockups look at the videos - see footnote 12). We describe the different points of views captured through the workshops or evaluations leading to them.

5.1   Food Registration

Meals are composed of food items or dishes, and the latter are composed of different ingredients. It is necessary to support the identification of all those elements for quantifying the nutritional composition of a meal. The co-design focused on UI elements to support easy registering of meals assuming the availability of an existing comprehensive food database. The UI elements include:

- Support for adding new food items by scanning their bar-code;
- Auto-complete search technology;
- Bookmarking favourite dishes and food items;
- Varied quantity units (e.g. grams or slices) and illustrative examples;
- Setting meals as recurrent;
- Creating variations of existing dishes.

Workshop participants often ate the same food, and suggested support for recurrent dishes and creation of variations of existing dishes. That would allow them to quickly register a new dish or meal instance. Another point requested by several patients was support for registering energy complements.

When it comes to quantifying food items, they suggested to provide units adapted to the type of food. For example, bread can be described in terms of slices and milk in terms of glasses. HPs suggested that non-standard units such as the ones above should be complemented with the equivalency to a standard unit such as grams or millilitres. HPs also suggested to size dish portions based on how much of a plate space they take, as illustrated in Fig. 1. **Evaluation** participants really liked this feature.

Overall, the UI elements for quick registration were highly rated in the questionnaires' answers and positively noted during the **Refinement Workshops**. The same applies for the food quantification, where all **Evaluation** participants thought they would be able to estimate the food amount with the App.

5.2   Enzyme Management

The enzyme management was presented as part of the Food Registration UIs as they go hand in hand. The quantity of recommended enzyme is displayed together with the meal items and a stepper control is presented so that the user can adjust the amount taken (as shown in Fig. 2). An important feedback was that different enzymes capsules or types contain different enzymes dosage, making it necessary configuration of the enzyme supplement. In addition, some patients suggested support for keeping track of the stock of enzyme capsules.

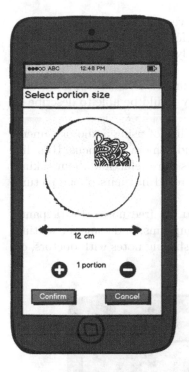

Fig. 1. Selecting a portion size   **Fig. 2.** Meal and enzyme overview

5.3   Recipe Book

Several participants often struggled to find energy rich recipes and welcomed advice for recipes. They suggested grouping recipes based on different characteristics: salty, sour, quick preparation, etc. They were also interested sharing recipes with other patients, commenting and rating. Dieticians in MyCyFAPP were however concerned that the App supports recipes curated by dieticians. They suggest a symbol to differentiate them from non-curated recipes.

Patients wanted the recipe book to be integrated with the food registration, so a dish could be registered directly from the recipe book. Patients would also like to create recipe variations and bookmark favourites.

5.4   Diary

A list of CF symptoms was developed with patients in the first workshops and validated by doctors. While patients consider all kinds of symptoms, HPs suggested to focus on gastrointestinal symptoms due to the scope of the project. The list from HPs included: pain in abdominal regions, diarrhoea, irregular stool, constipation, heartburn, vomiting and nausea. HPs stressed that context information should be defined for some symptoms. For example, for both heartburn and abdominal pain, it is important to know if it happens at night or before a meal.

The majority of the symptoms were suited for yes/no check-boxes and drop down menus covering simple additional context. However, for pain, patients in the **Initial Workshops** suggested to select the body area with pain from a body drawing, and, then set the intensity and frequency (as illustrated in Fig. 3). All **Evaluation** respondents supported the idea of clicking on a visual representation to localize pain, even if a few of them thought they would be able to describe it as well without the visual cue.

Patients and HPs were asked about the possibility of using audio or camera to record symptoms, such as audio for coughing and camera for mucus. HPs did not find it very useful for their assessment. Patients were reluctant about taking pictures of the mucus, and afraid they would be stored in theirs phone picture gallery.

The diary mockup also included a Notes field for free notes. Participants found it useful. Some would use it for detailing symptoms, and some for writing personal notes. The latter were not so keen about sharing notes with doctors, or between children and parents.

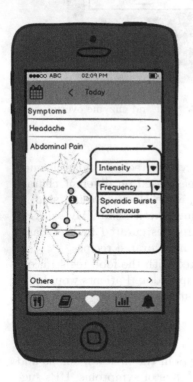

Fig. 3. Abdominal pain in diary

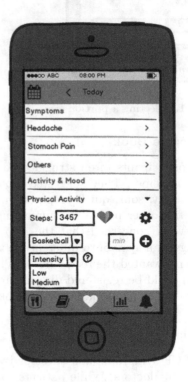

Fig. 4. Registering physical activity

5.5 Physical Activity Registration

Physical Activity Registration came out as a suggestion on the **Initial Workshops** in connection with food intake registration. Some HPs highlighted the importance of this feature for quantifying the calories expenditure and ensure that patients would eat enough to compensate for days of high physical activity. Some paediatrics did however not find it useful as it is difficult to quantify the activity of small children.

We designed the registration of physical activity as an entry in the diary which enabled the recording of multiple physical activities and steps (as illustrated in Fig. 4). Both steps and activities can be inserted manually or by connecting the App to a physical activity platform or device (such as Google Fit[13], FitBit[14], etc.). Some participants were users of such devices and appreciated such support.

Regarding the manual registration of physical activities, similarly to [9], parents suggested the inclusion of daily activities within the registry options. They suggested the inclusion of outdoor children games such as hide-and-seek and tag with the activities. During the talk-aloud experiment participants were unsure about which activity intensities theirs recent physical activity belonged to. Finally, they suggested to add an informative text that illustrates the types of activity intensity.

5.6   Goals

Most of the patients and parents were interested in following nutrition goals. Given that CF patients need to consume higher energy food to achieve theirs daily energy requirements, we expected that calories and fat would be the main concern. Indeed, some parents were concerned by high-energy intake. However, many parents and patients were more interested in ensuring a balanced diet. Some were also interested in other types of goals, such as goals related to sport and adhering to the treatment, in particular inhalations. Overall, participants stated that setting up goals and tracking them would motivate them to follow their treatment.

Some patients and parents were happy to receive goals from dieticians while some preferred to set up goals themselves. Dieticians on the other hand wished to curate goals or to be involved in the goal selection. They want not only to ensure that goals are sound and safe, but also adequate for a specific patient.

5.7   Treatment Explanation

Education was introduced in the App via explanation boxes attached to symptoms. The boxes were activated when pressing help buttons leading to a description of symptoms and possible causes. The information format was appreciated by parents, patients and HPs.

However there were different opinions about what content is useful between parents/patients and HPs. While patients and parents would like to receive feedback about how to remedy the symptom, HPs were not in favour of giving

---

[13] https://www.google.com/fit/.
[14] https://www.fitbit.com/.

recommendations. HPs argued that guidance can only be provided based on the whole patient context.

5.8 Health Visualization

Patients and parents were interested in visualizing both nutritional and health status over time. Most patients were satisfied of being able to visualize only the data they register. One parent also suggested access to the results from HPs examinations, such as bacteria infection levels.

Overall, they wished correlated aspects to be shown together, such as height, weight and nutrition. For those, they suggested that line graphs would be more suitable. For occurrence of symptoms, a tabular form was suggested. Each row would consists of a symptom, each column a calendar date and each cell a representation of that symptom in that date (colors or abbreviations could be used for the symptom state representation).

Participants expected to be able to select which data is displayed, and to zoom into periods, as well to access the details of a registration by selecting a value in the graphs.

5.9 Reminders

Patients and parents were interested in reminders for parts of the treatment not usual in the daily routine, such as new medication or consultation. They preferred reminders to be flexible to accommodate varied treatment aspects, rather than only support for medicine intake. They also favoured flexibility in the reminder creation to accommodate appointments with daily recurrence, end-dates or different medicine dosage. Most participants preferred to include reminders in the App rather than using the phone main agenda.

Regarding reminder alarms, participants wanted them to be discrete and easy to use. They wanted to be able to confirm the intake of medicine directly from the reminder notification; and to possibly snooze it (see Fig. 5).

5.10 Weight and Height Registration

Parents, and some patients, were especially concerned about height and weight recording since the malabsorption of nutrients by CF patients can affect the growth. However, HPs recommended to avoid recording weight every day because too much focus on growth is not good. They also would not use measurements done by patients themselves, because HPs could not verify how the measurement was done. Thus, they could not compare measurements done during consultations with those done by patients.

5.11 Sharing Data with Doctors

Both during our preliminary interviews (see Sect. 3) and the **Initial Workshops**, we noticed different views as for sharing data recorded by patients with

Fig. 5. Medicine notification

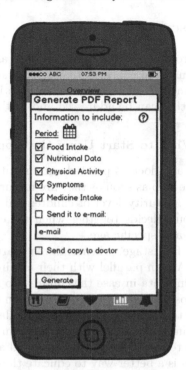

Fig. 6. Sharing data

doctors. Some patients and parents wanted to control what is shared while some wanted to share data automatically for simplicity, and because they expected that the shared data would allow HPs to make better diagnostics.

The designed solution allowed patients to decide which data to share, when to share and how to share it. The mockups enabled patients to share data in different ways. It allowed the automatically sending of data to HPs system, manually selecting which data and time range to send to HPs system or simply to generate a pdf containing the data (illustrated in Fig. 6). With the pdf option, the patient could send it to the doctor or choose what to print and bring to the consultation. This flexible approach was unanimously well received during the **Refinement Workshops** and **Evaluation**.

HPs underlined that patients should be informed that shared data would only be seen during consultations (around every 3 months). They claimed not being able to cope with real time follow-up, as similarly observed in [25]. As several patients and parents had expectation that HPs would contact them rapidly if data indicate some health issue, it is important that the App makes it clear to patients how and when doctors will use shared data.

6   Discussion

Apart from concrete design concepts and UI elements, the workshops uncovered transversal concerns that stretch across the different UIs and the CF self-management model. We present those in this section together with reflections on how they can be addressed and further investigated.

6.1   When to Start Using the App

Parents and doctors pointed out that it would be beneficial that children start using the App as soon as they are mature enough. When discussing, they agreed that the maturity level of children vary, and, therefore, parents, children and HPs should decide together when the children start using the App, instead of starting at a specific age.

In a first stage, when children start using the app, parents would like to use the App in parallel with their children in order to assume the responsibility for logging data in case the children do not. During the workshops, the concern about possible editing conflicts between parents and children was raised. Despite existing technical solutions to handle data conflicts, parents concluded that the best solution would be to refrain from editing data and rather talk with the children to clarify the discrepancy and ask the child to log data. Parents agreed that this is a better way to educate the children.

6.2   Customization

Both our initial interviews and the co-design workshops show a strong need for customization to different contexts and age groups. The knowledge about the disease increases as the patients grow up. At the same time, the health condition evolves leading to new requirements. Patients are different: some are compliant to the treatment, and some needs strong guidance. A factor that calls for customized support is that we target different user groups. While we initially consider two App user groups, i.e., parents managing the health of their children and patients managing their own health, we identified a new group, that of parents and children with CF cooperating.

Customization was proposed as a mechanism to simplify the UI allowing to include only the elements of interest. Some suggestions were selecting the order of the symptoms in the diary, removing symptoms, and selecting which data source to be present on the different graphs. Symptoms types and severity vary a lot from CF patient to patient and with the progress of the disease. For instance, some patients develop diabetes. The possibility to customize the symptoms in the diary would be especially important if the App is extended to include a complete list of symptoms, not only gastrointestinal symptoms.

The difference of age groups between users is also another aspect that calls for personalization. Growth tracking is important for children but it is not for adult patients. Younger users relate to mobile Apps differently. We noticed in our workshops that teenagers wanted to have a more playful interaction with the App. One of them, for example, expressed the wish to set the background colours of the App to match the ones of the football club he supports.

Participants voiced the importance of including all treatment aspects in a single App and customized for CF care. Patients described that they tried some of the available Nutritional Apps but gave up as the functionalities were directed towards weight loss and did not make sense for their case.

A special case of customization is that of parents with more than one child with CF. They would like to use the same App to manage both children.

When parents and their child are cooperating in health management, parents would like the child to receive reminders about medicine intake and, to receive themselves notifications that the child took the medicine. They also would like to configure the receipt of such notifications in case they become too annoying. The customization of what features are available in the App was also suggested as a mechanism to limit the App scope for children who start taking responsibility for self-management. In that way, new features could be unveiled little by little.

6.3   Data Quality and Control

During the co-design workshops, we noticed some divergences between patients and parents wish to decide on the management of their health, and HPs wish to curate the App content. While patients and parents wanted to freely define goals and create recipes, HPs wanted to ensure that those were medically valid. HPs were uncomfortable with the idea that an App would support goals and recipes that are not recommended by dieticians. Such divergence raises a compromise between supporting patients with their individual wishes that affect acceptance of the App, and the medical validity of the supported features. For recipes, HPs suggested to distinguish between dietician recommended recipes and user-generated recipes. For goals, HPs suggested that patients and parents could define those together with them during consultation.

HPs expressed some scepticism about the quality of the data entered by patients. They wanted patients to use an "I'm fine button" for days where they have no symptom, as to distinguish it from the absence of symptom registration. For the weight and height measurements, they would rather use the consultation measurements as they are performed on standard conditions (calibrated scale, without cloths, etc.).

Retrieving health information reported by patients out of the consultation and without being able to enquire about the patients context, introduces a situation to which HPs are not used to. It is important to further study how HPs will cope with this type of information, and to understand how recording can be useful without increasing the treatment burden for the patient.

6.4   Treatment Recommendation

During the workshops, most of the parents and patients voiced wishes of having treatment recommendations given by the App. They would like the App to indicate actions, such medicine intake, when symptoms are registered. They would also like the App to analyse the registered health patterns in order to detect correlations between events. HPs, on the other hand, were reluctant to such support. They argued that a lot of contextual information is needed to prescribe a treatment. They exemplified that several symptoms can be related to different diseases or conditions, and concluded that it can be dangerous to provide recommendations only based on the registration of symptoms.

7   Concluding Remarks and Future Work

The usage of co-design with multiple stakeholders involved in the self-management of CF enabled us to: (1) identify divergences between stakeholders and develop solutions that tackle these divergences; and (2) create design concepts for the core features effectively rooted in the functional requirements and non-functional requirements, such as privacy and time saving. The resulting mockups are consistent with design findings uncovered in similar research work and popular Apps cited here, but they also introduce elements which, as far as we know, have not been yet explored. For instance, we propose flexible mechanisms to share data and to create new instances of food intake from dish variations. At the same time, the mockups bundle together the specific and varied requirements for CF self-management in a mobile application.

Although the findings described here relate to the self-management of CF, the discussion in this article applies more generally to the introduction of a self-management mobile application in healthcare. Many aspects of the CF therapy, such as continuous medicine intake, regular physical activity and nutritional follow-up, are common to other chronic diseases, thus potentially making many of our findings directly applicable to other self-management applications. For example, findings about optimizing food registration confirm and complement those for diabetes [2] or obesity [22] Apps, but also shed light in different aspects of nutrition management as the nutritional context of CF patients differs from other chronic diseases.

The positive feedback and the participants willingness to try an App based on the mockups indicate that the design concepts are ready to be implemented. We will continue this research as we develop the App, and conduct a mid-term evaluation and later on assess the App in a clinical study. These evaluations will help us to understand the usability and acceptability of the design concepts.

Acknowledgments. Authors of this paper, on behalf of MyCyFAPP consortium, acknowledge the European Union and the Horizon 2020 Research and Innovation Framework Programme for funding the project (ref. 643806). Furthermore, we thank the participants to the workshops and the evaluation, and the project partners for the collaboration during participant recruitment and discussion of the results.

References

1. Living with CF: Treatments and therapies. https://www.cff.org/Living-with-CF/Treatments-and-Therapies/. Accessed 26 Sept 2016
2. Årsand, E., Tufano, J.T., Ralston, J.D., Hjortdahl, P.: Designing mobile dietary management support technologies for people with diabetes. J. Telemed. Telecare **14**(7), 329–332 (2008)
3. Arsand, E., Varmedal, R., Hartvigsen, G.: Usability of a mobile self-help tool for people with diabetes: the easy health diary. In: 2007 IEEE International Conference on Automation Science and Engineering, pp. 863–868. IEEE (2007)
4. Bate, P., Robert, G.: Experience-based design: from redesigning the system around the patient to co-designing services with the patient. Qual. Saf. Health Care **15**(5), 307–310 (2006)
5. Boren, T., Ramey, J.: Thinking aloud: reconciling theory and practice. IEEE Trans. Prof. Commun. **43**(3), 261–278 (2000)
6. Borowitz, D., Gelfond, D., Maguiness, K., Heubi, J.E., Ramsey, B.: Maximal daily dose of pancreatic enzyme replacement therapy in infants with cystic fibrosis: a reconsideration. J. Cyst. Fibros. **12**(6), 784–785 (2013)
7. Calvo-Lerma, J., Martinez-Jimenez, C.P., Lázaro-Ramos, J.P., Andrés, A., Crespo-Escobar, P., Stav, E., Schauber, C., Pannese, L., Hulst, J.M., Suárez, L., et al.: Innovative approach for self-management and social welfare of children with cystic fibrosis in europe: development, validation and implementation of an mhealth tool (MyCyFAPP). BMJ Open **7**(3), e014931 (2017)
8. Celler, B.G., Lovell, N.H., Basilakis, J., et al.: Using information technology to improve the management of chronic disease. Med. J. Aust. **179**(5), 242–246 (2003)
9. Consolvo, S., Klasnja, P., McDonald, D.W., Avrahami, D., Froehlich, J., LeGrand, L., Libby, R., Mosher, K., Landay, J.A.: Flowers or a robot army?: encouraging awareness & activity with personal, mobile displays. In: Proceedings of the 10th International Conference on Ubiquitous Computing, pp. 54–63. ACM (2008)
10. Consolvo, S., Klasnja, P., McDonald, D.W., Landay, J.A.: Designing for healthy lifestyles: design considerations for mobile technologies to encourage consumer health and wellness. J. Found. Trends Hum.-Comput. Interact. **6**(3–4), 167–315 (2014)
11. Dodd, M.E., Webb, A.K.: Understanding non-compliance with treatment in adults with cystic fibrosis. J. R. Soc. Med. **93**(Suppl 38), 2 (2000)
12. Free, C., Phillips, G., Galli, L., Watson, L., Felix, L., Edwards, P., Patel, V., Haines, A.: The effectiveness of mobile-health technology-based health behaviour change or disease management interventions for health care consumers: a systematic review. PLoS Med **10**(1), e1001362 (2013)
13. Fricke, L., Weisser, T., Floch, J., Grut, L., Vilarinho, T., Stav, E., Zettl, A., Schauber, C.: User needs in the development of a health app ecosystem for self-management of cystic fibrosis. Manuscript submitted for publication at JMIR mHealth and uHealth
14. Frøisland, D.H., Årsand, E.: Integrating visual dietary documentation in mobile-phone-based self-management application for adolescents with type 1 diabetes. J. Diabetes Sci. Technol. (2015). doi:10.1177/1932296815576956
15. Hardisty, A.R., Peirce, S.C., Preece, A., Bolton, C.E., Conley, E.C., Gray, W.A., Rana, O.F., Yousef, Z., Elwyn, G.: Bridging two translation gaps: a new informatics research agenda for telemonitoring of chronic disease. Int. J. Med. Inform. **80**(10), 734–744 (2011)

16. Hilliard, M.E., Hahn, A., Ridge, A.K., Eakin, M.N., Riekert, K.A.: User preferences and design recommendations for an mhealth app to promote cystic fibrosis self-management. JMIR mHealth uHealth 2(4), e44 (2014)

17. Kujala, S.: User involvement: a review of the benefits and challenges. Behav. Inf. Technol. 22(1), 1–16 (2003)

18. March, S.T., Storey, V.C.: Design science in the information systems discipline: an introduction to the special issue on design science research. MIS Q. 32(4), 725–730 (2008)

19. Nolte, E., McKee, M.: Caring for People with Chronic Conditions: A Health System Perspective. McGraw-Hill Education, London (2008)

20. Pearson, M.L., Mattke, S., Shaw, R., Ridgely, M.S., Wiseman, S.H.: Patient self-management support programs (2007)

21. Sanders, E.B.N., Stappers, P.J.: Co-creation and the new landscapes of design. Co-des. 4(1), 5–18 (2008)

22. Tsai, C.C., Lee, G., Raab, F., Norman, G.J., Sohn, T., Griswold, W.G., Patrick, K.: Usability and feasibility of PmEB: a mobile phone application for monitoring real time caloric balance. Mob. Netw. Appl. 12(2–3), 173–184 (2007)

23. Ward, B.W.: Multiple chronic conditions among US adults: a 2012 update. Prev. Chronic Dis. 11 (2014). https://www.cdc.gov/pcd/issues/2014/13_0389.htm

24. Webb, T., Joseph, J., Yardley, L., Michie, S.: Using the internet to promote health behavior change: a systematic review and meta-analysis of the impact of theoretical basis, use of behavior change techniques, and mode of delivery on efficacy. J. Med. Internet Res. 12(1), e4 (2010)

25. van der Weegen, S., Verwey, R., Spreeuwenberg, M., Tange, H., van der Weijden, T., de Witte, L.: The development of a mobile monitoring and feedback tool to stimulate physical activity of people with a chronic disease in primary care: a user-centered design. JMIR mHealth uHealth 1(2), e8 (2013)

26. Yach, D., Hawkes, C., Gould, C.L., Hofman, K.J.: The global burden of chronic diseases: overcoming impediments to prevention and control. JAMA 291(21), 2616–2622 (2004)

Even when Icons are Not Worth a Thousand Words They are Helpful in Designing Asthma mHealth Tools

Michael Lefco[1], Jensi Gise[2], Burton Lesnick[3], and Rosa I. Arriaga[1(✉)] (iD)

[1] Georgia Institute of Technology, Atlanta, GA, USA
arriaga@cc.gatech.edu
[2] Georgia State University, Atlanta, GA, USA
[3] Children's Healthcare of Atlanta, Atlanta, GA, USA

Abstract. Asthma is the most common childhood chronic illness. Its management requires that caregivers have access to a variety of information. For example, asthma action plans (AAP) are written instructions for responding to escalating asthma symptoms. Icons have been used to facilitate the accessibility of health information and we investigate whether they benefit parents of young children. We conducted a 4-part study with 36 participants where we (1) gathered requirements for an asthma management mHealth tool (2) assessed the comprehension of icons to be used in an AAP (3) compared the usability of a text-based (T-B) vs. icon-based (I-B) AAPs (4) and gathered feedback about an mHealth tool we designed. Results suggest that the icons we developed were highly matched to their meaning (92% translucency). Usability findings showed that in general both AAPs were equally matched. However, benefits accrued to I-BAAP users in relation to greater accuracy and speed of response in scenarios that required parents to identify asthma symptoms. Two-thirds of parents indicated that they would prefer to use the I-BAAP to manage their child's asthma. The remaining third preferred the T-BAAP because it contained more details. We conclude with recommendation on how designers and researchers can improve mHealth tools for caregivers of asthmatic children.

Keywords: Asthma · Asthma action plan · Icon-based asthma action plan · Asthma app · Mobile application · Mobile computing · mHealth · Application

1 Introduction

Asthma is a chronic respiratory condition. It is the most common disease among children with a 14% prevalence worldwide [33]. When not properly managed, asthma can lead to lessened quality of life and increased avoidable emergency department (ED) visits, hospitalizations, and deaths [31]. Asthma is a public health problem in both wealthy and developing nations [33]. Requirements for appropriately managing asthma are well known [6, 11]. Additionally, the Global Asthma Report indicates that health authorities in all countries should ensure that all patients are provided with a written asthma action plan (AAP) [6].

© IFIP International Federation for Information Processing 2017
Published by Springer International Publishing AG 2017. All Rights Reserved
R. Bernhaupt et al. (Eds.): INTERACT 2017, Part III, LNCS 10515, pp. 23–33, 2017.
DOI: 10.1007/978-3-319-67687-6_2

An AAP is a health management tool given to patients by their medical provider. It illustrates what actions to take at different levels of symptom severity from day-to-day (i.e., Green Zone) medication use to emergency situations (i.e., Red Zone). AAPs are important in enhancing the patient's or caregiver's understanding of the disease, encouraging self-management, [30] and creating a partnership between the physician and caregiver. Research suggests that this partnership coupled with strong communication between caregivers and physicians can lead to better medication adherence [1]. Furthermore, research has shown that children with written AAPs compared to those without AAPs are half as likely to be hospitalized or visit the emergency department [25].

Currently, AAPs given to children and caregivers are text-based paper documents. Studies have found that including icons and text (as compared to text alone) on documents may increase the likelihood that individuals being discharged from emergency rooms will read the information, do what was recommended [10] and retain the knowledge [4]. Houts et al. found that for the general public, pictures that are closely linked to text increase attention to and recall of health information better than text alone. They also found that pictures enhance adherence to health instructions and target behaviors for individuals with lower literacy [15]. These findings suggest that designers can positively impact health management by designing tools that include icons, pictures, and images in medical information.

Healthcare providers can encourage use of the AAP by reviewing it with the patient at each doctor visit and highlighting successful use as a way to control asthma symptoms. Ideally, self-management approaches should be tailored to the needs and literacy levels of patients and asthma management tools should be accessible at all points of care, from the hospital to the home [11, 14]. Usability and accessibility of an AAP are very important for the overall health of children with asthma. However, while 1 in 11 children in the United States have asthma, less than 1 in 2 children get an AAP [6]. Not having an AAP or not having access to one (e.g., because a parent did not send it to school) is a significant barrier to effective health management.

Our research has two goals. First, to investigate if using icons can help facilitate the asthma management of children with asthma. We addressed this goal by designing an icon-based asthma action plan (I-BAAP) using information from interviews with caregivers of children with asthma. Then we assessed mom's comprehension of asthma icons and finally we tested them on various scenarios using either an I-BAAP or a text based (T-B) AAP for correctness and speed of user response. This allowed us to assess any benefits of the I-BAAP over the T-BAAP for speed and accuracy of mom's response to common asthma symptoms. Our second goal is to investigate caregivers' receptiveness to using a mobile asthma management tool. We addressed this goal by designing a mobile I-BAAP and then gathering qualitative information from caregivers on its pros, cons, and usability. With our findings, we hope to bridge gaps in the literature regarding how icons, compared to text, can be of value for parents of children with asthma, and to better understand how mobile technology designers can improve usability of AAPs.

2 Related Works

There is a long history of studying the use of icons in HCI [13, 32] and health management [4]. There are few studies about the use of icons in asthma management tools. Adults have been the sole focus of research that has been done to study how images impact asthma management. Yin, et al. found that when physicians used an AAP with pictorial descriptions to provide asthma counseling in a patient-doctor scenario, these physicians provided clearer counseling than physicians who used a standard text-based AAP. The delivery of clearer communication and deeper coverage of content from physicians is believed to have a positive impact on asthma management [33]. Researchers have sought to leverage the positive outcomes found by including icons in health management material for adults with asthma. Roberts et al. examined benefits of a pictorial-based AAP among three different populations in the United Kingdom. The pictures used were well understood and the pictorial-based AAP was well received by participants. In this study, the adults with asthma were able to adequately recount appropriate actions to take in clinical scenarios using the pictorial-based AAP [27]. While this study shows the benefit of icons for physicians and adults with asthma, little research exists on how an icon-based, rather than text-based, AAP may help caregivers of young children with asthma deliver effective asthma care.

Asthma is a vibrant area of research in the mobile health (mHealth) space. This has run the gamut from design [20, 24], web-based technologies [3], instruments, [22, 23] to interventions [35–37]. Huckvale and colleagues have conducted a number of studies to investigate mobile asthma management tools [16–18]. In reviewing over 100 asthma apps they found that apps were not likely to provide information for self-care based on evidence in medicine, or focus on evidence-based interventions such as the use of an asthma action plan. However, a pilot study has found that adults with asthma perceived that a mobile application of a text-based asthma action plan could improve their ability to control their asthma [24].

Our study seeks to bridge three gaps in the literature review. First, rather than focus on adults with asthma we focus on the mothers of young children with asthma. Specifically, we investigate caregiver's use of an icon-based asthma action plan in asthma management scenarios for their young child. Second, while studies have investigated the benefit of icon-based AAPs, there is no study that actually compares them against traditional text-based AAPs. Third, while previous studies have focused on adults' perception of asthma action plan mobile applications, we will investigate mothers' attitudes toward using this technology to care for their child with asthma.

3 Methods and Results

We conducted a 4-part study with 36 total participants where we (1) gathered requirements for an asthma management mHealth tool (2) assessed the comprehension of icons to be used in an AAP (3) compared the usability of a text-based (T-B) vs. icon-based (I-B) AAPs (4) and gathered feedback about the mHealth tool we designed. Of the 36 participants, five participated in the first part of the study, 7 participated in the

2nd part of the study, and the remaining 24 participated in the 3rd, and 4th parts of the study. All participants provided informed consent before joining the study.

In part 1, we conducted interviews with 5 individuals including a pulmonologist (1), an asthma educator (1), nurse practitioners (2), and a parent (1) to design a mHealth tool. Interviews were focused on how medical professionals provide information and how parents receive it as well as important factors in asthma health management. The interviews were semi-structured to allow participants to drive the conversation towards the most important issues. Audio from the sessions was recorded. The interviews were professionally transcribed. Then 2 reviewers read through the transcription looking for design implications for the mobile I-BAAP. The 2 reviewers compared their notes to jointly confirm design ideas for the application. We used the gold standard of care for US, the National Heart, Lung, and Blood Institute's (NHLBI) asthma action plans (see Fig. 1A) to develop our paper-based I-BAAP. We designed our I-BAAP in paper-format because paper-based asthma action plans are the most common forms and it allowed us to test it against traditional text-based asthma action plans. A member of the research team designed the I-BAAP. He studied existing action plans and health iconography and used his design expertise in creating the paper I-BAAP (Fig. 1B). It is important to note that our goal with creating an asthma management tool was to develop a tool that included an AAP and other features to support parents. A prototype for the mobile health tool was built using the Twitter Bootstrap web framework (Fig. 1C).

A   B   C

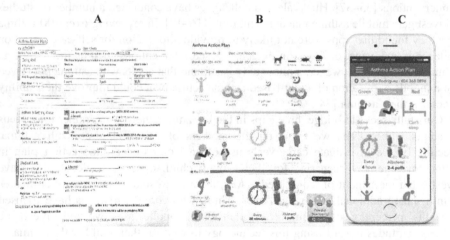

Fig. 1. Gold standard text (A)-, Icon (B)-based asthma action plan and (C) mobile tool

Interview analyses led to the inclusion of a number of features for the mobile application beyond the I-BAAP. Next, we provide a number of examples. The certified asthma educator recommended including notifications about asthma related events and reminders for medication refills and doctor appointments. Nurse practitioners advised that we distinguish between green and yellow zone medications, illustrate pre-treating before exercise, show alternative names of medicines, and enable a calendar tracker.

A pulmonologist suggested we display pictures of the asthma paraphernalia (e.g., the chamber and age related devices), and the mom we interviewed desired the ability to track symptom flare-ups in the app to be able to share with a doctor.

Only moms of children with asthma were present at the clinic where we recruited participants for this study. For the rest of the paper we refer to them interchangeably as "moms" or "participants." Thirty-one participants were recruited for Part 2–4 of the study in the waiting room of a local pulmonology clinic. Seven participated in part 2 of the study and the remaining 24 participated in parts 3 and 4 of the study. Since they all filled out the same survey we discuss those results first. We note, however, that some moms opted to forgo answering certain questions. Thus, there is not a complete set of answers for all items on the survey. On the survey we asked about demographic information, technology adoption, and questions related to the child's asthma management. Participants had at least 1 child with asthma (though some had multiple children with asthma, mean = 1.5). They were asked to report information for the child who was with them at the clinic. Participants had varying educational backgrounds ranging from leaving school in the 8th grade to a master's degree. Of the participants, 17 reported having public insurance, 7 had private, 4 had none, and 2 did not respond. Twenty-five participants were African American, 3 White, 1 Hispanic, and 1 did not respond. Demographics of the sample are representative of the moms and patients in the clinic on the days we recruited and conducted interviews.

Information on the participant's use of technology revealed 27/31 moms owned a smartphone and 23 surfed the Internet on their phone more than once per day. Nineteen/31 moms reported that they had not used technology to help manage their child's asthma. Mom's reported that they were very confident about their ability to control their child's asthma and their ability to provide a clear picture of their child's health to their doctor (avg. 4.41 (S.D. = 1.10) and 4.53 (S.D. = 1.08), respectively). These two survey items were on 5-point scale.

Survey responses revealed that the mean age of the child that was with them at the clinic was 8.25 years. Moms were asked to use the NHLBI severity index to indicate their child's asthma status. The severity level of the asthmatic children varied; 11 were reported as having severe asthma, 11 moderate, 4 low, and 1 did not respond. Twenty-six of 31 moms had an asthma action plan that they received in the last year and the rest did not remember getting one. Only 6 participants reported having the AAP with them (in their purse, child's book bag, etc.). Twenty-one/26 participants reported having shared their AAP with friends, family, or the child's school.

In Part 2 we tested the comprehension of the icons (with 7 moms). This was done using a paper evaluation in which users were presented with the icons (see in Fig. 1B and C) and asked to rate how well the icon matched our intended definition (translucency). Average translucency ratings for our icons were very high at 92%, or on average greater than 6.4 out of 7, and indicated that intended meanings match across the 11 icons. While the sample for testing icon comprehension was small, we found high agreement among the participants; because these results were similar to previous findings [27] we proceeded to the next phase of the study.

In Part 3, we investigated if icons could enhance participants' ability to manage their child's asthma symptoms. We did this by comparing text-based asthma action plans (T-BAAP, Fig. 1A) to icon-based asthma action plans (I-BAAP, Fig. 1B) using a scenario assessment test used in previous research [27]. We recruited 24 females who were randomly assigned to one of two groups (I-BAAP or T-BAAP). They were asked to use their AAP to explain how they would respond to 5 specific asthma-care scenarios [27], (see Table 1). The researcher recorded participants' responses and time taken to give the response. After each scenario, participants were asked about their confidence in answering the question and the ease of use of the AAP. At the end of the scenarios test, participants were shown the I-BAAP and the T-BAAP side by side and asked which they preferred to manage their child's asthma.

Table 1. Scenario questions and percentage correct (* indicates statistically different values for accuracy and $^\times$ indicates statistically faster responses for correct answers)

	N = 12 in each group	NHLBI	I-BAAP
Q1	Your child wakes up during the night coughing or wheezing. What actions should you take?	58%	*$^\times$92%
Q2	Are there any medications that your child should take every day? If so, what are they and when should they be taken?	92%	83%
Q3	When should you contact your doctor?	83%	$^\times$92%
Q4	Your child has had a cold for several days so you have started him on his quick relief medicine. You notice that he is still coughing and that his fingernails are a blue color. What action(s) should you take?	60%	*$^\times$75%
Q5	What is the name of the quick relief medicine?	66%	67%

Results from part 3 indicated that confidence in response and ease of use was basically at ceiling for both asthma action plans ($\sim$6.5/7 across all scenarios). Two-tailed t-tests were conducted to compare performance between the two AAP groups. Results showed that the difference in average speed for correct responses was significantly faster for I-BAAP users (M = 3.22, SD = 1.23) than for T-BAAP users (M = 6.21, SD = 4.43) (t (22) = 2.1572, p < 0.05, Cohen's d = 0.8807).

The two AAPs led to similar accuracy rates in 3/5 scenarios (see Table 1). However, there was a statistically significant difference between accuracy for scenarios 1 and 4. Results from a post-scenario test question about I-BAAP versus T-BAAP preference also showed that 15/24 participants thought that the I-BAAP would be more helpful in managing their child's asthma than the T-BAAP. All 24 moms were interested in "trying out" a mobile asthma health tool.

In part 4 moms in the waiting room of a local pulmonology clinic were presented with the mobile health (mHealth) tool we developed (Fig. 1C). The researcher instructed participants to explore the tool and to speak their thoughts as they interacted with it and to provide their general impressions of the tool. Each lasted approximately 10 min. Sessions were recorded for further analysis and feedback was organized into themes related to usability issues, reasons for use, understanding of asthma information and suggestions for improvement.

Part 4 data shows that there is general interest and receptiveness in using mHealth tools (all moms wanted to interact with it even if they did not have a smartphone). Part 4 also provided a set of recommendations for improvements to the mHealth tool. These included adding a medication alarm, the ability to personalize calendar information, the ability to send data in the application to their doctor as to give them a sense of how the child was doing before arriving for an appointment. These suggestions may all serve to improve the tool in future iterations. The biggest usability problems that emerged were that only 2/24 moms spontaneously found the navigation menu (which includes links to the triggers page, notifications, and the send plan feature) and the medication tracking feature in the AAP's "green zone".

4 Discussion

Our research bridged three gaps in the literature that can inform future mobile health tool development. First, we focused on mothers of children with asthma rather than adults with asthma [24, 27] or medical professionals [33]. Second, we compared the effectiveness of icon-based (I-B) asthma action plans (AAPs) versus text based (T-B) AAPs in terms of accuracy and speed of response to common asthma symptoms. Previous work had focused on designing I-BAAPs and testing their usability [15] but there had never been an exploration of the comparative strengths for managing asthma symptoms. Third, we gathered feedback for an mHealth tool for managing asthma that can serve to inform design and research with parents of young children.

In our study moms were presented with 5 different asthma management scenarios and provided either a T-BAAP or I-BAAP to answer questions related to these scenarios. We found that the I-BAAP had two main benefits over the T-BAAP. First, it facilitated identifying the relation between symptoms and medication. Images of figures that were coughing, wheezing, (scenario 1) or turning blue (scenario 2) allowed moms to easily identify the correct medicine to administer. Second, the I-BAAP led to significantly faster response times in 3 of the 5 scenarios and those faster speeds were associated with the correct response. Thus, moms that used the I-BAAP compared to moms' with the traditional AAP responded to asthma management scenarios more quickly and more accurately. We also found that the mom with the lowest educational level and lowest confidence in her ability to manage her child's asthma benefitted most by the I-BAAP.

The asthma management test indicated a trend where participants who used the I-BAAP had slightly lower accuracy on the question that asked for the name of the quick relief medication. This resonates with other health-related findings [4, 10, 15] that pairing text and images is helpful. This suggests that in future iterations of an I-BAAP, the medication icons should include larger or clearer text to make the medication name more identifiable.

Our study differed from other research that showed that icons had a profound impact on processing health information [4, 15]. This could be related to the fact that parents of children are more engaged in the management of their child's illness than adults are in their own health management. Support for this notion comes from that fact that moms in our study had high confidence in their ability to take care of their children and in their ability to communicate with the physicians. We also did not find that non-white participants benefited more from icon-based versus text-based health information [4]. This likely reflects that fact that education mediates the benefits of including icons in health information and our participants had high educational attainment.

Our study faces several limitations, which in turn provides ample opportunity for future research. While we did not intend to exclusively recruit females, however, only moms were present at the clinic where this study took place. There is no reason to believe that dads would have performed differently than moms but this is still an open question. Another limitation includes the small size and makeup of our sample population. Future studies should focus on participants with low literacy and low confidence in their ability to care for children with asthma (e.g., parents of newly diagnosed children or baby sitters or even the children themselves). Our results replicate findings that [27] I-BAAPs can be used to identify the correct actions to take when presented with asthma scenarios. However, there is no evidence that performance in the scenario test is related to asthma management in the real world. Future studies should deploy I-BAAP vs. T-BAAP and see if the advantages we noted (improved speed and accuracy) translate to dealing with asthma exacerbation at home or school.

Our study shows that while there may be a variety of mobile asthma tools [16–18] there is still much work for the HCI community in this space. For example, the technology utilization survey showed that while 66% of participants surf the web on their phone, only 10% use their phone to help manage their child's asthma. Likewise, 79% of the participants reported that their action plan was away from them, but 87% owned mobile phones. Thus, a mobile tool maybe a way to app could increase accessibility to the action plan. Our study shows that parents are open and receptive to mobile health tools that include both AAP and other features to manage their child's asthma and to share that information with other caregivers (teachers, other family members and doctors). These tools can also mediate communication between parents and doctors between scheduled visits. Previous research [34] showed that doctors communicate more clearly when using an I-BAAP than a T-BAAP. This maybe yet another reason to include I-BAAPS in the mHealth tool.

There are a number of implications from this study for both designers and researchers. One recommendation for icon designers is that they use Roberts et al.'s measure of translucency, how well icons matched their meaning [27]. This metric has now been successfully used across various patient populations in the UK and US. Our study also provides evidence that designers should include text to underscore important information in icon-based health tools. We found that some of the moms preferred the T-BAAP because it had more information than the I-BAAP. Likewise, we found that the one scenario where moms had to identify the name of the medicine was slower for the I-BAAP ground (where there were no labels). A take-away for researchers is that it is important to include both subjective and objective measures of usability. For example, we found ceiling effects for subjective measures "ease of use" even for scenarios where objective data (accuracy and response time) showed that parents were not answering accurately. Thus, it is not enough to ask users if a design or prototype works but to have them show you that they can use it.

5 Conclusion

Our study informs future directions for mHealth research with parents of children with asthma. The fact that two-thirds of the participants preferred the I-BAAP over the T-BAAP for managing their child's asthma suggests that this is an area rich with opportunities. Our study suggests that I-BAAPs may be beneficial in allowing parent to more quickly and accurately react to their child's asthma symptoms. Also, that it is important to include text in icon-based informational material. However, these results are limited by the fact that they were not conducted in the "real world". Broader implications include the fact that it is important for researchers to include both subjective and objective measure of usability. Specifically we found that self-report measures of "confidence" and "ease of use" were at times uncorrelated with accuracy of response.

Acknowledgments. We thank all of the participants for taking the time to aid us with our research.

References

1. Adams, R., Appleton, S., Wilson, D., Ruffin, R.: Participatory decision making, asthma action plans, and use of asthma medication: a population survey. J. Asthma, **42**, 673–678 (n.d.)
2. Annor, F., Bayakly, A., Vajani, M., Drenzek, C., Lopez F., O'Connor J., Yancey, M.: Georgia Asthma Prevalence Report. Georgia Department of Public Health, Health Protection, Epidemiology, Chronic Disease, Healthy Behaviors and Injury Epidemiology Section, December 2013
3. Arguel, A., Lau, A., Dennis, S., Liaw, S., Coiera, E.: An internet intervention to improve asthma management: rationale and protocol of a randomized controlled trial. JMIR Res. Protoc., E28 (n.d.)
4. Austin, P.E., Matlack, R., Dunn, K.A., Kosler, C., Brown, C.K.: Discharge instructions: do illustrations help our patients understand them? Ann. Emerg. Med. **25**, 317–320 (1995)
5. Cairns, P., Cox, A.L.: Research Methods for Human-Computer Interaction. Cambridge University Press, Cambridge (2008)
6. CDC, National Center for Environmental Health, Division of Environmental Hazards and health Effects: Asthma's impact on the nation - data from the CDC National Asthma Control Program (2015). www.cdc.gov/asthma. Also, Global Asthma report: http://ginasthma.org/wp-content/uploads/2016/04/GINA-2016-main-report_tracked.pdf
7. Chaudry, B., Connelly, K., Siek, K., Welch, J.: Mobile interface design for low-literacy populations. In: IHI 2012, 28–30 January 2012. Copyright 2012 ACM (2012)
8. Curtis, L., Wolf, M., Weiss, K., Grammer, L.: The impact of health literacy and socioeconomic status on asthma disparities. J. Asthma **49**, 178–183 (2012)
9. D'Auria, J.: All about asthma: top resources for children, adolescents, and their families. J. Pediatr. Health Care **27**(4) (2013)
10. Delp, C., Jones, J.: Communicating information to patients: the use of cartoon illustrations to improve comprehension of instructions. Acad. Emerg. Med. **3**, 264–270 (1996)
11. Expert Panel Report 3 (EPR-3): Guidelines for the diagnosis and management of asthma-summary report 2007. J. Allergy and Clin. Immunol. **120**(5) (2007)

12. Gillette, C., Carpenter, D., Ayala, G., Williams, D., Davis, S., Tudor, G., Yeatts, K., Sleath, B.: How often do providers discuss asthma action plans with children? Analysis of transcripts of medical visits. Clin. Pediatr. **52**, 1161–1167 (2013)

13. Gittins, D.: Icon-based human-computer interaction. Int. J. Man-Mach. Stud. **24**, 519–543 (1986)

14. Gupta, S., Wan, F., Hall, S., Straus, S.: An asthma action plan created by physician, educator and patient online collaboration with usability and visual design optimization. Respiration **85**, 406–415 (n.d.)

15. Houts, P.S., Doak, C.C., Doak, L.G., Loscalzo, M.J.: The role of pictures in improving health communication: a review of research on attention, comprehension, recall, and adherence. Patient Educ. Couns. **61**, 173–190 (2006)

16. Huckvale, K., Car, J.: Implementation of mobile health tools. J. Am. Med. Assoc. **311**(14) (2014)

17. Huckvale, K., Morrison, C., Ouyang, J., Ghaghda, A., Car, J.: The evolution of mobile apps for asthma: an updated systematic assessment of content and tools. BMC Med. **13**, 58 (2015)

18. Huckvale, K., Car, M., Morrison, C., Car, J.: Apps for asthma self-management: a systematic assessment of content and tools. BMC Med. **10**, 144 (2012)

19. Jeong, H.Y., Arriaga, R.I.: Using an ecological framework to design mobile technologies for pediatric asthma management. In: Proceedings of the 11th International Conference on Human-Computer Interaction with Mobile Devices and Services, p. 17 (2009)

20. Jeong, H., Yun, T., Sung, J., Abowd, G., Arriaga, R., Hayes, G.: Act collectively: opportunities for technologies to support low-income children with asthma. In: Proceedings of HCI 2011 - 25th BCS Conference on Human Computer Interaction, pp. 413–420 (2011)

21. Kascak, L., Rebola, C.B., Braunstein, R., Sanford, J.A.: Icon design to improve communication of health information to older adults. Commun. Des. Quart. **2**(1), 6–32 (2013)

22. Rivera, K., Cooke, N.J., Bauhs, J.A.: The effects of emotional icons on remote communication. In: Tauber, M.J. (ed.) Conference Companion on Human Factors in Computing Systems, CHI 1996, pp. 99–100. ACM, New York (1996)

23. Larson, E., Goel, M., Boriello, G., Heltshe, S., Rosenfeld, M., Patel S.: Spirosmart using a microphone to measure lung function on a mobile phone. In: Proceedings of the 2012 ACM Conference on Ubiquitous Computing, UbiComp 2012, pp. 280–289. ACM, New York (2012). http://dx.doi.org/10.1145/2370216.2370261

24. Licskai, C., Sands, T.W., Ferrone, M.: Development and pilot testing of a mobile health solution for asthma self-management: asthma action-plan smartphone application pilot study. Can. Respir. J. **20**(4), 301–306 (2013)

25. Lieu, T., Quesenberry, C., Capra, A., Sorel, M., Martin, K., Mendoza, G.: Outpatient management practices associated with reduced risk of pediatric asthma hospitalization and emergency department visits. Pediatrics **100**(3) (1997)

26. Ring, N., Jepson, R., Hoskins, G., Wilson, C., Pinnock, H., Sheikh, A., Wyke, S.: Understanding what helps or hinders asthma action plan use: a systematic review and synthesis of the qualitative literature. Patient Educ. Couns. **85**, E131–E143 (n.d.)

27. Roberts, N., Mohamed, Z., Wong, P., Johnson, M., Loh, L., Partridge, M.: The development and comprehensibility of a pictorial asthma action plan. Patient Educ. Couns. **74**, 12–18 (n.d.)

28. Rudd, R., Kirsch, I., Yamamoto, K.: Literacy and Health in America – Policy Information Report. Educational Testing Service (2004). www.ets.org/research/pic

29. Saver, C.: Overcoming low health literacy: helping your patient understand. OR Manag. **28**(6) (2012)

30. Tan, N.C., Chen, Z., Soo, W.F., Ngoh, A.H., Tai, B.C.: Effects of a written asthma action plan on caregivers' management of children with asthma: a cross-sectional questionnaire survey. Prim. Care Respir. J. **22**(2), 188 (2013)
31. United States Environmental Protection Agency. (N.D.) Children's Environmental Health Disparities: Black and African American Children and Asthma. permanent.access.gpo.gov. Accessed 22 Sept 2015
32. Worden, A., Walker, N., Bharat, K., Hudson, S.: Making computers easier for older adults to use: area cursors and sticky icons. In: Proceedings of the ACM SIGCHI Conference on Human factors in computing systems, CHI 1997 (1997)
33. World Health Organization statistics. http://www.who.int/respiratory/asthma/en/
34. Yin, H.S., Gupta, R.S., Tomopoulos, S., et al.: A low- literacy asthma action plan to improve provider asthma counseling: a randomized study. Pediatrics **137**(1), e20150468 (2016)
35. Yun, T.J., Joeng, H.Y., Hill, T.D., Lesnick, B., Brown, R., Abowd, G.D., Arriaga, R.I.: Using SMS to provide continuous assessment and improve health outcomes for children with asthma. In: Proceedings of the 2nd ACM SIGHIT International Health Informatics Symposium, IHI 2012, pp. 621–630 (2012). doi:10.1145/2110363.2110432
36. Yun, T.J., Arriaga, R.I.: A text message a day keeps the pulmonologist away. In: Proceedings of the SIGCHI Conference on Human Factors in Computing Systems, CHI 2013, pp. 1769–1778. ACM, New York (2013). doi:10.1145/2470654.2466233
37. Yun, T.J., Arriaga, R.I.: SMS is my BFF: positive impact of a texting intervention on low-income children with asthma. In: Proceedings of the 10th EAI International Conference on Pervasive Computing Technologies for Healthcare, Pervasive Health 2016 (2016). ISBN 978-1-63190-051-8

Keeping Children Safe Online: Understanding the Concerns of Carers of Children with Autism

Mike Just[⊠] and Tessa Berg

School of Mathematical and Computer Sciences,
Heriot-Watt University, Edinburgh, UK
{m.just, t.berg}@hw.ac.uk

Abstract. Children with autism spectrum disorder (ASD) have difficulty making sense of the world, and have an impaired ability to socially interact. This impacts their ability to understand inappropriate behaviour or recognize dangers online. Because of this, parent carers of children with ASD struggle to protect their children online. In this paper, we report on the results of two workshops with 16 parent carers of children with ASD in which we used rich pictures and group discussions to identify carers' concerns and protection methods. Our results indicate that carers have significant challenges with protecting their children, who they describe as "devious" and "obsessive", though also "clever" and "naive". In addition, carers often rely on physical controls and rules, which meet with limited success. From our results, we highlight the importance of educational approaches, and recommend the development of educational nudging tools to assist children, and to keep them safe online.

Keywords: Autism spectrum disorder, ASD · Carer · Caregiver · Safety · Security · Privacy · Protection

1 Introduction

Technology has advanced at a significant rate over the past few decades, and it is challenging for most people to understand what is required to protect themselves online [18, 32]. This rapid evolution can also make it difficult for older generations to keep pace with their younger counterparts. Within a family, it can therefore be challenging for parents to stay apprised of their children's activities, and especially, to ensure their protection. This is a particular challenge for parents when children have access to a wide range of Internet-enabled devices, and connect to a variety of people online [7]. These challenges can be further exacerbated for marginalised users [10], such as older people, and people with disabilities such as visual impairments or conditions such as autism spectrum disorder (ASD) [1, 6, 20]. According to Benford [4], autism affects an individual's social interaction, communication and imagination.

In this paper we study security concerns and protection needs (we define security broadly to include areas such as safety and privacy) of carers of children with ASD who access online services through home PCs, mobile phones, tablets, etc. Security

© IFIP International Federation for Information Processing 2017
Published by Springer International Publishing AG 2017. All Rights Reserved
R. Bernhaupt et al. (Eds.): INTERACT 2017, Part III, LNCS 10515, pp. 34–53, 2017.
DOI: 10.1007/978-3-319-67687-6_3

technologies that might otherwise be used by carers (e.g., parental controls) to protect their children are often designed for security, not usability [26], and therefore may not take into account the special needs of some users. With ASD, children can display obsessive behaviour with internet-capable technology and they are also particularly exposed to strangers misrepresenting themselves online. In addition, they can have difficulty predicting what the technology will do, the risks associated with sharing information, and how others may perceive shared information [4]. This makes ASD children a potential 'at risk', marginalised community of internet users. Responsibility for the protection of childrens' online activities remains solely with their carer, who undertakes this role, along with caring for their physical and emotional needs.

There has been significant research into the behaviour of children with ASD spanning over five decades [2, 13, 23] with more recent innovative research looking at technological solutions to aid well-being and experience [16, 17, 28, 29, 33]. In some cases, this has resulted in related benefits for parent carers, e.g., by showing parents a child's perspective [24]. Others have specifically examined the needs of carers of people with ASD, though this has tended to focus on specialist carers such as therapists [19]. Related work has investigated the needs of more informal carers, though not for ASD [30]. In terms of security protection, researchers have investigated options for helping people with special needs using assistive technologies, such as for people with ASD [20], for people with visual impairments [1, 9], and for older adults [6]. However, there is little research that focuses on understanding and supporting carers' security concerns for their children. One exception is studies on the relationship between parents and teens for security and privacy [7, 34]. Cranor et al. [7] investigated the different perspectives that parents and their teenage children have on privacy and technology, and they studied parents' use of some technology, such as monitoring software. However, in cases where children have special needs, such as children with ASD, there can be new challenges, and given the wide range of the autism spectrum, families could face unique challenges requiring varying levels of support.

Thus, our aim was to investigate the challenges of carers of children with ASD, and the methods they use to address these challenges in order to protect their children online. To achieve this aim we sought to answer the following research questions:

RQ1: How do carers characterise the online behaviour of their autistic children, and how do the characteristics affect the children's online security?
RQ2: What are the challenges to carers' ability to protect autistic children online?

To answer our research questions we conducted two workshops with 16 parent carers of children with ASD in which we used rich pictures (RPs) [3] and focus group discussions to gather carer responses. While our focus was on ASD, we felt that our results could be more broadly applicable. Our use of RPs to augment a traditional focus group discussion was motivated by similar approaches for novel user engagements to better understand their security and privacy needs [11, 14].

Our main contribution here is to provide novel insight into a carer's experience of, and perspective on the online activity of children with ASD. Additionally, and drawing partly on these insights, we discuss design implications for developing supportive tools for carers and children with ASD. We believe this to be the first study of the challenges of protecting an autistic child online from the perspective of a parent carer.

2 Background

Autism spectrum disorder (ASD) is a permanent developmental disability that affects all aspects of communication, usually resulting in an impaired ability to socially interact. People with ASD often have difficulty making sense of the world around them and thus can have a variety of care needs. Those with ASD often have an almost obsessive desire for 'sameness of environment' and a constant unchanging daily routine [2]. Many of those on the autism spectrum have unique and diverse abilities in visual skills, music and academic skills. Others have significant learning disabilities and are unable to live independently. People with ASD come from all nationalities and cultural, religious and social backgrounds. There are around 700,000 people in the UK diagnosed with autism with a majority of male over female [5]. Online communication devices, computer programs, apps and other technological resources can be extremely beneficial tools for individuals with autism. There has been considerable data collection and research into autistic online behaviour with evidence to suggest that the internet offers a 'comfortable space more suited to the autistic communication style' [13]. Benford [4] suggests that the introduction of the internet has encouraged the autistic community to better communicate with each other via chatrooms and bulletin boards and thus social isolation is reduced. However she also advises of negative issues for autistic people online suggesting they may be particularly vulnerable to individuals misrepresenting themselves or to the possibility of over-reliance on computer-mediated interaction resulting in an exacerbation of obsessive behaviour and withdrawal from face-to-face interaction. Davis [8] sees internet use as a continuum with healthy use on one side and pathological use on the other with problematic use of the internet being less of a product of the technology and rather the responsibility of the individual. Hartikainen et al. [15] suggest that restriction and monitoring controls are required however they stress the importance of a trusting parent-child relationship and collaboration of both parties for any design solution.

There are several studies that investigate the efforts of parents to protect their children's security and privacy online. Rode [25] performed an ethnographic study with 14 households and categorized the households based on how security roles were allocated in the family, and described a set of five rules that parents used to protect their children online. We identify similar rules in our study. Yardi and Bruckman [35] discovered a diversity of parental approaches, with parents often struggling to find the right balance between control and independence for their children. Cranor et al. [7] examined the different privacy perspectives of parents and their teens and found differences, especially for access to text messages. Further, they highlight communication problems as a key challenge, and for parents this often resulted from their lack of experience with some technology. Wisniewski et al. [34] examined the effects of different strategies by parents to protect their children's privacy, finding that direct intervention (e.g., using parental controls) reduced child risk but at the cost or limiting the benefits of a child's online interactions. However, the above research has not tended to focus on children with special needs, such as children with ASD.

In terms of caregiver support. Kientz et al. [19] focused on assisting caregivers with their support of children with ASD, where caregivers referred to therapists (e.g., behavioural, occupational, speech) who were external to the child's home and who are trained to treat children with ASD. They investigated technology solutions used to gather information about a child's behaviour (e.g., wearable sensors) in order to assist a caregiver in their treatment plan. Marcu et al. took a similar approach for families [24]. However, in general there is little focus on supporting family carers, especially in terms of their protection of children with ASD online.

3 Methodology

We recruited carers of children with ASD through a local autism support centre. The centre offers people with ASD, and their families, information, advice and local support. As well as acting as an information hub, the centre works closely with other groups and agencies, collaborating to understand and respond to the needs of the autism community. We advertised on the centre's Facebook page, inviting carers of children with ASD to one of two 1 to 1.5 h focus group sessions (early afternoon and late afternoon on the same day) on internet security in order to discuss the challenges they face with protecting their children online. Participants registered directly with the centre. Carers who participated in the workshop were compensated with the equivalent of about 30 US dollars. Prior to contacting the centre, our project was approved by our institution's ethics committee.

Each carer participated in one of two identically-run four-stage sessions. In Stage 1, once participants read a short project description and signed a consent form, we collected age and gender information, and asked participants to provide the age of the persons with ASD who they care for, and their relationship to them.

In Stage 2, we introduced the purpose of the session by presenting two questions that we wanted the carers to consider, under the heading "Internet Security":

- Q1: What are your concerns related to the security of the person you care for?
- Q2: What do you currently do to protect the person you care for?

To stimulate input we made some initial suggestions on areas that groups might consider exploring: passwords, sharing accounts, posting online, making friends and purchasing online. Carers were asked to respond to the questions by drawing their answers with pictures, and 2–3 examples of previous RPs (from areas unrelated to security or child protection) were briefly shown to participants. Participants were split into small groups of 3–4, lead to separate rooms in the centre, and they were provided with a number of coloured markers and a flip chart.

In Stage 3 each group of carers drew their rich picture (RP) responses to the two questions. A RP is a physical picture drawn by many hands which encourages discussion and debate supporting empathetic understanding within groups [3]. Groups were asked for all group members to draw on a sheet (size: 32 × 23") of poster paper at the same time. We facilitated the sessions with limited input to encourage discussion amongst group members, an approach termed 'eductive observation' [3]. An example of one of the RPs produced from the sessions is shown in Fig. 1.

In Stage 4 we brought all groups into in a single room, and asked each group to gather beside their pictures, which the facilitators had pinned to the wall, and discuss

Fig. 1. Rich picture (size: 32 × 23") example from workshops.

what they drew and why. Each group did this in succession. This discussion was facilitator-led with carers encouraged to share stories and verbally enhance their picture drawings. The discussion was audio recorded and later transcribed.

Analysis of transcripts (from Stage 4) and RPs (from Stage 3) was achieved by first logically separating the data for each into two key analysis themes, based on the two questions that we posed to the carers: carer concerns and carer protections. The transcripts were then analysed and coded using a grounded theory approach [12] with inductive content analysis [27]. Each of two researchers first independently reviewed and coded the transcripts in order to ensure inter-coder reliability [22], once for concerns and once for protections. The researchers then met to agree on a coding system, after which they re-coded the transcripts. The researchers met again to agree on the final transcript coding, afterwhich the final codes were recorded.

The RPs were also coded using the same coding system. Icons were isolated and categorised when they represented an issue, action or emotion that was particularly significant, expressive, sensitive or descriptive. One researcher took notes during the sessions that were later used to link each RP with different discussions from the transcript. As with Bell et al. [3] we looked specifically for instances where the pictures communicated additional knowledge to the transcribed description. For each transcript code, we recorded which had a RP associated with it, and which did not.

4   Results

In this section we discuss our participant carers, followed by results on Carer Concerns, Carer Protections, and Carer Rich Pictures. For our concerns and protections, we highlight some of the individual carer pictures in Figs. 2 and 3 (p. 14).

A total of 16 carers participated in the two sessions of our study (see Table 1), 14 of whom were female (88%). The seven carers from session 1 (S1) were split into two groups, while the 9 carers in session 2 (S2) were split into three groups. The most

Table 1. Workshop carers.

#	Session & Group #	Gender	Age range	Relationship between carer and child(ren) with ASD	ASD age
C1	S1, G1	F	41–50	Mother/Son	12
C2	S1, G1	F	51–60	Mother/Son	25
C3	S1, G1	F	31–40	Mother/Daughter	10
C4	S1, G1	F	41–50	Mother/Son	19
C5	S1, G2	F	41–50	Mother/Daughter	12
C6	S1, G2	F	41–50	Mother/Son	12
C7	S1, G2	F	41–50	Mother to 3 ASD/Unknown	9, 14, 16
C8	S2, G2	F	41–50	Mother/Son	8
C9	S2, G2	F	41–50	Mother/Son	14
C10	S2, G2	M	51–60	Grandfather/Granddaughter	9
C11	S2, G3	F	31–40	Mother/Son	11
C12	S2, G3	F	41–50	Mother/Son	16
C13	S2, G3	F	51–60	Grandmother/Granddaughter	9
C14	S2, G1	F	31–40	Mother/Son	9
C15	S2, G1	F	31–40	Step-Mother/Unknown	8
C16	S2, G1	M	41–50	Step-Father/Unknown	9

frequent age range for the carers was from 41–50 years with 9 carers. Most of the carer-child relationships were parent-to-child (12; 75%) with some step-parent (2; 12.5%) and grandparent (2; 12.5%). The carers were attending to the needs of 18 ASD young people between the ages of 8–25 (mean = 12, med = 11.5).

4.1 Carer Concerns Results Analysis

From the audio transcripts, we coded 103 concerns that we grouped into 5 categories (see Table 2). Below, we summarise the results for each category of concern.

Table 2. Carer concerns. 'RP' = # codes with rich pics; 'No RP' = # codes without rich pics

Category	Concern area	# of coded concerns	RP	No RP
Buying online	Inappropriate spending, getting access, independent spending	20	10	10
Meeting online	Meeting strangers, being bullied	15	11	4
Posting online	Posting inappropriately: family, friends, self	10	9	1
Lack of solutions	Lack of caregiver skill, inadequate solutions, unable to protect	26	11	15
Inappropriate behaviour	Inappropriate accounts, accessing material, & spending, posting	32	18	14

Buying Online. There were three concern areas for buying online with examples of inappropriate spending, and carer concern for children's spending (9 of 20 codes).

- C7: *"and my middle one had spent £2500 within 24 h on two separate cards of mine, on FIFA points."*
- C9: *"if my son had access I would be millions pounds in debt never mind thousands of pounds in debt."*

Further, carers noted examples of the persistent and addictive behaviour of their children to spend, even if unsuccessful, when the spend allowed them to meet other goals, such as the collection of points.

- C7: *"I cancelled my cards that day because at first I thought my card had been stolen. So it's still the wrong cards that are in, but he now I've realised [...] he's still buying transactions with the cards, the same cards, but they're failing. But he's found a glitch in the system where he then asks for a refund to get out of the fact that he's used a failed card, but the system still thinks it's OK for him to have the points so he's still getting the points."*

In these cases, it was difficult for children to understand the consequences of their actions, with carers highlighting the misunderstandings of their children, and the challenges of explaining some aspects of spending to a child with ASD.

- C14: *"I said to him 'you can buy this' and he wanted to get to the next stage, so he went and got it and bought it! And then I was like 'But [NAME], that is my money, where am I going to get that from?' and he goes 'It's ok mummy you get interest, cause if you leave your money in the bank the interest comes and you'll get it all back!' So a small piece of information that he's very right about doesn't mean what he thinks, it doesn't interpret the same way. So when you're speaking to him you have to be aware of that."*

Secondly, carers identified how their children gain access to spend (7 of 20 codes):

- C1: *"So one concern is buying things online, so [NAME]'s quite astute when it comes to the internet, so he could quite easily work out how to use a debit card or anything like that."*

Similar to their inability to understand inappropriate spending, carers noted their children's misconceptions for inappropriately accessing the carers' account information, and the further challenges for carers in terms of dealing with this behaviour:

- C14: *"And we've often been places, like in Asda and I'm putting in my PIN and he goes 'Mum, is your number still 1234?' And I'm like 'It WAS!' I stand there sometimes and think 'Oh, shit - I can't remember my number' - I've changed it that often, and you have to go back up to the bank [...] he just needs to see your fingers moving and he'll tell you what code it is. But he couldn't spell his surname."*

Thirdly, carers noted concerns regarding the ability of their older children to be able to independently spend in order to manage their well-being (4 of 20 codes).

- C7: *"look at the bigger picture for his future, and his own money in the financial sense, he could just go through any money he's got on this."*

Meeting Online. There were two concern areas related to meeting online. Firstly, carers expressed concern regarding who their children meet online (9 of 15 codes), particularly people who might impersonate young children.

- C8: *"my fear is that the hidden people, the deceit and danger that when they do go on they say that they are an eight-year-old the same as him."* (see Fig. 2(b2))

Carers also noted the particular vulnerability for their children as they are less capable to recognise such deceit (see Fig. 2(d2)).

- C13: *"It's [...] the vulnerability because there are people out here who know what they're doing - victimisation - and obviously our kids are an easy target."*

Secondly, additional concerns were raised regarding children socialising online, and the increased risk to their children of being bullied (6 of 15). One carer noted the challenges that their children have in terms of appropriately adding friends:

- C2: *"Basically what it is - if he's on Facebook and he has a load of friends on Facebook, and then he adds somebody and then there's somebody that wants to friend his friends. That's a danger because one was saying really inappropriate remarks and they were taking it out on him, defriending him because they had allowed somebody to friend him."* (see Fig. 2(f2)).

In another example, children became the target of ridicule based on material they posted (see Fig. 2(e1)).

- C12: *"You know, being the butt of the jokes, he tends to go on Instagram and again a lot of it's to do with cars, the Grand Prix etcetera, but there's grid girls, so they're quite, I mean they've got clothes on but some of them can be quite, you know. So somebody likes a lot of things, so when he's added friends from school, they've commented on how he likes that kind of thing."*

This has sometimes resulted in children being rejected online (C12: *"you know he's been booted offline"*, see Fig. 2(d1)).

Posting Online. In terms of posting online, concerns were raised about posting with regard to three groups of people: family, friends, themselves. Firstly, carers raised concerns about their children posting information, primarily photos, of family or friends (6 of 10 codes).

- C1: *"Yeah, I've said to her about those pictures - don't put pictures up."*
- C3: *"And also I said don't put pictures on of your friends because their parents might not want their child to be on."*

Secondly, carers noted concerns related to the availability of their children's own photos, and related information (e.g., emojis) that might be associated with the photos (4 of 10 codes):

- C3: *"And also Facebook, they were warned not to check in anywhere in case somebody sees their picture."*

Lack of Solutions. There were three concern areas related to a lack of solutions. Firstly, carers lamented their lack of skills and experience, especially when compared to their children (8 of 26 codes):

- C1: *"I stupidly don't know how to protect the account, thankfully her older sister does and she's sorted all that for me."*
- C4: *"I have difficulty with is I don't know enough about the security, and putting passwords in, it's such a vast thing that I don't know if that would be possible so that would be my concern."*

Secondly, carers highlighted the inadequacy of existing solutions, indicating that while they did implement some solutions, they were frustrated at their inadequacy, or their own inability to make the solutions work for them (12 of 26 codes). This was particularly evident in terms of various types of filters or parental controls.

- C7: *"so that's the only thing I can do, is switch off the WiFi."* (see Fig. 2(e2))
- C8: *"Some of these things are X-rated. How do you ... you can't control that. There's nothing you can ... There's no parental control you can put on a music video. So that's one of the things that affects me."*
- C11: *"all the links that come down the side - one day it was lesbians that came up and he clicked on the video. Now he was in the same room as us and we knew what it was and we could get it off him, but I don't even know how to set."*

One carer further highlighted the lack of standards across devices, and the negative impact this has for carers for remembering, and properly setting, privacy protections:

- C9: *"but then the phones have different privacy settings as well. So you can't access the same things on a phone that you can do on a computer."*

Thirdly, carers highlighted general concerns related to their difficulties with communicating with, or influencing their autistic children (6 of 26 codes):

- C1: *"Ben just doesn't seem to have a barrier, he'll speak to anybody, as long as it's not to peers."*
- C6: *"He's very very private, even with other people he doesn't like other people knowing, if he was doing a presentation in school about himself he'd refuse to do it, because he doesn't want people to know about him. So it's very difficult to keep tabs on what he's doing."*

Inappropriate Behaviour. We coded behaviours as inappropriate if the behaviour went against the stated wishes of the parent. This included codes for concerns already covered above (statements could be assigned multiple codes), related to inappropriate spending and posting of material online, and to two additional areas: creating accounts, and accessing inappropriate material. Whether the behaviour was intentional or not is difficult to determine, moreso for children with ASD.

Firstly, carers expressed concern about the ease with which their children could create online accounts, even if the child was forbidden to do so.

- C1: *"we disable a Google account but he just goes back in and can do another one. Or he can go and make another Facebook account. And he knows that if his date of birth doesn't work, he just puts my date of birth in!"*
- C9: *"Cos my sister in law set it up for and I was a wee bit, I wasn't very happy about it but my sister-in-law had it set up for her before I could even say I don't want that for her at this moment in time so."*

Secondly, carers expressed concern regarding the ability of their children to access to inappropriate material.

- C4: *"has access to all the information that's on the internet, including drugs, so we had a bit of a misfortune with that."*
- C5: *"And also, I drew a bunny rabbit because I can't draw Mario and Luigi! But you watch a video on YouTube of Mario and Luigi or something, quite innocent, and the language in the background by the men who are playing the game and demonstrating it is, absolutely horrendous. And swearing ... so you think it's something that's OK, but it's not."* (see Fig. 2(a2))
- C9: *"On my son's iPad which I didn't even think he'd be able to access [X-rated material]. And my mouth fell open. I was like that, oh my goodness."*

In some cases, in an attempt to convey a behaviour that is inappropriate to their children, parents can struggle with verbalising, though their thoughts were better captured by their picture.

- C5: *"Don't put on pictures that are not suitable of us, or don't look at pictures that are ... you know."* (see Fig. 2(a1))

Concerns Summary. In many cases, carers identified actions by their children for which the carers wanted more knowledge or control. Throughout, we asked carers to confirm that the challenges were specific to their children with ASD. This was confirmed by the carers, and while the concerns bear some resemblance to cases with children without ASD, carers noted clear differences, e.g., C7: *"I think the vulnerability, they just don't see danger, they can't sense danger. They can't see the big picture, because they tunnel-vision, it's black and white, no grey areas."* This should not be surprising and is reflective of the wide spectrum within ASD. The difference, in most cases, comes in terms of the challenges of protecting the child and influencing their behaviour, discussed further below.

4.2   Carer Protections Results Analysis

From the workshop transcripts, we coded 69 protections that we grouped into 3 categories (see Table 3). Below, we summarise the results for each protection category.

Control Access. Carers highlighted four approaches to controlling online access for their children. Firstly, carers indicated that they use physical controls in order to limit the online access of their children (10 of 27 codes), such as turning off WiFi hubs, and

Table 3. Carer protections. 'RP' = # codes with rich pics; 'No RP' = # codes with no pics

Category	Protection approach	# of coded protections	RP	No RP
Control access	Physical control, hidden information, filters, disable accounts	27	14	13
Monitor	Specific observation, shared space or passwords, first pass, general observation	21	6	15
Instruct	Rules, teaching, conditional	21	8	13

taking away devices such as smartphones and iPads so that they are not accessible in areas such as bedrooms and dinner tables.

- C1: *"how I protect my wee boy is I take the hub away. I have to take the internet hub off so I disconnect it."* (see Fig. 3 (a1))
- C5: *"We also do no iPads at the dinner table. We're all 5 of us at the dinner table, if they're on their own then that's fine but when we're having the 5 there's no iPads."* (see Fig. 3(d1))
- C7: *"my kids aren't allowed any gadgets - they've got no TVs, XBoxes or anything - in their rooms."*

With regard to controlling the use of devices, carers also highlighted some challenges in terms of maintaining control:

- C5: *"I have confiscated the iPad, so her answer was 'Well I'll just use YouTube and use the internet on my phone. So I confiscated the phone, so then on went the computer, at which point that had to be confiscated and she now has a Fire box on her TV so she can get YouTube on her TV!"*

Secondly, carers indicated that they try to hide information, such as passwords and bank card details, and also make use of one-time vouchers (6 of 27 codes).

- C5: *"When my kids use like iTunes or Google Play, I never ever put my bank account details in, I always use the cards, the vouchers."*
- C8: *"hidden passwords still work."*

Thirdly, carers indicated that they filter their children's access, either by content, or time-of-day (4 of 27 codes).

- C5: *"We have a thing set up where Netflix and things, that anything that's a PG is available all day but beyond 9 o'clock at night then my oldest daughter can access 15s and things. Which is good because it means we're not worrying about Netflix during the day."*
- C6: *"The settings on the iPad are all, he can't access anything 18-plus or anything like on YouTube."*

Fourthly, carers also indicated that they will sometimes disable their children's online accounts (2 of 27 codes), though these measures can have limited effects.

In the remaining cases (5 of 27 codes), carers indicated that they control access, but did not share a specific approach, e.g., C11: *"We've just got him off YouTube now"*.

Monitor. Carers described several ways in which they monitor their children that we grouped into four areas. Firstly, they will use (specific) observation of their children's devices (5 of 21 codes):

- C9: *"but I do now and again check his iPad to see what he's been up to, so far he's been all right. It's been fine."*

Secondly, carers use a shared space for their computers (4 of 21 codes), though this has some challenges in terms of maintaining consistent supervision.

- C7: *"but our main PC is downstairs in a communal area, and we all kind of share it."* (see Fig. 3(c1))
- C14: *"But even if you're in the same room with him - I'm probably in the next room bathing a child or out in the kitchen making something for tomorrow, so even though he's in a public area, I'm very rarely there, so he might as well be in his bedroom with the door closed at times."*

Carers also used shared passwords, where they knew the passwords used by their children (2 of 21 codes):

- C5: *"We also have it where I know all my childrens' passwords, and they don't know when I'm going to check but it's something we do."*

Thirdly, carers indicated that they will sometimes take a 'first pass' before their children visit a particular site, in order to ensure that it's appropriate (3 of 21 codes):

- C14: *"But before he does that, I have to sit through it to make sure there's no bad language, or there's nobody asking people to do anything."*

Fourthly, participants provided examples of general observations (7 of 21 codes), indicating that they intend to monitor their child, but were not specific about how:

- C12: *"it's about allowing him certain things because he is of that age but obviously we need to keep tabs on things."*

Instruct. Carers indicated that they would instruct their children in order to protect them, which took the form of rules, teaching, or establishing conditions. Firstly, carers indicated that they used rules (15 of 21 codes), which included the controlled use of devices (discussed under "control access" above), as well as in response to concerns related to meeting and posting online.

- C3: *"And also Facebook, they were warned not to check in anywhere in case somebody sees their picture."*

Secondly, there was also some indication from carers that they attempt to educate their children as well (3 of 21 codes), though no specific methods were given.

- C15: *"you try to teach them, but it's a hit or a miss whether they take in on board."*

Carers also tried to enforce conditional rules, rather than absolute rules.

- C14: *"If he wants to go on the iPad there's a few rules - homework has to be done, then he can have it."*

Protections Summary. Carers identified several protection measures, and highlighted their limited effectiveness. For the most part, the protections used by carers were rather one-sided, and did not always support a collaborative carer-child communication [7, 15]. For example, protections were often negative ("don't", "can't"), involved hiding or controlling information such as devices and passwords, and included secret monitoring of children's behaviour. There was some evidence of more progressive attempts by carers, including performing a "first-pass" review of an online site, and attempts to educate their children, though carers were only able to provide general approach descriptions.

4.3   Carer Rich Pictures

Of the 103 carer concerns we coded from the transcripts 57% (59/103) drew an image associated with the concern. Noticeably some concerns seemed simpler for the carers to illustrate visually whereas others seemed more complicated. In terms of posting online, of the 10 concerns coded, 9 had illustrated pictures (90%) suggesting that this particular concern may be more easily visualized. Meeting online concerns (73%) were also popular images to draw. The most difficult concern to visualize was a lack of solution (42%). In terms of protections, 40.5% (28/69) of the 69 protections that were coded from the transcripts had a rich picture associated with a protection. Controlling access protections were pictured by around half (52%) of the participant carers, while both monitoring (28.5%) and instructing (26%) protections had fewer associated pictures, suggesting they may be more demanding to illustrate.

Figures 2 and 3 represent image samples drawn within the six RPs from our workshops. There were some images that highlight and provide added insight to a concern or protection which was discussed orally. In some instances these images more readily offered enhanced clarity, more tacit understanding and stress the magnitude of the issue compared to the descriptive words. For example:

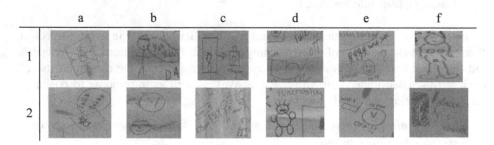

Fig. 2. Example concern images

- Figure 2(a1) is a prohibition image [3] representing a restriction (naked body images posted online) and the crossed sign through the circle shows the prohibition. The picture appears unambiguous and clear whereas the descriptive text appears more vague: C5: *"don't put on pictures that are not suitable of us, or look at pictures that are, you know."*

- Figure 2(d2) depicts a monster preying on the vulnerable. This is a powerful image that enhances the magnitude of the issue described vocally by C13 as *"there are people out there who know what they are doing, victimisation, and obviously our kids are an easy target."*
- Figure 3(b1) illustrates a child saying no when an iPad is confiscated. This illustrates high level anxiety and distress by the two layers of jagged red lines encompassing the child. The vocal description contributed by C5 was *"If I confiscate the iPad it's a minor explosion."*

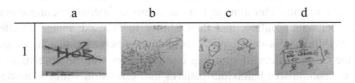

Fig. 3. Example protection images

Across the six RPs in this study we isolated 14 instances of prohibition [3]. For example, Figs. 2(a1) and 3(a1) show strong visual images that clearly, and with determination, show what is not allowed or desired. Figures 2(b1) and (c1) demonstrate highly visual examples of the pictures carers drew to illustrate inappropriate behaviour. Figure 2(b1) represents the dangers of a child discussing another person online. The blindfold, in this picture, illustrates the lack of face to face interaction and the concern of gossip. Figure 2(c1) depicts the inappropriateness of posting photographs of family members on Instagram. Meeting people online was illustrated very vividly. Images (a2, b2, c2, d1, d2, e1, e2, f1, f2) in Fig. 2 all represent the issues and challenges carers face, or worry about, when their children are online. Facebook icons (Figs. 2(c2) and (f2)) were a common image with many depicting the dangers of inappropriate remarks online and the ease with which a child can set up an account outwith the Facebook age restriction. Across all RPs we had two pictures depicting naked bodies (Figs. 2(a1) and (f1)) which, when described, allowed the carer to vocalise a private and possibly difficult concern to openly discuss with others in the workshop. Many of the images give very explicit visual depiction of the concern or protection. Other images were open to interpretation and we needed to code the transcript and pictures jointly to clarify the concern or protection.

5 Discussion

Below, we discuss the key results in terms of our two research questions.

RQ1: *How do carers characterise the online behaviour of their autistic children, and how do these characteristics affect the children's online security?*

Carers described their autistic children using a wide variety of expressive words such as "astute", "vulnerable", "private", "oblivious", "clever", "devious", "tunnel-visioned", "obsessed", "lonely", and "naïve". These adjectives show the diversity and indeed the paradoxical nature of characteristics that affect online behaviour and further indicates the range of contradictory difficulties carers have with keeping their children safe online. Further, though the categories and concern areas for children with ASD bear some resemblance to those for neuro-typical children, carers indicated greater concern for the risk to their ASD children, For example, carers gave very personal and alarming examples of extreme spending by their children, giving insight into the secretive and often devious nature of children with ASD. Carers noted that the abilities of their children, at least in terms of memory, contributed to their inappropriate behaviour online, and their ability to take advantage of their carers. Carers also highlighted issues relating to addictive behaviours and an inability to understand the consequences of spending online. Carers were in agreement regarding their children's compulsive behaviour patterns and obsession with online devices and certain websites. They shared stories concerning distressed emotional behaviours when children were prevented from being online.

Carers expressed strong concern regarding the ability of their children to distinguish strangers from friends due to an inability to detect falseness and deception. In particular, carers drew very expressive pictures about the vulnerability of their children and how they are less capable than their peers to recognise impersonators and the dangers associated with socialising online. Carers further suggested that their children may be more susceptible to behaviours such as bullying, when compared to other children, due to their inability to distinguish between sincerity and duplicity. Similarly, in terms of posting online, carers indicated that their children had difficulty with predicting the risks themselves and others with sharing personal pictures. Carers suggested their children had exceptionally high skills in some technical and memory areas, such as online gaming, setting up accounts and remembering passwords and very low social skills, such as understanding jokes, figures of speech or sarcasm.

The behaviour of children with ASD, combined with their increased vulnerability and inability to understand consequences makes them challenging to protect.

RQ2: *What are the challenges to carers' ability to protect autistic children online?*

Carers expressed frustration with their own technical inadequacy, the limitations of current technology, as well as the wider gap between them and their high performing children in terms of technical skill. Carers noted that some of their children possessed greater skills and had more technical knowledge than themselves, though carers also highlighted non-technical issues such as difficulties with communication and regulating parental controls. Some carers could illustrate their challenge in pictorial form better than, and with more clarity, words, such as drawing pictures of naked bodies to illustrate inappropriate online pictures. In terms of protections, carers often resorted to physical protections and rule setting. Physical protections seemed to work reasonably well, though not always (e.g., with children finding alternative ways online). Physical controls (such as confiscating a child's computing device) also exacerbated behavioural issues (e.g., C5: *"if I confiscate the iPad it's a minor explosion"*). Turning off the WiFi was another physical method to control access, though it has the effect of limiting service for the remainder of the family. One participant stated that she tapes off the camera on the laptop to stop webcam communication whilst another carer used a clock timer to limit internet use. Carers also highlighted several ineffective measures, such as disabling a child's account, since it was easy for children to set-up a new account and setting parental controls on streaming platforms such as Netflix when children would use clever solutions and ways to flout the limitation.

Rule setting, while seemingly easy for carers to establish and on which there seemed to be significant reliance, had low compliance. Some carers described improved compliance when they set conditions to the rules, such as homework to be completed before a device is allowed. The rule delivery, often in the form of an oral warning, was sometimes recognized as vague and open to interpretation by the child, requiring some carers to regularly repeat rules (C4: *"but we always keep reminding him"*). In some cases, rules were used to compensate for lack of knowledge and technical skill (C14: *"He's not allowed to go online, he's not allowed on chats because I wouldn't be able to control that, he'd be far more advanced than me."*).

Some of the carers discussed the challenges of monitoring technologies. A popular form of monitoring was to have communal areas for the family PC and another was to physically check what the child has been doing online, though both protections were difficult to consistently monitor and supervise. Another issue with maintaining observation was that children can set and change passwords to physical devices as well as to networks they are visiting online thus making supervision very problematic. This behaviour attests to the obsessive and somewhat devious nature of children with ASD.

Overall, carers provided more pictures to illustrate their concerns than their protections, and in some cases communication was enhanced by the pictures. Many of the stories the carers shared with us were private and personal and we found the pictures provided a safe and friendly platform for non-intrusive group engagement. In several cases, pictures said in one simple drawing what a carer struggled to articulate with words alone (see Sect. 4.3).

6 Design Implications

While recent research promotes the need for trusting relationships and collaboration, and good carer-child communication [7, 15], we found that most carers struggled to consistently influence and protect their children. In many cases, carers struggled with current technology, and with teaching their children. We suggest here some potential educational design approaches that draw upon our analysis of parent carer concerns and that could be explored further for assisting carers and their children.

One approach for directly addressing the behaviour of children with ASD online could be to support children in asking questions, similar to Hong et al.'s [17] use of social networks. Though in addition to relying on subjective advice, and requiring specialist knowledge, such an approach would require a child with ASD to first identify that there's an issue, and then pause their primary task in order to ask a question. Further, for the security challenges that we've identified, such an approach would need to ensure that it addresses related ethical and privacy concerns. We find this question/answer approach unsuitable for children with ASD as they are unlikely to be aware of danger or be able to identify possible future risk. To repeat from RQ1, our carers identified their children's online behavior as oblivious, and naïve. From our results, we envision two possible options to support the communication and collaboration between carers and children. Firstly, augmenting the work of Hong et al. [17], we suggest the design of collaborative tools in which children can ask questions of their carers, rather than asking on open social media. Carers could then provide a more informed response, possibly interacting with other carers for answers. This would enable people who know the child to assist them in managing their privacy while also giving them the ability to make their own decisions. Secondly, we suggest a tool that would enable a user to post content contingent on the approval of a trusted person, such as a carer. In cases where the action is appropriate, the posting decision can proceed without further involvement of the child. Alternative cases can be used to initiate a discussion between carer and child. Such tools would need to address several challenges, such as identifying adequate incentives to encourage use by children and carers, supporting privacy control for the child, and options for identifying subsets of posts for approval based on content.

In addition, we propose that an education-based approach could be used, drawing on previous use of comic strips for engaging children with ASD [21]. Such an approach could be investigated as a means to explain security issues that children with ASD might encounter online, and could leverage rich pictures. Also, approaches that could improve the awareness of possible posting issues, could help children with ASD to make more informed decisions. Wang et al. [31] have studied issues of posting online and regret, and investigated a nudging solution to help people to realise the potential audience of their post, prior to posting. In some cases, the solution was perceived as helpful, while in others, it was intrusive. However, the solution has not been evaluated with people with special needs. Taking into account the work of Lewandowski [21] and Wang [31] we suggest a combined approach to assist children with ASD online through the development of an intelligent educational nudging tool using, where possible, pictures to explain security issues. Similar to Wang et al. [31], nudges could provide additional information to a child about the reach of a potential post (e.g., this video post will be seen by strangers), where such information might be based on a set of rules established by carers (e.g., C3: *"don't put pictures on of your friends because their parents might not want their child to be on"*). This could allow an autistic child to follow home rules online. We envision such a nudging tool to be used primarily by the child but there is scope for carers to benefit from a tool that could warn them about possible security issues concerning their child.

From our workshops, we found that carers enjoyed sharing experiences with other carers, and learning the successes and failures of other carers, in a supportive sense, and to learn new protection approaches for caring for their own children, e.g., C7: *"I've learned an awful lot from different parents, more than I'd ever learn from the internet."* Carers identified a lack of technical knowledge, though they did not always recognise their inconsistent application of rules, which resulted in ineffective interactions and limited benefits for a child with autism. Tixier and Lewkowicz [30] identified similar benefits for older carers. As an unfortunate example of the current state of access to support for carers, the local autism centre used for our study has since lost its funding and closed. Thus, solutions that could support carers online potentially offer significant benefits. Drawing on these results, we propose the development of an online collaborative resource for carers of children with ASD.

7 Concluding Remarks

Children with ASD can introduce unique challenges for ensuring their protection online, and carers can struggle to find appropriate protection combinations. In this paper we identified challenges faced by carers for protecting their children online. In particular, carers struggle to consistently enforce protections, and to find ways to influence their child's behaviour. Drawing on the input from our carers, we suggest designs for several educational nudging tools to better support carers and to keep their children safe online.

For our future work, we plan to work directly with children with ASD, first to investigate more closely what they understand about security and privacy on line, and secondly to explore some of our educational approaches with families in order to influence children's behaviour, and hopefully ensure their online safety. We also plan to further explore the differences between ASD children and neuro-typical children.

Limitations. Our study was run from a parent carer perspective, with a limited set of carers from a particular geographic area so that studies with other carers and with children with ASD. would be helpful in order to confirm the identification of similar concerns. While our focus groups seemed helpful for allowing parent carers to interact and convey more information in some cases, interviews could also be used to elicit more specific concern and protection information.

References

1. Ahmed, T., Shaffer, P., Connelly, K., Crandall, D., Kapadia, A.: Addressing physical safety, security, and privacy for people with visual impairments. In: SOUPS 2016 (2016)
2. Baron-Cohen, S.: Do autistic children have obsessions and compulsions? Br. J. Clin. Psychol. **28**(3), 193–200 (1989)
3. Bell, S., Berg, T., Morse, S.: Rich Pictures: Encouraging Resilient Communities. Routledge, Abingdon (2016)
4. Benford, P.: The use of internet-based communication by people with autism. Doctoral dissertation, University of Nottingham (2008). http://eprints.nottingham.ac.uk/10661/1/
5. Brugha, T., Cooper, S., McManus, S., Purdon, S., Smith, J., Scott, F., Spiers, N., Tyrer, F.: Estimating the Prevalence of Austism Spectrum Conditions in Adults: Extending the 2007 Adult Psychiatric Morbidity Survey (2012). http://www.ic.nhs.uk/webfiles/publications/005_Mental_Health/Est_Prev_Autism_Spectrum/st_Prev_Autism_Spec_Cond_in_Adults_Report.pdf. Accessed 4 July 2016
6. Caine, K., Sabanovic, S., Carter, M.: The effect of monitoring by cameras and robots on the privacy enhancing behaviors of older adults. In: HRI 2012, pp. 343–350 (2012). http://dx.doi.org/10.1145/2157689.2157807
7. Cranor, L., Durity, A., Marsh, A., Ur, B.: Parents' and teens' perspectives on privacy in a technology-filled world. In: SOUPS 2014 (2014)

8. Davis, R.A.: A cognitive-behavioral model of pathological Internet use. Comput. Hum. Behav. **17**(2), 187–195 (2001)
9. Dosono, B.: Patron privacy: a luxury concern for marginalized internet users. In: iConference 2016 (2016). https://www.ideals.illinois.edu/handle/2142/89438
10. Dosono, B., Hayes, J., Wang, Y.: "I'm Stuck!": a contextual inquiry of people with visual impairments in authentication. In: SOUPS 2015, pp. 151–168 (2015)
11. Dunphy, P., Vines, J., Coles-Kemp, L., Clarke, R., Vlachokyriakos, V., Wright, P., McCarthy, J., Olivier, P.: Understanding the experience-centeredness of privacy and security technologies. In: NSPW 2014, pp. 83–94 (2014)
12. Glaser, B.: The Discovery of Grounded Theory: Strategies for Qualitative Research, p. 81. Wiedenfeld and Nicholson, London (1967)
13. Grandin, T.: My mind is a web browser: how people with autism think. Cerebrum **2**(1), 14–22 (2000)
14. Hall, P., Heath, C., Coles-Kemp, L., Tanner, A.: Examining the contribution of critical visualisation to information security. In: NSPW 2015, pp. 59–72 (2015)
15. Hartikainen, H., Livari, N., Kinnula, M.: Should we design for control, trust or involvement?: a discourses survey about children's online safety. In: Interaction Design and Children, pp. 367–378 (2016)
16. Hong, H., Yarosh, S., Kim, J., Abowd, G., Arriaga, R.I.: Investigating the use of circles in social networks to support independence of individuals with autism. In: CHI 2013, pp. 3207–3216 (2013). http://dx.doi.org/10.1145/2470654.2466439
17. Hong, H., Abowd, G., Arriaga, R.: Towards designing social question-and-answer systems for behavioral support of individuals with autism. In: PervasiveHealth 2015, pp. 17–24 (2015)
18. Ion, I., Reeder, R., Consolvo, S.: "… No one can hack my mind": comparing expert and non-expert security practices. In: SOUPS 2015, pp. 327–346 (2015). https://www.usenix.org/conference/soups2015/proceedings/presentation/ion
19. Kientz, J., Hayes, G., Westeyn, T., Starner, T., Abowd, G.: Pervasive computing and autism: assisting caregivers of children with special needs. IEEE Pervasive Comput. **6**(1), 28–35 (2007). http://dx.doi.org/10.1109/MPRV.2007.18
20. Kirkham, R., Greenhalgh, C.: Social access vs. privacy in wearable computing: a case study of autism. IEEE Pervasive Comput. **14**(1), 26–33 (2015)
21. Lewandowski, J., Hutchins, T., Prelock, P., Murray-Close, D.: Examining the benefit of including a sibling in story-based interventions with a child with asperger syndrome. Contemp. Issues Commun. Sci. Disord. **41**, 179–195 (2014)
22. Lombard, M., Snyder-Duch, J., Bracken, C.C.: Content analysis in mass communication: assessment and reporting of intercoder reliability. Hum. Commun. Res. **28**(4), 587–604 (2002)
23. Lovaas, O., Koegel, R., Simmons, J., Long, J.: Some generalization and follow-up measures on austic children in behavior therapy. J. Appl. Behav. Anal. **6**(1), 131–165 (1973)
24. Marcu, G., Dey, A., Kiesler, S.: Parent-driven use of wearable cameras for autism support: a field study with families. In: UbiComp 2012, pp. 401–410, September 2012. http://dx.doi.org/10.1145/2370216.2370277
25. Rode, J.A.: Digital parenting: designing children's safety. In: Proceedings of BCS-HCI (2009)
26. Sasse, A.: Scaring and bullying people into security won't work. IEEE Secur. Priv. **13**(3), 80–83 (2015). doi:10.1109/MSP.2015.65
27. Strauss, A., Corbin, J.: Basics of Qualitative Research, vol. 15. Sage, Newbury Park (1990)

28. Suzuki, K., Hachisu, T., Iida, K.: EnhancedTouch: a smart bracelet for enhancing human-human physical touch. In: CHI 2016, pp. 1282–1293 (2016). http://dx.doi.org/10.1145/2858036.2858439
29. Tentori, M., Escobedo, L., Balderas, G.: A smart environment for children with autism. IEEE Pervasive Comput. **14**(2), 42–50 (2015)
30. Tixier, M., Lewkowicz, M.: Counting on the group: reconciling online and offline social support among older informal caregivers. In: CHI 2016, pp. 3545–3558, May 2016
31. Wang, Y., Leon, P.G., Acquisti, A., Cranor, L.F., Forget, A., Sadeh, N.: A field trial of privacy nudges for Facebook. In: CHI 2014 (2014)
32. Wash, R.: Folk models of home computer security. In: SOUPS 2010, p. 11 (2010). http://dx.doi.org/10.1145/1837110.1837125
33. Washington, P., Voss, C., Haber, N., Tanaka, S., Daniels, J., Feinstein, C., Winograd, T., Wall, D.: A wearable social interaction aid for children with autism. In: CHI 2016 EA, pp. 2348–2354 (2016). http://dx.doi.org/10.1145/2851581.2892282
34. Wisniewski, P., Jia, H., Xu, H., Rosson, M., Carroll, J.: Preventative vs. reactive: how parental mediation influences teens' social media privacy behaviors. In: Proceedings of the 18th ACM Conference on Computer Supported Cooperative Work & Social Computing (CSCW 2015), pp. 302–316. ACM (2015)
35. Yardi, S., Bruckman, A.: Social and technical challenges in parenting teens' social media use. In: Proceedings of CHI 2011 (2011)

Mediating Interaction Between Healthcare Professionals and Patients with a Dual-Sided Tablet

Ashley Colley[✉], Juho Rantakari, Lasse Virtanen, and Jonna Häkkilä

University of Lapland, Rovaniemi, Finland
{ashley.colley, juho.rantakari, lasse.virtanen,
jonna.hakkila}@ulapland.fi

Abstract. We present and evaluate a functional prototype of a dual-sided tablet, where the back of the tablet presents complementary information to a patient during a medical consultation. Handheld tablet computers are nowadays part of the standard toolkit used by healthcare professionals, however, rather than supporting the interaction between the two parties, the device usage may create a communication barrier. Evaluation of the dual-sided tablet by healthcare workers and via an on online survey revealed that both groups considered the concept beneficial. Display of information on the medication, treatment timeline, and vital measurements (e.g. blood pressure, heart rate and temperature) on the patient side of the tablet were most valued. Additionally, patients felt increased assurance that their basic information was correct.

Keywords: Doctor-patient interface · Health informatics · Hospital information systems · Electronic health record · Dual sided display

1 Introduction

The interface between healthcare professionals and patients is critical in establishing a fluent communication channel between the two parties. In addition to the exchange of factual information, it influences the satisfaction of patients, and also clearly has an impact on the success of the medical care itself. For example, prior research has investigated the benefits of patient information displays and micro-explanations [12, 13]. Today, handheld tablet computers, such as Apples iPad, have become a daily working tool for many healthcare workers [2, 9]. In US hospitals 70% of physicians use smartphones or tablets as part of their daily working tools [14].

With the exception of repackaging to improve robustness or hygiene aspects, the majority of devices used are standard consumer devices, largely driven by their low price and familiarity of use. However, there is room to improve the human side of the technology, and optimize its design for situations where the healthcare professional is interacting with patients. With this motivation, we aim to create and evaluate a concept aiming to improve the patient experience by addressing the design of tablet computers used by healthcare professionals in a hospital environment. Specifically, we aim to address the challenge related to the device creating a barrier between caregiver and

© IFIP International Federation for Information Processing 2017
Published by Springer International Publishing AG 2017. All Rights Reserved
R. Bernhaupt et al. (Eds.): INTERACT 2017, Part III, LNCS 10515, pp. 54–61, 2017.
DOI: 10.1007/978-3-319-67687-6_4

patient, de-personalizing the interface, and the patient's feeling of not knowing what is happening whilst the doctor/nurse works with the tablet.

To address these challenges, we propose a dual-sided tablet, where the back of the device, i.e. that typically facing the patient, also contains a display. Thus, it can provide supporting visual information to the patient during the consultation (Fig. 1). This work extends the previous introduction of the concept of a dual-sided tablet a demo [1], by reporting on an evaluation by medical professionals and potential patients.

Fig. 1. The dual-sided tablet used in a hospital context. The front display shows electronic health record information, whilst the rear display provides the patient with visual information to support the consultation process.

2   Related Work

2.1   Use of Tablet Computers in the Hospital Domain

Prior art has studied the specific uses of tablet devices by hospital doctors, for example [10] reports that 30% of the clinicians in their study used tablets for sharing results with patients. The use of tablets to access Electronic Health Records (EHR) in the patient interface is highlighted as a core use case [2, 9]. Considering the use of tablets devices in the doctor's examination room, [9] concludes that the use of tablet computers was perceived positively by most patients. Based on the ubiquity of tablet device usage in today's hospital, it is well-motivated to try to improve the user experience in situations where the healthcare professional is interacting with the patient. Whereas the research on mobile technology usage in hospitals has been quite extensive, the concept of dual-sided tablets has not been previously examined.

2.2   Dual Display and See-Through Devices

Although a single-sided display is the default condition when interacting with computers, research has also addressed devices that include some form of display on two sides, and also some commercial examples exist. However, the examples are outside of medical domain. For example [6] present an implementation of a foldable display that may be configured such that it provides displays on front and back. Here, the focus is on the foldable interaction aspects rather than application contexts.

Considering touch input on one side of a device creating output on the reverse side, Lucid Touch [11] provides some insights, although with a totally different target than in our case. Devices with displays on two sides have been demonstrated in context of social use [3, 4]. In [3], a display attached to the back of the mobile phone shows which application the person is at the time using, and Kleinman et al. [7] have experimented with a laptop integrating a back-of-the-cover screen for self-expression with images and text. On a larger scale [8] present multi-user interaction on a 2-sided fog screen. The benefits of dual-sided see through displays for collaborative work are discussed by [5], concluding that it is an essential feature that each side of the display can display different content – a feature integrated into our concept. In the commercial sphere, Yota Devices (http://yotaphone.com/) produce a phone device with an e-ink display on the rear of the device, creating a dual display device. For example, when the camera application is active the rear display shows the text "smile" to the photograph's subject.

3   Dual-Sided Tablet Prototype and Evaluation

3.1   The Concept

Although the related work describes many positive sides of tablet use in the doctor-patient context, there is still further potential in improving the user experience and better mediate the communication between care personnel and patient. For instance, interaction ergonomics, trust, information visualization, and avoiding de-personalization of the patient experience can be better addressed. Currently, the patient is faced with the blank back of a tablet, whilst the caregiver attends to the tablet interface rather than the patient.

The front display of the dual-sided tablet is the healthcare professional's view. We envision this to be the current content used by medical professionals such as access to Electronic Health Record information and detailed data from the hospitals ICT systems. Additionally, the professional's view contains controls for the information that appears on the patient's view, e.g. a button to enable visibility. In this way, the healthcare professional is able to visually support his consultation with the patient.

3.2   Prototype Implementation

As a prototype implementation, we utilized two 10" Android tablets attached back-to-back in a 3D printed containing case we designed specifically for the purpose. Each tablet ran a custom developed Android application. The healthcare professional's view was implemented as a single page EHR type content with buttons in each section to switch on or off the display of the corresponding patient view on the opposite side of the tablet. As an extra feature, when the nurse or doctor views x-ray images and charts, we added the possibility to draw annotations on top of them, the result being also displayed on the patient's display. The annotation feature aimed to support the verbal consultation conversation e.g. by highlighting parameters as they are discussed. The upper display was interactive, i.e. a touch screen, and the interconnection between the two devices was made using Bluetooth. Our initial implementation and its usage are illustrated in Fig. 1.

Six different patient views were implemented (Fig. 2). These were selected to give a range of information types, from basic information, such as the patients' name and condition to information requiring more explanation, such as charts and x-rays.

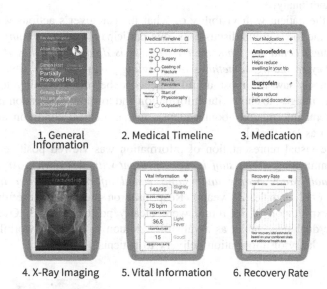

Fig. 2. The six patient side screens evaluated in the focus groups and survey.

3.3 Evaluation

As understanding the context of use is a critical part of identifying the potential value or problems of the dual-sided tablet, we create a video demonstrating its use in a hospital context. The video first showed the current experience using a traditional tablet and then the same scenario using the dual-sided tablet. Stills from the video are shown in Figs. 1 and 2. The video and static images of screens from the dual-sided tablet prototype (Fig. 2) were then used as source material for focus group sessions with healthcare professionals and an online survey. Additionally, the interactive prototype was presented in the focus group.

4   Results

4.1   Focus Group with Healthcare Professionals

We conducted four focus groups with altogether 25 participants (female = 22, male = 3), and 4–6 participants in each session. The participants were nurses, or student nurses close to graduation, who already worked closely with patients in a hospital setting. All 25 participants had previous experiences with electronic patient care records or other similar systems, 25/25 owned a smartphone and 16/25 a tablet.

The implemented demo and the video showing the use in a (simulated) hospital environment were shown. After viewing the video, the participants were directed to discuss each of the patient's screens in turn and asked to evaluate the various features presented in each. A researcher acted as moderator and the sessions were video recorded for later analysis.

Providing the patient with visibility of what the caregiver's actions was the main topic raised in the focus group discussions, one participant stating: *"I think it would be nice if the patient could see what their caregiver is doing. Then they don't get the feeling that they're hiding something or googling for symptoms"* (#9, female, 22 years). The nurses saw the most useful aspects to be, the capability to show and annotate X-Ray images, to show vital information and to show medication information. Providing general information about patient's name, medical condition and doctor's name was seen as less useful.

Overall the visual representation of information was viewed positively with one participant commenting: *"The staff is more present with this device. Also the information is visual! Many people understand visual information better than spoken information."* (#12, female, 24 years). Responses on the general usefulness of the concept and expectation of its future were clearly positive, Fig. 3. Overall nurses considered the dual-sided tablet as a valuable addition to the daily workflow and for improving the clarity of information delivery to patients.

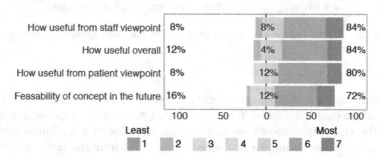

Fig. 3. Responses to the concept by nurses (n = 25). Percentage values indicate percentage of responses on negative, neutral and positive sides respectively.

4.2 Online Survey

With an online survey we aimed to gain the viewpoint of average people who would potentially be patients receiving care in a hospital. The survey the participants viewed the same concept video as used in the focus group sessions, and then proceeded to rate and give feedback on each of the features in concept. After removing 15 incomplete responses, the survey received 81 complete responses (67% female, 33% male), which were further analyzed.

Of the participants, 90% resided in [country removed for review], 96% owned a smartphone and 42% owned a tablet computer device. Considering their experience as a patient, 48% had been a patient in a hospital ward, 75% had experience a consultation with a doctor, and 43% had accessed their electronic medical records in some way.

Participants' feedback on a rating scale (Fig. 4) indicated the concept was considered *innovative* and *useful* with 65% and 62% of responses being on the positive side. Many participants noted the potential to enhance the communication channel between the doctor and patient, *"...engaging patients in real-time interaction with healthcare experts."* (#66, male, 26 years) and, *"Great idea! It offers more interaction and more comprehension for the patient. It also allows the doctor to read the information and maintain contact with their patient during the meeting."* (#74, female, 23 years). Potential problems with the concept were also noted, particularly related to the ergonomics of the patient viewing the content, *"The position of the patients' screen makes it difficult to read because of the typical way of holding a tablet."* (#48, male, 22 years).

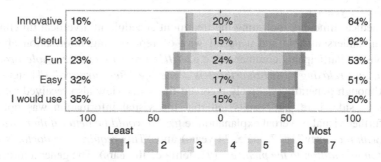

Fig. 4. Rating scale responses from the online survey on the overall opinion of the dual-sided tablet concept (n = 81). Percentage values indicate percentage of responses on negative, neutral and positive sides respectively.

Considering importance of the patient-side content (Fig. 5), participants felt that information on the medication prescribed was the most valued, with 64% rating this positively. In the freeform comments the participants commented on the legibility of the information: *"The medication information is given clearly and the purpose of each medication is explained well. Simply an efficient and a clear way to show information."* (#94, male, 26 years) Other participants commented on the reassuring effect the information about medication has on the patent: *"It answers a lot of questions, it's reassuring for the patient."* (#50, female, 22 years).

The value of the views showing vital information, medical timeline and x-ray imaging were all rated similarly with between 60% and 62% of participants giving rating on the positive side. The vital information view provided an overview of the current values basic measurements such as blood pressure, heart rate and temperature, together with an indication of the normal range. Generally, participants considered being able to read the information in addition to hearing it from the doctor was beneficial, *"It's good to have an overview of the vital information, so the patient can read it themselves."* (#75, male, 28 years). Considering the visualization, one participant commented, *"The*

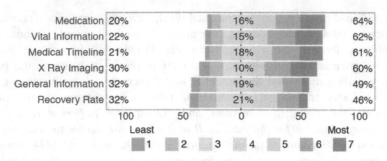

Fig. 5. Rating scale responses from the online survey on the usefulness of each patent view (n = 81). Percentage values indicate percentage of responses on negative, neutral and positive sides respectively.

colors help the patient understand what's happening. What is wrong and what is right." (#50, male, 22 years).

The medical timeline, indicating the treatment schedule in a vertical timeline, was seen as an understandable and a useful way of representing information about the hospital visits. Participants commented, e.g., "It's great to see the whole process of treatment, and relaxing to see that there is some life after surgery." (#1, female, 40 years). Although generally positively received the x-ray view also received ratings on the negative side, here participants felt that the visual information was not useful without further visual or verbal explanation, e.g., "It would be better if there was some analysis with the x-ray" (#17, male, 24 years) and "This requires the doctor's spoken explanation in addition to the picture." (#1, female, 40 years). The general information view aimed to reassure patients that their basic information was correct, e.g. that they were being treated for the correct illness, and this was commented accordingly: "I think it's important to see your own name, so you can make sure you are the correct patient, and the doctor's name. These create safety." (#2, male, 27 years). The concept also opened possibility for the patient to see new types of information: "Never seen a recovery visualized before" (#73, male, 23 years).

5 Discussion and Conclusion

To the best of our knowledge we present the first evaluation of a functional prototype of a dual-sided tablet for use in the clinical environment. Both medical professionals (n = 25) and potential patients (n = 81) considered the concept as useful. Communication of information that is difficult to understand purely verbally, such as medication names, numeric information and the treatment timeline, was identified as particularly enhanced by the visual support of the dual-sided tablet. Both medical professionals and potential patients considered information on medication, treatment timeline, and vital measurements (e.g. blood pressure, heart rate and temperature) as the most useful. From the patient's perspective, the dual-sided tablet also brought assurance that their basic data was correct, and offered a possibility to see new information types visualized.

We acknowledge that our work is limited by the facts that it is not carried out in a real clinical environment, and presents feedback from only one type of medical professional. As future work, we plan to extend our work and address these limitations.

References

1. Colley, A., Rantakari, J., Häkkilä, J.: Dual sided tablet supporting doctor-patient interaction. In: Proceedings of CSCW 2015 Companion. ACM (2015)
2. Duffy, M.: Tablet technology for nurses. AJN Am. J. Nurs. **112**(9), 59–64 (2012)
3. Jarusriboonchai, P., Malapaschas, A., Olsson, T., Väänänen, K.: Increasing collocated people's awareness of the mobile user's activities: a field trial of social displays. In: Proceedings of CSCW 2016, pp. 1691–1702 (2016)
4. Kao, H.L.C., Schmandt, C.: MugShots: a mug display for front and back stage social interaction in the workplace. In: Proceedings of TEI 2015, pp. 57–60. ACM (2015)
5. Li, J., Greenberg, S., Sharlin, E., Jorge, J.: Interactive two-sided transparent displays: designing for collaboration. In: Proceedings of DIS 2014, pp. 395–404. ACM (2014)
6. Khalilbeigi, M., Lissermann, R., Kleine, W., Steimle, J.: FoldMe: interacting with double-sided foldable displays. In: Proceedings of TEI 2012, pp. 33–40. ACM (2012)
7. Kleinman, L., Hirsch, T., Yurdana, M.: Exploring mobile devices as personal public displays. In: Proceedings of MobileHCI 2015, pp. 233–243. ACM, New York (2015)
8. Olwal, A., DiVerdi, S., Rakkolainen, I., Höllerer, T.: Consigalo: multi-user face-to-face interaction on immaterial displays. In: Proceedings of INTETAIN 2008. ICST Brussels, Belgium (2008)
9. Strayer, S., Semler, M., Kington, M., Tanabe, K.: Patient attitudes toward physician use of tablet computers in the exam room. Fam. Med. **42**(9), 643 (2010)
10. Walsh, C., Stetson, P.: EHR on the move: resident physician perceptions of iPads and the clinical workflow. In: AMIA Annual Symposium Proceedings, vol. 2012, p. 1422 (2012)
11. Wigdor, D., Forlines, C., Baudisch, P., Barnwell, J., Shen, C.: Lucid touch: a see-through mobile device. In: Proceedings of UIST 2007. ACM (2007)
12. Wilcox, L., Morris, D., Tan, D., Gatewood, J.: Designing patient-centric information displays for hospitals. In: Proceedings of CHI 2010, pp. 2123–2132. ACM (2010). http://dx.doi.org/10.1145/1753326.1753650
13. Wilcox, L., Morris, D., Tan, D., Gatewood, J., Horvitz, E.: Characterizing patient-friendly "micro-explanations" of medical events. In: Proceedings of CHI 2011, pp. 29–32. ACM (2011). https://doi.org/10.1145/1978942.1978948
14. http://mobihealthnews.com/38859/survey-almost-70-percent-of-clinicians-at-us-hospitals-use-smartphones-tablets/. Accessed 1 Feb

Stimulating Conversations in Residential Care Through Technology-Mediated Reminiscence

Francisco Ibarra$^{(\boxtimes)}$, Marcos Baez, Francesca Fiore, and Fabio Casati

University of Trento, Trento, Italy
{fj.ibarracaceres,marcos.baez,francesca.fiore,fabio.casati}@unitn.it

Abstract. In this paper we describe the design of a reminiscence-based social interaction tool, namely Collegamenti, that aims at stimulating conversations and a sense of mutual awareness in residential care. Unlike previous work, Collegamenti focuses on stimulating the different types of relationships that are relevant to the quality of life in residential care: interactions with primary family caregivers, contacts with the larger family, friendships with peer residents and interactions with the nursing home staff. We explore the needs and challenges of this scenario in terms of social interactions but also in terms of how to make the technology sustainable and well integrated with care practices and initiatives, and report on the findings from the qualitative studies and concept validation.

Keywords: Social interactions · Reminiscence · Older adults · Nursing homes

1 Introduction

Transitioning to long-term residential care demands major adjustments in the life of an older adult and his/her family [9]. In this scenario, connecting with family and peers is a key aspect contributing to adaptation, social integration, sense of belonging, and general wellbeing [4,6,17]. However, staying socially active can be challenging in this new environment where older adults are often placed without much choice for alternatives. Failing to remain socially engaged is known to have devastating effects on the nursing home (NH) life, contributing to feelings of loneliness, boredom, helplessness, declining mental health, reduced happiness, and increased mortality [3,5,14].

Despite efforts in promoting social activities in NHs, social isolation and loneliness are still main concerns in residential care [16]. The causes include different physical, psychological, and contextual factors that influence the opportunities and motivations of older adults to interact with others.

In this paper we describe the concept development of a reminiscence-based social interaction tool, called Collegamenti, that aims at stimulating conversations in residential care.

Reminiscence is the process of recollecting past memories, a practice that is common at all ages [20] and often conducted with older adults due to its

© IFIP International Federation for Information Processing 2017
Published by Springer International Publishing AG 2017. All Rights Reserved
R. Bernhaupt et al. (Eds.): INTERACT 2017, Part III, LNCS 10515, pp. 62–71, 2017.
DOI: 10.1007/978-3-319-67687-6_5

various functions and benefits. Webster [19] identifies eight particular functions: death preparation, identity, problem solving, teach and inform, conversation, boredom reduction, bitterness revival and intimacy maintenance. Thus, reminiscence serves an important social function in facilitating the sharing of personal memories with others, helping to create bonds between people [22].

In addition to lessons learned from existing reminiscence practices, our own preliminary surveys and visits (described later) identified a set of challenges that can be summarized in (i) creating bonds and friendships among residents in NHs, and (ii) facilitating and stimulating conversations with family members, especially the younger ones. We also understood that a solution is more likely to succeed if it fits into the processes and practices of the NH and its often overworked staff.

For these reasons, unlike previous research on the design of reminiscence applications (e.g., [1,10,11,21]), the goal is not only that of creating a digital archive that preserves memories or of reminiscing one's own life, but also that of using the information and media to discover and create connections among people (residents) who shared similar experiences, values and events, and to increase bonds with one's own family.

In the following we explore the challenges to the design of Collegamenti, describing the design process from the exploration of user needs and concept development to the early validations with nursing home stakeholders. From this research through design process [23] we derive lessons that contribute to the design of social interaction tools for NH residents.

2   Background

2.1   Related Work

Previous work on design for reminiscence and storytelling can be summarized in the following topics: facilitating usage by older adults, collecting memories, stimulating memory recall, and supporting conversations.

Using tangible interfaces is a prominent approach to facilitating the use of reminiscence solutions. Memento [21] uses scrapbooks and digital pens for memory collection and sharing, combining tangible scrapbooks that are already familiar to older adults with the benefits of online sharing. A similar setting - using physical albums and digital pens - was tested in [13] with positive results in terms of engagement and social interactions. The "Reminiscence Map" [7] is another example of a digital-physical interface but with a focus on stimulating memories around places. These are great examples of how familiar interfaces can facilitate usage by older adults. However, they do not facilitate the collection of pictures or stories, and offer no support for peer interaction and discovery.

Several solutions support the collection of pictures and stories. For example, PicMemory [11] facilitates memory collection by allowing family members of all ages to collect family stories collaboratively. It also provides a multi-modal interface to facilitate contributions by older family members. PicGo [10] proposes instead a solution to iteratively collect meaningful tags from pictures during reminiscence sessions (picture capturing and browsing) with older adults with dementia. These solutions point to the importance of collaboration and gathering context from stories. However, they do not address the challenge of creating bonds among older adults and limit the use of tags to browsing.

Facilitating social interactions is instead at the center of solutions such as digital photo frames [8]. The CIRCA project [1] explores the use of databases of video, music and photos to prompt conversations among carers, relatives and older adults in residential settings. CaraClock [18] facilitates instead browsing of collective memories via a clock-shaped digital photo albums that can be paired to show collective memories of a family from the perspective of each member. Virtual reality has also been explored with older adults affected by dementia, with interesting results for recreating past memories, although the support for group activities remains a challenge [15].

The above solutions provide valuable insights into the design of reminiscence technology, which we take as inspiration for Collegamenti. However, a major gap is still that of supporting social integration and bonding among residents, while also accommodating to the specific needs of older adults in residential care.

2.2   Our Preliminary Studies

To investigate the nature of relationships in residential care, we visited four nursing homes in northern Italy, in the spring and summer of 2016. During the visits, we conducted observations, semi-structured interviews and focus groups. All activities were attended by at least three researchers, in order to collect different perspectives and to reduce the chance of bias.

We found out that it is hard for residents to form friendships in NHs. The staff reports that **residents do not make friends**. In addition to the reasons mentioned in the introduction, budget and efficiency constraints sometimes interfere with fostering relationships. For example, allocation of residents is often based on the evolution of their health condition as well as organizational efficiency needs and not on their preferences.

Family members, especially the primary family caregiver (the spouse, a sibling or a child), visit very frequently, several times per week and, in some cases, every day. Young grandchildren also come along often, with some NHs even providing recreational spaces to encourage the visits, while young adults visit less frequently. This is not surprising, and is line with surveys to university students, who reported a very low frequency of interactions with their grandparents because of lack of time and common topics of conversation [2].

The NH staff organizes various activities to facilitate social interactions such as volunteering, cooking, handcrafting, religious and animation activities. While this works for some residents, especially those more independent and integrated, stimulating interactions and participation is still a challenge. As reported during a focus group *"At the end of the day, it is up to the ability and sensibility of the staff to identify opportunities for interaction and bringing residents closer"*.

Indeed an important take-home message from our preliminary studies is that there is plenty of space to improve the social interactions and the quality of

Fig. 1. Collage of pictures taken during the visits to the nursing homes.

relationships for people in nursing homes and their families, and to bring people together so that they can better integrate and feel part of the NH life. In this regard, **reminiscence provides a great opportunity**. Storytelling and past events are already a prominent theme in the NHs, not only as part of the reminiscence therapies for residents with dementia but as an integral part of the community as a whole:

- Corridors and shared spaces are decorated with old pictures of relevant places and news from the residents' lives (Fig. 1A, B).
- Documentaries and films related to the residents' lives are screened as part of the animation activities (Fig. 1C).
- Personal spaces feature pictures of family members, residents' important events and other mementos (Fig. 1E).
- Some initiatives such as "Memories in art" from one NH, aim at sharing residents' stories with the NH community (Fig. 1F).
- Social spaces allow for group activities as well as more intimate family interactions (Fig. 1D, G). Some group activities rely on technology support.

The challenge is then to build on the above practices, to support the social function of the reminiscence process, to (i) capture stories, taking them from the corridors to the virtual world, to involve more family members, especially younger generations; and (ii) use stories to start stimulating conversations, enriching family visits, bringing people together, and creating bonds among residents.

3 Collegamenti

Based on our preliminary studies, we developed the concept of a reminiscence-based tool, namely Collegamenti, that aims at stimulating conversations in residential care. It does so by enabling family members and friends to digitize pictures related to the life of the older adult, to then browse them together in a process that motivates social interactions while collecting stories and relevant information about the life of the person. This information can be used later to summarize important moments in the life of the person and to identify peers sharing similar life events and stories with the purpose of making new friends or reconnecting with old ones.

We based the design and usage scenario on the limitations of frail residents (which are the large majority in NHs), who are not really able to operate a tablet, making the interaction with Collegamenti assisted by family members and staff. Thus, the design allows for a multi-user interaction mode, optimized so that residents are able to see the content, while the family and staff drive the sessions. As seen in Fig. 2, Collegamenti builds on four main activities:

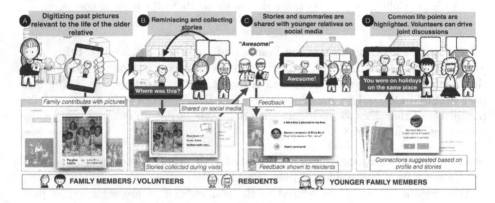

Fig. 2. Collegamenti concept and usage scenario.

- **Digitizing pictures.** Family members contribute by adding pictures and tags (place, date, people in the picture), and can even collaborate to collect relevant tags on each other's pictures. This alone allows the family to build an archive of relevant moments. Once digitized, pictures are automatically added to the resident's account, becoming available to all collaborators.
- **Reminiscing and collecting stories.** During the visits, family members (or staff) engage in reminiscence sessions with the residents. Digitized pictures are used as prompts to engage in meaningful interactions and to collect stories. At this phase, tags can also be refined with the help of the resident. The idea is to make visits more interesting, not only to collect information. Therefore, pictures and stories created can be revisited at any time, becoming a trigger for memories and conversation.
- **Engaging in online interactions.** The stories collected can be shared with the NH community and family members (on social media), which could derive in additional interactions, during visits and also online with the larger family. Residents (with the help of a facilitator) can access the feedback on his/her shared stories. Feedback from social media is captured and displayed in a format that facilitates the consumption and response. In the same way, residents

can access pictures and stories from other residents (friends) that could lead to face-to-face interactions. Thus, by enabling online interactions with family and peers we do not only aim at opening a communication channel, but at stimulating conversations.

– **Connecting with other residents.** The stories and tags collected are also used to find potential friends. Building on the homophily effect, which suggests that similarities among people lead to creating ties [12], Collegamenti would suggest friends based on common life events and their likelihood to create bonds. Suggestions include reasons for the connection, that aim at (i) introducing the other person, and (ii) highlighting the common aspects (e.g., "You and Gianni were born in Parma").

The above process relies heavily on the cooperation and interest of the NH staff and the primary family caregiver (on average 65 years old). This poses several challenges since we need to understand if such a solution is feasible in the NH context. Aspects that deal with the interaction design are not addressed in this paper, although the reader can refer to our low-fidelity prototype[1] for a close experience.

4 Methods

We conducted interviews with relatives of NH residents and members of the animation staff, and a work table with additional NH actors, aiming at:

– Assessing whether the concept and use of Collegamenti fits into current NH practices and activities performed by both relatives and staff
– Determining whether relatives and staff would be interested and able to perform the four main activities of Collegamenti (see Fig. 2)

Semi-structured Interviews were conducted by two researchers. We contacted one nursing home asking to interview relatives, and at least two members of the animation staff. The NH recruited both relatives and staff. We interviewed five relatives, each of a different resident, about Collegamenti's main activities (see Fig. 2) while, one volunteer and the coordinator of animation were interviewed on their current tasks and reminiscence related activities, and on the fitness of Collegamenti in the context of their work. Both interviews were complemented with a description and a storyboard of Collegamenti.

The Work Table was led by the same two researchers. Eighteen NHs in northern Italy were contacted to participate, among those willing to participate we chose randomly eight people, but ensured an equal number of men and women, and that no two participants belonged to the same NH. The table was attended by three NH directors, four coordinators (one of animation), and one relative.

---

[1] http://invis.io/USB4KFP7N.

Personas built from our preliminary studies were presented along with a storyboard and a prototype. Participants were asked to write down *challenges in the use of Collegamenti* and *reasons for not using it*, as well as *reasons for being used and liked.* Then, the four main activities were presented and participants were asked to write *challenges for their realization* and *current similar practices.*

5   Results

We have aggregated the feedback obtained from both the interviews and the work table, which were in a high level of agreement. Next we present the NH practices, and opportunities and challenges for Collegamenti's adoption.

5.1   Collegamenti in Nursing Home Practices

In some ways some of Collegamenti's activities are already conducted in NHs.

Digitizing Pictures. Some residents take their old pictures to the NH, and old pictures have already been used in past activities (*"I've brought photos from home for the story book"*). Moreover, the animation staff is familiar with digitizing pictures (*"now we take pictures of old photos"*) and some relatives would also be willing to help (*"I could scan the pictures... and send them by e-mail"*).

Reminiscence and Story Collection. We have identified many comparable activities, such as making the biography on entry to the NH, collecting residents' life stories and interests, and the existence of a NH newspaper about residents' stories and past (such as old traditions, or their old craft). It is worth mentioning that NH stakeholders value such activities (*"There is a therapeutic, rehabilitation aspect to it that is very useful"*), and note that they can help to increase residents self-worth and self-esteem. Moreover, participants observe that the involvement of relatives (in this case as facilitators during reminiscence sessions) would be beneficial since it increases the interactions between relatives and residents, and increases the trust towards the nursing home (*"Involving relatives improves the relation with the NH because they feel part of the care"*).

Sharing in Social Media is also done using NH websites or Facebook pages. Although content is mostly about current events, it was a pleasant surprise to find out that residents already have some sort of online presence. However, despite other means being used for online sharing (*"There is a digital version of the NH newspaper"*, *"We share pictures in Whatsapp"*), for residents most sharing still happens offline. The NH newspaper is printed and shared with relatives and within the NH community, and the collection of life stories is sometimes conducted as a group activity. Still, this is encouraging since it indicates a good disposition towards sharing.

Connecting with Other Residents. Residents can occasionally find out about common points (*"Sometimes we find common points while talking all together"*, *"[residents] already share -common points- autonomously or during the life sto-ries activities"*). Nonetheless, participants mentioned that these similarities are quite significant to generate interactions and rapport between residents (*"Com-mon interests are the spark to create a bond"*).

5.2 Challenges for Adoption

Despite the similarities between Collegamenti's main activities and current prac-tices in NHs, there are challenges to NH adoption of Collegamenti as a tool.

Workload of Facilitators. The main activities of Collegamenti can be time and effort consuming, and it is well known that the NH staff runs a tight work schedule. Clearly, residents will need support to use Collegamenti, and no one actor can support all the activities. Therefore, participants recognize the impor-tance of collaboration between the residents' relatives and the NH staff (*"A strong involvement of the relatives is needed"*).

Privacy Management. Participants noted that some of the information col-lected from pictures and stories can be considered as personal by residents (*"Res-idents are still very reserved. I see this more as a family thing"*). Participants emphasized that Collegamenti should allow to control which pictures and stories are available for sharing, as well as whom to share with. This becomes particu-larly important if sharing is automatic (e.g. on social media).

Residents Cognitive Skills. Despite the assistance of facilitators, not all res-idents would be able to use Collegamenti. Participants have pointed out that a part of the residents might not be able to remember facts about the picture (*"Only a small percentage of residents would be able to remember all this"*). Participants have highlighted the importance of identifying able and interested residents (as well as relatives who would act as facilitators).

6   Discussion and Future Work

The preliminary studies, along with the literature review, stress the need for promoting social interactions in residential care. This is a complex and challeng-ing problem, requiring the support and collaboration of the care network, since most residents are limited in their ability to seek opportunities on their own.

The studies reported in this paper point to the feasibility of using reminiscence-based technology as a sustainable instrument for promoting social interactions in residential care. The proposed concept of Collegamenti has received positive feedback in terms of (i) supporting current NH practices and activities from staff and family members, (ii) providing more opportunities, for interaction between the residents and relatives, and for collaboration between staff and relatives, and (iii) expanding the reach of reminiscence-based activities, by sharing in online channels to reach younger audiences, and evidencing com-mon life points between residents. However, these results should be interpreted within the studied cultural context. The challenges reported also indicate the need for additional features and further consideration to the process.

As for ongoing and future work, we are iterating on the design of the application, taking in consideration the aforementioned challenges, and planning experience prototyping sessions with residents and family members.

Acknowledgements. This project has received funding from the EU Horizon 2020 research and innovation programme under the Marie Sklodowska-Curie grant agreement No. 690962. This work was also supported by the "Collegamenti" project funded by the Province of Trento (l.p. n.6-December 13rd 1999).

References

1. Astell, A., Alm, N., Gowans, G., Ellis, M., Dye, R., Campbell, J., Vaughan, P.: Working with people with dementia to develop technology: the circa and living in the moment projects. PSIGE Newslett. **105**, 64–69 (2008)
2. Baez, M., Dalpiaz, C., Hoxha, F., Tovo, A., Caforio, V., Casati, F.: Personalized persuasion for social interactions in nursing homes. In: Persuasive Technologies 2016 (2016)
3. Berkman, L.F., Syme, S.L.: Social networks, host resistance, and mortality: a nine-year follow-up study of alameda county residents. Am. J. Epidemiol. **109**(2), 186–204 (1979)
4. Bradshaw, S.A., Playford, E.D., Riazi, A.: Living well in care homes: a systematic review of qualitative studies. Age Ageing **41**(4), 429–440 (2012)
5. Brummett, B.H., Barefoot, J.C., Siegler, I.C., Clapp-Channing, N.E., Lytle, B.L., Bosworth, H.B., Williams Jr., R.B., Mark, D.B.: Characteristics of socially isolated patients with coronary artery disease who are at elevated risk for mortality. Psychosom. Med. **63**(2), 267–272 (2001)
6. Friedemann, M.L., Montgomery, R.J., Maiberger, B., Smith, A.A.: Family involvement in the nursing home: family-oriented practices and staff-family relationships. Res. Nursing Health **20**(6), 527–537 (1997)
7. Huldtgren, A., Vormann, A., Geiger, C.: Reminiscence map-insights to design for people with dementia from a tangible prototype. In: ICT4AgeingWell, pp. 233–242 (2015)
8. Kim, J., Zimmerman, J.: Cherish: smart digital photo frames for sharing social narratives at home. In: CHI 2006 Extended Abstracts on Human Factors in Computing Systems, pp. 953–958. ACM (2006)
9. Lee, D.T., Woo, J., Mackenzie, A.E.: A review of older peoples experiences with residential care placement. J. Adv. Nurs. **37**(1), 19–27 (2002)
10. Lee, H.C., Cheng, Y.F., Cho, S.Y., Tang, H.H., Hsu, J., Chen, C.H.: Picgo: designing reminiscence and storytelling for the elderly with photo annotation. In: Proceedings of the 2014 Companion Publication on Designing Interactive Systems, pp. 9–12. ACM (2014)
11. Lee, H.C., Hsu, J.Y.J.: Picmemory: enriching intergenerational family interaction and memory collection. In: Proceedings of the 2016 CHI Conference Extended Abstracts on Human Factors in Computing Systems, pp. 3715–3718. ACM (2016)
12. McPherson, M., Smith-Lovin, L., Cook, J.M.: Birds of a feather: homophily in social networks. Annual Rev. Sociol. **27**(1), 415–444 (2001)

13. Piper, A.M., Weibel, N., Hollan, J.: Audio-enhanced paper photos: encouraging social interaction at age 105. In: Proceedings of the 2013 Conference on Computer Supported Cooperative Work, pp. 215–224. ACM (2013)

14. Seeman, T.E., Berkman, L.F., Blazer, D., Rowe, J.W.: Social ties and support and neuroendocrine function: the macarthur studies of successful aging. Ann. Behav. Med. **16**(2), 95–106 (1994)

15. Siriaraya, P., Ang, C.S.: Recreating living experiences from past memories through virtual worlds for people with dementia. In: Proceedings of the 32nd Annual ACM Conference on Human Factors in Computing Systems, pp. 3977–3986. ACM (2014)

16. Theurer, K., Mortenson, W.B., Stone, R., Suto, M., Timonen, V., Rozanova, J.: The need for a social revolution in residential care. J. Aging Stud. **35**, 201–210 (2015)

17. Thomas, W.H.: Life Worth Living: How Someone You Love Can Still Enjoy Life in a Nursing Home: The Eden Alternative in Action. VanderWyk and Burnham, Acton (1996)

18. Uriu, D., Shiratori, N., Hashimoto, S., Ishibashi, S., Okude, N.: Caraclock: an interactive photo viewer designed for family memories. In: CHI 09 Extended Abstracts on Human Factors in Computing Systems, pp. 3205–3210. ACM (2009)

19. Webster, J.D.: Construction and validation of the reminiscence functions scale. J. Gerontol. **48**(5), P256–P262 (1993)

20. Webster, J.D., Gould, O.: Reminiscence and vivid personal memories across adulthood. Int. J. Aging Hum. Dev. **64**(2), 149–170 (2007)

21. West, D., Quigley, A., Kay, J.: Memento: a digital-physical scrapbook for memory sharing. Pers. Ubiquit. Comput. **11**(4), 313–328 (2007)

22. Westerhof, G.J., Bohlmeijer, E.T.: Celebrating fifty years of research and applications in reminiscence and life review: state of the art and new directions. J. Aging Stud. **29**, 107–114 (2014)

23. Zimmerman, J., Forlizzi, J., Evenson, S.: Research through design as a method for interaction design research in HCI. In: Proceedings of the SIGCHI Conference on Human Factors in Computing Systems, pp. 493–502. ACM (2007)

Viability of Magazines for Stimulating Social Interactions in Nursing Homes

Valentina Caforio[✉], Marcos Baez, and Fabio Casati

University of Trento, Trento, Italy
{valentina.caforio,marcos.baezgonzalez,fabio.casati}@unitn.it

Abstract. Social isolation and loneliness have a strong negative impact on health and happiness. The correlation is present at all ages, but the risk of loneliness and isolation is particularly high in later life and when transitioning to residential care settings, where keeping in touch with the family, making new friends and integrating with the community in a new social context can be very challenging. In this note we report on our preliminary studies on the opportunity and feasibility of using custom, printed magazines for increasing feelings of connectedness and promoting meaningful interactions in nursing homes. The content and layout for the magazine are generated in an automatic or semi-automatic way and emphasize aspects that could lead to discovering connections or starting conversations. Initial findings point to the potential for such a magazine and lead to content guidelines that we elaborate in the paper.

Keywords: Older adults · Nursing homes · Social interactions · Loneliness

1 Introduction

Social isolation and loneliness are among the most dangerous and widespread diseases of modern times. Ample and concordant literature points to the lack of quality social interactions as a cause for declining mental health, lower happiness, and increased mortality, where the increase is comparable with those of alcohol and obesity [2,4,15].

Social interactions are also a key element in our well-being as we age and as we transition to long-term residential care [3,17]. In addition to the challenges posed by a new environment where we are often placed without much choice for alternatives, with age we tend to become more selective in our friendships [9–11] and less capable of regulating emotions from unpleasant friendship experiences [6].

Several studies have dealt with social isolation in older adults, proposing technological solutions to address the problem. Caprani et al. [5] propose a *reminiscence* device aimed at stimulating conversations and creating bonds among nursing home (NH) residents, but also at helping users living alone at home. A

© IFIP International Federation for Information Processing 2017
Published by Springer International Publishing AG 2017. All Rights Reserved
R. Bernhaupt et al. (Eds.): INTERACT 2017, Part III, LNCS 10515, pp. 72–81, 2017.
DOI: 10.1007/978-3-319-67687-6_6

low-fidelity prototype was evaluated on physical abilities, but results regarding the creation and enhancement of social bonds are not reported.

Santana et al. [14] devised a digital family newspaper aimed at supporting relationships between Mexican older adults and their younger relatives abroad. The newspaper is organized in sections, which can be populated by personal memories, anecdotes, events, pictures or videos uploaded by both young and old family members to maintain emotional closeness. In subsequent studies, the authors report that the system has been implemented and tested, with positive results regarding concept and perceived ease of use. The idea of sharing pictures in particular was well received, and the system was perceived as a possibility to enhance users' relationships [13].

Other solutions to enhance intergenerational family contacts include digital picture frames [7,8] for older adults, showing pictures sent by their younger relatives to provide topics of conversation and updates about their lives, as well as to create family cohesion.

Inspired by these attempts, in this work we explore the needs and possibilities for promoting social interactions in NHs in Italy. We believe insights and analyses can be generalized to many countries, but each nation - and sometimes each region - has specific NH populations and patterns in terms of, for example, family visits and interactions. Specifically, we aim at understanding the potential of leveraging a customized magazine as a vehicle for promoting interactions, and what the characteristics of such a publication should be.

In this paper we report on the preliminary studies we conducted to determine the feasibility and potential of such a publication. Specifically, for a magazine to be viable, we need to understand (i) if there is a friendship issue at all in NHs, (ii) if we can count on the help of staff and family members to guide the reading of the magazine and, very importantly, if magazine reading is an activity that is compatible with the practices in NHs, (iii) if the parties involved may have privacy concerns that would prevent us from collecting content, and (iv) which content, if any, would make the magazine interesting and appealing, if any. We next report on our study methods and findings in this respect.

2   Problem Analysis

To analyze the feasibility and determine a preliminary information design for such a magazine, we worked with six NHs in Italy, where we ran observations, interviews and focus groups that we detail in the following.

2.1   Methods

To investigate the nature of relationships in NHs we organized a set of visits to perform (i) ethnographic observations and (ii) semi-structured interviews with the staff (including volunteers in charge of entertainment activities) and relatives. The visits were conducted in the spring and summer of 2016 and attended by at least three researchers to collect different perspectives and reduce the chances of researcher bias [16]. These studies add to preliminary findings on the situation of intergenerational interactions in NHs [1].

Afterwards, in April 2017, we ran a focus group with representatives of each stakeholder (NH directors, coordinators, activity professionals and family representatives) of six different NHs, to discuss our initial findings and refine our insights. During the focus group, each participant was handed a card with a discussion topic and a specific finding. Each participant read aloud the topic and finding of her card, and the discussion was driven by the personal observations and experiences of each of the participants.

The observations were approved by the Ethical committee of "APSP Santo Spirito - Fondazione Montiel" of Pergine, Italy on the resolution of the 06/03/2016. The studies received ethical approval from University of Trento Committee on Research Involving Human Beings (Application N. 2017-003).

2.2   Results

The emergent themes from the observations and interviews are presented below, enriched with the discussions from the focus group:

Rather discouraging state of affairs for interactions. In most NHs, the staff reports that residents do not make friends, in part because of the concerns related to the efficiency of managing and running a NH with a tight budget, which is reported as sometimes getting in the way of relationships. For example, residents do not have the option of choosing their roommates, and the roommates also change quite often based on evolution in the health condition of the residents (in some NHs, different areas of the NH are dedicated to residents with different needs). Sometimes the division is in floors and, while there are common areas, the interaction among people living on different floors is less frequent. On the other hand, residents do seem to have the habit to sit with the same people during meals. It is not clear, however how such companies at lunch are formed and the friendship opportunities that this generates.

Facilitating interactions relies heavily on the Staff. In the focus group, a distinction was made by the participants between residents that are independent and cognitively able and those who are less so. Those independent have more opportunities to engage in social interactions, and need little help from the NH in this regard. Those who are less independent though - which are the large majority - do need help from the organization, and for this reason the NHs offer various animation activities. Still, *facilitating bonds depends heavily on the capabilities and wiseness of the Staff* in matching the residents and stimulating conversations.

Interactions with relatives are mostly centered around one family member. We learned that in all NHs the majority of residents have a person (typically the daughter) that comes very frequently to visit, often every day. *Interactions with the rest of the family are much less frequent*, and this is a source of frustration for the visiting family member, who often does what she can to involve the enlarged family. The focus group acknowledged that for logistic reasons the NHs interact with one reference person (usually the family member most involved) and this does not help in involving the larger family.

Grandchildren were cited as a frequent source of joyful visits, though mostly young children visit. Several NHs organize events and projects with younger people to make them interact with older adults and help both parts benefit from intergenerational contacts. During the focus group, it was observed by the participants that it is easier to interact with them for small children, who are spontaneous and don't fear the interaction. Not the same for older children and teens, who are less at ease and find it more difficult to interact.

Interactions with family, peers and staff are important. We emphasize that while family contacts are important and family members contribute to life satisfaction, friends contribute to affect [12]. Participants of the focus group stressed that friendships with other residents and with the staff are also crucial to facilitate adaptation in the RSA environment. In response to a concern of a family member participating in the focus group, about her mother and her difficulties in the transition to residential care, other participants mentioned how bonds help residents perceive the NH as a home.

In relation to the above challenges, NHs have already some practices and initiatives that can be taken as starting points on which solutions could be built (see Fig. 1, left side):

- Pictures and events from the past can be found in open and personal spaces (Fig. 1A), which shows ongoing practices of reminiscence in the NHs and an interest from residents.
- Reading magazines and newspapers is a recreational activity performed in all NHs (Fig. 1B), often with the help of staff and volunteers. Some NHs also act as daily recreational centers for a part of the population, in that case magazines are read daily.
- Posters and boards display pictures of the activities (Fig. 1C), as a way of informing visitors of the activities.
- In some NHs there are computers intended for Skype calls (Fig. 1D) for residents who have relatives far away, but it turns out they are not used much or not at all, also because of the lack of dedicated personnel to assist residents and organize calls. Some NHs have Internet points and allow their residents to use the computers, however residents are generally not digitalized.
- Memories from family members are treasured by residents (Fig. 1E), and are often drivers in conversations, even with the Staff.

In what follows we take these insights and opportunities into the design of a tool for promoting interactions among residents, family members and Staff, building on existing practices and mediums that are already widely used and accepted by our target population.

3   Customized Magazines Promoting Interactions

The studies and observations oriented us toward the idea of leveraging a traditional and accepted method for interaction, that is, a printed magazine[1] (called the *Collegamenti* Magazine - "connections" in Italian) as both a recreational activity and a vehicle to promote interactions. Reading a magazine is not only something people are already used to, but something NH residents regularly do and that is already integrated within the NH processes.

Fig. 1. Left: Collage of pictures from observations. Right: Magazine generation process.

The main idea is to include in the magazine personalized content contributed mainly by family members, and organized in such a way that it motivates interactions among residents and between residents and family members. In other words, we use technology to redesign the content over a traditional interaction method and to make the whole production cycle practical and sustainable (see Fig. 1), with the goal of keeping residents up-to-date with the life of the family and of creating topics of conversations between older adults, their younger relatives and their peers.

3.1   Magazine Content

The above opportunities can be leveraged by collecting interesting content about the past or about readers themselves, with the aim of providing a common ground readers can relate to, which can turn into new topics of conversation and opportunities for interaction. With this goal in mind, and building on our preliminary observations, we propose the following types of section:

– **Reminiscing**: Sections describing news, facts or people from the past. The goal is to create new topics of conversations and stimulate the cognitive and social abilities.

---

[1] Print-ready version of a prototype https://goo.gl/a3HSyu.

- **Bulletin boards**: Announcements and facts from residents and family. The goal of these sections is to create topics of conversations but also to provide a fun and interesting read for the residents, and for the larger family reading from home.
- **News from relatives**: Photos and activities collected from social media and other channels, to keep the residents informed and stimulate conversations.
- **Life in the NH**: Future and past NH events, with pictures and descriptions. The goal is to keep the larger family informed (and involved) and to create a new communication channel between the NH and the external world.
- **From the community**: News and obituaries to keep residents informed about what happens outside the NH, and to stimulate conversations.
- **Hobbies**: Articles about hobbies residents are interested in. The goal is to offer an interesting read that can stimulate conversations among residents.
- **Connections**: Sections showing what residents have in common. The goal is to help them know each other, stimulate conversations and shared activities.

The content is organized in sections using a design inspired by magazines for our target population, putting emphasis on pictures, showing connections among residents starting from the content and providing conversation triggers. This is important because, as we expect family members and volunteers to drive the reading sessions, we still enable residents—to the possible extent—to recognize the content and engage in the conversations.

3.2 Production Process

To make the process for generating the magazine sustainable, we devise an architecture and algorithms that could support increasing levels of human involvement in collecting, selecting and organizing the magazine content. As seen in Fig. 1 (Right), this is done by (A) reusing existing channels and content, (B) using back-end services and matchmaking algorithms based on ranking and (C) through an editorial tool for managing the magazine generation process. We stress that automation is very important as the generation requires the involvement of relatives and NH staff. Notice that professionals and relatives are indeed the persons we expect to be the main drivers of magazine reading, more so than the residents themselves, as newspaper reading is typically guided.

4   Early Evaluation

We performed two preliminary evaluations with relatives and staff members to first validate the concept of the magazine and its fit in the NH processes, and then to look specifically at each section. The relatives are heavily involved in our design and validation process because they are a central element in the life of a resident, and, given that they visit very frequently, they can also act as catalysts for interactions as well as help in the reading activities. In this sense, they are part of our population of target readers.

4.1   Concept Validation with Relatives and NH Staff

Methods. Two researchers conducted semi-structured interviews with the relatives of 5 residents from two NHs, and with 2 NH professionals responsible for the animation activities. The interviews took place inside the NHs and were done by first showing the magazine prototype and then explaining the concept with a storyboard. The objective was to obtain general feedback on the idea of the magazine and its applicability, in particular regarding its potential to create social interactions, to identify possible barriers, but also on the possibility to integrate it in the entertainment activities of the NH.

Results. Professionals rated the magazine positively, stating that (i) it can be beneficial for residents' social relationships, as it makes them feel at the center of the attention, and that (ii) even reading the magazine individually represents a form of social interaction, because it will make them more aware of each other. Importantly, professionals stated that the magazine can be integrated in the entertainment activities, and even proposed collaborative editing of the content.

One of the professionals mentioned the positive potential of the artifact even when residents already have friends, perceiving it also as a communication channel between the NH and the outer world. Feedback on the look and feel was positive but scant: essentially the staff assessed it positively citing the importance of large text and big images, as well as the quantity of the images, which were evaluated as engaging.

Regarding the feedback collected from relatives, one of the interviewees mentioned a possible barrier of refusal in the resident, due to physical impairments (poor sight). One of them mentioned that it could work more as a communication channel with those relatives who cannot visit often, which is indeed a main goal of the magazine. Interviewees did not think there would be a privacy concern for their children or grandchildren, as the information and pictures shown about them are generic and not intimate.

4.2   Content Validation with Different Stakeholders

Methods. The magazine was shown in a focus group with 9 representatives of stakeholders, including directors, coordinators and representatives of the relatives. We presented the concept and handed them copies of the artifact to browse. We went through the sections with them: we explained their content, how they were created and their objectives. Then, participants were asked to quantify on a 5-point Likert scale whether they believed each section achieved its objectives or not, also discussing their opinions with the group.

Results. The magazine had very positive feedback, with an average score of 4.1 (Min: 3.6, Max: 4.7). The results about each section are summarized below.

- **Reminiscing** (avg: 4.2). Participants agree that past memories are a recurrent topic in NH and have the potential to spark conversations.

- **Bulletin boards** (avg: 3.7). Announcements, facts and "gossips" were referred as of interest in the community, though on the specific case of gossips the consensus was that it should be consulted with the resident (or family).
- **News from relatives** (avg: 3.6). While participants agreed on the potential of these sections, they were concerned about the information automatically collected, suggesting to agree with the relatives beforehand on what type of information should and should not be disclosed with the resident.
- **Life in the NH** (avg: 4.3). Participants praised that this content would support some of the internal efforts to reach the larger family.
- **From the community** (avg: 4.3). News from the community are also a recurrent topic, though contrasting views were shared on whether to add obituaries. While it was considered *sad* by some participants, it was stressed that residents do check this section in newspapers.
- **Hobbies** (avg: 4.7). This section was very well received, participants stressing the interest in maintaining and discussing hobbies. This could also help in orienting animation activities and co-participation.
- **Connections** (avg: 3.9). This was well received, especially highlighting common aspects and featuring life stories, but it was pointed out that birthdays (part of this category) are not something residents are always happy to share.

On the concept of the magazine per se, it was generally agreed that a printed, "traditional" magazine can be a good solution for the target population in NHs. One participant mentioned that *"A printed magazine would help us record the history of the NH, a history we can revisit at any time"*. However, a digital version was also considered useful especially for displaying the latest updates.

In general, the feedback from directors, coordinators and family members tells us that the magazine structure and content has the potential to meet the objectives and be integrated into the practices of the NHs. However, they need to be personalized and calibrated on contexts and needs of residents and families.

5   Findings and Future Work

The studies we performed indicate that there is a significant portion of cognitively healthy individuals that reside in the NH for relatively long periods of time and that do not make friends. The studies also indicate that a physical, printed magazine oriented towards encouraging interactions fits into the NH processes and is accepted by the NH staff (otherwise it would be very hard to have an impact). The frequent presence of a family member on site can also facilitate the reading activities. Finally, interviews with staff and family members were insightful in identifying and validating content and structure. This enables us to tailor the design so to maximize the effect of the magazine. This is important because studies in NHs are often challenging and potentially distressing, so background work is essential. Forthcoming work involves the magazine production (with actual content) and distribution in the NHs.

Acknowledgements. This project has received funding from the EU Horizon 2020 research and innovation programme under the Marie Skodowska-Curie grant agreement No 690962. This work was also supported by the "Collegamenti" project funded by the Province of Trento (l.p. n.6-December 13rd 1999).

References

1. Baez, M., Dalpiaz, C., Hoxha, F., Tovo, A., Caforio, V., Casati, F.: Personalized persuasion for social interactions in nursing homes. arXiv preprint arXiv:1603.03349 (2016)
2. Berkman, L.F., Syme, S.L.: Social networks, host resistance, and mortality: a nine-year follow-up study of alameda county residents. Am. J. Epidemiol. **109**(2), 186–204 (1979)
3. Bradshaw, S.A., Playford, E.D., Riazi, A.: Living well in care homes: a systematic review of qualitative studies. Age Ageing **41**(4), 429–440 (2012). p. afs069
4. Brummett, B.H., Barefoot, J.C., Siegler, I.C., Clapp-Channing, N.E., Lytle, B.L., Bosworth, H.B., Williams, R.B., Mark, D.B.: Characteristics of socially isolated patients with coronary artery disease who are at elevated risk for mortality. Psychosom. Med. **63**(2), 267–272 (2001)
5. Caprani, N., Dwyer, N., Harrison, K., O'Brien, K.: Remember when: development of an interactive reminiscence device. In: CHI 2005 Extended Abstracts on Human Factors in Computing Systems, pp. 2070–2073. ACM (2005)
6. Charles, S.T., Leger, K.A., Urban, E.J.: Emotional experience and health: what we know, and where to go from here (2016)
7. van Dijk, B., Dadlani, P., van Halteren, A., Biemans, M.: Life changes, connection stays: photo sharing and social connectedness for people with special needs. In: Proceedings of the 28th Annual European Conference on Cognitive Ergonomics, pp. 135–142. ACM (2010)
8. Jeurens, J., van Turnhout, K., Bakker, R.: Family in focus: on design and field trial of the dynamic collage [DC]. In: Creating the Difference, p. 36 (2014)
9. Lang, F.R.: Endings and continuity of social relationships: maximizing intrinsic benefits within personal networks when feeling near to death. J. Soc. Pers. Relat. **17**(2), 155–182 (2000)
10. Lang, F.R., Carstensen, L.L.: Close emotional relationships in late life: further support for proactive aging in the social domain. Psychol. Aging **9**(2), 315 (1994)
11. Lang, F.R., Carstensen, L.L.: Time counts: future time perspective, goals, and social relationships. Psychol. Aging **17**(1), 125 (2002)
12. Pinquart, M., Sorensen, S.: Influences of socioeconomic status, social network, and competence on subjective well-being in later life: a meta-analysis. Psychol. Aging **15**(2), 187–224 (2000)
13. Rodríguez, M.D., Gonzalez, V.M., Favela, J., Santana, P.C.: Home-based communication system for older adults and their remote family. Comput. Hum. Behav. **25**(3), 609–618 (2009)
14. Santana, P.C., Rodríguez, M.D., González, V.M., Castro, L.A., Andrade, Á.G.: Supporting emotional ties among Mexican elders and their families living abroad. In: CHI 2005 Extended Abstracts on Human Factors in Computing Systems, pp. 2099–2103. ACM (2005)
15. Seeman, T.E., Berkman, L.F., Blazer, D., Rowe, J.W.: Social ties and support and neuroendocrine function: the macarthur studies of successful aging. Ann. Behav. Med. (1994)

16. Taylor, S., Bogdan, R., DeVault, M.: Introduction to Qualitative Research Methods, 4th edn. Wiley, Hoboken (2016)
17. Thomas, W.H.: Life Worth Living: How Someone you Love can Still Enjoy Life in a Nursing Home: The Eden Alternative in Action. VanderWyk & Burnham, St. Louis (1996)

Methods and Tools for User Interface Evaluation

A Model to Compute Webpage Aesthetics Quality Based on Wireframe Geometry

Ranjan Maity[(✉)] and Samit Bhattacharya

Department of Computer Science and Engineering,
Indian Institute of Technology, Guwahati, Guwahati 783019, Assam, India
{ranjan.maity, samit}@iitg.ernet.in

Abstract. Computational models of web page aesthetics prediction are useful for the designers to determine the usability and to improve it. Positional geometry of webpage objects (wireframe) is an important factor for determining the webpage aesthetics as shown in studies. In this paper, we propose a computational model for predicting webpage aesthetics based on the positional geometry. We have considered 13 features of positional geometry that affect aesthetics, as reported in literature. By varying these 13 features, we have designed 52 interfaces' wireframes and rated them by 100 users in a 5 point rating scale. Our 1 dimensional *ANOVA* study on users' rating shows, 9 out of the 13 features are important for webpage aesthetics. Based on these 9 features, we created a computational model for webpage aesthetics prediction. Our computational model works based on *Support Vector Machine* (*SVM*). To judge the efficacy of our model, we considered 10 popular webpages' wireframes, and got them rated by 80 users. Experimental results show that our computational model can predict webpage aesthetics with an accuracy of 90%.

Keywords: Computational model · Aesthetics · Features · Empirical study · Classification · ANOVA · Support vector machine

1 Introduction

With the advancement of technology, electronic devices like mobiles, laptops, i-pads etc. have become an essential part in our daily life. As a result, design of interfaces has become a vital issue for the researchers of Human Computer Interaction (HCI) community. Good interface design requires knowledge about people: how they see, understand and think [5]. Another important aspect of good design is how information is visually presented to the users or the *aesthetics* of the interface. According to the Oxford dictionary [17], *aesthetics* is "concerned with beauty and art and the understanding of beautiful things". It is argued that aesthetically pleasing interfaces increase user efficiency and decrease perceived interface complexity, which in turn helps in increasing usability, productivity and acceptability [15]. It has been also observed [2] that one redesigned graphical window, can save $20,000 of company during the first year of use. The general rule of thumb says every dollar invested in usability returns $10 to $100 [16]. So the current requirement of interface design is the design of aesthetically pleasing interface.

© IFIP International Federation for Information Processing 2017
Published by Springer International Publishing AG 2017. All Rights Reserved
R. Bernhaupt et al. (Eds.): INTERACT 2017, Part III, LNCS 10515, pp. 85–94, 2017.
DOI: 10.1007/978-3-319-67687-6_7

Thus, in general we can say that the interface aesthetics have an important role to play in determining usability. This is true particularly in the web page design. A webpage is composed of three different types of basic elements, or any combination of them, namely: text, image and short video/animation. Other webpage elements like: icon, table, and link etc. can also be approximated by text and image; like icon with image, table and link with text. The shapes of all the webpage elements can be approximated by rectangles. For example, a circular image can be treated as content of a rectangle (*wireframe*).

Since aesthetics is important in webpage design, it is necessary to measure it. Aesthetic measurement of webpage is considered to be *subjective*. Hence, the measure is primarily done through empirical means. A parallel research effort also attempted to develop computational models to evaluate aesthetics of the whole interface [12]. The advantage of computational model is the ability to evaluate interface aesthetics automatically, which in turn makes it possible to automate the design process itself, as demonstrated in [14].

Although a number of works [1, 4, 6–11] report on the contents of a webpage, Ngo et al. [12] found that the impacts of the contents on aesthetics are not important. Rather, the positional geometry of the webpage elements (wireframe) is strongly related with aesthetics. They proposed a computational model for webpage aesthetics based on the 13 positional geometry features of webpage elements. The average of these 13 feature values (termed as *order*) was used to judge the aesthetics of a webpage. Again Lai et al. [7] claimed that the *symmetry* feature had no relation with aesthetics. Finally, Ngo et al. [12] claimed that, their model may not be appropriate for the real webpages. So, we felt that there is a need to review the geometry related features and to develop a computational model for webpage aesthetics.

In this work, we re-examined the 13 best known features of webpage aesthetics, as reported in [12]. We created wireframes of 52 webpages and rated them by 100 participants. *ANOVA* study on the users' ratings revealed only 9 out of the 13 features are statistically significant for aesthetics measurement. Based on those 9 features, we developed a computational model to predict webpage aesthetics. Our model work based on the *linear kernel* of Support Vector Machine (SVM) [3]. To judge the efficiency of our model, we considered the wireframes of 10 real webpages, and rated them by 80 users. Experimental results show that our model can predict aesthetics with 90% accuracy. The details of the 13 positional geometry features, empirical data collections, the proposed model and analysis are described in this paper.

2 Empirical Study for Feature Identification

In order to find the impact of the 13 independent features associated with aesthetics [12], we performed an empirical study. We created 4 webpages for each feature by systematically varying the feature values. These webpages were rated by 100 participants. One dimensional ANOVA was used to find the impact of each feature, associated with webpage aesthetics.

For each feature, we created 4 webpages by varying the feature values systematically in 4 levels – *significant low* (SL), *low* (LO), *average* (AV), *high* (HI). Range for the feature values for each level is shown in Table 1. All these features are independent

Table 1. Four feature class with their range

Feature class	Min value	Max value	Feature class	Min value	Max value
SL	0	0.25	LO	>0.25	0.5
AV	>0.5	0.75	HI	>0.75	1

of each other, as reported in [12]. During the variation of each feature (in 4 different feature classes), we did not observe any significant variations in the other features, which may affect aesthetics.

Altogether, we designed 52 webpages wireframe models using Adobe Photoshop CS6™. The size of each model was 700 × 700 pixels. Figure 1 shows set of 4 such models, where the *unity* feature varies. All these 52 models were shown to the participants on PCs having 2.6 *GHz AMD Phenom II X3* 710, processor running on *Windows* 8. Each PC had a 23 in. wide viewing angle color display.

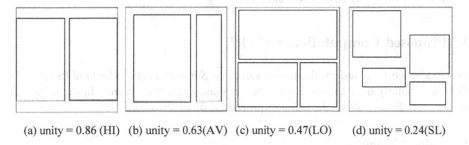

(a) unity = 0.86 (HI)   (b) unity = 0.63(AV)   (c) unity = 0.47(LO)   (d) unity = 0.24(SL)

Fig. 1. Wireframe models of webpages designed by varying the unity feature

One hundred participants took part in our study. Out of them, 20 were school students (average age 16 years), 60 were under and post graduate students (average age 22 years), and rest 20 were teachers (average age 36 years). All of them had normal or corrected-to-normal vision and none of them was colour blind (self reported). All of them were regular computer users. However, none was familiar with screen design concepts.

We created webpages' model of the 52 webpages without considering the contents of the webpage elements. All the 52 models were rated by 100 users in a five point rating scale (1–5); *five* denoted aesthetically pleasing webpage, and *one* denoted the aesthetically least pleasing webpage. A browser-based viewer was created for the users, with facilities to view previous/next sample and to rate a webpage model. After viewing each webpage model, participants rated it according to its *aesthetic appeal*. Each participant rated the 52 models assigned to him/her in two sessions (26 each) in a day. They were allowed to take breaks in each session. These measures were taken to avoid discomfort to the participants that might have arose due to the large number of webpages to be rated. To avoid the learning effect, we randomly varied the sequence of the webpage models shown to the users. Before data collection, we performed a small training sessions for the participants. In these sessions, participants were familiarized with the 5 point scale and the web interface by which they had to rate the webpage models.

Results and Analysis

We computed the feature values of the 52 webpages using the analytical expressions proposed by Ngo's work [12].

Based on the empirical results, we performed 13 independent 1 dimensional *ANOVA* (one for each feature) by using the *ANOVA1* command of *MATLAB 2014*. We observe that the p values are higher ($p > 0.05$) for the features - *density* (0.11), *economy* (.108), *rhythm* (.174) and *simplicity* (.0536). This implies that the variations of these feature values were not having statistically significant impact on the webpage aesthetics. On the contrary, the remaining 9 features – *balance, cohesion, equilibrium, homogeneity, proportion, regularity, sequence, symmetry* and *unity* were found to be statistically significant for the webpage aesthetics. So, we consider these 9 geometry features for webpage aesthetics. Accordingly, we propose a computational model based on these 9 features, as discussed below.

3   Proposed Computational Model

Our model works based on the *linear kernel* of *Support Vector Machine* (SVM) [3]. *SVM* is popularly used for solving the binary classification problems. In the following section, we discuss about the training procedure of our model.

3.1   Model Training

For the model training, we considered a subset of data (9 out of 13 features). It may be noted that we have 5200 ($100 \times 4 \times 13$) data points which are the ratings of 100 users on the 52 webpages; 4 webpages for each of the 13 features. Out of these 13 features, we considered 9 features for the training of our model. So, for these 9 features we have 36 webpages (4 for each feature) and their corresponding 100 users' ratings. Altogether, we have 3600 ($9 \times 4 \times 100$) training data points. In our model we consider 9 *SVM*s to predict the 9 features independently. Each of these 9 *SVM*s was trained by the 400 data points (100×4), which are the ratings of 100 users for the 4 different webpages of a particular feature. As, *SVM* works on labeled data, we converted all the 3600 unlabeled data to labeled training data by using the following logic.

```
Data Labeling
 Input:   36 feature values and their users' rating (100)
 Output: feature class (good or bad)

        if (feature value>= 0.5 and users rating >= 3)
                feature class = good (labeled by +1)
        else
                feature class = bad (labeled by -1)
        end if
```

A particular feature of a webpage was labeled as good (+1), only when an user gave a rating more than 2, in a 5 point scale, as well as the feature value was greater than or equals to 0.5 (computed by the Ngo's analytical expression [12]) in 0 to 1 scale. This was done to label almost half of the scale for aesthetically pleasing (good) feature and the rest was for aesthetically unpleasing feature. Based on these labeled data, we trained our model using the *SVMTRAIN* function of *MATLAB* 2014.

3.2 Empirical Study for Model Validation

The main objective of our model is to predict aesthetics for real webpages. For this purpose, we performed another empirical study on 10 real webpages. The details of the empirical study, along with the performance of our model are discussed below.

For model validation, we considered wireframes of 10 real webpages [18–27] (*home* pages of 10 websites). These webpages represent some popular domains, like – education, banking, e-commerce, social networking, entertainment, news and corporate sector. For all these webpages, we created the webpage models (constructed without considering the content of the webpage elements) by using *Adobe Photoshop* CS6™. Figure 2(b) shows the model of the *soundcloud* (Fig. 2(a)) page. These models were rated by the users in PCs, having 2.6 GHz AMD Phenom II X3 710 processor, running on *Windows* 8. Each PC had a 23 in. wide viewing angle colour display.

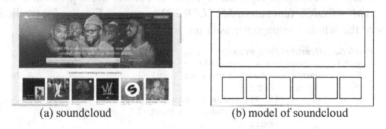

(a) soundcloud   (b) model of soundcloud

Fig. 2. Webpages and their model

All the 10 webpage models were rated by 80 new users. Out of them, 40 were male and the rest were female. Fifty participants were undergraduate students (average age 21 years), 20 users were postgraduate students (average age 27 years) and rest 10 were the faculty members (average age 40 years). All the participants were regular computer users but none of them had any knowledge about the website design principles. All the users had normal or corrected-to-normal vision and none of them was colour blind (self reported).

Each participant rated the 10 webpage models using the same browser-based viewer used in our previous study. After viewing each webpage model, they rated it according to its *aesthetic appeal* in the same 5 point rating scale, used in our previous study; 5 denoted aesthetically pleasing webpage, and 1 denoted aesthetically least pleasing webpage. To avoid the learning effect, we randomly varied the sequence of the webpage models shown to the users. A participant rated the 10 webpages assigned to her/him in one session in a day. Before data collection, we performed a small training sessions for the participants. In these sessions, participants were familiarized with the 5 point scale and the web interfaces by which they had to rate the webpages.

3.3 Results and Discussion

The 13 feature values and their average of the 10 webpage models were computed with the help of Ngo's [12] formulas. Although we selected the 9 features, but computation of these 13 feature values will help us to prove the efficiency of our model. Table 2 shows the *order* (average values of all the 13 features) of the 10 webpages' wireframes. Using these wireframes, we performed another empirical study. Results of the empirical study are shown in Table 2. The mode column of Table 2 denotes the rating, given by most of the users for a particular webpage. Based on the mode value, we classified the webpages in two classes – good or bad. For the binary classification we used the following logic.

```
if mode >= 3
        webpage class=good(aesthetically pleasing(+1))
else
        webpage class=bad(aesthetically unpleasing(-1))
```

We independently trained our *SVM*s to predict the feature class (good or bad) of the 9 features (for 10 webpages), reported in Table 2. Feature class prediction was done using the *SVMPREDICT* function of *MATLAB* 2014 version. Finally, for predicting the aesthetics of the whole webpage we used the following algorithm.

```
Prediction Algorithm for a webpage
Input:   9 feature class values (good or bad), count = 0
Output: webpage class (good or bad)
        for i = 1 to 9
                if (feature class == good)
                        count = count+1
                endif
                i=i+1
        end for
        if (count>=5)
                webpage class = good (labeled by +1)
        else
                webpage class = bad (labeled by -1)
        endif
```

The prediction algorithm shows, if most of the predicted features (5 out of 9) are aesthetically pleasing (good) then our algorithm (as mentioned above) predicts the webpage as good (aesthetically pleasing), otherwise it is treated as bad (aesthetically unpleasing).

We compared the predicted result of our model with the results obtained from empirical study. Using our model, we predicted the feature types of the 10 webpages as shown in Table 2. Then based on our webpage prediction algorithm we predicted the webpages as aesthetically pleasing (+1) or not (−1). The second rightmost column of the Table 2 shows the result of the webpage type (aesthetically pleasing or not) by the users' rating.

Table 2. Empirical study result vs. predicted result

| Website | Label predicted by our developed SVM | | | | | | | | | Model predicted webpage label | Mode of users' ratings | Users' choice webpage label | Order value based on Ngo [18] |
	Balance	Cohesion	Equilibrium	Homogeneity	Proportion	Regularity	Sequence	Symmetry	Unity				
CIT, Kokrajhar	−1	−1	+1	−1	+1	+1	+1	−1	−1	−1	3	+1	0.4706
Sound Cloud	+1	+1	+1	−1	+1	+1	+1	−1	+1	+1	4	+1	0.5216
SBI	−1	−1	+1	−1	−1	−1	−1	−1	−1	−1	2	−1	0.4334
Flipkart	−1	−1	+1	−1	−1	−1	−1	−1	−1	−1	2	−1	0.4775
Facebook	−1	−1	+1	−1	+1	+1	+1	+1	−1	+1	3	+1	0.4532
Amazon	+1	+1	+1	−1	+1	+1	+1	−1	+1	+1	4	+1	0.5133
NewsLive	−1	−1	+1	−1	−1	−1	−1	−1	−1	−1	2	−1	0.4520
Youtube	−1	−1	+1	−1	−1	−1	−1	−1	−1	−1	2	−1	0.4406
IIT Guwahati	+1	+1	+1	−1	+1	+1	+1	−1	−1	+1	4	+1	0.5003
TCS	+1	+1	+1	−1	+1	+1	+1	−1	−1	+1	4	+1	0.4581

Out of 10 webpages, our model accurately predicted 9 webpages. Thus, our model predicted webpage aesthetics with an accuracy of 90% (9 out of 10).

Ngo et al. [12] claimed that the *order* value may be a measure for aesthetics computation. However, in our study we observe that the *order* may not be relevant for real webpages. The *order* value of the 10 real webpages lied in the range from 0.43 to 0.52 as shown in Table 2, which is sorted based on the *order* value. It may be noted that, the order value of the *facebook* is 0.45 was treated by users as aesthetically pleasing webpage. In a contrary, the higher *order* value (than that of *Facebook*) of *Flipkart* 0.47 was treated as aesthetically unpleasing by the users. Again, the lower *order* value (than that of *Flipkart*) of *TCS* and *CIT, Kokrajhar* are 0.4532 and 0.4581 were marked as aesthetically pleasing webpages by the users. Even we can observe that the difference of the *order* value among the webpages *NewsLive* and *Facebook* is only 0.1%. But, still users find *facebook* as aesthetically pleasing, while the *NewsLive* as aesthetically unpleasing. Similarly, we observe the difference in the *order* value is only 0.7% among *CIT Kokrajhar* and *Flipkart*. But *CIT Kokrajhar* was treated as aesthetically pleasing, while the *Flipkart* was treated as aesthetically unpleasing.

Based on the above observations, we can claim that *order* is not a suitable metric for aesthetics computation of real webpages. In contrast, our model works based on *SVM*; which has the capability for solving binary classification problems with high accuracy.

SVM maps data into a higher dimensional input space and creates an optimal separating hyper plane in the higher dimensional space. As a result, two classes (good or bad) are created across the separating hyper plane. Then for a particular input, *SVM* predicts the corresponding class. We used this notion to predict the feature types of the 10 webpages. However, selection of *SVM* kernel is a tricky task. The general convention is to use the linear kernel first, as they are easier and faster than that of the others kernels, like *polynomial*, *RBF* and *Sigmoid* kernels. If the prediction result is satisfactory then *linear* kernel is the best option; otherwise, other kernels have to be used. Using this convention, we used the *linear* kernel of *SVM* in our model. We observed an accuracy of 90% in aesthetics prediction, which is good enough. So, we refrain to consider the other kernels. However, the performances of the other kernels in this context may be explored. In our model, we trained each *SVM* by 400 data. However, larger training data may improve the performance of our model.

Our model can predict webpage aesthetics in terms of two classes – aesthetically pleasing (good) or unpleasing (bad). It is the simplest type of classification and has the less chance of misclassifying than that of multiclass classifiers. Again, multiclass classifiers are more complex and consume more time for classification, than that of binary classifiers. So, for the devices, where time and computational power are the judgement factors, like – mobiles, PDAs etc., binary classifier is the best choice. In our study we collected the users' rating in a 5 point rating scale and predicted webpage aesthetics in two classes (good or bad). However, the performance of a model which can predict aesthetics in same scale (1–5) may be explored for further analysis.

Our computational model can help the designers to improve the design. For a particular webpage if our model predicts it as aesthetically unpleasing, then there is likely to be some problem with the design, which can reduce aesthetics and consequently, reduce usability of the design. Hence, the designer should take some corrective measures to improve the design. A designer can correct his/her design by considering the predicted *feature_class* values produced by our model. We can integrate our model with the webpage design guidelines or apply genetic algorithm based approach as reported in [14] to redesign webpage geometry. This redesign can improve aesthetic appeal; which in turn can increase usability.

In this work we have only considered the size and geometrical positions of the webpage elements for aesthetics. We have not considered the content of the webpage elements. But in some studies we observed that contents of webpage elements have impact on aesthetics. Our model may be combined with the models of short animations [14], text [10] and image model [9] to develop a complete computational model for evaluating aesthetic quality of a webpage. In our work, we consider the 4 variations of each feature. However, making more variations in each feature value may help us to develop a better model.

4   Conclusion

In this work, we reassessed the best known features for webpage aesthetics. We performed an empirical study and found that 9 features are important for aesthetics measurement. By considering these 9 features, we developed a computational model for aesthetics prediction. Our model works based on the *linear kernel* of Support Vector Machine. To judge the efficiency of our model, we performed another empirical study on real webpages, and found that our model can predict webpage aesthetics with a high accuracy of 90%. In future, we plan to refine and extend our model by more empirical data collection for model training and testing. We also try to combine our model with other predictive models for text, image and short animation aesthetics and develop a fully automated design environment. Investigation of more robust model based on other *kernels* of *SVM*s may also be explored. In our model we predicted aesthetics as good or bad. However, predicting aesthetics in the 5 point rating scale may also be an interesting topic. For each feature we considered only 4 variations. More variations in the feature values may help to build a more robust model.

Acknowledgement. We are thankful to all the participants who volunteered for the empirical studies.

References

1. Bansal, D., Bhattacharya, S.: Semi-supervised learning based aesthetic classifier for short animations embedded in web pages. In: Kotzé, P., Marsden, G., Lindgaard, G., Wesson, J., Winckler, M. (eds.) INTERACT 2013. LNCS, vol. 8117, pp. 728–745. Springer, Heidelberg (2013). doi:10.1007/978-3-642-40483-2_51
2. Cope, M.E., Uliano, K.C.: Cost-justifying usability engineering: a real world example. In: Proceedings of the Human Factors Society 39th Annual Meeting, vol. 39, no. 4, pp. 263–276. Human Factors Society, Santa Monica (1995)
3. Cortes, C., Vapnik, V.: Support-vector networks. Mach. Learn. **20**(3), 273–297 (1995)
4. Datta, R., Joshi, D., Li, J., Wang, J.Z.: Studying aesthetics in photographic images using a computational approach. In: Leonardis, A., Bischof, H., Pinz, A. (eds.) ECCV 2006. LNCS, vol. 3953, pp. 288–301. Springer, Heidelberg (2006). doi:10.1007/11744078_23
5. Galitz, W.O.: The Essential Guide to user Interface Design: An Introduction to GUI Design Principles and Techniques. Wiley, New York (1997)
6. Hill, A.: Readability of screen displays with various foreground/background color combinations, font styles, and font types. In: Proceedings of 11th National Conference on Undergraduate Research, vol. 2, pp. 742–746 (1997)
7. Lai, C.Y., Chen, P.H., Shih, S.W., Liu, Y., Hong, J.S.: Computational models and experimental investigations of effects of balance and symmetry on the aesthetics of text-overlaid images. Int. J. Hum. Comput Stud. **68**, 41–56 (2010)
8. Legge, G.E., Bigelow, C.A.: Does print size matter for reading? A review of findings from vision science and typography. J. Vis. **11**(5), 8 (2011)
9. Maity, R., Uttav, A., Verma, G., Bhattachariya, S.: A non-linear regression model to predict aesthetics ratings of on-screen images. In: OZCHI 2015, Melbourne, Australia, pp. 44–52 (2015)
10. Maity, R., Madrosia. A., Bhattachariya, S.: A computational model to predict aesthetics quality of text elements of GUI. In: IHCI 2015, Allahabad, India, pp. 152–159 (2015)
11. Miniukovich, A., Angeli, D. Computation of interface aesthetics. In: CHI 2015, Seoul, Republic of Korea, pp. 1163–1172 (2015)
12. Ngo, D.C.L., Teo, L.S., Byrne, J.G.: Modeling interface aesthetics. Inf. Sci. **152**, 25–46 (2003)
13. Shyam, D., Bhattacharya, S.: A model to evaluate aesthetics of short videos. In: APCHI, Matsue, Japan, pp. 315–324 (2012)
14. Singh, N., Bhattacharya, S.: A GA-based approach to improve web page aesthetics. In: Proceedings of 1st international conference on Intelligent Interactive Technologies and Multimedia (IITM 2010), pp. 29–32. IIIT Allahabad, India (2010)
15. Tractinsky, N.: Aesthetics and apparent usability: empirically assessing cultural and methodological issues. In: CHI 1997, New York (1997)
16. International Business Machines (IBM). Cost Justifying Ease of Use (2001)
17. http://www.oxfordlearnersdictionaries.com/definition/english/aesthetic_1

18. [CIT Kokrajhar] cit.ac.in
19. [IIT Guwahati] iitg.ac.in
20. [Facebook] facebook.com
21. [Sound cloud] soundcloud.com
22. [Youtube] youtube.com
23. [Flipkart] flipkart.com
24. [State Bank of India] onlinesbi.com
25. [Amazon] amazon.com
26. [Newslive] newslivetv.org
27. [TCS] tcs.com

Bringing Worth Maps a Step Further:
A Dedicated Online-Resource

Fatoumata G. Camara(✉) and Gaëlle Calvary

Univ. Grenoble Alpes, CNRS, Grenoble INP Institute of Engineering Univ.
Grenoble Alpes, LIG, Grenoble 38000, France
fatoumatag.camara@gmail.com, gaelle.calvary@imag.fr

Abstract. Worth Maps (WMs) are promising because they model interactive systems following different perspectives. Consequently, WMs support design in many ways. ARROW was introduced to provide designers with a systematic approach to worth mapping. However, the framework currently remains untested, which raises open questions about general applicability and relevance. In this work, we operationalize ARROW in additional design cases. With insights gained from the operational experience, we propose ARROWS (for ARROW-Support) as a refinement of the initial framework. ARROWS was assessed via a workshop with designers. Results highlight the need for appropriate resources supporting worth mapping. In order to fulfill this need, we have created and released a website providing designers with knowledge on ARROWS and WMs that follows a more practically oriented perspective.

Keywords: Worth-Centered Design (WCD) · Worth Maps (WMs) · ARROW · ARROWS · Online resource

1 Introduction

Since it is now clear that design must go beyond usability, we have witnessed the introduction of different approaches to designing for human-oriented attributes. For instance, the framework for positive experience [25] makes the assumption that the fulfillment of ten basic human needs leads to positive user experience (UX). These ten basic needs are: '*Security*', '*Keeping the meaningful*', '*Relatedness*', '*Popularity*', '*Competition*', '*Physical health*', '*Competence*', '*Influence*', and '*Stimulation*'. The framework for positive experience takes other aspects into account, such as usability and accessibility. Value-Sensitive Design (VSD) proposes including all values in design and especially those with moral import [15, 16]. In [16], Friedman and colleagues highlight a list of twelve values which are often implicated in interactive systems design. These twelve values are: '*Human welfare*', '*Ownership and property*', '*Privacy*', '*Freedom from bias*', '*Universal usability*', '*Trust*', '*Informed consent*', '*Accountability*', '*Courtesy*', '*Identity*', '*Calmness*', and '*Environmental sustainability*'. As witnessed by the aforementioned list, usability does matter in VSD. It is, however, differentiated from values and refers to criteria that characterize the system from a functional point of view.

© IFIP International Federation for Information Processing 2017
Published by Springer International Publishing AG 2017. All Rights Reserved
R. Bernhaupt et al. (Eds.): INTERACT 2017, Part III, LNCS 10515, pp. 95–113, 2017.
DOI: 10.1007/978-3-319-67687-6_8

Other work, with similar goals (i.e., designing for human-centered attributes), consider a larger scope of aspects. For instance, Almquist and colleagues [1] identified thirty elements of value coming into play when customers evaluate a product or service. These thirty elements are organized in a pyramidal hierarchy around four categories, which are (from bottom to top): '*Functional*' (14 elements) (e.g., '*Save time*', '*Sensory appeal*'), '*Emotional*' (10) (e.g., '*Nostalgia*', '*Design/aesthetics*'), '*Life changing*' (5) (e.g., '*Heirloom*', '*Self-actualization*'), and '*Social impact*' (e.g., '*Self-transcendence*'). Worth-Centered Design focuses on worth [6–8], defined as '*things that will motivate people to buy, learn, use or recommend an interactive product, and ideally most or all of these*' [8]. Worth can be modeled using Worth Maps as a connection between system-oriented and human-oriented elements. As such, from '*designing as crafting*' WMs shift design to '*designing as connecting*': they represent an interesting design tool.

This work is related to worth maps. The design tool has been investigated in several projects [2, 9, 11, 13, 14, 19, 27]. If there is a consensus on worth maps benefits for design, examples of existing WMs are more diverse in terms of constituent elements. In order to shape the content of WMs, Camara and Calvary [2] proposed the ARROW framework and illustrated it using a concrete case. However, beyond, the ARROW framework has not received yet much attention.

More precisely, this work addresses the general applicability and relevance of ARROW. Firstly, we have used the ARROW framework to create WMs in different project contexts. Secondarily, we have conducted a workshop with designers to assess insights gathered from the first worth mapping experience. Contributions are the following.

- We prove the applicability and relevance of ARROW.
- We present '*ARROW-Support (ARROWS)*' to propose refinements and extensions for the ARROW framework.
- We prove the understandability of ARROWS as well as, once more, the relevance of WMs for design.
- We propose an online resource dedicated to ARROWS and WMs.

The remainder is organized as follows: The next section discusses relevant literature associated with this work. Section 3 relates our worth mapping experience with a focus on Lyric, the illustrative case. Section 4 presents propositions of ARROWS for refining and extending the ARROW framework. Section 5 describes the assessment of ARROWS through a workshop conducted with designers. Section 6 presents the online resource dedicated to ARROWS and WMs. Finally, Sect. 7 concludes the paper and highlights directions for future work.

2   Literature Review

2.1   Worth Maps

WMs are inspired from Hierarchical Value Maps (HVMs) [21] used in marketing to study customers' motivations for purchase. HVMs combined separately elicited

Means-Ends Chains (MECs) together. MECs, in turn, connect (product) attributes (A) to (usage) consequences (C) and consequences to (personal) values (V): MECs are then formed of A-C-V chains [17].

WMs connect system-oriented attributes (also referred as 'design elements') to human-oriented ones (also referred as 'human elements'). Examples of design elements include materials and features; examples of human elements are usage impacts, feelings, and needs. WMs support three of the WCD meta-principles [12] ('*expressivity*', '*credibility*', and '*committedness*') and consider both positive and negative aspects related to the interactive system. Positive connections explain why users would buy, learn, use, and/or recommend the interactive system; negative ones explain factors that might hinder the use of the interactive system.

WMs have a vertical representation; the positive generally appears upwards while the negative appears downwards.

In interactive systems design, WMs were first called '*Worth/Aversion Maps (W/AMs)*'. W/AMs moved HVMs from release to early design stages (such as '*opportunity identification*' [7]) [10]. W/AMs also revisited HVMs in several points [10, 13].

- In HVMs, consequences can be functional or psychosocial; W/AMs refined and extended these with further types.
- In HVMs, values are restricted to the 18 instrumental and 18 terminal values from Rokeach's Value Survey [22]; W/AMs imposed no vocabulary in regards to values formulation.
- In HVMs, functional consequences must precede psychosocial ones; W/AMs do not impose such a rigid ordering.

In [13], W/AMs are revised and re-baptized '*worth maps*'. Changes mainly occurred regarding two points. Firstly, W/AMs had retained the two types of product attributes in HVMs: concrete and abstract attributes. WMs refined concrete attributes into two types: materials and features. Moreover, positive and negative abstract attributes are in WMs re-named respectively to qualities and defects. Secondarily, an alternative structure, handling user experience as interplay of feelings and actions, are used for usage consequences in WMs.

In [2], the authors relate their complete operationalization of the WCD framework through the development of Cocoon, phase by phase. In order to fulfill the lack of a concrete methodology for worth mapping, faced at '*design*' phase, the authors propose the ARROW (Appreciations, Requirements and Rationale Of Worth) framework, which also suggests different types of classes of elements and connections for WMs. The ARROW framework is at the core of this work and is described in more detail in the next section.

2.2 The ARROW Framework

ARROW (initially PEW [3]) was developed during the development of Cocoon, a mobile and context-aware application. The ARROW framework addresses worth as a twofold notion: '*Appreciated Worth*' vs. '*Requested Worth*' [2].

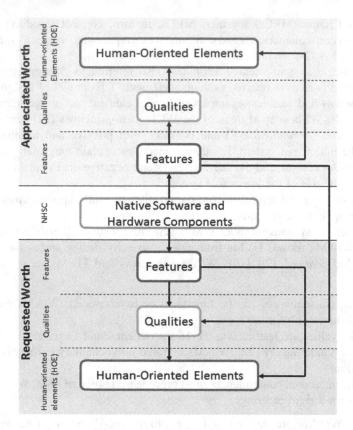

Fig. 1. The ARROW framework

Appreciated Worth represents the positive aspects of the interactive system (i.e., the strengths). By referring to worth definition, Appreciated worth highlights factors that motivate the user to buy, learn, use and/or recommend the interactive system.

Requested Worth overcomes the negative aspects of the interactive system (i.e., the weaknesses). In other words, through Requested worth, ARROW suggests that WMs rather highlight compensatory elements instead of negative aspects themselves. For instance, let's imagine that users point out information redundancy as a discouraging factor for the system use. Instead of representing 'information redundancy' in the worth map, ARROW suggests considering a means for controlling information frequency.

ARROW proposes that WMs are structured around Appreciated worth, Requested worth, and a third additional class of elements: '*Native Software and Hardware Components (NSHC)*' of the device(s) hosting interaction. The framework proposes further that both Appreciated worth and Requested worth consider three sub-categories of elements: '*Features*' (of the interactive system), '*Qualities*' (of Features), and '*Human-Oriented Elements (HOE)*' (impacted by interaction).

ARROW also suggests a vertical representation for WMs: Appreciated worth on the upper part, Requested worth on the lower part, and NSHC in the middle as they may support both appreciated and requested features.

2.3 WMs in Design

Previous work shows that WMs support design in several ways. In [13], authors conducted a field study with 11 families in order to investigate whether WMs could help highlight design solutions for family archiving purposes. In [14], sentence completion supported worth mapping with the aim to understand deeper motivations of online players. In both works, worth mapping has led to profitable outcomes for projects globally, worth mapping as an approach, and to WMs in terms of content.

Otero et al. conducted five semi-structured interviews to support the worth mapping process during the development of a digital public display for a teachers' common room [19, 20]. In conclusions, the authors state: '*The exercise of explicitly stating the connections between features, qualities, and higher-level constructs about use fostered critical thinking and search for alternative design solutions*'. Vu relied on a user study consisting of interviews to populate two WMs which were used for the main purpose of WMs: connect design sensitivities to human ones [27].

In [2] also, worth mapping is combined with other HCI techniques for data collection purposes: semi-structured interviews at the '*study of needs*' phase and a field study followed by group interviews at '*evaluation*' phase. Camara and Calvary showed that WMs could support: User Interface (UI) and interaction design, graphic design, and software implementation. In addition, because WMs based on ARROW are symmetric, the authors relied on an approach based on WMs comparison to support the evaluation of Cocoon. Finally, they highlight WMs as support to communication in heterogeneous design teams, thanks to their visual representation (i.e. *expressivity* of WMs).

WMs have evolved considerably over the time. Derived from HVMs, they were initially introduced as W/AMs, W/AMs were in turn refined and, more recently, ARROW was introduced as a framework dedicated to shape the content of WMs. If ARROW seems to be well suited for WMs in interactive systems, the framework presentation lacks detailed information regarding classes of elements and connections between them. Therefore, further goals of our work are to find out more about the ARROW classes and to understand the types of possible relationships that may link elements to each other.

3 Worth Mapping Beyond Cocoon

3.1 The Design Cases

The design cases considered for the worth mapping experience were selected in order to investigate worth maps in different application domains and design stages (see Table 1): Lyric[1,2] (a heating controller system), Colibri[3] (an advanced planning system) [4], FutureID[4] (an identity management system), and Cocoon (a mobile and

---

[1] https://www.youtube.com/watch?v=HU0y5vFdUz8.

[2] https://www.youtube.com/watch?v=yKKrFaJbRy8&feature=youtu.be.

[3] https://www.youtube.com/watch?v=Izc8HjeK3wQ&feature=youtu.be.

[4] http://www.futureid.eu/.

context-sensitive system) [2]. Furthermore, our literature review revealed that most worth mapping experiences relied on user-centered approaches to collect worth elements and understand connections between them (see Sect. 2.3). Yet, users' involvement requires resources (e.g., in terms of time and expertise) which may not be available in every project. Therefore, during this exercise, we have made the choice not to use any user-centered approach with the aim to test out whether worth mapping could be successful without support from users.

Here, we focus on our illustrative case, Lyric. Below, we describe the system as well as the worth mapping process and its outcomes. More information regarding the remaining cases is available in the online resource (see Sect. 6).

Table 1. Design cases characterization according to application domain and design stage.

Design stage	Domain			
	Lyric (Home Control)	Colibri (Suppy Chain)	FutureID (Identity)	Cocoon (Adaptation)
Opportunity identification		■		
Analysis				■
Design				■
Evaluation			■	■
Release	■			

3.2   Lyric: The Illustrative Case

Lyric is a heating system controller that offers a great deal beyond the primary functions of a thermostat through a distributed interaction between the Lyric device and the user's mobile devices (Smartphone and tablet). With Lyric, the user has the possibility to set the temperature to a desired value; the system takes different parameters (home temperature, humidity and outdoor weather) into account in order to perform the request. The user has also the possibility to set the thermostat to 'away'; the system knows then when the home is occupied vs. empty and uses the user's location to proceed to appropriate adjustments according to user's preferred settings ('Geofencing'). Additionally, Lyric allows the user to check the weather and create 'Shortcuts', which are easy to use custom settings (for instance, temperature at 60° on Fridays from 8:30 AM when the home is empty).

Lyric was chosen as an illustrative example because the heating controller system was used to motivate the first work around worth. Indeed, in [5], Cockton recalls reasons that might motivate for controlling heat in the home (e.g., money saving, care for the environment). Further, the author explains that existing systems (at that time) do not deliver the true worth by stating '*I know of no central heating controller that tells me how much money (and fuel) I've saved by setting a particular program*'. Therefore, more than ten years later, it would be interesting to see whether current systems address missing features to meet users' intrinsic motivations.

We have collected information from the Honeywell website and different videos to construct a worth map for Lyric. This information has allowed us to receive insights regarding Lyric features (as mentioned above) as well as regarding different aspects for populating the other layers of the worth map (NSCHs, qualities, and HOEs). It is, however, important to note that these sources mainly focus on positive aspects, corresponding only to the upper side of the worth map (i.e., Appreciated Worth). Nevertheless, it was straightforward to notice that Lyric does not let the user know the amount of money and/or energy s/he saved thanks to the effort put into programming the heating system. As a consequence, the 'Money/Energy savings computation' feature could be evidently considered as part of Requested Worth for Lyric. Additional research, supported by existing literature related to worth/values, has allowed us to identify additional Requested Worth elements.

The worth map for Lyric (see Fig. 2) diagrammatically summarizes the strengths of the thermostat. As such, it could support communication: proper advisement towards customers and efficient communication within the design team. Through identified missing aspects, the worth map also provides the design team with directions for improving the product during an iteration phase.

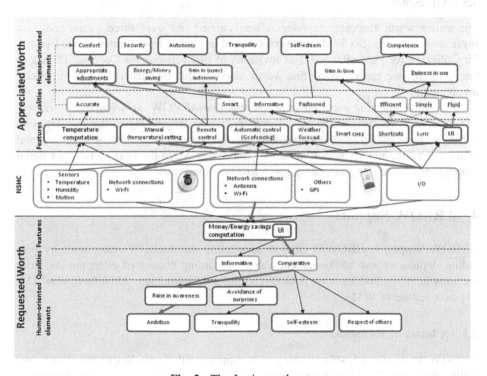

Fig. 2. The Lyric worth map

The NSHC layer illustrates modularization: native software and hardware components are grouped according to types of device.

The highlighted chains can be read as suggested below.

- Blue: the Geofencing feature relies on some network connections (the Wi-Fi of the Lyric device is highlighted here) for data exchange; the feature presents the quality of being smart as it knows when the house is empty or occupied and proceeds to appropriate adjustments accordingly; as such, the Geofencing feature contributes to energy and money saving, which may enhance financial security for the user.
- Pink: the manual setting feature allows the user to perform appropriate adjustments (thanks to input devices) and, therefore, allows her to experience physical comfort through adapted room temperatures.
- Gray: the Money/Energy saving computation component would rely on wireless network connections for data exchange; the feature should present the quality of being comparative, i.e., provide the user with comparable information (e.g., energy consumptions over the last three months, total of energy consumption over the last six months in comparison to the carbon footprint of a flight Paris-Berlin); such information might raise the users awareness of energy consumption and, consequently, create ambition for a change of habit.

3.3 Outcomes

The entire worth mapping experience was carried out over three years and four application domains. Six WMs were constructed in total: 4 from scratch (1 for Lyric; 2 for Colibri; 1 for FutureID) and 2 as revisions of first versions for Cocoon. Thanks to this outcome, we can conclude that worth mapping can be successful without users' involvement.

Our worth mapping experience also shows that ARROW, as originally described, can be applied to diverse domains. However, while progressing in the journey with WMs, we have gained more understanding on the framework and WMs in general and could, therefore, identify opportunities for improvement. In the next section, we detail propositions for refining/extending the ARROW framework.

4 ARROW-Support

ARROW-Support (ARROWS) aims at supporting the ARROW framework by providing definitions and additional knowledge regarding classes of elements and connections in WMs. Furthermore, ARROWS explicitly introduces '*Modularization*' [13, 14] as a feature of WMs.

4.1 Classes of Elements

ARROW defines three first-level categories: Appreciated Worth, Requested Worth, and Native Software Hardware Components (NSHC); both Appreciated and Requested worth are structured around three sub-classes: Features, Qualities, and Human-Oriented Elements (HOEs). ARROWS keeps the same classes of elements.

- **Native Software Hardware Components (NSHC)**: we define NSHC as peripheral components that can support the interactive system both from an internal (i.e., underlying processes) and an external point of view (i.e., the UI). Standard input and output (I/O) devices, such as the mouse, the keyboard, the camera, and the microphone, are generally part of NSHC. In the specific case of Lyric, we can, in addition, mention the GPS of the mobile device (considering that the system could rely on it to locate the user) as well as the Wi-Fi for data-exchange.

- **Features**: we propose considering the interactive system in detail by examining each feature individually, but, also globally by examining it as a whole. In the specific case of Lyric, examples of individual features include: the automatic temperature control by the system (Geofencing) as well as the manual temperature setting by the user. The global feature representing the system as a whole is named as the system, so '*Lyric*' in the illustrative example. Furthermore, ARROWS suggests paying a particular attention to the UI (and the associated interaction) by considering it as a sub-feature of each feature.

- **Qualities**: we propose that WMs distinguish four types of qualities:

- *UI and Interaction qualities* highlight dimensions of usability, ergonomic criteria as well as aesthetic aspects related to the interactive system. In Lyric, such qualities include: '*Simple*', '*Efficient*' or '*Fashioned*'.

- *Inherent qualities* result from the spirit of a feature or a concept. Inherent qualities can also be related to a company identity or culture and could, therefore, highlight dimensions of brand experience (BX) [23]. In the specific case of Lyric, '*Smart*' represents such a quality since the thermostat has initially been designed to be so.

- *Functional qualities* are related to underlying processes sustaining the UI and the interaction (e.g., data computation, database access). In the case of Lyric, '*Accurate*' belongs to functional qualities since the system takes different parameters into account in order to compute the temperature as accurately as possible. '*Instantaneous*' could also be part of Lyric (appreciated) functional qualities if changes requested remotely (from the mobile phone, for instance) are taken into account within a relative short period of time (e.g., 0.5 s).

- *Global qualities* reveal characteristics related to the interactive system considered as a whole (i.e., related to the global feature). Because only stability of many features makes a whole system stable, '*Stable*' can be considered a global quality in many cases, including the specific one of Lyric.

It is important to note that a global quality can be UI-related, inherent, or functional. In the case of Lyric, '*Fashioned*' is a UI-related global quality and '*stable*' could be considered as inherent-global one if the development team had the aim to design a system with an exceptional degree of stability and had, therefore, made effort to reach this goal, for instance, through specific testing strategies. In another example, '*Expensive*' could be considered as an inherent quality of Apple products since high cost seems to be part of the company's culture that contributes to the brand image (for ensuring high quality). However, since expensiveness is related to the product as a whole, '*Expensive*' would be a inherent-global quality.

It might be difficult sometimes to label a quality: there can be a fuzzy line between the aforementioned classes of quality. Therefore, we recommend practitioners rely on the three questions in order to determine more easily whether a quality is inherent, UI/Interaction-related, functional and/or global.

Table 2. Helper for determining qualities types

Inherent qualities		
Is the quality very specific to the context (e.g., system, project, company)?	Yes	
Some UI/Interaction-related and functional qualities		
Is the quality objectively measurable?	Yes	
Global qualities		
Is the quality related to a specific feature?		No

Table 2 highlights that inherent qualities are not generally objectively measureable, UI-related qualities can be objectively measurable and functional ones are generally objectively measurable. Additionally, we recommend practitioners proceed to qualities labeling according to: from inherent to UI-related/functional and from specific to global.

– **Human-Oriented Elements (HOEs)**: as in the initial framework, ARROWS represents human-oriented attributes under the name '*Human-Oriented Elements (HOEs)*'. User experience, understood as the result of direct interaction with a product or a service and indirect interaction (through a third party), is part of HOEs. It is important to note that interaction also includes here both anticipated and post usage. HOEs also encompass interaction consequences as well as higher-level elements impacted by interaction (though consequences or not), such as human needs and values.

  In the specific case of Lyric such elements include (financial) '*Security*' thanks to energy saving, (physical) '*Comfort*' thanks to appropriate temperature adjustments, and (feeling of) '*Competence*' since the user can easily reach his/her goals thanks to the simple and efficient UI.

4.2   Connections Between Elements

Let's consider that features, qualities, and human-oriented elements part of Appreciated worth are respectively represented by: AF ('Appreciated Feature'), AQ, and AHOE. The same naming rules apply to Requested worth. The types of connection depicted on the ARROW framework (see Fig. 1) can be textually translated as follows.

– (1) NHSC → AF → AQ → AHOE
– (2) NHSC → RF → RQ → RHOE
– (3) NHSC → AF → AQ
– (4) NHSC → RF → RQ
– (5) NHSC → AF → AHOE
– (6) NHSC → RF → RHOE

ARROW suggests full but also partial chains within WMs. If full chains make complete sense ((1), (2)), partial ones are more debatable since they assume that features with good qualities can contribute to worth even if they don't impact any HOE (i.e., (3), (4)) and that human-oriented elements can be directly impacted through features without intermediary qualities (i.e., (5), (6)).

Indeed, the worth mapping experience allowed us to understand that every feature presents one or more qualities and that every quality impacts human elements. As a consequence, WMs would only be composed of complete chains. Nevertheless, we could also admit that partial chains can be relevant in some cases: when the human-attribute element is reached though an expected quality (the connection between the quality and the HOE can be omitted) and when the human-attribute element is reached though an intrinsic (and not differentiating) quality (the connection between the feature and the quality can be omitted).

For instance, in the Lyric worth map (see Fig. 2), the quality 'Accurate' (of the feature 'Temperature computation') could be linked to the human-oriented element ('Comfort') considering that the user would be able to make good provisions accordingly. However, since accuracy would be expected from every thermostat, the impact in terms of HOE can be assumed as not significant and, as a consequence, the corresponding connection omitted.

4.3 Modularization

During the worth mapping exercise, we have understood that WMs can and should be modularized, both at elements and connections levels. Indeed, in [13], the authors grouped worth elements due a lack of space and, in [14], researchers use Microsoft Office Visio drawing layers to group complex connections. The worth mapping experience revealed that other reasons could, however motivate, modularity in WMs.

Worth maps can be rather big, which negatively impacts readability and understandability. Partial chains can already contribute to reduce complexity. Additionally, thanks to modularity, WMs could first give an overview before progressively disclosing details, as suggested by the information visualization mantra: 'overview first, zoom and filter, then details-on-demand' [24]. By doing so, WMs could also support the WCD meta-principles of 'inclusiveness' in an appropriate way by adapting information-level in the different layers according to stakeholders.

5 Workshop with Designers

To assess the meaningfulness and relevance of knowledge produced during the worth mapping experience, we conducted a one-day workshop, which provided us with the opportunity to introduce ARROWS and WMs to a group of practitioners.

5.1 Participants

Six people (4 female, 2 male) from a telecommunication company and all involved in interactive systems design participated in the workshop. The group of practitioners included: two human factors experts, a research project manager, an innovative service designer, a communication service architect, and a psychologist. According to data collected, participants had diverse backgrounds and played different roles in design.

5.2 Procedure

During the workshop, the participants were divided into two teams: the project manager, the innovative service designer, and one human factors specialist together in a first team; the communication service architect, the psychologist, and the other human factors specialist in a second team. The following activities were carried out (in the order they appear).

- Self-Introduction: participants as well as facilitators first built their personal and professional profile using Lego bricks. Then, each person commented on her tangible representation to introduce his/herself (Fig. 3).

Fig. 3. A group of participants building their profile with Lego bricks

- Refection on '*Worth*': each participant materialized '*worth*' using Lego bricks and, then, commented to share his/her perspectives on the notion with others.
- Design of the ideal thermostat: first, each team built an ideal thermostat using Lego bricks. Second, a team member described the resulting system from each side. Third, the two teams provided each other with feedback.
- Presentation of Lyric: the Lyric thermostat was introduced to participants through two videos.

- Introduction to ARROWS and WMs: WMs were first briefly defined. Then, ARROWS was introduced using Lyric. During the presentation, participants were allowed to interrupt the speaker to ask questions or to comment.
- Interactive Poster Session: WMs resulting from the worth mapping experience were presented during a poster session where participants and workshop facilitators could exchange. A poster representing each design case was presented. For each case, the poster described the project context and explained when (i.e., design stage(s)) and how they were used (i.e., purpose(s)).

The entire session was video-recorded. After the workshop, all the material used, including the posters, was sent to participants as attachment to a thank-you message. Participants were also invited to fill a questionnaire online, which was structured around three points.

1. Participants' data: to request information related to participants' gender, background, experience and roles in interactive systems design.
2. Worth maps: to assess the understandability of ARROWS and WMs as well as to collect participants' opinions regarding the relevance of worth maps for design and factors that could hinder their use in actual projects.
3. Lego bricks: to understand the gap that may exist between a representation built upon Lego bricks and information that can be captured from it.

This paper focuses only on the first two points. Related outcomes based both on information collected through questionnaires and insights gathered during the workshop are presented in the next section.

5.3   Outcomes

Participants' Profile
The collected data shows that workshop participants have diverse backgrounds. Thanks to their previous experiences, participants appeared to be equipped with different skills: strong technical ones but with a good understanding of Human Factors (HF) or the opposite. Finally, participants have declared taking part in different design stages, in which they play different roles.

Understandability of ARROWS and WMs
In order to verify that participants have fully understood information conveyed during the workshop, we have analyzed their definition of WMs. Only one participant (the architect) did not provide a (proper) definition for WMs. Instead, he formulated the following statement: *"It's complicated to define, however do we really need a well formalized definition?"*.
The other participants defined WMs as follows.

'A means for connecting users' primary needs to sensors and other technical components through intermediary features and qualities that foster paying attention to both existing and missing aspects (features, qualities, and values) and supports assessment of the interactive system's state at a given time' (human factors expert 1).

'*A cartography evolving over time and that represents the different values of a product/service and for monitoring possible improvements*' (project manager).
'*A good means of giving design a more profound dimension, thanks to the investigation beyond features and qualities*' (innovative service designer).
'*A more complete way to model and represent an interactive system; a means for addressing user experience more globally (not only focused on the UI)*' (human factors expert 2).
'*A cartography that allows to visualize relationships between the user's values and a product/service*' (psychologist).

Participants' definitions highlight that they have different perspectives on WMs, which is not surprising considering their different jobs and backgrounds. Nevertheless, the statements show that participants gained a good understanding of WMs as well as of the underlying ARROWS, providing that definitions surface: the structure using different layers, the focus on both design and human elements and the aim to connect them, and attention to aspects beyond the UI.

It is important to note that analysis of other answers from the architect show that he also understood well ARROWs and WMs. For instance, he wrote the following as a motivator for worth maps use: '*... because they highlight connections between the designed object and more profound values, both conscious and unconscious for the user*'.

Relevance of WMs for Design

Participants' motivations for WMs use highlight that they perceive the relevance of WMs for design. Indeed, participants would investigate worth maps because they would allow them to: visualize connections between design and human elements; identify strengths, weaknesses, and missing aspects; give attention to elements that are sometimes forgotten (such as emotions); prioritize features; test out something new (i.e., novelty).

In the questionnaire, participants were requested to identify design activities which can be well supported by WMs and explain how they would use them. Table 3 summarizes participants' responses.

Table 3. Design activities that can be well supported by WMs according to participants

Participant	Design stage					
	Opportunity identification	Study of needs	Software architecture	UI design	Graphic design	Evaluation
HF expert 1	Yes		Yes	Yes	Yes	Yes
Manager		Yes		Yes		Yes
Service designer	Yes	Yes				
Architect	Yes	Yes				Yes
HF expert 2	Yes	Yes				Yes
Psychologist	Yes	Yes			Yes	Yes

According to participants, WMs use is most relevant at '*Opportunity Identification*', '*Study of Needs*', and '*Evaluation*' phases. Participants also think that WMs could substantially support the creation of UI, as well as of graphic design. Software development-related activities are, according to participants, the ones that could be supported by WMs use in the less relevant way. Indeed, only one participant (i.e., one of the human factor specialists) pointed out that WMs could be used for the software architecture elaboration. It is important to note that this participant has a technical background. Furthermore, if the work in [3] highlights WMs as a means to support software implementation, according to our data, none of the participants would rely on WMs during software implementation. However, the project manager insisted on the fact that WMs could be well suited for agile developments as a monitoring tool from one sprint to another.

Our findings confirm that WMs can, indeed, support design in different ways. From our understanding, WMs can be seen as '*Boundary Objects*' [26] for multidisciplinary design teams, from which everyone can retrieve a minimum of information relevant to his/her concerns, and which contribute to enhancing understanding (and, therefore, designing worthwhile systems) and facilitating communication (and, therefore, reinforcing unity in heterogeneous settings).

Factors Hindering WMs Use

Participants' answers regarding factors that could hinder WMs use in actual design projects are the following.

'*Maybe the time required to set them up*' (human expert 1).

'*Difficulties and costs related to initial worth map creation; lack of explanations available for the entire project team; required additional costs and competencies*' (project manager).

'*We need to have time as well as necessary competencies for it*' (innovative service designer).

'*The time required to properly assimilate the concept and to get enough experience in order to take advantage of the method*' (service architect).

'*It doesn't seem easy to start from scratch for the design of a new system*' (human factors expert 2).

'*Cumbersome operationalization*' (psychologist).

Verbatims above show that the effort, in terms of time and intellectual demands, required for worth mapping might hinder use of WMs in actual design projects. Participants' statements also highlight uncertainties regarding the ability for an independent use of WMs (as already identified in [13]).

We believe that appropriate resources could help overcome these issues and, as a first step, we have designed and released a website dedicated to WMs. Next section presents this online resource for WMs.

6 The Online Resource

Our online resource is accessible at: http://phdgirl911.wixsite.com/arrows-and-wms. It provides designers with more practice-oriented knowledge on ARROWS and worth maps: the user walks through ARROWS step-by-step thanks to the Lyric example, which is introduced on a dedicated page. A particular section explains the benefits of WMs for design using concrete cases. In addition, the user is provided with the possibility to download the ARROWS template, examples of WMs, and the posters used during the workshop with designers (Fig. 4).

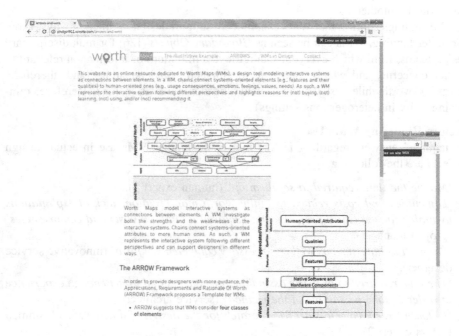

Fig. 4. The website dedicated to ARROWS and WMs

7 General Discussion and Conclusion

Based on the observation that the ARROW framework has not yet received much attention, we have engaged in the creation of WMs in different design projects using ARROW. This worth mapping experience provided us with more insights, which allowed us to refine/extend the ARROW framework and propose ARROW-Support (ARROWS). ARROWS was assessed through a workshop with designers. Concerns of participants of the workshop highlighted the necessity to make appropriate resources available in order to encourage the use of WMs. Therefore, we have designed and released a website to support designers getting started with WMs.

ARROWS defines the classes of elements that should be considered in WMs, details connections to be investigated between elements, and provides support for labeling qualities. Our experience shows that ARROWS is well appropriated for structuring worth maps in interactive systems design. Nevertheless, during the worth mapping experience, it was sometimes debatable whether a specific element belonged to a specific class or to another: the classification task was not always straightforward. Therefore, it is important to note that worth mapping should be flexible since the worth mapping process as well as worth maps (in terms of layout and content) can be sensitive to the design context. For instance, as highlighted in this paper, researchers' backgrounds (and maybe sensitivities also) can have an impact on worth elements naming and classification (see Sects. 1 and 4.1). According to Cockton and colleagues, the worth mapping process needs to be adapted to participants [13]. In our opinion, worth mapping and WMs could and should be adapted to a broader range of aspects (e.g., application domain, goals, people, and design phase).

Even though several factors can influence the worth mapping process and WMs, we believe that it exists a classification of worth elements (for instance, according to device types or application domains). However, only a more extensive use of worth maps could help elaborate such a classification (i.e., ontology for worth). In addition to allowing us to get a better understanding of worth, a worth ontology would support new areas of research, such as persuasive technologies [18], which rely on worth but suffer from the lack of visibility and maturity of methods and techniques for worth-centered developments.

Hopefully, our online resource will contribute to a broader use of WMs. However, due to the lack of an appropriate tool, the construction of WMs will probably still remain problematic. Therefore, in the future, we will focus on the development of a tool for an interactive creation of WMs. This tool will also offer features for copying, duplicating, and comparing WMs.

This paper presents a wide range of ways to use WMs in design. However, all of them suggest a use of WMs at design time. To the best of our knowledge, WMs have not been, so far, investigated at runtime. Therefore, in the future, we will also focus on WMs as support to adaptativity.

Acknowledgment. We warmly thank Orange Labs and Fraunhofer IAO for their participation and support.

References

1. Almquist, E., Senior, J., Bloch, N.: The elements of value. Harvard Bus. Rev. (2016). https://hbr.org/2016/09/the-elements-of-value

2. Camara, F., Calvary, G.: Worth-centered design in practice: lessons from experience and research agenda. In: Abascal, J., Barbosa, S., Fetter, M., Gross, T., Palanque, P., Winckler, M. (eds.) INTERACT 2015. LNCS, vol. 9299, pp. 123–139. Springer, Cham (2015). doi:10.1007/978-3-319-22723-8_10

3. Camara, F., Calvary, G., Demumieux, R.: The PEW framework for worth mapping. In: Kotzé, P., Marsden, G., Lindgaard, G., Wesson, J., Winckler, M. (eds.) INTERACT 2013. LNCS, vol. 8120, pp. 667–674. Springer, Heidelberg (2013). doi:10.1007/978-3-642-40498-6_59

4. Camara, F., Parmentier, T., Kharab, M.: Colibri: towards a new generation of advanced planning systems. In: 25me conférence francophone sur l'Interaction Homme-Machine, IHM 2013 (2013)
5. Cockton, G.: From quality in use to value in the world. In: CHI 2004 Extended Abstracts on Human Factors in Computing Systems, CHI EA 2004, pp. 1287–1290. ACM, New York (2004)
6. Cockton, G.: Value-centred HCI. In: Proceedings of the Third Nordic Conference on Human-computer Interaction, NordiCHI 2004, pp. 149–160. ACM, New York (2004)
7. Cockton, G.: A development framework for value-centered design. In: CHI 2005 Extended Abstracts on Human Factors in Computing Systems, CHI EA 2005, pp. 1292–1295. ACM, New York (2005)
8. Cockton, G.: Designing worth is worth designing. In: Proceedings of the 4th Nordic Conference on Human-Computer Interaction: Changing Roles, NordiCHI 2006, pp. 165–174. ACM, New York (2006)
9. Cockton, G.: Designing worth-connecting preferred means to desired ends. Interactions **15** (4), 54–57 (2008)
10. Cockton, G.: Putting value into e-valu-ation. In: Law, E.C., Hvannberg, E., Cockton, G. (eds.) Maturing Usability. Human-Computer Interaction Series, pp. 287–317. Springer, London (2008). doi:10.1007/978-1-84628-941-5_13
11. Cockton, G.: Sketch worth, catch dreams, be fruity. In: CHI 2008 Extended Abstracts on Human Factors in Computing Systems, CHI EA 2008, pp. 2579–2582. ACM, New York (2008)
12. Cockton, G.: Getting there: six meta-principles and interaction design. In: Proceedings of the SIGCHI Conference on Human Factors in Computing Systems, CHI 2009, pp. 2223–2232. ACM, New York (2009)
13. Cockton, G., Kirk, D., Sellen, A., Banks, R.: Evolving and augmenting worth mapping for family archives. In: Proceedings of the 23rd British HCI Group Annual Conference on People and Computers: Celebrating People and Technology, BCS-HCI 2009, pp. 329–338. British Computer Society, Swinton (2009)
14. Cockton, G., Kujala, S., Nurkka, P., Hltt, T.: Supporting worth mapping with sentence completion. In: Gross, T., Gulliksen, J., Kotz, P., Oestreicher, L., Palanque, P., Prates, R., Winckler, M. (eds.) INTERACT 2009. LNCS, vol. 5727, pp. 566–581. Springer, Heidelberg (2009). doi:10.1007/978-3-642-03658-3_61
15. Friedman, B.: Value-sensitive design. Interactions **3**(6), 16–23 (1996)
16. Friedman, B., Kahn, P.H., Borning, A., Huldtgren, A.: Value sensitive design and information systems. In: Doorn, N., Schuurbiers, D., van de Poel, I., Gorman, M.E. (eds.) Early Engagement and New Technologies: Opening up the Laboratory. PET, vol. 16, pp. 55–95. Springer, Dordrecht (2013). doi:10.1007/978-94-007-7844-3_4
17. Gutman, J.: A means-end chain model based on consumer categorization processes. J. Mark. 60–72 (1982)
18. Laurillau, Y., Foulonneau, A., Calvary, G., Villain, E.: Sepia, a support for engineering persuasive interactive applications: properties and functions. In: Proceedings of the 8th ACM SIGCHI Symposium on Engineering Interactive Computing Systems (EICS 2016), pp. 217–228. ACM (2016)
19. Otero, N., José, R.: Worth and human values at the centre of designing situated digital public displays. Int. J. Adv. Pervasive Ubiquitous Comput. **1**(4), 1–13 (2009)
20. Otero, N., Rego, A., José, R.: Considering the inclusion of worth and values in the design of interactive artifacts. In: Proceedings of the First International Conference on Integration of Design, Engineering and Management for Innovation (IDEMI 2009) (2009)

21. Reynolds, T.J., Gutman, J.: Laddering theory, method, analysis, and interpretation. J. Advert. Res. **28**(1), 11–31 (1988)
22. Rokeach, M.: The Nature of Human Values, vol. 438. Free Press, New York (1973)
23. Roto, V., Lu, Y., Nieminen, H., Tutal, E.: Designing for user and brand experience via company-wide experience goals. In: Proceedings of the 33rd Annual ACM Conference Extended Abstracts on Human Factors in Computing Systems, CHI EA 2015, pp. 2277–2282. ACM, New York (2015)
24. Shneiderman, B.: The eyes have it: a task by data type taxonomy for information visualizations. In: Proceedings of the 1996 IEEE Symposium on Visual Languages, VL 1996. IEEE Computer Society, Washington, D.C. (1996)
25. Sonnleitner, A., Pawlowski, M., Ksser, T., Peissner, M.: Experimentally manipulating positive user experience based on the ful_lment of user needs. In: Kotz, P., Marsden, G., Lindgaard, G., Wesson, J., Winckler, M. (eds.) Human-Computer Interaction INTERACT 2013. LNCS, vol. 8120, pp. 555–562. Springer, Heidelberg (2013). doi:10.1007/978-3-642-40498-6_45
26. Star, S.L., Griesemer, J.R.: Institutional ecology, 'translations' and boundary objects: Amateurs and professionals in Berkeley's Museum of Vertebrate Zoology. Soc. Stud. Sci. **19**(3), 387–420 (1989)
27. Vu, P.: A Worth-centered development approach to information management system design. Master's thesis, Aalto University (2013)

Extending Mobile App Analytics for Usability Test Logging

Xavier Ferre[1,2(✉)], Elena Villalba[2], Héctor Julio[2],
and Hongming Zhu[3]

[1] High-end Expert at Tongji University, Shanghai, China
`xavier.ferre@upm.es`
[2] DLSIIS, Universidad Politecnica de Madrid, Madrid, Spain
`evillalba@fi.upm.es, h.julio@icloud.com`
[3] School of Software Engineering, Tongji University, Shanghai, China
`zhu_hongming@tongji.edu.cn`

Abstract. Mobile application development is characterized by reduced development cycles and high time-to-market pressure. Usability evaluation in mobile applications calls for the application of cost-effective methods, specially adapted to such constraints. We propose extending the Google Analytics for Mobile Applications basic service to store specific low-level user actions of interest for usability evaluation purposes. The solution can serve both for lab usability testing, automating quantitative data gathering, and for logging real use after application release. It is based on identification of relevant user tasks and the detailed events worth gathering, instrumentation of specific code for data gathering, and subsequent data extraction for calculating relevant usability–related variables. We validated our application in a real usability test by comparing the automatically gathered data with the information gathered by the human observer. Results shows both measurements are statistically exchangeable, opening promising new ways to perform usability testing cost-effectively and at greater scale.

Keywords: Automated usability evaluation · Usability testing · Log file analysis · Usability evaluation of mobile applications

1 Introduction

Smartphones include the most advanced computing technology and are available to a growing user base. They combine a variety of sensors, high-speed Internet connection, good quality camera and touch-screen, offering additional possibilities for application developers. In 2015, 1.43 billion smartphones were shipped worldwide [1], while PC shipments amounted to a total of just 249 million [2]. Mobile apps give users the opportunity to carry out all sorts of activities on the move. In fact, they are coming to be the device that a rapidly growing user base chooses in order to use software and access the Internet. This is especially true in developing countries, where smartphones are the first Internet-connected computing device that a high number of citizens will have access to.

© IFIP International Federation for Information Processing 2017
Published by Springer International Publishing AG 2017. All Rights Reserved
R. Bernhaupt et al. (Eds.): INTERACT 2017, Part III, LNCS 10515, pp. 114–131, 2017.
DOI: 10.1007/978-3-319-67687-6_9

There are native and web-based mobile apps. Native apps are developed directly for a given platform, and, according to a mobile developer survey [3], they are developers' preferred option, whereas the use of web-based apps is declining [4]. There is a third option, hybrid apps, which wrap web content with native code. However, the main apps on the market are moving away from the hybrid to the native approach [5]. We will focus on native mobile apps in this paper. Henceforth, the term 'mobile app' refers to 'native mobile application'.

Usability and user experience (UX) are quality attributes with special relevance for mobile development, since competition in the app market is fierce: the two main mobile app stores, App Store for iOS and Google Play for Android, offer 2 and 2.2 million apps respectively [6]. Mobile software development teams face the challenge of this dynamic environment [7], with reduced time-to-market schedules and a continuous delivery paradigm to change and improve the app in order to get better user retention. Low-quality apps can have devastating consequences for mobile app development companies. As a result, there is a strong accent on usability testing [5].

User-centered design (UCD) is the approach applied to achieve a good level of usability in software systems [8]. There are a variety of UCD methods for achieving a good usability level (Ferre identified 95 different methods from six books [9]), most of them focused on usability evaluation. A careful selection of usability evaluation methods is essential in this field, as it faces the challenge of the changing and varied contexts of use: a mobile app can be used inside a building or outside under a very bright sunlight, with either no ambient noise or in a busy environment, and, possibly, the tasks can be interrupted and resumed several times before fulfilling the user objectives.

Traditional lab-based usability testing can offer valuable insight into possible usability problems in a pre-release stage, but it cannot possibly cover aspects of UX related to the changing contexts of use. Alternatively, field studies can offer rich and relevant findings [10], despite the challenge of measuring usability under real-life conditions in the mobile arena [11]. But the cost of field testing at a pre-release stage may be too high for average mobile development projects. Within this ongoing debate lab vs. field studies in the mobile usability evaluation community, we believe that field testing after release offers a compromise solution, and a complement to pre-release lab testing. Our proposal aims to cover these two evaluation approaches, with code instrumentation that serves both targets.

Field studies with selected users can consume a lot of resources. Automated usability evaluation is a potentially good alternative, offering the possibility to gather information from actual app usage. In particular, data capture for automated usability evaluation involves using software that automatically records usability data (e.g., logging UI usage) [12]. While usability testing provides timely feedback about user reactions to a new design in a controlled environment, automated usability logging can complement such basic method with evaluation in the actual context of use, shortening at the same time usability evaluation activities in the continuous delivery effort for mobile app development.

Google Analytics is a widely used cloud service offered by Google that tracks and reports website traffic, behaviors and purchases. It provides a limited web tool to access the reports and tracking data, but it also offers a public API to automate complex reporting and configuration. Such API can be used to extract the raw data and create custom reports, with some limitations in its Standard (free) version. This powerful tool is primarily designed for marketing purposes, such as the measurement of ad campaign success or ad revenue maximization. It also aims to measure UX aspects like user engagement, but it requires careful tweaking if it is to be useful for full-scale usability evaluation. In 2009, Google released a variant of this service specifically addressed to mobile apps: Google Analytics for Mobile Applications (GAMA) [13, 14].

We propose a logging mechanism for user actions that can serve both for usability testing and for continuous usability logging, based on GAMA. Our model is based on task modeling to establish the UI events to be tracked, automating the data capture side of usability evaluation, whereas the gathered data are analyzed and critiqued by usability experts.

In this paper, we present our logging mechanism and its validation in a lab usability test of a real application (available in both Google Play & iOS App Store).

Section 2 presents existing literature on the issue. Section 3 details the overall logging approach: (1) how task modeling and usability goal setting define the UI events to track; (2) the logging strategy injected into the application code; and (3) how lab usability testing is planned and the results of tests are interpreted. Section 4 details the results of the validation, where our proposed method has been applied for a usability test. Finally, Sect. 5 discusses the results obtained; and Sect. 6 outlines the conclusions and future lines of research.

2   Related Work

Usability evaluation is a cornerstone of the UCD process. In particular, according to ISO 9241-210 [8], feedback from users during operational use identifies long-term issues and provides input for future design.

Ivory and Hearst [12] presented the state of the art of automated usability evaluation back in 2001, classifying automated usability evaluation techniques into a taxonomy. They highlighted the fact that automation within usability testing has been used predominantly in two ways: automated capture of use data and automated analysis of these data according to some metrics or a model (log file analysis in Ivory and Hearst's terminology). They differentiated between methods for WIMP (windows, icons, pointer, and mouse) and for Web interfaces, but they did not take into account mobile interfaces. The first fully-fledged smartphone, the original iPhone, appeared in 2007. As Ivory and Hearst's survey was published well before this modern kind of mobile app came into being, it does not account for the peculiarities of this kind of software applications.

Automated website usability evaluation [15, 16] has been extensively applied to extract usability-relevant information from website logs. The reason is that web servers automatically log every single page access, creating a wealth of information for usability purposes. On the contrary, user events in mobile applications are not typically logged, except for some basic information gathered by GAMA for any mobile app using its services. Therefore, for a similar level of automated usability evaluation as in the web domain, additional explicit code instrumentation is needed. From the existing web mining strategies, our proposal goes in line with the web usage mining approach, where the steps are identification of users, identification of single sessions, and identification of the navigation paths within these sessions [15].

Every mobile platform offers a different UX [5, 17], and mobile UX has distinct features from the desktop experience [18]. Mobile usability and UX evaluation requires specific focus on issues like the changing context, smaller screen size, etc. For example, the number of clicks necessary to fulfill a task is very relevant as a usability attribute in the web domain, while number of taps is comparatively less important for mobile users (due to the much faster response times in mobile apps vs websites). For these reasons (among others), automated usability evaluation of mobile apps, while taking advantage of the wealth of experience distilled from years of application in the web and WIMP domains, cannot directly apply it to the mobile domain. It is necessary to carefully consider how traditional usability evaluation methods can be applied to mobile app development.

Paternò et al. [19] present an extension addressed to mobile apps of an existing tool that remotely processes multimodal user interaction in desktop applications. This extension allows remote evaluation of mobile applications, tracking both user actions and environmental conditions. It is based on a comparison of planned and actual user behavior, using CTT (Concurrent Task Trees) for task modeling.

Carta et al. offer a tool supporting remote usability evaluation of mobile websites [20]. They dismiss Google Analytics as being limited by the number of events that can be captured, which our approach has extended by means of custom dimensions (see Sect. 3.2.2). Carta et al. focus exclusively on the webpage interaction style, accounting mainly for page loads, whereas native mobile apps use a different method of interaction.

There exist a lot of services for automatic website usability evaluation, but only a handful for evaluation of native mobile apps in Android and iOS. Most of the latter ones, like validately.com or lookback.io, are based in video-recording of testing sessions, and they only offer remote usability testing (not evaluation of free use).

Balagtas-Fernandez and Hussmann present their EvaHelper tool and framework for collecting usability data in mobile apps [21]. It is based on generating usage logs stored in the mobile device. These logs are then processed to generate navigation graphs that can identify usability problems. Balagtas-Fernandez and Hussmann focus on the work of the developer to ensure adequate UI instrumentation. Kluth et al. [22] extend the Balagtas-Fernandez and Hussmann four-stage model considering an additional critique stage.

Lettner and Holzmann propose a toolkit for unsupervised user interaction logging in mobile apps oriented to usability evaluation [11]. They log user navigation between screens and on-screen interaction which is sent to a cloud-based web server for further analysis. They combine low-level metrics, like button-clicks, or session times, with device statistics. In this sense, their solution could have been applied using GAMA. But Lettner and Holzmann acknowledge that their approach has the limitation of not having pre-defined tasks.

Feijó et al. [23] propose a toolkit for automated emotion logging for mobile applications. It is able to trace emotional reactions of users during usability tests and relate them to the specific interaction that is taking place. These reactions are collected using the front camera of the mobile device.

Leichtenstern et al. [24] follow a similar approach, with their EVAL tool that records video-logs of users using a mobile application, and relates the videos to the specific screen that was being used at that time.

Porat et al. [25] present the MATE tool to support usability experts in the definition of the task scenarios to use in a usability test, allowing the combination of results of different kinds of usability testing methods across devices and operating systems. It is focused on performance metrics that they categorize as efficiency, effectiveness and frequency. The usability experts they have used for evaluation emphasize the need to particularize such metrics for each project.

According to Hulo and To [26], Sony has been using GAMA for some of their decoupled applications. Hulo and To's work extends GAMA basic service with a UsageTracker service that operates in the background to log UI events in the Telephone app of a Sony mobile phone. What they consider tasks are actually events or individual steps to log, therefore lacking a proper task analysis.

Of these proposals, only [21] and [22] actually record user events in a similar way to our approach. The EvaHelper tool [21] is very similar in terms of preparation difficulty to our approach, since it is necessary to include calls to an API. The gain in using GAMA as logging server is that it is very common that app development companies already use GAMA for its benefits in terms of marketing issues. Therefore, if GAMA is already used, the extra burden of using our instrumentation for specific usability-related event logging is lighter than when using an alternative API that requires handling the logging mechanism itself (starting the logging activity in the app, making sure the server is up and running, etc.).

About the second work, Kulth et al. [22] present a capture framework for just iOS, with no easy extension to Android, since it is based on specific characteristics of Objective-C programming language.

In short, while there exist other automated logging methods for desktop and web-based systems, to the best of our knowledge there are only 2 methods published for native mobile apps, and they either offer additional burden to our GAMA proposed approach, or they have not been applied to Android apps.

3   Our Logging Approach

Our approach for automated UI logging to support usability tests is based on considering tasks at the beginning of the process, and focusing the usability-related instrumentation and analysis on such tasks expressed as detailed use cases. This is combined with the usage of GAMA for the collection of relevant user events.

Our proposal is based on a three-stage approach (see Fig. 1):

1. **Identification of the user tasks of interest to be evaluated, task modeling and selection of the specific events to log in each task:** As part of the User & Task Analysis activity, user tasks are identified and prioritized, selecting the most relevant ones and building their task models. Such models are linked to specific

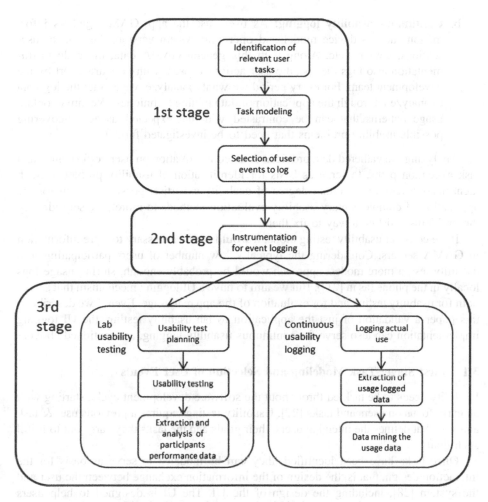

Fig. 1. Stages of the proposed logging approach

elements in the User Interface (UI). The usability evaluation strategy needs to be materialized in this stage, with the selection of specific events to be tracked through the logging mechanism.

2. **Instrumentation for event logging:** Implementation of the data gathering functionality in the app code to ensure that the selected events are logged in the GAMA servers. The UI is instrumented with calls to functions of the GAMA API (Application Programming Interface), sending the usability-relevant data gathered from user actions.

3. **Usability evaluation**

   a. **Lab usability testing:** First, it is necessary to plan the usability tests with specific instructions for test facilitators, so that each user task enactment is recorded and the User Unique IDentifier (UUID) is stored. After we carry out the usability test, we need to extract performance data from GAMA servers, differentiating the information corresponding to each test participant.

b. **Continuous usability logging:** As users use the app, GAMA gathers information such as device model and operating system version, duration of user sessions, country, etc. Along with this general GAMA data, the code instrumentation also logs the specific user actions chosen, with no extra effort by the development team. For every period we want to analyze, we extract the log data to analyze it through the application of data mining techniques. We aim to obtain usage patterns that can be contrasted with the expected usage, uncovering possible usability problems that need to be investigated further.

Analyzing the gathered data provides detailed information on user performance and task execution paths, to serve as basis for identification of usability problems. Such identification requires a certain degree of usability expertise, possibly calling for the application of complementary usability evaluation methods to more precisely identify the problems and find a way to fix them.

If we consider usability testing alone, it would not be necessary to store information in GAMA servers. Considering the typically low number of users participating in a usability test, a more modest approach would be probably enough, storing usage logs locally in the phone (as in [21]). But we aim to have a UI logging mechanism that serves both for usability testing and for evaluation of the app real usage. Even if we describe in this paper a validation of just the application to lab usability testing, the UI logging implementation can also serve for continuous usability logging, as mentioned above.

3.1   First Stage: Task Modeling and Selection of User Events

Usability needs to be tackled throughout the software development cycle, starting with an early focus on users and tasks [27]. Usability testing requires a previous user & task analysis that defines the intended users, their goals and the tasks they carry out to fulfill such goals.

Once tasks have been identified, they can be modeled to serve as basis for the interaction design, that is, the design of the information exchange between the user and the system [28], including the design of the UI. The UI is designed to help users perform the tasks of each major user profile.

Task models serve as the standard for optimal task execution from the designer point of view. When user actions depart from such path, it may be an indication of a divergence between the envisioned design model and the user mental model. The actual steps followed by a user to complete a task can be compared to the intended path of action detailed in the task model. Identified differences between both are relevant and must be studied in order to enrich the specification of the context of use and make design changes. We will call them in this paper 'user errors', to be in line with usability testing literature, understanding that they reflect possible design errors in any case.

Use case descriptions detail interaction design in term of user steps and system responses, and are built from the results of user and task analysis. Use cases are widely used in object-oriented design, but they also serve for UX design, according to Ivar Jacobson, the creator of the use case technique [29]. But we need UCD-oriented use cases that take into account user goals and usability, so they can serve as a basis for usability evaluation.

We have chosen use cases as technique for task modeling because they serve as an ideal bridge between HCI experts and developers. We need the detailed version of use cases (according to Constantine and Lockwood terminology [30]), so that user tasks are clearly linked to specific UI elements, and their activation can be adequately logged.

The different app screens are designed to comply with the design underlying the use cases. When changes are made in the actual UI code, use cases will have to be updated accordingly, to be able to maintain the coherence between model and code.

This stage identifies key information for usability purposes. If detailed usability goals are established, they are identified according to the tasks modeled, and they are taken as a basis for the identification of the UI elements to log. Usability test design will be then focused on measuring the variables that are described in the usability goals.

If no specific usability goals are considered, the UI elements to log are typically the ones that update the elements shown in a screen, or the ones that lead to a different screen.

Annotations are added to use cases stating the UI element that needs to be tracked, and the relevant context information to be considered. For example, it may be of interest for an application to know if the user moves repeatedly from one menu tab to another in a short period of time, because this may be a sign that the user does not know where to find the functionality that he or she is looking for. The elements to track and their interpretation in terms of usability will be specific to each project and domain. Figure 2 shows an example of an annotated use case for the app used in the validation (see Sect. 4).

3.2   Second Stage: Instrumentation for UI Logging

3.2.1   Google Analytics for Mobile Applications

The Google Analytics for Mobile Applications standard online tool offers aggregated data about screens traversed, scrolls, buttons tapped or similar actions. The GAMA services offer a report system that can serve to obtain the information of interest in a machine-readable format, but GAMA reports do not directly allow downloading any kind of information shown in the web tool. Particularly, they don't allow to download screen flow information.

Two main concepts of GAMA are dimensions and metrics. Dimensions are qualitative variables (e.g., city), while metrics are measurable quantitative values (e.g., total number of visits). We can combine at least one dimension and one metric to generate custom reports. Note that not every combination of dimensions and metrics is allowed. If we carefully choose the combination of dimensions and metrics, we can gather enough information for our purpose.

In our approach, annotated use cases serve as the basis for the instrumentation of the UI with appropriate calls to the tracking server (GAMA), providing details on key user actions, like buttons tapped or visited screens. We can use custom dimensions to include such information along with other basic information included in reports.

In any case, the screen flow information automatically tracked by GAMA is too coarse-grained for an accurate usability-focused analysis of usage interaction. We need a method for operating on aggregated data to identify unexpected patterns of usage, but we also need to be able to drill down to the log of actions carried out by specific

Use case: Search for a professor's email
User Profile: Student and Novice Student.
1.   The user opens the school app.
2.   The system displays the icons on the main screen.
3.   The user taps on "Subjects".
     Track user tap on the icon button.
4.   The system displays the list of subjects for the default degree[*].
5.   The user taps on the degree name.
     Track user tap on the spinner.
6.   The system displays a list with all the available degrees.
7.   The user selects a degree.
     Track user tap on a list item.
8.   The system displays the list of subjects for the chosen degree.
9.   The user taps on a subject.
     Track user tap on a list item.
10. The system displays information about the subject.
11. The user looks for the professor section and taps on the respective email
     address.
     Track user tap.

[*]: Users are not directly presented with a list of degrees, to save one tap for the users interested in the default degree (the main bachelor degree in the school where the majority of users are enrolled). The user needs to tap on the degree name to change to a different degree.

Fig. 2. Example of annotated use case used in the validation (*annotations highlighted in italics*)

individual users. We need both kinds of information (fine-grained and coarse-grained) to be able to apply data mining processes.

3.2.2   GAMA for Mobility Logging

Our proposal aims to carry out UI event logging for both lab usability testing reporting and for logging actual use, and both strategies can coexist in the same project. When the lab usability test is carried out after system deployment, the logging mechanism is already submitting usage information to GAMA servers, and we will then need to tell apart the usability test participants information from the gathered information about the rest of users. User identification plays an important role in this issue.

There are two GAMA parameters that we can use in order to identify specific user actions: Client ID and User ID. Both are unique user identifiers. While the Client ID is automatically assigned by GAMA and anonymous (using an UUID), the User ID is taken from the internal user profile and can be assigned by the app (in apps with a user profile). We have chosen Client ID as user identifier for our custom reports in order to keep the usability evaluation anonymous, and thus respect users' privacy rights. But having the user uniquely identified is not enough to analyze his/her steps when traversing the application. In order to complete our purpose, we need to add a timestamp as a second custom dimension. We use the current UNIX time in milliseconds as custom timestamp.

We use Client ID and our custom timestamp, combining them with other dimensions or metrics of interest, to define GAMA custom reports, thus obtaining user behavior flows and step-by-step user action tracking. These two custom dimensions are defined in the GAMA account in order to log usability-relevant actions. Every time information is sent to GAMA servers, the Client ID is specified and a timestamp is added. Figure 3 shows sample code for this kind of submission for Android. We can use this information to order user steps, allowing us to compare and analyze the paths and behaviors of test participants.

```
Tracker mTracker
= analytics.newTracker(R.xml.analytics_global_tracker);

String cid = mTracker.get("&cid");// Getting Client ID
String dimensionValue1 = cid;

Calendar c = Calendar.getInstance();
long ms = c.getTimeInMillis();
Log.i("TIME", Long.toString(ms));
String dimensionValue2 =  Long.toString(ms);

// Build and Send the Analytics Event.
mTracker.send(new
HitBuilders.EventBuilder().setCategory(category).setAction(action).setLa
bel(label).setValue(value).setCustomDimension(1,
dimensionValue1).setCustomDimension(2, dimensionValue2).build());
```

Fig. 3. Sample code for fetching Client ID and custom timestamp for the app Android version

3.3   Third Stage: Usability Evaluation

We will focus in this section in the application of the proposed logging mechanism just to lab usability testing, which is the option validated in the current paper.

It is typically recommended that usability testing not be carried out by a lone experimenter, but to involve more people that take care of the different roles. The two more common roles are data gatherer/note taker (to take relevant notes about user actions and errors), and time keeper (keeping track of each task starting and elapsed time) [31], and we aim to automate these two roles with the usage of our UI logging mechanism. Thus, with our approach only one usability expert is needed to take care of the usability test, acting mainly as facilitator [32].

But apart from having a proper code instrumentation, usability testing needs to be carefully planned to ensure that participants' tasks are correctly registered for further analysis.

3.3.1 Usability Test Planning

The tasks chosen for the usability test must have been between the ones modeled and instrumented for usage logging.

Apart from the task events instrumentation, there is a need for some special event that the test facilitator must activate when the task is about to start (for example going to the Home screen) and another special event to signal the end of the task. These actions must be logged as well, to be able to calculate the starting and ending time for each task in the subsequent test data extraction.

The test may be carried out on the participant's own mobile phone, to avoid user errors coming from lack of familiarity with the specific flavor of the operating system or device buttons. In such case, it is also necessary to access the mobile phone ClientID and register it for the later data extraction.

The test protocol must include the exact steps to be taken by the test facilitator to:

1. Install the app to test in the participant's mobile phone.
2. Ensure that the mobile phone has access to Internet, so that actions can be recorded in GAMA.
3. Register the device ClientID.
4. Indicate each task start and end.

3.3.2 Test and Interpretation of Logged Data

Tests are carried out, following the protocol previously established, and then the data logged needs to be extracted trough the GAMA API and analyzed.

We carry out the extraction of data through a set of Python language scripts that connect to GAMA servers and download the test data. The scripts query metrics and dimensions in a specific time interval for a ClientID.

In order to extract the path followed by the participant, the requested metric comprises all the events, and the specific dimensions are as follows:

- Our custom timestamp.
- ClientID.
- Event – Action.
- Event – Category.
- Day/Hour[1].
- Minute (See footnote 1).

---

[1] These two time-related dimensions are included just for manual double-check purposes, they are not strictly necessary if we have the timestamp.

We can order participant actions thanks to the timestamp. We then compare this course of actions with the optimal path previously identified in the use case, and the discrepancies are highlighted to identify possible design errors or different user behaviors that allow user analysis refinement. Lack of fluency in task enactment may also serve as an indicator of mismatch between the designers model and the user mental model. Task completion time is calculated subtracting the agreed upon task starting event timestamp from the ending event one.

Additional data can be collected, such as task completion rate and number of taps to complete the task. Optimal values for efficiency and effectiveness measures can be obtained from the measurement of designers performance with the application. Target values can be then defined considering such optimal values and the context(s) of use considered for the application. These values act as baseline measures for the usability test.

4 Validation Results

We validated our proposed logging mechanism by supporting a lab usability test for an app oriented to university students in our school, with more than 500 total installs in the Google Play store by the end of 2016.

A new map feature was designed for the app, and the usability test presents 6 tasks to carry out focused on such new feature. Code has been instrumented to ensure that such events are registered in the GAMA servers.

The usability tests have been carried out by a facilitator who measured time taken per task and number of user errors manually, as traditionally done in any usability test. Afterwards, both manually measured results and automatic measurements extracted from the logging mechanism have been compared using non-parametric tests (Mann-Whitney).

The usability test was announced through twitter and the forum of an HCI University course. Volunteers that participated in the test received a small gift.

29 participants were recruited, all of them University students between 18–25 years old and users of an Android phone. In the introduction to the usability test, participants were told that they could abandon the test at any time and they would still receive the gift.

4.1 Usability Test Procedure

For each test participant, the facilitator followed the following steps (trigger actions signaling task start and end appear highlighted in **bold face**):

1. Read the introductory text.
2. Install the app version to test in the participant's mobile phone, by activating the developer mode and the USB debugging mode in the phone, connecting it to the lab computer and running the test app.
3. Open the app and cancel the tutorial.
4. Go to the Settings section of the app and write down the ClientID displayed.

5. Read the task to the participant.
6. **Take the app to the screen where the task would be started** and ask the participant to carry out the task with the app. Start the manual timer at the same time.
7. When the participant says he/she has finished the task (or abandons), stop the timer and **go to Settings section of the app**.
   Steps 5–7 are repeated until all the tasks have been carried out.
8. Personal data and SUS (System Usability Scale) questionnaires are handed out to the participant to fill in.

The facilitator wrote down throughout the test task completion times, participant comments, relevant observations, number of participant errors, and if the participant successfully completed each task. Besides, test participants performance data were successfully recorded in Google Analytics servers, to be later compared to the manually registered data.

The ClientIDs registered for every participant served for the extraction of each test data from GAMA servers. All user events recorded in the logging mechanism were ordered by time using the timestamp custom dimension, and the special events used for signaling starting and ending time for each task were also looked for in the list of events. The start of the task was signaled by tapping the back button when in the Settings screen, and the end of the task was marked going to the Settings section when the participant says he/she had finished the task or abandoned. The timestamps of both events allowed for the calculation of task completion times.

4.2   Statistics Results

A total of 25 subjects were analyzed. 4 subjects' data were not included since the protocol was not strictly followed, or they did not complete the test.

First, a descriptive statistic analysis was done. Later, a non-parametric test (U test Mann-Whitney [33]) was used to determine if GAMA measurement is comparable to the gold standard of usability test, which is performed by a trained observer. Thus, our null hypothesis was that both distributions are replaceable. Significance was established at 0.05.

Tables 1 and 2 present the descriptive statistics of the time and errors, both manually and automatically measured through GAMA. Results are presented as average and standard deviation with a confident interval of 95%.

From the descriptive data we observe that per task both measurements are similar, both in terms of average measure and standard deviation. In order to test if they are statistically replaceable, we perform non-parametric tests, concretely U test Mann Whitney, since the distribution of data are not normal.

Table 3 shows the results of the p-values for all the models we fitted in the U test Mann Whitney. All p values are above 0.05, which is the threshold to consider that the null hypothesis is true. That is, that both distributions are equal in the time task and number of errors, implying that both methods to measure usability can be replaceable.

Table 1. Time to perform each task. Measured in seconds. CI: Confident interval. LL: Low level. UP: Upper level

	Average	CI 95%		Standard deviation
		LL	UL	
Manual Task 1	42.70	33.32	52.08	20.034
GAMA Task 1	49.00	35.80	62.20	28.200
Manual Task 2	49.25	36.36	62.14	27.535
GAMA Task 2	52.60	37.75	67.45	31.725
Manual Task 3	30.30	17.54	43.06	27.255
GAMA Task 3	28.80	17.59	40.01	23.955
Manual Task 4	47.75	35.64	59.86	25.872
GAMA Task 4	44.40	33.03	55.77	24.295
Manual Task 5	39.50	28.01	50.99	24.560
GAMA Task 5	39.70	28.66	50.74	23.591
Manual Task 6	41.90	32.40	51.40	20.300
GAMA Task 6	41.25	32.28	50.22	19.169
Manual total time	251.40	217.12	285.68	73.246
GAMA total time	255.75	225.70	285.80	64.206

Table 2. Number of errors per task. CI: Confident interval. LL: Low level. UP: Upper level

	Average	CI 95%		Standard deviation
		LL	UL	
Manual Task 1	1.75	1.18	2.32	1.209
GAMA Task 1	1.85	1.26	2.44	1.268
Manual Task 2	1.55	0.75	3.35	1.701
GAMA Task 2	1.60	0.76	2.44	1.789
Manual Task 3	0.50	0.03	0.97	1.000
GAMA Task 3	0.50	0.03	0.97	1.000
Manual Task 4	0.85	0.34	1.36	1.089
GAMA Task 4	0.85	0.36	1.34	1.040
Manual Task 5	0.75	0.16	1.34	1.251
GAMA Task 5	0.65	0.10	1.20	1.182
Manual Task 6	1.00	0.37	1.63	1.338
GAMA Task 6	1.15	0.47	1.83	1.461
Manual total error	6.40	4.90	7.90	3.202
GAMA total error	6.60	4.90	8.30	3.633

Table 3. Results of the U test Mann Whitney with a significant level 0.05

Time per task (seconds)		Errors per task	
Task 1	0.528	Task 1	0.603
Task 2	0.956	Task 2	0.981
Task 3	0.959	Task 3	0.926
Task 4	0.652	Task 4	0.962
Task 5	0.954	Task 5	0.982
Task 6	0.796	Task 6	0.875
Total	0.831	Total	0.799

5 Discussion

We have demonstrated through a non-parametric test that our automatic GAMA-based logging mechanism of user actions measurement and the traditional manual measurement are exchangeable. Usability testers of mobile apps can then profit of our logging approach to focus on observing user reactions, and thus avoiding the need to employ two experimenters for the test.

One of the test facilitators did not follow the protocol correctly, since he did not visit the Settings section of the app when appropriate (therefore his 4 tests were not included in the validation). This requirement might be too complicated for the test facilitator, as he/she does not receive any feedback from the app about the correct activation of the task starting and ending events. We need to explore the usability of this activation mechanism for test facilitators, and to provide an alternative way that is: (1) easier and faster; and (2) offers some user feedback.

We may use voice recognition for signaling task start and ending. In this case, the Settings section would have a way to turn on the testing mode, thus activating the voice recognition feature. A sound signal could be used for feedback in order to use the same channel of communication. A second option would be to use a non-common gesture (like a three-finger swipe) to indicate task start or ending. A screen blink could provide the user feedback in this case. We need to be very careful in the choice of the specific gestures for this purpose, because there is always the risk that they override a gesture already captured in the app to test.

Usability testing with usability experts will be necessary to establish the best way of signaling the start of the overall test and the start and ending of each task asked to the test participant.

For further analysis of our work, we have to refine the automated tracking mechanism to consider possible alternative paths. In most apps there is not only one way to carry out a task, but a variety of them which must be taken into account. Then, we can consider the number of user actions as an additional performance criterion. In this case, user actions departing from the optimal path would not be considered user errors if they follow an alternative success path.

Our logging mechanism serves both for lab testing and for evaluation of real usage. We have just tested the former application, lab usability testing, where user tasks are defined in advance. In the automated logging of user events on the field, a key issue for the analysis of the gathered data will be the identification of the user tasks.

We have started by gathering objective data related to basic usability attributes such as efficiency and effectiveness. However, additional variables could be studied in the future, such as advancement in the learning curve (how much usage time requires a user to reach a pre-defined level of performance), regularity/irregularity of app usage across time or number of times the help subsystem is accessed, or different paths users take to reach the same results.

Different variables are relevant depending on the stage of development the project is: defining the product concept, pre-release, or evolution of an already released app. Task completion times and number of errors may be variables of interest in the pre-release stage, while qualitative data may be more relevant in the early phases of development, or when the development team is working on a major redesign of an existing app.

UX also has a special relevance in mobile applications, and we intend to study how our proposed logging mechanism could gather data about additional variables affecting UX. When we have specific user profiles clustered and recognized through data mining, we will be able to include in the app code ad-hoc attitude questionnaires addressed to specific profiles.

6 Conclusions

We have presented a proposal for automated logging of UI events through the GAMA service for usability evaluation purposes, serving for both lab usability testing and for logging actual use. For lab usability testing it can allow for a higher number of participants or more ambitious test plans. When used for logging actual use, our GAMA-based proposal may allow for an easy management of a high volume of usage data, without the need of maintaining a dedicated server. The reduced cost of auto-mated or semi-automated solutions make them especially suited to the short devel-opment cycles present in mobile app development projects, increasing the cost-effectiveness of usability evaluation activities.

We have validated the logging mechanism applying it to lab usability testing of a real application, proving that the results of the automated version and the manual measurements are exchangeable. Despite this, some improvements are necessary to ensure that the test facilitator can more easily indicate to the logging mechanism when a new task is starting or ending.

We are currently working on the extraction and analysis of the user events logged through our proposed mechanism, applying data mining techniques in order to identify possible usability defects and specific user profile behavior. Validation of this alter-native application of our automated logging proposal will be necessary for fully acknowledging the advantages of the overall solution.

Extensive study of usage logs could provide an identification of typical usability problems in mobile apps, and possible solutions could be compiled in the form of guidelines for developers or interaction designers.

Finally, we plan to facilitate the task modeling and annotation for mobile app developers by building a plugin to ease use case annotation and code instrumentation.

Acknowledgements. We would like to thank the anonymous reviewers for their valuable feedback that allowed us to greatly improve the paper.

References

1. IDC: Apple, Huawei, and Xiaomi Finish 2015 with Above Average Year-Over-Year Growth, as Worldwide Smartphone Shipments Surpass 1.4 Billion for the Year (2016). http://www.idc.com/getdoc.jsp?containerId=prUS40980416
2. Gartner: Worldwide Device Shipments to Grow 1.9 Percent in 2016, While End-User Spending to Decline for the First Time (2016). http://www.gartner.com/newsroom/id/3187134
3. Appcelerator/IDC: Voice of the Next-Generation Mobile Developer, Appcelerator/IDC Q3 2012 Mobile Developer Report (2012). http://www.appcelerator.com.s3.amazonaws.com/pdf/Appcelerator-Report-Q3-2012-final.pdf
4. Flurry: Apps Solidify Leadership Six Years into the Mobile Revolution (2014). http://flurrymobile.tumblr.com/post/115191864580/apps-solidify-leadership-six-years-into-the-mobile
5. Joorabchi, M.E., Mesbah, A., Kruchten, P.: Real challenges in mobile app development. In: 2013 ACM/IEEE International Symposium on Empirical Software Engineering and Measurement, ESEM 2013, Baltimore, MD, USA, 10–11 October 2013, pp. 15–24. IEEE (2013). doi:10.1109/ESEM.2013.9
6. Statista: Number of apps available in leading app stores as of June 2016 (2017). https://www.statista.com/statistics/276623/number-of-apps-available-in-leading-app-stores/
7. Flora, H.K., Chande, S.V.: A review and analysis on mobile application development processes using agile method. Int. J. Res. Comput. Sci. **3**(4), 9–18 (2013). doi:10.7815/ijorcs.34.2013.068
8. ISO. 9241-210: Ergonomics of Human-System Interaction - Part 210: Human-Centred Design for Interactive Systems. ISO 9241-210 (2010)
9. Ferre, X., Juristo, N., Moreno, Ana M.: Improving software engineering practice with HCI aspects. In: Ramamoorthy, C.V., Lee, R., Lee, K.W. (eds.) SERA 2003. LNCS, vol. 3026, pp. 349–363. Springer, Heidelberg (2004). doi:10.1007/978-3-540-24675-6_27
10. Coursaris, C., Kim, D.: A meta-analytical review of empirical mobile usability studies. J. Usabil. Stud. **6**(3), 117–171 (2011)
11. Lettner, F., Holzmann, C.: Automated and unsupervised user interaction logging as basis for usability evaluation of mobile applications. In: Proceedings of 10th International Conference on Advances in Mobile Computing & Multimedia – MoMM 2012, vol. 118 (2012). doi:10.1145/2428955.2428983
12. Ivory, M.Y., Hearst, M.A.: The state of the art in automating usability evaluation of user interfaces. ACM Comput. Surv. (CSUR) **33**(4), 470–516 (2001). doi:10.1145/503112.503114
13. Path, M.: Introducing Google Analytics for Mobile Apps. Google Mobile Ads Team (2009). http://googlemobile.blogspot.com.es/2009/11/introducing-google-analytics-for-mobile.html
14. Google: Google Analytics for Mobile Apps. https://developers.google.com/analytics/solutions/mobile. Accessed 2017

15. Tiedtke, T., Märtin, C., Gerth, N.: AWUSA–a tool for automated website usability analysis. In: Proceedings of 9th International Workshop on Design, Specification and Verification DSV-IS 2002 (2002)
16. Ivory, M.Y.: Automated Web Site Evaluation. Researchers' and Practitioners' Perspectives. Springer Science+Business Media, Dordrecht (2003)
17. Angulo, E., Ferre, X.: A case study on cross-platform development frameworks for mobile applications and UX. In: Proceedings of XV International Conference on Human Computer Interaction - Interacción 2014, Puerto de la Cruz, Tenerife, Spain, pp. 1–8 (2014). doi:10.1145/2662253.2662280
18. Mendoza, A.: Mobile User Experience: Patterns to Make Sense of It All. Morgan Kaufmann, Waltham (2014)
19. Paternò, F., Russino, A., Santoro, C.: Remote evaluation of mobile applications. In: Winckler, M., Johnson, H., Palanque, P. (eds.) TAMODIA 2007. LNCS, vol. 4849, pp. 155–169. Springer, Heidelberg (2007). doi:10.1007/978-3-540-77222-4_13
20. Carta, T., Paternò, F., Santana, V.: Support for remote usability evaluation of web mobile applications. In: Proceedings of 29th ACM International Conference on Design of Communication - SIGDOC 2011, pp. 129–136 (2011). doi:10.1145/2038476.2038502
21. Balagtas-Fernandez, F., Hussmann, H.: A methodology and framework to simplify usability analysis of mobile applications. In: ASE2009 - 24th IEEE/ACM International Conference on Automated Software Engineering, pp. 520–524 (2009). doi:10.1109/ASE.2009.12
22. Kluth, W., Krempels, K.H., Samsel, C.: Automated usability testing for mobile applications. In: WEBIST, vol. 2, pp. 149–156 (2014)
23. Feijó Filho, J., Valle, V., Prata, W.: Automated usability tests for mobile devices through live emotions logging. In: Proceedings of 17th International Conference on Human-Computer Interaction with Mobile Devices and Services Adjunct (MobileHCI 2015), pp. 636–643. ACM, New York (2105). doi:10.1145/2786567.2792902
24. Leichtenstern, K., Erdmann, D., André, E.: EVAL-an evaluation component for mobile interfaces. In: Proceedings of 10th International Conference on Human-Computer Interaction with Mobile Devices and Services, pp. 483–484. ACM, September 2008
25. Porat, T., Schclar, A., Shapira, B.: Mate: a mobile analysis tool for usability experts. In: CHI 2013, Extended Abstracts on Human Factors in Computing Systems, pp. 265–270. ACM, April 2013
26. Hulo, A., To, J.: Developing real time tracking of user behavior, with Google analytics for mobile phone devices. Master thesis, Lund University (2015). https://lup.lub.lu.se/student-papers/search/publication/5305701
27. Rogers, Y., Sharp, H., Preece, J.: Interaction Design: Beyond Human-Computer Interaction, 3rd edn. Wiley, Chichester (2011)
28. Ferre, X., Juristo, N., Windl, H., Constantine, L.: Usability basics for software developers. IEEE Softw. 18, 22–29 (2001). doi:10.1109/52.903160
29. Jacobson, I., Spence, I., Kerr, B.: Use-case 2.0. Commun. ACM 59(5), 61–69 (2016). doi:10.1145/2890778
30. Constantine, L.L., Lockwood, L.A.D.: Software for Use: A Practical Guide to the Models and Methods of Usage-Centered Design. Addison-Wesley, New York (1999)
31. Rubin, J., Chisnell, D.: Handbook of Usability Testing. How to Plan, Design and Conduct Effective Tests, 2nd edn. Wiley, Indianapolis (2008)
32. Rettig, M.: Prototyping for tiny fingers. Commun. ACM 37(4), 21–27 (1994). doi:10.1145/175276.175288
33. Mann, H.B., Whitney, D.R.: On a test of whether one of two random variables is stochastically larger than the other. Ann. Math. Stat. 18(1), 50–60 (1947). doi:10.1214/aoms/1177730491

NexP: A Beginner Friendly Toolkit for Designing and Conducting Controlled Experiments

Xiaojun Meng[1(✉)], Pin Sym Foong[1], Simon Perrault[2],
and Shengdong Zhao[1]

[1] NUS-HCI Lab, National University of Singapore,
Singapore 117417, Singapore
{xiaojun, zhaosd}@comp.nus.edu.sg, pinsym@u.nus.edu
[2] Yale-NUS College, Singapore 138529, Singapore
simon.perrault@yale-nus.edu.sg

Abstract. In this paper, we introduce NexP (Next Experiment Toolkit), an open-source toolkit for designing and running controlled experiments. Unlike previous toolkits, it is targeted for the unmet needs of the beginners in experimental design, who may not have had prior statistical training, or experience in creating, implementing and executing controlled experiments. To accommodate such users, NexP features a hypothesis development process that scaffolds beginners into bridging the gap between daily language and formal statistical language. In our evaluation, we compared NexP against a state-of-the-art experimental design toolkit. Results showed that novices considered NexP more intuitive and easier to use. Users also reported that NexP helped them to better understand the experimental design process, making it a useful tool for both productivity and education.

Keywords: NexP · Controlled experiment · Toolkit · Design platform

1 Introduction

Controlled experiments are an important, widely-used research method in HCI to evaluate user interfaces, styles of interaction, and to understand cognition in the context of interactions with systems [6, 10]. Even for experienced researchers, designing a controlled experiment can be a tedious, multi-step process that is prone to errors.

To reduce the tedium involved in controlled experiment design, HCI researchers have proposed various toolkits to facilitate the design of controlled experiments [12, 17, 20]. Of these, only Touchstone [17] is a complete and functional general-purpose platform that facilitates exploring alternative designs of controlled experiments. It documents the experimental design in a shareable digital form to support replication and extension of previous research work in the HCI literature.

However, because of the complexity of controlled experimental design, existing toolkits continue to challenge beginner researchers. In our preliminary study with six beginner researchers, we saw that they had difficulty in identifying different factors

© IFIP International Federation for Information Processing 2017
Published by Springer International Publishing AG 2017. All Rights Reserved
R. Bernhaupt et al. (Eds.): INTERACT 2017, Part III, LNCS 10515, pp. 132–141, 2017.
DOI: 10.1007/978-3-319-67687-6_10

under a general research question, translating a research question into the appropriate variables and determining an appropriate arrangement of conditions, trials, blocks. It seems that beginners lack the ability to gradually refine questions from a rough inquiry to a robust, testable hypothesis.

There is evidence in pedagogical literature [1, 15] that these may not just be transient novice difficulties, but have an additional layer of conceptual difficulty associated with experimental design and statistical knowledge. In their statistical pedagogy textbook, Ben-Zvi and Garfield [1] identify a need for "selective, thoughtful, and accurate use of technological tools and increasingly more sophisticated software programs" that not only support doing the task, but support learning *about* that task.

Taken together, these beginner shortfalls run counter the usability of existing experimental design tools. Hence, we were motivated to create an experiment design tool that can better facilitate the learning of experimental design and is easier for users who might have a low understanding of statistical terminology and a low working understanding of the purposes and goals of experiment design.

We implemented our approach into a web-based open-source toolkit called NexP that has both design and execution platforms (Fig. 1). Compared with previous experimental design tools we introduced (1) a Question-Answer Structure that connects initial experimental concepts of a beginner researcher to the specialized domain of experiment design and (2) a streamlined step-by-step process to guide such users through complex process. With these two features, our goal was to enable users to explicitly link the final study design product with the study design decisions made previously.

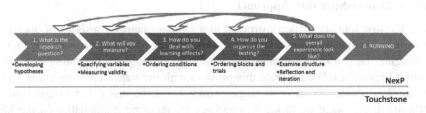

Fig. 1. Conceptual structure of NexP compared to touchstone. NexP scaffolds beginner researchers from ideation to implementation and back, while Touchstone mainly provides automation to experienced users in certain steps.

To evaluate the effectiveness of this design platform, we conducted a workshop study where experimental design novices compared the usage of NexP and Touchstone [17] in several experimental design tasks. We found that participants preferred NexP because of the guided process of hypothesis formulation. In addition, participants also indicated that NexP enhanced their understanding of the experimental design process. Overall, the contribution of this paper is the following:

(1) We propose a 5-stage approach using a Question-Answer Structure to enhance the users' understanding of experimental design by gradually guiding the beginner researchers from an initial idea to a concrete design. We implemented it into a web-based open-source toolkit NexP [8, 9].

(2) We evaluated NexP's experiment design process against an alternative toolkit with beginner researchers in terms of ease of use and learning facilitation for experimental design. Our results indicated that NexP is easier to use and better supports the participants' thinking and learning of experiment design.

2 NexP Structure

NexP's basic structure is a 5-stage process for designing experiments, with an additional 6th stage for running experiments. Much of the full process is detailed elsewhere in our 2-page implementation demo paper [18] and in our CHI course material [13]. Our current version transformed the previous template approach into the Question-Answer approach to better guide beginner users. It also incorporated a running platform into the previous implementation. This Question-Answer structure approach (elaborated below) is informed by the practice of scaffolding problem solving [7], and case of instructional design for complex domains [2, 11] Interim pilot testing showed that participants found this guidance useful. We adopted this approach for Stages 1–4.

As a result, the designing stages were focused on scaffolding the beginner researchers who may not understand statistical terms, or may not have had sufficient experience with experimental design to understand the purpose of such terminology. The elements of experiment design were deconstructed into 5 stages, and each deals with one section: Hypothesis, Variables and Measurements, Test Conditions, Test Order and Study Logistics.

Question-Answer-Structure Approach

Each of the first four stages is constructed in a similar manner – a series of questions, followed by a summary that restates the answers in more academic and statistical terms, thus bridging the gap from informal, non-scientific thinking, to generating formalized structured hypotheses. We illustrate this process with the transition from Stage 1 to 2.

Stage 1 is an ideation support stage, which helps the researcher in specifying a hypothesis. In this stage we tackle terminology by ignoring it altogether during ideation. Instead we begin by asking the evoking question "What is the general question that you want to answer in the study?" This is followed by unpacking the question further into smaller questions to elicit the comparative claim, the key task(s) involved, the measure used. Each step comes with explanations, help menus and loadable examples (Fig. 2). This step closes with a presentation of the answers in a structured 'research claim' statement, populated by the answers to the preceding questions:

> In my experiment, I want to hypothesize that for [target user] to do [task], the solution(s) [my idea] is better than [comparable idea]. To test this hypothesis, I will vary the [other contextual factors] and measure [measureable data].

At this point, the user is encouraged to make logical adjustments to their answers if they spot inconsistencies. Also, this is the first introduction to some experimental design terminology.

Stage 2 aims to connect the hypothesis to the variables in a controlled experiment. The terms that refer to the different types of variables, e.g. dependent/independent can

Fig. 2. Illustration of question-answer-structure approach to formalize the hypothesis.

be confusing, especially for beginners. Moreover, the specific terminology varies by research field, e.g. independent variable vs. factor. Therefore, in this step we explicitly make these connections by showing the claim statement from the first step as a point of comparison, but also sorting the individual elements into independent and dependent variables in this page, and labeling them as such. In effect the users' generic language statements are again re-structured into more formal statistical language. The user can freely modify these variables (add, remove, rename, reorder) and add test conditions with descriptions to each independent variable.

These two stages illustrate how the user is moved from a generic language statement into a claimable, provable claim statement in Question-Answer approach. The remaining stages proceed in a similar, linked manner.

Stage 3 presents both developed statements from Stage 1 and Stage 2, and presents the user with choices about the order of conditions. The terms 'between subjects', 'counter-balancing' for example require higher background knowledge than previous terms. As such, the help text for this stage is much more elaborate, and illustrates both pros and cons of each approach. This is one example of how NexP employs information redistribution to reduce cognitive load.

Stage 4 guides the experimenter to organize the structure of the experiment. It aids in balancing blocks and trials, and working through the timing of the entire experiment. Based on the existing design, NexP suggests the minimum number of participants for the experiment.

At the end of the 4th stage, the user is able to obtain an overview of the entire experiment (Fig. 3a). This overview acts a preliminary simulation of the entire experiment so that the design can be iteratively refined before deployment. In our evaluations, we found that this is the point at which most beginners realize that their experiment is far too elaborate, and they often returned to previous stages to adjust the parameters.

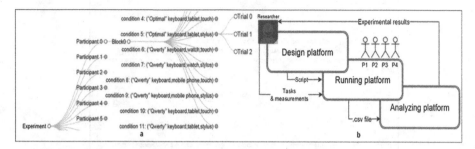

Fig. 3. (a) Simulation of the whole arrangement in the experiment; (b) summary of the design, running, and analyzing platform

Stage 4 is often the start of the iterative loop where users move between the stages freely to iterate the parameters and evaluate the results of their adjustments. It is in this iteration process that users experience the elaboration process that conveys the method of developing experimental design. The complexity of the dependent parts that have been distributed among the previous stages becomes clearer and users can freely iterate until the hypothesis, variables, conditions and trials come together in a viable experimental design.

Stage 5 of NexP guides the experimenter to set the instructions and detailed procedures for conducting the experiment, such as providing recruitment forms and consent forms templates. This stage also supports the experimenter in designing the pre-/post-questionnaires using Google Forms and later invokes the designed questionnaires in the running platform. The entire design can then be saved as either a summarized PDF report or a JSON file digitally, which can be imported and shared with other researchers for refinement and re-evaluation in the future.

Executing Experiments

In NexP, we implement a common platform for running different types of controlled experiments leveraging the browser. NexP can automatically read the experimental JSON file and output the whole web-based framework in the arranged order for running the experiment. Experienced programmers can modify the source code of this web framework according to their needs and implement tasks as they require. Figure 3b summarizes the relationship among design, execution, and experimental analysis stages. The design platform generates a script file that can be executed in the running platform. The measured data (e.g., pre-defined dependent variables) collected by the running platform are saved as CSV files, which can be further analyzed elsewhere.

3   Evaluation

To validate the ease of use and learning facilitation of NexP for people with limited knowledge of experimental design, we conducted a one-day workshop study to compare NexP with Touchstone [17].

Participants and Apparatus: 24 participants (8 females, 16 males) ranging from 21–50 years old (M = 29.2, SD = 6.9) attended this workshop. The participants included 3 faculty members, 5 researchers and 12 students from several universities, and 4 UX practitioners. All participants self-reported that they are not familiar with controlled experiments in HCI. None had any prior knowledge of either Touchstone or NexP. Participants were asked to bring their own laptop computers to the workshop, with installation instructions provided earlier.

Design and Procedure: The entire workshop lasted for 6 h from 10 am to 4 pm, spread over five sessions as described in Table 1. A within-subject design was used. Each participant replicated two tasks using both toolkits (NexP, Touchstone). The order of toolkit use was counter-balanced while the order of the replication tasks remained the same.

Table 1.   Design of the workshop.

1. Introduction (60 min)	Introducing experiment design (material from Scott MacKenzie's empirical evaluation book [3])
2. Prep and training (80 min)	Introducing and installing toolkits; Showing video tutorials and teaching on designing experiments using each toolkit
Lunch break (40 min)	Lunch provided
3. Replication task (100 min)	Participants replicate two existing controlled experiments, one for each toolkit.
4. Design task (70 min)	Participants design their own experiment based on a high level description, using a toolkit of their choice.
5. Debriefing (10 min)	Explain the purpose of the workshop; post-evaluation questionnaire

In session 3, each participant received soft copies of the original publications [16, 19] and a brief introduction on the replication tasks. Participants were randomly paired into groups of two to complete the tasks. We provided no additional help during this session. Each pair had to submit their resulting files generated by both toolkits to experimenters at the end of the session 3. For each replication task, participants were allowed to spend 35 min for a total of 70 min.

In session 4, the same participant pairs formed in session 3 were asked to perform the design task by using a preferred toolkit of their choice (either NexP or Touchstone). Finally, they were asked to each fill in the (7-point Likert scale) post-questionnaire based on Computer System Usability Questionnaire [5].

During the debriefing, we explained the complete purpose of the workshop and revealed that we were the authors of NexP. We finally asked participants to sketch features and suggest improvements on paper for an ideal experimental toolkit.

Tasks: *Training Tasks:* The purpose of the training task is to familiarize the participants with the two toolkits. To avoid bias, we created two video tutorials, one for each toolkit, demonstrating the step-by-step procedure to design an interaction technique experiment (Pie Menu vs. Linear Menu from [4]).

Replication Tasks: To minimize transfer of learning effect, participants were asked to replicate two controlled experiments from two CHI publications [16, 19], one for each toolkit. The first study investigated the noticeability of notifications under the influence of feedback modality and physical activity for interactive rings. The second study evaluated performance of different mode switching techniques for pen-based interfaces. We randomly chose those two studies as they provided clear and appropriate descriptions for HCI beginners to replicate.

Design Task: The purpose of the design task was to test how well the toolkits supported participants to design an open-ended controlled experiment. This design task was to compare ShapeWriter [14] to soft keyboards in terms of user performances.

Results

Replication Task: The 24 participants formed 12 groups to work on the replication tasks. 9 pairs (75%) were able to deliver a complete and correct experimental design using NexP, and 4 pairs (33.3%) were able to do so using TouchStone. Of the 3 groups that failed while using NexP, one failed to properly counterbalance the independent variables, another pair did not set the correct number of blocks and trials, and the last pair failed to define the correct independent variables with their levels. For the 8 groups that failed while using Touchstone, three were not able to define the dependent variables. One failed to define the correct independent variables with their levels. Two failed to define the correct counterbalancing strategy. Two were not able to finish on time and thus did not submit the TouchStone design files.

Design Task: When the participants were asked to choose their preferred toolkit for this task, 11 out of 12 pairs (91.7%) chose to use NexP. We did not measure the accuracy in this open task, because the detailed design was decided by the individual pairs.

Post-questionnaire: We compared quantitative feedback given on both toolkits using Wilcoxon signed-rank tests. For every affirmation of the questionnaire, the feedback was significantly more positive for NexP (all $p < .05$) than for TouchStone, except on the "It does everything I expect it to do" where NexP performs slightly, yet not significantly better than TouchStone ($M = 4.58$ vs. $M = 4.25$, $p = .17$).

The results of subjective preferences from the participants (Table 2), their choices of toolkit to use in session 4 and the success rate of replicating existing experiments in session 3, suggest that the scaffolding method embodied in NexP made it easier for non-expert users to use. It also indicates that despite their novice status, they are more capable of designing and presenting complete experimental designs using NexP.

Table 2. Summary of the post-workshop questionnaire. The values in second and third column are the median scores on a 7-point Likert scale for each toolkit. * and ** denote significance (p < .05 and p < .01).

Questions	NexP	TouchS	P
1. I became more productive with it	5.33	4.67	*
2. Easy to use	4.75	3.21	**
3. It does everything I expect it to do	4.58	4.25	
4. I can use it without written instructions	4	2.54	**
5. It requires the fewest steps to complete task	4.63	3.5	**
6. Using it is effortless	4.25	3	**
7. I quickly became skillful with it	5	3.83	**
8. It is easy to identify the hypothesis	5.29	3.21	**
9. It is easy to identify the independent variables	5.17	3.88	**
10. It is easy to arrange the order of the experimental conditions	5.25	4.25	*
11. I am satisfied with it	5	3.67	**
12. I would use it	5.29	3.63	**

4 Discussion and Implications

The workshop showed that NexP is a more beginner-friendly tool. Participants of the workshop found NexP easier to use and understand because it *"presents information more clearly"* (P3) and the *"terminology for NexP is easy to understand"* (P8).

We were particularly surprised when some participants mentioned that NexP has fewer steps as compared with Touchstone, because both toolkits actually have a similar number of steps for designing an experiment. Possibly, the perceived difference lies in the contrasting ways complex information is presented to users. NexP's use of scaffolding and information redistribution helped to break the experiment design process down to smaller sets of decisions. However, Touchstone relies on a different approach and aims at being as configurable as possible in order to fit the needs of expert users.

Participants also found that NexP provides better support for the thinking process of experiment design. Four participants particularly highlighted how NexP helped them identify and differentiate Independent and Dependent variables through the process of formulating the hypothesis. Participants (P6, P14) were impressed by *"the ability of NexP to convert the answers to [their] questions to independent and dependent variables"*. P12 stated that he liked *"the hypothesis feature of NexP, as it helps to break down the components of the research topic and quickly focus on the important aspects"*. Finally, participants P12 and P24 liked the *"tree structure simulation of NexP"*. The qualitative comments of the participants affirm the quantitative findings.

We conclude that of the major advantages of NexP is using the Question-Answer structure as well as providing a systematic and streamlined 5-stage approach to help users to think from a broad question to the final concrete design.

5 Conclusion and Future Work

In this work, we enhanced the original NexP with the Question-Answer structure to address the needs of beginner users. We evaluated this approach and found that NexP can help beginners to understand and execute controlled experiments better than a leading alternative. As observed by some our participants (P7, 17, 20, 24), NexP holds promise as a companion pedagogical tool to help instructors teaching controlled experiments. In addition, NexP provides the designing and running platform, as well as data support for analysis, making it one of the first attempts for an end-to-end solution. For future work, we would like to see NexP expanded as a learning support tool by conducting studies to further understand the needs of researchers who want to improve in their experimental design skills. We will also improve and publish the open-source NexP's design and running platform for the use of the community.

References

1. Ben-Zvi, D., Garfield, J.: The Challenge of Developing Statistical Literacy, Reasoning and Thinking. Springer, Dordrecht (2016). doi:10.1007/1-4020-2278-6. Accessed 1 Sept 2016
2. Jonassen, David H.: Instructional design models for well-structured and III-structured problem-solving learning outcomes. Educ. Tech. Res. Dev. **45**(1), 65–94 (1997). doi:10.1007/BF02299613
3. MacKenzie, I.S.: Human-Computer Interaction an Empirical Research Perspective. Newnes, Boston (2012)
4. Callahan, J., Hopkins, D., Weiser, M. Shneiderman, B.: An empirical comparison of pie vs. linear menus. In: Proceedings of SIGCHI Conference on Human Factors in Computing Systems, pp. 95–100 (1988). doi:10.1145/57167.57182
5. Lewis, J.R.: IBM computer usability satisfaction questionnaires: psychometric evaluation and instructions for use. Int. J. Hum.-Comput. Interact. **7**(1), 57–78 (1995). doi:10.1080/10447319509526110
6. Lazar, J., Feng, J.H., Hochheiser, H.: Research Methods in Human-Computer Interaction. Wiley, Hoboken (2010)
7. Rosson, M.B., Carroll, J.M.: Scaffolded examples for learning object-oriented design. Commun. ACM **39**(4), 46–47 (1996). doi:10.1145/227210.227223
8. NexP online access. www.nexp.site
9. NexP's design platform source code. https://github.com/mengxj08/webnexp, NexP's running platform source code: https://github.com/mengxj08/platformframework
10. Cairns, P., Cox, A.L.: Research Methods for Human-Computer Interaction. Cambridge University Press, New York (2008)
11. Cobb, P., McClain, K.: Principles of instructional design for supporting the development of students' statistical reasoning. In: Ben-Zvi, D., Garfield, J. (eds.) The Challenge of Developing Statistical Literacy, Reasoning and Thinking, pp. 375–395. Springer, Dordrecht (2004). doi:10.1007/1-4020-2278-6_16
12. Soukoreff, R.W, MacKenzie, I.S.: Generalized Fitts' law model builder. In: Conference Companion on Human Factors in Computing Systems - CHI 1995, pp. 113–114 (1995). doi:10.1145/223355.223456

13. Zhao, S., Meng, X., Foong, P.S., Perrault, S.: A Dummy's guide to your Next EXperiment: experimental design and analysis made easy. In: Proceedings of 2016 CHI Conference Extended Abstracts on Human Factors in Computing Systems (CHI EA 2016), pp. 1016–1019. ACM, New York (2016). doi:10.1145/2851581.2856675

14. Zhai, S. Kristensson, P.O., Gong, P., Greiner, M., Peng, S.A., Liu, L.M, Dunnigan, A.: Shapewriter on the iPhone - from the laboratory to the real world. In: CHI 2009 Extended Abstracts on Human Factors in Computing Systems, pp. 2667–2670 (2009). doi:10.1145/1520340.1520380

15. Malik, S.: Undergraduates' statistics anxiety: a phenomenological study. Qual. Rep. **20**(2), 120–133 (2015)

16. Roumen, T., Perrault, S.T, Zhao, S.: NotiRing: a comparative study of notification channels for wearable interactive rings. In: Proceedings of 33rd Annual ACM Conference on Human Factors in Computing Systems, pp. 2497–2500 (2015). doi:10.1145/2702123.2702350

17. Mackay, W.E, Appert, C., Beaudouin-Lafon, M., et al.: Touchstone: exploratory design of experiments. In: Proceedings of SIGCHI Conference on Human Factors in Computing Systems - CHI 2007, p. 1425 (2007). doi:10.1145/1240624.1240840

18. Meng, X., Foong, P.S, Perrault, S., Zhao, S.: Approach to designing controlled experiments. In: Buono, P., Lanzilotti, R., Matera, M. (eds.) Proceedings of International Working Conference on Advanced Visual Interfaces (AVI 2016), pp. 358–359. ACM, New York, 5 September 2016. doi:10.1145/2909132.2926086

19. Li, Y., Hinckley, K., Guan, Z., Landay, J.A.: Experimental analysis of mode switching techniques in pen-based user interfaces. In: CHI 2005, Proceedings of SIGCHI Conference on Human Factors in Computing Systems, pp. 461–470 (2005). doi:10.1145/1054972.1055036

20. Guiard, Y., Beaudouin-Lafon, M., Du, Y., Appert, C., Fekete, J.D, Chapuis, O.: Shakespeare's complete works as a benchmark for evaluating multiscale document navigation techniques. In: Proceedings of 2006 AVI Workshop on BEyond Time and Errors Novel Evaluation Methods for Information Visualization - BELIV 2006, p. 1 (2006). doi:10.1145/1168149.1168165

UX Metrics: Deriving Country-Specific Usage Patterns of a Website Plug-In from Web Analytics

Florian Lachner[✉], Florian Fincke, and Andreas Butz

LMU Munich, Human-Computer Interaction Group,
Amalienstr. 17, 80333 Munich, Germany
{florian.lachner,butz}@ifi.lmu.de, florian.fincke@campus.lmu.de

Abstract. Metrics for User Experience (UX) often involve traditional usability aspects, such as task success, but also mental aspects, such as interpretation and meaning. The actual experience of a user also highly depends on personal characteristics, such as the social and cultural background. In this paper, we investigate the relation between users' country of origin and their interaction patterns with an e-commerce website plug-in. We used a quantitative web analytics approach based on six UX-related metrics to evaluate the applicability of a quantitative UX evaluation approach in an international context. In a 34 day study we analyzed the usage patterns of 5.843 French, 2.760 German, and 5.548 Italian website visitors and found that they show significantly different patterns. This indicates that website metrics are a suitable means for cost-effective UX analysis on a large scale, which can provide valuable starting points for a further in-depth analysis.

Keywords: User experience · Cross-cultural design · User tracking · Data logging · Interfaces · Globalization · Localization

1 Introduction

The theory of User Experience (UX) goes back to the consideration of pleasure and emotions as part of a product's characteristics. Early approaches emerged from a user-centered design perspective, and the awareness of human factor professionals that user satisfaction is insufficiently considered in the concept of usability [26]. The consideration of pleasure and emotions was further increased by the focus on the interplay between affect and cognition. Due to this enhanced view on product design and development, aesthetics, pleasure, and usability became a balanced triad in the HCI community [40].

Nowadays, the primary goal of UX designers and engineers often is to create a pleasurable interaction between the user and the product that goes beyond traditional usability considerations [19]. It also has become common ground in the HCI community that experiences are subjective in nature and highly dependent

© IFIP International Federation for Information Processing 2017
Published by Springer International Publishing AG 2017. All Rights Reserved
R. Bernhaupt et al. (Eds.): INTERACT 2017, Part III, LNCS 10515, pp. 142–159, 2017.
DOI: 10.1007/978-3-319-67687-6_11

on the usage context [24, 32]. Hence, a user's experiences can be shaped and influenced based on his or her individual preferences (regarding aesthetics or ergonomics), mood, prior interactions, product brand, age, gender, and culture [7, 12, 16, 29, 30, 34, 42, 51, 52]. The cultural aspect becomes particularly interesting for global businesses, whose products or services can be accessed, evaluated, and purchased from all over the world [17, 37, 46, 61].

In order to ensure the intended quality of UX, measurement tools and methods represent a crucial resource in UX design and research processes. However, there is still an ongoing debate about the applicability and effectiveness of qualitative and quantitative approaches for UX measurement [6, 33, 57]. Furthermore, researchers and designers have to balance information value, cost efficiency, and expenditure of time when gathering attitudinal (e.g., through lab studies or surveys) or behavioral data (e.g., through data logging or time measurement) [50, 55, 56].

In this paper, we analyze the relationship between the country of origin and the usage behavior of users of a website plug-in (see Fig. 1). We base our analysis on quantitative behavioral data, gathered through user tracking, to draw a conclusion on the applicability of web analytics metrics. Our dataset stems from a data logging study of a plug-in that was implemented in an e-commerce website plug-in.

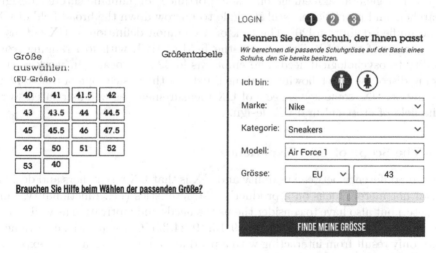

Fig. 1. Website plug-in (right) for shoe size recommendations and the link to it in the German online store (left).

Over the course of 34 consecutive days we tracked the behavior (i.e., plug-in interactions) of users located in France, Germany, and Italy based on six UX metrics, which we derived and adapted from the HEART framework of Rodden et al. [50]. Our study was motivated by the following research question:

*Which differences in the user experience of a website (plug-in) can we iden-
tify between French, German, and Italian users simply through web analytics
metrics?*

Consequently, the contribution of this paper is twofold: First, based on the
analysis of country-specific differences we identify associated relationships and
hence suitable levers to efficiently target further qualitative in-depth analyses.
Second, we adapt the quantitative UX framework of Rodden et al. [50] to our specific use case (i.e., e-commerce website plug-in) in order to examine the applicability of UX metrics that build upon large-scale website tracking data. Ultimately, we draw a conclusion how such a quantitative approach can support
designers in saving time and money for cross-cultural UX evaluation and potentially localized interface adaptions. For our analysis, we, therefore, exclude a supplemental investigation of further factors, such as gender differences or device
type. Our underlying goal is to foster an ongoing debate about cross-cultural
UX design and about an appropriate balance of qualitative and quantitative UX
measurement.

2   Background and Related Work

Despite the general agreement on its importance for human-centered design,
researchers and practitioners still struggle to narrow down the broad field of UX
to one unified definition [20]. The lack of a common definition of UX entails a
large variety of research directions in the field of HCI, with foci ranging from
usability to psychological needs and emotions [6,32]. To locate our work in this
ongoing discourse, the following sections illustrate the basic scope of (our understanding of) UX, some key aspects of UX measurement, as well as related work
in the field of cross-cultural UX design.

2.1   The Scope of User Experience

The main difference between usability and UX is that UX researchers and designers can not merely focus on a product's characteristics (i.e., functionality, purpose, etc.) but also have to consider the user's needs and motivation as well as the
context of use (i.e., the environment) [9,13,19,24,38]. Consequently, experiences
do not only result from interacting with a product but also from a user's expectations, others' opinions, or from experiences with related technologies before the
actual interaction. At the same time, experiences and associated feelings merely
evolve over time through reflection on previous interactions, advertisements, and
again through others' opinions [24,27,35,52].

The scope of UX becomes even more complex for globally acting businesses:
First, the concept of UX is differently understood between academia and industry
as well as between different countries [31,32]. Second, cultural differences in
language, values, or needs raise various questions regarding the suitability of
globally optimal or locally adapted designs of products and services [4,37,59].

In this paper, our goal is to analyze cultural differences in UX design. For this purpose, we simplify the origin of cultural differences to individual preferences caused by one's country of origin. Thus, we do not focus on further cultural allocations, such as age group or social background. Furthermore, UX in our context shall include both usability aspects as well as mental aspects, such as the interpretation of an e-commerce website plug-in. In order to answer our research question, we will, therefore, derive suitable web analytics metrics, which we call UX metrics.

2.2 Cross-Cultural Differences in UX Design

The need for cross-cultural considerations in interface design emerged more than two centuries ago, shortly after designers started to put an emphasis on the usability aspects of their designs (see [39]). Initial discussions mainly focused on the use of colors, language, as well as icons and symbols [5,53]. However, since then usability theories and measures in the HCI community rather marginally focused on cultural design preferences [14]. Nevertheless, with the further increasing interest in experiences of product interactions, researchers in the HCI community once again started to raise questions about cross-cultural design preferences (see [8,21,47]). In fact, various studies have already been able to identify cultural differences in UX design in different use cases.

Athinen et al. [1], for example, investigated culturally sensitive design for a mobile wellness application. In their study, they interviewed 16 people (8 from Finland and 8 from India) to identify similarities and differences in the understanding of wellness and its consequences for the design of a mobile application. They found that Finns and Indians have a different understanding of goal setting, which is an important aspect for the associated mobile application. Similarly, Walsh and Vaino [60] argue for cross-cultural UX considerations for mHealth applications, while Al-Shamaileh and Sutcliffe [2] demonstrate varying preferences in the design of health-related websites in the UK and Jordan.

Furthermore, Frandsen-Thorlacius et al. [14] were able to detect differences in the understanding of the concept of usability for Danish and Chinese users. Using a questionnaire survey, the authors were able to derive that Chinese users preferentially value visual appearance, satisfaction, and fun, whereas Danish users rather focus on effectiveness, lack of frustration, and efficiency. Reinecke and Gajos [48] were, likewise, able to analyze visual preferences of websites based on a comprehensive study of 2.4 million ratings from almost 40 thousand participants.

However, cultural differences are not limited to the evaluation of products and services. Lallemand et al. [31] point out discrepancies in the understanding of the concept of UX based on a survey amongst 758 researchers and practitioners from 35 nationalities. Gerea and Herskovic [15] additionally expand this study to Latin America. Nowadays, researchers want to further link cultural studies and product design, particularly through the integration of Hofstede's (see [22]) cultural dimensions in HCI [36,37,43,46,58].

2.3 Qualitative Vs. Quantitative UX Measurement

Because experiences are such a complex phenomenon, UX researchers and practitioners utilize a whole set of measurement approaches to anticipate, test, and improve a product's UX. However, there is no common agreement whether qualitative or quantitative approaches should be favored [6,33,49]. On the one hand, qualitative approaches (gathered through, e.g., interviews) provide rich and detailed insights for in-depth analysis [54], on the other hand, quantitative approaches (gathered through, e.g., questionnaires) can reduce costs and time effort [23,57].

Apart from this, UX measurement methods are primarily based on attitudinal data (i.e., data related to a user's feelings and emotions) [31,50]. In contrast, the HEART framework [50] represents a first step towards the integration of behavioral data (i.e., actual activities of users - traditionally used in usability testing, see [3,10,25,41]), in UX measurement. The framework includes five metrics, focusing on both usability and UX-related aspects [50]:

- *Happiness:* referring to, e.g., satisfaction and ease of use.
- *Engagement:* describing the user's level of involvement.
- *Adoption:* addressing customer acquisition.
- *Retention:* analyzing recurring users.
- *Task success:* covering traditional usability aspects.

The framework does not aim to describe UX as a whole but to strategically direct UX measurement processes based on large-scale data, particularly when working in teams. Therefore, one has to define a suitable measurement goal and approach per metric (e.g., the number of visits per week for *Engagement*, the error rate for *Task success*) depending on the respective product or service.

We understand their approach as an initial step towards including behavioral data from usability testing in UX measurement. Therefore, we aim to evaluate its applicability for our use case, i.e., the analysis of UX-related, country-specific usage patterns of French, German, and Italian users from web analytics. However, to ensure a suitable implementation of UX metrics in our collaboration partner's development process, we slightly customized our UX metrics based on the HEART framework.

3 Methodology and User Study

In order to examine the applicability of UX-oriented web analytics metrics for identifying country-specific user behaviors, we partnered with a company that provides a customizable website plug-in for online shoe stores. The plug-in allows customers to identify their correct shoe size based on the comparison with the size of another model.

3.1   Setting and Procedure

For our study, we tracked the plug-in interactions of a globally acting online shoe store. The analyzed plug-in (see Fig. 1 right) is integrated in the store's website and accessible through a link below the actual selection of the shoe size (see Fig. 1 left). The overall goal of the plug-in is that customers can enter information about a shoe that they already own in order to identify the correct size of the shoe they want to buy. To ensure a problem-free implementation in different countries, the plug-in was translated by professional translators for all countries.

Once a customer clicks on the link, the plug-in opens and asks for the customer's gender as well as the brand, category, model, and size of a comparative shoe (i.e., plug-in steps one to five). This information is used to identify the correct size for the customer depending on the shape and differences in size of the desired shoe. The comparative data is taken from our partner's internal database. As a sixth plug-in step, users can request (i.e., click) a shoe size recommendation. After receiving all the information, the recommended size is stored for 90 days and additionally displayed within the link's text label once a customer accesses the online store again. Thus, it is not necessary to open and use the plug-in repeatedly.

For post-hoc analysis, all tracked data points (plug-in openings, plug-in interactions, recommendation requests, and adding products to the website shopping cart) were anonymized and securely stored at our partner's server infrastructure for long-term evaluations through client-based tracking. Client-based tracking (i.e., Javascript-based for plug-in interactions and cookie-based tracking for long-term analysis of recurring users) was pursued to minimize data traffic in order to ensure a smooth and pleasant plug-in implementation. Shoe recommendations were tracked through server-based tracking. The country of origin was identified by the client's IP address.

3.2   Study Data and Analysis

Observations. We ran our study for 34 consecutive days. During this time, no special offer or promotion was announced at the client's online store in order to ensure the comparability of our analysis. Over the course of our study people from 200 countries visited the client's website, whereof people from 121 countries accessed the plug-in. For our investigation we focused on France, Germany, and Italy (277,551, 141,897, and 172,887 website loadings leading to 5843, 2760, and 5548 plug-in openings, respectively). Overall, about one third (31,4% in France, 30,4% in Germany, and 37,2% in Italy) of all website visitors per country accessed the website on a mobile device, two thirds (68,6% in France, 69,6% in Germany, and 62,8% in Italy) on a desktop device.

UX metrics. Our quantitative analysis of the plug-in interactions was based on six metrics (see Table 1) that we derived and adapted from the HEART framework [50]. Our metrics were consciously labeled with a distinguishing term in order to highlight the objective of each metric. Furthermore, the particular term allowed our collaboration partner to align strategic initiatives and development efforts.

Table 1. UX metrics used for the analysis of plug-in interactions.

UX metric	Definition and objective	see HEART [50]
Adoption	No. of openings (link clicks) to measure user acquisition	*Adoption*
Complexity	Time per data input to analyze complexity per plug-in step	*Engagement*
Task success	No. of total recommendations to track plug-in effectiveness	*Task Success*
Continuity	No. of successful inputs per step to retrace plug-in continuity	*Task Success*
Trust	No. of recommended orders to derive trust in suggestions	*Happiness*
Mastery	No. of suggested orders without plug-in opening (recurring users) to derive long-term trust	*Retention*

First of all, we tracked the user **Adoption**, i.e., the number of users that click on the link to the plug-in as well as the **Complexity** of the plug-in (based on the process time per plug-in step). In order to analyze the effectiveness of the plug-in, we defined the two metrics, **Task Success** (overall number of final recommendations) and **Continuity** (successful completions per plug-in step). These four metrics describe usability aspects of the plug-in.

For the interaction with the online shoe store plug-in, we wanted the associated UX to be a pleasant interaction with the service that results in a trustworthy shoe size recommendation. The goal of the plug-in recommendation, therefore, is that customers identify the correct size of a shoe and trust the plug-in even when the recommendation differs from the size of the comparative shoe. An additional feature of the plug-in is that the recommended shoe size is stored and shown in the plug-in link when users complete all plug-in steps and access the website again within 90 days (see Fig. 2).

Fig. 2. Link (in the German online store) to the plug-in without recommendation (left) and with recommendation for recurring users (right).

Against this background, we defined the metric **Trust** to understand if users rely on the shoe size recommendation of the plug-in (i.e., put the recommended shoe size into the website's shopping cart). We, therefore, only considered users who ordered a recommended shoe size that differed from the initially entered size of the comparative shoe and excluded users whose recommended size corresponded to the size of the selected comparative shoe. Thus, we could evaluate if users clearly relied on the plug-in's recommendation. We adapted the metric happiness from the HEART framework to our use case as it was not desired to establish a direct communication with the user. All users who successfully clicked through all steps received a recommendation whereas we defined a pleased user as a user that relied on the recommended size for his/her final order. In order to draw conclusions on the long-term experience with the recommendation service, we defined the metric **Mastery**. This metric refers to the number of orders (of recommended shoe sizes) from recurring users that did not open the plug-in again but relied on the suggestion of a suitable size based on their previously entered information. The information was stored in a client-side cookie for 90 days as described before. For this purpose, the recommended shoe size was shown in the link's text label. Once again, we only considered orders that included differing shoe sizes.

All in all, we see these metrics as suitable measuring points for the UX evaluation of equivalent recommendation plug-ins (with the objective to minimize recurring interactions) in an e-commerce context. In further use cases, researchers and designers will have to question their generalization and adapt the metrics accordingly (e.g., when a repetitious interaction is aspired).

Data analysis. We conducted a statistical analysis (using SPSS version 20.0) to identify varying usage behaviors between French, German, and Italian users. We used the Chi-Square Test in order to analyze the association between the country and the UX metrics of *Adoption*, *Task Success*, *Continuity*, *Trust*, and *Mastery*. In order to evaluate the UX metric *Complexity* we used two-way ANOVA and post-hoc Sidak as well as an ANOVA test. We excluded outliers in the process times for the analysis of the metric *Complexity* according to Grubbs [18]. An identified outlier was also excluded from the analysis of previous plug-in steps to ensure consistency within our results. For all analyses we defined a significance level of 5%.

4   Results

The analysis of our data set using the previously defined UX metrics yielded a number of differences in the usage behaviours of the website plug-in between French, German, and Italian users. Thus, we were able to derive significant differences in the adoption rate, dropout rate per plug-in step, the temporal usage patterns, and the reliance on recommendations as described below.

4.1 Country-Specific Adoption, Dropout, and Recommendation Rate

First of all, it should be noted that we found a relationship between the country of origin and the *Adoption* rate (see Table 2), i.e., number of plug-in openings to measure user acquisition ($\chi^2(2) = 714.327$, p = .000): 2.11% for French users (277,551 website loadings, 5,843 openings), 1.95% for German users (141,897 website loadings, 2,760 openings), and 3.21% for Italian users (172,887 website loadings, 5,548 openings).

The analysis of *Continuity* (i.e., number of successful inputs per plug-in step to retrace usage continuity) provided insights in the relationship between country of origin and successful completions per plug-in step. We found a relationship for the plug-in steps where users had to select their gender ($\chi^2(4) = 28.267$, p = .000), the brand of a comparative shoe ($\chi^2(4) = 10.166$, p = .038), an associated model ($\chi^2(4) = 22.019$, p = .000), and click to receive a shoe size recommendation ($\chi^2(2) = 6.781$, p = .034), as summarized in Table 2.

Except for the last step, where users had to click to receive a recommendation, we included users who successfully completed the respective step (success), closed the plug-in or browser (failure), and users who went back to the respective plug-in step after having already moved on to further plug-in steps (detour) in the analysis of the usage *Continuity*. Thus, we were able to derive usage patterns per plug-in step: Generally, in the first plug-in step (i.e., selection of the gender) users from all three countries showed the highest dropout rate (including only successful and failed completions): 22.51% for France (1315 failed users), 24.82% for Germany (685 failed users), and 26.71% for Italy (1482 failed users). In addition, most users who went back to a previous plug-in step chose to start from the beginning of entering the comparative data, more precisely by selecting the brand (the second plug-in step) of a comparative shoe (see Table 2).

In addition, we were able to identify a relationship of *Task Success* (i.e., number of total recommendations to understand plug-in effectiveness) and country of origin ($\chi^2(2)=13.332$, p=.001). Users from France showed the highest rate of successful recommendations (52% out of 5843 plug-in openings), followed by Germany (49% out of 2760 plug-in openings), and Italy (46% out of 5548 plug-in openings).

4.2 Divergent Temporal Usage Patterns

The goal of the metric *Complexity* was to identify temporal differences along the process steps in order to diagnose key hurdles of the plug-in. We used the z-score transformation to make the data normal before conducting the (two-way) ANOVA and post-hoc Sidak test, as our dataset (process time per plug-in step) did not represent a normal distribution according to the Kolmogorov-Smirnov test. We used post-hoc Sidak test as all users interacted with the plug-in independently. We then used the two-way ANOVA and a post-hoc Sidak test to analyze the effect of the country of origin on the time spent on each step along the plug-in process. Thus, we found out that there was an effect between country of origin and the process time per plug-in step ($F(10,2) = 10.427$, p = .000,

Table 2. Chi-Square results (χ^2) based on the UX metrics Adoption, Continuity, Task Success, Trust, and Mastery for French (FRA), German (GER), and Italian (ITA) users.

UX metric	Plug-In Step		Country of Origin				χ^2	Cramer's V
			FRA	GER	ITA	Total		
Adoption		Success	5843	2760	5548	14.151	714.327	.035
		Failure	271.708	139.137	167.339	578.184		
		Total	277.551	141.897	172.887	592.335	p = .000	
Continuity	Gender	Success	4528	2075	4066	10,669	28.267	.032
		Failure	1315	685	1482	3482		
		Detour	14	8	19	41		
		Total	5857	2768	5567	14,192	p = .000	
	Brand	Success	4105	1917	3733	9755	10.166	.022
		Failure	183	72	134	389		
		Detour	320	120	308	748		
		Total	4608	2109	4175	10.892	p = .038	
	Category	Success	3908	1797	3540	9245	4.218	n.s.
		Failure	312	155	283	750		
		Detour	178	87	196	461		
		Total	4398	2039	4019	10.456	p = .377	
	Model	Success	3354	1516	2906	7776	22.019	.034
		Failure	664	325	728	1717		
		Detour	27	18	44	89		
		Total	4045	1859	3678	9582	p = .000	
	Size	Success	3159	1417	2698	7274	8.256	n.s.
		Failure	213	108	228	549		
		Detour	6	4	12	22		
		Total	3378	1529	2938	7845	p = .083	
	Rec.	Success	3038	1350	2560	6948	6.781	.031
		Failure	125	70	145	340		
		Total	3163	1420	2705	7288	p = .034	
Task success		Openings	5843	2760	5548	14.151	13.332	.025
		Rec.	3038	1350	2560	6948		
		Total	8881	4110	8108	21.099	p = .001	
Trust		Yes	10	3	9	22	21.232	.193
		No	381	113	53	547		
		Total	391	116	62	569	p = .000	
Mastery		Yes	158	17	103	278	42.130	.136
		No	1094	421	500	2015		
		Total	1252	438	603	2293	p = .000	

$\eta^2 = .011$). In our study, Italian users significantly differed in their temporal usage patterns along all plug-in steps from French users (p = .000) as well as from German users (p = .022). French and Germany did not differ significantly (p > .050) (see Fig. 3).

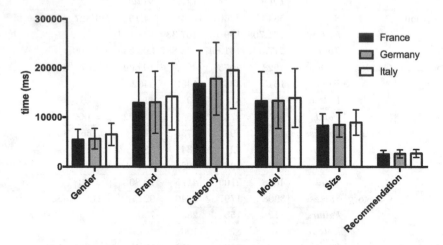

Fig. 3. Average process times for each plug-in step per country including the standard deviation.

Next, we conducted an ANOVA and post-hoc Sidak test to investigate whether the process times significantly vary per plug-in step. Thus, we found out that there is an effect of country of origin for the first plug-in step to select the gender ($F(12,2) = 10.774$, p = .000, $\eta^2 = .012$) as well as the third plug-in step to select a category of a comparative shoe ($F(12,2) = 6.342$, p = .002, $\eta^2 = .007$). For the other plug-in steps (i.e., brand, model, size, and recommendation) we could not identify significant differences (p > .050). More precisely, for the first step (i.e., gender) the process time (i.e., the mean) of Italian users differed from French users (p = .000) as well as from German users (p = .008). Furthermore, the mean of the process time of Italian users to select a category varied from the process time of French users (p = 0.001). On average, Italian users needed more time for each plug-in step.

4.3   Varying Reliance on Recommendations

Based on the two metrics *Trust* (number of recommended orders) and *Mastery* (number of recommended orders of recurring users without opening the plug-in) we analyzed the usage behaviors of plug-in users directly related to the recommendation service. The objective of these metrics is to understand whether the country of origin is related to the reliance of users on the shoe size recommendation as well as with the understanding of recurring users (who already successfully clicked through the whole plug-in process and should understand that their suitable size is directly represented in the plug-in opening link) that they do not have to open the plug-in again.

We found out that there is a relationship between country of origin and the *Trust* in the recommendation of the plug-in ($\chi^2(2) = 13.983$, p = .001). Furthermore, the country of origin is related to the understanding of the link's text label recommendation (*Mastery*) for recurring users ($\chi^2(2) = 42.130$, p = .000).

In our study, French and German users showed a comparable trust rate (i.e., number of users who ordered a differing shoe size based on the recommendation and excluding users whose initially entered shoe size equalled the recommended size hence no conclusion on the user's trust can be drawn) of 2.56% (FR: 10 out of 391, 114 additional users excluded) and 2.59% (GER: 3 out of 116, 60 additional users excluded). However, from 62 Italian users that got a differing recommendation, 9 users (14.52% excluding 27 additional users) relied on the plug-in and added a differing shoe size into the website's shopping cart (see Fig. 4).

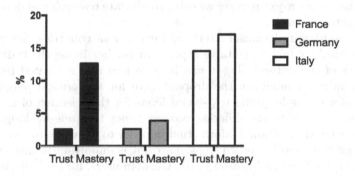

Fig. 4. Percentage of users per country who relied on the plug-in suggestion (Trust) or the suggestion in the link's text label (Mastery) when the recommended size differed from the comparative shoe size.

With regards to recurring users relying on the recommendation of the plug-in link, the number of French users (adding a differing shoe size into the website's shopping cart without opening the plug-in and once again excluding users for whom no conclusion can be drawn as the recommended size equalled the initially entered size) increased to 12.62% (158 out of 1252, excluding 486 additional users) and the number of reliant Italian users increased to 17.08% (103 out of 603, excluding 133 additional users). German users, however, remained at a rather low rate of 3.88% (17 out of 438, excluding 250 additional users) (see Fig. 4).

4.4 Summary and Interpretation

The analysis of UX metrics allowed us to understand country-specific usage patterns of French, German, and Italian users. Users from all three countries showed distinct adoption and dropout rates as well as, in particular, significant associations with the plug-in steps gender, brand, model, and recommendation. In addition, we identified significant differences in the overall task success rates. Furthermore, the country of origin is related to the temporal usage patterns along the plug-in steps, with Italian users being the slowest.

Finally, the analysis of the UX-focused metrics *Trust* and *Mastery* showed lower rates for French and German users compared to users from Italy. However, recurring users from France strongly increased their long-term trust rate (i.e., *Mastery*) due to the suggestion in the plug-in link's text label. The described UX metrics helped our project partner to efficiently focus on selected plug-in steps as the analysis highlighted country-specific relationships with a low effect size that are worth paying attention (Cramer's V between .10 and .20 and $\eta^2 = .01$) compared to country-specific relationships with a marginal effect size (Cramer's V between .00 and .10 and $\eta^2 < .01$) according to Rea & Parker [45] and Cohen [11]. The localization of all plug-in steps will increase development time and costs. Through the focus on selected and significant plug-in steps with at least low effect sizes, our project partner was able to allocate research and development resources more efficiently.

In order to identify localized interfaces for different countries, designers and researchers need to analyze suitable aspects in further in-depth studies. First, the interface of the website plug-in can be localized and evaluated recurringly for each country to minimize the dropout rate for the critical plug-in steps. One might, for example, prefer text-based icons for the selection of the gender. Second, with regards to the differing process times the plug-in design can be complemented with additional information in order to balance process times per step, dropout rate, and backward steps. Third, it is important to investigate the differences in the *Trust* and *Mastery* rate. German users, for example, might not want to receive suggestions within the link's text label but prefer to receive an individual recommendation each time. Thus, the overall plug-in and link design should be rearranged. Therefore, further qualitative in-depth investigations in the future will allow us to clarify our interpretations.

5   Conclusion, Limitation, and Future Work

In this paper, we demonstrated the applicability of web analytics metrics to analyze differences in the usage behavior and UX of an e-commerce website plug-in between French, German, and Italian users. We were able to identify significant relationships between the country of origin and the adoption rate as well as dropout rate of several plug-in steps. In addition, users from France, Germany, and Italy showed different temporal usage patterns as well as trust in the plug-in's recommendation. Although our work focused on the analysis of an e-commerce plug-in, further country-specific usage patterns have already been identified for Q&A websites such as Yahoo Answers (see [28]) as well as StackOverflow and Superuser (see [44]).

However, narrowing down the complex scope of UX to a selection of six customized website analytics metrics based on client-side user tracking can only be a first step. Overall, it will be necessary to further investigate and analyze the applicability of user tracking for UX measurement due to its quantitatively descriptive nature (see [24,32,41]. Inspired by traditional usability approaches (i.e., logging data) we see our work as a starting point to efficiently guide in-depth UX analyses, complementary to qualitative evaluations with a focus on attitudinal data. Additionally, client-based tracking might not holistically track all website visitors due to, e.g., blocked website cookies. It is, by nature, not possible to track how many website visitors block cookies. We, therefore, limited our analysis to recurring users of plug-in interactions and not website visits. Furthermore, the collaboration with our industry partner did not allow any modification of the original website. Consequently, it was not possible to add a registration process to track the user behavior across different devices.

Based on our research, future studies should add further metrics and qualitative in-depth analysis of country-specific usage patterns, test our findings through locally adapted user interface studies, and investigate the impact of server-based tracking on both the users' UX and the validity of web analytics metrics. Furthermore, the investigation of user-level data (i.e., the consolidated usage data of individual users) might allow conclusions about more detailed user behaviors. Ultimately, to set up a holistic UX-focused user tracking process, it is necessary to compare the effect of cross-country differences with and in contrast to further aspects, such as gender and device type.

We conclude that user tracking can be an efficient way to identify UX-related levers for culturally sensitive design adaptions of website plug-ins. At the same time, we agree with Vermeeren et al. [57] and Law et al. [33] that an exclusive focus on quantitative UX measurement (through, e.g., web analytics metrics) might ignore relevant insights of qualitative measurement approaches. Consequently a balance of various measurement tools and approaches should be promoted. In culturally sensitive development processes, the research and design team can implement UX-focused user tracking to identify suitable levers for country-specific design adaptions. Once significant differences in the usage behaviors for certain steps of a website plug-in have been identified, researchers and developers can, e.g., efficiently set-up subsequent A/B-tests and investigate the impact on the click behavior for different designs. This includes but is not limited to more or less information for such plug-insteps, different designs (colours, fonts, etc.) or simply a different user flow through the plug-in. Changes in the design can then be analyzed through further user tracking and supplemental qualitative evaluations.

In summary, our work was guided by the motivation to pursue a quantitative approach based on web analytics metrics to identify UX-related, country-specific usage behaviors of a website plug-in. We aim to foster an ongoing discussion about cross-cultural UX design as well as a suitable balance between qualitative and quantitative UX measurement - following up on the investigation of large-scale behavioral data. In particular, however, we want to emphasize that the challenging need of globally acting companies to analyze country-specific preferences and usage patterns requires cost-efficient and quickly adaptable UX

measurement tools. In this light, we perceive our work as a constructive starting point for further cross-cultural investigations based on large-scale behavioral
data.

References

1. Ahtinen, A., Ramiah, S., Blom, J., Isomursu, M.: Design of mobile wellness applications: identifying cross-cultural factors. In: Proceedings of the 20th Australasian
   Conference on Computer-Human Interaction (OZCHI), pp. 164–171. ACM Press
   (2008)
2. Al-Shamaileh, O., Sutcliffe, A.: Investigating a multi-faceted view of user experience. In: Proceedings of the 24th Australian Computer-Human Interaction Conference (OZCHI), pp. 9–18. ACM Press (2012)
3. Andreasen, M., Nielsen, H., Schrøder, S., Stage, J.: What happened to remote
   usability testing? An empirical study of three methods. In: Proceedings of the
   SIGCHI Conference on Human Factors in Computing Systems (CHI), pp. 1405–
   1414, ACM Press (2007)
4. Aykin, N.: Overview: where to start and what to consider. In: Aykin, N. (ed.)
   Usability and Internationalization of Information Technology, pp. 3–20. Lawrence
   Erlbaum Associates Inc., New Jersey (2005)
5. Barber, W., Badre, A.: Culturability: The Merging of Culture and Usability (1998).
   http://research.microsoft.com/en-us/um/people/marycz/hfweb98/barber/
6. Bargas-Avila, J., Hornbæk, K.: Old wine in new bottles or novel challenges? A
   critical analysis of empirical studies of user experience. In: Proceedings of the
   SIGCHI Conference on Human Factors in Computing Systems (CHI), pp. 2689–
   2698. ACM Press (2011)
7. Battarbee, K., Koskinen, I.: Co-experience: user experience as interaction. CoDe-
   sign 1(1), 5–18 (2005)
8. Beaton, J., Kumar, R.: Indian cultural effects on user research methodologies. In:
   Proceedings of the SIGCHI Conference on Human Factors in Computing Systems
   Extended Abstracts (CHI EA), pp. 4267–4271. ACM Press (2010)
9. Bjørneseth, F., Dunlop, M., Strand, J.: Dynamic positioning systems: usability
   and interaction styles. In: Proceedings of the 5th Nordic Conference on Human-
   Computer Interaction (NordiCHI), pp. 43–52. ACM Press (2008)
10. Chang, T.-H., Yeh, T., Miller, R.: GUI testing using computer vision. In: Proceed-
    ings of the SIGCHI Conference on Human Factors in Computing Systems (CHI),
    pp. 1535–1544. ACM Press (2010)
11. Cohen, J.: Statistical Power Analysis for the Behavioral Sciences. Academic Press,
    New York (1998)
12. Dunlop, M., Hamilton, I., Komninos, A., Nicol, E.: Shake 'N' Tap: a gesture
    enhanced keyboard for older adults. In: Proceedings of the 16th International Con-
    ference on Human-Computer Interaction with Mobile Devices & Services (Mobile-
    HCI), pp. 525–530. ACM Press (2014)
13. Dunlop, M., Mcgregor, B., Elliot, M.: Using smartphones in cities to crowdsource
    dangerous road sections and give effective in-car warnings. In: Proceedings of the
    SEACHI 2016 on Smart Cities for Better Living with HCI and UX (SEACHI), pp.
    14–18. ACM Press (2016)

14. Frandsen-Thorlacius, O., Hornbæk, K., Hertzum, M., Clemmensen, T.: Non-universal usability? A survey of how usability is understood by Chinese and Danish users. In: Proceedings of the SIGCHI Conference on Human Factors in Computing Systems (CHI), pp. 41–50. ACM Press (2009)

15. Gerea, C., Herskovic, V.: Measuring user experience in Latin America: an exploratory survey. In: Proceedings of the Latin American Conference on Human Computer Interaction (CLIHC). ACM Press (2015)

16. Gordon, M., Ouyang, T., Zhai, S.: WatchWriter. In: Proceedings of the SIGCHI Conference on Human Factors in Computing Systems (CHI), pp. 3817–3821. ACM Press (2016)

17. Gorman, T., Rose, E., Yaaqoubi, J., Bayor, A., Kolko, B.: Adapting usability testing for oral, rural users. In: Proceedings of the SIGCHI Conference on Human Factors in Computing Systems (CHI), pp. 1437–1440. ACM Press (2011)

18. Grubbs, F.: Procedures for detecting outlying observations in samples. Technometrics **11**(1), 1–21 (1974)

19. Hassenzahl, M., Tractinsky, N.: User experience - a research agenda. Behav. Inf. Technol. **25**(2), 91–97 (2006)

20. Hassenzahl, M.: User experience (UX): towards an experiential perspective on product quality. In: Proceedings of the 20th Conference on l'Interaction Homme-Machine (IHM), pp. 11–15. ACM Press (2008)

21. He, Y., Zhao, C., Hinds, P.: Understanding information sharing from a cross-cultural perspective. In: Proceedings of the SIGCHI Conference on Human Factors in Computing Systems Extended Abstracts (CHI EA), pp. 3823–3828. ACM Press (2010)

22. Hofstede, G., Hofstede, G.J., Minkov, M.: Cultures and Organizations. Software of the Mind. McGraw-Hill, New York (2010)

23. Hoßfeld, T., Keimel, C., Hirth, M., Gardlo, B., Habigt, J., Diepold, K., Tran-Gia, P.: Best practices for QoE crowdtesting: QoE assessment with crowdsourcing. IEEE Trans. Multimedia **16**(2), 541–588 (2014)

24. ISO DIS. 2009. 9241–210. Ergonomics of human system interaction-Part 210: Human-centred design for interactive systems. International Standardization Organization (ISO). Switzerland (2009)

25. Jewell, C., Salvetti, F.: Towards a combined method of web usability testing: an assessment of the complementary advantages of lab testing, pre-session assignments, and online usability services. In: Proceedings of the SIGCHI Conference on Human Factors in Computing Systems Extended Abstracts (CHI EA), pp. 1865–1870. ACM Press (2012)

26. Jordan, P.: Human factors for pleasure in product use. Appl. Ergon. **29**(1), 25–33 (1998)

27. Karapanos, E., Zimmerman, J., Forlizzi, J., Martens, J.: User experience over time: an initial framework. In: Proceedings of the SIGCHI Conference on Human Factors in Computing Systems (CHI), pp. 729–738. ACM Press (2009)

28. Kayes, I., Kourtellis, N., Quercia, D., Iamnitchi, A., Bonchi, F.: Cultures in community question answering. In: Proceedings of the 26th ACM Conference on Hypertext & Social Media, pp. 175–184. ACM Press (2015)

29. Komninos, A., Nicol, E., Dunlop, M.: Designed with older adults to SupportBetter error correction in SmartPhone text entry. In: Proceedings of the 17th International Conference on Human-Computer Interaction with Mobile Devices and Services Adjunct (MobileHCI), pp. 797–802. ACM Press (2015)

30. Lachner, F., Nägelein, P., Kowalski, R., Spann, M., Butz, A.: Quantified UX: towards a common organizational understanding of user experience. In: Proceedings of the 9th Nordic Conference on Human-Computer Interaction (NordiCHI). ACM Press (2016)

31. Lallemand, C., Gronier, G., Koenig, V.: User experience: a concept without consensus? Exploring practitioners' perspectives through an international survey. Comput. Human Behav. **43**, 35–48 (2015)

32. Law, E., Roto, V., Hassenzahl, M., Vermeeren, A., Kort, J.: Understanding, scoping and defining user experience. In: Proceedings of the SIGCHI Conference on Human Factors in Computing Systems (CHI), pp. 719–728. ACM Press (2009)

33. Law, E., Van Schaik, P., Roto, V.: Attitudes towards user experience (UX) measurement. Int. J. Hum Comput Stud. **72**(6), 526–541 (2014)

34. Lindley, S., Wallace, J.: Placing in age: transitioning to a new home in later life. Trans. Comput.-Hum. Interact. **22**(4), 1–40 (2015)

35. Lindley, S.: Making time. In: 18th ACM Conference on Computer Supported Cooperative Work & Social Computing (CSCW), pp. 1442–1452. ACM Press (2015)

36. Malinen, S., Nurkka, P.: The role of community in exercise: cross-cultural study of online exercise diary users. In: Proceedings of the 6th International Conference on Communities and Technologies (C&T), pp. 55–63. ACM Press (2013)

37. Marcus, A., Gould, E.: Crosscurrents: cultural dimensions and global web user-interface design. Interactions **7**(4), 32–46 (2000)

38. Mekler, E., Hornbæk, K.: Momentary pleasure or lasting meaning ? Distinguishing eudaimonic and hedonic user experiences. In: Proceedings of the SIGCHI Conference on Human Factors in Computing Systems (CHI), pp. 4509–4520. ACM Press (2016)

39. Nielsen, J.: Designing for international use (panel). In: Proceedings of the SIGCHI Conference on Human Factors in Computing Systems (CHI), pp. 291–294. ACM Press (1990)

40. Norman, D.: Emotional design. Ubiquity **45**(4), 1–1 (2004)

41. Obrist, M., Roto, V., Väänänen-Vainio-Mattila, K.: User experience evaluation - do you know which method to use?. In: Proceedings of the SIGCHI Conference on Human Factors in Computing Systems (CHI), pp. 2763–2766. ACM Press (2009)

42. Obrist, M., Wurhofer, D., Gärtner, M., Förster, F., Tscheligi, M.: Exploring children's 3DTV experience. In: Proceedings of the 10th European Conference on Interactive TV and Video (EuroiTV), pp. 125–134. ACM Press (2012)

43. Oliveira, N.: Culture-aware Q&A environments. In: Proceedings of DC CSCW Companion, pp. 101–104. ACM Press (2015)

44. Oliveira, N., Andrade, N., Reinecke, K.: Participation differences in Q&A sites across countries: opportunities for cultural adaptation. In: Proceedings of the 9th Nordic Conference on Human-Computer Interaction (NordiCHI). ACM Press (2016)

45. Rea, L.M., Parker, R.A.: Designing and Conducting Survey Research: A Comprehensive Guide. Wiley, Hoboken (2014)

46. Reinecke, K., Bernstein, A.: Improving performance, perceived usability, and aesthetics with culturally adaptive user interfaces. Trans. Comput.-Hum. Interact. **18**(2), 1–29 (2011)

47. Reinecke, K., Bernstein, A.: Predicting user interface preferences of culturally ambiguous users. In: Proceedings of the SIGCHI Conference on Human Factors in Computing Systems Extended Abstracts (CHI EA), pp. 3261–3266. ACM Press (2008)

48. Reinecke, K., Gajos, K.: Quantifying visual preferences around the world. In: Proceedings of the SIGCHI Conference on Human Factors in Computing Systems (CHI), pp. 11–20. ACM Press (2014)
49. Reyal, S., Zhai, S., Kristensson, P.: Performance and user experience of touchscreen and gesture keyboards in a lab setting and in the wild. In: Proceedings of the SIGCHI Conference on Human Factors in Computing Systems (CHI), pp. 679–688. ACM Press (2015)
50. Rodden, K., Hutchinson, H., Fu, X.: Measuring the user experience on a large scale: user-centered metrics for web applications. In: Proceedings of the SIGCHI Conference on Human Factors in Computing Systems (CHI), pp. 2395–2398. ACM Press (2010)
51. Rödel, C., Stadler, S., Meschtscherjakov, A., Tscheligi, M.: Towards autonomous cars: the effect of autonomy levels on acceptance and user experience. In: Proceedings of the 6th International Conference on Automotive User Interfaces and Interactive Vehicular Applications (AutomotiveUI), pp. 1–8. ACM Press (2014)
52. Roto, V., Law, E., Vermeeren, A., Hoonhout, J.: UX White Paper. Bringing clarity to the concept of user experience, Result from Dagstuhl Seminar on Demarcating User Experience (2011)
53. Sun, H.: Building a culturally-competent corporate web site: an exploratory study of cultural markers in multilingual web design. In: Proceedings of the 19th Annual International Conference On Computer Documentation (SIGDOC), pp. 95–102. ACM Press (2001)
54. Swallow, D., Blythe, M., Wright, P.: Grounding experience: relating theory and method to evaluate the user experience of smartphones. In: Proceedings of the 2005 Annual Conference on European Association of Cognitive Ergonomics (EACE), pp. 91–98. ACM Press (2005)
55. Tuch, A., Trusell, R., Hornbæk, K.: Analyzing users' narratives to understand experience with interactive products. In: Proceedings of the SIGCHI Conference on Human Factors in Computing Systems (CHI), pp. 2079–2088. ACM Press (2013)
56. Tullis, T., Albert, B.: Measuring the User Experience: Collecting, Analyzing, and Presenting Usability Metrics, 2nd edn. Morgan Kaufmann, Waltham (2013)
57. Vermeeren, A., Law, E., Roto, V., Obrist, M., Hoonhout, J., Väänänen-Vainio-Mattila, K.: User experience evaluation methods: current state and development needs. In: Proceedings of the 6th Nordic Conference on Human-Computer Interaction (NordiCHI), pp. 521–530. ACM Press (2010)
58. Walsh, T., Nurkka, P., Walsh, R.: Cultural differences in smartphone user experience evaluation. In: Proceedings of the 9th International Conference on Mobile and Ubiquitous Multimedia (MUM), pp. 1–9. ACM Press (2010)
59. Walsh, T., Nurkka, P.: Approaches to cross-cultural design: two case studies with UX web-surveys. In: Proceedings of the 24th Australian Computer-Human Interaction Conference (OZCHI), pp. 633–642. ACM Press (2012)
60. Walsh, T., Vainio, T.: Cross-Cultural Design for mHealth Applications. In: Proceedings of the 23rd Australian Computer-Human Interaction Conference (OZCHI). ACM Press (2011)
61. Yatani, K., Novati, M., Trusty, A., Truong, K.: Review spotlight: a user interface for summarizing user-generated reviews using adjective-noun word pairs. In: Proceedings of the SIGCHI Conference on Human Factors in Computing Systems (CHI), pp. 1541–1550. ACM Press (2011)

Multitouch Interaction

An Observational Study of Simultaneous and Sequential Interactions in Co-located Collaboration

Shuo Niu$^{(\boxtimes)}$, D. Scott McCrickard, and Steve Harrison

Computer Science Department, Virginia Tech, 2202 Kraft Drive,
Blacksburg, VA 24060, USA
{shuoniu,mccricks,srh}@vt.edu

Abstract. Large-scale multi-touch displays provide highly interactive spaces for small group activities. These devices feature the ability to detect concurrent touch inputs, which enable multiple co-located collaborators to manipulate virtual spaces in myriad ways. This paper explores two types of interaction, simultaneous and sequential, with regard to how people engage in shared virtual space during a collaborative ideation task. Our findings suggest that the two types of interactions present different patterns in both temporal and spatial dimensions. Sequential interaction is the major interaction technique, while the simultaneous interaction is actively used for information exploration and manipulating objects in personal space. Observation of semantic actions suggests that some behaviors are preferably performed in turns, while others are used more in simultaneous manner. The relationship between the two interaction types with regard to different collaboration factors is explored. We share lessons learned from the study and suggest design implications for multi-user touch interfaces.

Keywords: Simultaneous · Sequential · Turn-taking · Multi-user touch display · Collaboration · Coupling · Interaction stage · Territoriality · Semantic action

1 Introduction

Large-scale multi-touch displays are widely used in real-world practices to support various collaborative works [15, 16, 27, 36]. These displays detect concurrent multi-user touch inputs on a large space for information exploration and organization. They are targeted for workplaces that involve design and analysis activities [13, 17, 21, 26, 41]. In these contexts, the multi-user touch displays serve as platforms to facilitate creative activities, such as information exploration, idea generation and exchange, and decision-making.

Prior studies on contextual use of multi-user touch displays provide an understanding of interaction and collaboration styles. Two categories of interaction—simultaneous and sequential—are differentiated during collaborative use of virtual spaces [18, 20, 24, 27, 31, 34]. In *simultaneous interaction*, more than one person touches the display simultaneously to manipulate digital objects—for tasks that can be done in

© IFIP International Federation for Information Processing 2017
Published by Springer International Publishing AG 2017. All Rights Reserved
R. Bernhaupt et al. (Eds.): INTERACT 2017, Part III, LNCS 10515, pp. 163–183, 2017.
DOI: 10.1007/978-3-319-67687-6_12

parallel [27], or for collaborative tasks that require multiple users to complete [24]. In contrast, *sequential interactions* are guided by social protocols in which people negotiate and take turns using the device [28].

Clearly, simultaneous and sequential interactions afford certain tradeoffs. Simultaneous interactions support the distribution of tasks among people, opening possibilities to finish the task more quickly. But this task distribution may weaken awareness of others' actions. Sequential interaction can enhance awareness and build a sense of group cohesion by encouraging collaborators to observe and participate in actions, though it is unclear whether this sequentiality is the best use of time device interaction capability. Investigating factors that influence people's decisions to work simultaneously or sequentially—and roles and impacts of technology in encouraging their behaviors—will broaden our collective knowledge about ways in which technology can support collaborative efforts.

To better understand simultaneous and sequential interaction in creative collaboration with multi-user touch tabletops, we conducted an observational study of pairs and triads completing an ideation task on a 55" tabletop touch display. Ten design sessions are observed to investigate the patterns of the collaborative interaction. Four collaboration factors gleaned from prior research are investigated as factors in collaborative idea synthesis: *coupling style, interaction stage, territoriality,* and *semantic actions*. The four factors reflect workspace awareness knowledge [10] identified by Gutwin et al. and provide a platform for understanding how designers engage in collaborative tasks. Our research seeks to learn how users collaborate to foster future design of software and technology leveraging large multi-touch displays. The contributions of this work can be summarized as follows:

- Present four collaborative factors that influence simultaneous and sequential use of tabletop displays.
- Explain when and how interaction style influences collaborative factors.
- Identify how knowledge of simultaneous and sequential styles drawn from each collaborative factor provide recommendations for system design.

2 Related Work

The number of detected touch points technologically limited early studies on co-located collaboration with digital display tools. Single-touch devices based on fingertip or stylus input best support turn taking, not simultaneous collaboration [2, 35]. Thus, research on collaboration with these devices focused on social protocols for turn taking [32]. Advances in touch and gesture recognition technologies enable support for simultaneous interaction, raising questions about when and how to use it.

Both simultaneous and sequential interactions with large-scale multi-touch have been explored previously. The simultaneous and sequential nature of interaction techniques can be used to improve collaboration. For example, studies show that the walk-up-and-use nature of a public multi-touch display consists of both simultaneous and sequential interaction [15, 22, 27]. Information analysis and search tools on multi-user displays facilitate collaborative sense-making by supporting simultaneous and sequential use of the digital materials [18, 25]. Map and animation planning enforce simultaneous operations with gestures that have to be performed together to enhance group awareness [7, 24]. Interaction techniques such as virtual hands or arms are studied in terms of influences to the simultaneous and sequential interactions [4].

We introduced four factors in the introduction that have been used in prior work to observe and explain collaboration phenomena. Gutwin et al. explored workspace awareness and suggested five questions, with *who, where, what, when* and *how* as basic elements for workspace information [10] to guide identification of factors in a study. The four factors cover social, time, space and interaction aspects of co-located collaboration, giving a comprehensive examination of simultaneous and sequential interaction on tabletop displays (Table 1). *Coupling styles* capture how collaborators engage in mixed-focus collaboration, when people switch between individual and shared works [38]. It reflects the degree people are aware of others' presence and identity, as a part of the *who* question. Modes of *loose-* and *close-coupled* collaborations reflect social aspects of collaboration [10, 20, 21, 35, 42]. Understanding coupling styles is useful for understanding co-located groupware. *Interaction stages* describe temporal change in collaborative behaviors toward finishing an ideation task. Tabletop systems provide flexible ways for transitions between activities [35]. Collaborative design as a reflective and evolving process is generally described in terms of multiple steps or stages [33, 39]. In each, the nature of different activities influence *when* people collaborate with others and interact with digital artifacts [29, 33, 39]. *Territoriality* spatially probes how collaborators divide shared interaction space to organize ideas [11]. In *personal space*, individual ideas are engendered, while *shared space* is for idea exchange and integration [34]. Control and availability of digital objects in territories influences the arrangement of users and how individuals engage in personal and shared tasks [34, 35]. As an example of location and reaching issues, territoriality reflects information from *where* question. *Semantic actions*, concerning *what* actions are performed on *what* artifacts, bridge user cognition and interactive materials. Studies on interaction patterns with social meanings have evolved a gestural vocabulary with which users communicate with design objects [5, 30, 31]. These actions serve two purposes. Some gestures resemble interactions with physical objects and assist users in indicating relationships or similarities [8, 26]. Other gestures have social meanings; e.g., two corner-shaped hands which block other's view can convey privacy [44], and co-dependent gestures enhance awareness of joint actions [24]. Semantic actions influence interaction with shared materials and further coordinate simultaneous and turn-taking activities [35].

Technological advances, and accompanying tools, raise questions of when, where, and how simultaneous and sequential interaction are used effectively in collaboration. To further the knowledge on the collaborative interaction with multi-user touch display, this paper examines simultaneous and sequential interaction in a common goal-driven, free-form interaction ideation scenario using digital cards on a multi-user touch display. Multi-user multi-touch displays are increasingly used in design-related collaboration [9, 14, 21, 41]. Design tasks require participants to cooperate with each other in using digital materials, toward managing task progress and making decisions. Ideation tasks, seen in collaborative use of tabletop displays, involve activities like information gathering and decision-making [6, 7, 40].

3 Simultaneous and Sequential Interaction

Simultaneous and sequential interactions play different roles in the collaborative interaction with multi-user touch displays. Simultaneous input techniques support collaboration by giving each person equal opportunity for information access, and, accordingly, enhancing equality of participation across the group [16] and increasing cooperation [24]. In addition, when the interaction task consists of distributable work, simultaneous interactions allow collaborators to work on different parts of the task in parallel. However, simultaneous interaction may also result in interaction errors. Sequential input coordinated by social protocols is another collaboration approach with multi-user displays. Benefits lie in avoiding conflicts from simultaneous interaction [15], and sequential interaction also can enhance group awareness by leaving users sufficient time to observe each other's' activities [16]. But requirements of sequential use by a system or method might reduce efficiency by cutting down on opportunities for parallel activities [22, 27]. To provide a better understanding of the two interaction styles with the multi-user touch display, we focus on an ideation task to probe the patterns of collaborative activities in the four examined factors.

4 Collaboration Factors

We investigate two interaction styles through four collaboration factors in tabletop workspace. This section details the identification of these factors and discuss the sub-categories in each category (Table 1).

Table 1. Collaboration factors observed in this study

WA Info	Collaboration factors	Observed categories
Who (social)	Coupling style	Loosely-coupled, close-coupled
When (time)	Interaction stage	Browsing, organization, specification
Where (space)	Territoriality	Personal territory, group territory
What (interaction)	Semantic actions	Emphasizing, sorting, grouping, linking, deleting

4.1 Coupling Style

A group's collaborative coupling style describes the social manner in which individual collaborator participates the work. In collaborating through a multi-user display, some tasks benefit from joint attention and/or the joint action to complete, while other tasks can be done in parallel. Focused attention involves more verbal communications, usually centered on one or more digital objects. With distributed attention, communication is more occasional, and manipulations by different collaborators are not necessarily related. The group transits between focused and distributed attention, influencing manner of interaction with the display. We examine two types of coupling styles, *loosely-* and *close-coupled* collaboration [11, 18, 20, 38]. Communication and attention are the main indicators to distinguish coupling style. In close-coupled collaboration, the group has active discussions that focus on the same digital objects. In loosely-coupled collaboration, each group member focuses on objects in parallel without significant communication. Observing sequential and simultaneous interaction within each style will help understand how attention and conversation factors influence collaborative interaction.

4.2 Interaction Stage

This paper leverages three temporal stages of interaction which outline the design process, drawing primarily from the PIC-UP card set and the design tool [43], but prevalent across much of the design activities. We use *browsing, organization,* and *specification* as three interaction stages to observe the temporal changes of simultaneous and sequential interaction.

Browsing Stage is the initial step in using the interface to understand content in working space. When browsing, the group may not have a clear idea about the tool or task. Browsing gives users a perspective that helps to explore ways to use the system and understand the information provided by digital objects. Interactions when browsing are tentative and less coordinated, since attention and action of different users generally focus on their own interests. Parallel work helps users learn information and quickly identify ideas.

Organization Stage is associated with the arrangement of design materials toward deeper assessment of ideas from the browsing stage. The evolution of ideas from browsing to organization lie in relationships identified among digital elements. The group exchanges ideas and tries different combinations of the elements, to collaboratively make decisions on which elements to use. The shared display at this stage serves as a space to exchange the idea, so the interactions usually incorporate sharing or evaluating digital objects. These types of activities usually attract group attention, and the joint attention influences the manner of collaborative interaction.

Specification Stage involves refinements of the structure of the digital objects that comprise the design. As ideas are focused, details of digital elements and relationships among them are made more definite and clear. Activities in this stage include arranging elements and specifying relationships and interactions. Compared to organization, the arranging of the digital elements within this stage are no longer an attempt to find possibilities; they represent more certain and finalized modifications. As such, most interactions at this stage happen to nearly finished design through sequential access that help collaborators avoid mutual interference.

4.3 Territoriality

It has been widely observed that collaborators create *personal territories* and *group territories* in interacting with multi-user displays [4, 34, 41]. Personal territory is an area where an individual participant obtains digital resources and explores design alternatives. This area leaves collaborators a private space to clarify personal ideas before introducing them to the group. Group territory is a shared space to assemble ideas from each individual that serves as a space in which the group exchanges ideas and resources. The segmentation of the interaction space influences the manner of interaction. To further explore how territory influences the simultaneous and sequential interactions, we observe the two modes of collaboration within two types of territory. Personal territory interactions include activities within personal space, namely interactions to organize individual idea, or move interesting cards into the personal space. Group territory interactions consist of activities that happen in the group space, which are the modifications made to the ongoing design.

4.4 Semantic Actions

From creating a diagram to organizing data files with a multi-user touch display, collaborators need to annotate, sort, group, link and delete digital objects to make sense of the materials [8, 15, 16, 26]. This paper examines 5 semantic actions with the multi-user display—emphasizing, sorting, grouping, linking and deleting—gleaned from prior studies with interactive information synthesization that cover most design-specified actions [23, 26, 30]. When a user observes the object set and the elements are especially inspiring, the user may *emphasize* that object and share it with teammates with actions that include moving the object, pointing at it, and elaborating on an idea. After the user collects ideas, it is necessary to *sort* the digital objects and select suitable ones, perhaps by *grouping* similar or relevant information. By clustering digital objects, an idea group is used as an integrated entity to further connect to other materials. For key connections, collaborators *link* the feature pair by drawing lines between digital objects, or by positioning them closely. During organization of elements, if digital objects appear to be less important or relevant, users *delete* these elements through gestures such as moving them to the corner of the display.

5 Observational Study

This section describes our observational study of simultaneous interaction and sequential interaction in a small group design activity. Leveraging a card design system implemented on a multi-user tabletop display, 10 small groups of 2 or 3 collaborators created designs with digital materials. We chose a design task because it reflects the need to experience different coupling styles, to shift between creative design stages, to manage space utility, and to perform gestural actions, thereby fulfilling the goals of our observation.

The observational experiment was conducted with 19 undergraduate students between 18 and 30 years of age. To ensure the participants have basic design knowledge, participation was only open to students from two upper-level design-related classes: Human Computer Interaction (N = 16) and Information Design (N = 3). Students from the design classes are familiar with the nature of the task, which helps curtail the learning process and avoids confusion on task requirements. Participants worked in a team of 2 or 3 people, and they could take part in the study either once or twice. To help ensure diversity of ideas in the design process, no two participants could collaborate in a group more than once.

5.1 Multi-touch Supported Design Tool

The card-based multi-touch supported design tool used in this study is a design application [12] running on the Microsoft Perceptive Pixel (see Fig. 1). The Microsoft Perceptive Pixel is a 55-inch multi-touch display enabling simultaneous finger operations of different users like touching, pinching and dragging. The design application running on it consists of a blank working area in the center and design cards along each side (Fig. 3). Each design card can be moved, rotated and resized by different designers simultaneously with the fingertips. A toolbox, located on each side of the table, provides a drawing tools and a commenting tool. Using a pencil tool, users can draw lines of different colors and thicknesses with the finger. An eraser tool and an undo tool are provided for correction. A commenting tool creates a textbox and a virtual keyboard for editing the typed comments. Each textbox can also be moved, rotated and resized.

Fig. 1. Using the collaborative design tool on a Microsoft Perceptive Pixel system.

5.2 Collaborative Task and Digital Card Creation

The design task is to design a novel technology solution to help 5–7 year old children manage their emotions, such as anger and anxiety. The digital cards used in this study are created based on three workplace factors—social context, activities and artifacts—as described in the design requirements. Accordingly, we designed three types of cards corresponding to each of the dimensions: problem cards, activity cards and technology cards (Fig. 2). The 30 problem cards include emotional problems summarized from the Preschool Anxiety Scale (PAS) [37]. The problem cards aim to provide hints on the context of the design and help the designers understand the emotional problems of the children. 31 activity cards show common activities like reading, walking and listening to music with which the children can alleviate negative emotions. The technology cards have 37 popular digital devices like tablet, smartphone, and Google Glass.

Fig. 2. Examples of the three types of design cards. From left: problem card, activity card, technology card.

5.3 Process

19 participants formed 5 groups of 3 members and 5 groups of 2 members. Each group used the design system to complete the design task. First, the design task was described to the group. The method to manipulate the design card and draw the lines was demonstrated to the participants. Each participant then tried the system. After the participants became familiar with the tool, the group was informed that the design outcome should be presented in a form of design poster, and an example poster was shown and explained. An overhead camera looking the tabletop display (Fig. 3) recorded video of the entire design process. After finishing the design poster, each participant completed a 6-item questionnaire probing aspects of the experiment: using the interface, exploring the digital cards, organizing ideas, completing the design, collaborating with teammates, and general feedback. The questions include an open-ended writing portion to let participants leave their comments on each aspect.

During recruitment, we allowed participants to take part multiple times in the study. 6 students participated the study twice and the rest participated once. Repeated participation sought to explore whether participating multiple times would lead to

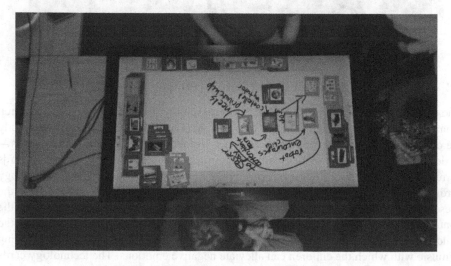

Fig. 3. Video screenshot of the investigation.

dominance and other changes in coupling styles, but the data and questionnaire shows that participants engage similarly each time, suggesting social conventions still guide the manner of collaboration [1].

5.4 Coding Method

To examine the relationships between the four collaboration factors and the simultaneous and sequential interaction, we first coded the video. Simultaneous and sequential interactions are determined by whether the participants touch the display at the same time. If two or more participants touch the display at the same time, that interaction period is tagged as simultaneous, otherwise as sequential.

The video clip was first divided into 3 parts according to 3 interaction stages. In the browsing stage of card-based groupware, the main task is observing the card set and discussing ideas over single or a small subset of the cards. We define the browsing stage as the period during which the most of, if not all, cards are browsed, ideas are brainstormed and useful or relevant design cards are selected. We use the time after which no cards being observed for the first time as the end of the browsing stage. The organization stage is a process of evaluating the initial ideas, make selection, and arrange the desired cards. A reversed observation method is applied to dissect this stage: the design result is referenced first, and second is the time when the final design plan is used, thus separating the organization stage and the specification stage.

We then used an event-based method to code the other 3 factors. Two research investigators reviewed the entire video separately. If the status of any factor changed, the investigator recorded the time stamp and the statuses of coupling style, territoriality and semantic actions according to the definition described above. For the coupling styles, if the participants communicate with each other (or keep silent) more than a short while (2–3 s), we consider them to be switched to close-coupled style (or loosely-coupled style, respectively). For territoriality, if a card is being or has been shown to all participants, and no user moves it back to his side, we consider this card to be in group territory. Interactions with shared cards are categorized as group territory activities. Otherwise the card is considered as personal card and interaction with it is categorized as personal territory activity. As mentioned previously, four semantic actions are coded based on the purpose of the interaction.

Emphasizing actions include pointing, scaling, or mentioning a single card to explain an idea. *Sorting* actions compare and select among cards and pick useful ones. *Grouping* actions move several cards together to form a card cluster. *Linking* actions align two cards together or draw lines between cards to show relationships. *Deleting* include actions which move the cards from the center to the corner.

Comments from the post-experiment questionnaire were analyzed with affinity diagramming. Comments were extracted from the questionnaire and placed on note card (181 cards in total), with one focused point on each card. 3 researchers, all with affinity diagramming experience, sorted the cards as a group, clustering and labeling related sets of cards as they emerged. The clusters of feedback are discussed in relation to the core themes of this paper.

6 Results

All groups successfully finished the design tasks and created a design poster, taking between 17 and 55 min. Average time taken was 33.12 min (SD = 11.26). Collectively, design groups showed good understanding of the content on the digital cards, with only two groups inquiring about two of the technology cards during the design period (about the MYO armband and the FuelBand). There were no major usability issues that interrupted the collaborations. Though several participants perform the task twice, they still followed similar progresses in the ideation task, suggesting that the influence did not significantly impact the results.

Overall, participants far more frequently interacted with the display sequentially than simultaneously. 10 groups spent an average of 1474.10 s (SD = 564.53) on sequential interaction and 513.10 s (SD = 214.84) on simultaneous interaction. The results revealed that the time on sequential interaction is longer than on simultaneous interaction.

Despite knowing that they can interact with the device simultaneously, the tabletop is used more in a turn-taking manner [31]. A typical design procedure is that the participant teams spent some time placing the cards around the table for better visibility, and spent the majority of the time discussing the cards, selecting useful elements, and taking turns organizing the cards. Results of each category are presented in Fig. 4.

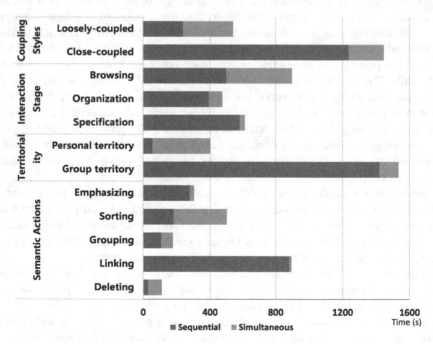

Fig. 4. Time of sequential and simultaneous interaction for four observed factors.

6.1 Interaction Modes with Coupling Styles

On average, the participant groups spent 24.08 min (SD = 12.67) designing closely together and 9.04 min (SD = 6.92) working independently. When focusing on the same set of digital objects (close-coupled), groups spent 1237.2 s (SD = 647.02) turn-taking with the table. The average time for simultaneous touch during close-coupled collaboration is 207.60 s (SD = 144.86), smaller than sequential. When groups focus on different objects and work in parallel (loosely-coupled), average times are 236.90 s (SD = 270.02) for sequential and 305.50 s (SD = 196.59) for simultaneous interaction.

In closed-coupled collaboration, collaborators often have tense communication and pay attention to the same design issue. These conversations are usually about suggesting and selecting ideas with the cards. Therefore it benefits participants to keep aware of each other's thoughts and behaviors to reach common ground. Compared to simultaneous interaction, sequential interaction results in more time to observe others' activity and evaluate ideas. Since simultaneous interaction with shared materials also might bring interference to conversation and action, participants generally apply sequential interaction to avoid potential conflicts. In loosely-coupled collaboration, participants deliberate and modify different parts of the design. Less mutual influence reduces the chance of conflict; therefore participants can use the card at the same time. We noticed that in loosely-coupled collaboration the sequential interaction time has similar range with the simultaneous interaction. From our observation, participants sometimes look at and think about different cards in parallel without actively moving the cards. The sequentially in this case is due to coincidental touch.

Results of the post-experiment questionnaire also imply that participants appreciate being able to access the table simultaneously, but still desire a close partnership found in sequential turn-taking. Regarding simultaneous access of the table, a participant in Group 6 (G6) noted *"I thought that the interface had a lot of options and free space which made me feel like I could do whatever I wanted."* A participant in G9 wrote *"I like how we were all able to stand up around the table and interact simultaneously on a single platform rather than individual screens."* The openness and equality of using the design table benefits the collaboration, since simultaneous use of the cards gives the participants room to think and work individually, while not blocking the channel for communication.

We also note a common concern on how cards scaffold idea exchange. For example, a participant of G1 commented on the system *"hard for some people to see cards of the people sitting opposite to them."* A G4 participant mentioned *"sharing cards with other group members is sometimes tedious due to having to rotate and re-rotate cards."* These concerns reflect that participants wish to know what others are doing and when they are willing to share ideas. These activities mirror the turn-taking observed in card processing. Though there could be a better method to share cards, the close-coupled collaboration helps the team share ideas and maintain mutual understanding of the task.

6.2   Interaction Modes in Three Stages

The average time span of the browsing, organization and specification design stages are 897.60 (SD = 390.58), 476.00 (SD = 286.71) and 613.60 (SD = 373.13) s. In the browsing stage, the times for sequential and simultaneous interaction have relatively close mean values of 499.30 s (SD = 297.95) and 398.30 s (SD = 145.37). However, in the organization stage, the average times for sequential and simultaneous interaction are 392.70 s (SD = 279.98) and 83.30 s (SD = 86.29), with the former higher than the latter. Moreover, in the specification stage, sequential interaction time (m = 582.10 s, SD = 351.41) is longer than simultaneous interaction time (m = 31.50 s, SD = 47.07).

The simultaneous interaction mostly happens at the browsing stage. This finding furthers the observation in [31] that simultaneous interactions were conducted merely at the beginning of the task. The exploration of the digital materials is the preparing phase through which collaborators become familiar with the design materials and collect initial ideas. Participants need time to browse the cards in parallel to clarify individual ideas, which leads to the simultaneous use of the cards. But when interesting ideas are identified, participants need time to briefly communicate and evaluate the idea; therefore sequential interaction also happens for similar time. In the organization stage, participants take turns proposing and evaluating ideas. The participant who suggests an idea usually takes control of the cards, and passes control of the cards to the next solver when finished. The specification stage has a clearer common goal in design. The changes and decisions made to the cards are important and definite. Therefore the simultaneous interaction in this stage is even less—collaborators need to pay attention when an idea is finalized; unexpected moves will distract the team and interfere with decision-making.

In completing the design task, interactions with cards reflect participants' thoughts on design. A participant (G5) commented on the browsing stage *"I felt cards on the table helped throw out a bunch of ideas, and the layout/tools along with the cards helped create an environment to nurture creativity and outside the box thinking."* Another participant (G6) noted during idea organization *"I was inspired to think of new ideas, by seeing all of the possible problems and technology that could detect such problem at once. It allowed me to quickly decide on a path to take."* But the number of the cards sometimes highlights problems with idea organization, since *"with all the cards however, sometimes the screen was a little bit chaotic and we would lose track of some of the cards"* (G10). Seeing and using the cards is a process of clarifying ideas [33, 39]. The phases of idea generation, synthesization, and specification reflect how participants use the design elements. Collecting possible ideas tends to be done in parallel, so cards are touched simultaneously in the browsing stage. Organizing and specifying relationships between ideas need joint attention, so card manipulations happen more in a turn-taking manner.

6.3   Interaction Modes in Different Territories

For the interaction in different territories, the average time participants spent in personal territory and group territory are 1584.60 (SD = 521.38) and 402.6 (SD = 197.89) s. The average time for sequential interaction and simultaneous interaction are 1417.90

(SD = 514.39) and 116.70 (SD = 112.57) s in group territory, with the former longer than the latter. When focusing on digital objects in personal territory, the average time is 56.20 (SD = 72.29) s for sequential interaction and 346.40 (SD = 167.53) s for simultaneous interaction. The simultaneous interaction in personal territory is longer than sequential interaction.

In personal territory, participants have free access to the cards and usually interact with them without concern for other participants. The simultaneous interaction in personal territory reduces the time to finish the parallel. Being able to work independently on different cards helps designers generate rich and diverse ideas. Another case of simultaneous use in personal territory is removing the less useful cards. Considering the number of the cards, the affordance of removing the card simultaneously reduces the time to narrow down the design options. The cards in group territory are shared by all members. The co-ownership of the design materials makes individual participant tend to acquire other's attention or consent before making changes. When working simultaneously in the group territory without proper awareness of each other's action, errors might be caused due to the conflict of operations.

Regarding transitions between two territories, the dragging and dropping feature of the digital cards gives the participants an easy way to integrate ideas. *"Integrating and changing our ideas was very simple, as we just had to drag cards around"* (G6) and *"it is easy to add/remove ideas and integrate them to the poster by moving the cards ... we can have a better view of all the technologies we want to use, so that we won't miss/forget something during the process."* (G8) However, some other features hinder free use of personal space. Some participants noted that the tool's moving and drawing modes block simultaneous use of the table: *"However, when drawing or commenting, it put the whole table in that mode (drawing mode) and the other person had to just watch. It would be great if one person could comment or draw, and the other people could still do other activities"* (G10) and *"if the group started working with one tool, and idea requiring the previous tool may be put on hold."* (G8) Participants wish to have the personal space always available even when others occupy the shared space to help quickly record ideas.

6.4 Interaction Modes with Semantic Actions

Five semantic actions are observed with different frequency of use. Linking of cards takes the longest time (m = 894.1 s, SD = 363.81), and deleting is the least performed action (m = 110.6 s, SD = 133.51). The average time for emphasizing, sorting, grouping are 303.6 (SD = 257.72), 502.6 (SD = 298.88), 176.3 (SD = 122.8) s. The five actions also show differences in terms of two modes of interaction. The result indicates that emphasizing and linking are performed more in turn-taking mode than simultaneous mode. Grouping and deleting, which are the two least used actions, show no significant differences with interaction mode. For the sorting, we noticed that average time in simultaneous interaction seems higher than that in sequential interaction. This is perhaps due to that group 7 spent nearly 15 min taking turns to evaluate and sort every one of the 98 design cards.

Our observation shows that different semantic actions are conducted with different interaction modes. Emphasizing one card denotes the discovery of an interesting idea.

Linking a pair of cards suggests designers identify or confirm an important relationship. These two actions usually involve pivotal ideas or decisions that inspire the team and push forward the design. As such they ask for joint attention and consensus from other members in the group. The necessity of group awareness makes the emphasizing and linking actions being conducted in a sequential manner. Different from emphasizing and linking, card sorting means ranking several cards based on some user-defined criteria. From our observation, most group members pick their own interesting cards and make the rest of the design grounded on the selected cards. So the sorting process is generally conducted in parallel in which participants can locate cards of individual interest very quickly. We also note that group 7 discusses and evaluates every card to decide which cards to use. The sequential reading and discussing of the cards increases the time to sort the ideas. Grouping and deleting are used less than the former three actions and are conducted both simultaneously and sequentially. Grouping was used to complement an idea by adding one or more cards to an existed card cluster. On the contrary, deleting happens when cards added previously appear to be less useful or irrelevant as the design evolves. In our study, the simultaneous adding or removing of cards usually happens when the target card does not impact the current design very much, while the sequential interplay of these actions usually involves cards of certain importance.

One noteworthy technique to emphasize and sort digital cards is enlarging or shrinking card, because "the resizing ability makes it easy to assign important/priority for each card" (G9) and *"being able to resize them gave us the ability to make certain cards appear as more important than other, which may be a desired ability in designing."* (G7) The resizable digital cards offer a unique affordance in contrast to paper cards: different sizes represent different importance, and the better visibility makes key elements easy to capture. Also, we observed that when a participant zoom the card to take up more screen space, the intentional or unintentional intrusion draws the group's attention, triggering a shift from simultaneous exploration to a turn-taking conversation.

The simultaneous dragging and dropping expedite creating card groups to cluster similar elements. The participants agreed that "it was very easy to share the cards or create groupings by dragging" (G3) and *"it was incredibly easy to create groupings, by simply dragging cards to their desired group."* (G6) But when the card group grows large, *"it would be great if there was a way to select cards and make them into a group, whenever you wanted to move a group of cards that you had related, you had to do it one by one".* (G10) These comments suggest that the participants adopt the provided touch interaction intuitively, but still wish the system to support new semantic actions for manipulating a group of digital artifacts.

7 Discussion

To expand the understanding of simultaneous and sequential interaction with multi-user touch display in creative design, our observational study examined interaction within a goal-oriented design task. Our findings suggest that simultaneous and sequential interactions are influenced by design-related activities including the deliberation, exchange, and integration of the group ideas, which form the main body of the collaborative task. Build on many previous studies on the collaboration over shared multi-touch devices (e.g. [19, 20, 36, 41]), our observation further looks into when and how people interact sequentially and simultaneously, particularly from social, spatial, temporal and gestural perspectives. Building on the analysis in the previous section of simultaneous and sequential interaction within the four collaboration factors, this section puts forth observations based on the findings.

7.1 Supporting Collaboration Techniques

Sequential interaction is the dominant collaboration technique for creative design with multi-user touch display. Participants spent more time on sequential interaction with the display compared to the simultaneous. The digital collaborative space is used as a supporting tool to help explain and exchange ideas. However, the conversations during the design, which mostly happens in a turn-taking fashion, influence the physical interactions.

Prior studies focus on the form of coupling styles [20, 38] or technology support for both close-couple and loosely-coupled collaboration [4, 19, 41]. This study further explores how coupling styles affect simultaneous and sequential use of the device. When closely collaborate with each other and have tense conversation, the participants tend to use the multi-user display in a sequential mode to avoid interference. But when working in distributed attention, collaborators are more flexible suggests that though the multi-user touch-sensitive device provides the ability to handle concurrent user inputs, the interaction manner does not totally lie on the affordances in selecting interaction manner. This implies that the influence of the social and attentional factors to the physical interaction is considerable.

The participants in our study perceive the openness and freedom of the interaction space as useful to foster creativity. The equal and simultaneous access to the touch table motivates participation, thereafter encourage making contributions. Also, the participants are ready to show their findings and learn what others are doing. Though resulting in the sequential interactions with the table, the close-coupled collaboration enhances the mutual awareness to each other's activities, and therefore builds the common ground to the collaborative task.

7.2 Supporting Task Change in Interaction Stages

Prior research gave general descriptions of when the simultaneous and sequential interactions happen in different contexts [7, 16, 31]. Grounded in these findings, this study conducted a deeper investigation of the two interaction modes in three interaction stages. Upon our observation, we notice that more frequently the simultaneous interactions happen at the browsing stage. In the organization and specification stage when the idea is getting more and more certain, collaborators do not interact with the display at the same time. This suggests that the simultaneous browsing helps collaborators quickly acquire enough information through exploration, and generate many potentially interesting if yet unclear ideas. Sequential interaction helps collaborators pay attention to each other and maintain the same understanding towards the decided plan.

Implications from this finding include the design of the groupware on the multi-user touch display should supports simultaneous information exploration and sequential decision-making. The interactive objects should be available to all collaborators for exploratory manipulation and the spatial interferences between them should be avoided. As the design becomes clearer, mechanisms to coordinate the turn-taking idea exchange and decision-making should be considered to facilitate mutual awareness.

Our participants took the digital cards as a media to forage and make sense with the design information. Building on prior knowledge on sense-making process [29] and reflective practices with the design materials [33, 39], our study suggests that different constitution and different interaction modes of the digital materials influence the path of design throughout the three design stages. When collaborating through groupware, providing abundant while simultaneously accessible materials at the beginning will expand the idea inventory. In completing the design, methods such as highlighting important objects and taking turns will encourage collaborators to focus more on the key thoughts and not diverging with too many unrelated ideas.

7.3   Supporting Interactions in Territories

Prior work has explored how collaborators work in personal and shared territories, and how technology can help and hinder work activities. When working on shared tasks, participants seemed to avoid touching the display at the same time, while when working separately they interacted with digital objects simultaneously. This observation of territoriality suggests that sequential use of the objects dominate interactions within group territory and the simultaneous interaction dominates personal space.

These interaction patterns suggest that collaboration tools should support transition between personal and group work, including by reflecting recent changes to assist collaborators in observing, evaluating, and responding to modifications [3]. Technology should enable collaborators to distribute work in the space and finish simultaneously to increase efficiency of collaboration and encourage balanced participation.

Control and availability of shared objects are critical for collaborative systems [34, 45]. In the context of co-located collaboration technologies, operations that interfere with personal control (e.g., mode switching) can cause interaction issues. Our observations showed that users might switch mode during personal work, ignoring global effects on others. Yet participants need availability of personal space: it facilitates idea organization, and allows the participants to work on their own subtask when others are editing the shared space. In crafting or choosing a collaborative digital table and software, one should consider ways to ensure an always-on personal space for each collaborator; or when the personal space is not available there should be proper support for awareness.

7.4   Supporting Semantic Actions

Some actions are better performed simultaneously, while others may be only suitable in turns. In the observation of the semantic actions, we noticed that activities like emphasizing one card or linking a pair of cards are conducted in turns. Some actions such as sorting the cards are usually performed in parallel. Other actions include grouping and deleting can be sequential or simultaneous, based on the content and importance of the target card.

Regarding relative utility, it would be beneficial to take the interaction mode into consideration when designing the interaction technique for the multi-user touch display. For example, in the gesture based collaboration system, gestures for sorting personal objects might be preferred to be performed simultaneously, so the system should be able to handle the simultaneous gesturing during these actions. Gestures for emphasizing or connecting the digital objects should be designed in a more noticeable manner to ensure group awareness of personal thoughts [44].

The digital cards capture most affordances of the paper cards, such as moving, rotating and clustering, but the malleable and distributable feature further enhance the co-located collaboration by helping idea exchange and integration. In our observational study, the resizing and the drag-and-drop action are used to communicate interesting cards and integrate group ideas. In addition to the semantic interactions that designed for object manipulation [5, 8, 24, 36], our study suggests that leveraging the communicational meaning of the semantic actions can also increase the mutual awareness of individual ideas and therefore reduce the effort to integrate group opinions. Other semantic actions on digital objects, such as the batch operations, should also be considered to facilitate organization and simplification of the design ideas.

8 Conclusions and Future Directions

This paper presents an observational study and its findings focused on collaborative interaction with the multi-user touch display. The simultaneous interaction and sequential interaction during the design activity are examined with four collaboration factors: coupling style, interaction stage, territoriality, and semantic action. The results suggest that in the design activity, sequential use of the digital objects is the major interaction manner with the multi-user touch display. Other results point to the understanding of the simultaneous and sequential patterns in different interaction stages, among different territories and upon actions with different semantic meanings. Main conclusions are as follows:

- Despite providing technology and encouragement in support of simultaneous interaction, in this study sequential interaction was the dominant collaboration technique with the multi-user touch display.
- The rich and simultaneously manipulable digital materials facilitate idea generation, but the organization and synthesization of the ideas require less interruptive and distractive approach to collaborate over the shared materials.
- The personal and collaborative spaces have their own characteristics of simultaneous or sequential access – personal space is preferred to be always and simultaneously available, while the collaborative space should be sequentially controlled.

Some actions are better performed simultaneously for efficient collaboration, while others may be only suitable to be performed in turns to better communicate ideas.

Attaching the communicational meanings to the semantic gesturing enhances the mutual awareness and mutual understanding.

With the prevalence of large-scale multi-touch displays, increasingly more collaborative work has potential to be supported by technology-enhanced materials and approaches. With the lessons learned in this study, future work should address the following topics.

First, an understanding of how simultaneous or sequential interactions affect collaborative activity is not yet clear. Future study should probe the two modes of the interaction by examining how each mode increases use of the actions, reduces the interaction error, enhances the awareness of other's activity, and so forth. The interactions probed in this study comprise basic and common touch gestures like moving, rotating and scaling the digital cards. Ways that other domain- or context-specific gesturing should be performed (and supported by digital tools) either simultaneously or sequentially needs more investigation.

Further, since sequential and simultaneous interaction plays different roles in design activities, better interaction techniques should be investigated to support the negotiations and mutual awareness among interactions with the different collaboration manners. For example, implementing semantically obvious and conflict-free gestures on the multi-touch display can help collaborators quickly understand each other's ideas with minimal interference. A deeper examination on the communicational meaning of touch gestures and designing notification support for sharing information with gestures will contribute to better collaborative touch interactions in the design and sense-making activities.

Also, collaborative interface bearing the simultaneous use of personal space and the turn-taking access to the shared objects should be explored and assessed. Possible solutions include dividing the interaction space into private and collaborative sections and providing specific control techniques (such as special gesturing or on-screen widgets) to coordinate the access and availability of different working spaces. The design of such techniques will also reflect the nature of the collaborative tasks in different activity stages. Inspiring ideas at the beginning and focusing the group on core components towards task completion should guide the design of collaborative interfaces for multitouch tables.

References

1. Bortolaso, C., Oskamp, M., Phillips, W.G., Gutwin, C., Graham, T.C.N.: The effect of view techniques on collaboration and awareness in tabletop map-based tasks. In: BT - Proceedings of the Ninth ACM International Conference on Interactive Tabletops and Surfaces, ITS 2014, Dresden, Germany, 16–19 November 2014 (2014)
2. Brandl, P., Haller, M., Hurnaus, M., Lugmayr, V., Oberngruber, J., Oster, C., Schafleitner, C., Billinghurst, M.: An adaptable rear-projection screen using digital pens and hand gestures. In: 17th International Conference on Artificial Reality and Telexistence (ICAT 2007), pp. 49–54. IEEE (2007)
3. Chewar, C.M., McCrickard, D.S., Sutcliffe, A.G.: Unpacking critical parameters for interface design. In: Proceedings of the 2004 Conference on Designing Interactive Systems Processes, Practices, Methods, and Techniques - DIS 2004, p. 279. ACM, Cambridge (2004)

4. Doucette, A., Gutwin, C., Mandryk, R.L., Nacenta, M.A., Sharma, S.: Sometimes when we touch: how arm embodiments change reaching and collaboration on digital tables. In: Proceedings of the 2013 Conference on Computer Supported Cooperative Work (CSCW 2013), pp. 193–202. ACM, San Antonio (2013)
5. Endert, A., Fiaux, P., North, C.: Semantic interaction for visual text analytics. In: Proceedings of the 2012 ACM Annual Conference on Human Factors in Computing Systems - CHI 2012, pp. 473–482. ACM, Austin (2012)
6. Evans, A.C., Wobbrock, J.O., Davis, K.: Modeling collaboration patterns on an interactive tabletop in a classroom setting. In: Proceedings of the 19th ACM Conference on Computer-Supported Cooperative Work & Social Computing, pp. 860–871. ACM, San Francisco (2016)
7. Fan, M., Antle, A.N., Neustaedter, C., Wise, A.F.: Exploring how a co-dependent tangible tool design supports collaboration in a tabletop activity. In: Proceedings of the 18th International Conference on Supporting Group Work (GROUP 2014), pp. 81–90. ACM, Sanibel (2014)
8. Frisch, M., Heydekorn, J., Dachselt, R.: Investigating multi-touch and pen gestures for diagram editing on interactive surfaces. In: Proceedings of the ACM International Conference on Interactive Tabletops and Surfaces (ITS 2009), pp. 149–156. ACM, Banff (2009)
9. Geyer, F., Pfeil, U., Hochtl, A., Budzinski, J., Reiterer, H.: Designing reality-based interfaces for creative group work (2011)
10. Gutwin, C., Greenberg, S.: A descriptive framework of workspace awareness for real-time groupware. Comput. Support. Coop. Work. 11(3–4), 411–446 (2002). (CSCW 2002)
11. Gutwin, C., Greenberg, S.: Design for individuals, design for groups: tradeoffs between power and workspace awareness. In: Proceedings of the Conference on Computer-Supported Cooperative Work, pp. 207–216. ACM, Seattle (1998)
12. Halskov, K., Dalsgård, P.: Inspiration card workshops. In: Proceedings of the 6th Conference on Designing Interactive Systems, pp. 2–11. ACM, University Park, Pennsylvania (2006)
13. Harris, A., Rick, J., Bonnett, V., Yuill, N., Fleck, R., Marshall, P., Rogers, Y.: Around the table: are multiple-touch surfaces better than single-touch for children's collaborative interactions? In: Proceedings of the 9th International Conference on Computer Supported Collaborative Learning, ISLS, Rhodes, pp. 335–344 (2009)
14. Hartmann, B., Morris, M.R., Benko, H., Wilson, A.D.: Pictionaire: supporting collaborative design work by integrating physical and digital artifacts (2010)
15. Hinrichs, U., Carpendale, S.: Gestures in the wild: studying multi-touch gesture sequences on interactive tabletop exhibits. In: Proceedings of the SIGCHI Conference on Human Factors in Computing Systems (CHI 2011), pp. 3023–3032. ACM, Vancouver (2011)
16. Hornecker, E., Marshall, P., Dalton, N.S., Rogers, Y.: Collaboration and interference: awareness with mice or touch input. In: Proceedings of the 2008 ACM Conference on Computer Supported Cooperative Work, pp. 167–176. ACM, New York (2008)
17. Hunter, S., Maes, P.: WordPlay: a table-top interface for collaborative brainstorming and decision making. In: Proceedings of IEEE Tabletops and Interactive Surfaces, pp. 2–5. IEEE (2008)
18. Isenberg, P., Fisher, D., Paul, S.A., Morris, M.R., Inkpen, K., Czerwinski, M., Paul, S.A., Morris, M.R., Inkpen, K., Czerwinski, M.: An exploratory study of co-located collaborative visual analytics around a tabletop display. In: 2010 IEEE Symposium on Visual Analytics Science and Technology (VAST), pp. 179–186. IEEE, Salt Lake City (2010)
19. Isenberg, P., Tang, A., Carpendale, S.: An exploratory study of visual information analysis. In: Proceedings of the SIGCHI Conference on Human Factors in Computing Systems, pp. 1217–1226. ACM, Florence (2008)

20. Jakobsen, M.R., Hornbæk, K.: Up close and personal: collaborative work on a high-resolution multitouch wall display. ACM Trans. Comput. Interact. **21**(2), 1–34 (2014)
21. Klemmer, S.R., Newman, M.W., Farrell, R., Bilezikjian, M., Landay, J.A.: The designers' outpost: a tangible interface for collaborative web site design. In: Proceedings of 14th Annual ACM Symposium User Interface Software Technology (UIST 2001), vol. 3, no. 2, pp. 1–10 (2001)
22. Marshall, P., Morris, R., Rogers, Y., Kreitmayer, S., Davies, M.: Rethinking "multi-user": an in-the-wild study of how groups approach a walk-up-and-use tabletop interface. In: Proceedings of the SIGCHI Conference on Human Factors in Computing Systems (CHI 2011), pp. 3033–3042. ACM, Vancouver (2011)
23. McCrickard, D.S., Abel, T.D., Scarpa, A., Wang, Y., Niu, S.: Collaborative design for young children with autism: design tools and a user study. In: 2015 International Conference on Collaboration Technologies and Systems (CTS), pp. 175–182. IEEE (2015)
24. Morris, M.R., Huang, A., Paepcke, A., Winograd, T.: Cooperative gestures: multi-user gestural interactions for co-located groupware. In: Proceedings of the SIGCHI Conference on Human Factors in Computing Systems (CHI 2006), pp. 1201–1210. ACM, Montréal (2006)
25. Morris, M.R., Lombardo, J., Wigdor, D.: WeSearch: supporting collaborative search and sensemaking on a tabletop display. In: Proceedings of the 2010 ACM Conference on Computer Supported Cooperative Work (CSCW 2010), pp. 401–410. ACM, Savannah (2010)
26. North, C., Dwyer, T., Lee, B., Fisher, D., Isenberg, P., Robertson, G., Inkpen, K.: Understanding multi-touch manipulation for surface computing. In: Human-Computer Interaction (INTERACT 2009), pp. 236–249. Springer, Heidelberg (2009)
27. Peltonen, P., Kurvinen, E., Salovaara, A., Jacucci, G., Ilmonen, T., Evans, J., Oulasvirta, A., Saarikko, P.: It's Mine, Don't Touch!: interactions at a large multi-touch display in a city centre. In: Proceedings of the SIGCHI Conference on Human Factors in Computing Systems (CHI 2008), pp. 1285–1294. ACM, Florence (2008)
28. Piper, A.M., O'Brien, E., Morris, M.R., Winograd, T.: SIDES: a cooperative tabletop computer game for social skills development. In: Proceedings of the 2006 ACM Conference on Computer Supported Cooperative Work (CSCW 2006), pp. 1–10. ACM, Banff (2006)
29. Pirolli, P., Card, S.: The sensemaking process and leverage points for analyst technology as identified through cognitive task analysis. In: Proceedings of International Conference on Intelligence Analysis, pp. 2–4 (2005)
30. Robinson, A.C.: Collaborative synthesis of visual analytic results. In: IEEE Symposium on Visual Analytics Science and Technology (VAST 2008), pp. 67–74. IEEE, Columbus (2008)
31. Rogers, Y., Hazlewood, W., Blevis, E., Lim, Y.-K.: Finger talk: collaborative decision-making using talk and fingertip interaction around a tabletop display. In: CHI 2004 Extended Abstracts on Human Factors in Computing Systems (CHI EA 2004), pp. 1271–1274. ACM, Vienna (2004)
32. Russell, D.M., Drews, C., Sue, A.: Social aspects of using large public interactive displays for collaboration. In: Borriello, G., Holmquist, L. (eds.) Proceedings of the 4th International Conference on Ubiquitous Computing (UbiComp 2002), vol. 2498, pp. 229–236. Springer, Heidelberg (2002). doi:10.1007/3-540-45809-3_18
33. Schon, D.A.: The Reflective Practitioner - How Professionals Think in Action, vol. 5126, pp. 1–8 (1983). Review
34. Scott, S.D., Carpendale, M.S.T., Inkpen, K.M., Sheelagh, M., Carpendale, T., Inkpen, K.M.: Territoriality in collaborative tabletop workspaces. In: Proceedings of the 2004 ACM Conference on Computer Supported Cooperative Work (CSCW 2004), pp. 294–303. ACM, Chicago (2004)

35. Scott, S.D., Grant, K.D., Mandryk, R.L.: System guidelines for co-located, collaborative work on a tabletop display. In: Kuutti, K. et al. (eds.) Proceedings of the Eighth European Conference on Computer Supported Cooperative Work (ECSCW 2003), pp. 159–178. Springer, Heidelberg (2003). doi:10.1007/978-94-010-0068-0_9

36. Niu, S., McCrickard, D.S., Nguyen, S.M.: Learning with interactive tabletop displays. In: 2016 IEEE Frontiers in Education Conference (FIE), pp. 1–9. IEEE (2016)

37. Spence, S.H., Rapee, R., McDonald, C., Ingram, M.: The structure of anxiety symptoms among preschoolers. Behav. Res. Ther. **39**(11), 1293–1316 (2001)

38. Tang, A., Tory, M., Po, B., Neumann, P., Carpendale, S.: Collaborative coupling over tabletop displays. In: Proceedings of the SIGCHI Conference on Human Factors in Computing Systems (CHI 2006), pp. 1181–1190. ACM, Montréal (2006)

39. Tholander, J., Normark, M., Rossitto, C.: Understanding agency in interaction design materials. In: Proceedings of the 2012 ACM Annual Conference on Human Factors in Computing Systems - CHI 2012, p. 2499. ACM, Austin (2012)

40. Tominski, C., Gladisch, S., Kister, U., Dachselt, R., Schumann, H.: A survey on interactive lenses in visualization. In: Eurographics Conference Visualization (2014)

41. Tse, E., Greenberg, S., Shen, C., Forlines, C., Kodama, R.: Exploring true multi-user multimodal interaction over a digital table. In: Proceedings of the 7th ACM Conference on Designing Interactive Systems, pp. 109–118. ACM, Cape Town (2008)

42. Vogt, K., Bradel, L., Andrews, C., North, C., Endert, A., Hutchings, D.: Co-located collaborative sensemaking on a large high-resolution display with multiple input devices. In: Campos, P., Graham, N., Jorge, J., Nunes, N., Palanque, P., Winckler, M. (eds.) INTERACT 2011. LNCS, vol. 6947, pp. 589–604. Springer, Heidelberg (2011). doi:10.1007/978-3-642-23771-3_44

43. Wahid, S., Branham, S.M., Cairco, L., McCrickard, D.S., Harrison, S.: Picking up artifacts: storyboarding as a gateway to reuse. In: Gross, T., Gulliksen, J., Kotzé, P., Oestreicher, L., Palanque, P., Prates, R.O., Winckler, M. (eds.) INTERACT 2009. LNCS, vol. 5727, pp. 528–541. Springer, Heidelberg (2009). doi:10.1007/978-3-642-03658-3_57

44. Wu, M., Balakrishnan, R.: Multi-finger and whole hand gestural interaction techniques for multi-user tabletop displays. In: Proceedings of the 16th Annual ACM Symposium on User Interface Software and Technology (UIST 2003), pp. 193–202. ACM, Vancouver (2003)

45. Yuill, N., Rogers, Y.: Mechanisms for collaboration: a design and evaluation framework for multi-user interfaces. ACM Trans. Comput. Interact. **19**(1), 1:1–1:25 (2012)

Dynamic UI Adaptations for One-Handed Use of Large Mobile Touchscreen Devices

Daniel Buschek$^{(\boxtimes)}$, Maximilian Hackenschmied, and Florian Alt

LMU Munich, Munich, Germany
{daniel.buschek,florian.alt}@ifi.lmu.de, m.hackenschmied@googlemail.com

Abstract. We present and evaluate dynamic adaptations for mobile touch GUIs. They mitigate reachability problems that users face when operating large smartphones or "phablets" with a single hand. In particular, we enhance common touch GUI elements with three simple animated location and orientation changes (*Roll, Bend, Move*). Users can trigger them to move GUI elements within comfortable reach. A lab study ($N = 35$) with two devices (4.95 in, 5.9 in) shows that these adaptations improve reachability on the larger device. They also reduce device movements required to reach the targets. Participants perceived adapted UIs as faster, less exhausting and more comfortable to use than the baselines. Feedback and video analyses also indicate that participants retained a safer grip on the device through our adaptations. We conclude with design implications for (adaptive) touch GUIs on large devices.

Keywords: UI adaptation · Reachability · One-handed use · Thumb · Touch · Mobile device

1 Introduction

Mobile devices today come equipped with increasingly larger touchscreens. Large screens are attractive for displaying photos, videos and websites. They also promise to ease input: Following Fitts' Law [7], large GUI elements (e.g. buttons, text links) are easier targets than smaller ones.

However, supporting and using a device with the same hand limits touch interaction to the use of the thumb. Thus, interaction with large screens suffers from the thumb's limited reach, both with respect to reachable distance and comfortably bendable angles [1]. Certain screen regions and thus GUI elements cannot be reached comfortably or even not at all.

Several UI adaptations have been proposed to address these problems. A popular approach implemented on devices on the market today shrinks and/or moves the displayed content to cover only that part of the screen which is easy to reach (e.g. "Reachability" on the iPhone[1], Samsung's "One-handed operation"

---

[1] http://appleinsider.com/articles/14/09/09/how-apple-made-the-iphone-6-and-iphone-6-plus-one-handed-use.

© IFIP International Federation for Information Processing 2017
Published by Springer International Publishing AG 2017. All Rights Reserved
R. Bernhaupt et al. (Eds.): INTERACT 2017, Part III, LNCS 10515, pp. 184–201, 2017.
DOI: 10.1007/978-3-319-67687-6_13

feature[2]). Other concepts change layouts (e.g. for keyboards[3]) or introduce new widgets (e.g. radial menus[4]).

Unfortunately, resizing the displayed content and input areas mitigates the benefits of a larger screen. Special widgets allow to keep the full screen area, but they must be introduced to the user, overlay existing content, or are difficult to integrate well into existing layouts (e.g. radial menu vs common box-layout of apps and websites).

To address these challenges and improve one-handed use, we investigate dynamic adaptations of common GUI elements (Fig. 1). We contribute: (1) four dynamic UI adaptations for three common main elements in mobile touch GUIs, (2) evaluated in a user study with 35 participants in the lab, (3) resulting in insights into one-handed use and relevant design implications for large mobile touchscreen devices.

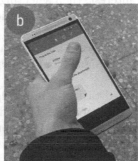

Fig. 1. In everyday life, (a) we often operate mobile devices with one hand. (b) On large devices, some screen regions cannot be reached comfortably. Here, the user struggles to touch the blue action bar at the top. (c) Rotating the bar to the left screen side renders it easily accessible. This may be triggered, for example, by "flicking", i.e. tilting the device to the left.

2   Related Work

The main problem with one-handed touch interaction on large devices is the limited range and flexibility of the human thumb [1]. Large screens may easily exceed the thumb's reachable area, yet one-handed use is often required in many every-day situations, for example when holding onto a rail or carrying other objects [15,23,24]. Users may cope by tilting the device to bring the far screen corner closer to the stretched thumb [5,22]. Besides the industry solutions

---

[2] http://www.androidcentral.com/how-set-your-galaxy-s5-better-one-handed-use.

[3] https://support.swiftkey.com/hc/en-us/articles/201457382-How-do-I-change-my-k eyboard-layout-with-SwiftKey-Keyboard-for-Android-.

[4] https://play.google.com/store/apps/details?id=jun.ace.piecontrol.

mentioned in the introduction, HCI research has proposed various approaches to improve one-handed mobile touch interaction:

TouchShield [12] allows users to bring up a new control widget with their thumb in the screen centre to facilitate a more stable grip. *ThumbSpace* [16, 19] introduced an easily reachable small proxy area to map touches to their corresponding location on the whole screen. Kim et al. [20] enabled users to (1) pan the screen content to move far targets towards the thumb, or to (2) summon a cursor that multiplies the thumb's movements to reach further. They used edge-swiping and "fat" touches to trigger these modes. In contrast, Chang et al. [5] triggered similar methods once the device's tilt indicated reaching for a distant target. While these methods can improve reachability and/or grip stability, many introduce indirect input [5,12,16,19,20], or require extra panning actions [5,20], which can slow down target selection.

Roudaut et al. [25] proposed a two-tap selection method – first triggering magnification of an area of interest, then selecting within the magnified display. They further proposed a magnetic target selection "stick" of sizeable length. Magnification might also move some targets within reach, and the "stick" can extend the thumb, but their goal was to improve target selection on *small* screens and thus the concepts were not designed and evaluated for improving reachability on large devices.

Other related work designed task-specific widgets for one-handed use, such as a radial contact list [13], an interface for video browsing [14], or an app-launcher [18]. While these designs can mitigate problems with reachability and precision, they are limited to their specific use-cases and thus in general not applicable across different tasks and applications.

Involving the fingers of the grasping hand on the back of the device [26–28] can also address reachability issues. However, this requires additional touch sensors on the back. Similarly, concepts envisioning a bendable device [8] cannot be realised with current off-the-shelf hardware.

Recent work has predicted front screen touches *before* the thumb hits the screen, based on grip changes during the reaching movement, registered with (1) back-of-device touch sensors [21] or with (2) device motion sensors [22]. While such methods could also be used to predict touch locations that users could actually never reach, it seems unlikely that users would even try to stretch towards obviously unreachable targets in order to enable such predictions in the first place.

Another line of research adapted underlying touch areas of on-screen keyboards to typing behaviour and hand posture without visual changes [4,9,11,29]. However, the main concern of these projects was typing precision, not reachability. In contrast, Cheng et al. [6] visually adapted keyboard shape and location to the user's grasp on a tablet, also to facilitate reachability. Similarly, we also follow the idea of adapting the location and shape of GUI elements to better suit the user's hand posture. Instead of keyboards for two-handed typing on tablets, we address main navigation elements and action buttons for one-handed use of large phones or "phablets".

In summary, related work (1) examined the thumb's limited reach [1], (2) motivated the support of one-handed use [15,23,24], and (3) proposed solutions which were either applied to the whole interface [5,16,19,20] or introduced new UI elements [5,13,14,18,20,25] and hardware [8,26–28]. In contrast, we investigate how one-handed use of mobile touch devices can be improved by adapting existing main GUI elements. In particular, we are interested in simple and easily understandable changes to UI layout, location and orientation.

3 Concept Development

Our design goal is to improve reachability of existing GUI elements – in contrast to related work that often invented new (task-specific) widgets. We decided to explore adaptations of the main elements of Google's Material Design[5] as an example of a popular modern design language for mobile touch GUIs. The following subsections describe our concept development process.

3.1 Brainstorming Session

We conducted a brainstorming session with colleagues and students from an HCI lab to generate ideas. No default GUI was given; rather, the task was to freely come up with ideas for adapting common mobile touch GUI elements to improve reachability in one-handed use. Clustering the ideas revealed design dimensions for adaptations: changing layouts globally (i.e. in GUI) and locally (i.e. within menu); changing alignment, orientation, shape, item arrangement; floating elements; and adding new elements.

3.2 Paper Prototyping

The generated ideas were captured as simple GUI sketches on paper, and shown to colleagues and students to gain early feedback. Ideas with moving elements were liked best overall. However, this step also revealed that, for further feedback, we needed to go beyond paper sketches.

3.3 App Prototyping

Hence, we moved from paper to phone. Integrating feedback from the discussions, we created click-through prototypes to be able to demonstrate the refined ideas on an actual device. We used the prototyping software *Sketch*[6] and *POP*[7]. We created 38 interactive mockup screens (like the ones in Fig. 2), showing the concepts embedded into a fake email client to give them meaningful application context.

---

[5] https://www.google.com/design/spec/material-design/, *last accessed 23rd Jan. 2017.*

[6] https://www.sketchapp.com/, *last accessed 22nd Jan. 2017.*

[7] https://popapp.in/, *last accessed 22nd Jan. 2017.*

3.4 Pre-study

We reduced the number of ideas to a feasible amount for a small study, based on another round of feedback from colleagues and guided by the previously identified design dimensions. We kept the six concepts shown in Fig. 2.

We employed them in a small user study to gather qualitative feedback on our ideas. We recruited four participants (three female, mean age 26, all right-handed). They were compensated with a €5 gift card for an online shop.

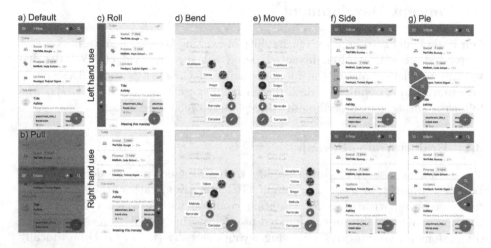

Fig. 2. Mockups showing (a) the unadapted UI, and the six adaptations evaluated in the pre-study: (b) *Pull:* users can pull down the action bar, it moves back up after using one of its buttons; (c) *Roll:* the action bar rotates around the screen corners into a vertical layout close to the holding hand; (d) *Bend:* the menu items bend to match the thumb's reachable angles; (e) *Move:* the button/menu is moved to the side of the holding hand; (f) *Side* and (g) *Pie:* redundant action bars can be swiped in from the screen edge. The top row shows the left-hand versions, the bottom row the ones for the right hand (exception: (b) *Pull* is pulled down for both hands). *Roll, Bend* and *Move* were selected for the final study.

Each participant tested all six concepts in random order. Participants were asked to fulfil simple tasks: opening an email, composing a new mail, deleting one. They were encouraged to think aloud during the tasks. After completing each task, they rated the current concept on a five-point Likert scale regarding eight items on aspects such as reachability, ease-of-use, understandability and distraction. In addition, they shared their thoughts verbally.

3.5 Selection of Concepts

The study revealed problems for: (a) *Pull* - pulling down the action bar merely reduces vertical distance to targets. Horizontally distant targets are still problematic. (b) *Side* - feedback revealed the importance of clear distinction between content and (adaptive) controls, which was problematic due to the transparency of *Side*. (c) *Pie* - Some participants were confused about redundant GUI elements. This was the case for both *Side* and *Pie*, which duplicate the action bar without hiding it. Hence, we decided against duplication. All other concepts received promising ratings and feedback and were thus selected for the main study: *Rolling Action Bar (Roll)*, *Moving Action Button/Menu (Move)*, and *Bending Action Menu (Bend)*

3.6 Final Concepts: Dynamic Adaptive UI

In summary, we propose four adaptations and an example trigger action.

Rolling Action Bar (Roll). An *Action Bar* is located at the top of most Android GUIs. It features buttons for navigation or main functionality in the current view. Triggering our adaptation rotates the bar around the screen corner (animated), changing it from its default location at the top to a left/right-aligned layout (see Fig. 2c). Triggering adaptation again moves it back to the default location at the top.

Moving Action Button/Menu (Move). The *Floating Action Button* is a single button "floating" on top of the view, often in the bottom right corner (see Fig. 2a). Our adaptation makes it movable: When triggering the adaptation, the button moves over to the left side of the screen (see Fig. 2e). This makes it easier to reach in left-hand use. Triggering the adaptation again moves it back to the right.

There is also a menu-version of this button, *Floating Action Menu*. Touching this menu button opens a floating menu (see Fig. 2e). As with the button, adaptation moves it to the other screen side, triggering again moves it back.

Bending Action Menu (Bend). Instead of moving the *Floating Action Menu*, this concept adapts the arrangement of its menu items. While the normal version displays menu items in a straight line, triggering our adaptation moves them into a curve to better fit the thumb's reachable area (see Fig. 2d). Repeated adaptation moves them back into a straight line.

Triggering Adaptations. Adaptations could be triggered explicitly or automatically. For our study, we implemented a simple explicit trigger: tilting the device in a short wrist turn (Fig. 3b). We decided not to use a touch gesture for the study to keep the trigger clearly distinguishable from the interactions, so that people could easily report feedback on adaptations and trigger separately. Tilting may also go well with the idea of movable elements – users can "flick" the UI elements to new locations. However, this trigger is an example, not part of our contribution.

4   User Study

To evaluate our adaptations, we conducted a repeated measures lab study. The independent variables were *device* (Nexus 5, HTC One Max), *hand* (left, right), and *concept* (four adaptive versions, plus the baseline versions of the three UI elements). We measured *completion time*, *device orientation*, and *reachability*, as well as user opinions on five-point Likert items.

4.1   Participants

We recruited 35 participants, mostly students, via a university mailing list and social media. 17 were female, 6 were left-handed. The average age was 24.7 years (range: 19–47). They received a €10 gift card for an online shop as compensation.

4.2   Apparatus

We used two devices to cover a range of interesting (i.e. "large") screen sizes, namely an LG Nexus 5 (4.95 in screen, $137.9 \times 69.2 \times 8.6$ mm), and an HTC One Max (5.9 in screen, $164.5 \times 82.5 \times 10.3$ mm). Our study app (Fig. 3c and d) showed the tested GUI elements. Menu elements had labelled buttons (e.g. "C1" to "C6", see Fig. 3c). The floating action menus/buttons were located near the bottom right screen corner (see Fig. 3d). A video camera captured the study, focusing on device and hands. Figure 4 shows a few selected scenes.

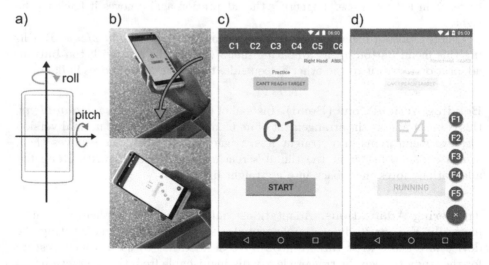

Fig. 3. This figure shows (a) roll and pitch measured relative to the device, (b) the trigger gesture, and example screens from the study app, (c) an *Action Bar* trial, and d) a running *Floating Action Menu* trial.

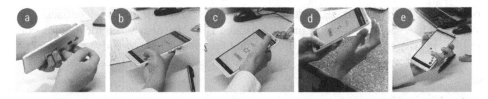

Fig. 4. Coping strategies: (a) tilting the device, (b) and (c) shifting the grip depending on the target location, (d) unstable grips, bringing the second hand close to "catch" the device if necessary, and (e) further strategies, such as using other fingers, reaching around the device.

4.3 Procedure

Each participant used both the left and right hand with both devices. For each device and hand, each participant completed seven tasks, namely using the four adaptations, plus the non-adaptive baseline versions of the three GUI elements. The order was varied using a Latin Square design. We explain the procedure by describing its three hierarchical components: tasks, trial sequences, and trials.

Tasks. Each task covered one GUI element and adaptation concept. We first explained the tested element and its adaptation, if available. A training trial sequence allowed participants to familiarise themselves with the task. They then completed six trial sequences.

Trial Sequences. Each trial sequence consisted of subsequently hitting five targets (for the *Floating Action Menu/Button*) or six targets (for the *Action Bar*). For the adaptive versions, adaptation had to be triggered at the start of the trial sequence; the element then stayed in its adapted state until the start of the next trial sequence. This procedure allowed us to analyse how many subsequent interactions were needed to compensate for trigger overhead (i.e. time required to trigger adaptation vs time saved by using the adapted element).

Trials. To start each trial within a sequence, participants had to touch a *"Start"* button with their thumb. The trial was over once they either had hit their target or a *"Can't reach"* button, to indicate that it was not possible for them to hit the target.

Two GUI elements featured multiple targets – the six buttons on the *Action Bar*, and the five menu options of the *Floating Action Menu*. In these cases, the app displayed the target label for the current trial in the screen centre (see Fig. 3c and d).

Subjective Ratings and Feedback. After each task, participants filled in a short questionnaire with five-point Likert items on perceived speed, comfort of reach, safe grip, and exhaustion. At the very end, qualitative feedback was gathered in a short semi-structured interview. Here, we also asked for opinions on explicitly triggered adaptations (i.e. manual trigger, as in the study) and implicit ones (i.e. automatic trigger, e.g. with a hand posture recognition system).

4.4 Limitations

Our lab study provides control and direct observation. However, future work should also evaluate acceptance in a field study over a longer period of time. Moreover, we chose a non-touch trigger (Fig. 3b) to keep it clearly separate from main interactions. Feedback suggests that turning a larger device in this way is not ideal for everyday use. Other triggers can be investigated, for example a touch swipe from the edge, a large touch [20], long touch, or implicit triggers. Finally, moving elements is only one way of adapting touch GUIs; our study does not include a comparison to other approaches, which we leave for future work.

5   Results

Results are reported per adaptation in comparison to the corresponding non-adaptive baseline element. For each element, we report on task completion time, device orientation, and reachability. Significance, tested where applicable, is reported at the 0.05 level. Further aspects of our evaluation and report are described as follows:

We first focus on data from the larger device (HTC One Max), and then provide a summarised comparison to the results obtained on the other device (Nexus 5). To evaluate the adaptations, we first analyse the data without the trigger. We then report on the influences of the trigger in a separate section. The elements' default versions are their right hand versions for all but the action bar (*Roll*) and the bending menu (*Bend*). Hence, if not stated otherwise, we report on the interesting *adaptation to the left hand*. We removed outliers (e.g. a participant interrupting the study in the middle of a trial).

Table 1 gives an overview, explained in detail in the following subsections.

5.1   Action Button – Fixed vs Move

We compared the fixed *Action Button* against the adaptive version (*Move*).

Time: Using the adapted version was significantly faster than the baseline ($t(28) = 3.11, p < .01$). Note df $= 28$ in this test, since three people decided to never use adaptation, and three others could not reach the baseline with their left hand at all.

Device Orientation: We found significantly less roll (Fig. 3a) with *Move* than in the baseline ($t(28) = 3.82, p < .01$).

Table 1. Results overview. The table shows the observed time and device roll when hitting the given targets on the HTC One Max, for both unadapted and adapted versions (adapted to left hand). Note that menu and action bar had multiple targets (i.e. menu items), hence we give ranges of values covering the target-specific values for these elements. We also measured pitch, but omit it here, since no significant differences were found for any element.

Element	Concept	Time (s)		Orientation (deg roll)	
		mean	sd	mean	sd
Action button	Unadapted	0.63	0.65	−11.70	16.28
Action button	Move	0.40	0.12	−0.71	4.10
Action menu	Unadapted	1.77–2.10	0.88–1.35	−23.87−−17.67	18.81–19.71
Action menu	Move	1.30–1.43	0.21–0.35	−5.97–2.92	3.94–5.85
Action menu	Bend	1.85–2.03	0.85–1.58	−13.87−−12.61	11.06–12.51
Action bar	Unadapted	0.72–2.35	0.20–2.25	−43.86−−19.75	14.67–18.29
Action bar	Roll	0.58–0.77	0.18–0.29	−10.94−−1.93	5.31–7.41

Reachability: Three people could not reach the baseline button with their left thumb. Observations and video analyses showed that many people required considerable effort and grip changes. *Move* could easily be reached by everyone.

5.2   Action Menu – Fixed vs Move or Bend

We compared the baseline *Action Menu* with two menu adaptations, moving (*Move*) and bending (*Bend*). All three menus featured five menu buttons as targets (Fig. 3d).

Time: Using the adapted version was only significantly faster than the baseline for moving the menu ($t(28) = 4.19, p < .001$), but not for bending it.

Device Orientation: We found significantly less roll for both adaptations than with the baseline (*Move:* $t(28) = 4.93, p < .001$; *Bend:* $t(29) = 3.72, p < .001$).

Reachability: Five people could not open the baseline menu with their left hand. The closed bended menu at the same location could not be reached by four people. This difference is explained by the coping strategies that some people invented but only employed in some cases. No reachability problems occurred for the movable menu.

5.3   Action Bar – Fixed vs Roll

We compared the static baseline *Action Bar* with the adaptive version (*Roll*).

Time: Using the adapted version (*Roll*) was significantly faster than the baseline for both the left hand ($t(34) = 6.12, p < .001$) and right hand ($t(34) = 7.36, p < .001$). We also found positive correlations between time taken and the reaching distance, that is the distance from the target to the screen edge of the holding hand (left hand: r = .445; right hand: r = .314). Standard deviation of time also correlated positively with reaching distance (left hand: r = .925; right hand: r = .788), indicating less controlled movements for further reaching.

Device Orientation: The adapted version had significantly less device roll than the baseline for both the left hand ($t(34) = 16.28, p < .001$) and right hand ($t(34) = 17.23, p < .001$).

Reachability: Many people struggled to reach the outer targets of the baseline action bar: Nine could not reach "6" and three could not reach "5" with their left hand (labels see Fig. 3c). With the right hand, seven could not reach "1" and two could not reach "2". *Roll* enabled everyone to reach all targets.

5.4 Trigger Overhead

Adaptations require time for trigger, animation, and users' reorientation. Repeated use of adapted elements might compensate for this. For our trigger we observed the following results:

The *Bending Action Menu* could not compensate for the trigger, taking up to 3.03 s longer than the baseline after the fifth target. The *Moving Action Button* almost reached zero, taking up to 0.43 s longer after the fifth target. The *Moving Action Menu* compensated for the trigger after three targets, leading to a mean advantage of 1.07 s after five targets. The *Rolling Action Bar* compensated for this after four interactions, leading to a mean advantage of 1.23 s after six targets. These values relate to our main adaptation scenario (default to left hand). We observed similar yet less pronounced results for right-hand adaptations.

5.5 Comparison of Screen Sizes

We have focused on the results from the larger device so far (HTC One Max, 5.9 in screen), since such large devices are the main target of our adaptations. To further evaluate benefits and limitations, we now compare the results to those obtained on the smaller device (LG Nexus 5, 4.95 in):

We found almost no effect of screen size on time with the adapted elements. However, the baseline elements strongly profited by the smaller screen. In consequence, the speed improvements achieved by using adapted elements almost disappeared on the smaller device. The smaller device required slightly less tilting than the larger one. Adapted elements still caused less tilting than non-adaptive ones. Reachability greatly improved on the smaller device. However, one person could still not reach the outermost target of the unadapted baseline *Action Bar*.

5.6   Reachability Coping Strategies

Our observations and video recordings revealed several coping strategies to deal with far targets: A main strategy was tilting the device, sometimes up to 90 degrees (Fig. 4a). Another common strategy was to move the hand along the edge of the device (Fig. 4b and c). This requires users to loosen their grip on the device. As a rough estimate from live/video observations, on average they moved approximately 2 cm along the edge to reach targets at the very top (on the HTC One Max). Some even moved the hand to the device's bottom, to enable their thumbs to better cover the full screen width. This was difficult and people often brought their second hand closer, ready to catch the device in case of a slip (Fig. 4d). Two tried reaching around the device with their fingers (Fig. 4e). This required considerable efforts and was reported as tiresome. These participants also stated that they probably would have involved their second hand instead in real-life use.

5.7   Subjective User Ratings

After each task, people rated the used element with four Likert items. All adaptive elements were perceived as faster, more comfortable to use, less exhausting to reach, and more grip safe, compared to their baselines for use with the left hand on the larger device. These differences were significant for all concepts apart from *Bend* (Bonf.-corrected Wilcoxon signed rank tests, all $p < .05$). For the right hand, *Roll* was also preferred over the baseline in all questions, since it had a right-hand adaptation as well (Fig. 2). Ratings for "It is exhausting to reach this element" had a moderate positive linear relationship with roll ($r = .511$). We also found weak to moderate negative relationships between roll and both comfort ($r = -.497$) and safe grip ($r = -.425$). On the smaller device, people did not feel at disadvantage with static GUIs, yet adapted UIs still had an advantage for comfort.

6   Discussion and Implications

6.1   Can Dynamic UI Adaptations Improve Reachability?

On the larger device, 25% of participants could not reach the (unadapted) *Action Bar*, 15% the *Floating Action Menu*, and 9% the *Floating Action Button*. Others struggled to reach some targets. In general, the thumb's functional area depends on the grip [1], which we did not keep fixed to avoid unnatural use. Our adaptations moved elements into the centre (*Bend* when opened), or closer to the thumb (*Move, Roll*), thus making them generally easier to reach.

Crucially, our adaptations enabled all participants to reach all targets. The only exception was the bended menu (*Bend*), which did not move the menu button itself and thus could not improve reachability for an unopened menu. Apart from this exception, our adaptations greatly improved reachability since they brought all targets into reach for everyone in our study.

Feedback, thinking-aloud, and Likert ratings further revealed that the majority of participants also found the adapted GUI elements less exhaustive and more comfortable to use.

Reachability was much less of an issue on a 4.95 in. device compared to the 5.9 in. one. In conclusion, we see the main applications of our adaptations for reachability improvements on the very large end of smartphones, as well as on "phablets".

6.2   Can Dynamic UI Adaptations Improve Speed?

The results show that our adaptations improve speed under certain circumstances. Firstly, adapted elements improved speed on the large device, yet this effect was marginal on the smaller one. This indicates that our adaptations are mainly beneficial on devices beyond the five inch mark. Secondly, the trigger plays an important role. Two of four adaptations could compensate for the ≈ 1.74 s overhead caused by our example trigger. Moving a single button or changing the shape of a menu could not compensate for the trigger, but relocating whole menus saved time after three to six interactions. We argue that such numbers of interactions without switching hand posture occur in many use-cases involving an action bar or menu, such as a browsing session.

Once adapted, all but one element (*Bend*) significantly shortened interaction time on the larger device. The exception for *Bend* is explained by the fact that the bended menu must still first be opened by reaching the menu button, as in the unadapted version.

Participants also subjectively rated these elements significantly faster than the baselines. Even moving a single important button could be worthwhile with a fast or automatic trigger (e.g. by inferring hand postures from preceding touch behaviour [2,10,29]). Finally, all adaptations were subjectively perceived as faster than the baselines where they mattered most, namely on the larger device when used with the left hand.

6.3   Can Dynamic UI Adaptations Facilitate a Safer Grip?

Device roll was significantly lower for elements adapted to the left hand, compared to the baselines. Pitch showed a similar yet non-significant tendency. The action bar's adaptation (*Roll*) also significantly reduced roll for the right hand. Less variance in targeting times suggests that *Roll* also resulted in more control, especially for the non-dominant hand. Since greater device tilting and movements may increase the risk of letting it slip, these results suggest that adaptations can facilitate a safer grip.

This conclusion is supported by participants' own perceptions: Regarding their grip on the device, they perceived the adapted elements as significantly safer than the baselines. This was revealed by the Likert ratings and was in line with further verbal feedback. Recorded sensor values and users' Likert ratings were also moderately correlated ($r = .4$ to $.5$): Less device tilt was associated with higher ratings on comfort and grip, and lower ratings on exhaustion.

6.4 Do Users Accept Dynamic UI Adaptations?

All adaptations received more positive ratings than the baselines. Most people elected the *Bending Action Menu* as their favourite adaptive UI element. Interestingly, this was the only adaptation that could not improve speed, even without the trigger overhead. However, people's comments suggest that they liked the feeling of "ergonomic optimisation". This was probably more visibly conveyed in the bended arrangement of the menu items than in location/rotation changes. Moreover, the bended layout matches the more comfortable movement directions, in which the thumb describes an arc instead of bending and extending (see [17]).

In conclusion, all GUI adaptations were well accepted by our participants. When asked about explicit/implicit triggers after the study, some participants said that they liked the explicit influence over the UI, yet the majority stated that they would prefer automatic adaptation, if it worked reliably.

6.5 Design Implications

We expect several observations, insights, and lessons learned from this project to be useful for designing adaptive touch GUIs for large devices beyond this work:

Reconsider Default Locations: Our baselines showed that users of larger devices can face serious reachability problems, even for UIs following a modern touch GUI design language. On devices beyond five inches and without dynamic adaptations, navigation and action bars would be easier to reach at the bottom of the screen, and action buttons can improve reachability for both hands by being centred horizontally.

Separate Controls from Content: Our pre-study revealed that it is difficult for users to understand and follow adaptive UI elements that are less clearly separated from the main content (e.g. due to transparency or overlays).

Avoid Introducing Redundancy: In our concept discussions and pre-study, we found that duplicating UI elements at easier reachable locations caused confusion due to the redundancy. Participants had to (1) understand that functionality had been duplicated and (2) mentally draw a connection between the new element and the normal one.

Make Explicit Adaptations "Sticky": We suggest that if adaptations are triggered by the user, they should not revert themselves after a single interaction. First, based on our speed and trigger-overhead analyses, keeping elements in their adapted state for subsequent actions helps to compensate for the time required by the trigger. Second, participants who would prefer an explicit trigger outside of the study indicated that they liked the feeling of control and changing the UI on their own command.

Adapt View Groups: Based on our analyses of trigger-overhead against saved time, we suggest to relocate multiple buttons at once (e.g. as in our moving menu and rotating action bar). This improves convenience and helps to compensate for trigger overhead, since users are then more likely to already find future actions within reach.

An "Ergonomic Look" Can Facilitate User Acceptance: Although bending the menu did not improve the quantitative measures, it looked ergonomically fitting for the thumb and the majority of participants highlighted this adaptation as their favourite.

6.6   Integration of Adaptations into Existing GUIs

Our non-adapted elements are simply the familiar elements from Material Design, not new ones. This makes it easy to integrate them into existing apps - simply replace the old version with an adaptive one; the visuals stay the same. On the other hand, this may make it hard for users to discover the new adaptive functionality. Ideally, the presented adaptations would be integrated into existing mobile interfaces by making them available on an operating system level. Thus, for example, all action bars would be adaptive ones. In contrast, integration into single apps might confuse users, since the GUI's behaviour then becomes less consistent across applications.

These issues can be addressed by explaining new adaptations to the user, for example with an overlay upon first use, similar to the commonly used app-introduction screens. More generally, new adaptiveness in any app or on OS level should be revealed and explained to avoid unexpected GUI behaviour from the users' point of view.

Finally, from a practical perspective, developers can realise adaptations like the ones presented here by making use of generalised frameworks that facilitate implementing adaptive GUIs (e.g. see [3]).

7   Conclusion and Future Work

While large mobile devices are attractive for displaying multimedia content, they also introduce reachability problems when users need to operate them with a single hand as required in many every-day situations. Some screen regions cannot be reached comfortably or not at all.

We have proposed dynamic adaptations of basic touch GUI elements to mitigate reachability problems for one-handed use of large mobile devices. A lab study ($N = 35$) showed that adapted elements improve reachability on a large device, and can reduce interaction time and device tilting. Moreover, using adaptations resulted in perceived higher comfort, less exhaustion, and a safer grip. We further derived lessons learned and implications for future design of adaptive mobile touch GUIs for large devices.

To take full advantage of dynamic GUI adaptations in practice, the next step is to investigate better triggers, including automatic ones. For example, adaptations could be triggered based on automatically inferred hand postures (e.g. [2,3,10,29]).

References

1. Bergstrom-Lehtovirta, J., Oulasvirta, A.: Modeling the functional area of the thumb on mobile touchscreen surfaces. In: Proceedings of the SIGCHI Conference on Human Factors in Computing Systems, CHI 2014, pp. 1991–2000. ACM, New York (2014). http://doi.acm.org/10.1145/2556288.2557354
2. Buschek, D., Alt, F.: TouchML: a machine learning toolkit for modelling spatial touch targeting behaviour. In: Proceedings of the 20th International Conference on Intelligent User Interfaces, IUI 2015, pp. 110–114. ACM, New York (2015). http://doi.acm.org/10.1145/2678025.2701381
3. Buschek, D., Alt, F.: ProbUI: generalising touch target representations to enable declarative gesture definition for probabilistic GUIs. In: Proceedings of the 2017 CHI Conference on Human Factors in Computing Systems, CHI 2017, pp. 4640–4653. ACM, New York (2017). http://doi.acm.org/10.1145/3025453.3025502
4. Buschek, D., Schoenleben, O., Oulasvirta, A.: Improving accuracy in back-of-device multitouch typing: a clustering-based approach to keyboard updating. In: Proceedings of the 19th International Conference on Intelligent User Interfaces, IUI 2014, pp. 57–66. ACM, New York (2014). http://doi.acm.org/10.1145/2557500.2557501
5. Chang, Y., L'Yi, S., Koh, K., Seo, J.: Understanding users' touch behavior on large mobile touch-screens and assisted targeting by tilting gesture. In: Proceedings of the 33rd Annual ACM Conference on Human Factors in Computing Systems, CHI 2015, pp. 1499–1508. ACM, New York (2015). http://doi.acm.org/10.1145/2702123.2702425
6. Cheng, L.P., Liang, H.S., Wu, C.Y., Chen, M.Y.: iGrasp: grasp-based adaptive keyboard for mobile devices. In: CHI 2013 Extended Abstracts on Human Factors in Computing Systems, CHI EA 2013, pp. 2791–2792. ACM, New York (2013). http://doi.acm.org/10.1145/2468356.2479514
7. Fitts, P.M.: The information capacity of the human motor system in controlling the amplitude of movement. J. Exp. Psychol. 47(6), 381–391 (1954)
8. Girouard, A., Lo, J., Riyadh, M., Daliri, F., Eady, A.K., Pasquero, J.: One-handed bend interactions with deformable smartphones. In: Proceedings of the 33rd Annual ACM Conference on Human Factors in Computing Systems, CHI 2015, pp. 1509–1518. ACM, New York (2015). http://doi.acm.org/10.1145/2702123.2702513
9. Goel, M., Jansen, A., Mandel, T., Patel, S.N., Wobbrock, J.O.: Contexttype: using hand posture information to improve mobile touch screen text entry. In: Proceedings of the SIGCHI Conference on Human Factors in Computing Systems, CHI 2013, pp. 2795–2798. ACM, New York (2013). http://doi.acm.org/10.1145/2470654.2481386
10. Goel, M., Wobbrock, J., Patel, S.: Gripsense: using built-in sensors to detect hand posture and pressure on commodity mobile phones. In: Proceedings of the 25th Annual ACM Symposium on User Interface Software and Technology, UIST 2012, pp. 545–554. ACM, New York (2012) http://doi.acm.org/10.1145/2380116.2380184

11. Gunawardana, A., Paek, T., Meek, C.: Usability guided key-target resizing for soft keyboards. In: Proceedings of the 15th International Conference on Intelligent User Interfaces, IUI 2010, pp. 111–118. ACM, New York (2010) http://doi.acm.org/10.1145/1719970.1719986

12. Hong, J., Lee, G.: Touchshield: a virtual control for stable grip of a smartphone using the thumb. In: CHI 2013 Extended Abstracts on Human Factors in Computing Systems, CHI EA 2013, pp. 1305–1310. ACM, New York (2013) http://doi.acm.org/10.1145/2468356.2468589

13. Huot, S., Lecolinet, E.: Spiralist: a compact visualization technique for one-handed interaction with large lists on mobile devices. In: Proceedings of the 4th Nordic Conference on Human-computer Interaction: Changing Roles, NordiCHI 2006, pp. 445–448. ACM, New York (2006). http://doi.acm.org/10.1145/1182475.1182533

14. Hürst, W., Merkle, P.: One-handed mobile video browsing. In: Proceedings of the 1st International Conference on Designing Interactive User Experiences for TV and Video, UXTV 2008, pp. 169–178. ACM, New York (2008). http://doi.acm.org/10.1145/1453805.1453839

15. Karlson, A.K., Bederson, B.B.: Studies in one-handed mobile design: habit, desire and agility. In: Proceedings of the 4th ERCIM Workshop on User Interfaces for All, UI4ALL 1998. Technical report (2006)

16. Karlson, A.K., Bederson, B.B.: One-handed touchscreen input for legacy applications. In: Proceedings of the SIGCHI Conference on Human Factors in Computing Systems, CHI 2008, pp. 1399–1408. ACM, New York (2008). http://doi.acm.org/10.1145/1357054.1357274

17. Karlson, A.K., Bederson, B.B., Contreras-Vidal, J.L.: Understanding single-handed mobile device interaction. In: Handbook of Research on User Interface Design and Evaluation for Mobile Technology, pp. 86–101 (2007)

18. Karlson, A.K., Bederson, B.B., SanGiovanni, J.: Applens and launchtile: two designs for one-handed thumb use on small devices. In: Proceedings of the SIGCHI Conference on Human Factors in Computing Systems, CHI 2005, pp. 201–210. ACM, New York (2005). http://doi.acm.org/10.1145/1054972.1055001

19. Karlson, A.K., Bederson, B.B.: ThumbSpace: generalized one-handed input for touchscreen-based mobile devices. In: Baranauskas, C., Palanque, P., Abascal, J., Barbosa, S.D.J. (eds.) INTERACT 2007. LNCS, vol. 4662, pp. 324–338. Springer, Heidelberg (2007). doi:10.1007/978-3-540-74796-3_30

20. Kim, S., Yu, J., Lee, G.: Interaction techniques for unreachable objects on the touchscreen. In: Proceedings of the 24th Australian Computer-Human Interaction Conference, OzCHI 2012, pp. 295–298. ACM, New York (2012). http://doi.acm.org/10.1145/2414536.2414585

21. Mohd Noor, M.F., Ramsay, A., Hughes, S., Rogers, S., Williamson, J., Murray-Smith, R.: 28 frames later: predicting screen touches from back-of-device grip changes. In: Proceedings of the SIGCHI Conference on Human Factors in Computing Systems, CHI 2014, pp. 2005–2008. ACM, New York (2014) http://doi.acm.org/10.1145/2556288.2557148

22. Negulescu, M., McGrenere, J.: Grip change as an information side channel for mobile touch interaction. In: Proceedings of the 33rd Annual ACM Conference on Human Factors in Computing Systems, CHI 2015, pp. 1519–1522. ACM, New York (2015). http://doi.acm.org/10.1145/2702123.2702185

23. Ng, A., Brewster, S.A., Williamson, J.H.: Investigating the effects of encumbrance on one- and two- handed interactions with mobile devices. In: Proceedings of the SIGCHI Conference on Human Factors in Computing Systems, CHI 2014, pp. 1981–1990. ACM, New York (2014). http://doi.acm.org/10.1145/2556288.2557312

24. Oulasvirta, A., Bergstrom-Lehtovirta, J.: Ease of juggling: studying the effects of manual multitasking. In: Proceedings of the SIGCHI Conference on Human Factors in Computing Systems, CHI 2011, pp. 3103–3112. ACM, New York (2011). http:// doi.acm.org/10.1145/1978942.1979402

25. Roudaut, A., Huot, S., Lecolinet, E.: Taptap and magstick: improving one-handed target acquisition on small touch-screens. In: Proceedings of the Working Conference on Advanced Visual Interfaces, AVI 2008, pp. 146–153. New York (2008). http://doi.acm.org/10.1145/1385569.1385594

26. Wigdor, D., Forlines, C., Baudisch, P., Barnwell, J., Shen, C.: Lucid touch: a see-through mobile device. In: Proceedings of the 20th Annual ACM Symposium on User Interface Software and Technology, UIST 2007, pp. 269–278. ACM, New York (2007). http://doi.acm.org/10.1145/1294211.1294259

27. Wolf, K., McGee-Lennon, M., Brewster, S.: A study of on-device gestures. In: Proceedings of the 14th International Conference on Human-computer Interaction with Mobile Devices and Services Companion, MobileHCI 2012, pp. 11–16. ACM, New York (2012). http://doi.acm.org/10.1145/2371664.2371669

28. Yang, X.D., Mak, E., Irani, P., Bischof, W.F.: Dual-surface input: augmenting one-handed interaction with coordinated front and behind-the-screen input. In: Proceedings of the 11th International Conference on Human-Computer Interaction with Mobile Devices and Services, MobileHCI 2009, pp. 5:1–5:10. ACM, New York (2009). http://doi.acm.org/10.1145/1613858.1613865

29. Yin, Y., Ouyang, T.Y., Partridge, K., Zhai, S.: Making touchscreen keyboards adaptive to keys, hand postures, and individuals: a hierarchical spatial backoff model approach. In: Proceedings of the SIGCHI Conference on Human Factors in Computing Systems, CHI 2013, pp. 2775–2784. ACM, New York (2013). http:// doi.acm.org/10.1145/2470654.2481384

Horizontal vs. Vertical: How the Orientation of a Large Interactive Surface Impacts Collaboration in Multi-surface Environments

Lili Tong[1($\boxtimes$)], Aurélien Tabard[2], Sébastien George[3],
and Audrey Serna[1]

[1] Univ Lyon, CNRS, INSA-Lyon, LIRIS, UMR5205,
69621 Villeurbanne, France
{lili.tong,audrey.serna}@insa-lyon.fr
[2] Univ Lyon, CNRS, Université Lyon 1, LIRIS,
UMR5205, 69622 Villeurbanne, France
aurelien.tabard@insa-lyon.fr
[3] UBL, Université du Maine, EA 4024, LIUM, 72085 Le Mans, France
sebastien.george@univ-lemans.fr

Abstract. Defining the form factor and set-up of surfaces, i.e., their size, position, and orientation, is one of the first decisions made when designing multi-surface environments (MSE). To support these choices, we conducted a study on how the orientation of a large display used alongside tablets impacts collaboration. Previous research involving only one interactive surface shows that display orientation changes how people interact with the display, the way they position themselves, or look at each other. Our study shows that in a MSE setting, the orientation of a large surface has a different impact: (1) it nuances previous results showing that horizontal surfaces are better for collaboration. (2) it impacts the way activities are conducted. The horizontal condition leads to more implicit coordination and balanced interaction with the large display, but to less structured work, while in the vertical condition, group coordination is more explicit and is structured around one main interactor. Compared to previous work, we also propose a more structured, comprehensive and detailed analysis grid for collaboration in MSE. Finally, based on our results, we derive recommendations for MSE design.

Keywords: Collaboration · Coordination · Multi-surface environments (MSE) · Tabletops · Tablets · Display orientation

1 Introduction

Multi-surface environments (MSE), i.e., the combination of devices into a seamless information space, have shown benefits for co-located collaboration [1]. Collaborative MSE are often composed of large displays acting as a shared space to coordinate efforts, and handheld devices used as personal spaces for individual tasks. The introduction of personal devices alongside large shared surfaces tends to improve efficiency of individual tasks within larger collaborative activities [32]. This has proved to be

© IFIP International Federation for Information Processing 2017
Published by Springer International Publishing AG 2017. All Rights Reserved
R. Bernhaupt et al. (Eds.): INTERACT 2017, Part III, LNCS 10515, pp. 202–222, 2017.
DOI: 10.1007/978-3-319-67687-6_14

especially useful in educational contexts [28], emergency response planning [6], and gaming [9, 26].

The form factor, i.e. size, orientation, overall shape, and configuration of surfaces in a MSE is generally decided early in projects. Yet these factors can have profound effects on how people interact in these environments. For instance, Zagermann et al. [35] recently showed that as the size of tabletops increases in a MSE, collaboration quality or sensemaking results decrease, since the larger screen diverts users' attention away from their collaborators and towards the shared display. Closer to our concerns, Rogers and Lindley [23] showed that horizontal displays supported a greater awareness of participants' activities compared to vertical ones.

In this paper, we investigate how the orientation of a large shared interactive display impacts collaboration in a Multi-Surface Environment. We revisit the question originally framed by Rogers and Lindley with a single surface, within a richer ecosystem of devices with more sophisticated inputs, i.e., multi-touch instead of a mimio pen. To understand the impact of display orientation, both on interaction and coordination aspects, we conducted a study in which twelve groups of three participants carried out a collaborative problem solving activity with tablets, associated with a 55" shared display, both in vertical and horizontal position (Fig. 1).

Fig. 1. A large interactive surface used alongside tablets in a problem solving activity. Left: the horizontal condition. Right: the vertical condition.

Our results show that multi-surface environments reduce the differences between the horizontal and vertical conditions compared to previous research studying group work with horizontal and shared surfaces [15, 22, 23]. Participants maintained a good level of awareness, created a similar amount of content and discussed in the same proportions in both conditions. However, we observed differences in activity organization between the two conditions. Participants in the horizontal condition acted more equally using both explicit and implicit coordination mechanisms, leading to anticipation, assistance and parallel work. In contrast, the vertical condition led to the emergence of a more structured activity with a main interactor and explicit distribution of labor among the group. We describe in detail the awareness mechanisms at play and their consequences on activity organization. Overall, our results weigh in, confirm, contradict, and extend previous work.

2 Related Work

We focus on collaboration in multi-surface environments. We are especially interested in understanding the interplay between the form-factors of devices, their affordances, and people's behaviors at both the individual and group level.

2.1 Multi-surface Environments

In a number of ways, Weiser's vision of ubiquitous computing environments in which people can seamlessly interact across devices [33], has made its way into our homes, workplaces, and learning environments [4]. These Multi-Surface Environments are particularly suited for conducting complex collaborative problem solving activities involving rich data exploration. Examples range from urban planning [28], to basin (oil/gas) exploration [25], as well as emergency response planning [6]. Games are another example of collaborative activities that can benefit from MSE [9, 26].

When looking at devices independently, commonly held views are that: (1) large shared surfaces are well suited to co-located collaborative activities [27]; (2) tabletops enable more equitable participation [20]; and (3) handheld devices support mobility with pervasive access to information, support planning and enable monitoring of activities [21]. However, the question of how to support effective collaboration in MSE is still open [5].

2.2 The Impact of Device Form Factors on Collaboration

When building MSE, decisions concerning the size, form and orientation of devices have to be made early on in the design process. These factors are often considered implicitly, or intuitively since data is scarce in the domain. The complexity of changing form factors may explain why few papers discuss their impact on interaction, even though these factors profoundly shape the affordances of devices. To mitigate this problem Inkpen et al. used a paper-based prototype to display orientation, size, and user arrangements [15]. They found that although participants felt the horizontal display was more natural and comfortable for collaboration, working with a vertical display tended to be more time-efficient.

Rogers and Lindley were among the first to study impact of device orientation on interaction and collaboration [23]. Through two experiments, they showed that horizontal displays are better at supporting collaboration, as they promote more suggestions and idea generation, while also leading to more role switches and greater awareness of others' actions. The authors proposed two reasons (1) the input device, a mimio pen, was easier to pass among users over the horizontal table, and (2) it was harder to input data on the vertical display while standing. More recent work by Potvin el al. [22] comparing vertical and horizontal multi-touch displays found that the horizontal surface encouraged more equal physical interactions among participants with the shared display, as well as equal verbal participation, which differs from Rogers and Lindley's study. Al-Megren et al. also showed that the vertical configuration was more likely to cause muscle fatigue comparing to the horizontal configuration [2].

All these previous studies focused on a single screen. Since Rogers and Lindley's study in 2003, large multi-touch displays, smartphones and tablets have become pervasive, raising the question of how people behave and collaborate in such Multi-Surface Environments. Compared to previous work, devices like smartphones or tablets make input much more efficient, which should change collaboration by distributing control more evenly. The same applies to input on large devices which is now fast, reliable and multi-touch, meaning that anybody can take control of a shared screen without any limitation.

2.3   Coordination Mechanisms

To effectively design collaborative activities in MSE, it is important to acquire a deep understanding of complex interactions occurring between users and devices, and individuals within a group [29]. In this context, coordination of individual actions within groups is crucial when pursuing collaborative activities. Malone and Crowston define coordination as "the act of managing interdependencies between activities performed to achieve a goal" [18]. In coordinated work, participants strive towards a shared goal dealing with time and organizational constraints. Several mechanisms are used in the coordination process such as awareness, regulation, information sharing and discussion.

Awareness of individual and group actions is crucial for a successful collaborative work. For Schmidt [24], awareness refers to actors "taking heed of the context of their joint effort". It also refers to monitoring practices of others and acting in a way that makes aspects of activity visible. Yuill and Rogers do not limit awareness to actions but extend it to situations where people "have ongoing awareness of the actions, intentions, emotions and other mental states of other interactants" [34]. In our work, we refer to awareness as a state of mutual consciousness allowing structuration of an activity, avoiding duplication of work and facilitating group progress and activity coordination. As Hornecker et al. state, with a good level of awareness, little verbal communication is used in coordinating activity, and assistance and anticipation actions arise [14]. On the contrary, a lack of awareness can negatively impact coordination. Interferences, "unintended negative influence on another user's actions" according to Hornecker et al. [14], can arise with multi-user devices when two or more participants try to perform incompatible actions (e.g. attempt to drag the same object, or select two inconsistent features).

Regulation builds upon awareness and relates to people's ability to plan, monitor, evaluate and regulate the joint activity [30, 31]. The concept of regulation is extensively used in the learning and psychology literature for analyzing collaborative behaviors [10]. In HCI, regulation is observed in terms of activity organization. Studies analyze the way group members elaborate strategies [35], adopt roles and distribute or share labor [23] to understand this meta-level of coordination and how it relates to the overall activity.

Finally, information sharing and discussions are also required in coordination processes. Information sharing involves building a common ground [7], which means that members collaborate in ensuring understanding and in grounding their mutual knowledge and assumptions. It also contains sharing information on physical objects such as documents and materials. The number and type of discussion occurring during group work are often considered for analysis of collaboration [8, 11].

2.4   Group Formations and Mobility in Collaboration

Physical formations also influence group behavior, which in turn shapes the physical formations. The notion of Facing formation, or F-formation, was introduced by Kendon [17] to describe how people adjust their position and orientation to interact together and jointly manage their attention. Although our study participants were not very mobile, we nonetheless paid attention to F-formations, proxemics [13], and the social interactions occurring in these arrangements. Here, the form factor and physical properties of artifacts also play a role in collaboration [16]. In their study on the use of paper documents, Paul and Luff emphasized particularly how form-factors would afford various levels of micro-mobility, e.g. tilting or flipping devices, which would then shape collaboration [16].

3   Study

We have shown that collaboration is important but very fragile and can be influenced by tiny details such as devices configurations, as shown during our case studies. We want to focus orientation to show that this little decision is already very impactful. Previous work [23] shows that horizontal displays offer better opportunities for equal interactions and distributed work coordination among participants. Our question is whether these observations still hold in MSE? In order to study this question, we designed a multi-surface application supporting problem-solving activities. A large surface displays the map, while tablets support information browsing, note taking and bookmarking favorite locations. For our experiment, we implemented a trip planning activity in the application.

3.1   Pre-study

In a preliminary study, we explored the impact of display orientation in MSE on individual and collaborative work. Our hypothesis was that the introduction of tablets would decrease the differences between horizontal and vertical conditions by enabling participants to carry out individual activities alongside. The study consisted of a collaborative problem-solving activity made up of an individual phase in which participants analyzed data on their tablets, followed by a collaborative phase in which participants discussed how to come to a collective decision.

The study lasted around 55 min. This included 5 min of task description and familiarization, 20 min for the task in one condition followed by a similar task in the other condition, and 10 min of debriefing at the end. We counterbalanced the orientation and the data presented to participants for the two conditions. Six groups of three people participated in the experiment. Within each group, participants knew each other.

Lessons from Pre-study

We found that the horizontal condition seemed to better support coordination among participants. Roles and tasks were most frequently distributed in this condition. Regarding individual tasks, participants inputted equal numbers of notes and arguments.

However, the structured nature of the activity constrained what participants could do. In practice, everyone had to analyze the same data in order to move to the next phase. Moreover, we noticed variations between the two sessions in terms of time spent to complete the task and also in the level of the discussions. Participants spent more time in the first session (mean = 19 min 24 s, SD = 3 min 54 s) than in the second session (mean = 11 min 36 s, SD = 4 min 24 s) with a statistically significant difference ($t(5) = 7.19$, $p = 0.0008$). Besides time duration, we also observed that participants discussed task strategy only in the first session and continued to use the same strategy in the second session. Both phenomena made it difficult to compare group behaviors and draw reliable conclusions.

3.2 Main Study

Based on the observations from the pre-study, we designed a task with fewer constraints and chose a between group experimental design. Our study configuration consisted of three participants, each with a tablet and sharing the multi-touch display. The collaborative activity, which consisted in planning a trip to New York, involved gathering information, analyzing it, and making group decisions.

3.3 Hypotheses

Based on the related work and our pre-study, we derived a set of hypotheses ranging from low-level interaction to high-level group organization. At a low-level, we focused on how people interact with devices in MSE while conducting collaborative activities, especially when creating and interacting with content. We hypothesized that:

- **H1**: the horizontal condition would lead to more balanced physical interactions with the large display within groups;
- **H2**: the difference in input levels (e.g., notes taken) between the two conditions would not be as pronounced as in prior work that did not include personal devices.

Our second set of hypotheses focused on higher-level activities related to group coordination:

- **H3**: the horizontal condition would support a higher level of awareness;
- **H4**: the horizontal condition would support more efficient activity organization;
- **H5**: the horizontal condition would encourage more communication and discussions.

3.4 Task Design

The task consisted in planning a trip itinerary to New York with a limited budget, comparable to that used by Rogers and Lindley [23]. Such an activity is open-ended enough to enable various types of group organization. While the task focused on trip planning, the same collaborative mechanisms are at play in any decision-making activities, which can be found in educational contexts (classrooms, museums), professional meetings or show rooms. We chose New York as the degree of knowledge of its landmarks was relatively similar in our target population. Based on their budget, participants had to agree on: how many days they would stay in the city; which hotel they would stay at; which activities they would do; and their itinerary for each day. Once finished, participants had to present the day-to-day outline of their trip.

The shared screen displayed a map with markers for 15 tourist attractions and 8 hotels (Fig. 2). Participants could push detailed information on their tablet by tapping their avatar on a marker (①). Information provided for each location included: description, price, rating, and feedback from other tourists (⑤). Using their tablets, participants could individually add locations to their favorites (⑥) and take notes (⑦). A card per location showed its favorites and notes on the shared screen (②). Four filter buttons on the shared screen were used to show/hide attractions, hotels, favorite locations, location cards (③). A timer in the top right corner reminded participants how much time was left (④).

Fig. 2. The application overview. Left: shared surface showing the map + favorite locations. Right: tablets content with details on an attraction.

3.5   Participants

We recruited 12 groups of three participants at our university. Group members knew each other. It amounted to 36 participants (24 males and 12 females). Participants were between 21 and 31 years old (mean = 26.1; SD = 3.28). They had different backgrounds including electronic engineering, biology and computer science. All used smartphones, but had never worked or participated studies in MSE.

3.6   Apparatus

We used a 55-in multi-touch display with a resolution of 1920 × 1080 pixels in both conditions. The tablets were Samsung Galaxy Note 8 with protective covers. The devices were wirelessly connected to the network. The MSE application was built with Web technologies, and devices communicated via websockets.

3.7   Procedure

Based on the literature and our pre-study, we chose a between-group design with the shared display orientation as an independent variable with two horizontal or vertical conditions. In both conditions, participants were standing (Fig. 1). In all we observed six groups of three participants in each condition, which is comparable to similar studies of collaborative work with tabletops [14, 35].

The experiment started with 5 min of task description and familiarization, and ended with 10 min of debriefing. The group had approximately 25 min to achieve the task, with a timer indicating the time left. However, the task instructions emphasized that the timer was an indication and that participants could spend more or less time depending on how the activity progressed.

3.8   Data Collection

We collected behavioral data through videos and logs. We used two cameras to record the sessions: one was placed near the ceiling to capture the activity on the shared surface, while the other was placed beside the shared surface to capture the group. We logged interactions with the shared display and the tablets, such as touch events on UI elements, dragging/zooming the map, choosing a location, submitting a note, etc.

4   Analysis Method

To analyze participants' behaviors, we defined a set of indicators detailed in Table 1 The indicators range from low-level actions, e.g. touch events, to higher-level coordination behaviors and group strategies.

Table 1. Indicators used to analyze participants' behaviors.

Behaviors	Data source	Indicators	
Interaction with device (H1 & H2)	Log	Notes/favorite locations/total number of touch events	
	Video	Touches on shared display per participant	
Awareness (H3)	Video	Positive	Reaction without request/complementary action
		Negative	Interference/verbal monitoring
		Neutral	Verbal shadowing
Activity organization (H4)	Log	Locations checked together at the same time/locations checked per person	
	Video	Discussion on strategy/duration of the whole task	
Discussion (H5)	Video	Discussion on hotels, attractions, budget and itinerary/sharing tablets for discussion	

4.1 Interactions with Devices

To analyze low-level interaction, we used log data to count touch events, how many notes participants submitted during the activity, and how many times they pressed the favorite button. We used video analysis to measure the number of touch events, e.g., tap, drag, or zoom, on UI elements of the shared display, in order to measure how active each participant was.

4.2 Awareness

To analyze group awareness, we used indicators from Hornecker's et al. model [14]. We took two positive indicators: reaction without explicit request and complementary action, which correspond to anticipation and assistance actions. Reaction without request is a proactive action that occurs when one participant reacts to, or helps, another without being explicitly asked. For instance, when a participant sends information about a location to his/her tablet and notices that another group member wants to check the same location, sending the information to him/her without being asked to is considered reaction without request. Complementary action occurred when participants were coordinating the task or distributing labor implicitly. We coded it when two or three participants were interacting together or alternately on the shared display without verbal coordination to achieve the same goal. For example, when two participants were sorting location cards together based on their itinerary, or when they were alternately dragging and zooming the map. These two indicators can be used to evaluate whether participants are aware of the on-going tasks taking place in the group.

We used two negative indicators of awareness: interference and verbal monitoring. Interference occurs when participants unintendedly interrupt or impede another person's actions. For example, when one person wants to choose a location while another accidentally drags the map, or when two participants are reaching for the same location card. Verbal monitoring occurs when a participant is inquiring about other persons' behaviors. For example, when one person is asking the other: "Which location are you checking?"

Finally, we used verbal shadowing to measure and assess how participants' maintained awareness [14]. We coded it when one person was describing or giving a running commentary about who is doing or going to do what. For example, when one person is saying: "I'm writing down the price of that hotel" or "I'll like that location".

4.3 Activity Organization

We analyzed activity organization in terms of group strategies, explicitly sharing labor, and roles taken by participants [23, 35], but also in terms of planning and monitoring [10]. We counted discussions related to activity organization when participants expressed strategies, such as deciding how to distribute labor, e.g. discussing the locations to explore. We also counted this indicator when participants were monitoring or planning these strategies. For example, when a group realized that nobody had favorited the locations explored, one participant stated: "one of us should 'like' the locations so we can filter the cards and find them easily", and another answered:

"yeah, you're right, I'll do that". To observe how groups shared labor, we counted parallel interactions, which occurred when participants were interacting together on the large surface for a different purpose.

We were interested in measuring whether the task was more efficient in one condition rather than the other. Quality of results could not be a good efficiency indicator since we proposed an open problem. The different results proposed by the groups all met the budget requirements. Thus, to measure the efficiency of group works, we analyzed the activity in terms of duration and exploration. We used our logs to compute the number of locations explored together and by each person.

4.4 Discussion and Information Sharing

We coded discussions in video based on the conversation topic. Each time participants talked about a topic within a continuous interval of time, we counted it as one discussion. If two topics were discussed during the same conversation, we counted one discussion per topic. The list of topics was set after the inter-rater reliability test of the two coders' observations. This list included *attractions*, when participants discussed about places to visit, *hotels* for discussions about the location of a hotel or room type, *budget*, when participants were discussing about ticket prices, and *itinerary* for their plan of the days.

To analyze how participants used their tablets during discussions and how information was shared among the group, we captured each time that they shared their tablets with others. Using a qualitative approach, we observed participants' movements and deictic gestures when exchanging ideas, or arguments when discussing collective decisions.

4.5 Video Analysis Process

Two coders analyzed the videos. We conducted an inter-rater reliability test before starting the analysis. We chose one group from each condition to carry out the test and picked two segments in each group: one at the beginning of the activity when participants were browsing locations, and the other at the end when participants started to discuss their final plan. Each segment lasted 2 min. We went through the video twice. In the first round, we noted all the interactions, such as dragging the map, touching cards, tapping the filter buttons, and the complementary or parallel interactions. In the second round, we conducted the verbal analysis, considering the awareness indicators described above, the different types of discussion, etc. In the end, the analysis had 96.46% agreements (Cohen's Kappa $\kappa = 0.88$). After we had clarified coding differences and refined our coding scheme, we analyzed all the videos.

5 Results

We present our results for each of our hypotheses and outline the main findings.

5.1   Interactions with Devices

We analyzed collaboration among groups from a low-level perspective to determine whether the orientation of the shared display impacted users' interaction. We emitted the hypotheses that horizontal shared display would allow more balanced interaction (H1), whereas combining tablets with the shared display would reduce the differences between conditions in terms of content created or modified (H2).

H1: More equality in physical interaction in the horizontal condition

To test this hypothesis, we calculated the percentage of touch events (tap, drag, etc.) per person within each group. We used the same formula as Marshall et al. [20] and Potvin et al. [22]. The inequality index is smaller in the horizontal condition (mean = 0.39, SD = 0.15) than in the vertical one (mean = 0.70, SD = 0.25) with a statistically significant difference (t (10) = −2.59, p = 0.027) (Fig. 3-left). In the horizontal condition, participants have more balanced interaction. On the other hand, in the vertical condition, groups were always organized around a main participant who had far more interactions than the others (Fig. 3-right), even though everyone had access to the surface. When the main interactor was interacting, others pointed at the surface to give suggestions or asked the interactor to interact

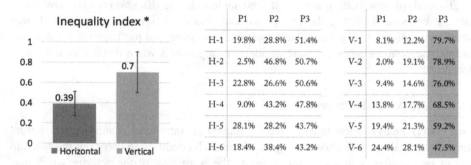

Fig. 3. More inequality of physical interaction in the vertical condition. Left: inequality index of physical interaction. Right: percentage of touch events per person in two conditions.

We observed behavioral differences on interacting with the large surface. Participants played with the display in the horizontal condition, such as zooming or dragging the map without a clear aim (something Zagermann et al. also noted in their study [35]). In contrast, in the vertical condition, interactions were goal-driven, with participants always touching the display for a specific purpose.

Finding 1: these observations validate H1. Large horizontal surfaces support more equality in physical interaction, whereas vertical surfaces lead to the emergence of a main interactor.

H2: Reduction of differences when creating and modifying content

To test this hypothesis, we measured the number of notes and favorite locations that each group submitted. The results showed no significant difference between two conditions in notes submitted (horizontal: mean = 16.3, SD = 6.62, vertical: mean = 11.3, SD = 8.66. t (10) = 1.12, p = 0.29), or in "Favorites" (horizontal: mean = 22.7, SD = 9.4, vertical: mean = 13.2, SD = 8.7. (t (10) = 1.81, p = 0.10). Unlike previous studies, we did not observe an effect of display orientation on content creation or interaction. Nevertheless, to validate statically this hypothesis, other experiments would need to be conducted with a 'no tablet' condition to compare against.

> **Finding 2**: these observations are in favor of H2, although more work would be required to validate this hypothesis. Combining tablets with a shared surface could reduce the differences between horizontal and vertical conditions, especially in the creation of and interaction with content, a fact which was highlighted in previous studies [23].

5.2   Group Coordination

To measure whether the orientation of the shared display impacts the way participants collaborate together from a meta-level, we analyzed group coordination according to awareness (H3), activity organization and exploration efficiency (H4) and communication and discussions (H5).

H3: Higher level of awareness in the horizontal condition

To test this hypothesis, we looked at several awareness indicators. Verbal monitoring is considered as a negative indicator of awareness [14] and occurs when participants want to know the current situation of the on-going activity, such as what a collaborator is doing or what stage the group is in. We observed few instances of verbal monitoring either in the horizontal condition (mean = 3, SD = 1.67) or the vertical condition (mean = 2.83, SD = 1.72) (Fig. 4-left). We observed significantly more verbal shadowing in the vertical condition (mean = 11.5, SD = 5.05) than in the horizontal condition (mean = 6, SD = 3.1; t (10) = −2.27, p = 0.046) (Fig. 4-right). In the vertical condition participants often gave cues to others, such as "I'm going to like that location", "I'll write down the price for that hotel", or "I'm going to look at this attraction to see if it's free"

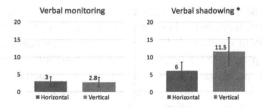

Fig. 4. Average number of *verbal monitoring* and *verbal shadowing* statements per condition (means with 95% CI).

In both conditions, groups maintained a good level of awareness, and participants did not feel the need to ask what the others were doing. However, in the vertical condition, participants had to make more efforts to maintain this high level of awareness, by explaining to the others what they were doing. This relates to *finding 1* and the presence of a main interactor, participants gave more verbal cues to each other to maintain awareness.

Regarding positive indicators of awareness, we observed more reaction without request in the horizontal condition (mean = 8, SD = 3.0) than in the vertical condition (mean = 3.5, SD = 2.1). The difference was statistically significant (t (10) = −3.01, p = 0.013) (Fig. 5-left). Participants maintained a better awareness of others and offered help without being explicitly asked. For example, in a horizontal condition group, one participant said: "OK, now we can check attractions". Another person then used the filter buttons on the menu bar to hide hotels and show attractions. There were also far more complementary actions in the horizontal condition (mean = 30.8, SD = 10.2) than in the vertical condition (mean = 9.2, SD = 3.9) with a statistically significant difference (t (10) = 4.85, p = 0.0008) (Fig. 5-middle). These actions could be, for example, handing over location cards or two participants dragging and zooming the map in turn. Complementary actions mostly occurred when participants were discussing the itinerary and sorting location cards according to their trip plan. More complementary actions suggest that participants were aware of the activity of other people anticipating actions and favoring higher implicit low-level coordination between people [12]. This finding is also related to the fact that there were more balanced interactions in the horizontal condition (Finding 1). As participants interacted equally, there were more chances of their having complementary actions.

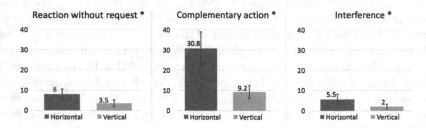

Fig. 5. Average number of *reactions without request, complementary actions*, and *interferences* per condition (means with 95% CI).

We observed a side effect of these balanced interactions in the horizontal condition, there was more interferences in the horizontal condition (mean = 5.5, SD = 3.39) than in the vertical condition (mean = 2, SD = 1.67). The difference is statistically significant (t (10) = 2.27, p = 0.048) (Fig. 5-right). As the horizontal condition fosters more balanced interaction, participants were all engaged in interacting, which can in turn cause more interferences: for example, when two participants wanted to drag the map or were reaching for the same location card. In the vertical condition, there was always one main interactor, a fact which prevented interference.

Finding 3: Groups maintained a good level of awareness in both conditions. In the vertical condition, even if participants made more efforts to maintain awareness, there was little occurrence of implicit coordination. This can be accounted for the emergence of one main interactor handling the large surface (Finding 1). With horizontal displays, participants are more likely to spontaneously help other group members or to finish the actions of others without verbal or explicit synchronization. Consequently, this can lead to more interference since participants interact more with the horizontal surface. Thus, our H3 hypothesis is partially validated. The horizontal condition offers a sufficiently good level of awareness for implicit coordination such as anticipation and assistance actions.

H4: More efficient activity organization in the horizontal condition

To test this hypothesis, we observed how participants organized themselves and discussed good practices, exploration strategies or division of labor

In both conditions, groups used explicit coordination to reach decisions about strategies or to organize work. We did not observe an impact of surface orientation on the number of discussions about strategies between the two conditions (horizontal: mean = 11, SD = 3.52; vertical: mean = 7.67, SD = 4.08; t (10) = 1.51, p = 0.16). However, we observed significantly more parallel actions in the horizontal condition (mean = 11, SD = 6.8) than in the vertical condition (mean = 4.2, SD = 2.99) (t (10) = 2.24, p = 0.048) (Fig. 6-first). For instance, in the horizontal condition, we observed several times a participant organizing the location cards while another person was checking the map. This can be related to our previous findings about balanced interaction (Finding 1) and awareness (Finding 3). Interestingly, in the vertical condition, the effort of maintaining a good level of awareness combined with the emergence of one main interactor for the shared surface did not do away with the need for explicit coordination among participants for strategy and activity organization. Moreover, the main interactor always took control of the activity, thus reducing the potential for parallel actions. In contrast, in the horizontal condition, participants interacted equally and needed to agree explicitly on the activity organization and their strategies. In this condition, more parallel actions were performed on the shared surface.

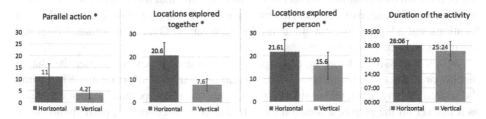

Fig. 6. Average number of *parallel actions, locations explored together* (excluding two opposite groups), *locations explored per person*, and *duration of the activity* (means with 95% CI).

Regarding exploration strategies and task efficiency, in the horizontal condition, participants preferred to check the same location together (5 out of 6 groups), while in the vertical condition, they distributed labor (5 out of 6 groups). Only one group in each condition did it in the opposite way. Excluding these two opposite groups, the number of location explored simultaneously in the horizontal condition is significantly higher than in the vertical condition. (respectively mean = 20.6, SD = 6.84, and mean = 7.6, SD = 3.29), (t (10) = 4.20, p = 0.005) (Fig. 6-second). The simultaneous exploration of locations in the horizontal condition led to significantly (t (34) = 2.53, p = 0.016) more locations explored per person in the horizontal condition (mean = 21.6, SD = 6.84) than in the vertical condition (mean = 15.6, SD = 7.4) (Fig. 6-third).

Finally, even though groups had different exploration strategies in the two conditions, we did not observe a significant difference regarding the time spent on the activity (in horizontal: mean = 28 min 06 s, SD = 3 min; in vertical: mean = 25 min 24 s, SD = 5 min 48 s; t (10) = 0.98 p = 0.35) (Fig. 6-fourth). This suggests that, in the horizontal condition, exploration of location was not as efficient as we expected. Even if participants checked more locations in this condition, they did not reach an agreement on their trip any quicker than in the vertical condition.

Finding 4: Our observations do not validate H4. Participants tended to use two different strategies in the two conditions. In the horizontal condition, groups explored the locations together and checked more locations. While in the vertical condition, participants distributed labor and each person explored fewer locations. In the end, the task duration was similar in both conditions. One strategy was not necessarily more efficient than the other.

H5: More discussions in the horizontal condition

To test this hypothesis, we analyzed how groups conducted discussions, how people shared information, the devices they used to support the discussion, etc. We analyzed both verbal cues and participants' formations

The number of discussions that participants had about hotels, attractions, budget and itinerary were similar in both conditions (horizontal: mean = 48.8, SD = 11.3, vertical: mean = 45.7, SD = 13.5). We initially thought that the design of the activity might have led to this similar number of discussions, and that this number was linked to the number of locations to check. However, participants explored different numbers of locations and adopted different strategies for exploration. Overall, orientation does not seem to influence group discussions.

When discussing a location, participants always used a device - either the shared display or a tablet - to support the discussion and bring in new information. When using the shared display, participants stood close to the screen and pointed at elements such as a marker on the map or a location card. In the vertical condition, participants faced the shared display in a line formation, while in the horizontal condition, they kept the same position throughout the activity. In five out of six groups, two participants stood on the long side and one stood on the short side. In the last group, all participants stood on one long side of the display.

Participants leveraged tablets to introduce new elements into the discussion. In the horizontal condition, probably due to their standing positions around the table, we mostly observed tablet sharing between two participants, such as one person holding his/her tablet towards another, or one person looking over the shoulder of the tablet's owner. We only observed once three participants sharing the same tablet. In the vertical condition, we observed more often three participants sharing the same tablet. Nevertheless, we found no significant difference in the number of times participants shared a tablet (horizontal: mean = 7.17, SD = 3.31, vertical: mean = 4.5, SD = 4.23; $t (10) = 1.22$, $p = 0.25$).

When the discussion did not rely on the shared surface, such as when participants calculated the cost of their trip, participants in the vertical condition always changed their position to a circular arrangement to maintain face-to-face discussion. Either the participant in the middle would step back, or the two participants on the side would step forward. In the horizontal condition, only the group with three participants standing in line changed its position, with the person in the middle stepping back a slightly. Other groups kept their former positions during the discussion.

Finding 5: We did not find a significant difference between the two conditions in the number of discussions within groups. This invalidates our hypothesis of discussions being better supported in the horizontal condition. In both conditions, participants used tablets for sharing information or individually exploring information, to bring arguments into the discussion. Furthermore, unlike in previous work [1], we observed participants re-arranging their formation, and forming more triad formations in the vertical condition.

---

6 Discussion

We studied the impact of display orientation in MSE by replicating and extending previous studies on single displays, in a realistic context, with modern high resolution multi-touch displays. Previous work on single displays is in places contradictory, our results weigh in, confirm or contradict them in places, and extend them (see Table 2). Building on our results and contrasting them to previous, we now look at how display orientation shaped collaboration. We use these results to draw implications for the design of collaborative activities in MSE.

6.1 Creating and Interacting with Content

Our study confirms previous results on the impact of display orientation on interaction [22, 23]. In the horizontal condition, physical interaction with the surface was more equally distributed among group members. The use of tablets does not seem to significantly impact direct interaction with the large surface. However, when looking at interactions that involved inputting information, tablets proved to be particularly beneficial in the vertical condition. Content creation trends toward similarity in the two

Table 2. Comparison of findings from former studies with ours. H and V respectively stand for horizontal and vertical conditions.

	Apparatus	Interaction (low-level)		Group coordination (high-level)		
		Physical interaction	Content creation	Awareness	Activity organization	Discussion / communication
Roger and Lindley 2004 [20]	Interactive tabletop and wall display	H: greater equality; V: main interactor	H: more notes; V: difficulty to write	H: higher level	V: the main interactor organized the task	H: more suggestions
Inkpen et al. 2005 [13]	Paper whiteboard	V: more body movements	V: more difficult to write	-	V: more focused on completing tasks	H: more on-task communication
Potvin et al. 2012 [19]	Paper whiteboard	H: slightly greater equality	-	-	-	H&V: similar number of discussions. V: slightly greater equality
Our study	Multi-surface environment	H: greater equality; V: main interactor	Reduction of difference between H&V	H&V: similar level. H: implicit coordination (assistance & anticipation); V: more efforts on maintaining awareness	H: parallel work; V: more structured & distributed work	H&V: similar number of discussions.

conditions. On a qualitative level, participants valued more the introduction of tablets in the vertical condition than in the horizontal condition. This suggests that MSE reduces differences previously observed in single shared display set-ups.

6.2 Similar Level of Awareness and Discussions

Awareness mechanisms and their consequences on the activity were ignored by Inkpen et al. and Potvin et al. [15], and only briefly analyzed by Rogers and Lindley [23]. In our study, we analyzed awareness in detail, distinguishing positive and negative indicators. Unlike in previous work [23], we found that participants maintained a good level of awareness in both conditions, as the low number of verbal monitoring suggests. However, in the vertical condition, this awareness came at a cost, as participants used far more verbal shadowing, i.e., announcing what they do. Moreover, they kept moving backward to observe the situation, before moving forward to analyze information on the shared display. In our study, the MSE set-up does not seem to impact communication with a number of discussions similar in both conditions (which contradict Rogers and Lindley [23] but confirms Potvin et al. [22]).

6.3 Surface Orientation Influences the Activity Organization

Compared to previous work, we observed more signs of implicit and explicit coordination in the horizontal condition. Participants were more inclined to anticipate the actions of others and to share and agree on strategies or good practices to conduct the task. The activity seemed to run far more naturally, as participants took upon themselves to visit locations and to support each other. However, participants had to make more efforts to ensure that they were in sync. In contrast, distribution of work seemed more efficient in the vertical condition. The person who interacted most with the display also distributed labor and sent information to others (also observed in Rogers and Lindley [23]). Even if participants took collective decisions all the same, the activity seemed more structured, with less interference than in the horizontal condition.

6.4   MSE Set-Ups Shape F-Formations

Our MSE set-up shaped how participants positioned themselves. In the horizontal condition, participants mostly maintained their formation, merely tilting their tablets to show their content to another participant. On the other hand, in the vertical condition, tablet sharing led to changes in position (often semi-circular or side-by-side formation). This suggests that bringing tablets could introduce freedom in group activities. Participants would have a personal workspace to conduct individual exploration, and join group discussions when needed.

6.5   Implications for Design

Our analysis indicated that the surface orientation induced participants to organize their activities in different ways. Horizontal surfaces seem to support more cohesive collaborative activities where participants go through the task together. On the other hand, vertical surfaces seem better suited to cooperative situations in which one person drives an activity and distributes tasks to others. Therefore, we suggest choosing a horizontal surface for activities that require equal participation, such as collaborative learning where participants have to acquire the same skills and knowledge [3]. We suggest using a vertical surface for the activities where one person takes control. Software features could also be considered to facilitate the task organization and distribution, such as providing opportunities for the main interactor to change the contents on others personal devices.

Incorporating indicators on the devices (e.g. showing who is exploring which location) could help improve awareness and decrease the amount of monitoring required. These visual feedbacks could also encourage participants to regulate their activity and mitigate the influence of screen orientation. Besides, if activities involve individual content creation, such as adding comments and doing individual exploration, then introducing handheld devices in complement to the shared surface should lead to more balanced contributions among participants.

In the end, building on the F-formations observed, we suggest to use proxemic interactions for the activities to support discussion, especially the activities involved with rich content or data. Cross-device interaction should support micro-mobile behaviors and support exchange of complex information across devices, such as transfer content or duplicate screens [19].

6.6   Limitations

The set-up used for our study is just one instance within the much wider space of MSE, and further studies are needed to build a solid body of knowledge on the topic. To reduce the number of confounding factors, all participants stood up. This could be questioned since tabletops might be used more widely in a seated position. Participants started the activity working side by side, and while UI elements could be rotated, they all had the same orientation to begin with.

7 Conclusion

MSE are particularly suited to supporting collaborative activities, enabling dynamic combination of devices to support group activities on large shared surfaces and individual activities on personal devices. Although there is a wealth of application examples demonstrating the benefits of MSE, the underlying collaborative dynamics are still unclear. We conducted a study showing that the orientation of a shared display in a MSE shapes group coordination. Our results show that MSE reduces differences between the horizontal and vertical conditions when it comes to create and interact with content. More importantly, it profoundly shapes the way collaborative activities are conducted: using a horizontal surface will lead to better equity of interaction and more cohesive activities. On the other hand, group coordination is more structured and is organized around a main interactor when a vertical display is used.

Acknowledgement. We thank all our participants. This work was partially funded by the China Scholarship Council Ph.D. program and the ANR project JENlab (ANR-13-APPR-0001).

References

1. AlTarawneh, R., Jaber, R.N., Humayoun, S.R., Ebert, A.: Collaborative position patterns for pairs working with shared tiled-wall display using mobile devices. In: Proceedings of the 2015 International Conference on Interactive Tabletops & Surfaces (ITS 2015), pp. 259–264. ACM, November (2015)
2. Al-Megren, S., Kharrufa, A., Hook, J., Holden, A., Sutton, S., Olivier, P.: Comparing fatigue when using large horizontal and vertical multi-touch interaction displays. In: Abascal, J., Barbosa, S., Fetter, M., Gross, T., Palanque, P., Winckler, M. (eds.) INTERACT 2015. LNCS, vol. 9299, pp. 156–164. Springer, Cham (2015). doi:10.1007/978-3-319-22723-8_13
3. Bachour, K., Kaplan, F., Dillenbourg, P.: An interactive table for supporting participation balance in face-to-face collaborative learning. IEEE Trans. Learn. Technol. **3**(3), 203–213 (2010)
4. Bell, G., Dourish, P.: Yesterday's tomorrows: notes on ubiquitous computing's dominant vision. Pers. Ubiquit. Comput. **11**(2), 133–143 (2007)
5. Campos, P., Ferreira, A., Lucero, A.: Collaboration meets interactive surfaces: walls, tables, tablets, and phones. In: Proceedings of the 2013 ACM International Conference on Interactive Tabletops and Surfaces (ITS 2013), pp. 481–482. ACM, October 2013
6. Chokshi, A., Seyed, T., Marinho Rodrigues, F., Maurer, F.: ePlan multi-surface: a multi-surface environment for emergency response planning exercises. In: Proceedings of the Ninth ACM International Conference on Interactive Tabletops and Surfaces (ITS 2015), pp. 219–228. ACM, November 2014
7. Clark, H.H., Brennan, S.E.: Grounding in communication. Perspect. Soc. Shar. Cognit. **13** (1991), 127–149 (1991)
8. DiMicco, J.M., Pandolfo, A., Bender, W.: Influencing group participation with a shared display. In: Proceedings of the 2004 ACM Conference on Computer Supported Cooperative Work (CSCW 2004), pp. 614–623. ACM, November 2004
9. Döring, T., Shirazi, A.S., Schmidt, A.: Exploring gesture-based interaction techniques in multi-display environments with mobile phones and a multi-touch table. In: AVI, vol. 10, p. 419, May 2010

10. Evans, A.C., Wobbrock, J.O., Davis, K.: Modeling collaboration patterns on an interactive tabletop in a classroom setting. In: Proceedings of the 19th ACM Conference on Computer-Supported Cooperative Work & Social Computing, pp. 860–871. ACM, February 2016

11. Fleck, R., Rogers, Y., Yuill, N., Marshall, P., Carr, A., Rick, J., Bonnett, V.: Actions speak loudly with words: unpacking collaboration around the table. In: Proceedings of the ACM International Conference on Interactive Tabletops and Surfaces (ITS 2015), pp. 189–196. ACM, November 2009

12. Gutwin, C., Greenberg, S.: A descriptive framework of workspace awareness for real-time groupware. Comput. Support. Coop. Work (CSCW) 11(3–4), 411–446 (2002)

13. Hall, E.T.: The hidden dimension. Doubleday, Garden City (1966)

14. Hornecker, E., Marshall, P., Dalton, N.S., Rogers, Y.: Collaboration and interference: awareness with mice or touch input. In: Proceedings of the 2008 ACM Conference on Computer Supported Cooperative Work (CSCW 2008), pp. 167–176. ACM, November 2008

15. Inkpen, K., Hawkey, K., Kellar, M., Mandryk, R., Parker, K., Reilly, D., Scott, S., Whalen, T.: Exploring display factors that influence co-located collaboration: angle, size, number, and user arrangement. In: Proceedings of HCI International, vol. 2005 (2005)

16. Luff, P., Heath, C.: Mobility in collaboration. In: Proceedings of the 1998 ACM Conference on Computer Supported Cooperative Work (CSCW 1998). ACM, New York, pp. 305–314 (1998)

17. Kendon, A.: Conducting Interaction Patterns of Behavior in Focused Encounters. CUP Archive, Cambridge (1990)

18. Malone, T.W., Crowston, K.: What is coordination theory and how can it help design cooperative work systems? In: Proceedings of the 1990 ACM Conference on Computer-Supported Cooperative Work (CSCW 1990), pp. 357–370. ACM, September 1990

19. Marquardt, N., Hinckley, K., Greenberg, S.: Cross-device interaction via micro-mobility and F-formations. In: Proceedings of the 25th Annual ACM Symposium on User Interface Software and Technology, pp. 13–22. ACM, October 2012

20. Marshall, P., Hornecker, E., Morris, R., Dalton, N.S, Rogers, Y.: When the fingers do the talking: a study of group participation with varying constraints to a tabletop interface. In: TABLETOP 2008 3rd IEEE International Workshop on Horizontal Interactive Human Computer Systems, pp. 33–40. IEEE, October 2000

21. Perry, M., O'hara, K., Sellen, A., Brown, B., Harper, R.: Dealing with mobility: understanding access anytime, anywhere. ACM Trans. Comput.-Hum. Interact. (TOCHI) 8, 323–347 (2001)

22. Potvin, B., Swindells, C., Tory, M., Storey, M.A.: Comparing horizontal and vertical surfaces for a collaborative design task. Adv. Hum.-Comput. Interact. 2012, 6 (2012)

23. Rogers, Y., Lindley, S.: Collaborating around vertical and horizontal large interactive displays: which way is best? Interact. Comput. 16(6), 1133–1152 (2004)

24. Schmidt, K.: The problem with 'awareness' introductory remarks on 'awareness in CSCW'. In: Computer Supported Cooperative Work (CSCW 2002), vol. 11, no. 3–4, pp. 285–298 (2002)

25. Seyed, T., Costa Sousa, M., Maurer, F., Tang, A.: SkyHunter: a multi-surface environment for supporting oil and gas exploration. In: Proceedings of the 2013 ACM International Conference on Interactive Tabletops and Surfaces (ITS 2013), pp 15–22. ACM (2013)

26. Scott, S.D., Besacier, G., Tournet, J., Goyal, N., Haller, M.: Surface ghosts: promoting awareness of transferred objects during pick-and-drop transfer in multi-surface environments. In: Proceedings of the Ninth ACM International Conference on Interactive Tabletops and Surfaces (ITS 2014), pp. 99–108. ACM, November 2014

27. Scott, S.D., Grant, K.D., Mandryk, R.L.: System guidelines for co-located, collaborative work on a tabletop display. In: Kuutti, K., Karsten, E.H., Fitzpatrick, G., Dourish, P., Schmidt, K. (eds.) ECSCW 2003. Springer, Dordrecht (2003). doi:10.1007/978-94-010-0068-0_9

28. Sugimoto, M., Hosoi, K., Hashizume, H.: Caretta: a system for supporting face-to-face collaboration by integrating personal and shared spaces. In: Proceedings of the SIGCHI Conference on Human Factors in Computing Systems (CHI 2004), pp. 41–48. ACM, April 2004

29. Vasiliou, C., Ioannou, A., Zaphiris, P.: An artifact ecology in a nutshell: a distributed cognition perspective for collaboration and coordination. In: Abascal, J., Barbosa, S., Fetter, M., Gross, T., Palanque, P., Winckler, M. (eds.) INTERACT 2015 Part I. LNCS, vol. 9297, pp. 55–72. Springer, Cham (2015). doi:10.1007/978-3-319-22668-2_5

30. Vauras, M., Iiskala, T., Kajamies, A., Kinnunen, R., Lehtinen, E.: Shared-regulation and motivation of collaborating peers: a case analysis. Psychologia 46(1), 19–37 (2003)

31. Volet, S., Vauras, M., Salonen, P.: Self-and social regulation in learning contexts: an integrative perspective. Educ. Psychol. 44(4), 215–226 (2009)

32. Wallace, J.R., Scott, S.D., Stutz, T., Enns, T., Inkpen, K.: Investigating teamwork and taskwork in single-and multi-display groupware systems. Pers. Ubiquit. Comput. 13(8), 569–581 (2009)

33. Weiser, M.: The computer for the 21st century. Sci. Am. 265(3), 94–104 (1991)

34. Yuill, N., Rogers, Y.: Mechanisms for collaboration: a design and evaluation framework for multi-user interfaces. ACM Trans. Comput.-Hum. Interact. (TOCHI) 19(1), 1 (2012). 25 p.

35. Zagermann, J., Pfeil, U., Rädle, R., Jetter, H.C., Klokmose, C., Reiterer, H.: When tablets meet tabletops: the effect of tabletop size on around-the-table collaboration with personal tablets. In Proceedings of the 34th Annual ACM Conference on Human Factors in Computing Systems (CHI 2016), vol. 13, pp. 53–67. ACM (2015)

Investigating Notifications and Awareness for Multi-user Multi-touch Tabletop Displays

Shuo Niu[✉], D. Scott McCrickard, and Steve Harrison

Computer Science Department, Virginia Tech,
2202 Kraft Drive, Blacksburg, VA 24060, USA
{shuoniu,mccricks,srh}@vt.edu

Abstract. Notifications seek to guide people's attention toward timely, relevant, and important tasks and interactions. This work considers situations in which multiple people are sharing a single large display, with collaborative notifications targeted at increasing team awareness of the joint goals, activities, and interactions. Notifications in recent studies show promise in enhancing awareness of the actions of co-located collaborators, but lacking is critical knowledge to guide the evaluation of the benefits and costs of collaborative activities. This paper presents a framework for notifications in a multi-user multi-touch context. The framework is explored for a card-sorting task performed by two people (a participant and a scripted confederate) on a shared tabletop display. Notifications highlight actions performed by each participant to understand changes in social, action, and activity awareness. Our study investigates individual work, social norms and team performance as three co-located factors that are affected by incorporating notifications.

Keywords: Awareness · Notification · Multi-user multi-touch · Social · Action · Activity

1 Introduction

Recent advances in multi-user multi-touch (MUMT) displays enable support for rich and complex simultaneous co-located collaboration. Multi-touch tabletop displays and wall-mounted displays provide collaborative spaces where people simultaneously interact with the digital content while being able to see and talk to each other, but use of these large displays introduce issues regarding how to support multi-person interaction. Distinguishing characteristics of tabletops, compared to other shared large displays, relates to the increased physical size and the support for multiple simultaneous touches. These differences allow users to establish their own personal spaces within the display and work on complex multi-handed tasks, with added potential to ignore the activities of others—necessitating awareness support such as notifications.

Prior studies have explored how visual designs and notifications influence awareness in collaboration [18, 20, 22]. Shared display notifications seek to address awareness problems, but studies suggest that incorporating notifications comes with attentional cost. Understanding and balancing such tradeoffs center the design and evaluation of notification techniques. Carroll et al. aggregated knowledge from prior

© IFIP International Federation for Information Processing 2017
Published by Springer International Publishing AG 2017. All Rights Reserved
R. Bernhaupt et al. (Eds.): INTERACT 2017, Part III, LNCS 10515, pp. 223–244, 2017.
DOI: 10.1007/978-3-319-67687-6_15

studies on collaborative awareness (e.g. [12, 16, 22]), concluding that collaborators' social, action, and activity awareness must be balanced by notifications [4]. This paper considers those three types of awareness, expanding their definitions to encompass the unique nature of MUMTs—highlighting the importance of awareness of shared activities in MUMT use.

We leverage the model identified by Carroll et al., expanding it into a framework that describes the effect of notification in tabletop-based co-located context. Individual work, social norms, and team performance are three collaboration factors in the framework, for which notifications have significant influence in social, action, and activity awareness. The framework provides an understanding of the effects of notifications—both benefits and costs—in influencing collaborative awareness over the MUMT display. The research outcome provides knowledge for MUMT designers to better use and evaluate notifications in supporting co-located awareness.

The framework is examined in a laboratory study with 61 participants. The study focused on a collaborative card-sorting task, exploring whether notifications that show collaborator activities affect awareness. The results consider two metrics for each of social, action, and activity awareness. The study demonstrates an increased awareness of the actions of others when using notifications, highlighting differences in social norm, task performance, and individual work. The results suggest a research agenda that encourages further investigation toward understanding not only how notifications affect social, action, and activity awareness, but also how notifications can be designed and used to encourage sharing and enhance communication.

2 Related Work

Prior work has highlighted the importance of awareness in collaboration and the value of notifications in helping to achieve awareness. This section examines arguments for why awareness is important, provides an overview of notification research, and describes how prior notification work has relevance to the emerging MUMT domain.

Situation awareness suggests that individual awareness of specific elements, team awareness of shared elements, and communication to share awareness information are critical to teamwork [13, 36, 53]. Understanding of personal workspace helps determine how team members make decisions and takes actions [12]. A high degree of team shared awareness implies collaborators' understanding of the shared elements, which is core to *common ground* [7, 41, 53]. Protocols to develop common ground is a part of social conventions in exchanging awareness information [4, 35, 50]. As such, maintaining awareness of others' actions has long been a topic of interest, including in Gutwin's framework for exploring workspace awareness [22] and Fussell's exploration of how visual cues help the conversational grounding and reduce the efforts to maintain situation awareness [18, 20].

Among the many techniques for awareness, notifications have been widely used to deliver information and achieve awareness [3, 4, 8, 46]. When working in a shared interaction space, people allocate attention to incoming notifications to maintain awareness of collaborators' presence, speech, and activities [22, 23]. The design of notifications for collaborative systems considers tradeoffs between utility benefits and attention costs [4, 6, 38]. Studies show that introducing notifications in groupware may heighten awareness of group work, but restrict individual progress [4, 11]. However, with the emergence of novel collaboration technologies like MUMTs, notification and awareness remain underexplored.

Existing MUMT research introduced (though did not always explicitly discuss) ways to support awareness in teamwork [37, 42, 56, 60]. Affordances of large interaction spaces, face-to-face communication, and simultaneously accessible multitouch not only support collaboration modalities [31, 59], but also provide ways to observe others' activities [31, 37, 55, 61]. As one would expect, efforts to make actions on MUMT displays visible to others lead to new awareness issues. For example, WeSearch and Cambiera integrated interactive visualization widgets to inform collaborators about searches and enhance the awareness of activities, though investigations of both tools suggest that awareness-enhancing widgets lack sufficient communicative benefits to support close collaboration [30, 42]. Pogat is an affective virtual agent that resides at the corner of MUMT tabletops to support affective awareness, resulting in extroverted personal feelings communicated by the tool that sometimes makes people uncomfortable [21]. SIDES uses co-dependent tangible tools to achieve action and activity awareness in a tabletop game, sometimes resulting in idea conflicts when children use the tool one at a time. [14]. Interactive maps OrMis and Canyon use secondary views to support mutual awareness in collaborative exploration, with study results suggesting people often work in turn-taking instead of simultaneously [3, 28]. Navi Badgeboard and Navi Surface use digital badges to increase the awareness of personal achievements and group activities, with a study implying that badges make the student hesitate to participate in collaboration without others' confirmation [5].

Problems with awareness-enhancing techniques in MUMTs are pertinent to individual and team awareness, particularly the effectiveness of communication. Utility and collaboration breakdowns stemming from notifications suggest a need to evaluate how MUMT affordances influence tradeoffs identified in traditional collaboration research. Carroll et al. drew from situation awareness, common ground and workspace awareness in suggesting that social awareness, action awareness, and activity awareness are core in notification design [4]. The model provides awareness breakdowns and suggests practical design strategies for notification systems. This work scopes how notifications may affect group activities, but the large interaction space [52], face-to-face communication [61], dynamic work styles [59], and multi-touch interactions afforded by MUMT displays introduce other factors unique to the MUMT-supported collaboration. The new contextual elements influence how collaborators perceive and react to notifications [12, 57].

Designing notifications for MUMTs needs a conceptual model to outline the benefits of raising collaborative awareness and the costs of interrupting individual tasks. Our research considers the contextual change in collaborative MUMTs, seeking to expand previous understanding of notifications in traditional computer-supported collaboration with the unique aspects of notifications on tabletop displays.

3   MUMT Displays and Collaborative Awareness

Staying aware of others' activities is a secondary but valuable part of co-located collaboration [4, 11]. When collaborating using a MUMT display, people monitor others' activities through multiple communication channels: listening to what others are saying, observing others' body gestures, seeing others' touch actions, and revisiting changes. Awareness on tabletop applications can be augmented with notifications showing others' activity, e.g., visual effects highlighting digital items. Notifications in the co-located workspace inform collaborators of prior group activities, but may influence individual activities and the manner in which collaborators participate group work. To connect prior work on notification design with practical application of MUMT notifications, we examine the use of co-located notifications with Carroll's awareness model. Carroll's model incorporates 3 high-level awareness types with a knowledge structure about notifications in collaborative systems. Action, social and activity awareness are refined from prior research on collaborative awareness, including situation awareness [12], workspace awareness [22, 24] and visual-based grounding process [16]. The model is rooted in practical use of collaborative notifications and clarifies the awareness categories that must be supported through notifications.

Action Awareness. Action awareness refers to the understanding of the ongoing actions carried out by collaborators. In collaborative applications, people know what objects are shared with others and who is modifying them through indicators on the screen. As a part of workspace awareness, these indicators reflect immediate and synchronous actions to the shared artifacts (e.g. *what* questions addressed by workspace awareness information), which influences one's own decision about the next action [12, 22]. MUMT displays provide large interaction space, enabling collaborators to work at different screen position while being able to see what others are doing. The division of screen space, referred as *territoriality* [54], reflects the space need for both individual and collaborative tasks. However, when observing actions in another's territory, awareness might be restricted by the form factors of the display [9, 33]. MUMT affordances influence factors such as *reaction* to the other's activity and *interruptions* to individual work. Direct touch affects how people react to others' actions, since responding in face-to-face collaboration is preferred to be timely, and body cues may attract others' attention. Due to large screen size, reacting to a notification and moving attentional focus requires cognitive effort. People usually defer or even completely leave their own ongoing work when they react to the notified item on the other side of the display [47]. The immediate reaction is a source of breakdowns and may cause interruptions to individual workflow.

Social Awareness. In CSCW, social awareness refers to knowledge of the presence of collaborators. Particularly in remote collaboration, people want to know about collaborators: anyone is available, who is around, who is doing the actions, and other social factors not visible to collaborators [22, 40]. These questions form people's understanding to the presence and identity of other collaborators, as well as the authorship of the actions [22]. Collaborators use language and other visual medium to maintain social awareness, which is a part social interactions for building common ground [7, 19, 20]. When collaborating using a tabletop display, however, issues of existence and engagement is different. The large interaction space affects social interaction. For example, recent study suggests that communication reduces with larger size of the shared display [61]. The introduction of MUMT technology for co-located presence makes mood-related factors such as *verbal communication* and *expressing disagreement* more important [31, 48]. In addition, social presence in a co-located context also encourages collaborators to react to each other or their digital representations (e.g. notifications) [49]. For example, responding to another's action with utterances or body cues shows awareness of other's thoughts and activities [26]. Giving an appropriate response can not only move forward the task, but also increase connectedness and build a closer working relationship. Asking about actions verbally helps capture others' purpose and plan in the collaborative task [22]. Awareness of the social context also influence the exchanging and merging of the individual awareness to develop common ground [53]. In co-located interaction with tabletops, the awareness to the other's social presence might influence people's willingness to consider different possibilities and express disagreements.

Activity Awareness. Activity awareness is the perception of collaborators' plans and motivations [4]. Activity awareness includes not only many aspects of social and action awareness through an understanding of the overall situation, but also a deeper understanding of the current and past workspace information throughout various collaborative events [22]. Activity awareness established from communication and shared views highly influence the effectiveness of collaboration [19, 20]. Higher activity awareness may simplify conversation and coordinate actions in the workspace [20, 22]. Establishing effective activity awareness on MUMTs is challenging. Collaborators are usually involved with others' work in different *coupling styles*—working separately in a *loosely-coupled* style or intensively with a *close-coupled* style [58]. Closer relationships improve collaboration outcomes, but people still need to work independently [30, 58]. Collaborators might be working in parallel during the collaboration, though the size and multi-touch capabilities can result in people not understanding others' activities. But others' activities in the collaborative task can affect individual work [29]. Awareness of the team situation influences the *utility* of the digital artifacts and the *effectiveness* of group work. Although most MUMTs are simultaneously accessible to all collaborators, people need to monitor other's actions on the shared items to decide the appropriateness one's own actions [53]. This understanding, which can be obtained from reading notifications, affects the utility of personal items. Failing to understand others' activities might lead collaborators to perform spurious work. Notifications indicating other's activities have promise in avoiding these problems and boost collaboration, but only if appropriately used.

4 Notification and Awareness

A *notification* is a way to "deliver the current, important information to users in an efficient and effective manner, without causing unwanted distraction to ongoing tasks" [40]. Notifications can heighten awareness of collaborators' activities, though they also introduce costs. Collaborative notification in our research has two characteristics: it presents an immediate alert after the partner makes an important change, and it provides enduring information about past activities. Previous knowledge of notification design and the unique form factors of MUMTs reveals three areas for which notifications affect awareness—individual work, social norms, and team performance—that help clarify the manner in which notifications affect collaborative awareness.

Individual Work. Individual situation awareness is the understanding to the status of the collaborative environment and leads to decision making and action execution [12]. Acting on items used by others, expressing diverse ideas, and pausing individual work to give responses are consequences of awareness to one's own responsibilities. During individual work, the degree for which each collaborator understands the impact of other's activities modifies the individual utility of the shared items. In MUMT collaboration, utility is embodied by which and how touch items are visited. An incoming notification distracts a user's attention from the current focus area to the notification. Given the large interaction space of MUMTs, moving attentive focus might interrupt individual actions, causing breakdowns in workflow. Disagreement may also be limited when notified that a different decision has already been made, for better or worse. Notifications in the face-to-face context heightening awareness of other's activities might enhance mutual understanding, but may also discourage individual thoughts.

Social Norms reflect conventions that affect the *grounding* process in which people communicate and exchange awareness information [7, 17, 20]. With MUMT notifications, collaborators obtain a way to acknowledge and respond to others' activities in the co-located space. Notifications serve as an embodiment of others' presence and activities. In addition to body cues, people can also acknowledge and react to others through interaction with notifications. But higher awareness of social presence may reduce verbal conversations. Notifications manifesting collaborators' past decisions may affect people's willingness to make changes, especially for items changed by others. These influences imply that notifications impact awareness of co-located social context and alter the social norms that guide co-located group work.

Team Performance. Notifications showing other's activities may potentially influence the performance of the collaborative task. Team performance in this study focus on how team situation awareness influence the overall utility and effectiveness of collaborative interaction. Notifications indicating the key changes assist the understanding of other's behavior. With higher awareness of other's actions and activities, people may simplify the face-to-face conversation to make the interaction more efficient [22, 34]. Notifications are also a part of the information upon which people make decisions on the next-up activities. Better understanding of others' activities helps people monitor the progress of the collaborative task, thereby increasing potential effectiveness of the collaboration. Notifications indicating the status of the digital objects help people decide which one to use and influence overall utility of the digital items on the MUMT display.

Framework of Notification and Co-located Awareness. Figure 1 summarizes how notifications impact different types of awareness, with individual work, team performance, and social norms as factors affected by notifications. The manner in which

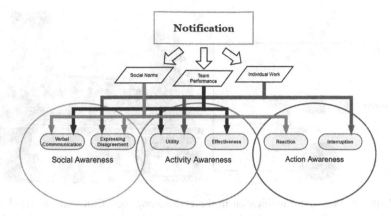

Fig. 1. Framework showing how notifications influence different types of awareness.

notifications influence social, action, and activity awareness comes from connections among factors and aspects in MUMT collaboration for each type of awareness. To better understand the role of notifications in co-located collaboration, a laboratory study is conducted with a collaborative card-sorting task on a MUMT display.

5 Supporting Card Sorting

Card sorting is a common method for organizing information in sense-making activities [27]. In this collaborative information organization activity, people explore a set of cards and sort them into categories. Each card contains an item, and cards in the same category share characteristics. In a card-sorting task, collaborators communicate to share thoughts, manipulate cards to explore the card content, and observe the card status to track the overall task progress. Analogous exploration and decision-making activities on MUMTs can be found in other examples [9, 25, 30, 43].

A card-sorting system is developed with Windows Presentation Foundation on a MUMT display. For our study, the system uses two identical sets of digital cards on two sides of the tabletop. Cards consist of text and pictures representing items to be sorted. Any card can be moved, rotated and zoomed with common multi-finger touch operations [60] by multiple people simultaneously. The system was designed with the guidelines proposed by Morris et al. [44] and Scott et al. [54, 55], replicating controls in each collaborator's personal space. Similar interface layouts can be seen in many other studies [29, 51, 61]. The color-coded category bins are in the center of the table. Users can drag and drop a card onto a bin to categorize it. The card background turns the same color as the bin when sorted. The notification used in the tool consists of an animation and a background color change (Fig. 2). When one user sorts a card into the bin, the card with the same content on his partner's side will shake for one second and then its background changes color. The animation informs the collaborator of an change, with the color indicating card category. Animated notifications have been shown to better attract user's attention compared to other generic notifications [2], which should help raise awareness when using large tabletop displays.

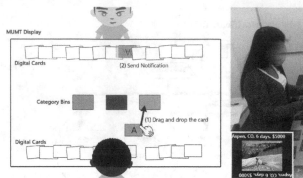

Fig. 2. Left: Interface and a notification in the card-sorting tool. Collaborators stand on two sides of the table and sort cards by dragging and dropping into category bins. Right: The experiment setup and an example card (inset).

6 Indicators of Awareness

There is no complete collection of metrics that fully reflect the different types of awareness, but we sought to identify a number of awareness indicators that reflect their core aspects [26] (Table 1). Carroll et al. defined social awareness as *people's understanding of the current social context*. The co-presence of users in tabletop collaboration affects the communication as well as recognition of communication between people. In the context of our experiment, we identify *verbal response* as the most indicative of social awareness more so than gaze, gesture and other social interaction. Verbal response implies the realization of the social presence of others, which may lead to ad-hoc communications as a part of grounding process [20]. No or few verbal responses in the co-located context suggests that participants are less ready to give feedback, or perhaps even a failure to realize a partner's decisions [49]. A second social awareness indicator, *category change,* is more indirect but interpretive, tying to the core activity of categorizing cards as required by this experiment. Awareness of social presence influences collaborator feelings about the card category. Understanding to the social context of the face-to-face collaboration indicates high social awareness, but may also discourage activities of individuals, such as expressing the intent to change the card sorted by another [11].

Action awareness refers to immediate reactions to others' actions on the shared objects categorized by a collaborator. In co-located collaboration, the moment-to-moment awareness of others' actions influences one's own decisions. Too much information about actions may tax users' ability to comprehend and excessively interrupt one's own activities. *Touch reaction* and *touch distance* were used as indicators of action awareness. Gestural behaviors on touch-enabled items reflect collaborators' cognitive flow [51, 58]. The immediate touch response to other's sorting actions indicates the perception of other's activities. Increased awareness of actions performed in the collaborative space enables participants to more easily identify changed items and understand how they influence their own tasks [22]. Touch distance

Table 1. Indicators of awareness

	Factor	Description	Examples
Social awareness	Verbal response	Collaborator gives feedback after seeing partner's activity	Acknowledgement of changes; Indicating awareness of other's presence and involvement; Verbal responses that initiate ad-hoc conversations and establish common ground
	Category change	Number of times a collaborator sorts previously sorted cards	Modifying others' sorting results; Reflecting level of concerns on other's past decisions; Category changes that indicate lower awareness of the authorship of actions or fewer concerns on changing other's decisions
Action awareness	Touch reaction	Collaborator identifies sorted card location and moves it to category	Reacting to or showing comprehension of other's actions through one's own actions; Touch reactions that influence one's own future actions on the shared items
	Touch distance	Accumulated distance between touch actions	Interruptions by the collaborator; Making effort to respond to other's actions; Increased hand move on the tabletop
Activity awareness	Item utility	Number of card movements per minute	Frequency of accessing different items; Stating or otherwise indicating knowledge of the item category
	Redundant Sort	Number of times collaborator sorts previously sorted cards	Statements reflecting lack of knowledge of other's repeated actions and implied intentions; Overlap in activities with collaborator

is used to evaluate interruption and distraction. We describe it as the accumulated spatial distance between every adjacent touch movement. Higher touch distance implies that the collaborator shifts attentional focus from one region to another. It might interrupt deliberation on the current card and break down card exploration.

Activity awareness influences the level of coordination in collaborative task. Higher activity awareness suggests that users accurately perceive others' goals and actions, and therefore adjust their own activities for higher teamwork effectiveness. Collaborators with higher activity awareness coordinate their own actions in accordance with the others' actions, not only lending more effort to unfinished tasks but also avoiding duplicated work. In this study, we examine activity awareness as it is reflected in item utility and number of times a collaborator sorts previously sorted cards to the same category (called redundant sort). Number of times the collaborator moves the cards reflects overall utility of the MUMT interaction space. With increased awareness of others' activities, we assume collaborators have less concern about interaction conflicts;

therefore more efforts can be spent on exploring the unused items [45]. Duplicating the sorting actions reflects people's knowledge about overall task progress. With low awareness of other's activities, a collaborator may not realize a card has been sorted and may perform a redundant action. Extraneous sorting behavior increases task burden and suggests low activity awareness, reducing task effectiveness.

7 Laboratory Study

Study participants were recruited from a community and university participant pool at our institution. During the experiment, a 55-in Microsoft Perceptive Pixel Display tabletop is placed in the center of a laboratory room with the participants standing on opposite sides (Fig. 2).

7.1 Research Setup

Each participant was assigned to an experiment group: the notification group or the control group. The notification group performed the card sorting task with notifications (see Fig. 2). The control group worked on a system without notifications—card-sorting actions were not reflected in the partner's cards. The task asks participants to sort up to 36 different travel destinations into 3 different categories representing 3 levels of visiting priorities: definitely visit, probably visit, possibly visit. The destinations are presented on 36 digital cards. Each card represents a well-known U.S. city (e.g., Boston, New York) with suggested days of travel and projected cost.

The participants were asked to sort the cards collaboratively with their partner, evaluating destinations as a team. To categorize a card, a participant drags and drops the card to a color-coded category bin. Each card can only be in one category. Once a card is sorted, the matching card on the partner's side reflects the new category. To measure the category change, the participants were notified that after the partner sorted a card and it is not necessary to sort it sorted again if there is agreement with the card category. For the notification group, sorting results in a highlighting notification on the same card on the partner's side and changes its background color. For the control group, sorting a card has no visual effect on the partner's card.

Participants were informed of the task requirements and system use and practiced with the system by moving and sorting an unrelated set of cards. The participants were told to sort around 15 cards based on the provided information on the card. They were also instructed that each category should contain at least 1 card, the task terminates if lasts longer than 20 min and one should not use the card on the partner's side. 61 participants (60 undergraduate and 1 graduate student, 37 females, mean age 19.9, SD 1.5) took part in the experiment. The participants had various majors: computer science (N = 9), psychology (8), biology (5) and neuroscience (4). 30 participants (19 females) were in the notification group and 31 (18 females) in the control group.

7.2 Experiment Confederate

Variables related to personality, aggressiveness, and preferences can greatly influence study results [32]. Because we were interested in comparing reactions to partner actions and system notifications, we chose to incorporate a research confederate. A *confederate* is a member of the experiment team who pretends to be a participant but who follows a pre-defined script. The confederate was instructed to perform identical actions for all participants. The confederate's script was developed with the following criteria to measure awareness factors: (1) For both groups, the confederate sorts the equal and reasonable number of cards (Verbal and Touch Response). (2) The participants' touch actions should not be greatly interfered by the partner (Item Utility and Touch Distance). (3) The partner sorted each designated card to the same category so that the two groups have the same situation to make changes (Category Change). The variable-controlled study influences the observation of the awareness indicators in two ways. First, since the confederate performs identical sorts for all participants, each participant receives same number of notifications, therefore the participants have equal chance to give verbal responses and touch reactions to the partner, with equal likelihood of interruption by sorting actions. This helps avoid cases of low notification count. Secondly, personal preference influences choices; use of a confederate ensures the two groups experience similar conditions. This helps avoid situations of participant reluctance to change category because the partner dominates collaboration.

An undergraduate research team member served as confederate and performed the card-sorting task with all participants. Participants did not know they would be working with a confederate before the study. If the participant asked questions or made a comment, the confederate gave brief feedback, but she did not engage directly with the participant's sorting activity. For example, if the participant asked "Do you want go to Boston?" The confederate will reply, "Yeah, you can sort it to whatever category you like." Before the actual experiment, the confederate practiced the task for 4 times with different persons for timing and quality.

To examine the awareness indicators under the same condition, the confederate followed the same pre-defined script across all sessions. A timer is provided at the corner of experiment room to let the confederate monitor the time. At the beginning of the task, the confederate suggests that they look at all the cards. Then after a period of time the confederate sorts one card to one category. The confederate sorts 12 cards in total. The order of the card sorting and categories where the cards were sorted were same with all participants, as showed in Table 2. When sorting 6 of the 12 cards, the confederate gives a verbal explanation. When sorting the other 6 cards, the confederate does not say anything (see column 4 in Table 2). If the confederate's sorting action conflicts with the participant's ongoing speech or actions, the confederate will delay her action a few seconds to let the participant finish. Since the confederate always sorts the same set of cards with the approximately same time interval, participants' verbal and gestural reactions to the confederate's sorting actions can be compared between groups.

Table 2. Confederate script. Column 1: time for each sort. Columns 2 & 3: card destination and category for each time. Column 4: whether confederate gives verbal explanation.

Time (MM:SS)	Card	Category	Verbal description
01:00	Boston	Definitely visit	Yes
01:30	Annapolis	Probably Visit	Yes
02:00	Washington	Possibly visit	No
03:00	Charleston	Definitely visit	No
03:30	Miami Beach	Probably visit	Yes
04:00	Napa Valley	Possibly visit	Yes
04:30	New Orleans	Definitely visit	No
05:00	Myrtle Beach	Probably visit	No
05:30	Richmond	Possibly visit	Yes
06:00	San Francisco	Definitely visit	No
06:30	San Antonio	Probably visit	No
07:00	Raleigh	Possibly Visit	Yes

7.3   Data Collecting Method

To quantify the awareness indicators in the study, we use 2 sources of data. An overhead camera over the center of the tabletop captured and saved all actions. The system also tracked and logged each touch movement performed on the MUMT display. Card movement records start at a touch on the cards and end when all fingers on that card leave the display, with collected attributes of each record including the card content, owner, current category, start and end point timestamps and pixel coordination, and whether the card is dragged and dropped into a bin and the category of the bin.

Video Data Analysis. The *verbal response* for the social awareness is reflected in reactions to confederate card sorting. We focus the video analysis of *card-sorting events*. 5 research team members independently transcribed card-sorting events in the video records. 12 events were identified in the video track first, then the research members took records of participant verbal feedback. 2 team members transcribed the notification group and another 2 transcribed the control group, while the lead researcher transcribed all videos in both groups. Each person worked individually without interaction. Thus, each record has 3 transcription records from 3 different team members. To ensure reasonable agreement, for each card-sorting event the participant is considered to give a verbal response if at least 2 records indicate an interaction.

Touch Data Analysis. The other 5 awareness indicators were quantified from touch logs. Each card movement performed by the participants were categorized into one of 3 touch categories – *moving touch* (MT), *sorting touch* (ST) and *awareness touch* (AT). MTs are the card movement before the card is sorted. STs are the actions of dragging-and-dropping the card into a category bin. ATs are the touch actions of moving the cards that already be sorted. *Touch reaction* is measured as the number of events for which the confederate sorted a card and the participant moved that card within 10 s. Item utility is the number of touch movements performed by the partici- pant, measured in touches per minute. The item utilities of the 3 touch types were measured separately. The card touching frequencies in each of the 12 card-sorting events intervals were calculated (from the beginning to the 1st card-sorting, and all 11 intervals between the 12 card-sorting events). Touch distance is calculated as the total distance between the start points of every pair of adjacent touch movements within the 10 s. 12 touch distance records are recorded for each of confederate card-sorting event. Category changes and redundant sort are the card-sorting events in which a participant sorts a card that has already been sorted, when the card is dragged-and-dropped into the different and the same category, respectively.

8   Results

One participant in the control group who did not work collaboratively as instructed and whose data was not considered in the analysis. Average task time for the notification group and the control group are 8.72 (SD = 9.55) and 9.55 (SD = 2.49) minutes, respectively. The participants in the notification group sorted 18.00 cards on average (SD = 7.64) and the control group sorted 18.83 cards on average (SD = 8.63). Since the two groups do not differ in task involvement, we focused on how notification affects the social, action and activity awareness. Differences for ANOVA tests for each of the awareness indicators is considered significant at a $p < 0.05$ level.

8.1   Verbal Response and Touch Reaction

Verbal response indicates participants' social awareness of giving feedback to the confederate and touch reaction indicates the action awareness of confederate's actions. These two awareness factors both measure immediate reactions to confederate's actions. The verbal response and touch reaction form 4 conditions: (A) the participant does not have any response behavior. (B) The participant gives a verbal response, but does not touch the sorted card. (C) The participant does not give a verbal response, but has an action to move the sorted card to a storage place. (D) The participant touches the sorted card and gives verbal response. Figure 3 shows the average numbers and standard deviations (in parentheses) of events in each condition.

When neither giving a verbal response to the confederate nor touching the card that was just sorted (condition A), the participant is less likely to notice nor is care about the confederate sorting behavior. In contrast, responding to the confederate's behavior and having some touch reactions (condition D) suggests that the participant paid attention to the confederate and acknowledges the idea or intent. In the study the notification group gives no response and both responses 3.5 times and 3.07 times respectively, compared to 4.33 and 1.97 for the control group in these conditions. The notification group responds significantly more times with both responses ($p = 0.0078$) and fewer times giving no response ($p = 0.0354$). The results suggest that the noti group has higher awareness of confederate's sorting behaviors than the control group.

Participants in the control group make a verbal utterance an average of 4.8 times, higher than the notification group's 2.8 times ($p = 0.0001$). The control group touches a card sorted by the confederate 0.9 times without a verbal reply, less than the notification group's 2.63 times ($p < 0.0001$). Considering events with both touch and

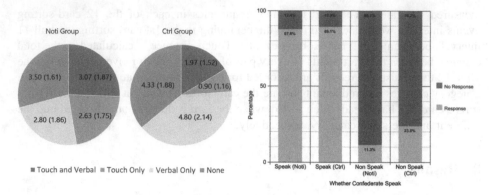

Fig. 3. Left: Numbers of confederate card-sorting events in 4 feedback conditions. Right: The 2 bars on left show percentage of events when the participant gives a verbal utterance in response to confederate verbal reasoning upon sorting. The 2 bars on the right show the percentages when the confederate sorts the card without saying anything.

verbal response, the notification group gave a verbal response 5.87 times and a touch reaction 5.7 times, compared to 6.77 and 2.87 times for the control group. The difference in condition (B) and (C) for the two groups suggests that the notification group was more likely to respond by moving a card rather than speaking to the confederate.

We further examined verbal communication based on when the confederate sorts a card. Figure 3 illustrates events when the confederate speaking resulting in participant verbal response. When the confederate said something while sorting the card, verbal replies were given almost 90% of the time regardless of group (two left bars in Fig. 3). The notification group gives fewer verbal responses (11.3%) when the confederate did not say anything, while the control group speaks to the confederate in 23.8% of the confederate's card-sorting events, a significant difference (p = 0.0146) (see Fig. 3, two right bars). This indicates that the notification group is less likely to initiate a conversation after capturing confederate's action. Comparing differences in immediate reactions between the two groups, the notification group has higher action awareness than the control group, but lower social awareness in giving verbal feedback.

8.2 Item Utility and Touch Distance

Item utility reflects activity awareness, influencing action performance. Touch distance reflects the effort participants spent in reacting to confederate's actions. Both indicators relate to action flow during sorting. Figure 4 shows average item utilities between confederate's card-sorting events. The two groups move cards at similar frequency until the confederate sorted the third card, when the control group moves unsorted cards at a lower frequency. The average moving frequency for the notification group is 19.72 (SD = 6.23) and control group is 16.14 (SD = 6.92), with former significant higher than latter (p = 0.0218). It implies that participants without notification were less effective in visiting unsorted cards, suggesting low activity awareness.

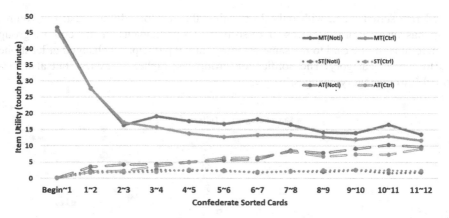

Fig. 4. Item utility of each touch type between the confederate card-sorting events.

Figure 5 shows average touch distance 10 s before and after each of the 12 confederate's card-sorting events, with notification group (52.31 in., SD = 3.20) larger than control group (41.28 in., SD = 3.20, p = 0.0188), suggesting that participants in the notification group have higher action awareness and are more likely to shift focus. After a notification, participants stop exploring the current area to focus on the highlighted card, and then resume work near the highlighted card. The cognitive breakdown resulting from high action awareness may interrupt ongoing thoughts and ideation.

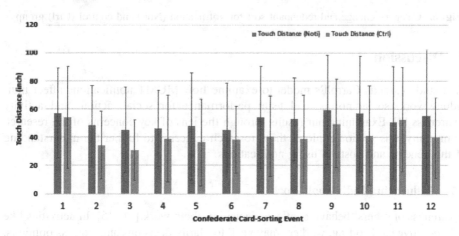

Fig. 5. The touch distances 10 s before and after each confederate card-sorting event. The distance is measured in inches. The error bars show ±1 standard deviation.

8.3   Category Change and Redundant Sort

Changing a card's category that was previously sorted by the confederate reflects either disagreement or lack of awareness, while unnecessarily sorting to the same category reflects low awareness. Figure 6 illustrates all category change and redundant sort instances. Only 4 participants in the notification group re-sorted cards after the confederate sorted them, with only 2 changing the category. In contrast, the control group has many more instances of re-sorting: 19 participants in the control group re-sorted at least one card to the same category, and 9 participants changed at least one card to another category. The notification group had higher awareness but also performed fewer category changes.

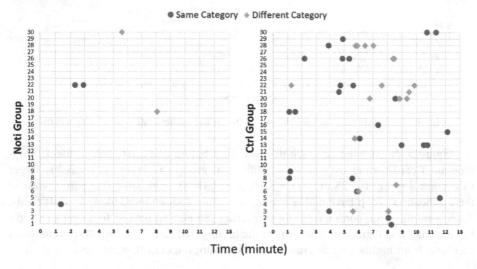

Fig. 6. Category change and redundant sort for notification (Noti) and control (Ctrl) groups.

9   Discussion

This study extends Carroll's model to examine how MUMT notifications affect individual work, social norms, and team performance for social, action, and activity awareness [4]. Examining our results through the lens of key concerns of the research community, this section explores these research concerns to further the understanding of the benefits and costs in using notifications.

9.1   Influencing Individual Work

Awareness of others' behaviors affects decisions about work [11, 36]. In activities like collaborative card sorting, workers may need to clarify decisions and express opinions. Our study shows how notifications can redirect individual work by affecting item utility, expressing disagreement, and causing interruptions. Notifications deliver awareness information into the personal space, resulting in others' actions exerting influence on individual work. In co-located teamwork, perceiving and understanding others' behaviors is indispensable to individual work [53]. Historically, this occurs through observation and conversation, but notifications provide an alternate awareness path. Our study reveals how connecting with others is important in raising awareness, drawing attention to others and their personal space [54]. With notifications, it is possible to recognize others' actions within one's own interaction space. Closer indicators of other's behaviors blend with items in the individual space, affecting individual task performance. Notifications influence how awareness information is delivered, necessitating decisions on how to craft notifications to encourage behavior. The attention-attracting nature of notifications encourages mental shifts—risking workflow breakdowns by redirecting attention and action.

When using notifications on tabletop displays, designers can employ notifications to complement collaborative awareness and intensify mutual influence between individual work, especially when collaborators engage in the personal space and risk awareness problems (e.g. opposite orientation [33] and long referring distance [9]). Users are likely to classify the items and tasks as "completed-by-others" and "to-be-finished", therefore lean more considerations and actions on the latter. Benefits include more attention on the unfinished work and better item utility, but it could weaken consideration of alternatives and interrupts personal work. **Designers need to consider appropriate ways to present notifications, realizing the tradeoff between intrusiveness to the individual's on-going task and increased understanding to alternatives and new possibilities brought by others' actions.**

9.2 Influencing Social Norms

Social norms play an important role in managing co-located work for MUMTs [1, 35]. In face-to-face design activities like card sorting, participants follow social conventions and protocols to communicate and conduct joint activities. Collaborators using tabletops become aware of others' actions in two ways: by observing another person perform an action and by observing the results of the action. Our results suggest that notifications heighten awareness of partner actions, changing participant behavior—though without discussion or comment as is the norm. Instead, reactions are directed toward the shared screen via lightweight touches. Even though the instigator of an action is present, people focus on technology rather than the collaborator.

This social norm finding furthers knowledge of grounding in co-located collaboration [7, 41]. Notifications can result in reluctance to express contrary thought: since they manifest others' activities, they may increase negotiation and persuasion costs. Contrary to the notion that face-to-face communication is considered a low-cost way to build common ground [41], understanding others through notifications may supersede a need to communicate—regardless of whether it leads to optimal outcome.

Notifications facilitate development of common ground, informing collaborators of others' activities. However, the ability to react by touch rather than verbally can result in an inability to gain confirmation [41], lessening connection found in verbal responses. When employing notifications, MUMT designers must consider the effects on face-to-face communication. In applications where collaborators benefit from verbal communication, our work suggests that notifications may create negative norms that discourage collaborators from talking about key issues. **Designers should leverage notifications to incite desired verbal communication while realizing the costs of the notifications: users working in parallel with notification-supported communication can increase efficiency of the collaborative task exchanges, but notifications may cause degradation in performance toward individual task goals.**

9.3   Influencing Team Performance

In face-to-face collaboration, perceiving and processing verbal and touch actions in co-located space is time-consuming. With notifications, participants have a path to recognize collaborators' thoughts and intentions, lessening perceived need to discuss the action. This can decrease time communicating with partners, smoothing the move to the next action and avoiding performing extra work. Our notifications seemed to reduce this need—though we acknowledge that other types of notifications might encourage verbal communication [43].

Salas et al. identify effects between individual and team situation awareness [53]. Awareness depends on environmental elements and collaborator communication [12, 53]. In MUMT-supported collaboration, these activities might be depressed by larger interaction space [61]. Notifications add flexibility to awareness management of co-located interaction. Instead of relying on body cues and conversation, well-designed notifications can tailor visibility and availability of information, providing more freedom to users in identifying others' activities. Flexibility in awareness management smooths simultaneous interaction by reducing conflicting actions (e.g. sorting a card to different category) so collaborators can work independently without intrusion [59].

Managing concurrent activities in co-located space influences participation and mutual awareness of collaboration [10, 15, 26]. In simultaneous interactions with MUMTs, availability of multi-touch interactions mean collaborators withdraw from interpersonal interactions and avoid conflicts by engaging in individual interactions—with the danger of reducing performance and awareness. Though interpersonal communication has long been recognized as the core to building common ground, notification-based understanding may provide enough grounding information in MUMT collaboration. **Tabletop designers could utilize notifications to improve collaborators' ability to work independently, especially for collaborative tasks that are suitable for divide-and-conquer, therefore improving team efficiency through simultaneous and synchronized work.**

10   Conclusions and Future Work

Notifications have been widely employed in supporting collaboration—they deliver current and important events in the collaborative space and heighten the awareness of other activities [4, 39]. Prior work on awareness-enhancing designs and tools on MUMTs focus on supporting the awareness for a single workspace element. This study expands previous knowledge by providing a critical understanding of using notifications in MUMT-supported collaboration. Three types of awareness are evaluated through a user study: social awareness, action awareness, and activity awareness. Our findings are grounded in contextual differences between traditional computer-supported collaboration and the action-highlighting collaboration on a shared tabletop display. Benefits and costs of using notifications are presented to foster future notification design for MUMT-based groupware.

Future work will investigate notification effect on personal and shared spaces in MUMTs. This research considered limited situations; it is important to consider approaches in which the style, number, and level of interaction differ. Also, notifications in this study affect interactions in limited ways, and it would be helpful to identify ways that notifications encourage and facilitate positive interpersonal communication.

References

1. Al-Qaraghuli, A., Zaman, H.B., Olivier, P., Kharrufa, A., Ahmad, A.: Analysing tabletop based computer supported collaborative learning data through visualization. In: Badioze Zaman, H., Robinson, P., Petrou, M., Olivier, P., Shih, T.K., Velastin, S., Nyström, I. (eds.) IVIC 2011. LNCS, vol. 7066, pp. 329–340. Springer, Heidelberg (2011). doi:10.1007/978-3-642-25191-7_32
2. Bartram, L., Ware, C., Calvert, T.: Moticons: detection, distraction and task. Int. J. Hum. Comput. Stud. **58**(5), 515–545 (2003)
3. Bortolaso, C., Oskamp, M., Phillips, W.G., Gutwin, C., Graham, T.C.N.: The effect of view techniques on collaboration and awareness in tabletop map-based tasks. In: BT - Proceedings of the Ninth ACM International Conference on Interactive Tabletops and Surfaces, ITS 2014, Dresden, Germany, 16–19 November 2014 (2014)
4. Carroll, J.M., Neale, D.C., Isenhour, P.L., Rosson, M.B., McCrickard, D.S.S.: Notification and awareness: synchronizing task-oriented collaborative activity. Int. J. Hum. Comput. Stud. **58**(5), 605–632 (2003)
5. Charleer, S., Klerkx, J., Odriozola, S., Luis, J., Duval, E., Santos Odriozola, J.L., Duval, E.: Improving awareness and reflection through collaborative, interactive visualizations of badges. In: ARTEL 13: Proceedings of the 3rd Workshop on Awareness and Reflection in Technology-Enhanced Learning, pp. 69–81. CEUR-WS (2013)
6. Chewar, C.M., McCrickard, D.S., Sutcliffe, A.G.: Unpacking critical parameters for interface design. In: Proceedings of the 2004 Conference on Designing Interactive Systems Processes, Practices, Methods, and Techniques - DIS 2004, Cambridge, MA, USA, p. 279. ACM (2004)
7. Clark, H.H., Brennan, S.S.E.: Grounding in communication. In: Perspectives on Socially Shared Cognition, pp. 127–149 (1991)
8. Van Dantzich, M., Robbins, D., Horvitz, E., Czerwinski, M.: Scope: providing awareness of multiple notifications at a glance. In: Proceedings of the Working Conference on Advanced Visual Interfaces, Trento, Italy, pp. 267–281. ACM (2002)
9. Doucette, A., Gutwin, C., Mandryk, R.: Effects of arm embodiment on implicit coordination, co-presence, and awareness in mixed-focus distributed tabletop tasks. In: Proceedings of the 41st Graphics Interface Conference, Halifax, Nova Scotia, Canada, pp. 131–138. Canadian Information Processing Society (2015)
10. Doucette, A., Gutwin, C., Mandryk, R.L., Nacenta, M.A., Sharma, S.: Sometimes when we touch: how arm embodiments change reaching and collaboration on digital tables. In: Proceedings of the 2013 Conference on Computer Supported Cooperative Work (CSCW 2013), San Antonio, Texas, USA, pp. 193–202. ACM (2013)
11. Dourish, P., Bellotti, V.: Awareness and coordination in shared workspaces. In: Proceedings of the 1992 ACM Conference on Computer-Supported Cooperative Work, pp. 107–114. ACM, New York (1992)
12. Endsley, M.R.: Toward a theory of situation awareness in dynamic systems. Hum. Factors J. Hum. Factors Ergon. Soc. **37**(1), 32–64 (1995)
13. Endsley, M.R., Robertson, M.M.: Situation awareness in aircraft maintenance teams. Int. J. Ind. Ergon. **26**(2), 301–325 (2000)

14. Fan, M., Antle, A.N., Neustaedter, C., Wise, A.F.: Exploring how a co-dependent tangible tool design supports collaboration in a tabletop activity. In: Proceedings of the 18th International Conference on Supporting Group Work (GROUP 2014), Sanibel Island, Florida, USA, pp. 81–90. ACM (2014)

15. Fischer, J.E., Reeves, S., Moran, S., Greenhalgh, C., Benford, S., Rennick-Egglestone, S.: Understanding mobile notification management in collocated groups. In: Bertelsen, O.W., et al. (eds.) ECSCW 2013, pp. 21–44. Springer, London (2013). doi:10.1007/978-1-4471-5346-7_2

16. Fussell, S.R., Kraut, R.E., Lerch, F.J., Scherlis, W.L., McNally, M.M., Cadiz, J.J.: Coordination, overload and team performance: effects of team communication strategies. In: Proceedings of the 1998 ACM Conference on Computer Supported Cooperative Work, pp. 275–284. ACM, New York (1998)

17. Fussell, S.R., Kraut, R.E., Siegel, J.: Coordination of communication: effects of shared visual context on collaborative work. In: Proceedings of the 2000 ACM Conference on Computer Supported Cooperative Work, pp. 21–30. ACM, New York (2000)

18. Gergle, D., Kraut, R.E., Fussell, S.R.: Action as language in a shared visual space. In: Proceedings of the 2004 ACM Conference on Computer Supported Cooperative Work, pp. 487–496. ACM, New York (2004)

19. Gergle, D., Kraut, R.E., Fussell, S.R.: Language efficiency and visual technology. J. Lang. Soc. Psychol. 23(4), 491–517 (2004)

20. Gergle, D., Kraut, R.E., Fussell, S.R.: Using visual information for grounding and awareness in collaborative tasks. Hum.-Comput. Interact. 28(1), 1–39 (2013)

21. Di Giacomo, E., Lubiw, A., Zimmer, B., Kerren, A., Cernea, D., Weber, C., Kerren, A., Ebert, A.: Group affective tone awareness and regulation through virtual agents. In: Bickmore, T., Marsella, S., Sidner, C. (eds.) IEEE Information Visualization, pp. 247–259. Springer, Heidelberg (2014)

22. Gutwin, C., Greenberg, S.: A descriptive framework of workspace awareness for real-time groupware. Comput. Support. Coop. Work (CSCW) 11(3–4), 411–446 (2002)

23. Gutwin, C., Greenberg, S.: Design for individuals, design for groups: tradeoffs between power and workspace awareness. In: Proceedings of the Conference on Computer-Supported Cooperative Work, Seattle, Washington, USA, pp. 207–216. ACM (1998)

24. Gutwin, C., Roseman, M., Greenberg, S.: A usability study of awareness widgets in a shared workspace groupware system. In: Proceedings of the 1996 ACM Conference on Computer Supported Cooperative Work, pp. 258–267. ACM, New York (1996)

25. Hinrichs, U., Carpendale, S.: Gestures in the wild. In: Proceedings of the 2011 Annual Conference on Human Factors in Computing Systems - CHI 2011, Vancouver, BC, Canada, p. 3023. ACM (2011)

26. Hornecker, E., Marshall, P., Dalton, N.S., Rogers, Y.: Collaboration and interference: awareness with mice or touch input. In: Proceedings of the 2008 ACM Conference on Computer Supported Cooperative Work, pp. 167–176. ACM, New York (2008)

27. Hudson, W.: Card sorting. In: The Encyclopedia of Human-Computer Interaction, 2nd edn. (2013)

28. Ion, A., Chang, Y.-L.B., Haller, M., Hancock, M., Scott, S.D.: Canyon: providing location awareness of multiple moving objects in a detail view on large displays. In: Proceedings of the SIGCHI Conference on Human Factors in Computing Systems - CHI 2013, Paris, France, p. 3149. ACM (2013)

29. Isenberg, P., Elmqvist, N., Scholtz, J., Cernea, D., Ma, K.-L., Hagen, H., Kwan-Liu Ma, K.-L., Hagen, H.: Collaborative visualization: definition, challenges, and research agenda. In: Information Visualization, pp. 310–326. SAGE Publications, London (2011)

30. Isenberg, P., Fisher, D., Paul, S.A., Morris, M.R., Inkpen, K., Czerwinski, M., Paul, S.A., Morris, M.R., Inkpen, K., Czerwinski, M.: An exploratory study of co-located collaborative

visual analytics around a tabletop display. In: 2010 IEEE Symposium on Visual Analytics Science and Technology (VAST), Salt Lake City, Utah, USA, pp. 179–186. IEEE (2010)

31. Isenberg, P., Tang, A., Carpendale, S.: An exploratory study of visual information analysis. In: Proceedings of the SIGCHI Conference on Human Factors in Computing Systems, Florence, Italy, pp. 1217–1226. ACM (2008)

32. Kohn, M.L., Schooler, C.: Work and Personality: An Inquiry into the Impact of Social Stratification. Ablex Publishing, Norwood (1983)

33. Kruger, R., Carpendale, S., Scott, S.D., Greenberg, S.: Roles of orientation in tabletop collaboration: comprehension, coordination and communication. Comput. Support. Coop. Work 13(5–6), 501–537 (2004)

34. Lee, J., Tatar, D., Harrison, S.: Micro-coordination: because we did not already learn everything we need to know about working with others in kindergarten. In: Proceedings of the ACM 2012 Conference on Computer Supported Cooperative Work (CSCW 2012), Seattle, Washington, USA, pp. 1135–1144. ACM (2012)

35. Mark, G., Fuchs, L., Sohlenkamp, M.: Supporting groupware conventions through contextual awareness. In: Hughes, J.A., Prinz, W., Rodden, T., Schmidt, K. (eds.) Proceedings of the Fifth European Conference on Computer Supported Cooperative Work, pp. 253–268. Springer, Dordrecht (1997). doi:10.1007/978-94-015-7372-6_17

36. Mark, G., Kobsa, A., Gonzalez, V., Clark, H.H., Brennan, S.E., Endsley, M.R., Robertson, M., Rittenbruch, M., Salmon, P.M., Stanton, N.A., Walker, G.H., Baber, C., Jenkins, D.P., McMaster, R., Young, M.S.: What really is going on? Review of situation awareness models for individuals and teams. In: Proceedings of Sixth International Conference on Information Visualisation, vol. 14, no. 2, pp. 127–149 (2002)

37. Marshall, P., Hornecker, E., Morris, R., Dalton, N.S., Rogers, Y.: When the fingers do the talking: a study of group participation with varying constraints to a tabletop interface. In: 3rd IEEE International Workshop on Horizontal Interactive Human Computer Systems (TABLETOP 2008), pp. 33–40 (2008)

38. McCrickard, D.S., Abel, T.D., Scarpa, A., Wang, Y., Niu, S.: Collaborative design for young children with autism: design tools and a user study. In: 2015 International Conference on Collaboration Technologies and Systems (CTS), pp. 175–182. IEEE (2015)

39. McCrickard, D.S., Chewar, C.M.: Attuning notification design to user goals and attention costs (2003). http://portal.acm.org/citation.cfm?doid=636772.636800

40. McCrickard, D.S.S., Czerwinski, M., Bartram, L.: Introduction: design and evaluation of notification user interfaces. Int. J. Hum. Comput. Stud. 58(5), 509–514 (2003)

41. Monk, A.: Common ground in electronically mediated communication: Clark's theory of language use (2014)

42. Morris, M.R., Fisher, D., Wigdor, D.: Search on surfaces: exploring the potential of interactive tabletops for collaborative search tasks. Inf. Process. Manag. 46(6), 703–717 (2010)

43. Morris, M.R., Lombardo, J., Wigdor, D.: WeSearch: supporting collaborative search and sensemaking on a tabletop display. In: Proceedings of the 2010 ACM Conference on Computer Supported Cooperative Work (CSCW 2010), Savannah, Georgia, USA, pp. 401–410. ACM (2010)

44. Morris, M.R., Paepcke, A., Winograd, T., Stamberger, J.: TeamTag: exploring centralized versus replicated controls for co-located tabletop groupware. In: Proceedings of the SIGCHI Conference on Human Factors in Computing Systems, Montréal, Québec, Canada, pp. 1273–1282. ACM (2006)

45. Morris, M.R., Ryall, K., Shen, C., Forlines, C., Vernier, F.: Beyond "social protocols": multi-user coordination policies for co-located groupware (2004)

46. Paul, C.L., Komlodi, A., Lutters, W.: Interruptive notifications in support of task management. Int. J. Hum. Comput. Stud. **79**, 20–34 (2015)
47. Peltonen, P., Kurvinen, E., Salovaara, A., Jacucci, G., Ilmonen, T., Evans, J., Oulasvirta, A., Saarikko, P.: It's Mine, Don't Touch!: interactions at a large multi-touch display in a city centre. In: Proceedings of the SIGCHI Conference on Human Factors in Computing Systems (CHI 2008), Florence, Italy, pp. 1285–1294. ACM (2008)
48. Piper, A.M., O'Brien, E., Morris, M.R., Winograd, T.: SIDES: a cooperative tabletop computer game for social skills development. In: Proceedings of the 2006 ACM Conference on Computer Supported Cooperative Work (CSCW 2006), Banff, Alberta, Canada, pp. 1–10. ACM (2006)
49. Reeves, B., Nass, C.: How People Treat Computers, Television, and New Media Like Real People and Places. CSLI Publications and Cambridge University Press, Cambridge (1996)
50. Rittenbruch, M.: Atmosphere: a framework for contextual awareness. Int. J. Hum.-Comput. Interact. **14**(2), 159–180 (2002)
51. Rogers, Y., Hazlewood, W., Blevis, E., Lim, Y.-K.: Finger talk: collaborative decision-making using talk and fingertip interaction around a tabletop display. In: CHI '04 Extended Abstracts on Human Factors in Computing Systems (CHI EA 2004), Vienna, Austria, pp. 1271–1274. ACM (2004)
52. Ryall, K., Forlines, C., Shen, C., Morris, M.R.: Exploring the effects of group size and table size on interactions with tabletop shared-display groupware. In: Proceedings of the 2004 ACM Conference on Computer Supported Cooperative Work - CSCW 2004, Chicago, Illinois, USA, p. 284. ACM (2004)
53. Salas, E., Prince, C., Baker, D.P., Shrestha, L.: Situation awareness in team performance: implications for measurement and training. Hum. Factors J. Hum. Factors Ergon. Soc. **37**(1), 123–136 (1995)
54. Scott, S.D., Carpendale, M.S.T., Inkpen, K.M., Sheelagh, M., Carpendale, T., Inkpen, K.M.: Territoriality in collaborative tabletop workspaces. In: Proceedings of the 2004 ACM Conference on Computer Supported Cooperative Work (CSCW 2004), Chicago, Illinois, USA, pp. 294–303. ACM (2004)
55. Scott, S.D., Grant, K.D., Mandryk, R.L.: System guidelines for co-located, collaborative work on a tabletop display. In: Kuutti, K., et al. (eds.) ECSCW 2003, pp. 159–178. Springer, Dordrecht (2003). doi:10.1007/978-94-010-0068-0_9
56. Niu, S., McCrickard, D.S., Nguyen, S.M.: Learning with interactive tabletop displays. In: 2016 IEEE Frontiers in Education Conference (FIE), pp. 1–9. IEEE (2016)
57. Smith, K., Hancock, P.A.: Situation awareness is adaptive, externally directed consciousness. Hum. Factors J. Hum. Factors Ergon. Soc. **37**(1), 137–148 (1995)
58. Tang, A., Pahud, M., Carpendale, S., Buxton, B.: VisTACO: visualizing tabletop collaboration. In: ACM International Conference on Interactive Tabletops and Surfaces, Saarbrücken, Germany pp. 29–38. ACM (2010)
59. Tang, A., Tory, M., Po, B., Neumann, P., Carpendale, S.: Collaborative coupling over tabletop displays. In: Proceedings of the SIGCHI Conference on Human Factors in Computing Systems (CHI 2006), Montréal, Québec, Canada, pp. 1181–1190. ACM (2006)
60. Wobbrock, J.O., Morris, M.R., Wilson, A.D.: User-defined gestures for surface computing. In: Proceedings of the SIGCHI Conference on Human Factors in Computing Systems, Boston, MA, USA, pp. 1083–1092. ACM (2009)
61. Zagermann, J., Pfeil, U., Rädle, R., Jetter, H.-C., Klokmose, C., Reiterer, H.: When tablets meet tabletops: the effect of tabletop size on around-the-table collaboration with personal tablets. In: Proceedings of the 2016 CHI Conference on Human Factors in Computing Systems, Santa Clara, California, USA, pp. 5470–5481. ACM (2016)

New Interaction Techniques

Comfort: A Coordinate of User Experience in Interactive Built Environments

Hamed S. Alavi[1,2]($\boxtimes$), Himanshu Verma[1], Michael Papinutto[1,3],
and Denis Lalanne[1]

[1] Human-IST Research Center, University of Fribourg, Fribourg, Switzerland
{hamed.alavi,himanshu.verma,michael.papinutto,denis.lalanne}@unifr.ch
[2] Swiss Federal Institute of Technology (EPFL), Lausanne, Switzerland
[3] Visual and Social Neuroscience Unit, University of Fribourg, Fribourg, Switzerland

Abstract. Comfort as a technical term in the domain of architecture has been used meticulously to describe, assess, and understand some of the essential qualities of buildings, across four dimensions: visual, thermal, acoustic, and respiratory. This body of knowledge can be drawn upon to shed light on the growing branch of HCI that pursues a shift from "artifact" to "environment" (and from "usability" to "comfort"). We contribute to this conceptual-contextual transition in three consecutive steps: *(1)* sketch the outline of comfort studies in the scholar field of Architecture and the ones in Human-Computer Interaction, *(2)* propose a schematic model of comfort that captures its interactive characteristics and, *(3)* demonstrate an interactive tool, called ComfortBox, that we prototyped to help answer some of the research questions about the perception of comfort in built environments.

Keywords: Human-Building Interaction · Comfort · Adaptive architecture

1 Introduction

Interaction design and architecture have a two-decade-long history of mutual influence and dialogue. From one side, interaction design has drawn on architectural concepts and reflections in multitude of endeavours, namely, in the reification of "Ubicomp" vision and the physical embodiment of computing [1], in the amalgamation of function and form [2], in the development of interaction design patterns [3], and in studying the symbiosis of people and artifacts [4]. From the other side, in architecture, numerous attempts strove to understand the integration of digital elements in buildings and urban design [5,6]. Despite these instances of mutual learning, it has been argued that the depth and breath of concrete collaborations between architects and interaction designers are far from the ideal [7]. The cases where interaction designers or HCI researchers engage in an architectural project are rather rare [8]. Instead, in the current scenarios, technology is typically retrofitted onto a new or existing building, to

© IFIP International Federation for Information Processing 2017
Published by Springer International Publishing AG 2017. All Rights Reserved
R. Bernhaupt et al. (Eds.): INTERACT 2017, Part III, LNCS 10515, pp. 247–257, 2017.
DOI: 10.1007/978-3-319-67687-6_16

perform functions that were previously done "less efficiently". The evolution of windows exemplifies this scenario. Window is a remarkably sophisticated architectural element with physical, spatial, and social affordances, which have been the subject of creative design for many years. With the recent ecological and energy concerns, the efficiency of operable windows has been criticized, leading to the situation where in modern buildings the interconnected functions of window are separated and each assigned to one building automation component (e.g. automated shading, ventilation, air conditioning). These components (functions) have been occasionally re-envisioned with a user-centered approach, and substituted by interactive technological innovations such as Nest learning thermostat[1], Comfy App[2] ventilation, and context-aware shading and lighting. Questioning this retrofitting model against the ideas of embodiment and the vision of "profound technolgies" in Ubicomp, the notion of Human-Building Interaction (HBI) [9] has proposed an alternative scenario, in which interaction design, and more broadly HCI, have an early interwoven engagement in the design, construction, and evaluation of built environments. This, nevertheless, entails constructing a common grounding about what it means to design user experience with and within built environments, of which comfort is a key coordinate.

Given this background, we present an elaboration on the concept of comfort. The ultimate goal is to create practical knowledge and tools that can support HBI design research. In this paper, we, first, summarize how comfort is studied in architecture, identifying the broad research questions that have been widely investigated, and the ones that are currently the topic of scientific explorations. Second, we propose a model that illustrates the relationships between the components that are found relevant in the existing studies, but also highlights the significance of HBI design and the processes through which comfort is achieved in interaction with the environment. This model has inspired the design of a tool that we prototyped to facilitate the data collection process in comfort studies. The tool, called ComfortBox, is described in the third part of this paper.

In the interest of clarity, we restrain our discussion within the scope that has been well-established in the domain of architecture, covering the four dimensions of thermal, visual, acoustic, and respiratory comfort. In the following text, whenever we use the term "comfort", we refer to only these four dimensions, unless it is explicitly stated otherwise.

2   Comfort Studies in Architecture

Gaston Bachelard in his book *La Poétique de l'Espace* (The Poetics of Space) has compared comfort - in its broadest sense - to the 'lived experience' within architecture as its phenomenological consequence. Similar philosophy has been adopted since the early 21st century to investigate the relationship between

---

[1] https://nest.com/uk/thermostat/meet-nest-thermostat/.
[2] https://www.comfyapp.com/.

human health & well-being and the physical characteristics of the indoor environment - temperature, air, light and sound [10]. Subsequently, the description of comfort was encapsulated into four respective dimensions (thermal, respiratory, visual, and acoustic), and remained the basis for further design and studies until the present time [11].

The rest of this section aims to chart the outline of the research landscape that investigates these dimensions. This is done through, first and foremost, stating the very broad research questions that have been raised about comfort in the domain of architecture. The answers that we present for each of these questions demonstrate a summary of the influential and iconic works in the respective field, and contribute to our discussion by giving insight into the commonly applied methodologies and the scientific language, which notably differ from those of interaction design research.

Q1. **What environmental attributes influence the occupant's comfort?**
Thermal comfort has been found to be percieved in relation to the ambient air temperature, humidity, and air-flow. Fanger [12] in his highly influential set of studies used thermal chamber to examine participant's reaction to different thermal conditions. He created a model called the Predicted Mean Vote and Predicted Percent Dissatisfied (PMV/PPD), which led to the standardization of building thermal conditions by the International Organization of Standardization (ISO). Hopkinson [13] has illustrated the different surface and material characteristics that can be used to assess the *visual* comfort. These characteristic parameters are *(a)* the amount of light on the surface (i.e. *illuminance*), *(b)* the intensity of light reflected by the surfaces (i.e. *luminance*), *(c)* temperature of light, and *(d)* glare. Intensity of noise (in db) and its frequency in Hertz (Hz) determine the levels of *acoustic* comfort [11]. Finally, the effects of different constituents of air on human health have been examined, but since some studies have found inconclusive results with regards to different pollutants [14,15], *respiratory* comfort is predominantly associated to the concentration of CO_2 (in *ppm* - Parts Per Million).

Q2. **In what *delineated* ranges of environmental attributes are buildings perceived as comfortable?**
Despite the large amount of research conducted to find the ranges of acceptable thermal condition, it has remained the topic of discourse and only two standards (ASHRAE[3] 55 and EN15251) have reached a consensus, recommending the operative temperature range from 21 °C to 24 °C in winter and from 22 °C to 25 °C in summer [16–18]. Visual comfort is a task-dependent quality; the amount and type of light that is needed depends on the task that the occupant is engaged in. The high precision tasks, for instance, require higher level of illuminance and luminance without glare. CEN [19] provided recommendations regarding glare, colour index and lightning level in an office space (illuminance near 500 lux, luminance in the range [32, 130] lux). Different building characteristics such as the location and the type of building have been considered as the factors that define the acceptable

---

[3] American Society of Heating, Refrigerating and Air-Conditioning Engineers.

acoustic conditions. These characteristics are quantified via the levels of the Noise Ratio (NR), which varies for different buildings. For example, the recommended Noise Ratio level for an office is defined as 35 [20]. Finally, Multitude of research on air-quality levels, and its subsequent standardization for habitable buildings by ANSI[4]/ASHRAE [21], has specified the recommended concentrations of CO_2 levels to be below 1000 ppm for a higher respiratory comfort.

***Q3*. How do the individual and cultural characteristics influence these ranges?**
Surprisingly, the study of comfort as a subjective phenomenon has been delayed until the 21st century. Brager and de Dear in their 2007 book, Buildings, Culture and Environment: Informing Local and Global Practices, state that "comfort is not just an outcome of the physical environment but it is our very attitudes about comfort both on an individual and cultural scale" [22]. Two recent studies by Chappels and Shafaghat uncover the intra-individual and inter-individual variability, indicating differences of comfort sensations depending on culture, experience, age, and education [23,24].

***Q4*. How can a built environment be assessed in terms of comfort?**
Post-Occupancy Evaluation (POE) is a commonly used method to assess buildings in terms of their inhabitants' comfort and living experiences, after they have been occupied [25]. Questionnaires have often been used to evaluate occupants' perceived comfort along the aforementioned dimensions, and consequently identify different kinds of architectural or constructional flaws [26,27]. In a lab setting, other methods such as the analysis of physiological responses have been increasingly incorporated to speculate the level of experienced comfort. For instance, Yao and his colleagues demonstrated that different physiological indicators such as skin temperature, heart rate, and electroencephalography (EEG) can be used as reliable predictors of perceived thermal comfort [28,29].

3   Comfort Studies in HCI

Driven by the move towards sustainable habitation, studies focusing on occupants' comfort have been a relatively recent trend in HCI and Ubicomp. *Thermal* comfort, amongst the different dimensions, has been the popular subject of investigation because of the *(a)* perceived lack of control and engagement within tightly controlled, automated buildings; and *(b)* enhanced measures to conserve energy through contextual optimization of HVAC[5] systems. These aspects have significantly pronounced the role of HCI in Sustainability [30], and driven the research agenda towards the design of many user-oriented interactive artifacts, where thermal comfort and awareness about energy utilization are (strongly) coupled and contextualized. Milenkovic et al. [31], for example, have demonstrated an energy-awareness system called POEM (Personal Office Energy Monitor) that also enables occupants within offices to notify the BMS or a building

---

[4] American National Standards Institute.
[5] Heating, Ventilation, and Air-Conditioning.

manager about the state of their thermal comfort and consequentially suggest necessary actions. Furthermore, motivated by the same paradigm and to support the differential pricing due to renewable energy supply, Alan et al. [32] conducted a field study with three smart thermostat prototypes in 30 UK residences to comprehend the mental models and expectations about inhabitants' thermal comfort. Costanza et al. with their Temperature Calendar [33] - an ambient visualization of thermal variations in workplaces - have used these displays as a medium for occupants to engage with the policy makers, and collectively appropriate workplaces that offer higher thermal comfort while optimizing energy resources.

Respiratory comfort corresponding to the surrounding air quality, has been examined with (quite some) urgency in the last several years, primarily to mitigate the adverse effects of air pollution in urban environments, and to support occupants' "right to awareness" about the healthiness of their surroundings. Within buildings, awareness systems that register and visualize the levels of Particulate Matter (for example, *inAir* [34, 35]) and Carbon Dioxide - CO_2 - (for example, *MAQS* [36]) have been designed and evaluated. In addition to monitoring, the weather station developed by Frešer et al. [37] also recommends the relevant future actions to ensure a healthy environment by additionally accounting for the number of occupants within a room and the current state of windows.

The main track of comfort research in architecture differs markedly from the perspective of HCI and its emphasis on the active role of occupants in achieving their comfort. The schema that we demonstrate in the next section provides a bigger picture that incorporates components relevant to both perspectives while articulating the distinctions.

4   Occupant-Centered Model of Comfort

In the model that we illustrate in Fig. 1, the individual occupant (user) seeks comfort in continuous interaction with her environment. The environment consists of the physical situation, but also the social setting, that is, the other occupants are considered as part of the environment. The model can be best understood by tracing two processes of comfort evaluation, which we discuss in the following as *Involuntary* and *Voluntary*:

1. **Involuntary Evaluation - Autonomic Response:** A continuous sensing process monitors the part of the physical environment inside occupant's receptive field (e.g. intensity of light in her field of view, temperature in her micro-environment). This is done by the human's sensory system, which consists of several components: the sensory endings (e.g. photoreceptors in retina, thermoreceptors in skin), neural pathways, part of the brain that perceives the transduced sensory information, and a transient sensory memory (e.g. iconic memory, haptic memory) [38]. Depending on the external situation perceived in the environment and the internal state of the occupant (physiological and psychological), comfort at that moment is evaluated involuntarily.

Consequently a set of regulatory actions take place, in order to maintain a relatively constant condition for the inner organs. These actions are autonomic and may be in the form of *(a)* physiological responses (e.g. retina size change, squinting, sweating, shivering, heart rate change), and/or *(b)* impact on the psychological state (e.g. annoyance), which may trigger a "waking signal", calling for (sub)conscious evaluation of situation and behavioral response.

2. **Voluntary Evaluation - Behavioral Response:** There are occasions when comfort fades into our conscious or subconscious attention. This may stem from the fact that involuntary responses have not been sufficient (as mentioned above), but also due to external triggers such as being the subject of a comfort study and asked to rate it, or even at a meta-cognition level, for example, when reading this text. Several parameters may impact our voluntary judgment of comfort: *(a)* the physiological and psychological state (e.g. sweating, being annoyed by noise), *(b)* sensory information, and also *(c)* the mental model of the environment related to the level of expectations and tolerance. The outcome may appear as interaction with the built environment (e.g. opening a window, closing the shutter).

These actions are intended to make modification in body's immediate environment and may update the occupant's mental model of her environment and how it reacts to various manipulations.

Without aspiring to delineate these mechanisms (some of which are still open scientific questions), we argue that by recognizing the distinction between the Involuntary and Voluntary states, the model highlights points that are of special interest to the discussion of comfort in the context of Human-Building Interaction.

In addressing an HBI design question such as "what style of interaction with a window-like element can enhance the occupant's comfort?" what is at stake is the moments when a transition from Involuntary to Voluntary occurs, leading to a behavioral response that may be in the form of interacting with the designed element. While a *performant* building should minimize the instances when comfort becomes a (sub)conscious concern, the role of interaction design is to serve those moments, to understand the occupant's physical and mental state in those situations, to create appropriate space of possible actions, to offer "usable" interactivity, and to help the concern of comfort fade back to the Involuntary state.

HBI studies must be able to capture (or deliberately generate) the situations where comfort is in the Voluntary state. They must also be able to understand the possible correlations between the alternative design choices and the user behaviour in those situations. However, for the sake of (holistic) completeness, it is critically (and yet equally) important for an HBI researcher to create a full understanding of episodes that lead to the transitions to and from the Involuntary state. Consequently, a contextualized, sensitized, and localized understanding of each individuals' surroundings and physiological measurements, might allow for inference of ones' level of comfort - information that can be queried in the findings reviewed in Sect. 2 (especially the answers to the broad questions *Q1* and *Q4*). We continue discussing this model in the next section, by explaining two methodological concerns that it uncovered, motivating the design of ComfortBox.

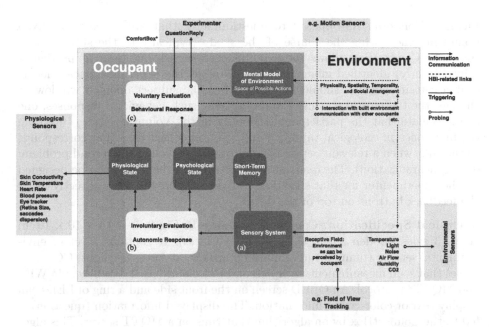

Fig. 1. Comfort is achieved in interaction with the built environment, through an iterative process in which the occupants (a) observe the environmental condition with their sensory receptors, (b) evaluate it involuntary, and accordingly change physiological and/or psychological state, and if remarkable discomfort is observed, (c) (sub)consciously acts upon it, given the space of possibilities that the occupants believe they have. The adaptation action may make a change in the environment objectively and in the occupants' perception. The "Voluntary Evaluation" state may also be triggered by an external factor such an experimenter asking the occupants to reflect about their comfort.

5   ComfortBox as a Research Tool

Motivation. The model pronounces two methodological concerns in conducting comfort surveys, when asking the subject of the study, for instance, "how do you rate your thermal comfort?" *First*, our sensory memory is highly transient, and the participants' answer to that question would reflect only their experience in the last moments before the question was asked. Given that, the answer to a question such as "how do you rate visual comfort during the last week?" is highly unreliable. This makes aligning the questionnaire data with the observed user's behaviour to be practically impossible, especially in longitudinal studies. On the other hand, frequent prompting could not be an appropriate solution, as it creates annoyance and itself affects comfort and the way it is reported. *Second*, when the experimenter asks the study subjects to rate their comfort, this prompting triggers the Voluntary process of comfort evaluation. Activating the Voluntary process is part of the biological mechanism to call for behavioral response. An external (artificial) trigger might raise concerns about the ecological-validity of the study, and might simply result in exaggerated responses.

Design Concept. As opposed to questionnaires that are collected at fixed points in time during the course of the study (typically at the start and/or the end), ComfortBox allows the experimenters to ask questions at particular "(intelligently) identified moments". For example, the experimenter can decide that a certain question should be asked when the subject opens a window or changes the thermostat setting. From observing such behavioral responses, one can speculate that the participant is already in the Voluntary state, (avoiding the first concern: ecological-validity), and also can collect data that corresponds to the time when a relevant action is monitored (addressing the second problem: data synchronization). The question that appears on the screen can be designed by the experimenter for that situation and the answers are given directly using the feedback buttons on top of the device.

Technical Specification. ComfortBox, shown in Fig. 2, is a $10 \times 10 \times 10$ cm cube (3 sides wooden and 3 sides mirror surfaces). It contains a set of environmental sensors (temperature, humidity, airflow, air pressure, light, CO_2, and noise) that send measurements every second to a cloud-based database, via WiFi and MQTT[6] protocol. An OLED screen on the front side and a ring of LEDs can display text or color-coded information. The displayed information (question) is fed to the ComfortBox by an algorithm that runs on a MQTT server. This algorithm is tinkered by the experimenter and can work with input variables from the ComfortBoxes' sensor measurements, but also from other sensors used in the study. The buttons on top of the box allow for answering the posed questions.

API for Researchers. A programming interface based on Node-RED[7] is provided. The experimenter designs a user scenario which determines the opportune circumstances under which a specific question can be asked, and particular information to be provided to the user.ComfortBox is currently being used by the

Fig. 2. ComfortBox is an interactive research tool designed to facilitate data collection in lab and in-situ comfort studies. The physical design is intended to help blend into the desktop setting and stay in the periphery of attention when not used.

---

[6] http://mqtt.org/.
[7] https://nodered.org/.

Human-IST research center, in University of Fribourg, Switzerland, in two ongoing research projects that aim to address the impact of "agency" and "awarness" on the perception of comfort. ComfortBox contributes to the model (illustrated in Fig. 1) at the same position as the "Experimenter" component. It substitutes (or supports) the survey mechanism, with the possibility to connect to the other sensing systems (e.g. physiological, environmental, and motion sensors).

6 Conclusion

At the core of this contribution, our proposed model extends the generally accepted view in architectural studies which considers comfort as a "quality of building", and suggests that comfort is also an "objective for occupants", to be achieved in interaction with the built environment. It illustrates that besides the involuntary physiological and psychological processes, an independent yet communicating conscious process contributes to the accomplishment of comfort. And finally, of high relevance to Human-Building Interaction discourses, the model recognizes that comfort has autonomic but also behavioral manifestations; that it is part of our interactive experience with the built environment and entails design attempts that account for its full picture.

References

1. Dourish, P.: Where the Action is: The Foundations of Embodied Interaction. MIT Press, Cambridge (2004)
2. Ingram, B.: Feature-learning from architecture. Interactions **16**(6), 64–67 (2009)
3. Alexander, C., Ishikawa, S., Silverstein, M., i Ramió, J.R., Jacobson, M., Fiksdahl-King, I.: A Pattern Language. Gustavo Gili, Barcelona (1977)
4. Brand, S.: How Buildings Learn: What Happens After They're Built. Penguin, Westminster (1995)
5. Mitchell, W.J.: City of Bits: Space, Place, and the Infobahn. MIT Press, Cambridge (1996)
6. Spiller, N., et al.: Digital Architecture now: A Global Survey of Emerging Talent. Thames & Hudson, London (2008)
7. Alavi, H.S., Churchill, E., Kirk, D., Nembrini, J., Lalanne, D.: Deconstructing human-building interaction. Interactions **23**(6), 60–62 (2016)
8. Verma, H., Alavi, H.S., Lalanne, D.: Studying space use: bringing HCI tools to architectural projects. In: Proceedings of CHI 2017, ACM (2017)
9. Alavi, H.S., Lalanne, D., Nembrini, J., Churchill, E., Kirk, D., Moncur, W.: Future of human-building interaction. In: Proceedings of CHI 2016 Extended Abstracts. ACM (2016)
10. Hawkes, D.: The environmental Imagination: Technics and Poetics of the Architectural Environment. Taylor & Francis, Milton Park (2008)
11. Bluyssen, P.M.: The Indoor Environment Handbook: How to Make Buildings Healthy and Comfortable. Earthscan, Abingdon (2009)
12. Fanger, P.O.: Thermal Comfort. McGraw-Hill, New York (1970). Danish tec edition
13. Hopkinson, R.G.: Architectural physics: lighting (1963)

14. Bornehag, C.G., Sundell, J., Weschler, C.J., Sigsgaard, T., Lundgren, B., Hasselgren, M., Hagerhed-Engman, L.: The association between asthma and allergic symptoms in children and phthalates in house dust: a nested case-control study. Environ. Health Perspect. **112**(14), 1393–1397 (2004)
15. Fisk, W.J., Lei-Gomez, Q., Mendell, M.J.: Meta-analyses of the associations of respiratory health effects with dampness and mold in homes. Indoor Air **4**, 284–296 (2007)
16. De Dear, R.J., Brager, G.S., Reardon, J., Nicol, F., et al.: Developing an adaptive model of thermal comfort and preference/discussion. ASHRAE Trans. **104**, 145 (1998)
17. ASHRAE Standard. Standard 55–2013. Thermal environmental conditions for human occupancy (2013)
18. CEN. Indoor environmental input parameters for design and assessment of energy performance of buildings addressing indoor air quality, thermal environment, lighting and acoustics. European Committee for Standardization, Belgium (2007)
19. CEN. Light and lighting-lighting of work places-part 1: Indoor work places. European Committee for Standardization, Brussels, Belgium (2002)
20. EN CEN. Acoustics - description, measurement and assessment of environmental noise - part 1: basic quantities and assessment procedures. European Committee for Standardization, Brussels, Belgium (2016)
21. Janssen, J.E.: Ventilation for acceptable indoor air quality. ASHRAE J. **31**(10), 40–48 (1989)
22. Cole, R., Lorch, R.: Buildings Culture and Environment. Wiley, Hoboken (2007)
23. Chappells, H., Shove, E.: Debating the future of comfort: environmental sustainability, energy consumption and the indoor environment. Build. Res. Inf. **33**(1), 32–40 (2005)
24. Shafaghat, A., Keyvanfar, A., Ferwati, M.S., Alizadeh, T.: Enhancing staff's satisfaction with comfort toward productivity by sustainable open plan office design. Sustain. Cities Soc. **19**, 151–164 (2015)
25. Preiser, W.F., White, E., Rabinowitz, H.: Post-Occupancy Evaluation (Routledge Revivals). Routledge, Abingdon (2015)
26. Wagner, A., Gossauer, E., Moosmann, C., Gropp, T., Leonhart, R.: Thermal comfort and workplace occupant satisfaction results of field studies in German low energy office buildings. Energy Build. **39**(7), 758–769 (2007)
27. Bluyssen, P., Aries, M., Dommelen, P.: Comfort of workers in office buildings: the European HOPE project. Build. Environ. **46**(1), 280–288 (2011)
28. Yao, Y., Lian, Z., Liu, W., Shen, Q.: Experimental study on physiological responses and thermal comfort under various ambient temperatures. Physiol. Behav. **93**(1), 310–321 (2008)
29. Yao, Y., Lian, Z., Liu, W., Jiang, C., Liu, Y., Lu, H.: Heart rate variation and electroencephalograph-the potential physiological factors for thermal comfort study. Indoor Air **19**(2), 93–101 (2009)
30. DiSalvo, C., Sengers, P., Brynjarsdóttir, H.: Mapping the landscape of sustainable HCI. In: Proceedings of CHI 2010, pp. 1975–1984. ACM (2010)
31. Milenkovic, M., Hanebutte, U., Huang, Y., Prendergast, D., Pham, H.: Improving user comfort and office energy efficiency with POEM (personal office energy monitor). In: CHI 2013 Extended Abstracts. ACM (2013)
32. Alan, A.T., Shann, M., Costanza, E., Ramchurn, S.D., Seuken, S.: It is too hot: an in-situ study of three designs for heating. In: Proceedings of CHI 2016, pp. 5262–5273. ACM (2016)

33. Costanza, E., Bedwell, B., Jewell, M.O., Colley, J., Rodden, T.: 'A bit like British weather, i suppose': design and evaluation of the temperature calendar. In: Proceedings of CHI 2016, pp. 4061–4072. ACM (2016)
34. Kim, S., Paulos, E.: InAir: measuring and visualizing indoor air quality. In: Proceedings of UbiComp 2009, pp. 81–84. ACM (2009)
35. Chen, X., Zheng, Y., Chen, Y., Jin, Q., Sun, W., Chang, E., Ma, W.Y.: Indoor air quality monitoring system for smart buildings. In: Proceedings of UbiComp 2014, pp. 471–475. ACM (2014)
36. Jiang, Y., Li, K., Tian, L., Piedrahita, R., Yun, X., Mansata, O., Lv, Q., Dick, R.P., Hannigan, M., Shang, L.: Maqs: a mobile sensing system for indoor air quality. In: Proceedings of UbiComp 2011. ACM (2011)
37. Frešer, M., Gradišek, A., Cvetković, B., Luštrek, M.: An intelligent system to improve T-H-C parameters at the workplace. In: Proceedings of UbiComp 2016 Adjunct, pp. 61–64. ACM (2016)
38. Krantz, J.: Experiencing Sensation and Perception. Pearson Education (US), New York (2012)

Designing Smart Shoes for Obstacle Detection: Empowering Visually Challenged Users Through ICT

Vikram Singh Parmar[✉] and Krishna Sai Inkoolu

National Design Business Incubator, National Institute of Design,
Ahmedabad, Gujarat, India
Vikram_p@nid.edu, m.saik@yahoo.com

Abstract. The paper presents a case of Smart Shoes that uses ultrasonic sensors to detect the obstacle in front of the user. Additionally, this shoe signals a user by tapping at the foot arch. An evaluative study of the Smart Shoes was conducted with (n = 31) users; (17) blind people, (9) low vision and (5) non-disabled users. The study was conducted to judge reliability of the Smart Shoes by evaluating it from (a) ratio of obstacles identified to total obstacles encountered, (b) distance of obstacle apprehension and (c) response time. The study was conducted in a controlled and definite environment. The results from the study illustrate this footwear to be 89.5% effective in detecting obstacles such as vehicles, people, furniture, footpaths, poles, and miscellaneous obstacles with a mean response time of 3.08 s. Users average distance of obstacle apprehension was 108 cm in regular mode and 50 cm in the crowd mode. The future research & evaluative studies will be conducted in actual operational/moving environments.

Keywords: Design · Blind people · Low vision · Non-disabled · Visual Impairment · New Product Development · Mobility

1 Introduction

Worldwide, it is estimated that approximately 285 million people are visually impaired out of which 39 million are blind [1]. India accounts for 20% of world's blind population. Mobility is an important aspect of human life and is adversely affected in people with visual disability. To overcome this limitation, they turn towards assistive devices to take a step closer to independent mobility. Most common and the oldest conventional device aiding them in mobility is the Hoover cane. Other options such as guide dogs, GPS and other Tech Gizmos have been continuously evolving to make these users independent [2]. The design and evaluative study of smart shoes reported in this paper is an effort to leapfrog current assistive devices' development process for people with visual Impairment.

© IFIP International Federation for Information Processing 2017
Published by Springer International Publishing AG 2017. All Rights Reserved
R. Bernhaupt et al. (Eds.): INTERACT 2017, Part III, LNCS 10515, pp. 258–266, 2017.
DOI: 10.1007/978-3-319-67687-6_17

The long Hoover cane is one of the world's oldest products. While Hoover cane has been a widely accepted mobility-aid, there has not been any significant innovation in this domain since last few decades. In analyzing the existing Hoover cane, we came across few limitations needed to be addressed to improve the existing mobility of its users. For instance, users get feedback about the obstacles only when the cane touches it. This means a small range of obstacle detection (the length of the cane) [3], and consequently less time to react to the obstacle. It can prove to be dangerous when it comes to obstacles like moving vehicles etc. Also, using aids like Hoover cane, guide dogs or some other technologically advanced hand-held gadgets to navigate in domestic environment keeps one hand always occupied in holding the aid, which otherwise can be used for purposes like safeguarding during an accident.

Many people without disabilities perceive an assistive mobility aid as an indicator of the physical disability and they either get out of the way or rush to help the user, out of pity. What people don't realize is that these are the means used by them to be more independent. This stigma created in the society against the aids and the visually challenged have perpetuated a myth of helplessness for long and have kept them away from achieving the first-class status. In studying most of the accidents [4] among people using Hoover cane, we found that one of the primary reasons usually is the short or long length of the cane not being able to provide adequate information in time and lack of training.

With reference to Neurophysiology, humans are sight dependent [5]. 30–40% of our cerebral cortex is devoted to vision, as compared to 8% for touch or just 3% for audio [6]. To compensate for our most dominant sense, providing the feedback tactilely [7] is an efficient and effective mechanism when coupled with vibrations. We do acknowledge that prolonged exposure to vibrations could cause problems like tactile hallucinations ("Phantom Vibrations") and Whole-Body/Hand-Arm Vibration Syndrome [8].

For blind people, hearing and touch become the major senses, respectively [9]. Considering the noise pollution level of private or public spaces in India, tap (tactile) emerges as a promising tool to communicate with aforementioned users. The Smart Shoes presented in this paper explores the potential of tap in alerting users about the obstacles in front through a novel (and innocuous on prolonged usage) feedback mechanism. This footwear employs a novel method of providing feedback and has a long and customizable range of detection that can aid in independent mobility. The remaining sections will describe the design of the Smart Shoes, methods followed in conducting user testing, results of this on-going study, followed by conclusion indicating future research plans for this project.

2 Design

The design of Smart Shoes is our effort to serve visually impaired people by facilitating their mobility. It detects obstacles in a customizable range of up to 2 m by making use of an ultrasonic sensor and providing the feedback to user through a tapping mechanism at the foot-arch. The footwear employs a directional ultrasound sensor that is continuously transmitting and receiving sound waves to detect the obstacles in front of the user. The intensity of the tapping varies based on the distance between the user and the obstacle. This feedback mechanism has been developed meticulously so as to be effective and at the same time, not to have any ill effects on the user's health, in case of long term product usage. The footwear works in two modes; (a) Regular mode - This is the 'by-default' mode detecting obstacles present in a range of 0–2 m. (b) Crowd mode- It has a range of 0–1 m and is suitable for surroundings with frequent obstacles. Figure 1 depicts the design of Smart Shoes. Figure 2 depicts positioning of the ultrasound sensor.

Fig. 1. Depicts ultrasound sensor that detects the obstacles (left). Depicts design of the Smart Shoes prototype (right).

Based on the mode selected, processor sends the signal to arch-pad to initiate tapping with computed intensity. Ease of usability is what the user interface is based on. The users don't have to remember any complex button combinations nor do they need an extensive training to operate the device. There are two buttons; (a) Power button: This button is used for powering the system on/off, (b) Mode button: The footwear can be used in any of the two modes using the mode button. When it is pressed, the buzzer present in the system indicates current mode. Figure 3 depicts two modes of the Smart Shoes and the two buttons.

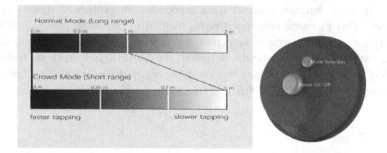

Fig. 2. Depicts two modes of the Smart Shoes and power button

The system is powered by using a rechargeable Lithium-ion battery. Battery level is indicated by the buzzer when switching on the system. Once fully charged the system can work for at least 5 h. The pleasant aesthetics of the footwear helps in diminishing the prejudice held by the society against the assistive devices.

3   Method

3.1   User Group

A total of (n = 31) users participated in the study where 17 users were Blind People, 9 Low vision [10] and 5 non-disabled users (see Fig. 3). Non-disabled and low vision users were included in the study to understand if presence of sense of sight affects the usage of the product. These users were blindfolded during the testing. Of the 26 users with visual disability, 20 users had it since birth (of which 8 had low vision) and the rest 6 users from time ranging from 4 years ago to 22 years ago. The users were distributed into the age group of 16 to 35 years old, 45% users falling in the age group of 16–20 years old, 35% in the age group of 21–25 years old, and 10% in the age group of both 26–30 years old and 31–35 years old each. 9 users out of the total had undergone a cane-training course. All the users volunteered for the study and were associated with Blind People's Association (BPA), Ahmedabad, Gujarat.

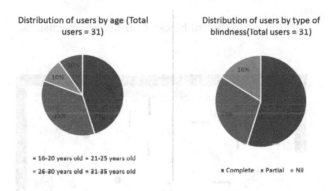

Fig. 3. Depicts distribution of user age and level of blindness

3.2   Experiment Design

To assess the effectiveness of Smart Shoes in detecting the obstacles, definite control trials with (n = 31) users were conducted on an artificial obstacle course. The course was designed in such a way so as to emulate the obstacles encountered in day-to-day life. All the visually impaired users (n = 26) were selected from BPA, Ahmedabad and were from different backgrounds (age, educational qualification, profession etc.). All these participants were using different modes of navigation from one place to another (cane, human aid etc.). However during the testing they were asked to use only smart shoes to navigate among the obstacles. The non-disabled users (n = 5) belonged to Ahmedabad, Gujarat and were happy to volunteer by themselves on seeing the experiment.

Before the testing, each user was introduced to the Smart Shoes and its functionality for an average of 5 min. They were shown a demonstration of the Smart Shoes; they were asked to be stationary and one team member from development team moved in front of them; changing the distance between them and allowing them to get a feel of the tapping and its varying intensity. The simple UI of the Smart Shoes allowed the users to get acquainted with it relatively quickly and ready for the test.

The testing took place in the campus of BPA, Ahmedabad, Gujarat. A parking space of 12 × 6 m was used as the test arena where all the frequently encountered obstacles (such as vehicles, people, footpath, poles, pillars, furniture and other miscellaneous obstacles) were re-created artificially (see Fig. 4). The obstacles were categorized as follows:

- Vehicle: Motorbike, Car, Cycle, Rickshaw, Three-wheeler, Carts, Bus.
- People: Our team members tried to simulate the encounters such that the user might have in their daily life with fellow human beings (stationary and moving of 3 & 2 people respectively, refer Fig. 5).
- Footpath: Peripheral walls of the obstacle course ranging from 15 cm to 45 cm high.
- Pole: Electric poles, PVC pipes (diameter 20 cm), cylindrical pots.
- Furniture: Chair with cylindrical thin legs with the ground clearance of more than 45 cm, Sofa, etc.
- Miscellaneous Obstacles: Cardboard blocks of different dimensions.

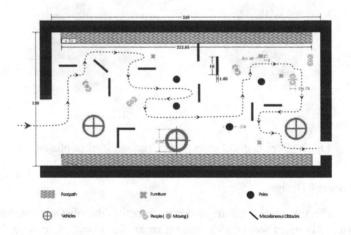

Fig. 4. Depicts artificial obstacle course

All the obstacles were of different dimensions and users encountered one obstacle at a time. To ascertain the ability and effectiveness of the Smart Shoes, the following performance indicators were studied:

The Ratio of Obstacles Identified to Total Obstacles Encountered: Out of all the obstacles that were encountered by the user while navigating the course, how many were detected before coming in contact with the obstacle. A high ratio indicates a high awareness about the obstacle presence in the environment. This will also reflect the collision rate of a user with the obstacles when he was mobilized using the Smart Shoes. The relation being inversely proportional to the metric studied.

The Distance of Obstacle Apprehension: The distance between the user and the obstacle when it was detected with the help of the smart shoes. A large distance means early detection, alerting the user about the obstacle just in time to take effective measures to avoid it.

Response time: Response time is characterized as the time between the user stopping due to an obstacle detection using the Smart Shoes and starting to walk again, assuming that an obstacle-free path has been identified. A low response time means that the user has adapted well to the ways of the Smart Shoes and is able to quickly ascertain the free path when encountered with an obstacle.

4 Results

The results showed that the users were able to detect 89.5% obstacles out of all encountered obstacles with a mean response time of 3.08 s. Users' average distance of obstacle apprehension was 108 cm in regular mode and 50 cm in the crowd mode. Sample image shown in Fig. 5.

Fig. 5. User navigating through the obstacle course wearing the Smart Shoes

4.1 Ratio of Obstacles Identified to Total Obstacles Encountered

The overall ratio of the obstacles identified, against the total obstacles encountered were 0.8948. Users encountered up to a maximum of 40 obstacles during the experiment in the obstacle course. The responses were manually scored and the collisions with the obstacles were noted down during the experiment. The ratio of obstacles identified to total obstacles encountered was calculated post-experiment from the data (see Table 1).

Table 1. Ratio of obstacles detected to total obstacles encountered

Total obstacles	Obstacles detected	Obstacles hit	Obstacles detected
17.12	15.32	1.8	0.8948

4.2 Distance of Obstacle Apprehension

The Smart Shoes has two modes: Regular mode (range 0–200 cm) and crowd mode (0–100 cm). The average distance of early detection was 108 cm in regular mode with a standard deviation of 21.49 and 50 cm in crowd mode with a standard deviation of 7.89 (see Table 2).

Table 2. Average distance for obstacle apprehension

Mode	Distance of obstacles apprehension	Standard deviation
Regular (0–200 cm)	108 cm	21.49
Crowd (0–100 cm)	50 cm	7.89

4.3 Response Time

The average response time was 3.08 s. Prolonged usage of the product may result in a shorter response time for the user. The responses were manually scored meticulously from a thorough study of the video recordings of the experiments post testing (see Table 3).

Table 3. Average response time

Average response time	3.08 s

4.4 Other Observations on the Use of the Smart Shoes

The users were skeptical about the feedback mechanism of the Smart Shoes in the beginning of the experiment leading to a cautious gait. As they became familiar with the product usage and understood how the feedback works, their walking resumed to normal and had a better understanding of the change in the tapping intensity. The users became more confident as the experiment went on and they were able to check for an obstacle-free path using the Smart Shoes more efficiently. In rare cases, users went astray and needed experimenter's intervention to get back on course.

5 Conclusions

This paper presented an obstacle detection system embedded Smart Shoes that enabled people with visual impairment to identify obstacles in advance. Quantitative controlled trials conducted on (n = 31) users in an artificially designed obstacle course showed that the system is able to detect the obstacles with an efficiency of 89.5%. Users' average distance of obstacle apprehension was 108 cm in regular mode and 50 cm in the crowd mode. The average response time of users was 3.08 s. The study was conducted on an artificially designed obstacle course. The obstacle course was designed carefully with a wide variety of obstacles. Obstacles present in the experiment replicated most commonly encountered hindrances in the daily lives of users. Users with blindness had an average obstacle detection ratio of 0.889 with an average response time of 2.54 s. Their average distance of obstacle apprehension was 108.88 cm in regular mode and 51.49 cm in crowd mode. Users with low vision had an average obstacle detection ratio of 0.91 with an average response time of 3.23 s. Their average distance of obstacle apprehension was 116.21 cm in regular mode and 48.11 cm in crowd mode. The users without disability had an average obstacle detection ratio of 0.89 with an average response time of 4.65 s. Their average distance of obstacle apprehension was 84.8 cm in regular mode and 48.4 cm in crowd mode.

The results reflected that the non-disabled users had the longest response time and the least distance of obstacle apprehension when it comes to using the Smart Shoes. It may have happened due to their sudden loss of sense of sight, implicitly relating this finding to the recently turned blinds. Further study including recently turned blind users will be able to reflect more on the same. Low vision users had the highest obstacle detection ratio. This may have happened due to their self-confidence in their mobility that their residual sight gives them even when they are blind-folded. They may also be dependent on their other senses for mobility that may have led to a high obstacle detection ratio using the Smart Shoes. From this study, we conclude that the Smart Shoes could be used by the blind and low vision users to enhance their visibility in daily life. In future, longitudinal research would be required to judge if the Smart Shoes would be able to augment their conventional way of mobility, thereby make them independent after prolonged usage. Next evaluative studies will be conducted in actual operational/moving environments.

Acknowledgement. The research team would like to acknowledge Mr. Anip Sharma's contribution for his support in building the prototype and assist us in conducting the field experiment.

References

1. World Health Organization. Visual Impairment and Blindness statistics: Fact sheet No. 282, August 2014
2. Tebo, L.R.: OTR/L. ATP, A Resource guide to assistive technology for students with visual impairment

3. Staffordshire   University.   http://blogs.staffs.ac.uk/profdavidclarkcarter/2014/10/21/why-would-a-blind-person-not-use-a-white-stick/
4. Manduchi, R., Kurniawan, S.: Mobility-related accidents experienced by people with visual impairment. AERJOURNAL-D-10-00048R1, February 2011
5. NORA Neuro-Optometric Rehabilitation Association. https://nora.cc/vision-a-brain-injury-mainmenu-64.html
6. Biological exceptions. perspective on our senses, September 2011
7. Pundlik, S., Tomasi, M., Luo, G.: Evaluation of a portable collision warning device for patients with peripheral vision loss in an obstacle course. Invest. Ophthalmol. Vis. Sci. **56**, 2571–2579 (2015). doi:10.1167/iovs.14-15935
8. World Health Organization. Occupational exposure to vibration from hand-held tools: The effects on human performance: risk assessment and prevention, vol. 03, pp. 16–20
9. Velázquez, R.: Wearable assistive devices for the blind (Chap. 17). In: Lay-Ekuakille, A., Mukhopadhyay, S.C. (eds.) Wearable and Autonomous Biomedical Devices and Systems for Smart Environment: Issues and Characterization. LNEE, vol. 75, pp. 331–349. Springer, Heidelberg (2010). doi:10.1007/978-3-642-15687-8_17
10. Disabilities, Opportunities, Internetworking, and Technology (DO-IT). http://www.washington.edu/doit/how-are-terms-low-vision-visually-impaired-and-blind-defined

Effects of Haptic Feedback in Dual-Task Teleoperation of a Mobile Robot

José Corujeira[1,2(✉)], José Luís Silva[2,3], and Rodrigo Ventura[4]

[1] Instituto Superior Técnico, Universidade de Lisboa, Lisbon, Portugal
jose.corujeira@tecnico.ulisboa.pt
[2] Madeira-ITI, Funchal, Portugal
Jose.Luis.Silva@iscte.pt
[3] Instituto Universitário de Lisboa (ISCTE-IUL), ISTAR-IUL, Lisbon, Portugal
[4] Institute for Systems and Robotics, Instituto Superior Técnico,
Universidade de Lisboa, Lisbon, Portugal
rodrigo.ventura@isr.tecnico.ulisboa.pt

Abstract. Teleoperation system usage is challenging to human operators, as this system has a predominantly visual interface that limits the ability to acquire situation awareness, (e.g. maintain a safe teleoperation). This limitation coupled with the dual-task problem of teleoperating a mobile robot, negatively affects the operators cognitive load and motor skills. Our motivation is to offload some of the visual information to a secondary perceptual channel (haptic), by proposing an assisted teleoperation system. This system uses haptic feedback to alert the operator of obstacle proximity, without directly influencing the operator's command inputs. The objective of this paper, is to evaluate and validate the efficacy of our system's haptic feedback, by providing the obstacle proximity information to the operator. The user experiment was conducted to emulate the dual-task problem, by having a concurrent task for cognitive distraction. Our results showed significant differences in time to complete the navigation task and the duration of collisions, between the haptic feedback condition and the control condition.

Keywords: Teleoperation · Human-robot interaction · Haptic feedback · Mobile robots

1 Introduction

Teleoperation of mobile robots is performed in non-line-of-sight conditions. It consists in a human operator controlling, through an interface, a mobile robot that is in a remote environment. As such, the teleoperation system interface becomes the only link between a human operator and the mobile robot, and its environment [1]. This means the interface is responsible for providing the necessary information about the robot status (e.g. camera position, battery life, sensors) and its surrounding environment (e.g. orientation, location, obstacles) [2, 3]. Hence, the capacity for the interface to provide relevant information in context, at the right moment and correct modality impacts the performance of the human operator, and his/her ability to acquire situational awareness [4].

© IFIP International Federation for Information Processing 2017
Published by Springer International Publishing AG 2017. All Rights Reserved
R. Bernhaupt et al. (Eds.): INTERACT 2017, Part III, LNCS 10515, pp. 267–286, 2017.
DOI: 10.1007/978-3-319-67687-6_18

Most of teleoperation interfaces are predominantly visual (e.g. [5–7]). This imposes perceptual limitation, and originates a decoupling of the physical environment from the natural human perceptual processing by compromising the human perception of affordances, scales, and motion [2]. This decoupling further affects the operator's ability to control the robot, and acquire situational awareness (e.g. building mental models of remote environments, distance estimation and obstacle detection). Consequently, human operators usually feel a high level of disorientation, and are unable in most cases to discern the robot's distance from an obstacle, leading to collisions [8, 9]. Therefore, teleoperation of mobile robots is challenging.

There has been research (e.g. [7], [10–13]) concerned with how to mitigate this decoupling, between the physical environment, where the robot is operating and the human perception of that environment. In order to improve human operators' performance and lower their cognitive workload, while teleoperating the mobile robot. Particularly, in the field of haptic-feedback interfaces for mobile robot teleoperation. In the Lee et al. [14] study, it was shown that a combination of environmental and collision-preventing force significantly reduced the number of collisions compared to no haptic feedback stimulus, in both virtual and real environments. This combination of forces was also responsible for higher distance maintained from obstacles and lower average speeds on collision by participants, in both virtual and real environments. A study by Hacinecipoglu et al. [10] also showed a reduction in the number of collisions and time to complete the task. They also evaluated cognitive workload, with haptic feedback leading to a reduction of mental and temporal demand, as well as reducing the level of effort and frustration felt by participants. Their haptic feedback implementation actively adjusted the steering wheel to correct the navigation course of the mobile robot.

In Barros and Lindeman [15] research, the authors used a vibro-tactile feedback belt in the participant's torso, as a haptic feedback, instead of the more widely used method of applying counter forces on the input control device. This vibro-tactile feedback belt was activated when the distance of an obstacle was $d \leq 1.25$ m. Alerting participants of the direction and imminence of robot collision through vibration (intensity or frequency) on a specific region in the belt. Their results showed a significant decrease in the number of collisions with the vibro-tactile belt in comparison to not having haptic feedback.

In Brandt and Colton [16] one of the force feedback algorithms used was the Dynamic Parametric Field (DPF), which has four zones (safe, warning, transition, collision), these determine the force applied to the haptic input device. They defined these zones as:

- *Safe Zone* – no haptic feedback is applied at a distance greater than d_{max};
- *Warning Zone* – force feedback increases from 0% to 60% for $d_{mid} < d < d_{max}$;
- *Transition Zone* – force feedback from 80% to 100% for $d_{min} < d < d_{mid}$;
- *Collision Zone* – 100% force feedback for $d < d_{min}$.

As with the previously mentioned work, this implementation of haptic feedback led to lower number of collisions and duration of collisions when compared to no feedback.

The current scientific understanding indicates that haptic feedback improves mobile robot teleoperation, in basic navigation tasks. By improving the situational awareness and performance of a human operator, which helps mitigate the decoupling of the physical environment from the natural human perceptual processing. Yet all these studies required specialized and prototypical devices to provide haptic feedback, with most of them acting directly on the operator's input controllers. And they do not tackle the impact of using haptic-feedback in a typical dual-task set-up of mobile robot teleoperation [3].

Has stated, mobile robot teleoperation is typically a dual-task activity, be it in Urban Search and Rescue [17], surveillance and target acquisition [3], or explosive ordnance disposal [18]. This dual-task activity is comprised of:

- controlling the robot - maintain operational effectiveness, avoid obstacles, check robot status, etc.;
- accomplishing the objective - covers all aspects regarding the objectives for which the robot is being used (e.g. finding victims, defuse a bomb, search for target, etc.) [3].

With this paper, we first aim to describe our haptic feedback teleoperation system, that alerts a human operator of obstacle direction and proximity. This system relies on a modified DPF and a dynamic limitation algorithm of a robot's maximum velocity. It also relies on a commercially available consumer gaming controller to provide input commands and haptic feedback information. This means the system is portable, and does not directly act upon the input controls that the operator uses. The rationale behind this implementation, is to allow operators, through the modulated haptic feedback, to quickly identify crucial obstacle distance zones, and let them decide what is the appropriate course of action. While the system mitigates the possible collision damage of the robot, and gives more time for the operator to make that decision.

The second purpose of this paper, is to evaluate and validate the efficacy of our developed haptic feedback system. In providing the obstacle proximity information to the operator, within the context of a dual-task mobile robot teleoperation. Based on previous results from other research, our hypothesis is that participants using the haptic feedback system will have an increase in navigational performance (shorter time to complete the task, lower number of collisions, and shorter duration of collision).

This paper's novelty, lies in the fact that we test the impact of haptic feedback in human performance, in a mobile robot dual-task teleoperation activity. It also, contributes to the scientific understanding, that haptic feedback is beneficial without directly acting upon the input controls. As well as, proposing a hardware agnostic haptic feedback teleoperation system.

The paper is structured as follows. Section 2 discusses an overview of the proposed haptic feedback teleoperation system. Section 3 presents the experimental set-up and procedure of our user study with the proposed haptic feedback teleoperation system. The results of the user study are presented in Sect. 4. Sections 5 and 6 are the discussion of the results and the conclusion, respectively. There is also an appendix section with material used in the user study.

2 System Overview

This section describes both maximum velocity limitation (collision mitigation) algorithm, and haptic feedback feature (modified DPF and directional haptic feedback), of our teleoperation system. The collision mitigation is responsible for reducing the mobile robot's maximum velocity, to increase the time a human operator has to avoid an obstacle. And in the eventuality of a robot colliding reduce the damage that occurs to the robot and environment. The haptic feedback feature is responsible for warning the human operator of obstacle proximity and direction to the mobile robot, so a human operator can safely navigate through an environment.

2.1 Collision Mitigation

This teleoperation system incorporates an active collision mitigation feature, that works for a priori known obstacles. The feature consists in limiting the robot's maximum velocity in accordance to a modified dynamic parametric field (DPF). The idea is to give human operators increasingly more time to make a movement correction, since the maximum allowed velocity diminishes per shorter obstacle distances. And if a collision happens, it will be at lower velocities, thus in theory not causing major damage to the robot, nor the environment.

The active collision mitigation feature uses potential fields generated by the saturated variation of Fast Marching Square (FM^2) [19], as a parameter in the velocity limitation algorithm. FM^2 was chosen as it gives us the capacity to define propagation viscosity zones, on our initial tests, for a known environment. We modified the parameters of how the slowness map is generated, to make our system agnostic to the mobile robot platform.

We first use a modified DPF to define zones of viscosity, for the wave propagation of the saturated slowness map (SSM). The DPF is composed of three distinct propagation viscosity areas (Fig. 1), with obstacles as source of the wave:

- *Collision Zone* – for $d \leq d_{min}$ the wave propagation velocity is 1/4.
- *Warning Zone* – for $d_{min} < d \leq d_{max}$ the wave propagation velocity is 3/4.
- *Safe Zone* – for $d > d_{max}$ the wave propagation velocity is its maximum.

where d is the distance from an obstacle,

$$d_{min} = \text{robot width} + k_{buffer}, \tag{1}$$

k_{buffer} being a constant buffer distance, and

$$d_{max} = 3 \times d_{min}. \tag{2}$$

We chose these dimensions as they provide a reasonable influence space to warn the operator of obstacle proximity. These dimensions also allow us to easily set-up the system to any ground mobile robot, without the need to calculate the robot kinematics

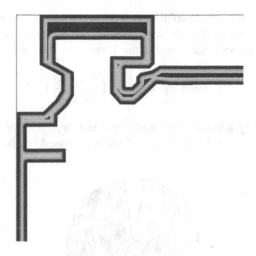

Fig. 1. Example of a saturated slowness map; *Collision Zone* – blue, *Warning Zone* – green-yellow, *Safe Zone* – red (Color figure online)

each time, as our intention is to obtain a closely related hardware agnostic system. The second modification of the SSM, is the saturation value for the *Safe Zone*,

$$T_{saturated} = k_{buffer} + T_{d_{max}},$$ (3)

where $T_{d_{max}}$ is the time needed for the wave to reach d_{max}, and $T_{saturated}$ is the saturation value at each it is safe to navigate the robot.

To compute the maximum allowed velocity, we pair the SSM with the robot's estimated position. We take a pessimistic approach to the location estimation uncertainty, by choosing the closest point to an obstacle boundary (from the location estimation point cloud), that returns a non-zero T value. Thus, maximum allowed velocity is given by

$$V_{max} = \frac{V_{RM} \times T}{T_{saturated}},$$ (4)

where V_{RM} is the robot's specified maximum velocity.

2.2 Haptic Feedback

The haptic feedback feature of our proposed teleoperation system builds on the DPF implementation proposed by Brandt and Colton [16]. As well as, directional force feedback proposed by Barros et al. [20].

1. *Dynamic parametric field* (DPF): As with [16], our system begins to apply haptic feedback at distances equal or less than d_{max} from obstacles. And uses the DPF and SSM previously defined in the collision mitigation section, with two variations. The first variation is to obtain the T value, where we use the most probable estimated

position for the robot. This variation is so that the haptic feedback intensity may reflect the actual distance that the robot is from the obstacles more accurately. The second variation proportionally inverts the T value for the haptic feedback intensity.

$$\text{Intensity} = 100 - \left(\frac{T \times 100}{T_{\text{saturated}}}\right), \tag{5}$$

2. *Directional haptic feedback*: The haptic feedback was divided in three quadrants (Fig. 2): left, centre and right, instead of the 8 proposed in [20].

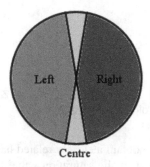

Fig. 2. Directional haptic feedback quadrants: left and right total angle is $\pi - 0.18$ rads, Centre is 0.18 rads

We made this decision based on the static nature of the obstacles, and to simplify the operator's awareness of obstacle direction in relation to the robot's direction of motion. Therefore, the haptic feedback direction is computed by

$$|\nabla\text{SSM}| = |\nabla\phi| = \frac{1}{F(x,y)}, \tag{6}$$

$$\alpha_{\text{HF}} = (\pi - \text{atan2}(\nabla\phi)) - \theta_{\text{robot}}, \tag{7}$$

with x, y being the current robot's estimated position, $\nabla\phi$ is the Eikonal equation for the SSM [19], and θ_{HF} is the robot's current orientation.

An advantage of this haptic feedback teleoperation system is it opens the possibility to use robots that do not have proximity and range sensors (e.g. sonar, laser), and still provide directional haptic feedback to the human operator.

3   Experiment

To test our haptic feedback system an experiment was performed. To evaluate whether using haptic feedback to indicate obstacle proximity, improves the effectiveness of teleoperating a mobile robot, in a teleoperation dual-task activity. In this experiment the operator must navigate the mobile robot while concurrently performing a cognitive distractor task. In particular, we evaluated the *time to complete the navigational task*, the *number of collisions*, and *duration of collision* (duration the robot stays in contact with an obstacle). This setup is intended to simulate normal teleoperation activity of mobile robots, where operator focus is the mission objective (e.g. defuse a bomb, find victims, or target acquisition), with the navigation being a secondary task to accomplish the mission [3].

– *Hypothesis*: Participants using the haptic feedback system will have an increase in navigational performance, compared to not having haptic feedback.

The details of the experimental setup are described in the following sections.

3.1 Participants

Twenty people voluntarily participated in the experiment. They were not compensated. Participants were aged between 17–40 (10 males, 10 females), where 4 completed high-school, 6 bachelor's degree, 6 master's degree, 2 doctoral degree, and 2 did not respond. Sixteen participants had driver's license, with experience between 0.5–15 years. Seventeen participants had more than 5 years of experience playing videogames, one participant had between 2 to 5 years of experience with videogames, one participant 1 year experience of playing videogames, and one participant had never played any videogame prior to the experiment. In regards to current videogame playing frequency, 10 participants play irregularly, 3 play once every 6 months, 1 plays once a month, 2 participants play weekly, and 3 play videogames daily. All participants have had experience playing videogames with a gamepad. Two participants use a gamepad every time they play, 13 play with a gamepad sometimes, and 4 participants have played few times with a gamepad.

3.2 Design

The experiment involved one independent variable: feedback type (two levels: with haptic feedback (HF), no haptic feedback (NHF)). This was presented using an independent measures design – each participant was assigned randomly to one of the two conditions, while guaranteeing each group had a homogeneous distribution of gender. All participants were given a 10-min trial run to learn how to teleoperate the robot in a test map, prior to beginning the experiment.

3.3 Apparatus

Implemented System. Our haptic feedback teleoperation system is implemented on the Robot Operating System (ROS) framework [21]. We use the Stage Robot Simulator [22] to simulate the mobile robot and the experimental environments. The simulated mobile robot is a Turtlebot2 from Open Source Robotics Foundation [23], by using the turtlebot_stage ROS package. For robot localization, we selected the Adaptive Monte Carlo Localization (amcl) package. The teleoperation system is running on Ubuntu 16.04 distribution with ROS Kinetic Karma.

The DPF values are: d_{min} = 50 cm = 35.4 + 14.6, d_{max} = 150 cm. We modified the Turtlebot2 maximum velocity to V_{RM} = 3 m/s, to increase the probability of collisions and shorten the run time of the trial.

Simulation Environment. We used two environment maps in this experiment. For the learning run the map used is 47.175 × 47.425 m, representing a 123.8 m long corridor with 10 easy bends. The corridor has a minimum width of 1.925 m and a maximum width of 5.125 m (Fig. 3).

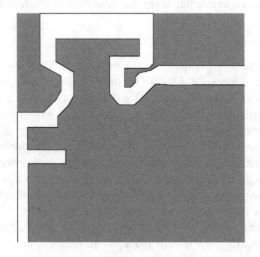

Fig. 3. Learning map

These dimensions were chosen so participants could easily and confidently learn how to control the Turtlebot2 robot. In the trial run, the map has 30 × 43.75 m, representing a cramped winding 131.625 m long path, where the narrowest part is 0.75 m and the widest part is 5.875 m (Fig. 4).

This map was chosen to provide a challenging course for participants, with multiple turns and narrow passages.

To show participants the simulated environments Rviz was used (Fig. 5), with the following view settings: left and right panes collapsed; third person follower camera; *yaw* = π; *distance* = 0.58; *focal point* (x = 0.48, y = 0, z = 0.06); *focal shape size* = 0.25 and fixed; *near clip distance* = 0.01; *target frame* = base_link.

Display System. To provide the operator with visual feedback the simulated environment is shown on a LG M2262D-PZ. This device features a screen with a diagonal size of 55.88 cm, and a resolution of 1920 × 1080. The simulation software was shown in full screen mode.

Input Device. To teleoperate the simulated robot an Xbox One S Wireless Controller was used. It has 4 independent vibration motors, with 2 distinct vibration modes (rumble and impulse). So, when the Turtlebot2 robot was in the *Safe Zone* no vibration was felt on the controller. Within the *Warning Zone* the impulse vibration was activated

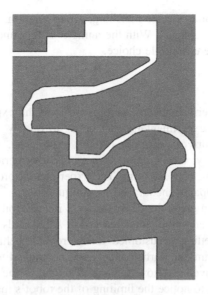

Fig. 4. Trial map

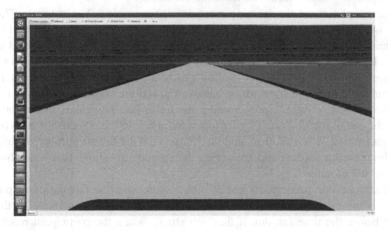

Fig. 5. Rviz view

on the respective side(s) (left, right, or both left and right corresponding to front or back). When in the *Collision Zone* the rumble vibration would also kick in, with the same distribution as the *Warning Zone*.

Physical Environment and Props. The experiment took place in a meeting room, this space was selected to minimize outside distractions. The concurrent task was performed with the aid of printed 19 aptitude questions[1]. Testing numeric ability, abstract

---

[1] http://web.tecnico.ulisboa.pt/jose.corujeira/PDFfiles/Study_Psychometric_Test.pdf.

reasoning, and spatial ability (shape matching, group rotation, 2D shape combination, 3D cube views, and solid shapes). With the numeric ability and shape matching being open answer, the rest were multiple choice.

3.4 Procedure

Participants met the experimenter and were escorted to the experiment room. Participants then received the experimental instructions[2] to review, and filled basic demographics (gender, age, driver's license, driving experience, videogame experience, videogame play frequency, videogaming with gamepad experience, and gamepad use frequency), and recording consent form. The experimental procedures were also discussed orally and participants encouraged to ask questions.

Participants were then given the Xbox One S Wireless Controller and reviewed the control scheme to teleoperate the simulated robot. Afterwards, participants begun the 10-min learning run, getting accustomed to the robot's behaviour with their input commands. Within the run, the participants were encouraged to collide with a wall to learn how the robot behaved and how they could get out of the situation. The intention was also for participants to notice the limiting of the robot's maximum velocity, when they approached a wall. And if participants were from the HF group, they would feel the corresponding haptic feedback from the controller.

Upon completion of the learning run participants took a 1 min break. This was done so we could set up the trial run environment. Prior to beginning the trial run the video camera was set to record, and the run procedure was again explained to participants. It constituted in pressing the "view" button on the controller to begin the run, maintain pressed the "left shoulder" button to activate the Turtlebot2's motors, use the "left thumbstick" to move forwards or backwards, and the "right thumbstick" to rotate the Turtlebot2 left or right. Upon crossing the finish line press the "menu" button to indicate the end of the trial run. Participants were also told the objective was to perform the navigation task, in the shortest amount of time with the fewest number of collisions. While simultaneous reading and answering the aptitude questions that were shown by the side of the monitor (Fig. 6).

For each question participants had 30 s to answer, after the fact the participant had to move to the next question. Participants also had the option to move to the next question before the time ran out, if they felt stuck. When the participant reached the final question, we would go back to the first unanswered question and continue from there, with this process being repeated until the finish line was reached.

After ending the trial run, participants filled out a post-experiment questionnaire handed to them.

3.5 Measures

The primary measures used in this study were, *completion time of trial run*, *number of collisions*, and *duration of collision*, with secondary measure being the *post-experiment*

---

[2] http://web.tecnico.ulisboa.pt/jose.corujeira/PDFfiles/Study_Instructions.pdf.

Fig. 6. Trial run - experiment set-up

questionnaire. A third measure was *the score of correct answers* given in the con-current task (aptitude test), and the *number unanswered questions*. Within each trial run, the simulation system would log the beginning and end time of the run, as well as the position of each collision and timestamps for the duration of each collision. These were measured in seconds of elapsed time. The *post-experiment questionnaire* was composed of 8 questions. The first 7 questions with answers being provided by a semantic differential rating scale that range from 1 (very negative opinion) to 7 (very positive opinion). These questions ranged from collision awareness, turning awareness, location awareness, and usefulness of limitation of maximum velocity (see Appendix). The eighth question was for comments and opinions. The aptitude test *answer scores* were:

- complete correct answer - 1 point;
- incomplete correct answer for a question with multiple answers - (number of correct answers)/(total number of answers) points;
- wrong answer – 0 points.

4   Results

A bilateral Mann-Whitney U analysis of the two groups demographic information showed they are equivalent ($p_{genre} = p_{academic\,level} = p_{driver\,license} = p_{plays\,vg} = p_{time\,playing\,vg} = p_{vg\,g} = 1$, $p_{age} = 0.5401$, $p_{driver\,time} = 0.715$, $p_{vg\,frequency} = 0.703$, $p_{vg\,gamepag\,frequency} = 0.607$).

Analysing the trial run *completion time* (Fig. 7) led to significant differences between conditions (t_{18} = 2.654, p = 0.016; 97% CI, 23.6–413.1).

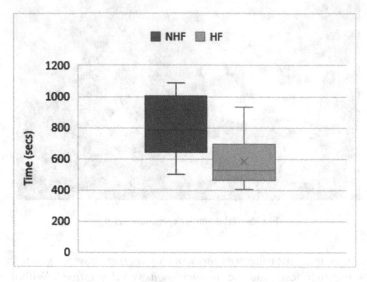

Fig. 7. Time to complete the trial run

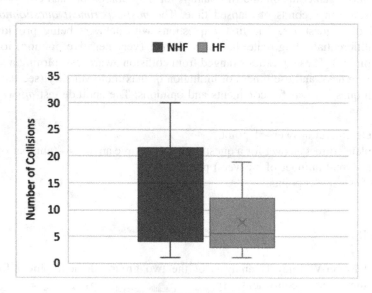

Fig. 8. Number of collisions

We used an independent measures T-test, with grouping variable *feedback type*, as we can assume sample normality for HF condition $\left(W_{(10)} = 0.904, p = 0.245\right)$ and NHF condition $\left(W_{(10)} = 0.945, p = 0.6097\right)$ from the Shapiro-Wilk W test [24]. The average completion time for participants in the HF condition was 3 min and 38 s faster than the average completion time for participants in the NHF condition.

The *number of collisions* (Fig. 8) did not led to any significant differences between the HF and NHF groups $(U = 32.5, n_{HF} = n_{NHF} = 10, p = 0.0987)$, in one-tailed Mann-Whitney U test for discrete values [25]. Yet, a trend was observed, where participants of the HF group had fewer collision (median = 5.5) than those of NHF group (median = 15).

In our *duration of collision* sample data (Fig. 9) we have some outliers in both conditions, these are valid dataset occurrences. The outliers happened due to the complete loss of awareness by the participants, and on which way they should move the robot to stop colliding with the wall. The outliers also took place when the participants were not being aware of colliding with the wall, thus continuing to touch the wall while moving through the path. These outliers compromise the comparison

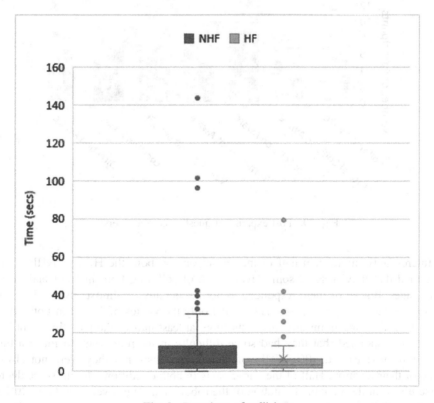

Fig. 9. Durations of collisions

between the HF and NHF conditions, with that in mind we used the simple approach of not considering them for the analysis. We labelled the outliers for HF (Lower bound = −7.8 s, Upper bound = 13.8 s) and NHF (Lower bound = −17.415 s, Upper bound = 29.565 s) with a multiplier of g = 2.2 [26, 27]. We cannot assume sample normality for HF condition ($W_{(10)} = 0.872$, $p < 0.001$) and NHF condition ($W_{(10)} = 0.841$, $p < 0.001$) from the Shapiro-Wilk W test. The analysis of *duration of collision* shows a significant difference between HF and NHF (U = 3397.5, $n_{HF} = 71$, $n_{NHF} = 128$, p = 0.0016), in one-tailed Mann-Whitney U test [25]. Where the HF group had a significant shorter *duration of collision* than the NHF group.

Analysing the post-experiment questionnaire answers (Fig. 10) there is no visible difference between the HF and NHF group responses.

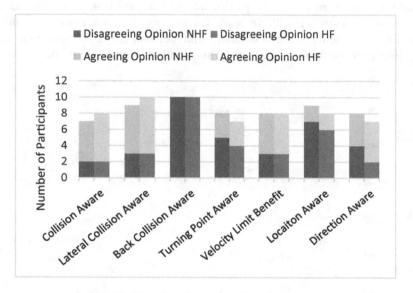

Fig. 10. Post-experiment questionnaire answers

Interestingly, more than half of the participants in both the HF and NHF groups responded that they were at some level aware of colliding both in front and on the lateral sides. But all of them responded to not having any or almost any level of back collision awareness (participant answers had only the values of 1 or 2 in both conditions). In the turning point awareness question, at least half of the participants in both conditions responded that they had some difficulty in judging when to make a turn. Sixty percent (HF) and 70% (NHF) of participants answered they were not always aware of their location. Half of the participants in both conditions, found some degree of usefulness in the variable limitation of the robot's maximum velocity. Only 20% of the HF participants responded that they were mostly not aware of the direction of travel, which contrasts with 40% of the participants in the NHF group.

A between groups analysis of the *aptitude scores* and *number of unanswered questions* was not possible, as there exists an association between the two measures ($r_{HF} = 0.933$ and $r_{NHF} = 0.324$) (Fig. 11).

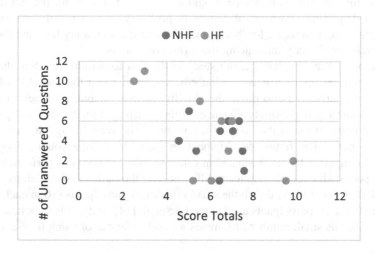

Fig. 11. Relation between aptitude scores and number of unanswered questions

From the trial run *completion time* and *duration of collision* significant results, we can substantiate our hypothesis. As a result, adding haptic feedback to inform the operator of wall proximity, significantly improves the time to complete a navigation task and diminishes the duration of collisions, when the focus is on a concurrent task.

5 Discussion

The current study sought to investigate the efficacy of indicating obstacle proximity through haptic feedback, in a teleoperation activity where the operator's focus of attention is on a secondary task (answering an aptitude questionnaire). By making a comparison with a control condition where haptic feedback is absent. The choice of this experimental setup, was motivated by the scenarios of mobile robotic teleoperation in bomb disposal, urban search and rescue, and target acquisition.

Our findings confirm our hypothesis, the inclusion of haptic feedback to inform the operator of obstacle proximity improves navigational task performance. Our results showed a significant reduction of navigation completion time, in average by 3 min and 38 s compared to the NHF condition. As well as, decreasing the amount of time that the operator's robot stays in collision with a wall. These results can be explained by an augmentation of situation awareness provided by the haptic feedback, while the visual focus is on the concurrent task. Thus, we corroborate the findings in [14–16]. In contrast with these previous study findings, our results did not show any significant difference in the number of collisions between groups. But a trend can be observed that points towards it. On the other hand, our results led to a significant improvement of task completion time in line with Hacinecipoglu et al. [10], but was not present on these studies [14–16]. This inversion of results is probably due to the difference in the experimental setup and haptic feedback, since we added a secondary task and the haptic feedback was not directly influencing the input commands.

To the best of our knowledge, our study is the first to demonstrate that the haptic feedback improves operator teleoperation efficacy, even when the operator's focus is on a concurrent task. We also prove the viability of using haptic feedback to indicate obstacle direction and proximity distance, without acting directly on the input commands (but rather through the body of a commercially available gaming controller). Our results can drive future development in portable mobile robot teleoperation interfaces to integrate haptic feedback, in order to increase operator performance.

The reported absence of significant differences in the number of collisions between HF and NHF, is most likely due to the small number of participants (10 in each group), as opposed to the 20 participants used in the Lee et al. [14] study. It is important to note that even with this small number of samples a trend in favour of using haptic feedback emerged.

The absence of any significant difference in the post-experiment survey between groups, might be due to participants giving more focus to the concurrent task, and thus feeling they were consciously out of touch with what was going on with the robot. Another possibility is participants did not experience both conditions, thus did not have any prior frame of reference to compare with.

The aptitude test results were not viable for analysis, due to the inconsistent nature of the process. Since participants had the option of moving to the next question, and thus being able to revisit those questions multiple times, it also meant that some participants saw more questions and had more accumulated time with each question due to their longer trial run time. In contrast, the opposite happening to the participants with shorter trial run times, who never saw all the questions. This was a shortcoming of the experimental setup, with no clear way of solving it. Nevertheless, it is important to mention that all participants tried to answer the highest number of questions possible, their focus of attention throughout the trial run was the aptitude test. Thus, the aptitude test was a successful distractor task.

Our findings indicate a time benefit for completion of task and duration of collisions, when wall proximity haptic feedback is present in a static dual-task teleoperation activity.

6 Conclusion

Within this paper, we presented the implementation of our haptic feedback teleoperation system. Which warns a human operator of obstacle direction and proximity, through the vibration in a gaming controller. We also describe the user study and respective results, done on the efficacy of the haptic feedback teleoperation system, in a dual-task teleoperation scenario.

Our system has the advantage of being hardware agnostic. Meaning it can be used with most ground mobile robot platforms, even if they do not have proximity nor range sensors. And can also be used with a large variety of haptic feedback devices. The approach we took to implement a collision detection system can be easily applicable in telepresence scenarios, where a mobile robot is used within an office space, since the environment is mostly static and known (e.g. Double robot from Double robotics).

We then tested the effectiveness of our system, through a teleoperation dual-task user study in a simulated virtual environment. To our knowledge, this is the first study that tested the effectiveness of haptic feedback in a dual-task teleoperation condition. From the user study, we conclude that haptic feedback improves human operator performance, in dual-task teleoperation activities where the remote environment is static. Furthermore, the navigational performance improvement, both in task completion time and in collision duration reduction, occurs in a situation where participant focus is in a distractor task and has no prior knowledge of the remote environment (in our case a static environment).

As an initial study on the use of haptic feedback in a dual-task teleoperation activity, this paper's results support the hypothesis that haptic feedback is beneficial to human operator safe teleoperation of robots. The work presented on this paper will serve as a basis for our future work. Our next steps will be to adapt the current system to be used in an unknown dynamic remote environment. To accomplish this, we intend to use a Simultaneous Localization and Mapping algorithm coupled with the mobile robot's laser and odometry, to obtain in real time the layout of the remote environment and obstacles. Then with each update to the generated map, we will run the Fast Marching Square (FM^2) algorithm to generate a Saturated Slowness Map. With this approach, it will be possible to test our system in real world situations where the environment is previously unknown and dynamic.

Acknowledgment. The work described in this paper was carried out with the support of ARDITI – Agência Regional para o Desenvolvimento da Investigação Tecnologia e Inovação under Project M1420 - 09-5369-FSE-000001- PhD Scholarship, whose support we gratefully acknowledge. This work was also supported from Fundação para a Ciência e a Tecnologia (FCT, Portugal), through project UID/EEA/50009/2013. This research has been funded through ERAChair Grant Agreement 621413.

Appendix

Post-experiment Questionnaire

1. How aware were you of the robot colliding?

| Not Aware | 1 | 2 | 3 | 4 | 5 | 6 | 7 | Very Aware |

2. How aware were you of a possible lateral collision?

| Not Aware | 1 | 2 | 3 | 4 | 5 | 6 | 7 | Very Aware |

3. How aware were you of a possible back collision?

| Not Aware | 1 | 2 | 3 | 4 | 5 | 6 | 7 | Very Aware |

4. How easy was it to know when to turn?

| Very Hard | 1 | 2 | 3 | 4 | 5 | 6 | 7 | Very Easy |

5. How useful was the limitation of maximum velocity, when getting close to a wall?

| Not Useful | 1 | 2 | 3 | 4 | 5 | 6 | 7 | Very Useful |

6. I was always aware of the robot's location.

| Strongly Disagree | 1 | 2 | 3 | 4 | 5 | 6 | 7 | Strongly Agree |

7. I was always aware of which direction I should move to.

| Strongly Disagree | 1 | 2 | 3 | 4 | 5 | 6 | 7 | Strongly Agree |

8. Comments and Opinions

_____

_____

_____

References

1. Bejczy, A.K.: Teleoperation, telerobotics. In: The Mechanical Systems Design Handbook, Pasadena, California, vol. 3, no. 2, pp. 205–214 (2001)
2. Chen, J.Y.C., Haas, E.C., Barnes, M.J.: Human performance issues and user interface design for teleoperated robots. IEEE Trans. Syst. Man Cybern. Part C (Appl. Rev.) 37(6), 1231–1245 (2007). doi:10.1109/TSMCC.2007.905819
3. Trouvain, B.: Teleoperation of unmanned vehicles: the human factor (2006)

4. Adamides, G., Christou, G., Katsanos, C., Xenos, M., Hadzilacos, T.: Usability guidelines for the design of robot teleoperation: a taxonomy. IEEE Trans. Hum.-Mach. Syst. **45**(2), 256–262 (2015)
5. Sanguino, T.J.M., Márquez, J.M.A., Carlson, T., Millán, J.D.R.: Improving skills and perception in robot navigation by an augmented virtuality assistance system. J. Intell. Robot. Syst. Theory Appl. 1–12 (2014)
6. Chua, W.L.K., Johnson, M., Eskridge, T., Keller, B.: AOA: ambient obstacle avoidance interface. In: Proceedings of IEEE International Workshop on Robot and Human Interactive Communication, vol. 2014, no. October, pp. 18–23 (2014)
7. Reveleau, A., Ferland, F., Labbé, M., Létourneau, D., Michaud, F.: Visual representation of sound sources and interaction forces in a teleoperation interface for a mobile robot. J. Hum.-Robot Interact. **4**(2), 1 (2015)
8. Yanco, H.A., Drury, J.: 'Where am i?' acquiring situation awareness using a remote robot platform. In: 2004 IEEE International Conference on Systems, Man and Cybernetics (IEEE Cat. No. 04CH37583), vol. 3, pp. 2835–2840 (2004)
9. Nielsen, C.W., Goodrich, M.A., Ricks, R.W.: Ecological interfaces for improving mobile robot teleoperation. IEEE Trans. Robot. **23**(5), 927–941 (2007)
10. Hacinecipoglu, A., Konukseven, E.I., Koku, A.B.: Evaluation of haptic feedback cues on vehicle teleoperation performance in an obstacle avoidance scenario. In: 2013 World Haptics Conference, WHC 2013, pp. 689–694 (2013)
11. Dragan, A.D., Srinivasa, S.S.: Online customization of teleoperation interfaces. In: Proceedings of IEEE International Workshop on Robot Human Interactive Communication, pp. 919–924 (2012)
12. Quintas, J., Almeida, L., Sousa, E., Menezes, P.: A context-aware immersive interface for teleoperation of mobile robots (2015)
13. Hou, X., Mahony, R., Schill, F.: Comparative study of haptic interfaces for bilateral teleoperation of VTOL aerial robots. IEEE Trans. Syst. Man Cybern. Syst. **46**(10), 1352–1363 (2016)
14. Lee, S., Sukhatme, G., Kim, G.J., Park, C.-M.: Haptic teleoperation of a mobile robot: a user study. Presence Teleoperators Virtual Environ. **14**(3), 345–365 (2005)
15. de Barros, P.G., Lindeman, R.W.: Multi-sensory urban search-and-rescue robotics: improving the operatoror's omni-directional perception. Front. Robot. AI **1**, 1–15 (2014)
16. Brandt, A.M., Colton, M.B.: Haptic collision avoidance for a remotely operated quadrotor UAV in indoor environments. In: 2010 IEEE International Conference on Systems, Man and Cybernetics, pp. 2724–2731 (2010)
17. Casper, J., Murphy, R.R.: Human-robot interactions during the robot assisted urban search and rescue response at the world trade center. IEEE Trans. Syst. Man Cybern. Part B Cybern. **33**(3), 367–385 (2003)
18. Ryu, D., Hwang, C.S., Kang, S., Kim, M., Song, J.B.: Wearable haptic-based multi-modal teleloperation of field mobile manipulator for explosive ordnance disposal. In: IEEE International Workshop on Safety, Security and Rescue Rototics, pp. 98–103 (2005)
19. Valero-Gomez, A., Gomez, J.V., Garrido, S., Moreno, L.: The path to efficiency: fast marching method for safer, more efficient mobile robot trajectories. IEEE Robot. Autom. Mag. **20**(4), 111–120 (2013)
20. De Barros, P.G., Lindeman, R.W., Ward, M.O.: Enhancing robot teleoperator situation awareness and performance using vibro-tactile and graphical feedback. In: Proceedings of 2011 IEEE Symposium on 3D User Interfaces, 3DUI, pp. 47–54 (2011)
21. Quigley, M., Conley, K., Gerkey, B., Faust, J., Foote, T., Leibs, J., Berger, E., Wheeler, R., Mg, A.: ROS: an open-source robot operating system. ICRA **3**(3), 5 (2009)

22. Hedges, R.: Stage (2008). http://playerstage.sourceforge.net/index.php?src=stage. Accessed 24 Sept 2016
23. Open source robotics foundation: TurtleBot (2016). http://www.turtlebot.com/. Accessed 24 Sept 2016
24. Royston, J.P.: Algorithm AS 181: the W test for normality. Appl. Stat. **31**(2), 176 (1982)
25. Conover, W.J.: Practical nonparametric statistics. Statistician **22**, 309–314 (1971)
26. Tukey, J.W.: Exploratory data analysis. Analysis **2**(1999), 688 (1977)
27. Hoaglin, D.C., Iglewicz, B.: Fine-tuning some resistant rules for outlier labeling. J. Am. Stat. Assoc. **82**(400), 1147–1149 (1987)

Effects of Human Cognitive Differences on Interaction and Visual Behavior in Graphical User Authentication

Marios Belk[1,4(✉)], Christos Fidas[2], Christina Katsini[3],
Nikolaos Avouris[3], and George Samaras[4]

[1] Cognitive UX GmbH, Heidelberg, Germany
belk@cognitiveux.de
[2] Department of Cultural Heritage Management and New Technologies,
University of Patras, Patras, Greece
fidas@upatras.gr
[3] HCI Group, Department of Electrical and Computer Engineering,
University of Patras, Patras, Greece
katsinic@upnet.gr, avouris@upatras.gr
[4] Department of Computer Science, University of Cyprus, Nicosia, Cyprus
cssamara@cs.ucy.ac.cy

Abstract. This paper discusses two user studies to investigate whether human cognitive differences affect user interaction and visual behavior within recognition-based graphical authentication tasks. In order to increase external validity, we conducted the studies with separate user samples. In the first study ($N = 82$) which embraced a longitudinal and ecological valid interaction scenario, we examined whether field dependence-independence (FD-I) differences have an effect on their login performance. During the second study ($N = 51$) which embraced an in-lab eye tracking setup, we investigated whether FD-I differences of participants are reflected on their visual behavior during graphical key creation. Analysis of results revealed interaction effects of users' FD-I differences which indicate that such human cognitive differences should be considered as additional human design factors in graphical user authentication research.

Keywords: Human cognition · Graphical passwords · Usability · Eye tracking

1 Introduction

Graphical passwords have been proposed as viable alternatives to traditional textual passwords since: *(a)* they leverage the picture superiority effect, claiming that pictures are better recalled by the human brain than text information [1, 3]; and *(b)* they leverage new interaction design capabilities (*e.g.*, selecting images through finger touch on the screen) [1, 4]. Graphical passwords are now being widely adopted in real-life use, *e.g.*, PassFaces [2], Android Pattern Unlock, and Windows 10 Picture Authentication.

Graphical mechanisms can be classified into three primary categories [2, 11]: *recall-based mechanisms* that require users to memorize and draw a secret pattern [5–7];

© IFIP International Federation for Information Processing 2017
Published by Springer International Publishing AG 2017. All Rights Reserved
R. Bernhaupt et al. (Eds.): INTERACT 2017, Part III, LNCS 10515, pp. 287–296, 2017.
DOI: 10.1007/978-3-319-67687-6_19

cued-recall-based mechanisms that require users to identify particular locations on an image which serve as cues to assist the recall process [8, 9]; and *recognition-based mechanisms* that require users to create a graphical key by memorizing a set of images, and then recognize those among decoys [2, 4, 10].

Recognition-based mechanisms necessitate from humans to perform visual search and visual memory processing tasks, aiming to view, recognize and recall graphical information. Researchers have examined the effects of various individual differences on graphical passwords such as age, gender and language differences [12], cognitive disabilities [13] and verbal/imager style differences [14, 15]. In addition, given that humans do not embrace similarities in visual search strategies and capacity of visual memory, different studies investigated the effects of human memory on various types of graphical passwords [11], image type (*e.g.*, faces *vs.* single-object images) and grid size in recognition-based graphical passwords [4, 33], usage of multiple graphical passwords [16], frequency and interference [17], and image distortion [18, 19].

Research Motivation. Bearing in mind that recognition-based graphical authentication tasks are in principle cognitive tasks which embrace visual search and visual memory processing of graphical information, we further investigate the effects of individual differences in such tasks by adopting Witkin's *field dependence-independence theory (FD-I)* [20, 21]. The FD-I theory suggests that humans have different habitual approaches, according to contextual and environmental conditions, in retrieving, recalling, processing and storing graphical information [20], and accordingly distinguishes individuals as being field dependent and field independent. *Field dependent (FD) individuals* view the perceptual field as a whole, they are not attentive to detail, and not efficient and effective in situations where they are required to extract relevant information from a complex whole. *Field independent (FI) individuals* view the information presented by their visual field as a collection of parts and tend to experience items as discrete from their backgrounds.

With regards to visual search abilities, evidence has shown that FI individuals are more efficient in tasks that entail visual search than FD individuals since they are more successful in dis-embedding and isolating important information from a complex whole [21, 22]. With regards to visual working memory abilities, research has shown that FI individuals have more enhanced working memory abilities than FD individuals since viewing shapes is primarily a visuospatial function, and the cognitive ability of extracting embedded shapes out of a complex whole involves the use of central executive functions, such as monitoring [23].

To the best of our knowledge, the effects of FD-I towards interaction and visual behavior in recognition-based graphical authentication has not been investigated.

2 Method of Study

2.1 Hypotheses

H_1. There are differences in interaction behavior (task efficiency and effectiveness) during graphical login between FD and FI users, by also considering the device type.

H_2. There are differences in visual behavior (fixation count and duration) during graphical key selection between FD and FI users, by also considering the device type.

2.2   Research Instruments

Human Cognitive Factor Elicitation Tool. Users' FD-I was measured through the Group Embedded Figures Test (GEFT) [24] which is a widely accredited and validated paper-and-pencil test [21, 22]. The test measures the user's ability to find common geometric shapes in a larger design. The GEFT consists of 25 items; 7 are used for practice, 18 are used for assessment. In each item, a simple geometric figure is hidden within a complex pattern, and participants are required to identify the simple figure by drawing it with a pencil over the complex figure. Based on a widely-applied cut-off score [22], participants that solve 11 items and less are classified as FD, participants that solve 12 items and above are classified as FI.

Eye Tracking Device. A wearable eye tracking device was used; Tobii Pro Glasses 2 [25], which has 4 eye cameras and a 100 Hz gaze sampling frequency.

Recognition-Based Graphical Authentication Mechanism. A recognition-based graphical authentication mechanism was designed and developed following guidelines of well-cited graphical schemes; Passfaces [2], DejaVu [10] and ImagePass [4]. During user enrolment, users created their authentication key by selecting a fixed number of 5 single-object images out of 120 images in a specific order. The same image could not be selected multiple times in a single key. The provided policy was based on existing approaches and is typical in recognition-based graphical authentication [1, 13].

Interaction Devices. The graphical authentication mechanism was deployed on two types of devices; *desktop computers* (Intel core i7 with 8 GB RAM, 21-inch monitor, standard keyboard/mouse) and *mobile touch-based devices* (Samsung P1000 Galaxy, with a 7" screen size and Apple iPad 3, with a 9.5" screen size). In both device types, the grid of images was visible in a single screen view without requiring scrolling.

2.3   Procedure

In order to thoroughly investigate the effects of FD-I, we conducted two user studies with separate user samples; Study A investigated FD-I effects on *graphical login performance over time*, and Study B investigated FD-I effects on *visual behavior during graphical password creation*.

Study Design A. The graphical authentication mechanism was applied in the frame of a University laboratory course in which students would authenticate through a login form for accessing their daily course's material (*i.e.*, daily lab exercise). Main aim was to increase ecological validity since students would use the authentication mechanism as part of a real-life laboratory course. The study lasted for four months based on a between-subjects study design. The first month was dedicated for classifying the participants into FD and FI groups. Several controlled laboratory sessions were conducted in which users solved the GEFT. Then, participants created their graphical key and further interacted with the graphical authentication mechanism to access their course material throughout the semester (three months). Half of the participants interacted on desktop computers and the other half interacted on mobile touch devices. The allocation was based on both FD and FI groups so that the devices were balanced across user groups. To control the frequency of access and prevent user interactions with other types of devices, the users' IP addresses were monitored so that they would access the authentication mechanism only through the devices located at the laboratory room. The users' interactions with the authentication mechanism were recorded for three months (two sessions per week; a maximum twenty-four sessions for each user). Client-side and server-side scripts were developed that measured the total time to login (seconds) for each user session and the number of attempts required to login.

Study Design B. The graphical authentication mechanism was applied in the frame of an enrolment/registration process of a real-life service in order to increase ecological validity. The study was conducted in a quiet room in the lab where each participant was asked to sit in front of a computer at about 40 cm away from the screen. Initially, the participants were introduced to the procedure of the study and familiarized with the eye tracking equipment. Participants wearing glasses were allowed to wear the eye tracking equipment on top of their glasses. Participants first solved the GEFT aiming to classify them into FD and FI groups. Next, participants enrolled in the service in which they had to create a graphical key through the graphical authentication mechanism. The grid of images was constantly the same for all participants. Since the participants were not familiar with recognition-based graphical mechanisms, we provided guidelines related to the applied policy and participants were free to ask any questions before proceeding with the key creation task. Half of the participants interacted on a desktop computer and the other half interacted on a mobile touch device. The allocation was based on both FD and FI groups so that the devices were balanced across groups. Raw eye tracking data were recorded, *i.e.*, fixation count and duration.

2.4   Participants

In Study A, 82 individuals (40 females, 42 males) participated in the study, ranging in age from 18 to 25 ($m = 20.46$; $sd = 3.82$). Based on their scores on the GEFT; 39 participants (47.5%) were FD; 43 participants (52.5%) were FI. In Study B, 51 individuals (16 females, 35 males), ranging in age from 18 to 40 ($m = 29.29$; $sd = 5.76$), participated in the study. Based on the users' scores on the GEFT, 25 participants (49%) were FD; 26 participants (51%) were FI. All participants had prior interaction experience with desktop and mobile devices. No participant was familiar with recognition-based graphical authentication and the GEFT. All participated voluntarily and could opt out any time they wished. To avoid bias, no details were provided about the research.

3   Analysis of Results

3.1   Interaction Behavior Analysis During Graphical Login (H_1)

We compared the *time to login* (task efficiency) and the *number of attempts* (task effectiveness) to successfully login based on 1854 recorded login sessions[1].

Task Efficiency. For time to login, we performed a mixed effects analysis[2]. As fixed effects, we entered the interaction device type (desktop and mobile) into the model, and as random effects, we used subjects to account for non-independence of measures (24 sessions). To account for multiple testing, we adjusted the alpha level with the Dunn-Sidak correction and accordingly report the corrected *p*-values in the analysis[3]. *P*-values were obtained by likelihood ratio tests of the full model with the effect in question against the model without the effect in question [29]. Visual inspection of residual plots revealed that linearity and homoscedasticity were violated. Thus, we performed a log transformation on the dependent variable (time to login), and further inspected residual plots, histograms and Q-Q plots of the residuals, indicating that there were no obvious deviations from linearity, homoscedasticity and normality. In the analyses, we report descriptive statistics and comparisons based on the non-transformed data, whereas significance testing is performed on the transformed data. Figure 1 illustrates the login time per device type across all the sessions of the study.

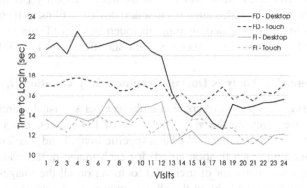

Fig. 1. Login time comparisons between FD and FI users over the three-month study [32].

The analysis revealed that users' FD-I affected the time needed to login ($\chi^2(1) = 20.599$, $p < .001$), as FI users were overall significantly faster in completing the login task than FD users. On desktop interactions, FI users were faster than FD users by 5.4 s $\pm$ 1.01 (standard errors (*SE*)), while on touch interactions, FI users were again faster by 3.74 s $\pm$ .99. The main effect of device type on time needed to login is

---

[1] For a more detailed analysis on the users' interactions and feedback, please see [32].

[2] For the analysis, we used *R* [26] with the *lme4 package* [27].

[3] Using the *dunn.test package* in *R* [28].

not significant, nor is the interaction between FD-I and device. The analysis also revealed a main effect of session trials on the time to successfully login indicating that time to login improves as users gain more experience ($\chi^2(1)$ = 205.36, $p < .001$). FD users recorded the highest times on both desktop and touch devices throughout the 24 sessions compared to FI users. Nevertheless, while FD users needed more time to login than FI users in the initial sessions, as they gained experience, time difference between FD-FI users notably decreased (Fig. 1).

Table 1. Failed attempts (out of 1854 sessions) per FD-I group and device type.

Overall	Desktop-FD	Touch-FD	Desktop-FI	Touch-FI
288	80	90	71	47
Total	170		118	

Task Effectiveness. The number of sessions with failed attempts was counted. A session is considered as failed in case the participant needed more than one attempt to successfully login. Over the span of 24 sessions for each user, we entered a flag indicating whether the session was a successful or a failed attempt. We performed a mixed logistic regression with the task effectiveness (successful *vs.* failed) as the dependent variable. The independent variables were used as fixed effects (FD-I, device type), and the subjects as random effects. Among 1854 sessions, 288 attempts failed (15.53% overall error rate). Most failed sessions were caused by FD users (80 failed attempts in desktop and 90 failed attempts in touch devices). FI users recorded 71 failed attempts in desktop and 47 failed attempts in touch devices (Table 1). However, the analysis revealed that these differences were not significant ($\chi^2(1)$ = 5.06, $p = .17$).

3.2 Visual Behavior Analysis During Graphical Key Creation (H_2)

Given that the graphical password creation embraces per se visual search analysis and comprehension, we analyzed the visual behavior of FD-I users, in terms of *fixation count* (the number of times a user looked at a specific image) and *fixation duration* (the number of milliseconds each fixation lasted) for each image in the grid. Accordingly, we analyzed the visual behavior of users: *(a)* focusing on all the images of the image grid during key creation; and *(b)* on the chosen images of the graphical key.

Cumulative Visual Behavior During Graphical Key Creation. To study the effect of FD-I on visual behavior during graphical key creation, a two-way MANOVA was run with two independent variables (FD-I and device type) and three dependent variables (total fixated images, mean fixation count and mean fixation duration per image). There was a linear relationship between the dependent variables, and no evidence of multicollinearity. There were no univariate and no multivariate outliers in the data. Data were normally distributed. There was homogeneity of covariance matrices and variances. Table 2 shows the cumulative fixation count and duration per group.

Analysis revealed a statistically significant main effect of FD-I on the combined dependent variables ($F(3,45)$ = 4.393, $p = .009$, *partial η^2* = .227). Further analysis of the main effects revealed a statistically significant difference between FD-I for desktop

Table 2. Cumulative fixation count and duration per FD-I group and device type.

Median	Desktop-FD	Desktop-FI	Touch-FD	Touch-FI
# of images fixated	40	*56.36*	39	*61.08*
Fixation count	1.50	*2.07*	2.46	2.25
Fixation duration	.41	.55	.61	.58

interactions on the total fixated images ($F(1,47)$ = 4.728, p = .035, *partial* η^2 = .091), and touch interactions on the total fixated images ($F(1,47)$ = 8.323, p = .006, *partial* η^2 = .150). FI users fixated on significantly more images than FD users. A statistically significant difference between FD-I for desktop interactions on the fixation count was revealed ($F(1,47)$ = 4.760, p = .034, *partial* η^2 = .092), with FI users having a significantly larger fixation count than FD users. However, the difference was not significant for touch interactions ($F(1,47)$ = .676, p = .415, *partial* η^2 = .014). No significant differences were found between FD-I for desktop and touch interactions on fixation duration.

Visual Behavior per Selected Image of the Graphical Key. We performed a similar analysis as the previous focusing on the fixation count and duration of each image that was selected for the graphical key. All assumptions were met for conducting the test. We run a two-way repeated measures MANOVA test with two independent variables (FD-I and device type), and two dependent variables (fixation count and duration per selected image in the graphical key). Table 3 summarizes the median fixation count and duration of the selected images of the graphical key.

Table 3. Median fixation count and duration for selected images in the graphical key.

Median	Desktop-FD	Desktop-FI	Touch-FD	Touch-FI
Fixation count	2.00	2.16	2.1	2.69
Fixation duration	1.32	1.43	1.58	2.39

There was a statistically significant effect of FD-I on the combined dependent variables ($F(4,44)$ = 3.164, *Wilks'* Λ = .777, p = .023), with FI users fixating more time on the selected images than FD users. The interaction effect between FD-I and device type was not statistically significant ($F(1,44)$ = .990, *Wilks'* Λ = .917, p = .083).

4 Discussion of Main Findings

Finding 1 – FD-I differences affect task login efficiency over time in graphical passwords across device types. FI users needed significantly less time to complete the graphical login task compared to FD users over the whole period of the three-month study (supporting H_1). From a theoretical point of view, given that FI users have enhanced analytical abilities and dis-embedding skills, and an enhanced visual working memory in contrast to FD users [23], FI users might have been positively affected in graphical login tasks since the images are processed through the visual working memory sub-system.

Finding 2 – FD-I differences affect task login effectiveness over time in graphical passwords. FI users needed less attempts to complete the graphical login task compared to FD users (supporting H_1). This can be due to the stimuli and interaction design of the graphical mechanism, *i.e.*, in the case of graphical login, homogeneous objects and structure are illustrated to the users, in which the surrounding framework might dominate the perception of the aiming items. Accordingly, when FD users interact with these stimuli, they might find it difficult to locate the information they are seeking because other information might mask what they are looking for. In contrast, FI users find it easier to recognize and select the essential information from its surrounding field due to improved dis-embedding skills and visual search abilities [21].

Finding 3 – FD-I differences affect visual behavior during graphical password creation. FI users fixated cumulatively on more images across device types, and had a significantly higher fixation count on desktop computers than FD users. In addition, an analysis per selected image has shown that FI users fixated more time on their chosen images than FD users across device types (supporting H_2). Since FI users are analytical and pay attention to details through deeper processing of visual information [20–23], hence they spent more time to process the images in the grid during and prior selection. Such a behavior could have an effect on memorability, in favor of FI users who, as analyzed in Finding 1 and Finding 2, had an increased efficiency and effectiveness in login time and attempts compared to FD users. In addition, FD users fixated on, and selected from a smaller subset of the image grid than FI users, thus affecting practical security entropy of the graphical authentication scheme as shown in [30].

5 Design Implications and Conclusion

The findings underpin the value of considering human cognitive differences as a design factor, in both design and run-time, to avoid deploying graphical authentication schemes that unintentionally favor a specific group based on the designer's decisions.

From a designer's perspective, all findings underpin the value for versatility in the design and development of graphical authentication schemes by taking into account human cognitive differences in information processing. Currently, human cognitive characteristics are not considered as human design factors of graphical user authentication schemes and thus we hope that our work will inspire similar research endeavors (e.g., see the approach discussed in [32] on how human cognitive factors can be incorporated in personalized user authentication schemes). Furthermore, since FI users tend to scan the whole grid of images prior selecting their key, while FD users tend to scan a smaller subset prior selecting their key, an intelligent mechanism could assist FD-I users to reach an improved equilibrium between security and usability, e.g., by illustrating multiple, smaller grids of images to FD users. In addition, low-level eye metrics (fixation count and duration on specific areas of interests) could be used at run-time for user classification and modeling (e.g., [31]), to scaffold users during graphical key creation tasks.

A limitation of the eye tracking study relates to its limited ecological validity which is inherent to the nature of in-lab experiments that was necessary to run the eye tracking setup. Another limitation concerns that only one particular graphical authentication mechanism was investigated although a variety of other genres and mechanisms exist (*e.g.*, Windows 10 Picture Authentication, Android Pattern Unlock, etc.).

References

1. Biddle, R., Chiasson, S., van Oorschot, P.: Graphical passwords: learning from the first twelve years. ACM Comput. Surv. **44**(4), 41 p. (2012)
2. Passfaces Corporation: The Science Behind Passfaces. White paper (2009). http://www.passfaces.com/enterprise/resources/white_papers.htm
3. Paivio, A., Csapo, K.: Picture superiority in free recall: imagery or dual coding? Cogn. Psychol. **5**(2), 176–206 (1973)
4. Mihajlov, M., Jerman-Blazic, B.: On designing usable and secure recognition-based graphical authentication mechanisms. Interact. Comput. **23**(6), 582–593 (2011)
5. Jermyn, I., Mayer, A., Monrose, F., Reiter, M., Rubin, A.: The design and analysis of graphical passwords. In: Proceedings of the USENIX Security Symposium (Security 1999). USENIX Association (1999)
6. Gao, H., Guo, X., Chen, X., Wang, L., Liu, X.: YAGP: yet another graphical password strategy. In: Proceedings of the Conference on Computer Security Applications, pp. 121–129. IEEE Computer Society (2008)
7. Tao, H., Adams, C.: Pass-Go: a proposal to improve the usability of graphical passwords. Netw. Secur. **7**(2), 273–292 (2008)
8. Wiedenbeck, S., Waters, J., Birget, J., Brodskiy, A., Memon, N.: Authentication using graphical passwords: effects of tolerance and image choice. In: Proceedings of the Symposium on Usable Privacy and Security (SOUPS 2005), pp. 1–12. ACM Press (2005)
9. Chiasson, S., Forget, A., Biddle, R., van Oorschot, P.: Influencing users towards better passwords: persuasive cued click-points. In: Proceedings of the Conference on People and Computers, pp. 121–130. British Computer Society (2008)
10. Dhamija, R., Perrig, A.: DejaVu: a user study using images for authentication. In: Proceedings of the USENIX Security Symposium. USENIX Association (2000)
11. Stobert, E., Biddle, R.: Memory retrieval and graphical passwords. In: Proceedings of the Symposium on Usable Privacy and Security (SOUPS 2013), article 15, 14 p. ACM Press (2013)
12. Nicholson, J., Coventry, L., Briggs, P.: Age-related performance issues for PIN and face-based authentication systems. In: Proceedings of Conference on Human Factors in Computing Systems (CHI 2013), pp. 323–332. ACM Press (2013)
13. Ma, Y., Feng, J., Kumin, L., Lazar, J.: Investigating user behavior for authentication methods: a comparison between individuals with down syndrome and neurotypical users. ACM Trans. Access. Comput. **4**(4), Article 15, 27 p. (2013)
14. Belk, M., Fidas, C., Germanakos, P., Samaras, G.: Security for diversity: studying the effects of verbal and imagery processes on user authentication mechanisms. In: Kotzé, P., Marsden, G., Lindgaard, G., Wesson, J., Winckler, M. (eds.) INTERACT 2013. LNCS, vol. 8119, pp. 442–459. Springer, Heidelberg (2013). doi:10.1007/978-3-642-40477-1_27
15. Belk, M., Fidas, C., Germanakos, P., Samaras, G.: A personalized user authentication approach based on individual differences in information processing. Interact. Comput. **27**(6), 706–723 (2015). Oxford University Press

16. Chowdhury, S., Poet, R., Mackenzie, L.: A comprehensive study of the usability of multiple graphical passwords. In: Kotzé, P., Marsden, G., Lindgaard, G., Wesson, J., Winckler, M. (eds.) INTERACT 2013. LNCS, vol. 8119, pp. 424–441. Springer, Heidelberg (2013). doi:10.1007/978-3-642-40477-1_26

17. Everitt, K., Bragin, T., Fogarty, J., Kohno, T.: A comprehensive study of frequency, interference, and training of multiple graphical passwords. In: Proceedings of the Conference on Human Factors in Computing Systems (CHI 2009), pp. 889–898. ACM Press (2009)

18. Hayashi, E., Dhamija, R., Christin, N., Perrig, A.: Use your illusion: secure authentication usable anywhere. In: Proceedings of the Symposium on Usable Privacy and Security (SOUPS 2008), pp. 35–45. ACM Press (2008)

19. Hayashi, E., Hong, J., Christin, N.: Security through a different kind of obscurity: evaluating distortion in graphical authentication schemes. In: Proceedings of the Conference on Human Factors in Computing Systems (CHI 2011), pp. 2055–2064. ACM Press (2011)

20. Witkin, H.A., Moore, C.A., Goodenough, D.R., Cox, P.W.: Field-dependent and field-independent cognitive styles and their educational implications. Educ. Res. **47**(1), 1–64 (1977)

21. Angeli, C., Valanides, N., Kirschner, P.: Field dependence-independence and instructional-design effects on learners' performance with a computer-modeling tool. Comput. Hum. Behav. **25**(6), 1355–1366 (2009)

22. Hong, J., Hwang, M., Tam, K., Lai, Y., Liu, L.: Effects of cognitive style on digital jigsaw puzzle performance: a GridWare analysis. Comput. Hum. Behav. **28**(3), 920–928 (2012)

23. Rittschof, K.A.: Field dependence-independence as visuospatial and executive functioning in working memory: Implications for instructional systems design and research. Educ. Tech. Res. Dev. **58**(1), 99–114 (2010)

24. Witkin, H.A., Oltman, P., Raskin, E., Karp, S.: A Manual for the Embedded Figures Test. Consulting Psychologists Press, Palo Alto (1971)

25. Tobii Pro Glasses 2. http://www.tobiipro.com/product-listing/tobii-pro-glasses-2/#Specifications. Accessed 19 Sep 2016

26. R Core Team: R: a language and environment for statistical computing. R Foundation for Statistical Computing, Vienna, Austria (2015). https://www.R-project.org/

27. Bates, D., Maechler, M., Bolker, B., Walker, S.: Fitting linear mixed-effects models using lme4. J. Stat. Softw. **67**(1), 1–48 (2015)

28. Dinno, A.: dunn.test: Dunn's Test of Multiple Comparisons Using Rank Sums. R package version 1.3.1 (2015). http://CRAN.R-project.org/package=dunn.test

29. Winter, B., Grawunder, S.: The phonetic profile of Korean formality. J. Phon. **40**, 808–815 (2012)

30. Katsini, C., Fidas, C., Belk, M., Avouris, N., Samaras, G.: Influences of users' cognitive strategies on graphical password composition. In: Extended Abstracts of the Conference on Human Factors in Computing Systems (CHI 2017), pp. 2698–2705. ACM Press (2017)

31. Raptis, G., Katsini, C., Belk, M., Fidas, C., Samaras, G., Avouris, N.: Using eye gaze data and visual activities to infer human cognitive styles: method and feasibility studies. In: Proceedings of the Conference on User Modeling, Adaptation and Personalization (UMAP 2017). ACM Press (2017, to appear)

32. Belk, M., Fidas, C., Germanakos, P., Samaras, G.: The interplay between humans, technology and user authentication: a cognitive processing perspective. Comput. Hum. Behav. (2017, to appear)

33. Belk, M., Pamboris, A., Fidas, C., Katsini, C., Avouris, N., Samaras, G.: Sweet-spotting security and usability for intelligent graphical authentication mechanisms. In: Proceedings of the Conference on Web Intelligence (WI 2017). ACM Press (2017, to appear)

Pupil-Assisted Target Selection (PATS)

Christoph Strauch[✉], Jan Ehlers, and Anke Huckauf

Department of General Psychology, Ulm University, Ulm, Germany
{christoph.strauch,jan.ehlers,
anke.huckauf}@uni-ulm.de

Abstract. Physiological signals such as pupil size changes promise improvements for human-computer-interaction. However, the pupil response is known to be rather slow and unspecific. This hinders its application in target selection up to now. Nevertheless, there are indications for fast diameter changes accompanying cognitive processing already at early stages so that pupil effects can even precede psycho-motor activity. Building on these findings, we investigated the potential of short-latency pupil size changes for improving target selection in a search and select task. Pupil assisted target selection (PATS) was shown to be competitive to both, purely pupil-based and to dwell-time based selection modes in regard to selection times, but at the cost of more false positives than for a dwell-time approach in a search and select task. This demonstrates the usefulness of PATS as a means for target selection. The observed pupil dynamics correspond to early signal courses in basic research. Pupil dynamics also suggest room for further improvements of the integrated concept of pupil-assisted target selection.

Keywords: Gaze-based interaction · Cognitive pupillometry · Physiological computing · Eye-tracking

1 Introduction

1.1 Physiological Interaction

Current multimodal systems vary in respect of number and kind of input channels. The growing field of physiological computing extends parameterization by providing human-computer interfaces (HCI) with physiological information [1]. Physiological data includes information on the psychophysiological state of the user and is usually applied to derive emotional features and to make systems aware of a user's (cognitive) condition. However, one vision of physiological computing frameworks is that the corresponding information (e.g., pupil dynamics, electrodermal activity changes or heart rate variability) can even be transferred into active control signals. Explicit commands (voice commands, gestures or keystrokes) could be supported through a broader range of signals or would become obsolete to a certain degree [2]. Furthermore, directly accessing input channels via implicit information may extend communication to a variety of devices for which standard interfaces are not suitable. For example, virtual-reality headsets could be operated by tracking pupil size. Including physiological data might also lead to more inclusive interfaces which can be used by all, healthy persons as well as severely disabled people [3].

© IFIP International Federation for Information Processing 2017
Published by Springer International Publishing AG 2017. All Rights Reserved
R. Bernhaupt et al. (Eds.): INTERACT 2017, Part III, LNCS 10515, pp. 297–312, 2017.
DOI: 10.1007/978-3-319-67687-6_20

Recent studies on physiological computing include a variety of physiological variables that contain relevant information on a user's cognitive and affective state [3]. However, the depicted signals are usually diffuse and emerge as unspecific functions of autonomic activity changes. E.g. pupil size changes may indicate the amount of cognitive load just as various levels of affective processing [4]. This low specificity has so far prevented a straight forward application of physiological variables in HCI. Furthermore, most parameters are characterized by rather long latencies that prevent from a direct application. However, changes in pupil diameter constitute one of the fastest psychophysiological variables, with latencies below 500 ms after stimulus onset [5]. There is also evidence that diameter changes not only accompany, but to some extent precede psychomotor processing [6, 7]. Early pupil size changes that reliably occur during target selection may therefore be used as a predictor and thus as an implicit command for target selection. The current work introduces a target selection procedure that combines gaze information and pupil dynamics to implement a new concept of eyes-only interaction in HCI.

2   Related Work

Pupil size is determined by two antagonistic muscle groups, governed by the sympathetic and parasympathetic division of the autonomous nervous system. An increase in physiological activity is associated with an enlargement of pupil size, whereas low autonomic arousal correlates with reduced pupil diameter. Thus, pupil size is not exclusively adjusted by changes in illumination but also provides a valid measure of a subject's cognitive and affective state [8]. The amount of mental workload is reflected in an enlargement of pupil diameter [9] such as the dilation in response to emotionally arousing sounds [5]. Attentional processes may also be investigated by deconvoluting the pupillary signal [10] just as decision processes in binary tasks [7, 11] or the decision to click on a website [12]. Even hunger is reported to affect baseline pupil sizes [13]. Furthermore, detecting and recognizing perceptual stimuli is known to evoke pupil dilations [8]: The so-called "navigational intent", refers to a state in which subjects try to get an overall picture of an image. During this period, pupil size is lower compared to phases of "informational intent", in which the user searches for a particular object [14]. To the present day, pupil size changes are mainly used as a passive indicator for cognitive processing; however, there is evidence that the corresponding dynamics can be deliberately influenced and may serve as an active information channel [4].

Pupil sizes are obtained with camera systems; the associated dynamics are reported to entail latencies of about 0.5 s. As reaction to emotionally charged sounds, a maximum pupil dilation about 2–3 s after stimulus onset is reported [5]. The human pupil size varies from under 1 mm to over 9 mm, psychologically evoked diameter changes are rather small and reported to amount up to 0.5 mm [8]; however, [4] report pupil size changes of up to 1 mm in an active biofeedback application.

Changes in pupil diameter are therefore of central interest for physiological computing systems. However, underlying mechanisms are not always clearly distinguishable and may reflect similar operating principles. Hence, it is necessary to disentangle the associated dynamics and to identify specific signal courses that can reliably be assigned to definable cognitive processes.

2.1 Pupil Size Changes as an Active Information Channel in HCI

In HCI, pupil sizes changes are usually applied to derive mental effort on-line [15]; only few studies are known to utilize pupil dynamics as an active input channel for HCI [16–18].

A recently introduced pupil-based interaction concept [17] builds on the finding that pupil diameter can be subject to voluntary control albeit via cognitive strategies and could be used as an input mechanism to HCI [4, 19, 20]. Here, the induction of cognitive load enabled locked-in patients to communicate on the basis of changes in cognitive load. Different arithmetic problems were successively displayed on a screen in conjunction with the words "yes" or "no". Participants select the response options by processing the displayed task and hereby increase pupil diameter via cognitive load in one of the two phases. The slope of a regression then indicated which answer was envisaged to be selected. The reactions to questions with obvious solutions enable to check for error rates. This approach is especially promising, since it may be applied to clinical subjects outside the laboratory. However, error rates are still high and, more importantly, selections are only binary and take several seconds to be completed. Moreover, data could only be analyzed post-hoc so that live communication was not possible and explicit mental arithmetic is necessary to operate the system [17]. [16] make use of pupil size changes during target selection. In this setting, targets slowly oscillate with different frequencies, whereas pupil dynamics adapt to the flickering source. Here, the number of different options is limited by the number of frequencies in the lower range that can reliably be distinguished from each other. Similar to the aforementioned, this selection mechanism takes several seconds to complete a selection.

Taken together, current approaches that apply pupil dilation for active target selection are associated with overly long selection times and partially high error rates. Hence, pupil-based target selection seems to be unsuitable for real time computer input in end-user applications. However, for scenarios, such as the operation of cognitively demanding tasks, also active pupil size manipulation should be considered [18].

2.2 Selection-Associated Pupil Size Changes

However, besides the mentioned slow changes in pupil size with mental load, also motor actions and their precedent decision processes are reported to be accompanied by pupil size changes [6, 7, 21]. According to [7, 12, 21], one might expect that the decision to select a certain object affects pupil size: more concretely, when a user fixates an attracting target, pupil size should be expected to even precede or occur within few hundreds of milliseconds. In line with these findings, finding a target during visual search is associated to a fast dilation in contrast to fixations off-target [22, 23]. However, in a machine learning approach, pupil size variation only slightly contributes to post-hoc classification of user intent in addition to other variables derived by eye-tracking [24]. For objects, which are not considered as potential target by the user, pupil size should be expected to vary within its standard noise. Up to now there is no research examining such early pupil size in applied scenarios. Still, such early signal changes may provide a new approach for pupil-based target selection. Based on these signal dynamics, we developed an eyes-only interface for a pupil assisted target selection (PATS) mechanism that aims to equally reduce selection times and error rates.

2.3   Research Aims

- Investigate the potential of using pupil size changes to improve target selection at an early stage
- Compare PATS with standard gaze-based dwell-time approaches
- Assess early pupil dynamics during target selection.

3   Methods

3.1   Pupil Assisted Target Selection (PATS)

PATS integrates pupil size changes with information on gaze behavior as two central input variables. Implemented as a usual dwell-time approach, target selection may either be achieved by a simple fixation duration or else through pupil enlargement beyond a predetermined threshold, whichever is reached first. The selection process was thereby accompanied by feedback. Fixated objects were consistently highlighted. However, PATS was assessed in two versions, differing in the pupil feedback provided for the user. As a comparison for PATS, a purely dwell-time selection approach was used in which users had to fixate a target for a eye-typing novice dwell-time (1000 ms) [25]. In addition, a pupil size-based selection mechanism was implemented, in which a calibrated increase in pupil size over 667 ms was the criterion for object selection. Window length was chosen based on the dynamics reported in [7, 22]. In both papers, considerable increases are registered within lower than 1 s. This length corresponded to 40/60 Frames. The deviation between beginning and end of the 667 ms was calculated continuously and started when a new trial was presented. That is, objects did not have to be fixated. Hereby, also fixation slightly preceding dilations [7, 22] could be used. For all modes, an initial dwell-time of 500 ms was necessary to enable selection.

3.2   Task

The system was evaluated employing a search and select task: several targets are arranged in a circle. One of the circularly arranged objects serves as target. The target is defined via its similar shape to a centrally placed object. Figure 1 illustrates the task layout. In the depicted example, the object at 8 o'clock corresponds to the central object and would thus have to be selected.

Error rates and selection times were assessed in order to determine effectiveness and efficiency, respectively. Error rates are computed as the sum of false positive non-intended selections and time-out errors. A trial was counted as time-out when users

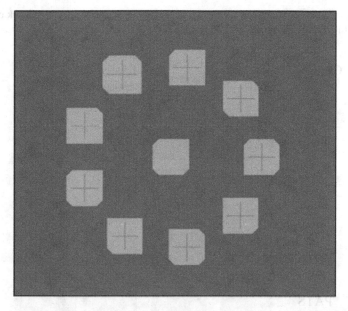

Fig. 1. Search and select task with nine circularly arranged objects including one target corresponding to the reference object in the center.

did not select a target within 20 s. The selection time is the time from first fixating the intended target until selection. User satisfaction was assessed with the "system-usability scale" (SUS), ranging from 0 (no user satisfaction) to 100 (perfect user satisfaction). The SUS also measures learnability by determining how difficult it is to adapt to a system's set of rules [26].

3.3 Feedback and Selection Modes

Selection performance using PATS was assessed in two ways that varied with regard to the kind of feedback. Both approaches were compared to a purely pupil-based and a purely fixation (dwell-time)-based selection mode. All four concepts are illustrated in Table 1.

When fixated, every object was highlighted in light blue. Unattended objects were displayed in yellow as depicted in Fig. 1. For the selection mode purely based on pupil size changes, a dark grey circle appeared 500 ms after a target was fixated. A bright grey circle visualizing the criterion for selection was shown within the fixated target. The size of this circle was meant to illustrate the increase in pupil size over 667 ms required for selection, a threshold which was determined during calibration before each block. Within this circle, a light grey circle dynamically represented the current increase in pupil size pupil diameter within this time window. As soon as the outer circle was filled, the target was selected. Subsequently, the associated target was framed with a blue line to indicate a successful selection for 2 s. Each trial was followed by a pause of 1 s.

Table 1. Presentation of target and feedback for the four selection modes. Feedback circles were dynamically filled until the target was selected.

Objects	Target not fix-ated	Target fixated	Target fixated >500 ms	Target selected
Pupil Size				
Dwell-Time				
PATS				
PATS Reduced FB				

The sequence of events in the dwell-time selection mode was the same as for the purely pupil-based selection, except the following differences: As soon as gaze entered the object, a light grey circle was displayed in the object. It was filled clockwise by a brighter circle. After fixating the object for a period of 1000 ms, the light circle was completely filled and the object was selected.

The PATS selection mechanism combines the purely pupil-based and the dwell-time based approach. A static light grey circle appeared within the dark grey circle. For PATS with reduced feedback, only the gaze-based highlighting was applied. The sequence of events is illustrated in Table 1 separately for all four selection modes.

3.4 Apparatus

Pupil size and gaze were tracked using a SMI iView XTM Hi Speed 1250 eye-tracker (SensoMotoric Instruments GmbH, Teltow) positioned 65 cm from the screen (BenQ XL2720Z 1920 * 1080 Pixels, 60 Hz). For the experiment, the eye tracker was also set to a sampling rate of 60 Hz. Data were collected using iViewX 2.8.43 software. Following the manufacturer, tracker precision is better than 0.01° visual angle, precision for pupil size estimation is 0.01 mm or better. Diameter was calculated using a pixel to mm conversion by the manufacturer. A chin rest secured the constant distance and position of the seated participants' heads and eyes to both, eye-tracker and screen. The task, presentation of visual stimuli, the underlying selection modes, as well as data savings, were implemented using PsychoPy version 1.81.02 [27].

3.5   Sample

24 users participated in the experiment, all of them were students at Ulm University (female = 18, M_{Age} = 24.08). All users reported normal or corrected to normal vision. All participants reported to not having consumed drugs or medication prior to the experiment, no neuronal diseases or traumatic brain injuries were reported; and all participants were asked to stay absent from coffee for at least one hour prior to the experiment. Participants signed an informed consent and took part in the study on a voluntary basis. They received either course credits or a present containing a set of glittering unicorn-stickers and wiggle eyes as a reward.

3.6   Procedure

Experiments were carried out in a laboratory with constant brightness of 38.0 lx obtained at the eyes' position. After having signed the informed consent, users filled a questionnaire to assess demographic variables and a confidential questionnaire assessing potential traumatic brain injuries, the usage of illegal substances and neuronal diseases. This took about ten minutes. The users were then instructed about the search and select task using a printed screenshot. Users were informed that looking at the objects they intend to select was a prerequisite for selection. However, it was not explained how exactly a selection could be performed; meaning that the role of pupil size changes was not mentioned. In addition, participants were told that they will use different selection modes and were explained that they would have to evaluate them after the tasks. Additional questions were answered if occurred.

Users took a seat in front of the monitor in the eye-trackers' chin rest. It was ensured that pupils and the corneal reflexes could be registered reliably in all gaze positions. Then the automatic SMI calibration started: 13 points were displayed systematically on the screen to calibrate the gaze position mapping. Another 13 points appeared in order to validate the gaze-mapping. Users could access a keyboard with their right hand, which enabled to push ← and → . After calibration of the eye tracker, threshold for pupil-based selection was calibrated. Therefore, participants had to complete thirty trials of the search and select task employing the pupil selection mechanism. It was constantly determined whether pupil diameter enlarged for more than 0.2 mm within the foregoing 667 ms. If so, targets were selected; however, only after a minimum dwell-time of 500 ms. Whenever a target was selected correctly, the criterion diminished by 2%. In case of a false positive selection, the criterion increased by 5%, in case of a time-out error, the criterion diminished by 5%. The resulting criterion after thirty trials was then further used during the pupil-based or assisted target selection.

After calibrations, users performed twenty trials of the search and select task with each of the four selection modes. The serial order of the modes was fully permutated in six sequences; each sequence was completed by four participants. The PATS mode with reduced feedback was consistently applied last, since it was assumed that subjects needed training in order to be able to work with an input mode which displays only little feedback. After completing a selection mode, a short information was given that the next run is starting soon so that participants were able to distinguish the different concepts from another. Within each selection mode twenty trials of the search and select task with randomized target shapes were to be performed. After each target selection, a screen was presented: "Wolltest Du dieses Objekt auswaehlen? (nein = ← , ja = →). (Did you intend to select this object (no = ← , yes = →))". If 20 s were exceeded during a selection process, the respective trial was aborted, and "time out error" was displayed on the screen. Such a trial was counted as time-out. After pushing either ← or → , the next trial started after a one second-break. After three blocks with varying order of selection modes, the reduced-feedback selection mode was performed as a last condition. Finally, participants were asked to answer one SUS for each selection method and received their reward.

4   Results

Twentyfour users completed the study. Since the search and select task comprised twenty trials for each selection mode, error rates and selection times were calculated on the basis of 480 trials per selection mode. For PATS, 45.63% of selections were performed using the pupil size selection mechanism and 54.37% using dwell-time. For PATS with reduced feedback, 40.83% of targets were selected with the pupil, while 59.17% were selected by dwell. A summary of key usability parameters is depicted in Table 2. All dependant variables were analyzed employing ANOVAs for repeated measures. Whenever sphericity could not be assumed, Greenhouse-Geisser correction was applied. Post hoc comparisons were analyzed via Bonferroni corrected contrasts.

Table 2. Key usability statistics separately for the four selection modes pupil, dwell, PATS and PATS with reduced feedback. Usability and learnability were assessed using the SUS; that is, the range of usability and learnability is 0–100, hereby 100 marks the best possible evaluation.

Selection mode	False positives M	Time-out M	Selection times M	Usability rating M	Learnability rating M
Pupil	4.58%	0.83%	1.48 s	65.63	75.52
Dwell	0.63%	0.21%	1.00 s	76.56	83.54
PATS	6.88%	0.00%	0.82 s	75.26	72.92
PATS reduced FB	5.40%	0.00%	0.84 s	75.26	79.69

4.1   Error Rates

Among the four selection mechanisms, error rates were lowest for the dwell-time selection mechanism with .84% errors ($SE = 0.39\%$). But, also pupil-based selection (5.41%, $SE = 1.34\%$), PATS (6.88%; $SE = 1.27\%$), and PATS with reduced feedback (5.41%, $SE = 1.47\%$) produced error rates that still allow task operation. A significant difference between selection modes could be found ($F_{(2.21,\ 50.78)} = 6.24$; $p < .01$ $\eta^2_{part} = .21$). Post-hoc comparisons reveal that only dwell-time differed significantly from all other modes.

4.2   Selection Times

Selection times were longest for the pupil selection mechanism (1.48 s, $SE = 0.15$ s). However, it is important to note that observed average selection times for twelve of the 24 users are comparable to the dwell-time of 1000 ms or lower (Median = 1.13 s). PATS (0.82 s, $SE = 0.01$ s) and PATS with reduced feedback (0.84 s, $SE = 0.01$ s) produced lower selection times than the dwell-time of 1000 ms and merely pupil-based selection. Average selection times were comparable between subjects except for the pupil selection mechanism, for which individual differences were monitored. The distribution of selection times is depicted in Fig. 2.

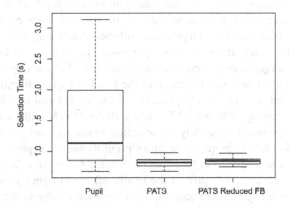

Fig. 2. Distribution of selection times for pupil based, PATS and PATS with reduced feedback selection modes.

Taken together, effectivity for purely pupil-based selection mode was lower than for dwell time selection. However, effectivity as well as efficiency were shown to be best for PATS and PATS with reduced feedback. All selection modes but PATS and PATS with reduced feedback differ from another significantly with regard to selection times (($F_{(1.02,\ 23.46)} = 17.46$, $p < 0.001$, $\eta^2_{part} = .43$).

4.3   User Satisfaction and Learnability

For usability, no significant differences in ratings were found ($F_{(2.25,51.66)} = 2.310$, $p = .10$, $\eta^2_{part} = .09$). However, descriptively, usability was rated worst when targets were selected utilizing the purely pupil selection mode (65.63, SE = 4.49) and almost similar for dwelling (76.56, SE = 3.85), PATS (75.26, SE = 4.13) and PATS without feedback (75.26, SE = 4.01). Following [28], these evaluations are all above the critical value for the 2nd quartile; dwelling, PATS and PATS with reduced feedback were even rated within the third quartile, indicating a good usability.

Similarly, learnability ratings did not differ significantly ($F_{(1.90,43.62)} = 2.77$, $p = .08$, $\eta^2_{part} = .11$). Descriptive statistics show that learnability was rated worst for PATS (72.92, SE = 5.30) and for the purely pupil-based selection mode (75.52,

SE = 4.96). PATS with reduced feedback (79.69, SE = 4.87) and dwell-time based selection (83.54, SE = 3.65) received higher ratings.

Overall, usability (71.29, SE = 2.73) and learnability (77.99, SE = 4.02) scores reveal that users generally evaluated the selection modes as usable and learnable [28]. Effectivity, efficiency, and usability all indicate that PATS, especially PATS with reduced feedback, can be used for active target selection, although the implemented dwell-time based selection could not be outperformed.

4.4   Signal Dynamics

In order to examine the dynamics of pupil signals prior to and subsequent to target selection, respective signals were further analyzed. Firstly, pupil signals in all trials in which selections were confirmed as unintended by the user were excluded in further analysis. Then, all trials in which targets were selected faster than 1.5 s after task onset were excluded. This was done, so that a proper in-task baseline could be registered and the second before target selection could be analyzed for all remaining trials. Data were normalized with a local baseline: the mean of the first 0.5 s of each trial was subtracted from each data point. For the purely pupil-based mode, 411 out of 480 trials met the criteria, 444 for dwelling, 406 for PATS, and 410 for PATS with reduced feedback. The signals were averaged separately by selection mode for each user. Users' means are depicted in Fig. 3. The graph gives mean pupil dynamics separately for selection modes, starting 1 s before entering the finally selected target until 2.5 s after entering the target. That is, the event of entering the finally selected target by gaze is set to 0 s.

As can be seen in Fig. 3, there seems to be a common course in the pupil dynamics for all selection modes: two local maxima, one at about 0.4 s, one at about 1.5 s, and one local minimum at about 0.8 s are recognizable for all pupil dynamics. This is even true for the dwell-selection mode, which did not require pupil size changes.

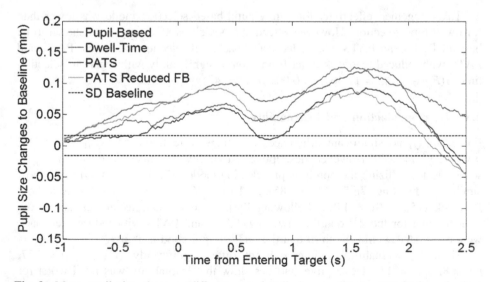

Fig. 3. Mean pupil size changes (differences to baseline) over time separately for selection modes. 0 s represents the time when the finally selected target was entered by gaze.

The maximum pupil response at about 1.5 s might be interpreted as a pupillary response to the load associated with the ongoing selection process, the feedback and the confirmation of successful selection. However, even before entering the target, mean pupil size rises considerably and independently from the selection mode. This signal course corresponds to the course reported in [7] but is even clearer. The signal shows a comparable dilation as in [22], however, additionally, a subsequent constriction is found. Figure 4 depicts the mean pupil size changes during the PATS mechanism together with a functional 95% confidence interval calculated on the basis of 24 mean signal dynamics. Thus, for every averaged data point a confidence interval was calculated on the basis of the 24 mean-constituting data points. The functional confidence interval can thus also illustrate the significant changes to baseline occurring at about 0.4 s and 1.5 s [4].

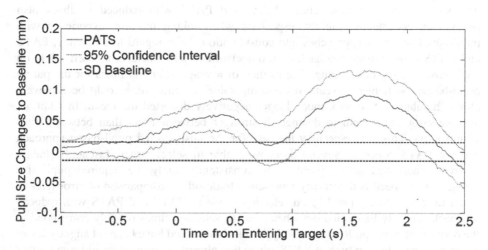

Fig. 4. Dynamics of mean pupil size changes (differences to baseline) during PATS. 0 s represents the time when the finally selected target was entered by gaze.

Could the illustrated pupil size changes be elicited by the timing of the task, e.g. the foregoing pause and/or task onset alone instead of target selections? In order to investigate this question, we compared long and short trials, assuming that longer trials should be robust regarding carry over effects from foregoing events. For 980 out of 1651 trials, subjects needed 3 s or more until fixating the correct object (<3 s: 671 trials). We find almost identical signal properties for long as for short task completion times entailing maxima at about 0.4 s and 1.5 s and a minimum at about 0.8 s.

5 Discussion

The current investigation aims to evaluate the potential of pupil size changes to actively support target selection. The integrative interaction concept PATS combines the benchmarking dwell-time approach with the newly developed concept of a purely pupil-based selection mode. Therefore, we assessed effectiveness, efficiency, and user satisfaction, as well as early pupil size courses that accompany object selection in a search and select task. Signal dynamics were analyzed from 1.5 s prior until 2.5 s after the first fixation of an intended target. The classical dwell-time selection mode was associated with highest accuracy rates; PATS (and PATS with reduced feedback) appeared to be less effective but entailed considerably shorter selection times. Key usability parameters were rated positively for all four evaluated selection modes. The tracked pupil sizes show early pupil size changes that accompany and precede the first fixations of intended selections.

In an interface that uses first settings for the crucial parameters, brightness, window length and deviation criterion, we assessed usability for PATS in a search and select task. Key-usability variables show that PATS is possible. Effectiveness, measured as percentage of incorrect answers, is best for the dwell-time approach; however, unsupported pupil-based selection, PATS, and PATS with reduced feedback also provide an acceptable usability, especially when taking the low experience with pupil-based selection approaches into consideration. With regard to efficiency, PATS and PATS with reduced feedback even outperformed target selection based solely on pupil size changes or dwelling. The median of average selection times for the purely pupil-based mechanism reveals that a comparable selection time could be achieved, although subjects who took much longer negatively distorted the mean. In addition, average error rates seem to distinguish stronger between users than between trials within users. This was especially the case for the unsupported pupil-based approach and the PATS concepts: several users were able to select targets fast and reliably, whereas others had severe problems to consistently apply the required pupil size changes. But, speed and accuracy represent a trade-off. A comparison of error rates in dwell time and purely pupil-based selection mode to PATS and PATS with reduced feedback can only be carried out when average selection times roughly correspond to the dwell-time concept. Retrospectively, dwell-time should have been set slightly lower to the average selection time of PATS, given that almost no errors were observed. Error rates for dwelling might change if the dwell-time was reduced to the average selection times of PATS, this should be focused on in further studies in order to allow an adequate judgement of the competitiveness of dwell and pupil enhanced dwell-times.

Usability ratings did not differ significantly. This must not mean that they are in fact comparable. On a descriptive basis, usability of the dwell-time approach and the PATS concepts, were rated comparably good. However, merely pupil-based selection was evaluated worse than all other modes. Also in learnability, there were only minor differences, and dwell-time and PATS with reduced feedback receiving the highest ratings. One might speculate that the intuitive dwell-time feedback facilitates operability whereas feedback on pupil size changes appeared mostly too short and couldn't fulfill its actual function. User reports subsequent to the testing match the assumption that feedback in PATS and during unsupported pupil-based selection mode was disturbing and unhelpful. The rated learnability is on average higher than the usability evaluation. Subjects had to complete only 20 trials per selection mode, whereas one turn lasted for about 5 min. Given the short operation time, overall performance might be better in a longer experiment, since subjects were generally optimistic to further improve the ability to operate the system.

Pupil dynamics were comparable for each selection method. The obtained signal courses reveal two local maxima, 0.4 s and 1.5 s after target entry and irrespective of the applied selection mechanism. In PATS and purely pupil-based selection, an increase in pupil size can be expected as the selection principle also depends on the slope of the signal. However, the depicted signal courses can also be observed during dwell-time selection mode, for which pupil size changes are irrelevant for selection. Hence, one might suggest that this pupil dynamic accompanies target selection in general and can thus be used for further improvements and enlargements of PATS.

Concerning the second peak at about 1.5 s, one might assume that either the processing of the feedback information, and/or of the successful selection, might have caused this pupil reaction. But, there is also a first peak at about 0.4 s revealing a considerable increase in pupil size even before the target is fixated. In order to use respective signal dynamics for further application, it would be necessary to know more about their causes.

Early peaks in pupil size changes have already been reported: The decision to select a target (or information leading to this decision) is reflected by pupil size changes occurring even before looking at the target. Indeed, the pupil dynamics observed in our current study correspond to pupil size changes reported by [7] in a cognitive decision task and also to diameter changes reported when spotting an intended objects during visual search [22, 23]. However, in addition, a subsequent constriction was observed. This constriction could also carry information on the certainty of the foregoing decision and could be included in more sophisticated future selection criteria [29].

Nevertheless, it is still unclear under which circumstances such changes in pupil diameter linked to mental decision processes can be observed. Whether the local minimum may be attributed to constrictions associated with fixations [30], or to decisional processes described by [7] or certainty of choice [29], has to be examined in further studies. For now, these observed signal dynamics provide a promising way to improve human-computer interaction using pupil size changes.

The present data suggest that respective processes are inherent in search and select tasks. For further application, it would be important to know whether similar signal changes could also be obtained when subjects face unintended objects. For example, [31] report considerably larger pupil sizes for targets envisaged to be selected compared to rejected objects; this supports the assumption that pupil dilations selectively accompany intended behavior. However, due to the variety of factors that influence pupil dynamics it is difficult to assign specific characteristics in the signal course to definable cognitive processes. Taken together, although still unclear, early effects regarding pupil size changes which are associated with intentions support our assumption that pupil-size changes can be applicable for active human-computer interaction. The window lengths and thresholds of the pupil-based selection criteria might be modified based on the presented data, e.g. by customizing window length, pupil-based selection times could show less variance than in this experiment; performance in further investigations could be improved.

The current results show for the first time that an implicit physiological event (pupil size changes) can successfully support active target selection in an adequate speed-accuracy tradeoff. Selection times are consistently below one second with accuracy rates being comparable or even better than common approaches [16, 17]. But, in this first approach, PATS did not outperform the benchmarking dwell-time. Including pupil size might improve common ways of computer input, like it has been demonstrated for gaze [32]. Further research has to demonstrate to which extent key usability parameters and the observed pupil dynamics can be replicated and generalized onto different environments and frameworks. Apart from gaze, PATS may be combined with other additional input modalities. Machine learning techniques fitted to the observed signal properties might be able to detect additional signal characteristics that allow both faster and more reliable processing [24]. Further analyses might also determine signal components that provide a valid distinction between pupil size changes that accompany intended and non-intended behavior patterns. Similar to the already existing purely pupil-based HCI input mechanisms, we show that pupil size is a useful variable in order to improve target selection.

6 Conclusion

The integrative interaction concept PATS enriches the established gaze-based target selection procedure with implicit information on pupil diameter. PATS although not outperforming a standard dwell-time approach, was shown to produce only slightly worse target selection performances with regard to effectivity, efficiency, and usability. A detailed analysis of involved pupil dynamics reveals that early pupil size changes accompany selections in a search and select task. Utilizing these early components in an integrative approach suggest that selection times might be reducible to substantially under 1 s. Summing up, pupil size changes underline the potential of implicit signals even for active target selection in HCI.

Acknowledgements. We thank all the volunteers. We would also like to thank Teresa Hirzle in particular for her extraordinary valuable technical assistance and discussions. This study was supported by the SFB 62 by the Deutsche Forschungsgemeinschaft (DFG).

References

1. Jacucci, G., Fairclough, S., Solovey, E.T.: Physiological computing. Computer **48**, 12–16 (2015)
2. Byrne, E.A., Parasuraman, R.: Psychophysiology and adaptive automation. Biol. Psychol. **42**, 249–268 (1996)
3. Allanson, J., Fairclough, S.H.: A research agenda for physiological computing. Interact. Comput. **16**, 857–878 (2004)
4. Ehlers, J., Strauch, C., Georgi, J., Huckauf, A.: Pupil size changes as an active information channel for biofeedback applications. Appl. Psychophysiol. Biofeedback **41**(3), 1–9 (2016)
5. Partala, T., Surakka, V.: Pupil size variation as an indication of affective processing. Int. J. Hum. Comput. Stud. **59**, 185–198 (2003)
6. Richer, F., Beatty, J.: Pupillary dilations in movement preparation and execution. Psychophysiology **22**, 204–207 (1985)
7. de Gee, J.W., Knapen, T., Donner, T.H.: Decision-related pupil dilation reflects upcoming choice and individual bias. Proc. Nat. Acad. Sci. **111**, E618–E625 (2014)

8. Beatty, J., Lucero-Wagoner, B.: The pupillary system. Handb. Psychophysiol. **2**, 142–162 (2000)
9. Hess, E.H., Polt, J.M.: Pupil size in relation to mental activity during simple problem-solving. Science **143**, 1190–1192 (1964)
10. Wierda, S.M., van Rijn, H., Taatgen, N.A., Martens, S.: Pupil dilation deconvolution reveals the dynamics of attention at high temporal resolution. Proc. Natl. Acad. Sci. **109**, 8456–8460 (2012)
11. Simpson, H.M., Hale, S.M.: Pupillary changes during a decision-making task. Percept. Mot. Skills **29**, 495–498 (1969)
12. Slanzi, G., Balazs, J.A., Velásquez, J.D.: Combining eye tracking, pupil dilation and EEG analysis for predicting web users click intention. Inf. Fusion **35**, 51–57 (2017)
13. Pittino, F., Mai, S., Huckauf, A., Pollatos, O.: Effects of hunger on sympathetic activation and attentional processes for physiological computing. In: Proceedings of the 3rd International Conference on Physiological Computing, pp. 542–546 (2016)
14. Jang, Y.-M., Mallipeddi, R., Lee, S., Kwak, H.-W., Lee, M.: Human intention recognition based on eyeball movement pattern and pupil size variation. Neurocomputing **128**, 421–432 (2014)
15. Pomplun, M., Sunkara, S.: Pupil dilation as an indicator of cognitive workload in human-computer interaction. In: Proceedings of the International Conference on HCI (2003)
16. Mathôt, S., Melmi, J.-B., van der Linden, L., van der Stigchel, S.: The mind-writing pupil: a human-computer interface based on decoding of covert attention through pupillometry. PLoS ONE **11**, e0148805 (2016)
17. Stoll, J., Chatelle, C., Carter, O., Koch, C., Laureys, S., Einhäuser, W.: Pupil responses allow communication in locked-in syndrome patients. Curr. Biol. **23**, R647–R648 (2013)
18. Ehlers, J., Strauch, C., Huckauf, A.: A view to a click: pupil size changes as input command in eyes-only human-computer interaction. Int. J. Hum.-Comput. Stud. (submitted)
19. Ekman, I., Poikola, A.W., Mäkäräinen, M.K.: Invisible eni: using gaze and pupil size to control a game. In: Proceedings of the 2008 CHI Conference on Human Factors in Computing Systems. ACM (2008)
20. Ekman, I., Poikola, A., Mäkäräinen, M., Takala, T., Hämäläinen, P.: Voluntary pupil size change as control in eyes only interaction. In: Proceedings of the Symposium on Eye Tracking Research and Applications ETRA, pp. 115–118 (2008)
21. Einhäuser, W., Stout, J., Koch, C., Carter, O.: Pupil dilation reflects perceptual selection and predicts subsequent stability in perceptual rivalry. Proc. Natl. Acad. Sci. **105**, 1704–1709 (2008)
22. Klingner, J.: Fixation-aligned pupillary response averaging. In: Proceedings of the 2010 Symposium on Eye-Tracking Research and Applications, pp. 275–282. ACM (2010)
23. Privitera, C.M., Renninger, L.W., Carney, T., Klein, S., Aguilar, M.: Pupil dilation during visual target detection. J. Vis. **10**, 3 (2010)
24. Bednarik, R., Vrzakova, H., Hradis, M.: What do you want to do next: a novel approach for intent prediction in gaze-based interaction. In: Proceedings of the Symposium on Eye Tracking Research and Applications, pp. 83–90. ACM (2012)
25. Majaranta, P., Ahola, U.K., Spakov, O.: Fast eye-typing with an adjustable dwell time. In: Proceedings of the 2009 CHI Conference on Human Factors in Computing Systems. ACM (2009)
26. Lewis, J.R., Sauro, J.: The factor structure of the system usability scale. In: International Conference on Human Centered Design (2009)
27. Peirce, J.W.: PsychoPy—psychophysics software in Python. J. Neurosci. Methods **162**, 8–13 (2007)

28. Sauro, J., Lewis, J.R.: Correlations among prototypical usability metrics: evidence for the construct of usability. In: Proceedings of the 2009 CHI Conference on Human Factors in Computing Systems, pp. 1609–1618. ACM (2009)

29. Urai, A.E., Braun, A., Donner, T.H.: Pupil-linked arousal is driven by decision uncertainty and alters serial choice bias. Nat. Commun. **8** (2017)

30. Mathôt, S., Melmi, J.-B., Castet, E.: Intrasaccadic perception triggers pupillary constriction. PeerJ **3**, e1150 (2015)

31. Jadue, J., Slanzi, G., Vel, J.: Web user click intention prediction by using pupil dilation analysis. In: Proceedings of the 2015 IEEE/WIC/ACM International Conference on Web Intelligence and Intelligent Agent Technology (WI-IAT), pp. 433–436 (2015)

32. Zhai, S.: What's in the eyes for attentive input. Commun. ACM **46**, 34–39 (2003)

Personalisation and Visualisation

Grab 'n' Drop: User Configurable Toolglasses

James R. Eagan[✉]

LTCI, Télécom ParisTech, Université Paris-Saclay, Paris, France
`james.eagan@telecom-paristech.fr`

Abstract. We introduce the *grab 'n' drop toolglass*, an extension of the toolglass bi-manual interaction technique. It enables users to create and configure their own toolglasses from existing user interfaces that were not designed for toolglasses. Users compose their own toolglass interactions at runtime from an application's user interface elements, bringing interaction closer to the objects of interest in a workspace. Through a proof-of-concept implementation for Mac OS X, we show how grab 'n' drop capabilities could be added to existing applications at the toolkit level, without modifying application source code or UI design. Finally, we evaluate the power and flexibility of this approach by applying it to a variety of applications. We further identify limitations and risks associated with this approach and propose changes to existing toolkits to foster such user-reconfigurable interaction.

Keywords: User interfaces · Toolglasses · Instrumental interaction · Polymorphism

1 Introduction

Toolglasses [4] are a bi-manual interaction technique in which users click through movable controls to apply their operations to the target below. They have been shown to be useful in a variety of contexts, from drawing applications [4] to debugging tools [13] to editing colored Petri nets [2].

In the nearly 25 years since toolglasses were initially proposed, multiple pointing devices have become increasingly common. While still not the norm, many laptop users, for example, work with an external mouse, effectively providing a second pointing device in addition to the laptop's integrated pointer.

Despite their utility, few applications provide support for toolglasses. In this article, we show how existing user interface (UI) toolkits could be updated to provide support for user-configurable toolglasses, without requiring application programmers to update their code. Users can then assemble and configure their own toolglasses from existing applications. We introduce the *grab 'n' drop toolglass*, a proof-of-concept implementation for Mac OS to explore what existing toolkit features help make this kind reconfiguration feasible, where they are insufficient, and how toolkits could be modified to better support such reconfiguration. The running toolglass prototype probes where, in real applications,

© IFIP International Federation for Information Processing 2017
Published by Springer International Publishing AG 2017. All Rights Reserved

R. Bernhaupt et al. (Eds.): INTERACT 2017, Part III, LNCS 10515, pp. 315–334, 2017.
DOI: 10.1007/978-3-319-67687-6_21

this approach breaks down. While this implementation is in the context of Mac OS, it uses principles that are generalizable across most common UI toolkits. We further explore several ways that users might be able to extend such reconfigurable interfaces and discuss design limitations in current toolkits that limit the kinds of extension possible.

The contribution of this work is thus (1) an interaction technique for assembling user-created toolglasses from existing interface elements in existing applications and (2) a technical contribution of how existing toolkits could be updated to better support such toolglasses. We evaluate the grab 'n' drop toolglass not from a usability point of view but in terms of the technical feasibility of transforming interaction by users.

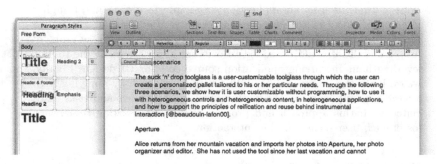

Fig. 1. The grab 'n' drop toolglass in Pages. The toolglass, floating on the top left, contains three empty buckets on its bottom, right. The remaining buckets contain the extracted actions from various widgets visible in the toolbar and styles list on the left. The user has just grabbed the "Heading 1" style.

Initially, a grab 'n' drop toolglass provides a collection of empty buckets (Fig. 1). When the user clicks through an empty bucket onto a widget, the toolglass stores the action associated with that widget (grab). When the user subsequently clicks through the toolglass, it applies that action to the object under the toolglass (drop). As such, a user can add and configure toolglass interactions, even in applications not designed for such interaction.

Furthermore, these toolglasses can be polymorphic. For example, a user may reconfigure a grab 'n' drop toolglass created in one application to perform analogous operations in another. A polymorphic operation is a logical operation that is realized differently depending on some combination of the control, the target object, and its context. For example, applying a heading style to some text in a word processor might set a named style to the text; in an HTML or LaTeX editor, it might wrap it in markup; in an email message it might set it to bold and change its size. A single logical operation—make this text a header—may be implemented using different underlying functional operations depending on the context.

2   Related Work

The grab 'n' drop toolglass builds on toolglasses, certainly, but also on work in runtime, third-party program modification, on end-user customization, and on user-interface toolkits and interactions.

Toolglasses and magic lenses [4] were first proposed by Bier *et al.* in 1993 as a general-purpose interaction technique, a new style of widget that programmers could add to their toolbox. Various extensions have been proposed, including toolglasses for debugging [13] and visualization [11]. Moreover, they act as a strong complement to other tools, such as floating palettes and marking menus [20].

Perhaps the closest in spirit to our proposed technique is the style toolglass in Beaudouin-Lafon and Mackay's CPN2000 [3]. Initially, empty items in the toolglass act as a style picker, extracting attributes such as color and thickness. They then become style droppers, applying those attributes to target objects. We extend CPN2000's notion of picking (grabbing) and dropping styles beyond an application's domain objects to its interface elements.

Other approaches let users modify a program's interface: Tan *et al.*'s Win-Cuts [27] let users trim away irrelevant portions of windows to their context. Hutchings and Stasko's window snipping extends this notion to provide for live interaction with trimmed windows [14]. Pushing the farthest, Stuerzlinger *et al.*'s user interface Façades [26] treat the interface itself as a modifiable object, letting the user recompose those elements to create new palettes or even replace tools with functional equivalents. While they do enable users to convert entire tool pallets and toolbars into toolglasses, they does not describe support for more general composition from more primitive widgets. We generalize this approach to individual widgets and extend it beyond command-then-object interactions.

Program Modification. Various approaches have been taken to enabling third-party modifications to software. Cypher *et al.* edit a good overview of such modifications for the web [6], where a strong mash-up culture has evolved. On the desktop, tools such as Dixon and Fogarty's Prefab [8] offer the possibility to "make every application open source" by identifying the user interface components in the pixels drawn to the screen. Such approaches are surprisingly powerful, despite only having access to rendered pixels and user input events. Other approaches involve varying degrees of access to or integration with source code. Eagan *et al.* provide an overview of such techniques [10]. Each of these approaches aims to provide developers with the means to add new functionality or behaviors to existing software.

End-User Customization. Non-programmer end-users have a long history of customizing their software to suit their own particular needs [19]. With sufficient scaffolding and motivation, they can even go as far as to program [9,22], and even construct sharing communities [12,17], with different users assuming different roles to encourage and foster such customization [12].

Our work draws inspiration from these approaches. In this context, our goal is to enable users to compose new interactions from existing program functionality without requiring them to program or manipulate complex configuration dialogs. As such, we draw inspiration from programming by demonstration [7]: a user simply clicks through interface elements to construct a personal toolglass. Grab 'n' Drop toolglass do not, however, attempt to infer intent from user's actions. As such, they could best be described as employing configuration by demonstration rather than programming by demonstration.

Finally, Ponsard and McGrenere propose Anchored Customization [23], which modifies the preferences panels of existing applications to enable users to access preference settings directly from the user interface elements involved. This approach is similar in two primary ways: in both cases, the proposed technique brings the user's interaction and attention to the relevant widgets; and both techniques were grafted into existing applications by means of a hack that is independent of the technique itself.

3   Four Scenarios

The grab 'n' drop toolglass is a user-customizable toolglass through which the user can create a personalized pallet tailored to his or her particular needs. Through the following scenarios, we show how it is user customizable without programming, how to use it with heterogeneous controls and heterogeneous content, in heterogeneous applications, and how to support the principles of reification and reuse behind instrumental interaction [2].

3.1   Aperture

Alice returns from her mountain vacation and imports her photos into Aperture, her photo organizer and editor. She has not used the tool since her last vacation and cannot remember the keyboard shortcuts when operating in full-screen mode, so she creates a new grab 'n' drop toolglass in standard, windowed mode. Into four empty buckets, she clicks through the toolbar buttons for the straighten, crop, redeye, and retouch commands. She then enters full-screen mode, which hides all controls but the cursor and her toolglass, and expands the photo to fit to the undecorated screen. She clicks through the crop toolglass to re-compose the image, perhaps refining the crop by moving the toolglass out of the way. She then clicks through the red-eye reduction tool to hide the effects of the flash.

3.2   Styles in Pages

Bernard and Charlie are collaborating on an article for Interact, and Charlie has composed an unformatted first-draft of the article. In order to apply the correct styles to the article in Pages, Bernard must first select the relevant text or paragraph, then select the appropriate style in a list on the side of the screen. Systematically applying these styles thus involves repeatedly scrolling and precisely pointing in the document, then precisely pointing in the list on the side, alternating attention and focus between the content and the styles palette (Fig. 1).

Bernard creates a new grab 'n' drop toolglass and clicks through empty buckets to add the section, subsection, and other styles from the styles panel to the toolglass. He then closes the styles panel and clicks through to the bold and italic toolbar buttons to add them to the toolglass. He can then use this toolglass to systematically apply the appropriate styles to the document by scrolling and clicking through the toolglass within the document view, maintaining his attention on the text content without the back-and-forth from before.

3.3   Styles in Mail

Some time later, Bernard is working in Mail and wants to style a rich-text email message he is composing. He loads the toolglass that he created in Pages. Although Mail does support rich text, it does not use the same styles functionality as Pages. As a result, Bernard must first re-define each of the grab 'n' drop buckets in the toolglass by clicking through on the relevant controls in Mail. He holds the shift key to combine (or stack) multiple actions and clicks through the Helvetica font pull-down button, the bold button, and the 12-point font selector. Once defined, clicking on a particular style in the toolglass in Mail will apply a similar styling to text in a mail message as it would to text in his word processor.

3.4   Lab Notebook

Denise is documenting a lab procedure in an email. In the control software for a piece of lab equipment, she creates a new toolglass for the procedure and clicks through each of the relevant controls to extract its associated action. She then switches to her email message and command-clicks the controls in the toolglass to drop their stored screenshot as a rich-text attachment, integrating screenshots of the configured controls into the text of the procedure.

Some time later, Eric reads the procedure and command-clicks through an empty bucket onto the image of one of the controls embedded in the document in order to grab it into the toolglass. He then command-clicks through the bucket onto the relevant control to apply the state described in the image to the underlying control.

4   Grab 'n' Drop

The grab 'n' drop toolglass is based on traditional toolglasses, initially proposed nearly 25 years ago [4]. As with traditional toolglasses, it uses two pointing devices, such as an integrated trackpad in a laptop and a wireless mouse. The left (non-dominant) hand controls the position of the toolglass, while the right (dominant) hand controls the position of the pointer.

With the grab 'n' drop toolglass, the user can compose new toolglasses from the existing functionality exposed through the application's existing interface, even in applications that do not currently support toolglass-based interaction. (Our prototype implementation is built on Mac OS X and integrates with arbitrary Cocoa applications using the Scotty toolkit [10].)

Initially, the toolglass is populated with empty controls, or buckets (Fig. 1). These buckets can be filled by positioning an empty bucket on top of a clickable control, such as a button, segmented control, list item, or toolbar item. When the user clicks through the empty bucket, the toolglass inspects the underlying control to extract its associated action. (We describe this process in more detail in the implementation section.) Once the bucket has "grabbed" the associated action, it draws itself with a copy of the control's on-screen representation.

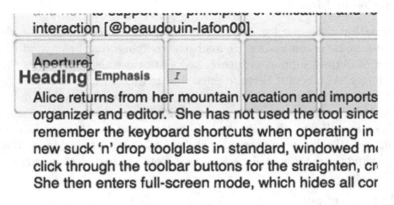

Fig. 2. Dropping an action in Pages. The user has just selected the word "Aperture" through the "Heading 2" bucket of the toolglass. As soon as she releases the mouse, the style will be applied.

By selecting a collection of desired controls, a user can create his or her own custom toolglass. Furthermore, by storing the control's target and associated action, the source control itself need not continue to exist. If, for example, the user populates one of the buckets with a control in a palette and later closes the palette, the bucket will continue to function.

When the user clicks on a filled bucket, the toolglass passes the click through to whatever window is underneath (Fig. 2). The press, any subsequent drag events, and the release are all passed through the toolglass to the underlying window. Each bucket can either trigger the associated action either just before relaying the user's initial press to the region below the toolglass or just after the user releases the mouse. Activating the control before passing-through mouse events is useful for controls that activate modes (command-then-target), whereas the latter option is appropriate for controls that operate on a selection (target-then-command). If the user drags beyond an individual toolglass item, such as when highlighting a long sentence, the command used is that that was under the initial mouse press.

Toolglasses can be saved and restored in future invocations of the application, allowing for use for both one-off tasks and for co-adaptive behaviors [18]. In this way, a user can propose new interactions with an existing interface, making the application better fit his or her particular needs. Furthermore, he or she is likely to adapt his or her behavior as the interface itself now supports new kinds of interaction.

4.1 Polymorphic Toolglasses

Beyond inherently polymorphic commands, such as copy and paste, the grab 'n' drop toolglass supports polymorphism across applications by letting the user re-configure a toolglass for use in another application.

A toolglass loaded from another application will keep the same buckets, with each bucket showing the control's icon from the application in which it was initially created. Because each application is different, however, the controls themselves may or may not exist. As such, the bucket invalidates its references to the underlying control actions when loaded into a new application and draws itself in an inactive state. When the user attempts to use such an inactive bucket in a new application for the first time, the application prompts to reconfigure it for the new application by grabbing a new control. Holding the shift key appends additional controls.

In this way, the user can create a toolglass whose functionality adapts itself to the particular application in question. For example, applying a header style from the toolglass in a word processor might change a style by applying its word-processing concept of a style. In an HTML editor, it might trigger a command to wrap that text in a header tag. In a Mail client, it might make the text bold and change its size. In this way, a single bucket with a single logical function may trigger different underlying functionalities depending on the particular program.

4.2 Command Syntax

As the name suggests, there are two primary interactions associated with the grab 'n' drop toolglass: *grab* and *drop*. As described above, the grab operation extracts the associated action (and state, if applicable) of a control into the toolglass. The drop operation applies that action (including the associated state, if any) to the subject of the interaction with the underlying window below the toolglass. There is additionally a toggle to configure the *drop* operation to apply its associated action *before* or *after* the user interaction has occurred.

In the current proof-of-concept implementation, we use modifier keys at the time of the grab operation to regulate this mode. We plan to replace this interaction with something more intuitive in a future prototype. A modifier-less click applies the operation after passing through user interactions to the underlying window, as for a control that operates on a selection. Holding down the option key during a grab operation will cause the drop operation to apply before passing along the interactions, as suitable for a mode-switching control such as a control pallet item.

Normally, once a command has been grabbed into a bucket, subsequent clicks on that bucket are treated as drops. A user can combine multiple commands, however, by holding the shift key to grab additional controls into the toolglass. When a bucket contains multiple controls, a drop operation applies each action in the order in which they were grabbed.

Finally, holding the command-key during a drop causes the toolglass to drop the captured human-readable image of the control instead of applying the action. This image contains a serialization of the stored data in its meta-data, such that the image actually contains the same machine-readable data stored in the toolglass. A command-drop on a control, on the other hand, reconfigures the state of the control to reflect that stored in the toolglass. Holding the command-key during a grab operation causes the operation to look for such meta-data in an image under the mouse instead of looking for a widget at the click location.

4.3 Live Screenshots

The typical use of grab 'n' drop toolglasses is to compose a personal toolglass out of existing widget components, effectively treating the program's interface as malleable and re-composable. We further extended the toolglass to support treating the live interface as an embeddable object in a document. As such, the user can drop the captured screenshot of the widget in a bucket into a document, as in the lab procedure scenario described above. Indeed this scenario itself comes from Klokmose and Zander's work with scientists on laboratory notebooks [16].

When the user command-drops a bucket, the toolglass passes the click through to the underlying window, then inserts a screenshot of the widget as if pasted from the clipboard. In the meta-data of the image, the toolglass writes the same information that would be serialized for subsequent program invocations (described in more detail in the following section). As such, the dropped image contains both a human-readable representation of the associated widget, but also a machine-readable description sufficient to re-connect the image to the associated widget, similarly to how Kato *et al.* encode robot pose data in images embedded in source code [15].

Because all of the machine-readable information necessary to link the image to the widget is stored in the meta data of the image, any existing document or image editor that preserves the embedded meta-data can be used to edit that document. Re-establishing the link requires only that the toolglass be able to map a click to the image, which is currently implemented using the Mac OS X Cocoa rich text editing APIs.

4.4 Serialization

Once the user has created a personal toolglass, such as the styles toolglass, she can save that toolglass for later. Saving a toolglass causes each bucket's screenshot, associated action, and any state information about the widget to be serialized and stored in a file on disk. On a subsequent invocation of the application, the user can then load the toolglass to restore these links. Because the application was not designed for this kind of interaction in mind, re-establishing this link can be potentially fragile and does not work in all cases. We describe the details of this process in the Implementation section, and focus on specific edge cases in the Discussion section, below.

Serialization for Other Applications. In some ways, loading a saved tool-glass in another application is more straight-forward. The grab 'n' drop toolglass relies on references to the underlying callback controllers of an application. With the exception of standard, toolkit-level actions, any two arbitrary applications are unlikely to use the same callbacks, even for logically-equivalent commands. As such, it is generally not possible to re-link a toolglass bucket from one application to a new application. For this reason, buckets loaded from another application are initially disabled. Effectively, these buckets are like empty buckets: a click through the bucket will grab the action off the target widget.

Unlike empty buckets, however, the bucket will still contain the original widget's screenshot and will keep that screenshot even after being re-linked in the new application. We chose not to replace the screenshot so as to maintain a more consistent representation across applications. For example, a styles toolglass is a styles toolglass, regardless of the particular operations necessary to realize it in the host application.

5 Implementation

We have created a proof-of-concept implementation of the grab 'n' drop tool-glass as a Scotty [10] plugin for Mac OS X Cocoa applications. Eagan *et al.*'s Scotty uses runtime toolkit overloading to enable the modification of third-party applications without access to their source code[1]. Scotty plugins run inside the host program and thus have access to its internal classes and objects, including documents, views, and their controllers.

While this proof-of-concept implementation is effectively a Mac OS X hack using Scotty, neither the concept of the grab 'n' drop toolglass nor the overall implementation approach is dependent on the Mac. Rather, this approach enabled us to effectively extend the Cocoa toolkit to provide a set of generally reusable components that could be provided by other toolkits such as Java Swing or Windows .Net using analogous capabilities in those toolkits.

5.1 Requirements

There are four principal challenges in implementing grab 'n' drop toolglasses:

- Extracting and invoking a widget's associated action.
- Handling state and other side-effects.
- Managing object-then-action and action-then-object command syntaxes.

---

[1] We will make the source code available at `code.eagan.me`.

- Serializing these extracted data for subsequent program invocations.
- Embedding serialized data in dropped images.

We address these challenges in the remainder of this section.

Creating Toolglasses. We have implemented toolglasses in Mac OS X using the Cocoa Human Interface Device APIs. When a toolglass is first created, the list of available input devices is polled. By default, when more than one mousing device is present, the first one is bound to the toolglass and the remaining mice control the standard system pointer. Thus, if only one mouse is present, toolglass interaction is disabled, falling back on traditional interactions. On laptops, the builtin trackpad is generally the first mouse found and is bound to the toolglass.

The toolglass itself is an undecorated, focus-less window with a mostly transparent background. It is then filled with buckets, which are simply standard widgets (`NSView`), with all input redirected into a state machine using a Scotty event funnel [10]. In order to pass events to the underlying window, the toolglass clones the currently handled event and injects it into the system event queue (using a Cocoa event tap). That event can then be either consumed or propagated to the standard event stream. It is essential that the state machine for the toolglass preserve standard event symmetry invariants, such as press/release pairing and that drag events always occur between a press and a release. If these invariants are not respected, the program may enter into an undefined state.

Widget Design Patterns: (Controllers, Target-Action). Cocoa applications are typically developed using a model-view-controller (MVC) architecture [24], where event handlers are typically implemented in a controller object associated with the interface. Widgets, in turn, use a target-action pattern to designate their controller (the target) and the message[2] to send to the target (action). Other toolkits typically use a similar mechanism to handle callbacks, signals, or event handlers: when a widget is triggered, the system executes some bit of code with an event describing what happened and what was triggered. In Cocoa, when a widget is triggered, such as by clicking a button or pressing return in a text field, the widget sends its action message to its target with itself as the sole parameter: the sender.

Grab: Extracting a Widget's Action. Grabbing a widget's "callback" thus entails simply storing a reference to its target and action, and storing a reference to the widget itself. We also create a copy of its backing image in order to store its on-screen representation in the toolglass bucket. Invoking a previously grabbed command whenever it is dropped through the toolglass is then as simple as invoking the *action* on the *target* with the source widget as the *sender* (*e.g.*, `target.invoke(action, from: sender)`). This action will then typically operate on the user's current selection in the application.

---

[2] Objective-C uses message-passing to invoke methods.

Special Cases: State, Subclasses, Side-Effects. Some controls may be stateful. For example, a compound control, such as a list or a segmented toolbar control, may perform some form of "backchannel" communication beyond the standard target-action invocation model. An action method might, for example, query its sender to identify which list item or segment was clicked.

For such stateful controls, it is necessary to capture that state. We create a proxied copy of the control to be used as the sender in place of the original widget. This proxy is a Scotty object proxy [10]. An object proxy is a *metaclass*[3] whose instances are subclasses of the class of the object to be proxied. An instance of this metaclass stores a copy of the source object to be proxied. Methods invoked on it can then be forwarded to the underlying object, creating a sort of man-in-the-middle stand-in for the original widget. We have implemented proxy classes for the standard outline/list view, popup button, and segmented control classes.[4]

When invoking a control, the toolglass uses this proxy as the sender instead of the original control. Thus, if the action method queries the control for one of these overridden methods, the captured state is used instead of the current state.

Drop: Invoking a Stored Action. When the user performs a drop, she clicks through the toolglass, possibly dragging, before eventually releasing. Toolglass buckets may be configured to trigger their action either before passing the initial click to the window below, as in the case of a command mode (*e.g.* the redeye tool), or after the terminating mouse release, as in the case of an operation on a selection (*e.g.* the styles chooser).

As shown above, actually triggering the callback associated with the source widget is straight-forward and simply involves sending the action message to the target with either the source widget or its proxy as the sender parameter.

Serializing the Grab 'n' Drop Toolglass. Initially identifying a widget, its target, and its action during a grab operation is easy: they come from the clicked widget. But in order to serialize toolglasses across invocations of the application, we need a way to find these same objects in a new application instance, without a user's click to identify the widget. Furthermore, when loading a previously serialized toolglass, the program may be in a different state. The interface may be in a different configuration and the relevant objects might not have been created.

During serialization, we need to construct a path from a known, fixed reference point to the widget. To construct this path, we use three starting points:

---

[3] A metaclass is a class of classes. Whereas an instance of a class is an object, an instance of a metaclass is itself a class.

[4] The first two simply override the `clickedRow` and `selectedItem` methods, respectively, to return whatever value was active when the control was grabbed. For segmented controls, there are two methods that need to be overridden: `selectedSegment` and `isSelectedForSegment:`, which are actually independent methods that handle multiple segments.

the current document, the current window, and the application's master controller. We then use the reflection APIs to conduct a breadth-first search using the attributes of each of these controllers to find a shortest path to the target objects. If none of the controller's instance variables matches the target widget, we expand the search to any controllers or delegate objects that it may reference. Unfortunately, controllers and delegates are merely design patterns; there is no formally-expressed relationship in the code itself. By convention, however, in Cocoa, such attributes typically have names ending in delegate or controller, as in `windowDelegate` and `playbackController`. Other conventions apply in other toolkits. We consider any such non-nil variables to be valid search candidates.

Finally, we fall back to the view hierarchy itself. We avoid using the view hierarchy because it is more likely to change between application launches. Nonetheless, it is sometimes the only available path to a particular controller. As such, any time we encounter an `NSView` instance, we add that to the search.

If no valid path is found at the end of this breadth-first search, it will not be possible to serialize that particular control for future use. In such a case, the bucket can still be used during the current session, but it will not be possible to save it and restore it later. If there are multiple paths, we use the first (shortest) path, preferring to avoid any paths involving the view hierarchy if possible.

In order to avoid unforeseen side effects, we look only at instance variable when searching for serialization paths. Comparing the values of two variables is safe. We ignore methods, since they may have unanticipated effects. For example, in some applications, calling the accessor for the current print job could potentially trigger a print job if one does not exist.

When loading in a new application instance, however, those attributes might not yet have been initialized. Thus, when deserializing, we prefer to use those very same accessors that we avoided during serialization.

In Java and other languages, accessors typically start with `get`. In Cocoa, methods and attributes are in different namespaces. We therefor look for a method with the same name, or with any leading underscores or a single m removed and re-camel-cased. This strategy relies on programming conventions and is thus inherently fragile.

Embedding Serialized Data in Dropped Images. Once the functionality for serializing a bucket between applications exists, embedding that serialized data in an image is easy. Furthermore, during a grab operation, we store a screenshot of the target widget.[5]

6   Discussion

6.1   Leveraging Design Patterns: Controllers, Target-Action

In the general case, giving the user complete control over all aspects of the user interface and functionality is almost certainly infeasible. Software applications

---

[5] The current implementation uses Cocoa's `CGImageProperties` APIs to read and write the serialized bucket into the screenshot's metadata.

are frequently complex, and user interfaces particularly so. Nonetheless, certain common design patterns in the development of user interfaces are particularly helpful at enabling the runtime modification of interaction and functionality. We rely on three design patterns in particular:

- The Model-View-Controller (MVC) programming model,
- Callback-bindings for widgets, and
- Dynamic dispatch in object-oriented programming languages.

The first of these, *MVC* [24], reflects the separation between interface, application functionality, and the link between the two. Views, or widgets, are typically programmed using standard classes in a toolkit library, although they are frequently customized through inheritance. The model is effectively opaque and may even be implemented in another programming language, but it is linked to the interface through the controller, which maps widget events to operations on the model. Different programs follow more- or less-clean implementations of this separation, and frequently the *PAC* model [5] under the guise of MVC. Regardless of the particular implementation, analyzing the controller provides a foothold into the underlying functionality of the program, and the links into the operational interface that controls it.

Callback-bindings are the linking mechanism between a widget and the controller. In Cocoa, these are implemented using the *target–action* model where a widget event, such as a button press, triggers an *action* on its associated *target*. The target is typically the associated controller, and the action is the associated method. The grab 'n' drop toolglass relies on being able to thus map widgets to their associated controllers and event handlers. Other user interface toolkits use different design patterns to express callbacks, but the overall result is similar: linking a widget to an event handler on some object. In Java Swing, this link is performed using a *listener* pattern; in Qt (C++), this binding is performed using *signals* and *slots*.

The last of these patterns, *dynamic dispatch*, is the process by which the programming language chooses, at runtime, what code to execute when a program invokes a method on an object. In most object-oriented programming languages, such as Objective-C, Java[6], C++[7], JavaScript, and Python, a dynamic component performs a mapping between an object and the particular method to execute. Our proof-of-concept implementation works by analyzing these mappings for a particular class to create an object proxy capable of standing-in for an existing object but with an overloaded or overridden implementation. This pattern is not strictly necessary to implement user-configurable toolglasses. If the target-action model were extended to provide for target-action-state, then applications could express their functionality entirely with such components. There would no longer be a need for proxy objects to, *e.g.*, hard-wire the selected item in a list or segmented button.

---

[6] for non-`final` methods.
[7] for all `virtual` methods.

6.2   The Interface as a Lens into the System

The human-software interface, of its nature, is designed to be understood by the human user of the software. As such, the interface exposes the core functionality of the system in a human-understandable fashion. While the design of the grab 'n' drop toolglass enables the user to transform the interaction around which the system was designed, it does not require a deep understanding of that system. Instead, it draws upon the user's understanding of what different controls do, of the user's own situated context, to re-assemble the underlying functionality into new controls. The only system knowledge necessary to implement the toolglass is that of the general design patterns described in the previous section.

More generally, other tools beyond the grab 'n' drop toolglass may be able to take similar advantage of the human user's understanding of the interface to make extensive modifications to the underlying functionality possible. The grab 'n' drop toolglass does so without programming, but tools such as Yeh et al.'s Sikuli [28] offer a glimpse into ways that end-users might be able to reprogram existing software applications, creating a sort of situated macros or software extensions to existing application interfaces. Sikuli relies exclusively on the surface representation of the application, but a hybrid approach that offers a similar degree of high-level interaction with existing components combined with direct access to their underlying functionality offers an exciting potential.

On the more advanced end of the spectrum, programmable tools in the spirit of Maclean et al.'s Buttons [21, 25] could help make it possible for richer expressivity with underlying software functionality. With a sufficiently scaffolded environment, many kinds of programming tasks may become accessible even to end-user programmers [22].

6.3   End-User Programming

The grab 'n' drop toolglass aims to provide a programming-free means of letting a user adapt an existing user interface to her own needs. Tools such as Sikuli [28], Prefab [8], and Scotty [10], among many others, provide tools for programmers to alter software interfaces or functionality. Between these two ends of the spectrum lie more advanced end-user programming techniques, aiming to increase raise the ceiling of expressivity while maintaining a low threshold to entry.

For example, by using a model of intentionality based on some combination of the user's context and the widgets he or she grabs into the toolglass, the toolglass could potentially provide more seamless interaction without explicit programming. For richer control, EUD environments such as Sikuli could enable the user to go beyond simply extracting existing widgets to including new interactions and functionalities. Under the current proof-of-concept implementation, the user explicitly configures each bucket to control only the order of operations for dropped actions.

6.4   Design Opportunities

Under normal usage, an application's interface provides its own set of widgets—
which may potentially be instruments—through which the user interacts with
associated domain objects. For most typical users, this exposed interface should
be sufficient most of the time (assuming any reasonably well-designed application). For those users or those situations where that interface is not sufficient,
however, the user may wish to act not on the domain objects but rather with
the application itself. We have created the grab 'n' drop toolglass as a first step
in this direction: the creation of a class of interactive tools to allow an end user
to operate on an application's underlying interface and functionality, similarly
to how Façades let a user modify an application's interface [26].

This type of interaction is common in physical interactions with real-world
tools, where a master craftsman might typically use standard off-the-shelf tools
to practice her trade. But when confronted with a particular need, she might
create an adapter, or modify the tool in some way to better satisfy her special
case. Should that adapter or modification be particularly useful, she might share
it with others, possibly even becoming a new member of a standard toolbox, as
we have seen with a wide variety of now standard tools: needle-nose pliers, 90-
degree screwdrivers, *etc.*

This type of interaction offers an exciting design opportunity to create a
broad class of tools. One need not necessarily look as far as the real world to
identify these kinds of practices. Unix users have a long and well-documented
history of customizing their software with Unix dotfiles [19], whether for functional reasons, to work around compatibility issues, or even for self-expression.
Furthermore, sharing cultures [12,17] arising around such customizations have
even led to entire communities, with customizations being produced and shared
by expert programmers and tinkerers alike [21].

Furthermore, when confronted with a relevant problem within one's domain,
with sufficient motivation, even regular end-users may program extensive customizations for their own particular needs. For example, spreadsheet software
has led to vast collections of complex logic programmed by secretaries and other
non-computing professionals [22], while artists have formed communities around
the development and exchange of Photoshop plugins and customizations [9].

6.5   Generalizability Across Applications

In order to understand the generalizability of the grab 'n' drop toolglass, we
conducted a survey of different applications in addition to Aperture, Pages, and
Mail, used in the scenarios: Keynote, Pixelmator, OmniGraffle, and Preview.

While the grab 'n' drop toolglass is able to bring toolglass interaction to
applications that were not designed with such interaction in mind, not all interactions are compatible. Moreover, current designs of applications that would
be amenable to toolglasses, *e.g.*, drawing applications, may use an unsuitable
interaction vocabulary.

The grab 'n' drop toolglass works well with command-then-action or action-then-command interactions, such as toolbar buttons that operate on a selection. However, many buttons may not interact directly with a selection. For example, drawing in Keynote would be a perfect application for a traditional toolglass. However, its interaction model is such that, when the user creates a shape, it is dropped on the canvas at an arbitrary position. The user then resizes and re-styles that object. As such, it is possible to click through the toolglass to create a shape, but that shape is placed independent of where the user has clicked. As such, the user can compose a personal toolglass, but it's utility degrades to that of a toolbar.

Similarly, OmniGraffle allows the user to click and drag out rectangles, but not other forms. The user must draw a rectangle, then change its form with a separate control. Moreover, it provides a list of forms that have been used in that document. As such, the list of pertinent forms depends on the current document and is thus inconsistent throughout the application. In this case, the user may expect to draw a circle, but instead find a cloud or a rounded rectangle because the captured state varies between documents.

On the other hand, applications with a more traditional modal palette inter-action style, such as Pixelmator for drawing or Preview's annotations toolbar, provide compatible interface elements. Creating, for example, an annotation toolglass with differently-colored highlighters or an underline thus behaves as expected.

Finally, our proof-of-concept is implemented as a hack on the system using Scotty [10]. As each new version of Mac OS introduces stricter sandboxing restrictions, fewer and fewer applications remain compatible. While this will prevent deployment of the prototype as-is, our contribution is an interaction technique for user-composable toolglasses, not a hack on Cocoa. For example, if Cocoa provided its own grab 'n' drop toolglass, there would be no need to break into the sandbox and into an application's runtime.

6.6   Limitations and Fragility

We have successfully used grab 'n' drop toolglasses in a variety of Mac OS X Cocoa-based applications, including Pages (word processor), Keynote (presenta-tion tool), Mail, Aperture (photo manager), and others. Additionally, we have used the toolglass on a variety of widgets, both standard and custom, includ-ing standard buttons (*e.g.* OK), toggle buttons (*e.g.* on/off switch), segmented buttons (*e.g.* unified bold/italic/underline button), pull-down menus (*e.g.* font button), and lists.

Nonetheless, any time one modifies the behavior of an existing program, espe-cially without knowledge of its underlying design and implementation, there is a non-insignificant risk of breaking any hidden assumptions and thus introducing instability. Such instability may range from mild, such as a user expecting an action to make something bold but seeing it turn italic instead, to severe, such as corrupting or losing data or crashing.

In our use of the grab 'n' drop toolglass, we have not observed data corruption. The worst we have seen has been unexpected program termination (*i.e.* a crash) induced by a bug (since corrected) in the implementation of the toolglass prototype that injected an extraneous mouse press event or suppressed a mouse release event, breaking the system's underlying assumptions about the symmetry of press/release events.

The most common sort of non-bug-related unexpected behavior that we have observed in our testing relates to uncaptured state leading to hidden behavior not exposed by the standard callback model. As we have seen earlier, in the standard target-action design pattern, a widget invokes its target's action method with itself as the sole parameter, the sender, whenever a widget event is triggered (*e.g.* a button is clicked). For a button, this is the end of the widget's involvement, but for other widgets, such as a list or a segmented control, the action method *may* query the sender for its state, such as the item selected. Or it may even interact with any other arbitrary part of the system to determine its behavior. We are not aware of a robust, automatic solution to capture and model such hidden interactions. If the behavior of a triggered action depends on such hidden interactions, then the toolglass might end up triggering a different, unexpected behavior.

We have implemented proxies for the following standard widgets:

- NSOutlineView to capture the clicked row
- NSPopUpButton to capture selected item
- NSSegmentedControl to capture the selected or clicked segment.

The grab 'n' drop toolglass uses these proxies any time one of these widgets or any of its subclasses is grabbed. Although our current implementation has worked in our usage, there is a risk that a subclass may only re-use other aspects of the parent class' behavior and may re-implement or bypass the captured behavior of the proxy. In these cases, the resulting behavior is difficult to predict.

We have also created a SNDTracerProxy that logs all method calls to the console before forwarding them to the proxied object. This proxy is useful for a programmer to probe any hidden interactions that may involve the proxied object but is beyond the scope of normal user interaction with the toolglass.

It may be possible to resolve much of this fragility by extending the target-action design pattern to more fully express some of these relationships. Such extensions, however, would require that programmers change the way that they develop software. Furthermore, if these patterns do not fully integrate with the tools to implement the software functionality, then they could add a similar burden as AppleScript [1] or other extension interfaces, which provide a second, parallel API for developers to maintain.

Even with strong design patterns, not all software is well-designed. Certain applications do not adequately follow recommended design patterns or even misuse them, resulting in applications that may be difficult to maintain even with access to their source code. Augmenting their existing behavior or interaction may further exacerbate such fragility.

7   Conclusions and Future Work

The grab 'n' drop toolglass provides a relatively simple interaction technique through which end-users can modify the underlying interaction of existing applications without access to their source code. In many cases, it lets user create new, customized toolglasses suited to their own particular needs without programming and without special support by the underlying application. We have demonstrated a proof-of-concept implementation for Mac OS X Cocoa applications, but variations of this technique should be compatible with other graphical environments.

We view the grab 'n' drop toolglass as part of a larger class of user-programmable interactions, wherein the underlying software functionality and interaction is malleable. We plan to continue our work in this area, investigating a combination of novel programming models and interactions techniques to increase the flexibility and control over the software without requiring extensive programming on the part of the user. Of particular need are richer design patterns to better express the currently-hidden assumptions behind the interactions between the user interface and the application functionality.

Additionally, there is currently no effective way for an end user to adequately gauge the fragility and risk associated with performing certain operations. It may not be fully necessary to fully insulate the user from all risk so long as she may be able to make her own informed decision as to whether to assume it. In future work, we plan to explore such trade-offs.

References

1. Apple Computer Inc.: AppleScript Language Guide. Addison-Wesley Longman Publishing Co., Inc., Boston (1994)
2. Beaudouin-Lafon, M.: Instrumental interaction: an interaction model for designing post-WIMP user interfaces. In: CHI 2000: Proceedings of the SIGCHI Conference on Human Factors in Computing Systems, pp. 446–453. ACM, New York (2000)
3. Beaudouin-Lafon, M., Mackay, W.E.: Reification, polymorphism and reuse: three principles for designing visual interfaces. In: AVI 2000: Proceedings of the Working Conference on Advanced Visual Interfaces, pp. 102–109. ACM Press (2000)
4. Bier, E.A., Stone, M.C., Pier, K., Buxton, W., DeRose, T.D.: Toolglass and magic lenses: the see-through interface. In: SIGGRAPH 1993: Proceedings of the 20th Annual Conference on Computer Graphics and Interactive Techniques, pp. 73–80. ACM, New York (1993)
5. Coutaz, J.: PAC: an object oriented model for implementing user interfaces. SIGCHI Bull. **19**(2), 37–41 (1987). http://doi.acm.org/10.1145/36111.1045592
6. Cypher, A., Dontcheva, M., Lau, T., Nichols, J.: No Code Required: Giving Users Tools to Transform the Web. Morgan Kaufmann Publishers Inc., San Francisco (2010)
7. Cypher, A., Halbert, D.C., Kurlander, D., Lieberman, H., Maulsby, D., Myers, B.A., Turransky, A. (eds.): Watch What I Do: Programming by Demonstration. MIT Press, Cambridge (1993)

8. Dixon, M., Fogarty, J.: Prefab: implementing advanced behaviors using pixel-based reverse engineering of interface structure. In: CHI 2010: Proceedings of the 28th International Conference on Human Factors in Computing Systems, pp. 1525–1534. ACM, New York (2010)
9. Dorn, B., Tew, A.E., Guzdial, M.: Introductory computing construct use in an end-user programming community. In: Proceedings of the IEEE Symposium on Visual Languages and Human-Centric Computing, VLHCC 2007, pp. 27–32 (2007). http://dx.doi.org/10.1109/VLHCC.2007.33
10. Eagan, J.R., Beaudouin-Lafon, M., Mackay, W.E.: Cracking the cocoa nut: user interface programming at runtime. In: Proceedings of the 24th Annual ACM Symposium on User Interface Software and Technology, UIST 2011, pp. 225–234. ACM, New York (2011). http://doi.acm.org/10.1145/2047196.2047226
11. Fishkin, K., Stone, M.C.: Enhanced dynamic queries via movable filters. In: CHI 1995: Proceedings of the SIGCHI Conference on Human Factors in Computing Systems, pp. 415–420. ACM Press/Addison-Wesley Publishing Co., New York (1995)
12. Gantt, M., Nardi, B.A.: Gardeners and gurus: patterns of cooperation among cad users. In: Proceedings of the SIGCHI Conference on Human Factors in Computing Systems, pp. 107–117. ACM, New York (1992)
13. Hudson, S.E., Rodenstein, R., Smith, I.: Debugging lenses: a new class of transparent tools for user interface debugging. In: UIST 1997: Proceedings of the 10th Annual ACM Symposium on User Interface Software and Technology, pp. 179–187. ACM, New York (1997)
14. Hutchings, D.R., Stasko, J.: Quantifying the performance effect of window snipping in multiple-monitor environments. In: Baranauskas, C., Palanque, P., Abascal, J., Barbosa, S.D.J. (eds.) INTERACT 2007. LNCS, vol. 4663, pp. 461–474. Springer, Heidelberg (2007). doi:10.1007/978-3-540-74800-7_42
15. Kato, J., Sakamoto, D., Igarashi, T.: Picode: inline photos representing posture data in source code. In: Proceedings of the SIGCHI Conference on Human Factors in Computing Systems, CHI 2013, pp. 3097–3100. ACM, New York (2013). http://doi.acm.org/10.1145/2470654.2466422
16. Klokmose, C.N., Zander, P.-O.: Rethinking laboratory notebooks. In: Lewkowicz, M., Hassanaly, P., Wulf, V., Rohde, M. (eds.) Proceedings of COOP 2010, pp. 119–139. Springer, London (2010). doi:10.1007/978-1-84996-211-7_8
17. Mackay, W.E.: Patterns of sharing customizable software. In: Proceedings of the 1990 ACM Conference on Computer-Supported Cooperative Work, pp. 209–221. ACM Press, New York (1990)
18. Mackay, W.E.: Users and Customizable Software: A Co-Adaptive Phenomenon. Ph.D. thesis, Massachusetts Institute of Technology (1990)
19. Mackay, W.E.: Triggers and barriers to customizing software. In: CHI 1991: Proceedings of the SIGCHI Conference on Human Factors in Computing Systems, pp. 153–160. ACM Press (1991)
20. Mackay, W.E.: Which interaction technique works when?: floating palettes, marking menus and toolglasses support different task strategies. In: AVI 2002: Proceedings of the Working Conference on Advanced Visual Interfaces, pp. 203–208. ACM, New York (2002)
21. MacLean, A., Carter, K., Lövstrand, L., Moran, T.: User-tailorable systems: pressing the issues with buttons. In: CHI 1990: Proceedings of the SIGCHI Conference on Human Factors in Computing Systems, pp. 175–182. ACM Press, New York (1990)
22. Nardi, B.A.: A Small Matter of Programming: Perspectives on End User Computing. MIT Press, Cambridge (1993)

23. Ponsard, A., McGrenere, J.: Anchored customization: anchoring settings to the application interface to afford customization. In: Proceedings of the 2016 CHI Conference on Human Factors in Computing Systems, CHI 2016. pp. 4154–4165. ACM, New York (2016). http://doi.acm.org/10.1145/2858036.2858129

24. Reenskaug, T.: Models—views—controllers. Technical report, Xerox PARC, December 1979

25. Robertson, G.G., Henderson Jr., D.A., Card, S.K.: Buttons as first class objects on an X desktop. In: Proceedings of the 4th Annual ACM Symposium on User Interface Software and Technology, pp. 35–44. ACM Press, New York (1991)

26. Stuerzlinger, W., Chapuis, O., Phillips, D., Roussel, N.: User interface façades: towards fully adaptable user interfaces. In: UIST 2006: Proceedings of the 19th Annual ACM Symposium on User Interface Software and Technology, pp. 309–318. ACM, New York (2006)

27. Tan, D.S., Meyers, B., Czerwinski, M.: WinCuts: manipulating arbitrary window regions for more effective use of screen space. In: CHI 2004 Extended Abstracts on Human Factors in Computing Systems, pp. 1525–1528. ACM, New York (2004)

28. Yeh, T., Chang, T.H., Miller, R.C.: Sikuli: using GUI screenshots for search and automation. In: UIST 2009: Proceedings of the 22nd Annual ACM Symposium on User Interface Software and Technology, pp. 183–192. ACM, New York (2009)

Shelves: A User-Defined Block Management Tool for Visual Programming Languages

Sheng-Yi Hsu[(⊠)], Yuan-Fu Lou, Shing-Yun Jung, and Chuen-Tsai Sun

National Chiao Tung University, Hsinchu, Taiwan (R.O.C.)
{syhsu, yflou, syjung, ctsun}@cs.nctu.edu.tw

Abstract. Block editors such as the one used in Scratch are now found in many visual programming languages (VPLs). While considered user-friendly for non-programmers or program learners, they have at least three important display limitations: readability, program structure, and re-use. To address these issues we have developed block shelves, a formatting and organizing tool in support of user-defined VPL structures. Usability experiment results indicate that block shelves can significantly enhance block code navigation and searches, as well as project structure clarification. In the interest of improving project collaboration and code re-use, users can utilize the extensible markup language file format to export/import shelves, and thereby share block codes between projects. Features designed for shelves and the experiment findings are value for course design in project-based learning and future block editor interface improvements.

Keywords: Human-computer interaction · Computer education · Visual programming languages · Code usability · Project-based learning

1 Introduction

As tools for reducing barriers for non-programmers or for program teaching for children, visual programming languages (VPLs) are currently in widespread use (Fig. 1). Scratch [16], MIT App Inventor [15], and Alice [5] are three examples of VPLs that have been created to help learners create their own programs. The list of software tools that contain VPLs as alternate programming environments include Orange [6] for data mining, Modkit [13], and LabVIEW [9] and Quite Universal Circuit Simulator [3] for circuit simulation, among others. Compared to text editors, VPLs are considered much more intuitive and user-friendly due to their drag-and-drop feature. A user first drags a block from a toolbox, which is normally categorized with the block functions, and then drop the block in the block editor. The event-first programming characteristic makes block location irrelevant to compiled project/program results [17].

However, Weintrop and Wilensky [19] pointed out that the recognition that longer blocks-based programs can be difficult to manage. Meanwhile according to Okerlund and Turbak [14], more than 50% of all MIT App Inventor projects consist of more than 30 blocks, which indicates that a user of MIT App Inventor has a more than 50–50 chance of referencing a project having 30+ blocks. In short, the higher the number of functions, the greater the number of blocks shown in the editor, the larger the canvas

© IFIP International Federation for Information Processing 2017
Published by Springer International Publishing AG 2017. All Rights Reserved
R. Bernhaupt et al. (Eds.): INTERACT 2017, Part III, LNCS 10515, pp. 335–344, 2017.
DOI: 10.1007/978-3-319-67687-6_22

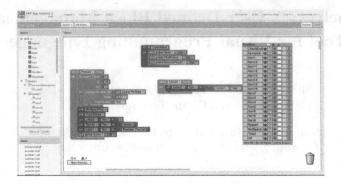

Fig. 1. Screenshots of block editor in MIT App Inventor with block shelves.

size, and the greater the potential for degraded block code readability. Thus, the users of many block editors must make tradeoffs between block code readability and canvas size. Another problem is the lack of block search functions in any of the currently available block editors—this despite the importance of search and navigation support tools for professional developers, who spend at least one-third of their time on redundant but necessary navigation between code fragments [10]. Clearly there is a need to keep track of all blocks during a project and to ensure that each block is easily identifiable. A related issue involves the tracing or reading of blocks when opening projects managed by others for review or adaptation, or when workshop/class instructors want their students to locate specific blocks in their block editors. In sum, VPLs may be very effective tools for lowering barriers to program learning and development, but they are less useful in terms of reading, tracing, and maintenance.

Block editor issues can be categorized as readability, program structure, or block code reuse problems. To address all three issues we have developed a block tagging, formatting, and organizing tool that we call block shelves. The basic idea is that users can arrange block codes on shelves that are labeled as "function," "usage," "execution process order," and so on. Users can re-arrange blocks at any time without deconstruction until they identify the most suitable classification method. Our goal in this paper is to provide a detailed explanation of our proposed tool using a review of related works, a design overview, a quantitative evaluation, and a conclusion.

2   Related Works

Until recently, most approaches to improving code readability and usability have been created in support of text-based programs. Some of the most common involve indentation [4], coding style [12], variable naming [16], modulation [8], and the application of context to improve productivity [10]. Most current block editors provide 4 primary block functions for managing project complexity [15, 16, 18]. However, more and more projects are block-based, and therefore entail four primary block functions:

1. Commenting. This is considered the most common method for improving code readability. Not only do comments help others understand the program creator's ideas, they are also useful for keeping track of one's own projects. However, none of the block editors currently in use have comment search functions, thus forcing users to check blocks individually.
2. Block collapsing. Originally created as a method for keeping screen real estate small, this feature also helps to reduce block code complexity while navigating. After applying this feature, each group of connected blocks is displayed as a single block on a canvas, thereby reducing the overall number of blocks that are shown.
3. Sort by category. After sorting, blocks can be lined up according to category. However, even though block collapsing and sorting can make block layout simple and clean, it still lacks structure or a system for code tracing.
4. Block duplicating. This operation allows users to copy and paste individual or multiple selected blocks. However, this operation is limited to individual projects. Users who want to use the same blocks in other projects must re-build them from the beginning.

In addition to providing block functions, some VPLs also provide a conceptual structure for project managements. The methods used for conceptual structure design can be divided into two categories:

1. Design a strict coding style. This method requires users to follow certain rules to program, which improves the readability and the structure, but not block re-use, in block editors. In Pencil Code, blocks are only allowed to connect vertically, which is clear, easy, straightforward for first-time programmers to use [2].
2. Design "containers" to organize blocks. Most VPL adapt this method to design editors; Scratch [16], Stencyl [11], Gameblox [7] are well-known examples for this type of design. In such editor environment, containers can be designed according to objects (Scratch), behaviors (Stencyl), or user-customized purposes (Gameblox). Taking Scratch as an example, each sprite is a container for anchoring blocks designed for the sprite.

Introducing a conceptual structure for managing a project is indeed helpful for readability. However, the current methods don't provide extra functions for making good use of the conceptual structure; for example, users can't enable or disable all actions designed in some container once. Therefore, besides designing block shelves as containers to organize blocks, we also design a toolbox, shelfBox, for showing shelves and providing extra shelf functions to utilize the shelves defined by users.

3 Design Overview

We chose MIT App Inventor 2 (AI2), which combines the Javascript-based Google Blockly with the Google App Engine, to demonstrate our proposed tool. Accordingly, all modifications for shelf demonstration were created using Google Blockly.

As shown in Fig. 2a, adding blocks to a shelf is similar to other AI2 block-related processes. Right mouse clicks are used to add blocks to a shelf within a project. The

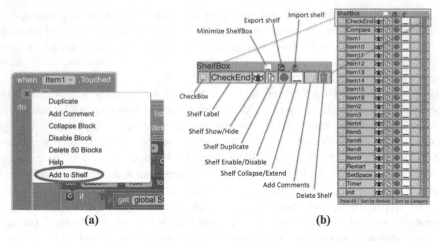

Fig. 2. (a) Menu for adding a shelf, and (b) an example of the ShelfBox toolbox. In 2b, Left: detailed interface descriptions. Right: 21 block shelves used for the posttest involving Pusheen the Cat.

primary functions designed for each shelf are shown on the left hand side of Fig. 2b. Added shelves are shown on the right hand side. There are seven primary shelf functions:

1. Show/hide (👾/👾). This function allows users to hide or show blocks placed on a selected shelf. In addition to saving screen space, this feature controls the number of blocks shown in the block editor. Take Fig. 1 bottom as an example: the editor would merely show the connected block group of <Restart> in the canvas, that is, the groups of <Clock2> and <to ClearStates> are hiding from the canvas, when the show button in the shelf of "Restart" is clicked.
2. Collapse/expand (_/□). This feature allows users to control the number of blocks shown in a block editor. Applying this feature, the blocks in the same shelf would collapsed into one single block. Unlike in the visibility function, users can still see each collapsed block in the editor.
3. Enable/disable (●/●). Since "breakpoint" isn't implemented in current editors, this feature is used to enable or disable all block codes on a selected shelf. Instead of enabling/disabling blocks one-by-one, this feature allows users to enable/disable entire shelves, thus making functional checking/debugging more efficient. Unlike shelf collapse/expand, this function traces codes by checking block functions.
4. Duplicate (🅑). This function duplicates all blocks on a selected shelf, which is useful when creating similar programs or testing block codes without wanting to change the originals.
5. Comment (▨). This feature allows users to add detail to their shelf titles/ descriptions as displayed on the shelfbox.
6. Delete (🗑). This feature deletes existing shelves without affecting blocks in the editor. However, users need to be careful when using this function due to the lack of a mechanism for recovering deleted shelves.

7. Shelf export/import (⬈/⬋). This feature supports block sharing between projects. Users can export/import selected shelves using the extensible markup language (xml) file format. This function is useful for co-designers, who can work in separate locations and send their contributions to a central organizer.

4 Experiment Design and Procedure

To measure code reading and navigation, we used block search and reading time as measures of differences between block editors with and without block shelves [1]. We tested whether block shelves improved block code navigation, improved block code reading, and/or helped users understand project structure in terms of implementing VPL project functions. Our primary goal was not to determine whether the proposed block shelves system improved bug-fixing efficiency, but whether it improved block code understanding. For each task, participants were given full information as well as hints to help them understand task requirements. At various debugging stages we measured the time that each participant required to locate target blocks after reading a task, and reading time required to locate bugs after locating a target block. Debugging in the current block editor necessitates locating target blocks before replacing, updating, and adding blocks or values. Task requirements were analyzed as one of two types: requiring one or more changes to a single existing block, or duplicating existing block codes before changing corresponding blocks to prevent users from creating their own block codes during the experiment.

A total of 60 graduate and undergraduate students were recruited from National Chiao Tung and National Tsing Hua Universities in Taiwan (mean age 23, maximum age 38, minimum age 18). None of the study participants had ever used a VPL, but all had taken computer introduction and programming courses. Participants were randomly divided into experimental (MIT App Inventor 2 with block shelves) and control groups (original MIT App Inventor 2) of equal size.

The experiment consisted of three stages: tutorial, pre-test, and post-test. During the 40-min tutorial stage we introduced Android front-end design and block code design apps. The tutorial project consisted of 197 blocks and 6 screens to show users how to add a gadget to the mobile phone interface, and how to use block codes to control them (e.g., how to add buttons, canvases, balls, timers, graphs, and text tags). All participants took the pretest after the tutorial course. The 250-block calculator was added to the pretest to determine whether the two groups' coding abilities were identical. To minimize the effect of imprinting, the number of blocks for the posttest project was increased by a factor of 4.2 (1,045 blocks). Pusheen the Cat, a pelmanism game that requires players to remember the locations of icons, was used to determine whether the block shelves improved user performance. All trials were conducted using the Windows 7 version of the Chrome browser, and recorded with oCam v23.0 video capture software. Meanwhile all participants were given 10 min to practice using their respective apps on Xiaomi Redmi 1 mobile phones.

All participants didn't require to start from scratch but to debug from a base of block codes in both pretest and posttest. The task descriptions used in the pretest and in the posttest are listed in Table 1 respectively. For pretest tasks 1 and 2, participants were asked to add block codes for division and the number 9 by respectively referencing existing arithmetic operations and numbers. For tasks 3, 4 and 5, they were required to locate and fix bugs in a target block. For the posttest, block shelves used by the Pusheen group were constructed prior to the experiment (shelf labels are shown in Fig. 2(b). Also for tasks 1 and 3, participants were asked to add and correct block codes by referencing other items; for tasks 2, 4 and 5 they were instructed to locate and repair a target block.

Table 1. Pretest and posttest tasks.

Task	Calculator (pretest)	Pusheen the Cat (posttest)

1	**Add a division function.** Hint: Add block code for "div" by referencing "mul" or "sub."	**Add the item 7 function.** Hint: Add the "item7" block code by referencing the block codes of other items, except for "item5."
2	**Add a 9 function.** Hint: Add block code for "num9" by referencing block codes for other numbers, except for "num9" or "num5."	**Correct condition for checking if two selected icons are identical.** Hint: Find the "compare" block code and correct the condition (FirstPicture + SecondPicture ==17) in the if-statement.
3	**Correct the + function.** Hint: Find the "add" block code and modify the function by referencing the block codes of other operations.	**Correct the "cat5" icon display after selecting item5.** Hint: Find the "item5" block code and modify the display function by referencing other items.
4	**Correct the 5 function.** Hint: Find the "num5" block code and modify the function by referencing the block codes of other numbers.	**Correct the timer displayed in the bottom-right corner after hitting Restart.** Hint: Find the "Restart" block code and set the "Label2" variable to 0.
5	**Correct the = function.** Hint: Find the "equ" block code and set result.text to get the variable "global result."	**Correct the text alert for the end of a game.** Hint: Find the "CheckEnd" block code and set the "Label1" variable to "win."

5 Results and Analysis

All search and reading times while performing calculations and Pusheen the Cat tasks were measured and listed in the Table 2. Pretest search and reading time data were used to compare the programming abilities of control and experimental group participants. No significant differences between the two groups were observed for search time (control group M = 207.53, SD = 62.21; experimental group M = 212.2, SD = 49.78; t_{58} = −0.321, p = .750), reading ability (control group M = 317.67, SD = 17.12; experimental group M = 316.83, SD = 18.83; t_{58} = .033, p = .974), or completion time (control group M = 525.2, SD = 14.40; experimental group M = 529.03, SD = 20.82; t_{58} = −1.41, p = .888). Next, we used completion time differences between pretests and posttests for all participants to measure improved performance associated with block shelves. The data indicate a significant difference ($F_{1,58}$ = 53.757, p = .000 < .05), with mean completion time for the experimental group (M = −9.567, SD = 27.89) significantly better than for the control group (M = 285.2, SD = 28.95). Combined, these results suggest that the experimental group participants benefited from the block shelves feature.

Table 2. Descriptive statistics (M ± SD) for search time and reading time.

Study Group	Task1	Task2	Task3	Task4	Task5
		Calculator (Pretest)			
		Search Time (Sec.)			
Control	84.67±43.61	27.73±16.50	24.50±13.12	20.13±12.89	50.50±28.14
Experimental	71.20±38.97	33.07±15.51	31.07±14.99	22.43±13.27	54.43±34.05
		Reading Time (Sec.)			
Control	60.47±49.01	21.97±14.21	12.37±16.28	7.53±7.05	215.33±98.52
Experimental	68.93±59.73	15.87±14.78	17.77±22.33	7.87±9.89	206.40±98.10
		Pusheen the Cat (Posttest)			
		Search Time (Sec.)			
Control	61.57±33.10	124.13±59.72	44.27±26.47	55.97±39.87	64.87±51.51
Experimental	14.23±6.73	20.73±20.74	10.90±6.65	11.33±7.61	11.57±6.31
		Reading Time (Sec.)			
Control	140.93±64.80	135.30±73.73	68.07±60.63	73.57±49.13	41.73±28.99
Experimental	116.73±57.80	141.43±60.15	56.60±25.30	89.97±49.18	45.97±25.55

Search and reading time differences were also respectively used to determine whether the block shelves helped users with block code navigation and reading tasks. Our data indicate a significant improvement in block code navigation ($t_{52.33}$ = 14.159, p = .000 < .05), with the experimental group (M = −143.43, SD = 62.64) outperforming the control group (M = 143.27, SD = 88.17). However, no significant improvement was found for block code reading time (experimental group, M = 133.87, SD = 151.02; control group M = 141.93, SD = 151.04; t_{58} = .207, p = .837). Reading time is associated with the time used to locate a program bug after identifying a target block, but debugging ability is strongly correlated with a user's familiarity with block code grammar. Since none of the study participants had ever used a block editor or read block code prior to our experiment, it is understandable that no difference was noted between the two groups.

The data also confirm a decrease in VPL project readability as the number of blocks increased. As stated in the Experimental Design section of this paper, the Pusheen the Cat block number was four times greater than the number for the calculator, thus reducing the potential for imprinting. Control group participants spent significantly more time on code navigation during the posttest compared to the pretest ($t_{29} = -8.9$, $p = .000 < .05$). Both control ($t_{29} = -5.147$, $p = .000 < .05$) and experimental group participants ($t_{29} = -4.855$, $p = .000 < .05$) used significantly more reading time during the posttest compared to the pretest. Even though project complexity increased for the posttest, experimental (block shelf) group members used significantly less search time finding the blocks they wanted to reference and/or change ($t_{29} = 12.542$, $p = .000 < .05$).

For the posttest, all participants had 10 min to use the app before dealing with the assigned tasks. That practice period, plus experience from the tutorial and pretest, meant that every participant had at least some ability using the app components and mechanisms (e.g., buttons and basic functions). For posttest task 1, participants were told to reference other items to reconstruct <item 7>. We intentionally deleted all blocks programmed for <item 7> as a means of testing whether the block shelves helped users understand the VPL project structure. Further, experimental group participants dealt with a shelfbox from which <item 7> had been deleted (Fig. 2b). Still, average search time for the experimental group participants for task 1 was 4 times faster than for the control group, suggesting that the shelves shown in the shelfbox were sufficient for the experimental group users to quickly understand what was required of them. A more detailed experiment is needed to determine just how much the experimental group participants understood, as well as to determine how much a similar control group might improve with greater time spent practicing. Our data indicate significant improvement for control group users between tasks 1/2 and tasks 3/5.

6   Conclusion

The experiment data indicates that the proposed block shelves tool[1] significantly improved project readability, that the shelfbox feature provided users with fast global views of projects, and that visible shelfbox features allowed users to select shelves for checking, which improved their understanding of block code navigation and VPL project structure. Once users understood how blocks were organized on block shelves, they could easily understand which blocks they wanted to check/add, even though the shelves in question may not have been listed in the shelfbox. The results suggest that code block understanding increases, even for large projects, when users organize block shelves with clear titles and comments.

---

[1] Source code can be downloaded at https://github.com/syhsu/appinventor-shelves.

References

1. Bragdon, A., Zeleznik, R., Reiss, S.P, Karumuri, S., Cheung, W., Kaplan, J., Coleman, C., Adeputra, F., LaViola Jr., J.J.: Code bubbles: a working set-based interface for code understanding and maintenance. In: Proceedings of SIGCHI Conference on Human Factors in Computing Systems, vol. 2, pp. 2503–2512. ACM (2010)
2. Bau, D., Bau, D.A., Dawson, M., Pickens, C.S.: Pencil code: block code for a text world. In: Proceedings of 14th International Conference on Interaction Design and Children (IDC 2015), pp. 445–448. ACM, New York (2015)
3. Brinson, M.E., Jahn, S.: Qucs: a GPL software package for circuit simulation, compact device modelling and circuit macromodelling from DC to RF and beyond. Int. J. Numer. Model. Electron. Netw. Devices Fields 22(4), 297–319 (2009)
4. Clifton, M.H.: A technique for making structured programs more readable. ACM SIGPLAN Not. 13(4), 58–63 (1978)
5. Cooper, S., Dann, W., Pausch, R.: Alice: a 3-D tool for introductory programming concepts. J. Comput. Sci. Coll. Consort. Comput. Sci. Coll. 15, 107–116 (2000)
6. Demšar, J., Curk, T., Erjavec, A., Gorup, Č., Hočevar, T., Milutinovič, M., Možina, M., Polajnar, M., Toplak, M., Starič, A., Štajdohar, M., Umek, L., Žagar, L., Žbontar, J., Žitnik, M., Zupan, B.: Orange: data mining toolbox in Python. J. Mach. Learn. Res. 14, 2349–2353 (2013)
7. Du, E.: Gameblox flexidor: adding flexibility to blocks based programming environments. Master thesis, Massachusetts Institute of Technology (2015)
8. Eick, S.G., Graves, T.L., Karr, A.F., Marron, J.S., Mockus, A.: Does code decay? Assessing the evidence from change management data. IEEE Trans. Softw. Eng. 27(1), 1–12 (2001)
9. Elliott, C., Vijayakumar, V., Zink, W., Hansen, R.: National instruments LabVIEW: a programming environment for laboratory automation and measurement. J. Assoc. Lab. Autom. 12(1), 17–24 (2007)
10. Kersten, M., Murphy, G.C.: Using task context to improve programmer productivity. In Proceedings of 14th ACM SIGSOFT International Symposium on Foundations of Software Engineering (SIGSOFT 2006/FSE 2014), pp. 1–11. ACM, New York (2006)
11. Liu, J., Lin, C., Wilson, J., Hemmenway, D., Hasson, E., Barnett, Z., Xu, Y.: Making games a "snap" with Stencyl: a summer computing workshop for K-12 teachers. In: Proceedings of 45th ACM Technical Symposium on Computer Science Education (SIGCSE 2014), pp. 169–174. ACM, New York (2014)
12. Miara, R.J., Musselman, J.A., Navarro, J.A., Shneiderman, B.: Program indentation and comprehensibility. Commun. ACM 26(11), 861–867 (1983)
13. Millner A., Baafi, E.: Modkit: blending and extending approachable platforms for creating computer programs and interactive objects. In: Proceedings of 10th International Conference on Interaction Design and Children, pp. 250–253. ACM (2011)
14. Okerlund, J., Turbak, F.: A preliminary analysis of APP Inventor blocks programs. Poster presented at Visual Languages and Human Centric Computing (VLHCC), pp. 15–19 (2013)
15. Pokress, S.C., Veiga, J.J.D.: MIT APP Inventor: enabling personal mobile computing. arXiv preprint arXiv:1310.2830 (2013)
16. Resnick, M., Maloney, J., Monroy-Hernández, A., Rusk, N., Eastmond, E., Brennan, K., Millner, A., Rosenbaum, E., Silver, J., Silverman, B., Kafai, Y.: Scratch: programming for all. Commun. ACM 52(11), 60–67 (2009)

17. Turbak, F., Sherman, M., Martin, F., Wolber, D., Pokress, S.C.: Events-first programming in APP Inventor. J. Comput. Sci. Coll. **29**(6), 81–89 (2014)
18. Roque, R.V.: OpenBlocks: an extendable framework for graphical block programming systems. Master thesis, Massachusetts Institute of Technology (2007)
19. Weintrop, D., Wilensky, U.: To block or not to block, that is the question: students' perceptions of blocks-based programming. In: Proceedings of 14th International Conference on Interaction Design and Children (IDC 2015), pp. 199–208. ACM, New York (2015)

Text Priming - Effects of Text Visualizations on Readers Prior to Reading

Tilman Dingler[1]([⊠]), Dagmar Kern[2],
Katrin Angerbauer[1], and Albrecht Schmidt[1]

[1] VIS, University of Stuttgart, Stuttgart, Germany
{tilman.dingler,katrin.angerbauer,albrecht.schmidt}@vis.uni-stuttgart.de
[2] GESIS Leibniz Institute for the Social Sciences, Cologne, Germany
dagmar.kern@gesis.org

Abstract. Living in our information society poses the challenge of having to deal with a plethora of information. While most content is represented through text, keyword extraction and visualization techniques allow the processing and adjustment of text presentation to the readers' individual requirements and preferences. In this paper, we investigate four types of text visualizations and their feasibility to give readers an overview before they actually engage with a text: word clouds, highlighting, mind maps, and image collages. In a user study with 50 participants, we assessed the effects of such visualizations on reading comprehension, reading time, and subjective impressions. Results show that (1) mind maps best support readers in getting the gist of a text, (2) they also give better subjective impressions on text content and structure, and (3) highlighting keywords in a text before reading helps to reduce reading time. We discuss a set of guidelines to inform the design of automated systems for creating text visualizations for reader support.

Keywords: Priming · Reading interfaces · Comprehension · Text visualization

1 Introduction

Reading is an activity needed in most facets of our daily life. By reading, people gather information from text, extract meaning, build knowledge and foster other cognitive abilities, such as reasoning [38]. The information age changes our reading behavior. With an abundance of information made available through the Internet and accessible on electronic devices, reading becomes a ubiquitous activity and the overall time spent reading increases [29]. However, the activity of reading on computers and other electronic devices tends to be shallower than on conventional media [12] and the skill to quickly scan a document in order to get the gist of its content becomes important.

Visualizations can be used to make readers quickly filter out the essence of a text and help with the decision on whether a text is worth reading in the first

© IFIP International Federation for Information Processing 2017
Published by Springer International Publishing AG 2017. All Rights Reserved
R. Bernhaupt et al. (Eds.): INTERACT 2017, Part III, LNCS 10515, pp. 345–365, 2017.
DOI: 10.1007/978-3-319-67687-6_23

place [28]. Understanding the gist of a text supports overall text comprehension and allows readers to process a text's content and meaning in more detail. By facilitating text reading in this way, people could manage their daily readings more effectively by reducing overall reading time or increasing reading volume.

In this work, we investigate the use of text visualizations to support reading activities on electronic devices with a special focus on effective gist extraction, comprehension, and perceived usefulness. Here, we make use of the *Priming Effect* – a concept taken from psychology that describes an implicit memory effect: by exposing users to a current stimulus, a response to another stimulus is triggered in the future [4]. We base our use of the term on the more conceptual definition of how the exposure to one stimulus influences the perception of a subsequent one. While this is barely a recognition task in the range of milliseconds, we use it to investigate an effect in higher-level cognitive tasks by applying the effect to reading. Therefore, we launched an investigation into the utility and effects of four different text visualizations: word cloud, highlighting, mind map, and image collage. After having conducted an initial focus group, we collected both quantitative and qualitative results in a comprehensive user study with 50 participants. Results show the feasibility of using mind maps and text highlights as primers. Based on our findings we derive requirements for building automated text visualizations for reading on electronic devices. The contribution of our work is as follows:

1. We show that text visualizations can be used to get the gist of a text prior to reading.
2. We compare four visualization types with regard to their utility, finding that mind maps are most useful in aiding understanding.
3. We provide insights into how highlighting can help to reduce reading time by giving readers a better text understanding and to go through text quicker.
4. We present an architecture for an automated system to support readers on electronic reading devices through visualizations.

2   Background and Related Work

Our research combines aspects of different research fields. In this section, we provide same insights into reading behavior and how it has changed as well as reading comprehension. Furthermore, we introduce the priming effect and provide information about text summaries and visualizations.

2.1   Reading Behavior

Cunningham and Stanovich [38] speak of the *Matthew's Effect* when describing a 'rich get richer, poor get poorer' - phenomenon for reading. The ability to comprehend and read large volumes creates a reciprocal relationship: readers with a broader knowledge base carry out a smaller amount of effort while gaining a more positive experience than readers who struggle to comprehend text [10].

Positive experiences can be a great motivation which puts avid readers into a positive feedback loop, which eventually affects vocabulary development, abilities of expression, and reasoning. Liu [29] investigated the effects the information age has had on people's reading behavior: with more information constantly available, the time spent on reading increased, specifically the amount of work related reading. On the other hand, reading patterns get more shallow and fragmented as people read in less depth. This seems to be a coping mechanism through which people get through the high amount of daily readings and only read a text in detail if it is assumed to be highly relevant. The ability to scan and browse text for pointers to valuable information becomes increasingly important.

2.2   Reading Comprehension and Recall

Reading comprehension is essential to extract meaning from text. Comprehending a text is a combination of recalling what has been read and the understanding of the underlying concepts [31]. Therefore, the text needs to be interacted with on a mental level and connected to the reader's existing knowledge of the world [1]. Being aware of the context instead of just the meaning of single words is also crucial for understanding. Federmeier and Kutas [17] showed that words are often predictable in sentence contexts and that sentence contexts can facilitate comprehension. Bransford and Johnson [8] investigated the role of contextual knowledge where comprehension often results from the context. In their experiments, they showed that participants who had to comprehend a text passage without being provided with the appropriate context did worse in comprehension tests than those who had been provided with the context. Another result of their experiments is that prior knowledge alone is not always helpful for the comprehension process but that it has to be activated first through some stimulus. Text comprehension and memory are deeply intertwined. Kintsch [24] explicitly contrasted remembering and learning, where remembering entails the process of simply reproducing the information of a text. This requires a shallower form of comprehension, whereas if a reader has effectively learned from a text, she can apply that knowledge to new situations. Reading comprehension is therefore a multi-faceted measure, which often is assessed by the reader's ability to recall what is stated in the text (literal comprehension), interpret the text's meaning by connecting rather implicitly stated information (inferential comprehension), or to relate the text's content to prior experiences and knowledge (evaluative comprehension) [7]. Learning has occurred, if a reader has been able to build a well-structured representation of the text and connect this representation to the background knowledge she possesses [30].

2.3   The Priming Effect

When a stimulus subconsciously influences the processing of the following stimulus, psychologists speak of a *Priming Effect*. Influencing stimuli, the so-called *primes*, can have an effect on memory processing tasks [4]. Research in psychology has confirmed this effect for reading activities. Typical implicit memory testing methods include word primes, such as, for example for the prime 'apple' [33]: for word stem completion, such as A P _ _ _, for word fragment completion: _ P _ L _, for anagram solving: 'plape', and word identification tasks.

Rajaram and Roediger [33] apply these tasks with different primes in different modalities (auditory or visual priming), forms (word or picture) and typefaces to evaluate the magnitude of priming effects. Their findings show that for modalities showing visual primes for visual tasks and auditory primes for auditory tasks is recommendable. Hence, we were interested in whether this effect can be used when using text summary visualizations as primers before reading a text to foster text comprehension and recall.

2.4 Text Summaries

Related work about text summaries belongs to the field of text mining. Text mining, in general, describes the process of extracting high-quality information from documents (see [22] for an overview). In this work, we focus on extracting keywords from text and make use of the term-frequency-inverse document frequency (tf-idf) method [34]. This method determines the relevance for each term by combining the term frequency (tf) of a term (a term with a high frequency in a document is probably more important than a term with a low frequency) with the inverse document frequency (a term that has a high frequency over all documents is less descriptive for a particular document). For example, the frequency of the term *"and"* is high in a single document as well as in a set of documents. Therefore, the tf-idf score is quite low. Whereas, the term *"priming"* has a high frequency in one document but not in the set of specific documents the tf-idf score is high and indicates an importance of this term. To reduce the impact of larger tf-idf values, a log-scale is applied:

$$tf - idf_{t,d} = tf_{t,d} \times log(\frac{N}{df_t})$$

Here, t stands for the term under investigation, d for the document in a corpus t belongs to. N depicts the total number of documents in the corpus which is divided by the number of documents containing the term df_t.

2.5 Text Visualization

Banas and Brown [5] define visualization as "the conversion of information to a symbolic representation of a particular idea, concept, or data object". Hence, representations can reveal patterns, relationships, and concepts helping observers to new understandings and deeper comprehension of text. Text visualizations also convey information quickly and efficiently and generally aim to make the comprehension of aspects easier. Kalmane [23] stresses the potential of online visualization tools to assist reading comprehension, especially for language learners.

Adding context-relevant images, for example, helps understanding and learning overall [11]. In traditional textbooks, visualizations were often crafted for illustrative purposes, which were rather laborious to create. Now it is pragmatical to generate visualizations automatically and support readers in-situ. A lot of research has been carried out to automatically generate text visualizations. The complexity of these text visualizations ranges from visualizing single documents (see, *e.g.*, [21,40]) over visualizing the context of a book (see, *e.g.*, [14,32]) to visualizing documents and their relationships in digital libraries (see, *e.g.*, [42]). Comprehensive overviews of different text visualization techniques are provided by Alencar et al. [2] or Kucher and Kerren [25]. In our work, we focus on single document visualizations based on their relation to a corpus of related documents.

3 Visualizations for Text Priming

We decided to investigate four different types of text visualizations with different characteristics regarding their effects on reading activities: word cloud (representing all extracted words), highlighting (representing keywords in their context), mind map (representing selected keywords and their connections to each other), and image collage (representing a couple of keywords in a more abstract form). We chose these common visualization types as they are rather well-established representations of texts. With regard to our user study, we thereby attempted to minimize possible novelty effects. In the following section, we describe these four visualization types, discuss why we think that they are worth considering for invigorating priming effects and how we designed them for our user study. In all cases, we build upon the 50 most relevant keywords extracted from a text through tf-idf.

3.1 Word Cloud

A set of visually presented words arranged in a cloud is commonly known as a "tag cloud". If the content of a text is summarized, it is also often called a "word cloud", which is the term we will use throughout this paper. Viegas and Wattenberg [41] provide a comprehensive overview of the history and different types of tag or word clouds. Such word clouds have been widely used for teaching and learning (see, *e.g.*, [6]), which is why we are interested in their feasibility to prime a reader for a text. We apply a simple design for visualizing the 50 most descriptive keywords of a text by varying font sizes according to keyword's importance and a color scheme that does not distract the reader but fosters readability. In our design, size and color reflect the importance of a word. The sequential word order of the keywords aims to mirror the text's structure. Figure 1A shows a word cloud, which we used in our study.

3.2 Highlighting

Printed text often contains in-text highlights in the form of keywords marked by being given a background color. Different studies showed the positive effects

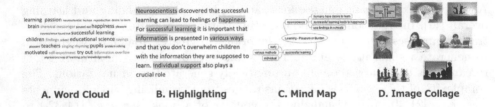

A. Word Cloud   **B. Highlighting**   **C. Mind Map**   **D. Image Collage**

Fig. 1. Visualizations used in our user study summarizing a text about learning.

highlighting has on text retention (see, *e.g.*, [18,19]), whereby actively highlighting, performed by the reader herself during reading is considered more effective than pre-existing highlights [19]. However, there are also studies that conclude that reading a text that has been highlighted by expert readers improves recall of the highlighted text passage [13,15]. This also implies that the quality of the highlighting plays an important role, as inappropriate highlighting can have negative effects on reading comprehension [20,37]. The highlighting approach in contrast to using word clouds retains the context in which the word occurs and may provide more information at a glance. According to the guidelines on text highlighting techniques in [39], we chose to color the background of the 50 most relevant keywords in yellow. Figure 1B shows an extract of a highlighted text, which we used in our study.

3.3   Mind Map

Mind maps [9] are often used for organizing information by grouping important aspects into clusters and thereby have the ability to structure the information [43]. Structured information can be learned better and is processed more efficiently [4,26]. We assume that due to the visualized connection, the gist of a text might be derivable and prime the reader for the text. The mind maps used in our studies are manually created, and we concentrate only on a few keywords and their relation to each other, to make the mind maps clear and usable. During initial trials we found about 15 keywords to be appropriate to represent our study texts whose length varied between 500 and 600 words. Some of them are grouped together to describe a single concept, *e.g.*, the keywords "successful", "learning" and "happiness" are part of the concept: "successful learning leads to happiness". Figure 1C shows a summary of one of the texts used throughout our study.

3.4   Image Collage

Following the ancient proverbs "every picture tells a story" or "a picture says more than thousand words", an image collage seems to be a suitable way to summarize text visually. Results of studies performed throughout the 1990s support this assumption as they have shown that depictive images aid the learning process [11]. Zhu et al. [44] presented a Text-to-Picture system capable of creating an Image Collage of short texts. The images are synthesized from some of the text's most relevant keywords. Another method was introduced by Aramini et al. [3]: their system generates unsupervised and automatically visualization of shortened texts using images that can be found on the Web. We pursue a similar approach and search for suitable images corresponding to important keywords on creative common image portals like *Flickr* or *Google Creative Commons Image Search*. Not all of the 50 keywords can be well represented by an image. For creating the image collages for our user study, we analyzed the keywords regarding their metaphorical expression. We conclude that for each text eight pictures representing the main keywords can be chosen (see Fig. 1D).

4 Pre-study

To collect initial qualitative feedback on our general approach we conducted a pre-study in the form of focus groups.

4.1 Methodology and Procedure

We held two focus groups with four participants (3 females) each lasting about 90 min. All participants were university students with different backgrounds and between 19 and 24 years old ($M = 22.25, SD = 1.67$). The native tongue of everyone was German. We chose four texts with different text styles (fiction, news and science) and created four visualizations whereby the word cloud visualized a fictional text, highlighting was used for an abstract of a scientific paper, the mind map summarized a news article and the image collage a scientific article. Discussions were recorded in a written protocol, after which the participants' comments were sorted into categories. Both visualization and text were in German and printed on paper. The main part of the focus group comprised discussions on the four visualizations regarding their usage and utility before, during and after reading the text. The four visualizations were discussed one after the other, and in the end, general design aspects of such visualizations were debated.

Results and Discussion. From the discussions and preliminary design explorations we derived ideas for using visualizations as pre-, during-, and after-reading support.

Pre-reading. Before diving into the actual text, participants found the visualizations helpful in general but mind map and image collage in particular. On the other hand, however, they were sometimes confused as some content in the visualizations did not make immediate sense to them. In some cases, the keywords were even found misleading. Furthermore, it was mentioned that visualizations could also help deciding whether a text is relevant to a certain topic.

During-Reading. Having visualizations accessible during reading, participants found it easier to keep an overview of the structure of the text. One participant stated that the mind map visualization helped to structure the text while another said the highlighting helped to pay attention to important parts of the text.

Post-reading. All participants found the visualizations to be very helpful in the post-reading phase, especially as memory aids when they needed to retain the texts' contents. One participant had doubts about the usefulness of pictures as a memory aid after a long period and supposed textual cues would be more helpful. Another participant found post-reading support more important than pre-reading support.

In general, participants preferred getting a quick overview of a text. If a lot of time was required to look at a visualization to make sense of it, it was regarded as less beneficial. Participants said they had to spend the most time trying to figure out text contents from the word cloud, whereas the content of the image collage visualization was perceived quickest. During the study, no clear preference for one type of visualization could be observed. Especially the use of images as cues was controversial: some participants stated they found images most helpful, while others considered them least informative and preferred textual cues. Because no clear preferences for one of the visualization could be determined within the focus groups, we designed a user study for investigating all four visualizations. We set out to research the effect of such visualizations on the reader before, during and after reading. We start with the before-reading phase and present this user study as well as its results in the following sections.

5   User Study

With the goal of investigating the feasibility and appropriateness of our four text visualizations to prime readers for going through a text on electronic devices, we conducted a user study. As the Priming Effect is complex and cannot be regarded as a unitary effect [35] we focus on different aspects to approximate it:

1. The first impression the reader gets about the text after seeing the visualization but before reading it.
2. The effects on reading comprehension and time spent reading.
3. The subjective utility of visualizations and how they help readers gain an overview of a text and its content.

5.1   Apparatus

As reading material, we chose five standardized texts from the Institute for German as a Foreign Language (TestDaF). Since we expected participants to be native German speakers, we selected texts in German dealing with issues of general interest (*e.g.*, "*Earthquakes*" or "*The effect of nuts on health*"). Text lengths ranged between 500 and 600 words. Each text came with ten multiple choice questions, each with three possible answers for assessing reading comprehension. For each text we extracted the 50 most relevant keywords: each text was preprocessed with *TreeTagger* [36]. From its output, we only considered nouns, verbs, and adjectives as well as removed frequent stopwords. For tf-idf calculations, we used the *gensim* library[1] and used a corpus consisting of 500 articles, which we took from *SSOAR*[2], a freely accessible paper platform for social sciences. For creating the word clouds we used JavaScript. Highlighting visualizations were manually created based on the words extracted from our system. The image collage was also manually created and used the eight most important keywords, for which we searched images through Google Images. The mind map was manually generated, too, but was oriented on the text's structure and keywords. Keyword extraction, as well as the creation of the visualizations, was done independently from the comprehension tests in order to not induce any researchers' bias. Figure 1A–D shows visualizations used for the text *"Learning-Pleasure or Burden"*. Since our investigation focuses on reading on electronic devices, we conducted the study on desktop PCs and therefore created a comprehensive online survey using *Limesurvey*[3]. Hence, multiple participants could take part in the study at the same time under our supervision.

5.2   Methodology

Data collection took place from August to September of 2016 at a university and a research institute where multiple participants could be processed simultaneously. We followed a within-subject design approach with the texts and the visualizations being the independent variables in five conditions: the four different visualizations, plus one text without visualization as a baseline condition. As dependent measures, we collected Likert-style ratings, comprehension scores, measured reading time, and free-form text comments.

5.3   Procedure

At both locations, the study took place at a computer lab under controlled conditions without distractions on 13 in. displays showing the texts with a 12px font size. All participants followed the following procedure: we explained the purpose of the study and asked each participant to sign a consent form. Then, we handed out a paper with the URL to the online survey, which they could fill in at one of the workstations in the lab. Participants were randomly but equally assigned to five different surveys. Each survey employed a different order of conditions as well as different allocations between the condition and underlying text. Participants were assigned to the surveys following a counterbalanced measures design via Latin Square. The surveys were divided into steps in a series of self-directed webpages (see Table 1). It started with an introduction and questions about

---

[1] https://pypi.python.org/pypi/gensim.
[2] http://www.ssoar.info/.
[3] https://www.limesurvey.org/.

Table 1. Structure of the survey. In the baseline condition (no visualization) only the steps 'Text' and 'Comprehension questions' were utilized in section B.

A	Introduction
	Demographic questions
	Questions on reading behavior
B *repeated for each visualization and the baseline condition*	Visualization of the text (visible for 1 minute)
	Question "What do you think the text is about?"
	Text
	Evaluation of the visualization according to the following characteristics on a 5-point Likert-scale from "I disagree" (1) to "I strongly agree" (5): 1. The visualization helped me to understand the text. (**Comprehension**) 2. The visualization helped to get the gist of the text. (**Gist**) 3. The visualization reflected the content of the text comprehensively. (**Fit**) 4. The visualization provided an overview of the text structure. (**Structure**)
	Comprehension questions
C	Final ratings: Which is the most helpful visualization? Which visualization do you like most regarding design? And why?

demographic information and reading behavior. Afterwards, the visualization of the text was shown for one minute. All visualizations except for highlighting were fully visible. For highlighting participants could freely scroll the text. Participants were allowed to progress with the study before one minute was over by clicking on "next". A question about the content of the text followed before the actual text was presented to participants. There was no time-limit for reading the text. Then, questions about the visualization were asked, before ten comprehension questions had to be answered. This step B (see Table 1) was repeated for each visualization and the baseline condition. In the baseline condition, participants had only to read the text and to answer the comprehension questions. The study took about 45 min for each participant.

5.4 · Participants

We recruited 50 participants (15 females) with their age ranging from 18 to 60 ($M = 27.7, SD = 6.19$). 32 were university students from different fields of study, while 10 were researchers and the remaining seven worked as software developers or secretaries. 45 participants stated German to be their mother tongue, and the others spoke German fluently. 21 participants were considered to be frequent readers (more than seven hours reading time per week), 12 to be casual readers (between four and six hours reading time per week) and 17 to be scarce readers (less than three hours reading time per week).

6   Results

In the following, we present our results from the subjective assessments, pre-impression analysis, comprehension tests, reading time, and free commenting.

6.1   Quantitative Measures

User Ratings. For the following analysis, we applied Friedman tests followed by Wilcoxon signed-rank tests with a Bonferroni correction applied, which resulted in a significance level of $p < 0.008$. Figure 2 contains an overview of all subjective ratings with regard to each visualization and the four characteristics: Comprehension, Gist, Fit and Structure as shown in Table 1.

Looking at the subjective user feedback regarding the utility of the visualizations, there was a statistically significant difference in perceived **comprehension** with regard to visualization type, $\chi^2(3) = 33.725$, $p < 0.001$. Median perceived comprehension ratings for word cloud, mind map, highlighting, and image collage were 2 (1 to 3), 4 (2.75 to 4.25), 3.5 (2 to 4), and 2 (1 to 3), respectively. There was a statistically significant difference in perceived comprehension in favor of mind map over word cloud ($Z = -4.36$, $p < 0.001$) and over image collage ($Z = -4.022$, $p < 0.001$). Also, highlighting was rated significantly higher than word cloud ($Z = -2.636$, $p = 0.008$) and image collage ($Z = -3.344$, $p < 0.001$).

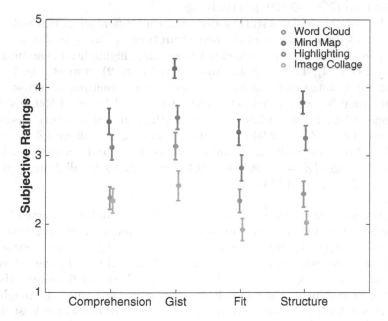

Fig. 2. Subjective user ratings (mean and standard errors) for each visualization type with regard to their utility for supporting text *comprehension*, understanding the *gist* of a text, its *fit* to reflect the text's content and its adequacy to reflect the text's *structure*.

As for perceived text content overview—*i.e.*, getting the **gist** of a text—there was a statistically significant difference in how much of the different visualization types conveyed, $\chi^2(3) = 38.173$, $p < 0.001$. Median perceived content overview ratings for word cloud, mind map, highlighting, and image collage were 4 (2 to 4), 5 (4 to 5), 4 (3 to 4), and 2 (1 to 4), respectively. Post-hoc tests showed a statistically significant difference in how well the visualizations provided a content overview with mind map being rated best over word cloud ($Z = -4.336$, $p < 0.001$), image collage ($Z = -4.534$, $p < 0.001$), and highlighting ($Z = -2.806$, $p = 0.005$). Highlighting was better received than image collage ($Z = -3.998$, $p < 0.001$). No statistically significant difference was found between highlighting and word cloud ($Z = -1.496$, $p = 0.135$) and between word cloud and image collage ($Z = -1.678$, $p = 0.093$).

There was a statistically significant difference in how comprehensive the corresponding visualization **fit** the text content, $\chi^2(3) = 36.491$, $p < 0.001$. Median perceived ratings for word cloud, mind map, highlighting, and image collage were 2 (1 to 3.25), 4 (2 to 4), 3 (2 to 4), and 2 (1 to 2), respectively. There were statistically significant differences with mind map being rated better than word cloud ($Z = -3.822$, $p < 0.001$) and image collage ($Z = -4.627$, $p < 0.001$). Also, highlighting was better perceived to comprehensively reflect the content than image collage ($Z = -3.719$, $p < 0.001$). No statistically significant difference was found between highlighting and word cloud ($Z = -1.984$, $p = 0.47$), image collage and word cloud ($Z = -1.921$, $p = 0.055$) or between highlighting and mind map ($Z = -2.169$, $p = 0.03$).

Finally, results yielded a statistically significant difference in how well visualization provided an overview of the text **structure**, $\chi^2(3) = 48.850$, $p < 0.001$. Median perceived ratings for word cloud, mind map, highlighting, and image collage were 2 (1 to 4), 4 (3 to 5), 4 (2 to 4), and 2 (1 to 2), respectively. Post-hoc tests showed a statistically significant difference in structural overview ratings with mind map be being rated better than word cloud ($Z = -4.599$, $p < 0.001$) and image collage ($Z = -5.224$, $p < 0.001$). Highlighting was better perceived than word cloud ($Z = -2.940$, $p = 0.003$) and image collage ($Z = -4.670$, $p < 0.001$). No statistically significant difference was found between word cloud and image collage ($Z = -1.965$, $p = 0.49$) or between highlighting and mind map ($Z = -2.136$, $p = 0.033$).

Pre-impressions. After being shown each visualization and before actually being presented the full text, participants were asked about their pre-impression, *i.e.* what they thought the text's content was about. We had three independent researchers assess each comment according to how well they fit the actual text content on a school grading scale from 1 (being best) to 6 (being mislead). Therefore, we instructed the researchers to assign grade 4 when the rough topic was identified, 5 when the topic was incorrectly identified but was at least similar, and 6 when the participant's assumption did not match the content of the text at all. Grades from 1 to 3 depended on the level of detail. We then calculated a mean inter-annotator agreement score for each pre-impression statement and performed a Friedman test on the resulting final grade. There was a statistically significant difference in calculated grades based on the quality of participants' pre-impressions, $\chi^2(3) = 47.730$, $p < 0.001$. Median perceived ratings for word cloud, mind map, highlighting, and image collage were 4 (3 to 4.25), 3 (2 to 4), 4 (3 to 4), and 4 (4 to 5), respectively. There were statistically significant differences with mind map leading to most accurate pre-assessments compared to tag cloud ($Z = -3.820$, $p < 0.001$), highlighting ($Z = -3.987$, $p < 0.001$), and image collage ($Z = -5.393$, $p < 0.001$). Also, tag cloud performed better than image collage ($Z = -3.053$, $p = 0.002$), so did highlighting ($Z = -4.046$, $p < 0.001$). Highlighting and tag cloud seemed to perform similarly resulting in a non-significant difference ($Z = -0.767$, $p = 0.443$).

Comprehension Scores and Time Spent Reading. For comprehension scores, a one-way repeated measures ANOVA with a Greenhouse-Geisser correction yielded no statistical significance between conditions ($F(3.314, 162.402) = 1.086$, $p = 0.36$). We looked at how much time it took participants to read the prospective texts followed by studying the visualizations for 60 seconds. Most participants took full advantage of this time interval. Hence, there was no statistically difference in visualization viewing time ($F(1.158, 56.731) = 0.296$, $p = 0.622$). With regard to time spent reading the full text, there was a significant difference based on which visualizations participants studied beforehand ($F(3.335, 163.435) = 3.087$, $p = 0.024$). Post hoc tests using the Bonferroni correction revealed that readers spent less time reading after a highlighting visualization compared to viewing an image collage ($Z = -3.384$, $p = 0.001$). On average, readers who viewed a highlighted version of the text were 24.9 seconds (*i.e.*, 12.1%) faster than when viewing an image collage (compared to word cloud: 10.4%, mind map: 5.5%, and without visualization: 9.2%) No other pairwise comparisons yielded any statistically significant results, however there is a tendency of highlighting to help reduce reading time as compared to word clouds ($Z = -2.736$, $p = 0.006$) and reading without any prior visualizations ($Z = -2.667$, $p = 0.008$).

6.2   Qualitative Measures

Participants were asked which visualization they found most appealing and most helpful (see Fig. 3). They were encouraged to provide explanations of their assessment, which we analyzed by dividing them into single statements and assigning them to respective visualizations. Altogether, we collected 32 statements regarding appeal and 52 statements regarding helpfulness. In the following, answers given by more than one participants are listed and the number of occurrences is shown in brackets after each provided statement: the image collage was described as a simple and clear design, but at the same time with a lack of expressivity (N = 3). It is clearly arranged (N = 3), arouses interest to read the text (N = 2), is good to remember things (N = 2) and helps to formulate a mental image of the content (N = 2). On the other hand, participants pointed out that "Pictures are open to interpretation, therefore, they might mislead the reader." (N = 2). Highlighting provides the structure of the text (N = 5)

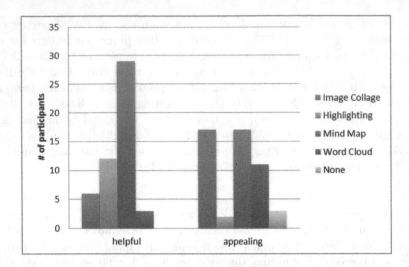

Fig. 3. Participants' ratings of different visualization types regarding appeal and helpfulness.

and shows the words in their context (N = 4). However, two subjects were overstrained by the volume of text. Comments for the mind map were predominantly positive. It was stated as clearly and logically structured (N = 9). It summarized the essential information of the text (N = 11), shows connection between the information (N = 10), allows recognizing the structure of the text (N=9) and contributes to the understanding (N = 4). Participants appreciated the word cloud for providing the most important words (N = 4) in a pretty way (N = 3). But the word cloud was also considered as too overloaded (N = 2). In general, there was a perceived benefit of looking at text visualizations before reading a text. This is supported by the fact that nobody answered the question "Which visualization do you find most helpful?" with *none*.

7   Discussion

The initial focus group gave us insights into the applicability of visualizations before, during, and after the actual reading process. Due to the feedback, we set out to assess the feasibility of using text visualizations as primers to improve text reading. Therefore, we conducted a user study examining the utility of four different visualizations types.

We could not confirm an objective effect difference on comprehension between those visualizations. When designing studies around reading it is crucial to not only pay attention to the nature of the texts used, but also to the difficulties of measuring text comprehension. We opted for a solution in which the texts came with pre-defined comprehension tests as they were commonly used in current language proficiency assessments. Hence, they often required not only literal translation, but also transfer skills. When reviewing the test results, we noticed that many participants had difficulties with these type of questions resulting in a rather homogeneous distribution of mean comprehension scores, which is why we also analyzed the subjectively perceived effects that visualizations had on readers. Here, we found effects on subjective perception of using visualizations before reading with regard to their utility to convey the text's content and structure. The mind map was rated most helpful in providing an overview and getting the gist of a text. Its nature allows communicating content and structural information more comprehensively since the mind map's visual design often reflects semantic and structural relationships in the text.

Also, highlighting lead to better subjective text comprehension. By studying highlighted keywords of a text before reading it was shown in our study to give readers an impression of the text's gist. We also found that it reduced the actual reading time by up to 12.1%. This could be due to the readers already being exposed to the entire text beforehand, where participants were able to read ahead. However, some of the participants claimed that due to the time limit of 60 seconds they had problems to capture all of the highlighted keywords, which might be an argument against the premature detailed reading.

By objectively assessing the quality of participants' presumed text summaries prior to reading, we find that visualizations can give readers a good first impression of the content. Mind maps—due to being rich in structure and content information—helped participants' most in grasping the text content, while highlighting and word cloud performed better than image collage. These findings show the usefulness of visualizations, such as mind maps, to allow readers to skim and possibly disregard a text quickly. This skill is especially useful in situations or jobs, where people need to process a lot of text.

We were further able to relate effects of inappropriate highlighting to participants' feedback stating that visualizations could be misleading. One participant pointed out that highlighting a verb without its negation might be interpreted completely different. The benefit of highlighting is strongly dependent on the quality of the underlying keyword extraction. As Silvers and Kreiner [37] showed that inappropriate highlighting could have negative effects on reading comprehension, merely using tf-idf scores might be too simplistic. More sophisticated topic models, such as Latent Dirichlet Allocation (LDA), need to be exerted in order to extract meaningful keywords and therefore convey text context more accurately to support comprehension. Image collages also bear the risks to prime the user in different directions. This is caused by the rather ambiguous nature of images since they often trigger different associations, which is challenging to design for deliberately.

During the pre-study, we identified three strands of application scenarios, namely using visualizations as primes before reading, as an aid to keep an overview during, and as a summary support for after reading. A combination of those could have profound effects on readers' ability to quickly get the gist of a text in order to decide on its relevancy. Then during reading contextual graphics are provided to aid readers' sense of text position and sequence of argumentation. And afterwards, having a summary highlighting the text essence to be committed to long-term memory. Specific visualizations during each of these stages can differ due to their utility, which is why we investigated the first stage with all four visualization types mentioned. Further studies will need to be conducted to get insights into their specific design, most effective content generation, and application cases. For now, we have been focusing on the pre-reading phase and the use of such visualizations to prime readers. Based on our quantitative and qualitative findings we derive a set of implications in the following and introduce our vision for an automated system that takes text cues from a user's reading device and provides effective visualizations tailored to the reader to support the reading experience.

8   A System to Support Readers Through Visualizations

In our study of visualizations, we found that prior viewing impacted the readers' ability to make out the gist of a text and in the case of highlighting reduced the actual reading time. Mind maps, on the other hand, were best fit to convey the structure and the essential content of a text.

In the following, we apply our findings into a vision of an automated system capable of providing such visualizations on the fly as users deal with their daily readings. Thereby, not only the text at hand needs to be considered, but also the reading goal. Visualizations, for example, can help readers disregard or engage with a text in more detail based on their pre-assessment. Further, as discussed by our focus groups, visualizations can serve different purposes based on whether they are being used before, during, or after reading. A system that takes a text as an input and creates visualizations on the fly can tailor to those requirements. Figure 4 shows an overview of the key components of such a system, which takes text from the reader's device as cues to generate visualizations while considering the user's reading goal and characteristics (such as background knowledge and reading habits). From our results, we derived the following important aspects that we propose to be considered while creating such a system.

Extraction. An automated system for reader support through visualizations needs to comprise a representative corpus to ensure a reliable keyword extraction. The extraction itself and its quality are vital for the utility of the system, as we have learned from the participants' feedback who were not always able to connect the topics presented in some visualizations, especially in image collages, which mislead some readers. A reliable keyword extraction then informs the system which images to look for in order to enhance visualizations or build the corresponding image collages.

Visual Clues. Providing visual clues about the semantic link between the keywords is crucial since we have learned that keywords on their own are not meaningful enough. Such links can be of structural nature, as the mind maps showed to be more effective when conveying text overview. Such links—also to externally related sources—can help readers understand content since providing context increases text comprehension [8].

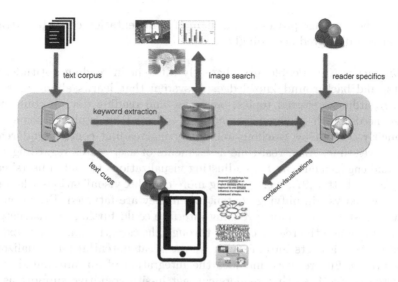

Fig. 4. System pipeline for supporting in-situ text visualizations: a central instance collects available texts, processes them, links them to additional content, such as relevant images, and creates visualizations taking into account readers' preferences and the devices' attributes on which these visualizations are being rendered.

Image Selection. Images are appealing and can be useful to motivate readers to read a text, but bare little insights about the gist of a text and can even be misleading. For an automated system, there are two important aspects:

(1) filtering out meaningful keywords that describe a text in its essence, and (2) a comprehensive image database that contains a well-indexed pool of images to avoid ambiguities. In the study presented, we focused on the applicability of image collages as primes, hence we opted for manual image selection, but sophisticated tagging and visual processing algorithms might automate this process in the future.

Address Information Overload. For pre-assessments of text, highlighting of most relevant text aspects is vital to convey the gist of a text effectively. Avoiding clutter is crucial since otherwise the visualization overloads the reader and loses its merit alongside the text. In our study, it became clear that mind maps conveyed a stronger structural overview as compared to word clouds, which were more likely to be perceived as cluttered. The hierarchical structure of mind maps helps to highlight important concepts where details can be pushed further down the branches.

Text Structure. Conveying a text's structure helps readers orient themselves in the text and allows them to follow the string of argumentation. The mind maps used during our study conveyed that structure, which leads to increased overview of structure and content. The simple structure is given by text flow, but using semantics and language processing, a chain of argumentation could be extracted from text and displayed accordingly.

User Characteristics. People are inherently different in reading aptitude, their interests, and background knowledge. A system that learns about user preferences regarding preferred topics, language, and reading device, could adapt to these needs. Such preferences could be collected by explicit user settings or implicitly derived by tracking and analyzing reading content and reading behavior over time. Also, real-time assessments of user states regarding visual fatigue and engagement can help adjusting visualizations to match users' cognitive capacities better [27], *e.g.*, creating more complex visualizations when readers are engaged vs. simplifying content when they are fatigued. Based on such internal user states, a dynamic reading interface could further be instructed by the system to guide the reader quicker through the essential parts of a text [16].

Taking these aspects into account, we see great potential for visualizations as text primes. Future work includes the integration of an automated system as depicted in Fig. 4, so that readers can get in-situ cognitive support as they deal with their daily readings on electronic devices. By receiving visualizations that break down the gist of a text into small, digestible chunks. Such visualizations can guide readers through the string of argumentation and support text comprehension.

9   Conclusions

In this paper, we focused on the use of visualizations as primers to support reading. In a comprehensive user study with 50 participate we investigated in what way four types of text visualizations were useful to convey text content and structure before reading. Comparing word cloud, highlighting, mind map and image collage we found that mind maps were rated best to support comprehension and structure of a text. Highlighting, on the other hand, showed that readers who study keywords in their context later require less time spent reading.

We conclude with a proposed design of a system that receives a text and provides context-specific visualizations. Context includes text cues produced by keyword extraction, the combination of different sources (e.g., image databases), and taking into account specific goals and characteristics of the reader. This could allow visualizations not only to serve as text summaries but further convey text structure and provide enhancements through images. Our study showed that readers were able to pre-assess the content of a text based on visualizations— foremost through mind maps, which allowed them to absorb the gist of a text quickly. With the growing demands of our information society to keep up with daily readings, visualizations can help readers making quick and informed decisions about the utility and content of a text prior to reading.

Acknowledgments. We thank our study participants and acknowledge the financial support of the Future and Emerging Technologies (FET) programme within the 7th

Framework Programme for Research of the European Commission, under FET grant number: 612933 (RECALL).

References

1. Ahmadi, A.: Comprehension of a non-text: the effect of the title and ambiguity tolerance. J. Pan-Pac. Assoc. Appl. Linguist. **15**(1), 163–176 (2010)
2. Alencar, A.B., de Oliveira, M.C.F., Paulovich, F.V.: Seeing beyond reading: a survey on visual text analytics. Wiley Int. Rev. Data Min. Knowl. Disc. **2**(6), 476–492 (2012). http://dx.doi.org/10.1002/widm.1071
3. Aramini, S.A., Ardizzone, E., Mazzola, G.: Automatic illustration of short texts via web images. In: Proceedings of 6th International Conference on Information Visualization Theory and Applications, IVAPP, (VISIGRAPP 2015), vol. 1, pp. 139–148. INSTICC, ScitePress (2015)
4. Baddeley, A., Eysenck, A., Anderson, M.: Memory. Psychology Press, New York (2009)
5. Banas, J.R., Brown, C.A.: Web 2.0 visualization tools to stimulate generative learning. pp. 77–90. IGI Global (2012)
6. Baralt, M., Pennestri, S., Selvandin, M.: Action research: using wordles to teach foreign language writing. Lang. Learn. Technol. **15**(2), 12–22 (2011)
7. Basaraba, D., Yovanoff, P., Alonzo, J., Tindal, G.: Examining the structure of reading comprehension: do literal, inferential, and evaluative comprehension truly exist? Read. Writ. **26**(3), 349–379 (2013)
8. Bransford, J.D., Johnson, M.K.: Contextual prerequisites for understanding: some investigations of comprehension and recall. J. Verbal Learn. Verbal Behav. **11**(6), 717–726 (1972)
9. Buzan, T.: Make the Most of Your Mind. Simon and Schuster, New York (1984)
10. Caillies, S., Denhière, G., Kintsch, W.: The effect of prior knowledge on understanding from text: evidence from primed recognition. Eur. J. Cogn. Psychol. **14**(2), 267–286 (2002)
11. Carney, R., Levin, J.: Pictorial illustrations still improve students' learning from text. Educ. Psychol. Rev. **14**(1), 5–26 (2002)
12. Carr, N.: The Shallows: What the Internet is Doing to Our Brains. WW Norton & Company, New York (2011)
13. Cashen, V.M., Leicht, K.L.: Role of the isolation effect in a formal educational setting. J. Educ. Psychol. **61**(6p1), 484 (1970)
14. Collins, C., Carpendale, S., Penn, G.: Docuburst: visualizing document content using language structure. In: Proceedings of 11th Eurographics/IEEE - VGTC Conference on Visualization, The Eurographs Association, EuroVis 2009, pp. 1039–1046. Wiley, Chichester (2009). http://dx.doi.org/10.1111/j.1467-8659.2009.01439.x
15. Crouse, J.H., Idstein, P.: Effects of encoding cues on prose learning. J. Educ. Psychol. **63**(4), 309 (1972)
16. Dingler, T., Shirazi, A.S., Kunze, K., Schmidt, A.: Assessment of stimuli for supporting speed reading on electronic devices. In: Proceedings of 6th Augmented Human International Conference, AH 2015, pp. 117–124. ACM, New York (2015). http://doi.acm.org/10.1145/2735711.2735796
17. Federmeier, K.D., Kutas, M.: A rose by any other name: long-term memory structure and sentence processing. J. Mem. Lang. **41**(4), 469–495 (1999). http://www.sciencedirect.com/science/article/pii/S0749596X99926608

18. Foster, J.J.: The use of visual cues in text. In: Kolers, P.A., Wrolstad, M.E., Bouma, H. (eds.) Processing of Visible Language, vol. 13, pp. 189–203. Springer, Boston (1979). doi:10.1007/978-1-4684-0994-9_12

19. Fowler, R.L., Barker, A.S.: Effectiveness of highlighting for retention of text material. J. Appl. Psychol. **59**(3), 358 (1974)

20. Gier, V.S., Herring, D., Hudnell, J., Montoya, J., Kreiner, D.S.: Active reading procedures for moderating the effects of poor highlighting. Read. Psychol. **31**(1), 69–81 (2010). http://dx.doi.org/10.1145/223904.223912

21. Hearst, M.A.: Tilebars: Visualization of term distribution information in full text information access. In: Proceedings of SIGCHI Conference on Human Factors in Computing Systems. CHI 1995, pp. 59–66. ACM Press/Addison-Wesley Publishing Co., New York (1995). http://dx.doi.org/10.1145/223904.223912

22. Hotho, A., Nrnberger, A., Paas, G.: A brief survey of text mining. LDV Forum - GLDV J. Comput. Linguist. Lang. Technol. (2005)

23. Kalmane, R.: Improving Reading Comprehension with Online Text Visualization Tools. Lulu Press, Morrisville

24. Kintsch, W.: Text comprehension, memory, and learning. Am. Psychol. **49**(4), 294–303 (1994)

25. Kucher, K., Kerren, A.: Text visualization techniques: taxonomy, visual survey, and community insights. In: 2015 IEEE Pacific Visualization Symposium (PacificVis), pp. 117–121 (2015)

26. Kudelic, R., Konecki, M., Malekovic, M.: Mind map generator software model with text mining algorithm. In: Proceedings of ITI 2011 33rd International Conference on Information Technology Interfaces (ITI), pp. 487–494, June 2011

27. Kunze, K., Sanchez, S., Dingler, T., Augereau, O., Kise, K., Inami, M., Tsutomu, T.: The augmented narrative: toward estimating reader engagement. In: Proceedings of 6th Augmented Human International Conference, AH 2015, pp. 163–164. ACM, New York (2015). http://doi.acm.org/10.1145/2735711.2735814

28. Li, Z., Shi, S., Zhang, L.: Improving relevance judgment of web search results with image excerpts. In: Proceedings of 17th International Conference on World Wide Web, WWW 2008, pp. 21–30. ACM, New York (2008). http://doi.acm.org/10.1145/1367497.1367501

29. Liu, Z.: Reading behavior in the digital environment: changes in reading behavior over the past ten years. J. doc. **61**(6), 700–712 (2005)

30. McNamara, D.S., Kintsch, W.: Learning from texts. Eff. Prior knowl. Text Coherence **22**, 247–288 (1996)

31. Morineau, T., Blanche, C., Tobin, L., Guéguen, N.: The emergence of the contextual role of the e-book in cognitive processes through an ecological and functional analysis. Int. J. Hum.-Comput. Stud. **62**(3), 329–348 (2005). http://www.sciencedirect.com/science/article/pii/S1071581904001089

32. Paley, W.B.: Textarc: showing word frequency and distribution in text. Poster Presented at IEEE Symposium on Information Visualization, vol. 2002 (2002)

33. Rajaram, S., Roediger, H.L.: Direct comparison of four implicit memory tests. J. Exp. Psychol. Learn. Mem. Cogn. **19**(4), 765 (1993)

34. Ramos, J.: Using tf-idf to determine word relevance in document queries. In: Proceedings of 1st Instructional Conference on Machine Learning (2003)

35. Ratcliff, R., McKoon, G.: A retrieval theory of priming in memory. Psychol. Rev. **95**(3), 385 (1988)

36. Schmid, H.: Treetagger—a language independent part-of-speech tagger. Institut für Maschinelle Sprachverarbeitung, Universität Stuttgart 43, p. 28 (1995)

37. Silvers, V.L., Kreiner, D.S.: The effects of pre-existing inappropriate highlighting on reading comprehension. Lit. Res. Instr. **36**(3), 217–223 (1997)
38. Stanovich, K.E., Cunningham, A.E.: What reading does for the mind. J. Direct Instr. **1**(2), 137–149 (2001)
39. Strobelt, H., Oelke, D., Kwon, B.C., Schreck, T., Pfister, H.: Guidelines for effective usage of text highlighting techniques. IEEE Trans. Vis. Comput. Graph. **22**(1), 489–498 (2016)
40. Strobelt, H., Oelke, D., Rohrdantz, C., Stoffel, A., Keim, D., Deussen, O., et al.: Document cards: a top trumps visualization for documents. IEEE Trans. Vis. Comput. Graph. **15**(6), 1145–1152 (2009)
41. Viégas, F.B., Wattenberg, M.: Timelines: tag clouds and the case for vernacular visualization. Interactions **15**(4), 49–52 (2008). http://doi.acm.org/10.1145/1374489.1374501
42. Wise, J.A., Thomas, J.J., Pennock, K., Lantrip, D., Pottier, M., Schur, A., Crow, V.: Visualizing the non-visual: spatial analysis and interaction with information from text documents. In: Proceedings of 1995 IEEE Symposium on Information Visualization, INFOVIS 1995, p. 51–. IEEE Computer Society, Washington, DC (1995). http://dl.acm.org/citation.cfm?id=857186.857579
43. Zhang, F.: The application of visualization technology on knowledge management. In: Proceedings of 2008 International Conference on Intelligent Computation Technology and Automation, ICICTA 2008, vol. 02, pp. 767–771. IEEE Computer Society, Washington, DC (2008). http://dx.doi.org/10.1109/ICICTA.2008.479
44. Zhu, X., Goldberg, A.B., Eldawy, M., Dyer, C.R., Strock, B.: A text-to-picture synthesis system for augmenting communication. In: Proceedings of 22nd National Conference on Artificial Intelligence, AAAI 2007, vol. 2, pp. 1590–1595. AAAI Press (2007). http://dl.acm.org/citation.cfm?id=1619797.1619900

The Panta Rhei: Modernizing the Marquee

Megan Monroe[✉] and Mauro Martino

IBM Research, Boston, MA, USA
`madey.j@gmail.com`

Abstract. Many multimedia visualizations abstract the underlying content into aggregate displays, requiring user interaction in order to expose the original text, images or video. The drawback of this approach is that unlike traditional, numerical data, multimedia data is readily interpretable. Users can catch an image or phrase out of the corner of their eye an immediately understand the content. However, this passive discovery cannot take place when content is only exposed through direct interaction. In this paper, we present the Panta Rhei, a peripheral display designed to avoid this pitfall by surfacing original content when the user is not actively engaged with the application. We provide the full implementation details, including the many ways in which the underlying parameters can be tuned to suit various objectives. Since the display can easily support text, images or videos, our goal is to enable more widespread discussion and experimentation involving this technique for multimedia visualization.

Keywords: Visualization · Animation · Passive · Engagement-versatile

1 Introduction

This work began as a larger project to visualize the news in real time. The goal was for users to understand which events were trending, who was involved, and which stories were sneaking under the radar. Accordingly, a number of visualization strategies were employed to extract and link entities [8], to identify keywords and concepts [13, 14], and to gauge sentiment [6]. However, there were two critical drawbacks to these aggregate displays:

1. Without interaction, the display remained relatively unchanged until the next big news story broke.
2. Without interaction, and with limited screen space, only one article was being displayed in detail at any given time.

In this paper we present the Panta Rhei (Greek for "everything flows"), a web-based animation that scrolls article titles across the browser window as an infinite, mesmerizing stream. The Panta Rhei is triggered when there has been no interaction for a set period of time. It demands no active attention or interaction, and yet was surprisingly adept at triggering serendipitous discovery from the periphery during its initial deployment [9].

The contribution of this paper is primarily technical. We detail the Panta Rhei's scrolling mechanism, which allows developers to feed in customized content without

© IFIP International Federation for Information Processing 2017
Published by Springer International Publishing AG 2017. All Rights Reserved
R. Bernhaupt et al. (Eds.): INTERACT 2017, Part III, LNCS 10515, pp. 366–373, 2017.
DOI: 10.1007/978-3-319-67687-6_24

substantial code modifications. We test and report on the small number of underlying parameters that can be tuned to achieve a wide array of functional and aesthetic objectives, including piquing the user's attention when the display is receiving only peripheral attention.

2 Background

Many text and multimedia visualizations dedicate the majority of screen space to computed abstractions of the underlying content [1, 3, 7]. Even so, the seeming consensus is that the original content must be accessible to prevent misinterpretation [15]. This is typically accomplished through active interaction [10]. This work explores the other side of this equation, mapping the exposure of original content to physical time when interaction is not taking place or has become undirected.

The Panta Rhei is intended to serve as a periphery-passive or focus-passive display in an engagement-versatile application. However, unlike Tanahashi's Stock Lamp [12], the Panta Rhei displays unabstracted content. When a particular image or phrase catches the user's eye, they are seeing the *actual thing* that is interesting, not an abstracted aggregate. The Panta Rhei is also unique in that it is designed to be reusable. It is structured to allow developers to flexibly feed in any combination of text, images, and videos. The display can simply be plugged into existing applications to make them more engagement-versatile. Though its design adheres closely to related work involving ambient displays [5, 11], the aesthetic details are beyond the scope of this paper.

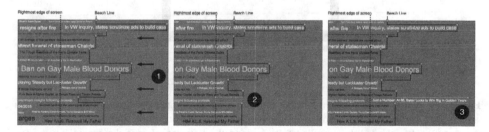

Fig. 1. The beachLine sits just offscreen (note that the dotted line represents the end of the screen) and works to ensure a steady stream of content. (1) Content scrolls steadily onto the screen, moving from right to left (2) when a tick has scrolled fully onto the screen, the beachLine is notified to backfill the empty space (3) a new tick is added to the beachLine, which is adjusted by the width of that tick.

3 Implementation

The Panta Rhei modernizes the classic news ticker marquee with inspiration from Steven Fortune's sweepline algorithm [4]. The web-based implementation scrolls a tightly-packed grid of heterogenous content across the browser window (or a specified <div> of the browser window). Each item of content, referred to as a "tick", is contained in a <div> and can thus be comprised of any web element (image, video, text). This paper will focus on text, and consequently, a right-to-left scrolling such that the beginning of the text leads onto the screen. The display is powered by a data structure called the beachLine, a set of points that descends vertically from the top of the screen to the bottom. Each of these points keeps track of a tick that is currently in the process of scrolling onto the screen. Conceptually, the beachLine sits just out of view, beyond the rightmost edge of the screen, and is updated every time a tick scrolls fully into view (see Fig. 1).

New ticks are added to the display in a just-in-time fashion. That is, ticks are created such that their leftmost edge is flush against the rightmost edge of the screen and they immediately begin their scroll across the display. When a tick is created, it is armed with two future actions. First, the tick will notify the beachLine when it has scrolled fully onto the screen. This is the beachLine's cue to backfill the space that the tick is leaving in its wake. Second, the tick is set to remove itself from the page entirely once its rightmost edge has scrolled beyond the left side of the screen. This prevents the visualization from queuing up undue memory usage. These three stages of a tick's lifecycle are depicted in Fig. 2.

Fig. 2. (1) A new tick is created with its leftmost edge flush against the rightmost edge of the screen (2) once the tick has scrolled fully onto the screen it notifies the beachLine to add new content (3) when the tick has scrolled fully beyond the leftmost edge of the screen it removes itself from the page entirely.

3.1   Updating the beachLine

The beachLine is comprised of a set of points that descend vertically down the screen, each consisting of an x-coordinate, a y-coordinate, and the id of the tick that generated it. However, as it is shown in Fig. 1, it is easier to think of the beachLine as a series of vertical facings against which new content can be aligned. These facings can simply be extrapolated from the points.

When a newly created tick has scrolled fully onto the screen, it notifies the beachLine by submitting its y-coordinate (i.e. its vertical position on the screen). This initiates a two-phase process in which the beachLine first locates and determines the height of the facing on which that y-coordinate falls. This height is served to the developer, who in turn supplies any <div>, or tick, that does not exceed the allotted height. Thus, developers can employ a variety of content and layout strategies by customizing only a single function, getNewTick(), which is shown in Fig. 4. They can return a tick that exactly fits the space. They can return a smaller, vertically centered tick. They can add multiple ticks. Or no ticks at all.

The new content, consisting of zero or more ticks, is then is fed back to the beachLine to be incorporated into its point system. This is done by increasing the x-coordinates of the beachLine points by the width of the new ticks, and adding points as necessary. The four possible reconfigurations of the beachLine that can result from adding a new tick are shown in Fig. 3. What is critical to note about these updates is that, while the y-coordinates of each beachLine point represents a true y-position on the screen, the x-coordinates continue to increase monotonically as new ticks are added to the beachLine. Thus, the x-coordinate of a beachLine point represents only its *relative* x-position compared to the other points on the beachLine. Each new tick is also added to a pool of activeTicks, which indicates that the beachLine is expecting to eventually receive its backfill request. Ticks are removed from the pool as these requests are received.

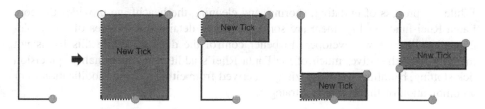

Fig. 3. Given a vertical facing on the beachLine, which is defined by two consecutive points (left), a new tick can be added in any of the four ways shown on the right.

3.2   Maintaining the beachLine

The continual updating of the beachLine eventually results in an extremely ragged edge, with vertical facings too short for the intended content. To account for this, two operations are performed on the beachLine each time a backfill/update call is made.

Shoring the beachLine: As discussed in the previous section, developers do not need to fully fill an open facing when it becomes available. However, the space that is not filled (now its own facing) becomes an empty section of the screen without an active backfill timer. If left unchecked, these unused facings slowly consume the entire screen.

Because the x-coordinates of the beachLine points are relative, we do not know the absolute position of the beachLine at all times. However, we can infer it momentarily when a backfill request is initiated because such a request means that the rightmost edge of a tick, and thus its corresponding beachLine facing, is flush with the rightmost edge of the screen (see Stage 2 of a tick's lifecycle in Fig. 2). By obtaining the x-coordinate of this beachLine point, we can infer which sections of the screen have gone unfilled because their x-coordinates will be lower, meaning that these facings have already scrolled onscreen. Thus, when a backfill request is received, these empty facings can be reclaimed by pushing their x-coordinates up to match facing being backfilled, a process referred to as "shoring" the beachLine.

Cleaning the beachLine: Once the beachLine has been shored, adjacent sections can be merged together to form larger facings, a process referred to as "cleaning" the beachLine. This process is dictated by a single parameter that tells the beachLine how close the x-coordinates of adjacent facings must be in order to be merged, which can be tuned to produce larger or smaller facings. When two facings are merged, the new facing assumes the larger of the two x-coordinates, which prevents ticks from overlapping, and the tick id associated with lower x-coordinate is removed from the activeTicks pool in order to prevent a duplicate backfill. Shored facings will always be merged when they are adjacent to the facing that generated the backfill request, since their x-coordinates will be equal. Thus, the core Panta Rhei algorithm is a self-perpetuating process of updating, shoring, and cleaning the beachLine. The pseudocode for this entire process is presented in Fig. 4.

4   Extensions and Control

While the process of updating, shoring, and cleaning the beachLine provides the core Panta Rhei functionality, there are some additional details and features of the implementation that allow developers to better control the display. While this list is not meant to be exhaustive, much of the Panta Rhei's additional functionality (precision tick slotting, handling screen resizing) is derived from either a slight modification to or a combination of the following strategies.

Override Backfills: For a number of reasons, it is necessary to backfill a section of the screen even if there is no corresponding entry in the activeTicks pool. This can be done by incorporating an "override" id into the checkActiveTicks() function that will always allow the backfillTick() function to proceed. In particular, this tactic is used to initialize the display.

Pausing and Restarting: Pausing the Panta Rhei's scrolling is accomplished with two actions. First, the activeTicks pool is emptied, ensuring that no new content will be added to the display when the backfill timers fire. Second, the animation assigned to each tick is halted and removed. Restarting the display then, requires an analogous process. First, every tick on the screen is reissued an animation that will complete its scrolling and remove it from the display. Second, any tick that is intersecting the rightmost edge of the display is reissued a backfill timer that will go off when the remainder of the tick has scrolled onto the screen.

Splitting the Stream: This feature was originally requested so that news headlines pertaining to multiple entities could be compared. Splitting the stream is accomplished by adding points of the form {x: -1, y: *y-positionOfSplit*, id: "split"\} to the beachLine. A "split" point acts like a pillar, shoved into a riverbed - content is forced to flow around it. The shoring and cleaning functions are updated to skip over any beachLine points with the "split" id and, similarly, the getFacing() function returns a

```
function backfillTick (id, y){
  //MAINTAIN BEACHLINE
  shoreBeachLine();
  cleanBeachLine(mergeDiff);

  if( ! checkActiveTicks(id) ) return;

  //GET FACING HEIGHT
  var facing = getFacing(y);
  var currY = facing.top;

    while(currY < facing.bottom){
      var height = facing.bottom - currY;

      //CREATE A NEW TICK
      var tick = getNewTick(height, currY);
      tick.setPosition(screen.width, currY);
      var tickID = tick.id;
      var tickW = tick.width;

      //UPDATE BEACHLINE
      updateBeachLine(tick);

      var phase2 = tickW / scrollSpeed;
      var phase3 = (tickW + screen.width)
                             / scrollSpeed;

      //BACKFILL TIMER
      setTimeout( backfillTick(tickID, y),
        phase2);

      //ANIMATION AND REMOVAL TIMER
      newTick.animate({ left: -tickW
          }, phase3, "linear", function() {
            $(this).remove(); });

      currY += tickH;
    }
}
```

Fig. 4. The self-perpetuating backfillTick() function drives the display using the beachLine and the activeTicks pool.

facing of 0 height if its parameter lands on a "split" facing. To remove a split, the id of the corresponding beachLine point needs only to be set to null. The negative x-value then ensures that the facing will be reclaimed during the next beachLine shoring.

Discovery: Our goal was for the Panta Rhei to function in the periphery, enabling serendipitous discovery without requiring interaction. This is accomplished with a patiently-paced animation, a non-intrusive color scheme, and a visual randomness to how the content is packed into the stream. However, the display can also demand the user's attention more actively when necessary. A particular headline, displayed in a unique color, in isolation, or in a rigid grid that defies the typical heterogeneity of the display all succeeded in our initial testing at piquing the user's attention even when they are not paying direct attention to the display. These three tactics are shown in Fig. 5.

Fig. 5. The Panta Rhei can draw attention to a particular tick using color (top), uniformity (middle), or isolation (bottom). (Color figure online)

5   Conclusion

The Panta Rhei is a reusable, peripheral display that surfaces original content comprised of text, images, or any other element that can be placed within a web-based <div>. It's initial deployment within a corporate communications team, tasked with tracking online media, yielded a surprising array of immediate and actionable insights. "Most of our tools don't bring light to a story until it is trending, so since [this article] was not trending yet we had not noticed it on any other tool in the room," a team member reported of one particular instance when she spotted a headline in which the purchase price of a recent acquisition had been misprinted. The responsible publication was immediately contacted to have the misprint corrected. Going forward, the Panta Rhei will be subjected to more formal testing in order to quantify its ability to generate such insights with more empirical rigor.

References

1. Collins, C., Carpendale, S., Penn, G.: Docuburst: visualizing document content using language structure. In: Proceedings of the Eurographics/IEEE-VGTC Symposium on Visualization (EuroVis), vol. 28, no. 3, pp. 1039–1046 (2009)
2. D3.js - Data Driven Documents. http://d3js.org/. Accessed 23 Mar 2016
3. Eler, D.M., Nakazaki, M.Y., Paulovich, F.V., Santos, D.P., Andery, G.F., Oliveira, M.C.F., Neto, J.B., Minghim, R.: Visual analysis of image collections. Vis. Comput. 25(10), 923–937 (2009)
4. Fortune, S.: A sweepline algorithm for voronoi diagrams. In: Proceedings of the Second ACM Symposium on Computational Geometry, pp. 313–322 (1986)

5. Jafarinaimi, N., Forlizzi, J., Hurst, A., Zimmerman, J.: Breakaway: an ambient display designed to change human behavior. In: CHI EA '05 CHI '05 Extended Abstracts on Human Factors in Computing Systems, pp. 1945–1948 (2005)
6. Pang, B., Lee, L.: Opinion mining and sentiment analysis. Found. Trends Inf. Retrieval 2(1–2), 1–135 (2008)
7. Rao, D., McNamee, P., Dredze, M.: Newslab: exploratory broadcast news video analysis. In: IEEE Symposium on Visual Analytics Science and Technology, pp. 123–130 (2007)
8. Rao, D., McNamee, P., Dredze, M.: Entity linking: finding extracted entities in a knowledge base. In: Poibeau, T., Saggion, H., Piskorski, J., Yangarber, R. (eds.) Multi-source, Multilingual Information Extraction and Summarization. Theory and Applications of Natural Language Processing, pp. 93–115. Springer, Heidelberg (2012). doi:10.1007/978-3-642-28569-1_5
9. Rosenman, M.F.: Serendipity and scientific discovery. J. Creative Behav. 22, 132–138 (1988)
10. Shneiderman, B.: The eyes have it: a task by data type taxonomy for information visualizations. In: IEEE Symposium on Visual Languages, pp. 336–343 (1996)
11. Skog, T., Ljungblad, S., Holmquist, L.E.: Between aesthetics and utility: designing ambient information visualizations. In: Proceedings of the 9th Annual IEEE Conference on Information Visualization, INFOVIS 2003, pp. 233–240 (2003)
12. Tanahashi, Y., Ma, K.L.: Stock lamp: an engagement-versatile visualization design. In: Proceedings of the 33rd Annual ACM Conference on Human Factors in Computing Systems, CHI 2015, pp. 595–604 (2015)
13. Viégas, F.B., Wattenberg, M., Feinberg, J.: Tag clouds and the case for vernacular visualization. In: ACM Interactions, vol. XV, no. 4, July/August (2008)
14. Viégas, F.B., Wattenberg, M., Feinberg, J.: Participatory visualization with wordle. IEEE Trans. Vis. Comput. Graph. 15(6), 1137–1144 (2009)
15. Yatani, K., Novati, M., Trusty, A., Truong, K.N.: Review spotlight: a user interface for summarizing user-generated reviews using adjective-noun word pairs. In: CHI 2011 Proceedings of the SIGCHI Conference on Human Factors in Computing Systems, pp. 1541–1550 (2011)

Your Data, Your Vis: Personalizing Personal Data Visualizations

Hanna Schneider[✉], Katrin Schauer, Clemens Stachl, and Andreas Butz

LMU Munich, Munich, Germany
Hanna.schneider@ifi.lmu.de

Abstract. Personal Visualizations (PV) provide visual feedback on personal data, e.g., regarding physical activity or energy consumption. They are a vital part of many behavior change technologies (BCT) and Personal Informatics tools. Feedback can be presented in various ways, for example using counts and graphs, stylized displays, metaphoric displays, narrative information, data physicalisations, or even living plants. The properties of a PV are likely to influence its effectiveness towards reaching a goal. However, users' perceptions and preferences regarding different PVs seem to vary strongly, rendering a one-size-fits-all approach unsuitable. To investigate whether preferences for certain PVs coincide with personality or gender, we conducted a lab study with three example PVs: *Donut*, *Glass*, and *Creature*. Indeed, the results of our lab study are a first indicator that there is a relationship between personality traits and preferences for different PVs. High scores on extraversion and openness, for example, positively correlated with a preference for *Creature*. In contrast, high scores in conscientiousness negatively correlated with a preference for *Creature*. Further research is necessary to better understand how truly personalized PVs can be realized, which, in turn, might fit better into people's lives and thereby be more effective.

Keywords: Personal informatics · Visualization · Personality · Behavior change

1 Introduction

Collecting and tracking personal data is becoming increasingly popular in various domains, ranging from physical activity (e.g., FitBit) to sleep (e.g., SleepCycle), food and water consumption (e.g., MyFitnessPal), and financial expenses (e.g., Mint) [18]. Tracking personal data can support people in becoming more aware of their habits and behaviors, changing their behavior, or reaching specific goals (such as spending less money or being more physically active) [8]. These systems are often called behavior change technologies (BCT) [25]. An important part of many BCTs is the way in which they present feedback, often delivered through personal visualizations (PVs). One of the main challenges that PVs face is the diverse personalities and contexts that they should cater for [26]. As an example,

© IFIP International Federation for Information Processing 2017
Published by Springer International Publishing AG 2017. All Rights Reserved
R. Bernhaupt et al. (Eds.): INTERACT 2017, Part III, LNCS 10515, pp. 374–392, 2017.
DOI: 10.1007/978-3-319-67687-6_25

for some users direct feedback, e.g., on the amount of weight gained or the amount of energy consumed, might induce negative feelings such as guilt or shame, while other users might appreciate the honesty of the technology and feel motivated. Several studies have reported that PVs provoked negative feelings among some users [28,39]. These negative experiences are named as a reason for the limited success of persuasive technologies, particularly in the long run [6]. One way to address this problem is to adapt the design of PVs to the individual needs and preferences of a user.

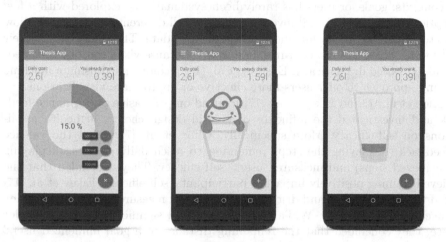

Fig. 1. Screenshots of the *Donut* (left), *Creature* (middle) and *Glass* (right) personal data visualization in the liquid-intake tracking application developed for our study.

In this work, we therefore tried to gain a better understanding of how preferences for PVs correlate with stable, well-researched personal traits based on the established *Big Five* personality theory. We developed three sample visualizations to convey users' daily liquid intake based on a review of existing liquid intake tracking applications: a plain visualization (*Donut*), and two decorated visualizations – namely a visualization based on the metaphor of a glass (*Glass*), and a visualization based on the metaphor of a creature (*Creature*) as depicted in Fig. 1. We chose liquid intake as an example tracking metric because a broad range of users can relate to this use case. In a lab study, 36 participants were introduced to the three visualizations, conducted a personality test, and rated each visualization with respect to its attractiveness, its motivating or deterring effect, and their interest in its state.

Our hypothesis was that depending on the user's personality visualizations that make use of metaphors such as *Creature* and *Glass* might either be perceived as more engaging or deterring. Our results support this hypothesis. This paper reports the correlations between preferences for visualizations and personality traits and discusses directions for future research.

2   Related Work

2.1   Personal Visualizations (PVs)

Huang et al. [26] defined the field of personal visualizations (PV) as "the design of interactive visual data representations for use in a personal context". Examples for PVs range from counts, graphs, and tables [11,18] via stylized displays [12,30], watchfaces [21] and narrative information [40] to data physicalisations [38] and living plants [5]. However, the suitability of different PVs for different contexts, goals, or users has rarely been systematically explored with a few exceptions: Epstein et al. [18] investigated how well different "visual cuts" allow users to explore their location and physical activity data. The visual cuts in their study were tables, graphs, captures, and maps. Because visualizations that people valued varied dramatically, Epstein et al. [18] recommended using a machine learning approach to offer users more effective or appropriate visualizations.

Choe et al. [7] and Eikey et al. [17] focused on persuasive performance feedback and investigated the influence of several design choices in health applications on self-efficacy. More specifically, Choe et al. [7] varied the valence of feedback (displaying the steps remaining to reach daily goal vs. displaying the achieved steps) and measured users' self-efficacy. They concluded that the achieved framing positively impacted participants' self-efficacy. Eikey et al. [17] varied the effect of color and distance to a goal and measured users' self-efficacy for accomplishing a goal. While they did not find significant results for color choice, they concluded that the remaining distance to a goal influenced users' self-efficacy.

While these studies revealed interesting results about the design of progress bars and text feedback, our study relates users' personalities and gender to their preferences for plain (*Donut*) and decorated visualizations (*Glass*, and *Creature*). Several researchers have explored potential advantages of decorative elements in charts, including for example memorability of charts, as examined by both Bateman et al. [4] and Li and Moacdieh [31]. While Bateman [4] concluded that visualizations with decorative elements were more memorable and preferred by most participants, Li [31] presented more ambiguous results: Some people perceived the decorative elements as inefficient, unprofessional and overloaded, while others perceived them as cute, attractive, and interesting. However, we do not yet understand, which users prefer what kind of visualization and in what context.

There is a lack of studies looking at users' preferences for decorative elements in PVs with respect to their individual differences. However, the idea of adapting visualizations has been applied to other types of visualizations under the name of user-adaptive visualizations.

2.2   User-Adaptive Information Visualization

Several researchers (e.g., [9,10,23,46]) investigated the idea of user-adaptive visualizations, which are visualizations tailored in real-time to the needs and abilities of each user [9]. Existing work in this area has investigated the influence of both cognitive abilities [10,41] and personality traits [22,46] on the effectiveness of visualizations. Early results support the hypothesis that adapting visualizations to individual differences increases performance and satisfaction with visualizations significantly. However, existing studies focused on expert visualizations with the goal to extract complex information as quickly as possible. In contrast, the goal of the PVs used in our study is to motivate users to monitor their own data and work towards a goal. As discussed by Huang et al. [26], the nature of PVs is very different from expert visualizations. We are not aware of any studies that investigate how to adapt PVs to users' personality to motivate them towards reaching a goal.

2.3 The Influence of Personality

One possible source of influence on the perception of different types of data visualizations roots in users' personality dispositions. In psychological science, the dominant personality theory is the lexically derived *Big Five* personality trait theory [13,20]. In this theory personality is described by five broad traits, each of which consists of six sub-facets representing more narrow aspects of the personality. Below, we briefly summarize the *Big Five*:

People scoring high on *extraversion* are more sociable, lively, risk-taking, dominant, and in general prefer being in company with others over being alone. People scoring low on this personality trait are usually described as more reserved, reflected, and do not find much pleasure in spending time with many people [3]. People scoring high on *emotional stability* experience less negative emotions, feel more evenly-tempered, less impulsive, and also less responsive to stress. Low scores in emotional stability correspond to more negative feelings and longer durations of those [2]. *Conscientiousness* is a personality trait that describes how dutiful, self-disciplined, organized and deliberate someone is [32]. People scoring low on this dimension are typically more laid-back, less urged towards achievement, less goal-oriented, and less driven by success. This personality trait is closely related to academic as well as work place performance, and is therefore often assessed in job interviews [45]. The personality trait of *Agreeableness* is important for inter-personal relationships and describes how kind, sympathetic as well as helpful and considerate someone is. People with low scores usually are not very concerned about the feelings of people and are less likely to help others generally preferring competition over cooperation [27]. *Openness* is the personality trait that in general describes how curious someone is towards new experiences, feelings and attitudes. People with low values on this trait are generally described as more traditional, conservative and less flexible in their thinking and behavior. *Openness* is also correlated with intelligence and creativity [15].

We assume that users' preference for certain PVs might correlate with certain personality traits and sub-facets

3   Prototype

For our lab study, we chose liquid intake as an example for self-tracking because the recommendation to drink a certain amount of liquid every day is wide-spread and well-known. Moreover, liquid volume is a simple metric to represent.

Instead of developing our own visualizations, we wanted to pick up state-of-the-art visualizations that are already being used in applications today. Hence, we reviewed applications in app stores and found three broader visualization categories: those using plain charts and graphs, those using non-living metaphors (such as glasses and bottles) and those using living metaphors (such as plants and animals). As depicted in Fig. 2, we picked a plain visualization (*Donut*) and a living metaphor (*Creature*) as the two ends of a spectrum as we expected that users' personality might influence their preference for one or another. We added a non-living metaphor (*Glass*) as a third visualization to see whether it would be perceived similarly to the living metaphor.

Fig. 2. Sketches of the three different concepts for visualizing liquid intake status compared in our study (left: *Donut*, middle: *Creature*, right: *Glass*).

3.1   Donut Chart

Donut is based on PVs often used by commercial tracking software such as Fitbit[1], Jawbone Up[2], Withings[3], or the water consumption tracker "Hydrate Daily". Before any liquid intake was recorded, the circular bar chart is completely grey. When the user adds predefined amounts of liquid to the counter, the blue bar grows clockwise, filling up the circular bar to represent the user's progression towards the daily liquid goal (see Fig. 2 left).

3.2   Creature Metaphor

Creature makes use of the metaphor of a living plant. Empathy and compassion can be strong motivators and might therefore be used to foster behavior

---

[1] https://www.fitbit.com.
[2] https://jawbone.com/up.
[3] http://www.withings.com/.

change [19]. There is evidence that users can emotionally engage with artificial pets and in many cases these emotions have therapeutic effects [34]. Botros et al. [5] used this effect by linking the well-being of a real plant to the physical activity of a user. Related, *Creature* displays a creature that suffers and is afraid to die of thirst when users themselves do not drink enough water. When a user adds predefined amounts of liquid, the creature becomes happier to represent the user's progression towards the daily liquid goal (see Fig. 3). Hence, the user is now responsible for the well-being of another virtual being. Several apps in the app store such as "Plant Nanny" use a similar concept.

Fig. 3. *Creature* visualizes a user's intake of predefined liquid amounts with its progressing states of happiness.

3.3   Glass Metaphor

To allow the comparison between living and non-living metaphors, we introduced *Glass*, as shown in Fig. 2 right. It uses the metaphor of a glass, just as several apps in the app stores do (e.g., "Daily Water Free"). Again the water level (similar to the blue bar in *Donut*) fills up with the percentage of the daily liquid goal that has already been consumed.

4   Method

We ran a mixed between-within-subjects design with a 3 *Concepts* (*Donut* vs. *Glass* vs. *Creature*) × 2 *Gender* (*male* vs. *female*) design and counterbalanced *Concepts* with a Latin Square for each *Gender*. We chose a lab setting for this initial exploration (instead of a field study) to reduce the influence of the context of use on our results.

4.1   Evaluation Metrics

As Huang et al. [26] pointed out, the evaluation of PVs presents a new challenge because typical visualization metrics (time and error rate) do not suffice and no best practices exist. They suggest "ease" as a new metric that defines how easily a tool fits into one's daily life, habits, and routine. "Ease" can, therefore, only be measured in long-term studies, in which participants use the PV in their daily life. Even though this is an important aspect of PV evaluations, we wanted to measure immediate aspects of the user experience that influence whether users feel inclined to use a PV again. Guided by literature on effects of design and information presentation on engagement [24,35], motivation [14, 38], and self-efficacy [7,17], we decided to use attractiveness, motivating effect, interest in its state, and deterring effect as dependent variables. To measure the dependent variables, we asked participants to express their agreement to the following statements on 7-point likert scales (statements translated from German):

attractiveness: "I perceive the visualization as attractive."
motivating effect: "I feel motivated to drink more water after looking at the visualization."
interest in its state: "I'm interested in the state of the visualization. I would look at it throughout the day."
deterring effect: "I perceive the visualization as deterring."

In Addition, we included three questions to validate whether all data visualizations and tasks were easy to understand.

4.2   Task

The purpose of the study task was that participants understood the three distinct concepts for visualizing liquid intake goals. Therefore, we asked participants to add predefined amounts of liquid to the liquid intake counter using the buttons provided and to verbalize their thoughts and questions using a think-aloud technique. The researcher who conducted the experiment took notes of all comments and questions. Afterwards, participants were asked whether they understood the concept of the visualizations and any remaining questions were clarified. This procedure took between 3 and 10 min for each visualization.

4.3   Personality Test

We measured participants' personality traits using the *Big Five* Personality Inventory (BFSI) [1] in a laboratory setting. Performing the test took 18 min on average. We selected the BFSI for personality assessment due to its short length as well as its favorable psychometric properties.

4.4   Procedure

Our study set-up consisted of seven main steps: (1) informed consent (2) exploring the interactive prototype, (3) individual rating of each concept, (4) enforced ranking of all three concepts, (5) post-questionnaire about smart-phone usage, attitude towards tracking liquid intake, and demographics, and (6) personality test. Finally, (7) participants had the chance to express their opinions verbally, comments were noted down, clustered by researchers and considered in the analysis in addition to quantitative results. We used a unique identifier to link the different anonymized data types from questionnaires and personality test.

4.5 Participants

We recruited 36 paid (7.50 €) participants (18 female) through university mailing lists and social networks. Most participants were bachelor, master and PhD students with 44% studying Computer Science or similar subjects. Almost all participants (94%) were smart-phone users with 45% having used smart-phones for at least three years. The majority of participants (72,2%) had "tried to drink a certain amount of liquid every day before" confirming the relevance of the chosen scenario.

4.6 Data Analysis

To examine all possible relationships between personality, gender and preferences, we took an exploratory approach in our study design and data analysis. Due to the exploratory nature of our study, we report 95% confidence intervals (CI) instead of p-values [36]. Confidence intervals not only provide information about the estimated range of the true values in the population (e.g., with repeated measures the CI would contain the correlation value of the population in 95% of the cases), but they also inform about significance in hypothesis testing research (not significant if the CI contains zero). In other words, CIs inform about the precision of the obtained estimator (narrow is good, wide is bad). These values inform hypotheses to be tested in future studies and should not readily be interpreted as established facts. Since we measured preferences for visualizations in ordinal scores, we used Spearman correlations to analyse correlations between ratings and personality dimensions [44]. Since scores on personality dimensions were normally distributed for both genders in our sample, we used Pearson product-moment correlation for correlations between predictor variables (see Fig. 4).

4.7 Limitations

Our study design has the following limitations: (1) Personality is a very complex phenomenon to study. Hence, it needs more than one study to build up an understanding of how individual differences are connected with preferences for visualizations. This study, therefore, can only present a starting point. As the study took on average 45 min to complete, we had to limit the number of PVs to three and restrict the amount of participants (N = 36). Due to these restrictions, correlations have to be interpreted with caution. More example PVs need to be tested to be able to generalize our results. However, given that many correlation coefficients feature medium effect sizes (above a threshold of .30) and given that many correlations are in line with psychological literature, we believe that the results provide first insights into the relationships between personality, gender and preferences for PVs.

(2) Arguably, the scales, underlying the visualizations we used in our study, differ in their nature: *Donut* and *Glass* are based on a donut and a bar chart and can therefore easily be used as linear scales. Using *Creature* as linear scale is

more difficult as value differences can not be clearly mapped to pixels: small differences in the gesture and facial expression of the creature might have a smaller or bigger effect on its expression and are open to interpretation by their users. To avoid issues with just noticeable differences we implemented the three visualizations as ordinal scales in our study (users could only add predefined amounts of liquid with provided buttons and those amounts were mapped to distinct states). Although the focus of our study was to compare three general visualization ideas and not on how these visualizations precisely progress, we conducted a prestudy to confirm that the different states of *Creature* were readable and clearly ordered in the eye of potential users. Therefore, we are confident that the differences of underlying scales did not affect our results. Nevertheless, readers should be aware of the potentially different perceptions of the scales underlying our visualizations.

(3) In line with Eikey et al.'s [17] approach, we measured participants' perceptions via self-report as this research is in a too early state to measure actual behavior. As we measured perceived attractiveness and interest in the state of the visualizations, we think the results of our study could inform a broader set of personal visualization systems and therefore have an impact beyond behavior change. We chose a controlled lab experiment to ensure the validity of the personality test and to minimize the influence of other contextual factors. However, whether long-term preferences differ (or not) needs to be tested in a long-term study. This will also allow to verify effectiveness towards behavior change, the main goal PVs for behavior change.

5   Results

We will first describe correlations between predictor variables and overall ratings of PVs in *descriptive statistics*. Next, we will describe correlations between preferences and personality traits.

5.1   Descriptive Statistics

Personality and Gender. For completeness, we report correlations between predictor variables. There were no significant correlations between gender and the Big Five personality factors. However, there were correlations between several Big Five personality factors (as shown in Fig. 4). The highest correlation was observed between extraversion and emotional stability ($\rho = 0.639$, $p < 0.001$). We calculated variance inflation factors (VIF) for both extraversion (VIF $= 1.5$) and emotional stability (VIF $= 2.1$). As the VIF was smaller than 4 in both cases, we proceeded with the analysis [16].

Overall Ratings of PVs. All three concepts received ratings of four or higher on attractiveness by a majority of participants (*Donut*: 75%, *Glass*: 61.1%, *Creature*: 75%). *Creature* was most often perceived as motivating (*Donut*: 44.4%,

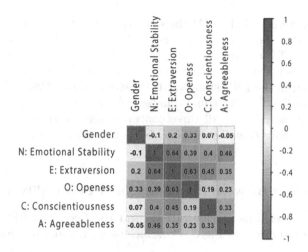

Fig. 4. Pairwise Pearson correlations between the predictor variables, namely, the *Big Five* measures and gender. Negative values mean a negative correlation, positive values a positive correlation. Gender is encoded as 0:=male, 1:=female.

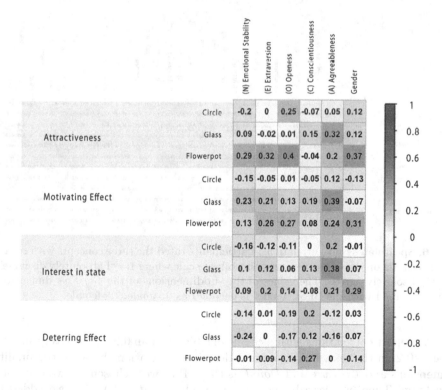

Fig. 5. Spearman's rank correlations: Participants rated the three concepts with regard to the criteria on the left on a seven-point Likert scale where 1:="I absolutely disagree", 7:="I absolutely agree". The values of the *Big Five* dimensions were measured with the BFSI, gender is encoded as 0:=male, 1:=female.

Glass: 52.8%, *Creature*: 61.1%). At the same time, the motivating effect of *Creature* also seemed to be more controversial (*Donut*: M=4.17, SD=1.46, *Glass*: M=4.58, SD=1.40, *Creature*: M=4.67, SD=1.97). Moreover, more women perceived *Creature* as motivating than men (w: 72,2%, m: 50,0%). The percentage of people interested in the PV's state was highest for *Glass* (*Donut*: 55.6%, *Glass*: 72.2%, *Creature*: 58.3%). An equal number of men and women was interested in the state of *Glass* (72%). All three concepts were perceived as deterring by only one participant: *Donut* and *Glass* by a female, and *Creature* by a male participant.

5.2 Correlations Between Preferences and Personality Traits

Correlations between Likert scale ratings and the five main BFSI personality dimensions are visualized in Fig. 5. Correlations with subdimensions are shown in Fig. 6.

		N1: Anxiety	N2: Angry Hostility	N3: Depression	N4: Self-Consciousness	N5: Impulsiveness	N6: Vulnerability	E1: Warmth	E2: Gregariousness	E3: Assertiveness	E4: Activity	E5: Excitement Seeking	E6: Positive Emotions	O1: Openness to Fantasy	O2: Openness to Aesthetics	O3: Openness to Feelings	O4: Openness to Actions	O5: Openness to Ideas	O6: Openness to Values	C1: Competence	C2: Order	C3: Dutifulness	C4: Achievement Striving	C5: Self-Discipline	C6: Deliberation	A1: Trust	A2: Straightforwardness	A3: Altruism	A4: Compliance	A5: Modesty	A6: Tender-Mindedness	Gender
Attractiveness	Circle	-0.21	-0.22	-0.15	-0.15	-0.01	-0.21	-0.09	-0.04	-0.03	0.1	0.17	-0.11	0.04	0.35	0.2	0.09	0.19	0.22	-0.13	-0.18	0	0.03	-0.04	-0.11	0	0	0.15	0.1	-0.26	0.1	0.12
	Glass	0.1	0.07	0.08	0	0.32	0	0.1	0.03	-0.1	0.01	-0.15	0.01	-0.16	0.13	0.19	-0.31	0.15	0.1	0.02	0.13	0.15	0.15	0.31	0.19	0.02	0.39	0.29	0.13	0.17	0.23	0.12
	Flowerpot	0.28	0.27	0.32	0.23	-0.02	0.08	0.35	0.2	-0.01	0.25	0.37	0.36	0.27	0.43	0.24	0.34	0.45	0.38	-0.01	-0.16	-0.17	-0.03	0.24	-0.01	0.17	0.31	0.06	0.38	-0.21	0.15	0.37
Motivating Effect	Circle	-0.16	-0.05	-0.3	0.01	-0.03	-0.13	0.2	0.14	-0.15	-0.09	-0.1	-0.09	-0.02	0.04	0.11	0.03	-0.1	0.03	-0.13	-0.13	0.07	0.23	-0.01	-0.14	-0.02	0.04	-0.22	0.1	0.35	0.06	-0.07
	Glass	0.28	0.06	0.23	0.3	0.2	0.1	0.32	0.19	0.03	0.21	-0.04	0.25	-0.18	0.04	0.23	0.08	0.26	0.24	0.19	0.07	0.23	-0.01	0.37	0.24	-0.01	0.51	0.45	0.06	0.18	0.26	-0.07
	Flowerpot	0.17	0.09	0.17	0.12	0	-0.09	0.35	0.22	0.03	0.2	0.2	0.23	0.09	0.29	0.23	0.29	0.47	0.23	0.14	-0.12	-0.07	0.09	0.36	0.18	0.21	0.31	0.19	0.22	-0.1	0.17	0.31
Interest in PV's State	Circle	-0.29	0	-0.15	-0.16	0.01	-0.2	0.1	0.03	-0.19	-0.11	-0.29	-0.01	-0.28	0.1	0.14	-0.21	-0.09	-0.08	-0.13	-0.07	0.08	0.06	0.04	0.01	0.02	0.1	0.3	0.1	0.02	0.28	-0.01
	Glass	0.02	0.04	0.1	0.1	0.2	-0.08	0.29	0.19	0.09	0.12	-0.16	0.16	-0.2	0.2	0.33	-0.09	0.12	0.18	0.09	0.05	0.2	0.1	0.26	0.08	-0.05	0.4	0.43	0.08	0.25	0.35	0.07
	Flowerpot	0.04	0	0.18	0.17	-0.08	-0.17	0.36	0.16	-0.09	0.09	0.05	0.28	-0.02	0.35	0.22	0.13	0.18	0.19	-0.04	-0.19	-0.1	-0.15	0.14	0.01	0.09	0.27	0.25	0.11	-0.13	0.16	0.29
Deterring Effect	Circle	-0.14	-0.16	-0.17	0	-0.05	-0.07	-0.11	0.04	0.1	-0.05	0.07	-0.07	0	-0.01	-0.07	-0.16	-0.21	-0.24	0.15	0.16	0.18	0.14	-0.05	0.08	-0.06	-0.19	0.02	-0.03	-0.13	-0.04	0.03
	Glass	-0.27	-0.22	-0.27	-0.01	-0.11	-0.21	-0.11	0.06	0.13	-0.05	0.11	-0.1	0.07	0	-0.05	-0.11	-0.24	-0.28	0.1	0.07	0.09	0.06	-0.17	0.08	-0.12	-0.21	-0.11	-0.06	-0.14	0.01	0.07
	Flowerpot	0	0.04	-0.1	-0.12	0.19	-0.02	-0.1	-0.1	0.12	-0.09	-0.08	-0.15	-0.06	-0.17	0.04	-0.13	-0.1	-0.12	0.28	0.2	0.19	0.25	0.06	0.25	-0.08	-0.13	0.04	-0.03	0	0.11	-0.14

Fig. 6. Spearman's rank correlations: Participants rated the three concepts with regard to the criteria on the left on a seven-point Likert scale where 1:="I absolutely disagree", 7:="I absolutely agree". The values of the subdimensions of the *Big Five* dimensions were measured with the BFSI, gender is encoded as 0:=male, 1:=female.

We report correlations with a coefficient bigger than 0.2, respectively smaller than −0.2, in the text. Below, we first describe correlations between personality dimensions and *Creature* and *Donut* as these PVs were chosen as two ends of a spectrum. Then, we describe correlations with *Donut*, a PV that we added to contrast *Creature* with a non-living metaphor. Finally, we describe correlations with gender.

Creature Metaphor. High scores in openness, extraversion, agreeableness, and emotional stability positively correlated with perceptions of *Creature* as attractive and motivating while high scores in conscientiousness correlated with perceiving *Creature* as deterring. More details on correlations between ratings of *Creature* and the main and subdimensions of personality, including 95% confidence intervals, are displayed in Fig. 7.

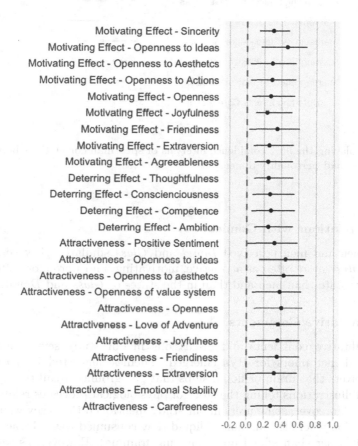

Fig. 7. Displaying the 95% confidence intervals of spearman correlations between ratings of Creature and personality dimensions

Donut Chart. Correlations between personality and ratings of *Donut* were generally very small. Only openness to aesthetics, a subdimension of openness, correlated with higher ratings of *Donut* as attractive.

Glass Metaphor. Higher scores on agreeableness correlated with higher interest in the state of *Glass*, and with higher ratings of *Glass* as attractive and as motivating. Lower scores in emotional stability correlated with higher ratings of

Glass as deterring. More details on correlations between ratings of *Glass* and the main and subdimensions of personality, including 95% confidence intervals, are displayed in Fig. 8.

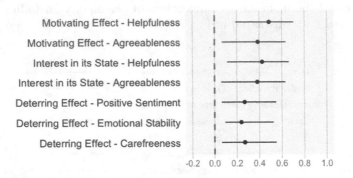

Fig. 8. Displaying the 95% confidence intervals of spearman correlations between ratings of Glass and personality dimensions

5.3 Correlations with Gender

Both women and men perceived *Donut* and *Glass* similarly. However, women rated *Creature* more often as attractive, motivating, and were more often interested in its state than men and than in the states of *Glass* and *Donut*.

5.4 Qualitative Comments

From qualitative comments and discussions in our study several alternative themes and metaphors for PVs emerged. Themes suggested by participants included rivers that drain or flood, ships that go aground or sail through heavy swell, and illustrations telling the story of physiological processes related to liquid intake. Moreover, some users in our study mentioned that they would prefer a visualization where the amount of liquid they consumed was subtracted of the daily goal rather than added up (remaining framing). However, as we did not collect preferences on the valence of feedback by all participants, we were not able to investigate if preferences coincide with users' personality or gender.

6   Discussion and Future Work

We see three main takeaways of our study: (1) It seems likely that preference and aversion for PVs coincide with users' personalities as measured with the Big Five personality questionnaire. (2) To create PVs that are as engaging as possible, they need to be adapted to suit users preferences. This might be achieved in several ways. (3) Finally, our work provides guidance on how personalized PVs can be evaluated in future research.

6.1 Personality and Preferences for PVs

In our study, especially the personality traits openness (openness to new ideas, aesthetics, and openness of value system), extraversion (love of adventure, friendliness, and joyfulness), and agreeableness correlated with positive ratings of *Creature*. This observation is in line with previous research, that associated these personality traits with a need for affect [33]. People with a high need for affect tend to choose, for example, emotional movies or to become involved in an emotion-inducing event [33]. Hence, it seems plausible that related personality traits correlate with a preference for PVs, which make use of decorative elements and metaphors. Moreover, we found a tendency that conscientious people (described as dutiful, organized, self-disciplined, and deliberate) found *Creature* more deterring. In previous research conscientiousness was negatively associated with internet use [29] and playing videogames [43]. Hence, it seems plausible that more conscientious people are less drawn towards entertaining and decorating elements and prefer clean and plain visualizations. Correlations between perceptions of *Glass* and personality traits were somewhat similar but less and weaker than correlations with perceptions of *Creature*. Moreover, in our study, women tended to rate *Creature* more positively than *Donut* and *Glass*. These findings bring a new perspective to discussions of the usefulness of decorative elements in charts. It seems likely that such decorative elements can make PVs more engaging especially for users with a certain personality. However, future research is necessary validate these findings with more users and to explore a wider set of visualizations.

6.2 Design Space of Personalized PVs

We limited the set of PVs in our study to three, in order to keep the length of the experiment reasonable. These visualizations are examples taken from a rich design space. This design space encompasses, for example, different themes and metaphors not limited to plants and animals. Even for the relatively simple example of liquid intake visualizations, a variety of themes and metaphors emerged during our study in qualitative comments and discussions with participants. Future work should further analyze and explore this design space, e.g., in participatory design sessions and investigate how preferences are connected with users' individual differences.

6.3 Evaluation of Personalized PVs

To explore the design space of PVs and the suitability of visualizations for different users and user groups, it is necessary to define evaluation criteria. Established evaluation metrics for visualizations - such as time and error rate - are, however, unsuitable for PVs. Rather than efficiency, the user experience is more likely to influence whether the PV is adopted and used over a longer period of time. In this study, we therefore used attractiveness, motivating effect, deterring effect, and interest in its state as evaluation metrics. However, even though these metrics allowed us to gain a first understanding of users' perceptions, they are tentative and most certainly need to be rethought in future studies. Beyond these, there are likely other relevant metrics, e.g., related to user experience or retention. If PVs are part of BCT actual behavior change is an important metric to measure in the long term. Future work should expand and explore the set of evaluation techniques used for PVs including the use of PVs in context and in the long term.

6.4   Adaptive vs. Adaptable PVs

Once a better understanding of the connection between users' individual differences and preferences for PVs is established, an important question to explore is how PVs could be adapted to better suit users' individual needs. As for all personalized systems, two general ways to achieve this personalization are to allow users to explicitly choose preferred visualizations (e.g., with a flexible framework that helps people design visualizations for themselves, as suggested by Huang et al. [26] or automatic adaptation. Automatic adaptation requires a user model that includes relevant characteristics of the user - in our case personality traits. These parameters might for example be inferred from mobile phone usage behaviors. Other trait-like factors such as cooperation have already been successfully predicted [37]. As data sets that contain both smartphone usage and personality data have already been collected from over 40.000 users, predicting personality traits based on mobile phone usage in the near future seems feasable [42]. However, some questions need to be answered before automatic adaptation becomes an option: When and how is a visualization adapted? How can adaptations be suggested without annoying or irritating the user?

7   Conclusion

There are many ways to visualize a user's personal data. PVs can be plain and direct like counts and graphs or more abstract like stylized displays or data physicalizations. Previous research showed that users seem to perceive different kinds of PVs very differently. To shed light on potential relationships between personality, gender, and preferences for PVs, we conducted an exploratory lab study with three example PVs. According to our results, preferences for PVs do indeed coincide with personality: For example, participants who scored high on openness and extraversion were more likely to prefer the PV with a living metaphor, while participants who scored high on conscientiousness rated it more negatively. Our results are in line with previous psychological research. Therefore, we are confident that our results provide promising insights into the relationships between personality and preferences for PVs. However, our research can not be more than a starting point at this stage and further validation of our findings is needed.

References

1. Arendasy, M.: BFSI: Big-Five Struktur-Inventar (Test & Manual). SCHUHFRIED GmbH, Mödling (2009)

2. Asendorpf, J.B., Neyer, F.J.: Psychologie der Persönlichkeit. Springer, Berlin (2012)
3. Ashton, M.C., Lee, K., Paunonen, S.V.: What is the central feature of extraversion? Social attention versus reward sensitivity. J. Pers. Soc. Psychol. **83**(1), 245–252 (2002)
4. Bateman, S., Mandryk, R.L., Gutwin, C., Genest, A., McDine, D., Brooks, C.: Useful junk? The effects of visual embellishment on comprehension and memorability of charts. In: Proceedings of the SIGCHI Conference on Human Factors in Computing Systems, CHI 2010, pp. 2573–2582. ACM, New York (2010). http://doi.acm.org/10.1145/1753326.1753716
5. Botros, F., Perin, C., Aseniero, B.A., Carpendale, S.: Go and grow: mapping personal data to a living plant. In: Proceedings of the International Working Conference on Advanced Visual Interfaces, AVI 2016, pp. 112–119. ACM, New York (2016). http://doi.acm.org/10.1145/2909132.2909267
6. Brynjarsdottir, H., Håkansson, M., Pierce, J., Baumer, E., DiSalvo, C., Sengers, P.: Sustainably unpersuaded: how persuasion narrows our vision of sustainability. In: Proceedings of the SIGCHI Conference on Human Factors in Computing Systems, CHI 2012, pp. 947–956. ACM, New York (2012). http://doi.acm.org/10.1145/2207676.2208539
7. Choe, E.K., Lee, B., Munson, S., Pratt, W., Kientz, J.A.: Persuasive performance feedback: the effect of framing on self-efficacy. In: AMIA Annual Symposium Proceedings, vol. 2013, p. 825. American Medical Informatics Association (2013)
8. Choe, E.K., Lee, N.B., Lee, B., Pratt, W., Kientz, J.A.: Understanding quantified-selfers' practices in collecting and exploring personal data. In: Proceedings of the SIGCHI Conference on Human Factors in Computing Systems, CHI 2014, pp. 1143–1152. ACM, New York (2014). http://doi.acm.org/10.1145/2556288.2557372
9. Conati, C., Carenini, G., Toker, D., Lalle, S.: Towards user-adaptive information visualization (2015). http://www.aaai.org/ocs/index.php/AAAI/AAAI15/paper/view/9933
10. Conati, C., Maclaren, H.: Exploring the role of individual differences in information visualization. In: Proceedings of the Working Conference on Advanced Visual Interfaces, AVI 2008, pp. 199–206. ACM, New York (2008). http://doi.acm.org/10.1145/1385569.1385602
11. Consolvo, S., Klasnja, P., McDonald, D.W., Landay, J.A.: Designing for healthy lifestyles: design considerations for mobile technologies to encourage consumer health and wellness. Found. Trends Hum.-Comput. Interact. **6**(3–4), 167–315 (2014). http://dx.doi.org/10.1561/1100000040
12. Consolvo, S., McDonald, D.W., Toscos, T., Chen, M.Y., Froehlich, J., Harrison, B., Klasnja, P., LaMarca, A., LeGrand, L., Libby, R., Smith, I., Landay, J.A.: Activity sensing in the wild: a field trial of ubifit garden. In: Proceedings of the SIGCHI Conference on Human Factors in Computing Systems, CHI 2008, pp. 1797–1806. ACM, New York (2008). http://doi.acm.org/10.1145/1357054.1357335
13. Costa, P.T., McCrae, R.R.: Four ways five factors are basic. Pers. Individ. Differ. **13**(6), 653–665 (1992). http://www.sciencedirect.com/science/article/pii/019188699290236I
14. Deci, E.L.: The relation of interest to the motivation of behavior: a self-determination theory perspective (1992)
15. DeYoung, C.G.: Openness/intellect: a dimension of personality reflecting cognitive exploration. In: Mikulincer, M., Shaver, P.R., Cooper, M.L., Larsen, R.J. (eds.) APA handbook of personality and social psychology, Volume 4: Personality

processes and individual differences, pp. 369–399. APA handbooks in psychology, American Psychological Association, Washington (2015)

16. Dormann, C.F., Elith, J., Bacher, S., Buchmann, C., Carl, G., Carré, G., Marquéz, J.R.G., Gruber, B., Lafourcade, B., Leitão, P.J., Münkemüller, T., McClean, C., Osborne, P.E., Reineking, B., Schröder, B., Skidmore, A.K., Zurell, D., Lautenbach, S.: Collinearity: a review of methods to deal with it and a simulation study evaluating their performance. Ecography **36**(1), 27–46 (2013). http://dx.doi.org/10.1111/j.1600-0587.2012.07348.x

17. Eikey, E., Poole, E., Reddy, M.: Information presentation in health apps and devices: the effect of color, distance to goal, weight perception, and interest on users' self-efficacy for accomplishing goals. In: iConference 2015 Proceedings (2015)

18. Epstein, D., Cordeiro, F., Bales, E., Fogarty, J., Munson, S.: Taming data complexity in lifelogs: exploring visual cuts of personal informatics data. In: Proceedings of the 2014 Conference on Designing Interactive Systems, DIS 2014, pp. 667–676. ACM, New York (2014). http://doi.acm.org/10.1145/2598510.2598558

19. Goetz, J.L., Keltner, D., Simon-Thomas, E.: Compassion: an evolutionary analysis and empirical review. Psychol. Bull. **136**(3), 351 (2010)

20. Goldberg, L.: Language and individual differences: the search for universals in personality lexicons. Rev. Pers. Soc. Psychol. **2**, 141–165 (1981). Beverly Hills, CA

21. Gouveia, R., Pereira, F., Karapanos, E., Munson, S.A., Hassenzahl, M.: Exploring the design space of glanceable feedback for physical activity trackers. In: Proceedings of the 2016 ACM International Joint Conference on Pervasive and Ubiquitous Computing, UbiComp 2016, pp. 144–155. ACM, New York (2016) http://doi.acm.org/10.1145/2971648.2971754

22. Green, T.M., Fisher, B.: Towards the personal equation of interaction: the impact of personality factors on visual analytics interface interaction. In: 2010 IEEE Symposium on Visual Analytics Science and Technology (VAST), pp. 203–210. IEEE (2010)

23. Green, T.M., Fisher, B.: Impact of personality factors on interface interaction and the development of user profiles: next steps in the personal equation of interaction. Inf. Vis. **11**(3), 205–221 (2012). http://dx.doi.org/10.1177/1473871612441542

24. Haroz, S., Kosara, R., Franconeri, S.L.: Isotype visualization: working memory, performance, and engagement with pictographs. In: Proceedings of the 33rd Annual ACM Conference on Human Factors in Computing Systems, pp. 1191–1200. ACM (2015)

25. Hekler, E.B., Klasnja, P., Froehlich, J.E., Buman, M.P.: Mind the theoretical gap: interpreting, using, and developing behavioral theory in hci research. In: Proceedings of the SIGCHI Conference on Human Factors in Computing Systems, CHI 2013, pp. 3307–3316. ACM, New York (2013)

26. Huang, D., Tory, M., Aseniero, B.A., Bartram, L., Bateman, S., Carpendale, S., Tang, A., Woodbury, R.: Personal visualization and personal visual analytics. IEEE Trans. Vis. Comput. Graph. **21**(3), 420–433 (2015)

27. Jensen-Campbell, L., Graziano, W.G.: Agreeableness as a moderator of interpersonal conflict. J. Pers. **69**(2), 323–361 (2001)

28. Kuznetsov, S., Paulos, E.: Upstream: motivating water conservation with low-cost water flow sensing and persuasive displays. In: Proceedings of the SIGCHI Conference on Human Factors in Computing Systems, CHI 2010, pp. 1851–1860. ACM, New York (2010). http://doi.acm.org/10.1145/1753326.1753604

29. Landers, R.N., Lounsbury, J.W.: An investigation of big five and narrow personality traits in relation to internet usage. Comput. Hum. Behav. **22**(2), 283–293 (2006). http://www.sciencedirect.com/science/article/pii/S0747563204001128

30. Lane, N.D., Lin, M., Mohammod, M., Yang, X., Lu, H., Cardone, G., Ali, S., Doryab, A., Berke, E., Campbell, A.T., Choudhury, T.: Bewell: sensing sleep, physical activities and social interactions to promote wellbeing. Mob. Netw. Appl. **19**(3), 345–359 (2014). http://dx.doi.org/10.1007/s11036-013-0484-5
31. Li, H., Moacdieh, N.: Is "chart junk" useful? An extended examination of visual embellishment. In: Proceedings of the Human Factors and Ergonomics Society Annual Meeting, vol. 58, no. 1, pp. 1516–1520 (2014). http://pro.sagepub.com/content/58/1/1516.abstract
32. MacCann, C., Duckworth, A.L., Roberts, R.D.: Empirical identification of the major facets of conscientiousness. Learn. Individ. Differ. **19**(4), 451–458 (2009)
33. Maio, G.R., Esses, V.M.: The need for affect: individual differences in the motivation to approach or avoid emotions. J. Pers. **69**(4), 583–614 (2001). http://dx.doi.org/10.1111/1467-6494.694156
34. Marti, P., Pollini, A., Rullo, A., Shibata, T.: Engaging with artificial pets. In: Proceedings of the 2005 Annual Conference on European Association of Cognitive Ergonomics, EACE 2005, pp. 99–106, University of Athens (2005). http://dl.acm.org/citation.cfm?id=1124666.1124680
35. Norman, D.: Emotion & design: attractive things work better. Interactions **9**(4), 36–42 (2002)
36. Jaeger, R.G., Halliday, T.R.: On confirmatory versus exploratory research. Herpetologica **54**, S64–S66 (1998). http://www.jstor.org/stable/3893289
37. Singh, V.K., Agarwal, R.R.: Cooperative phoneotypes: exploring phone-based behavioral markers of cooperation. In: Proceedings of the 2016 ACM International Joint Conference on Pervasive and Ubiquitous Computing, UbiComp 2016, pp. 646–657. ACM, New York (2016) http://doi.acm.org/10.1145/2971648.2971755
38. Stusak, S., Tabard, A., Sauka, F., Khot, R.A., Butz, A.: Activity sculptures: exploring the impact of physical visualizations on running activity. IEEE Trans. Vis. Comput. Graph. **20**(12), 2201–2210 (2014)
39. Thieme, A., Comber, R., Miebach, J., Weeden, J., Kraemer, N., Lawson, S., Olivier, P.: "we've bin watching you": designing for reflection and social persuasion to promote sustainable lifestyles. In: Proceedings of the SIGCHI Conference on Human Factors in Computing Systems, CHI 2012, pp. 2337–2346. ACM, New York (2012). http://doi.acm.org/10.1145/2207676.2208394
40. Tollmar, K., Bentley, F., Viedma, C.: Mobile health mashups: making sense of multiple streams of wellbeing and contextual data for presentation on a mobile device. In: 2012 6th International Conference on Pervasive Computing Technologies for Healthcare (PervasiveHealth) and Workshops, pp. 65–72, May 2012
41. Velez, M.C., Silver, D., Tremaine, M.: Understanding visualization through spatial ability differences. In: IEEE Visualization, VIS 2005, pp. 511–518. IEEE (2005)
42. Welke, P., Andone, I., Blaszkiewicz, K., Markowetz, A.: Differentiating smartphone users by app. usage. In: Proceedings of the 2016 ACM International Joint Conference on Pervasive and Ubiquitous Computing, pp. 519–523. UbiComp 2016. ACM, New York (2016). http://doi.acm.org/10.1145/2971648.2971707
43. Witt, E.A., Massman, A.J., Jackson, L.A.: Trends in youth's videogame playing, overall computer use, and communication technology use: the impact of self-esteem and the big five personality factors. Comput. Hum. Behav. **27**(2), 763–769 (2011). http://www.sciencedirect.com/science/article/pii/S0747563210003237 web 2.0 in Travel and Tourism: Empowering and Changing the Role of Travelers
44. Yarkoni, T.: Personality in 100,000 words: a large-scale analysis of personality and word use among bloggers. J. Res. Pers. **44**(3), 363–373 (2010). http://www.sciencedirect.com/science/article/pii/S0092656610000541

45. Ziegler, M., Bensch, D., Maaß, U., Schult, V., Vogel, M., Bühner, M.: Big Five facets as predictor of job training performance: the role of specific job demands. Learn. Individ. Differ. **29**, 1–7 (2014)
46. Ziemkiewicz, C., Kosara, R.: Preconceptions and individual differences in understanding visual metaphors. In: Proceedings of the 11th Eurographics/IEEE - VGTC Conference on Visualization, EuroVis 2009, pp. 911–918. The Eurographs Association, John Wiley and Sons Ltd., Chichester (2009). http://dx.doi.org/10.1111/j.1467-8659.2009.01442.x

Persuasive Technology
and Rehabilitation

A Technology for Prediction and Prevention of Freezing of Gait (FOG) in Individuals with Parkinson Disease

Megh Patel[1(✉)], Gottumukala Sai Rama Krishna[1], Abhijit Das[2], and Uttama Lahiri[1]

[1] Department of Electrical Engineering,
Indian Institute of Technology Gandhinagar, Gandhinagar, India
megh2301@gmail.com, {gottumukala.sai,
uttama.lahiri}@iitgn.ac.in
[2] AMRI Institute of Neurosciences, Kolkata, India
abhijit.neuro@gmail.com

Abstract. External cueing in the form of visual, auditory or vibratory cue is useful to avoid freezing of gait (FOG) problem commonly experienced by individuals with Parkinson Disease (PD). The currently available technology-assisted solutions are of limited help because of two main issues: (i) the use of accelerometer or gyro-based wearable sensors for prediction of FOG are noise prone and (ii) deliver external cues without any individualization. In our present research, we have designed a low-cost system that can be attached as an add-on module on ordinary walking stick that can (i) predict freezing of gait (ii) deliver visual, auditory and/or vibratory cues in an individualized manner. We conducted a preliminary study with one PD participant. The preliminary results show potential of our system to reduce freezing counts, increase average step length and walk speed of the participant.

Keywords: Parkinson's Disease (PD) · Cues · Freezing of gait(FOG) · Gait analysis

1 Introduction

Globally, approximately 1% of individuals older than 60 years are reported to be suffering from Parkinson's Disease (PD) [1] which turns out to be more than 10 million people worldwide [2]. Gait abnormality is a hallmark of this disease which is attributed to loss of neurons in substantia nigra of basal ganglia, responsible for generation of dopamine [3]. Freezing of gait (FOG) is a common and debilitating, but largely mysterious, symptom of Parkinson disease with limited treatment options [3]. FOG is characterized by varying combinations of start hesitation, hesitation while walking through narrow spaces and at the time of turning, stop hesitation or hesitation at any point while walking, which often results into fall [3]. Thus, often, the PD individuals suffering from FOG, become dependent on caregivers for community ambulation, thereby adversely affecting their independent community living and overall quality of life.

© IFIP International Federation for Information Processing 2017
Published by Springer International Publishing AG 2017. All Rights Reserved
R. Bernhaupt et al. (Eds.): INTERACT 2017, Part III, LNCS 10515, pp. 395–403, 2017.
DOI: 10.1007/978-3-319-67687-6_26

Technology-assisted solutions that provide external cues, have been reported to improve walk pattern with reduced/no FOG occurrence during walking in PD patients [4, 5]. External cues in the form of visual, auditory or vibratory cues are delivered either in isolation or in combination. Visual cues in the form of transverse lines on the floor [6], 3D staircase painted floor [7], curved end of an inverted walking stick [8], laser lines projected on floor by foot-mounted wearable device [9] have been reported to be useful in improving walk pattern of individuals with PD. Combination of Visual and Auditory cues given by augmented reality based Google glass has also been found to be useful for avoiding FOG in individual with PD [10]. Auditory cues generated by Listenmee mobile based application has been shown to be useful in improving the walk pattern of individual with PD [11]. The Vibratory cue has been shown to contribute to significant improvement in step synchronization in individuals with PD suffering from FOG [12]. For example, Step-synchronized vibratory cue applied to one's feet, such as in PD shoes, has been reported to improve one's walking ability [12].

These currently-existing technology-assisted solutions often suffer from the protocol of delivery of the external cues and/or usage of wired systems. Specifically, most of the systems delivering Visual, Auditory, and/or Vibratory Cues, generate these cues either individually or in combinations continuously, instead of assist-as-needed. For example, most systems generate Vibratory cue in a continuous manner (irrespective of whether this cue is required or not) and delivered alternately to both legs of a person that is often irritating and/or distracting to the person. Additionally, given the spectrum nature of the disorder, often the manifestation of the PD symptoms is highly variable even in an individual, [13] which calls for personalization. There is no existing system to our knowledge that can trigger combinations of the three external cues in an integrated and assist-as-needed manner that is individualized to each person's walking capability. Again, researchers have often used wearable sensors attached to the hands [14] or feet [15] for sensing gait abnormalities. However, the attachment of these sensors can (i) bring in a feeling of being wired, affecting the freedom of movement of the user and (ii) pose a possibility of adding signal noise on account of movement artifacts that may not be associated with one's walking.

Thus, given these limitations, we have designed a Smart Walking Aid System that can be fitted as an add-on module on an ordinary available walking stick and wirelessly trigger peripheral modules to deliver Visual, Auditory and/or Vibratory cues in an integrated, assist-as-needed and individualized manner. Additionally, our proposed system does not use any wearable sensors to sense gait abnormalities of the user. Instead, this intelligently monitors one's walking stick movement profile to predict one's possibility of freezing of gait.

1.1 Objectives and Scope

The objectives of this paper are two-fold: (i) present the design of the Smart Walking Aid System and (ii) preliminary validation study with one PD participant. This paper is organized as follows: Sect. 2 describes the system design Sect. 3 presents Experimental Setup for our study with proposed system, Sect. 4 presents the results obtained in our study and discussion based on the obtained result. Section 5 presents conclusion and limitation.

2   System Design

Our Smart Walking Aid System is composed of two sub-modules, namely (1) Master Controller Module and (2) Vibratory Belt assembly.

2.1   Master Controller Module

The Fig. 1 shows the Smart Walking Aid System with Master Controller Module (MCM) mounted on an ordinary walking stick at a height of x cm from the bottom tip of the stick. The MCM module is a micro-controller based unit operated by a 5 V regulated supply. MCM receives pulses from two Proximity Sensors (US1 and US2). The US1 is mounted at the bottom of the MCM module and it is used to sense the distance of the stick tip from the ground surface. The US2 is mounted at the stick tip and it is used to sense the user's foot. The MCM module triggers three output peripheral devices, namely, (i) Laser Line Generators to deliver Visual cue by projecting two parallel red colored laser lines (Line1 and Line2) on the floor (ii) Piezo-electric Buzzer to deliver Auditory cue and (iii) Vibratory Belt assembly to deliver Vibratory cue. There are two laser line generators attached in holders for laser line generators as shown in Fig. 1 and piezoelectric buzzer is mounted inside MCM.

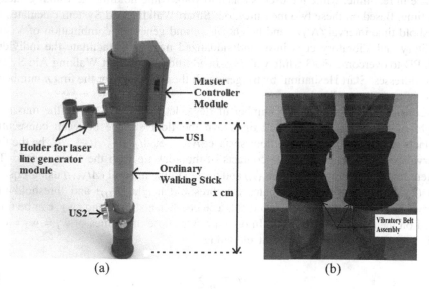

Fig. 1. Smart walking aid system comprising of (a) Master Controller Module (MCM) attached on ordinary walking stick and (b) Vibratory belt assembly to be worn on calf muscles.

2.2   Vibratory Belt Assembly

The Vibratory Belt assembly is a microcontroller based unit that houses a vibrator unit with Bluetooth connectivity that needs to be wrapped on the calf muscle. The Bluetooth receiver attached with Vibratory Belt Assembly communicates wirelessly with

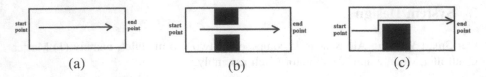

Fig. 2. (a) Layout 1 (straight walking path), (b) Layout 2 (walking path with narrow passage), (c) Layout 3 (walking path requiring one to turn)

the Bluetooth transmitter of the MCM module to trigger the delivery of vibratory cue based on assist-as-needed.

2.3   Operation Rationale

Occurrence of FOG in an individual with PD, while walking is often accompanied with small shuffling steps along with freezing being experienced in hand which in turn changes hand movement profile while walking [14]. Thus, our Smart Walking Aid System computes (i) the time interval between two consecutive contacts of stick tip with the floor surface and (ii) the maximum height (from the floor surface) of the envelope of the profile of the stick tip between two consecutive contacts with the floor surface in real-time, while the user is asked to walk while holding the walking stick in real-time. Based on these two measures, our Smart Walking Aid System calculates the threshold time interval (Δt_{TH}) and height (h_{TH}), and generates combination of Visual, Auditory and Vibratory cues in an individualized manner to facilitate the individual with PD to overcome FOG while walking. In addition, our Smart Walking Aid System also addresses 'Start Hesitation' by triggering all the three cues for the first n number of steps in an individualized manner.

Consider that for the first n number of steps, let $h_1, h_2, h_3, \ldots h_n$ be the maximum height of the profile of the stick tip above the floor surface between consecutive contacts of the stick tip with the floor surface. Also, let $\Delta t_1, \Delta t_2, \Delta t_3, \ldots, \Delta t_n$ be the time interval between the consecutive contacts of the stick tip with the floor surface. The system finds the average height (h_{AVG}) and average time interval (Δt_{AVG}) using Eqs. (1) and (2). Then the system computes the threshold height (h_{TH}) and threshold time interval (Δt_{TH}) by using Eqs. (3) and (4). The coefficients, 'w_1' and 'w_2' can be tuned based on the therapist's feedback. In our case, we chose the values of $w_1 = w_2 = 0.25$ which can be different for different individual.

$$h_{AVG} = \frac{1}{n} \sum h_n \tag{1}$$

$$\Delta t_{AVG} = \frac{1}{n} \sum t_n \tag{2}$$

$$h_{TH} = (w_1) * (h_{AVG}) \tag{3}$$

$$\Delta t_{TH} = (w_2) * (\Delta t_{AVG}) \tag{4}$$

While the user walks with the walking stick and the stick tip touches the floor surface, our Smart Walking Aid System projects two red colored laser lines (Line$_1$ (near the stick tip perpendicular to the stick and in front of user) and Line$_2$ (offset by z units from Line$_1$ and parallel to Line$_1$)) on the floor. When, the stick tip touches the floor surface, auditory cue as a beep-like sound is generated which works as step initiation cue. When the user steps on Line$_1$, Auditory cue as a coin drop sound is generated which works as feedback cue for correct step.

While the user walks with the walking stick, our Smart Walking Aid System computes instantaneous values of Δt and h and checks whether,

$$\Delta t_{AVG} - \Delta t_{TH} \leq \Delta t \leq \Delta t_{AVG} + \Delta t_{TH} \tag{5}$$

$$h_{AVG} - h_{TH} \leq h \leq h_{AVG} + h_{TH} \tag{6}$$

Based on these conditions (Eqs. (5) and (6)), our Smart Walking Aid System predicts abnormality in one's gait pattern. In turn, it triggers Vibratory cue (in an individualized manner) to the user's calf muscles alternatively for the next n steps along with Visual and Auditory cues. That is when person puts walking stick on the floor, system gives one vibratory pulse on one leg and after detection of leg placing on first laser line by US2, system gives vibratory pulse on another leg using Vibratory Belt assembly and that continues until the conditions (5) and (6) are satisfied.

3   Methods

3.1   Participant

We designed a study in which one male PD participant aged 52 years took part. This participant was recruited from the Civil Hospital, Ahmedabad. He was suffering from PD for the last 10 years with frequent freezing of gait, and was found to be at Stage 3 of the Hoehn and Yahr (H&Y) scale [16]. The participant was asked to use a walking stick integrated with the smart walking aid system while walking.

3.2   Experimental Setup

Our experimental layout was carefully selected to investigate whether our smart walking aid system was capable to address issues of (i) start hesitation, (ii) hesitation while walking through narrow pathway and (iii) hesitation while the user needs to deviate from the straight path. The pathway was 10 m long. The experimental layout was of three different types, namely, (i) a 3 m wide straight pathway with no narrow passages and no turns (layout 1), (ii) 3 m wide straight pathway with a narrow passage of length 0.5 m and width 1 m at a distance of 4.5 m from the start point (layout 2) and (iii) straight pathway of width 3 m with an obstacle at a distance of 4.5 m from the start point (layout 3). For layouts 1 and 2, the participant was asked to walk along the straight pathway without turning. For layout 3, the participant was asked to deviate from the straight pathway by taking two turns and walk alongside the obstacle while avoiding it.

The layouts 1, 2 and 3 are shown in Figs. 3(a), (b) and (c). For each layout, there were three walk conditions, such as, walk with smart walking aid system with (i) only visual cue (C1), (ii) combination of visual and auditory cues (C2) and (iii) combination of visual, auditory with vibratory cues (C3). For each condition corresponding to each layout, we computed three indices such as, (1) number of times of freezing of gait (Freezing count), (2) average step length and (3) walking speed.

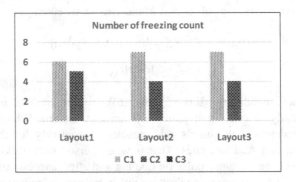

Fig. 3. Implication on number of freezing counts.

4   Results and Discussion

Our results are discussed below.

4.1   Implication on Freezing Counts

The number of freezing counts reduced from C1 to C2 to C3 with no freezing being observed with all the three cues applied simultaneously by our Smart Walking Aid system. Figure 3 shows the number of freezing counts observed in different layouts and different conditions (C1, C2 and C3) while our participant walked with the smart walking aid. This possibly infers that vibratory cue delivered in an individualized manner in conjunction with visual and auditory cues have contributed to complete reduction of the freezing for this participant irrespective of start hesitation, hesitation for moving through narrow spaces and turn hesitation.

4.2   Implication on Average Step Length

Previous research confirms that person with Parkinson's disease have fundamental problem in regulating the step length (in meter) during walking, which ultimately results in reduced average step length [18]. The average step length of the PD participant has increased for C3 compared to that for C1 and C2 irrespective of the experimental layout (Fig. 4).

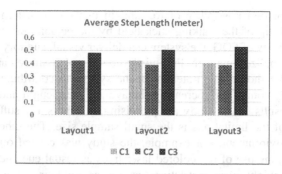

Fig. 4. Implication on average step length

4.3 Implication on Walking Speed

We also found that C3 results in improved walking speed which was better than C1 and C2 irrespective of the study layout (Fig. 5).

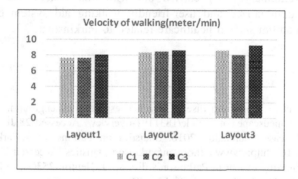

Fig. 5. Implication on walking speed

Thus for all layout, C3 results in reduction in Freezing count, Increase in Step Length and Walking Speed which shows capability of our proposed walking aid system to improve walking pattern of PD Participant.

5 Conclusion

Freezing during walking is one of the most disabling features of individuals with PD [17]. This often gets manifested in terms of reduced average step length (shuffling of steps) along with reduced walking speed. Reduction in freezing counts during walking can improve the gait performance of the individual. In turn, this can lead to increased step length and walking speed. In our present study, we have designed a smart walking aid system that can be connected as an add-on module onto an ordinary walking stick.

The system can predict possibility of freezing in one's gait pattern by sensing the profile of the stick tip of the walking stick held by the person during walking. Upon detection of possibility of FOG, the system can deliver visual, auditory and/or vibratory cues in an individualized manner. Preliminary results of a study carried out with a participant with PD showed the potential of the system to contribute to reducing the number of freezing counts and increasing the average step length and walk speed.

Though the results of our study are promising, yet the study suffers from certain limitations. One of the limitations is the small sample size. The other limitation was restricted study environment. For example, the study was carried out indoors. Thus, questions such as, the use of red colored laser lines as visual cue and intensity of the audio tone used might pose restrictions as far as outdoor study environment is concerned.

In future, we plan to have a randomized and controlled study with a larger number of participants for a longer duration. Also, we plan to use our system outdoors where we might need to replace red-colored laser lines with different colored lines, tune the intensity of audio tone to be audible even in the noisy surroundings, as specified by the user. Also, we plan to make provision of delivering the audio cue to the user using a headset.

From the preliminary study carried out with this system, we hope that the cost-effective, individualized and user-friendly walking aid system can potentially bring about a paradigm shift in healthcare related to Parkinson.

References

1. Hauser, R.A., et al.: Parkinson disease: practice essentials, background, anatomy (2016). http://emedicine.medscape.com/article/1831191-overview. Accessed 28 June 2016
2. Parkinson's Disease Foundation 2016. Statistics on Parkinson's - Parkinson's disease foundation (2016). http://www.pdf.org/en/parkinson_statistics. Accessed 28 June 2016
3. Okuma, Y.: Freezing of gait in Parkinson's disease. J. Neurol. **253**(7), vii27–vii32 (2006)
4. Rubinstein, T.C., Giladi, N., Hausdorff, J.M.: The power of cueing to circumvent dopamine deficits: a review of physical therapy treatment of gait disturbances in Parkinson's disease. Mov. Disord. **17**(6), 1148–1160 (2002)
5. Lim, I., van Wegen, E., de Goede, C., Deutekom, M., Nieuwboer, A., Willems, A., Jones, D., Rochester, L., Kwakkel, G.: Effects of external rhythmical cueing on gait in patients with Parkinson's disease: a systematic review. Clin. Rehabil. **19**(7), 695–713 (2005)
6. Lewis, G.N., Byblow, W.D., Walt, S.E.: Stride length regulation in Parkinson's disease: the use of extrinsic, visual cues. Brain J. Neurol. **123**(10), 2077–2090 (2000)
7. Soneji, M.: Empathy is the key to great innovation. Video, February 2015. https://www.ted.com/speakers/mileha_soneji. Accessed 12 Sept 2016
8. Dietz, M.A., Goetz, C.G., Stebbins, G.T.: Evaluation of a modified inverted walking stick as a treatment for parkinsonian freezing episodes. Mov. Disord. **5**(3), 243–247 (1990)
9. Zhao, Y., Ramesberger, S., Fietzek, U.M., D'Angelo, L.T., Lüth, T.C.: A novel wearable laser device to regulate stride length in Parkinson's disease. In: 35th Annual IEEE Conference of the Engineering in Medicine and Biology Society (EMBC), pp. 5895–5898. IEEE (2013)

10. McNaney, R., Vines, J., Roggen, D., Balaam, M., Zhang, P., Poliakov, I., Olivier, P.: Exploring the acceptability of Google glass as an everyday assistive device for people with parkinson's. In: 32nd Annual ACM Conference on Human Factors in Computing Systems, pp. 2551–2554. ACM (2014)
11. Lopez, W.O.C., Higuera, C.A.E., Fonoff, E.T., de Oliveira, C., Souza, U.A., Martinez, J.A. E.: Listenmee® and Listenmee® smartphone application: synchronizing walking to rhythmic auditory cues to improve gait in Parkinson's disease. Hum. Mov. Sci. 37(2014), 147–156 (2014)
12. Winfree, K.N., Pretzer-Aboff, I., Hilgart, D., Aggarwal, R., Behari, M., Agrawal, S.K.: The effect of step-synchronized vibration on patients with Parkinson's disease: case studies on subjects with freezing of gait or an implanted deep brain stimulator. IEEE Trans. Neural Syst. Rehabil. Eng. 21(5), 806–811 (2013)
13. Parkinson's Disease Foundation. http://www.pdf.org/en/symptoms
14. Mazilu, S., Blanke, U., Tröster, G.: Gait, wrist, and sensors: detecting freezing of gait in Parkinson's disease from wrist movement. In: IEEE International Conference on Pervasive Computing and Communication Workshops, pp. 579–584. IEEE (2015)
15. Jovanov, E., Wang, E., Verhagen, L., Fredrickson, M., Fratangelo, R.: deFOG—A real time system for detection and unfreezing of gait of Parkinson's patients. In: IEEE Annual International Conference of the Engineering in Medicine and Biology Society, pp. 5151–5154 (2009)
16. Bhidayasiri, R., Tarsy, D.: Parkinson's disease: Hoehn and Yahr scale. In: Movement Disorders: A Video Atlas, pp. 4–5. Humana Press (2012)
17. Lamberti, P., Armenise, S., Castaldo, V., de Mari, M., Iliceto, G., Tronci, P., Serlenga, L.: Freezing gait in Parkinson's disease. Eur. Neurol. 38(4), 297–301 (1997)
18. Williams, A.J., Peterson, D.S., Earhart, G.M.: Gait coordination in Parkinson disease: effects of step length and cadence manipulations. Gait Posture 38(2), 340–344 (2013)

Designing User Interfaces
in Emotionally-Sensitive Applications

Alistair Sutcliffe[(✉)]

Manchester Business School, University of Manchester, Booth Street West,
Manchester M15 6PB, UK
a.g.sutcliffe@manchester.ac.uk

Abstract. A method for analysing emotion and motivation for design of affective user interfaces is described. Theories from psychology of emotion and motivation are applied in user-centred design to analyse desired influences on users, and plan appropriate UI features, based on a scenario-based approach that analyses affective situations. The method informs design of multimedia and agent-based user interfaces for persuasive technology applications and domains where the user interface may have emotive effects. Use of method is illustrated with a case study in health informatics for a persuasive technology application.

Keywords: Emotion · Motivation · Scenarios · Interactive agents · Persuasive technology · Health informatics

1 Introduction

Although emoticons are an established part of the HCI vocabulary, designing user interfaces when emotional reactions are critical is less well understood. The importance of emotion in design of character-based user interfaces has been established by Picard [36], while manipulation of user emotion also plays a central role in games design [7, 26]. ECA (Embodied Conversational Agents) and Human Robot Interaction have used a limited range of emotions, by applying rules linking facial expressions, gaze and body posture [5, 10, 34, 35]. While these areas of HCI provide the means of realising emotion in design they do not advise on how to plan the effect of affect for interactive situations, i.e. how emotional response by users may be anticipated from the affective expressions of agents, and how emotional responses from multimedia content may be anticipated. Design of affective user interfaces has been implicit in games applications, although explicit methods and heuristics to guide designers are not widespread. For example, Callele et al. [7] proposed scenario sketches annotated with emotional effects, while Benford et al. [4] included emotional incidents in their trajectories approach to scripting interaction. However, no systematic taxonomy or heuristics advising on how to apply emotions in design have been proposed. This paper addresses these concerns by proposing a method for analysing affective scenarios and advises on the use of emotional expression in user system interaction. It focuses on identifying the likely emotional state of the user in a given application context, and then user interface design to adapt to the user's emotion.

© IFIP International Federation for Information Processing 2017
Published by Springer International Publishing AG 2017. All Rights Reserved
R. Bernhaupt et al. (Eds.): INTERACT 2017, Part III, LNCS 10515, pp. 404–422, 2017.
DOI: 10.1007/978-3-319-67687-6_27

Emotions are becoming important in a growing class of applications which relate to individual people [30]. Design of persuasive user interfaces may also involve anticipating users' emotional responses to praise and empathetic messages [18]. Further motivation to consider human emotion within the design process arises from the rapid growth of social software; for example, design principles for e-community sites [37] draw attention to social emotions of responsibility and encourage a sense of belonging. Considering emotion *a priori* enables designers to anticipate human emotional responses and mitigate their downsides, for example by providing sympathetic advice to defuse frustration [27, 33] or adapting content and messages to avoid disappointment.

Many advisory or explanatory systems aim to influence human behaviour; for example, e-health systems may attempt to influence users towards improving their lifestyles. These applications, frequently described as persuasive technology or captology [18], incorporate design features which play on people's emotions. The CASA (Computer As Social Actor) effect [38], which demonstrates that people tend to react to even minimal human presence on computers (i.e. virtual agent, character or even a photograph of a person) as if it were a real person, has been influential in guiding the choice of media, characters, and dialogue content to evoke emotional responses. Although some methods for using affect in persuasive applications have been developed [19], no general approach for affect-based UI design has been proposed.

A systematic approach is therefore needed to address how people may react to potentially affect-laden situations and to plan productive design influences on human emotion while avoiding adverse responses. This paper proposes a model and process for analysing the role of emotion in interactive, user-centred applications, with design advice directed towards agent-based interfaces and social software. In the next section, previous literature in HCI and related disciplines is reviewed. In Sect. 3, models and theories of motivation and emotion are briefly reviewed, with their relevance to UI design. A process of analysing emotional responses by stakeholders and specifying requirements for affective applications in described in Sect. 4, followed by an illustration of the process in a persuasive e-health application case study. The paper concludes with a discussion of the prospects for affective UI design.

2 Related Research

Emotional response to user frustration by providing sympathetic messages has been demonstrated to improve performance and user attitudes [27, 33], while affective design has been widely applied in ECAs [35, 36] and robotics, where use of emotions portrayed by non-verbal communication has been shown to persuade users more effectively [10]. Emotion and motivation are key features of emotional design methods; for instance, manipulation of hope/fear or social acceptance/rejection [19], and guidelines in many persuasive design methods are based on manipulating users' affect either via CASA principles [38], or by rhetorical argument applied to dialogue design [39]. Design guidelines for achieving affect in character-based interfaces can be based on taxonomies of facial expressions and voice prosody effects as well as use of colour and selection of media for mood manipulation [6]; however, analysing users' responses and design of affective user interfaces has received less attention.

A method for designing for affect in games applications has been proposed by Callele [7], as a process of scripting with storyboards and scenarios for planning user interaction. Design effects to evoke emotions such as surprise and fear were annotated on to drawings of the game world; however, no particular model of emotion was proposed. Value-based design [21] elicits user feelings and attitudes to potential systems by presenting cue cards associated with possible emotional responses and user values. Scenarios and storyboarding techniques are used to elicit stakeholder responses, but value-based design does not focus directly on user emotions; instead, it aims to elicit users' attitudes and feelings about products and prototypes as an aid towards refining requirements with human-centred values. Values and affective responses have been investigated by Cockton et al. [11] in worth maps, which attempt to document stakeholders' views about products or prototypes. Worth maps may include emotional responses, but their main focus, similar to value-based design, is to elicit informal descriptions of potential products expressed in stakeholders' language of feelings, values and attitudes. User Experience (UX) has described affective aspects of products [25], drawing attention to aesthetics and enjoyable properties of interactive applications, but no guidelines have been proposed about how to analyse UX or for designing features to deliver an enjoyable user experience.

The role of emotion in user-centred design of products was highlighted by Norman [31], who argued that good design should inspire positive emotional responses from users, such as joy, surprise and pleasure; however, Norman was less forthcoming on how to realise affect-inducing design, beyond reference to the concept of affordances, intuitively understandable user interface features. Techniques for exploring affect in requirements include use of personas, pen portraits of typical users, with their feelings and possibly emotion in their personalities [12]. Personas were developed further into extreme characters [15] as a means of eliciting stakeholders' feelings to provocative statements about designs, although neither of these techniques considered the role of emotion explicitly. Requirements for emotion are tacitly included in design of embodied conversational agents [5, 9] as scripts for controlling facial expression, posture and gaze of virtual agents; however, the ECA literature contains few techniques for eliciting or specifying desired emotional responses.

3 Theories of Emotion and Motivation

As Brave and Nass [6] point out, affect-oriented design concerns users' needs as well as their emotions. Two areas of psychology are relevant to personal needs: first, motivation theory, which explains deep-seated goals or drives which determine our behaviour; and secondly, emotions, which characterise our automatic reactions to events and situations. The intention is to augment user-centred design (UCD) with knowledge from psychology about users' goals which are tacit (motivation), and reactions that may arise when goals or motivations are frustrated (emotions). Psychologists distinguish between emotions, which are specific responses, and moods, which reflect more general good or bad feelings. Moods are general states, whereas emotions are part of our cognitive response and persist as memories of responses to events, objects and people. Emotions may be either positive (pleasure and joy) or negative (fear, disgust) and may have a force, e.g. worry or anxiety is a mild form of fear. There are many theories of emotion; however, three have received more attention in the design of software systems. First, Norman's model [31] divides emotional responses into three layers: the visceral layer which produces psychosomatic responses to fear and anger; a behavioural layer that dictates actions in response to emotion, such as rejecting a product; and finally a reflective layer in which emotional responses are rationalised, e.g. disappointment in a product after a poor user experience. Norman advises that software design should encourage emotions of pleasure, joy and surprise for positive behavioural and reflective responses, but gives little advice on how to achieve such responses in a design. Second, ECA designers have favoured Ekman's theory [16] which characterises a simple set of basic emotions: anger, disgust, fear, sadness and surprise, which are communicated by facial expressions. The third more comprehensive theory is the OCC (Ortny, Clore, Collins) model [32] which contains a taxonomy of 22 emotions, classified into reactions to events, agents (other people) and objects, and which may be either positive or negative. A simplified view of the OCC taxonomy is shown in Fig. 1. Reaction to events depends on whether the consequences concern oneself (+ve hope, -ve fear) or others, and then the impact of the event (satisfaction, fears confirmed/relief, disappointment). Responses to objects may either be mild (like or dislike) or stronger (love/hate). Emotional response to agents' actions depends on who the action relates to (self, others, group) and then the perceived effect of the action and whether it was positive, such as pride as a positive response to one's own action, or reproach as a negative reaction to another person's action. Event-related emotions are

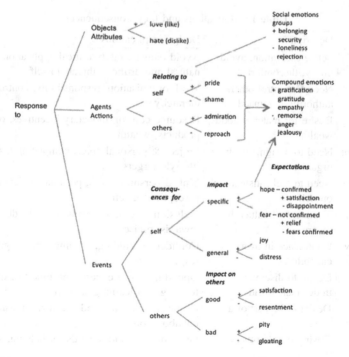

Fig. 1. OCC model decision tree for classifying emotions; augmented with social emotions

responses to situations and changes in the environment and related either to oneself or others in terms of consequences and impact. For example, joy is a positive assessment of an event (e.g. birthday party) relating to oneself with a general impact, and hope is the positive emotion in a specific response to getting a present, which may than happen (satisfaction) or not (disappointment). Some emotions, such as gratification, remorse, gratitude and anger, are complex responses to events and agents/objects. Even though the OCC model is comprehensive it does not account for social emotions such as empathy (+ve reaction to an agent) and belonging (+ve reaction to group membership) [3]. In spite of these limitations the OCC model is suitable for application to requirements analysis since the event/agent/object taxonomy and decision tree can be applied to analysing emotional reactions. Individual stakeholders may experience emotions in response to events, objects or agents produced by the software system, or which may be a consequence of events and objects in the system environment. Once a range of "emotion inducing" states has been identified, responses to them can be planned for software agents and multimedia systems.

3.1 Motivation Analysis

Motivations were classified by Maslow [28] into levels ranging from basic bodily needs such as hunger and thirst, to higher-level needs for security, comfort and safety, and finally socially related motivations of self-esteem and altruism. Table 1 summarises the more important motivations for requirements analysis, synthesised from

Table 1. Motivations and their consequences

Motivation	Description	Design implications
Safety	Self preservation, avoid injury, discomfort	Avoid danger: safety critical applications; avoid natural and artificial threats to self
Power	Need to control others, authority, command	Work organisation, responsibility, control hierarchy
Possession	Desire for material goods, wealth	Resource control, monetary incentives, ownership, products, wealth
Achievement	Need to design, construct, organise	Project & personal goals, completing tasks, lifestyle targets
Self-esteem	Need to feel satisfied with oneself	Linked personal goals, personal achievement, also perception of self
Peer-esteem	Need to feel valued by others	Inclusion in groups, teams social feedback and rewards, praise
Self-efficacy	Confidence in own capabilities	Confidence building, training, encourage responsibility
Curiosity, learning	Desire to discover, understand world	Opportunities to experiment, time to explore, self tutoring and learning support
Sociability	Desire to be part of a group	Group membership and social relationships, collaboration in work
Altruism	Desire to help others	Opportunities and rewards for helping, selfless act

Maslow's motivation theory. Column 2 describes the motivation as hints for analysis questions, some of which are suggested by the motivation type itself, i.e. questions about interest in learning, or willingness to help others. Column 3 suggests high-level UI or socio-technical design implications for each motivation type; for example, self-efficacy, curiosity and learning point towards the need for opportunities to experiment which may suggest end-user development facilities.

Safety subsumes basic physiological motivations to satisfy hunger, thirst, and protect oneself. Power, possession and achievement are all related directly to personal goals, although in different ways. Power is manifest in actions and social relationships, and is associated with responsibility, trust, and authority. Possession is more personal, concerning goals to own resources, wealth or products. Achievement (or failure) is the end state of most goals, although in motivation theory it spans many personal goals as a lifetime ambition. Self- and peer-esteem concern personal perceptions of self and of self by others, which may indirectly be related to goals if achievement is frustrated, leading to a decline in self-esteem. Motivations of achievement, self- and peer-esteem are important in persuasive technology design to suit individual needs; for instance, in e-commerce, marketing tools can be customised to praise customers [18, 19] and thereby improve their self-esteem (positive well being).

Self-efficacy is realising one's potential, hence increasing abilities and responsibility. Altruism and sociability are social motivations driving group behaviour, the need to belong to groups and undertake selfless acts, which incidentally increases peer esteem and hence the sense of belonging to the group. People with high sociability motivation will collaborate and cooperate with others in group working. Motivations can be measured by questionnaires; however, simple checklists of motivations are sufficient to direct analysis in most applications.

4 Applying Emotions and Motivations in UCD

The taxonomies of emotions and motivations are used as tools for thought in scenario-based design (SBD) [8]. Motivational analysis extends analysis of users' needs in personae and SBD; in contrast, emotions are reactions, and consequently these fit as a means of assessing the implications of situations. The affective UCD process is summarised in Fig. 2.

The process follows two related pathways: first, the analysis path that starts from users' needs where the motivation component in the EUCD method is applied; then, affective situations are considered by identifying scenarios for the user roles and stakeholders who may experience significant emotions, followed by analysis of the situations and events that may lead to emotional experiences. Barriers to achieving personal goals and motivations are investigated in "what if" scenario analysis, as well as problems in achieving the desired emotional reaction. The second planning path has its origins in design goals to influence users and their personal goals. System agents and actions are specified in response to anticipated situations. The two pathways interact: the system goals planning pathway suggests situations for follow-up analysis, while affective situations identified in the domain may alter plans and system goals. Analysis of affect may be stimulated by the type of application; for example, games and

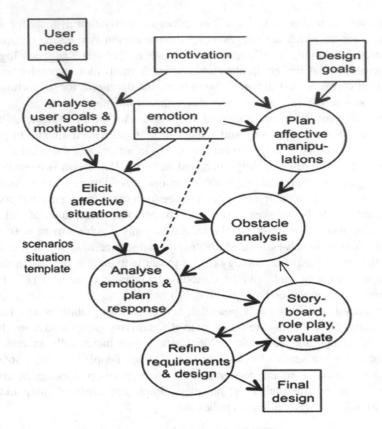

Fig. 2. Summary of the Emotional UCD process

entertainment applications aim to manipulate user emotions, while e-commerce applications have design goals to influence decisions of individual stakeholders and user groups.

Design goals may arise from the need to motivate users to change their behaviour or persuade them towards certain decisions in applications such as healthcare (lifestyle behaviour), marketing e-commerce (purchasing decisions) or social e-communities (persuade people to participate).

4.1   Analysing User Goals and Motivations

Analysis of users' goals follows conventional interviews and scenario-based techniques augmented with motivation analysis using the taxonomy. For example, personal goals to improve one's diet and take exercise will be related not only to achievement but also to self-esteem (feeling good about oneself) and peer esteem (improved standing among friends having lost weight). Barriers to personal goals may have motivational implications such as frustrated achievement, power and possession, which in turn may have knock-on effects on self-esteem and peer-esteem. Since emotional responses are frequently related to motivations as well as to our short-term goals and aspirations, analysis of motivations, goals and emotions is inevitably intertwined. A summary of motivations and possible barriers to their realisation, and emotional responses to frustrated motivation, is given in Table 2.

Table 2. Motivations, obstacles and responses

Motivation	Barriers/threats	Possible emotional response and (mitigation)
Safety	Dangerous events, malevolent agents	Fear, hate (remove cause or relocate user, add defences and counter measures to events)
Power	Change to authority, responsibility	Anger, shame, resentment (compensation, change people, relationships)
Possession	Reduced resource control, monetary incentives	Anger, jealousy, resentment (reallocate resources, responsibilities, change people)
Achievement	Constraints on goals, actions	Anxiety, frustration resentment (change goals, remove constraints)
Self-esteem	Adverse events, goals not achieved	Shame, anger (re-focus goals, emphasise other achievements)
Peer-esteem	Adverse interactions, events	Rejection, loneliness (focus on +ve social relationships)
Self-efficacy	Limitations on actions and responsibilities	Disappointment, distress (improve opportunities, challenges)
Curiosity, learning	Excessive workload, time, resources	Disappointment, reproach (provide time, change workload)
Sociability	Group conflict, personality and authority clashes	Rejection, resentment, loneliness (negotiate problems, change group membership, responsibilities
Altruism	Limitations on actions	Distress, disappointment (provide opportunities, rewards)

The motivations and emotions listed in Table 2 can be used to prompt questions in both directions. Emotional reactions to a scenario may indicate motivational problems, while barriers to personal goals and related motivations indicate emotional consequences which will need to be addressed either in the social system or design of information content and artificial agents.

4.2   Identifying Affective Situations

The first step is to identify the range of potential affective situations, then to trace the source responsible for emotional reactions in the system content or environment. Situation analysis is directed towards identifying the possible emotional response and its source, then establishing requirements for system agents and responses using the template illustrated in Table 3.

Table 3. Affective situation requirements template, with notes

Application	Situation ID
Agents & actions	People in the scenario, possible actions and communication
Objects	Objects and design artefacts
Events (previous)	Expected events in the environment, with their source, when known. User memory of previous events
Expected emotion	As identified from the above and obstacle analysis
System response	Remove cause, mitigate effect
Agent requirements	Agents' actions for mitigation
Other requirements	Non-agent responses, avoid cause, etc.

Scenarios, use cases and storyboards, all commonly practised UCD techniques, can be adapted for "affective situation" analysis with stakeholder groups and individual users. Scenarios describing potential emotion-invoking incidents may be elicited from stakeholders or created by analysts to explore user reactions to personal goals and design features. Storyboards and sketches are used to illustrate scenarios and are presented to users to capture their responses. Since agent-based technology is now cheap and easy to use, lightweight prototypes can be developed to explore design options with a range of emotional expressions by agents [2]. Some examples of facial expression of emotions using agent prototyping tools are illustrated in Fig. 3.

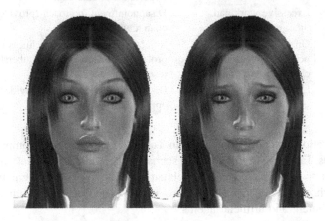

Fig. 3. Expression of emotion by agent's face with dialogue excerpts. Left: "You seem to have problems; can I help you?"; Right: "… all is ok; please continue".

Facial expression alone is somewhat ambiguous, as might be discerned from Fig. 3, so it needs to be combined with dialogue, for example "you seem to have difficulty in placing this order, please select the product again" and "thank you for you order, please proceed to payment" in a typical e-commerce sequence. Emotional expression is even more effective when prosody (voice tone) is used, and text to speech output with limited tonal expression is provided by agent development tools.

4.3   Analysing Situations and Emotions

Tracing the source of emotions follows the template and OCC decision tree to elicit the reasons for the response, then identifying the source in the system environment, content or the design itself. The OCC decision tree helps to identify potential emotions and their causes by asking questions about the source of the problem (agents' actions, objects' attributes, events), who it affects (self, other stakeholders), and the consequences and impact of the problem as well as any previous related experiences (expectations). Affective reactions may be caused either by the system design, the content of the design, agents, especially people and other stakeholders, actions, or events in the system environment the user has to deal with. Poor implementation of requirements or missing requirements may evoke frustration and anger in more extreme cases. User reaction to the content of applications and websites may be more complex as the response may be caused by information and messages conveyed by text or speech, images of people or natural phenomena, or even sounds and music. Situations involving the system environment range from other people in computer-mediated communication and social software, to events in the world or user goals that the system has to respond to by advising, persuading or directing the user to take action.

Anger tends to be associated more closely with agents and people, so the presentation of characters, opinion and values that clash with the stakeholder's viewpoint should be investigated. Fear is related to events as well as to specific agents, so events in the system environment or described in the system content (e.g. website information) should be questioned. Disgust is a strong, visceral emotion usually associated with content, for example images of putrefying food. Socially oriented emotions have roots in reactions to people and events, so in this case the stakeholder's relationship with others may need to be investigated, through the history of events involving the user and others in the system environment. Social emotions are also important considerations in social computing applications, with privacy and security implications. For example, disclosure of secrets may cause shame (in own behaviour), jealousy (in others) remorse (in injudicious actions which have offended others) and so on. Scenarios of information disclosure and privacy controls can explore the types and strengths of emotional responses.

4.4   Scenario-Barrier Analysis

Planning system responses to user emotions can be helped by analysing obstacles to motivations and personal goals. If responses can invoke appropriate user motivations then potential negative emotions might be deflected or converted into positive responses (e.g. convert dislike into like by changing an object or design). Since motivations are long-term goals, barriers will tend to be more general and persistent than may be expected for short-term personal goals. Table 4 gives some guidance in analysing possible reasons for affective reactions for a sub-set of OCC negative emotions.

The causes (agents, people, events, etc.) may hinder the achievement of personal goals while column 3 gives limited guidance on countermeasures. Motivational consequences may be mitigated by design in the social system, for example, poor

Table 4. Emotions, possible causes and responses

Emotion	Barriers, causes	Possible responses/mitigations
Hate	Actions of people or things, value clashes	Remove object, agent; change focus to self-achievement
Anger	Offensive events, people, things, values	Remove cause, mitigate reasons
Fear	Threats to self, dangerous objects, situations	Remove threat or user from situation, add protection
Disgust	Offensive objects, people	Remove cause, change location
Jealousy	People's actions, objects	Mitigate reasons, change focus to self
Shame	Own actions self-image	Analyse reasons, change focus to achievement

self-esteem arising from a lack of achievement may be alleviated by improving training, changing the organisation of work, or re-setting targets to make them more achievable. Emotional responses indicated from the motivation barrier analysis suggest further scenarios where the implications can be explored by role-playing situations in which the generic obstacles are made more realistic and concrete, e.g. being turned down for promotion frustrates achievement and has a negative impact on self-esteem.

4.5 Planning Responses

The source of the emotional response is traced back to the agent, action or event, and response scenarios are planned to mitigate the anticipated negative emotion. Once the source is known, responses to deal with the situation can be specified. There are three main routes: first to remove the source; secondly to reassure the users and diffuse the emotion by reducing the significance or impact of the reaction; and finally planning a system response to change negative affect into its related positive emotion, e.g. fear is converted into relief by explaining that the event's consequences are not what the user expected. Removing the source in content can be achieved by editing to remove the offending image, text or event; however, changing sources in the system environment may not be an option, so a mitigation strategy may be necessary. For example, if resentment is felt in response to the success of others, then a better outcome might be to convert this into satisfaction or deflect the negative emotion by urging the user to reflect on their own achievements. Resentment might be reduced by counselling the user to ignore the event as unimportant or reflecting on their own success rather than envying others.

Hate and its milder manifestation (dislike) may be encountered as a response to missing requirements, poor user interface design, or when users are frustrated by poor design. With content, the causes may arise from a clash between the user's beliefs and values and information or opinions expressed in the content. Adverse reaction to personalities is another likely cause. Emotional responses to products and designed artefacts are usually easier to deal with since these can be traced back to the feature causing dislike. Disliked features indicate poor design or missing/inappropriate requirements.

Positive emotions are less of a concern in situation analysis since there are fewer implications for system requirements, although when goals for influencing user behaviour are present, then scenarios need to be developed that describe the desired positive emotion, e.g. pleasurable experience for persuading users. To illustrate, in an e-commerce application selling high-quality design goods such as jewellery, the system goal is to influence the user to buy the product. The user is a member of the public, objects are the jewellery products, and the intended emotions are curiosity, pleasure and desire. Requirements for a sales agent's virtual character are to empathise with the user, using a smiling facial expression to communicate interest and pleasure in explaining the product, followed by actions to demonstrate product qualities, and use of gesture and gaze to draw attention to these features. In games applications a sequence of affective situations will lead the user-player through interactive episodes with agents and events to evoke fear, anxiety, surprise and relief as the game sequence unfolds. Action scripts and sketches of the game's virtual world amplify the requirements described in the template.

5   Case Study Application of EUCD

In this section, use of the Emotional UCD process in a persuasive technology application in e-health is described.

5.1   Detecting Early Onset of Cognitive Impairment

The system is intended to help early diagnosis of cognitive dementia and Alzheimer's disease among the elderly. Unfortunately, Alzheimer's disease is diagnosed too late in too many people, by which time there is little that medical science can do to help; however, if the disease is detected early, then treatments can delay its onset and ameliorate its symptoms. Early onset can be detected by memory tests, patterns of word use and motor reaction times, so the high-level system goal is to remotely and unob-trusively monitor people's use of home computers and text-based messaging via e-mail and social networking sites. There are many complex requirements involving data and text mining to produce early onset diagnostic indicators, which do not concern this paper; instead, analysis of the users' possible reactions to the system are described, with the aim of persuading elderly users to self-refer for follow-up tests and appropriate medical treatment.

The users' motivation is safety, to avoid Alzheimer's disease if possible; with personal goals to participate as volunteers in the trial for altruistic reasons. Affective situations in this case are an obvious consequence of the design goal to warn the user. The affective UCD problem is to analyse people's potential reaction to system diag-noses. The diagnostic part of the system will not be perfect, hence there is uncertainty about the results and the danger of false positive diagnoses, which could provoke fear about the consequences. Scenarios based on these assumptions were explored. If the system detected signs of dementia then this information could be distressing to the user. This raises questions about how the information should be communicated to the user, and the appropriate system response to different diagnostic signs. Using the OCC model, the source of anticipated emotions of fear and distress are the event (message), which has consequences for self (the user) with a specific impact when the feared expectation (diagnosis of dementia) is confirmed. Relief or fear confirmed are also possible depending on the results of follow-up tests. This may also have a general impact leading to distress and fear of the future. This is summarised in the template shown in Table 5.

Table 5. Situation template: cognitive impairment diagnosis. Situation: diagnosis of problems, low confidence

Agents & actions	User, possibly their kin
Objects	Text, graphs feedback presentation
Events (previous)	Message warning about possible cognitive impairment (patient history)
Expected emotions	Anxiety, fear, distress, relief
System response	Mitigate consequences, reassure user, empathise
Agent requirements	Agent sympathises with user, communicates
Other requirements	Supplementary information, communication with doctors, kin and friends

The next step is to specify the system response. In this case the mirror emotion (relief) can be explored since the diagnosis is uncertain, so suggestions for follow-up tests can be specified to confirm or negate the initial diagnosis with reassuring messages that many initial signs turn out to be false alarms.

Consulting medical experts with explanations of tests in memory clinics is another system response. The social emotion of empathy is another means of dealing with distress, hence requirements for social support might be explored, for instance the acceptability of letting close friends know via a social network. A range of scenarios (see Fig. 4) were developed to explore different means of communicating the potentially distressing message, with system responses ranging from no emotion (just the facts), to expression of empathy by agent characters. Other design options involved

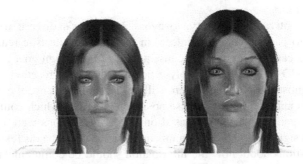

Fig. 4. Scenario and agent storyboard for the weak diagnostic signs situation

choice of media to deliver the message (text, voice, agent character plus voice/text), as well as the content and format of the message (polite, sympathetic tone).

Scenario: You are presented with evidence of memory problems from the computer monitor. How would you feel about the messages presented, and the follow-up advice to complete more self assessment tests?

Agent: " Sorry to disturb you, but I have found a few signs of problems with your memory. These might not be significant but I think it would be helpful to try a few follow-up tests: see the following link."

These scenarios of personal goals and motivations were investigated to identify possible barriers to system goals (to encourage self-referral for follow-up tests), for example self-denial that the user has a medical problem. Analysis of the storyboard scenarios showed individual differences in affective responses. Some users preferred simple factual communications, whereas others liked the empathetic agent. Older characters were suggested to match the user audience, also using a doctor to evoke more trust. Content options included simple explanations of the reasons for diagnosis, with limited disclosure of the information to close friends or kin in the user's social network. All users felt that, apart from letting their very best friend know if the follow-up tests did confirm the problem, any disclosure would cause them distress and unnecessary fear among friends.

Scenario analysis also produced insight into ethical concerns with use of e-mail content for text mining. Analysis scenarios presented fictitious e-mails with varying degrees of affective content which were then personalised for each individual or used more general language. Privacy/safety motivations and distress/fear emotional responses underpinned these scenarios since if access to e-mail content were not possible this could hinder the diagnostic ability of the system. Users were willing to allow access to e-mail content in general terms, but personalised emotive content raised anxieties and privacy fears. The problem of replies to e-mail becoming part of the content emerged during these scenarios as users pointed out that this potentially involved others and raised the question about how permission would be sought when it would be difficult to predict which friends or kin they would exchange messages with. The conclusion was to design filters so only user-authored content would be accessible.

5.2   Evaluation

The prototypes were evaluated in five workshops with a total of 24 participants (14 male, 10 female, age range 60–75, median 66), with a median four participants/session plus two facilitators. Prototype UIs presented feedback messages communicating potential early onset dementia to elicit users' reactions, feelings and ethical issues. Three prototype versions were presented in workshops and interviews: (i) the agent character interface produced using the method described in this paper, (ii) a minimal text message interface, using empathic text that closely matched the agent speech, and (iii) a minimal text interface with additional explanation justifying the feedback mes-sage. The additional information showed graphs based on fictitious recording of user behaviour, indicating where the threshold had been exceeded to trigger the feedback message. Time constraints imposed by the research project on the evaluation session precluded a conventional experimental design with use of usability/user experience questionnaires, so only limited quantitative data could be recorded. Problems raised in the workshops were explored further in 13 interviews following a similar approach. Questions in the interviews also probed users' reactions to fears/barriers for adopting the system and taking follow-up action after an alert message. Respondents (4 male, 9 female), ranging from 67 to 89 years old (median 72), were all interviewed in their own homes, apart from three sessions carried out in a community centre.

There was no consensus on choice of the design option (text/augmented text/agent), although a majority in all workshops favoured provision of more detail and the availability of regular reports (content). Use of the agent was favoured in all workshops as a backup to text, where participants suggested that self-help (how to cope) and explanation (dementia mitigation treatments) could be important motivators for persuading them to take follow-up action. Reaction to the agent design was mixed, with approximately 60% of the participants agreeing that the message spoken by the agent was more sympathetic that plain text, although several participants commented that the facial expression was difficult to interpret. In the interviews most respondents (8/13) favoured the plain text alert message over other design options, although a majority (11) agreed that the agent could be a useful supplement to the plain text, and 10/13 preferred supplementary information to be presented by the agent rather than graphs. Consistent with the interviews, the value of the agent was seen to be in delivering additional information. The facial expression was interpreted by 10 participants as being empathetic and showing mild disappointment, although 3 could not discern any particular expression. Reaction to the agent designs was mixed. Overall, text was preferred, although the agent presentation was considered to be a useful supplement if it added value by providing more information. Design of the empathetic message may be more important that conveying emotion by facial expression. We did not test a non-empathetic version of the feedback message; however, all participants agreed that the tone of the message was appropriate. The choice of agent character (young female) was considered appropriate by most participants although several interviewees (7) preferred an older character, closer to their age group.

5.3   Lessons Learned

The design produced by the method was moderately successful. However the evaluation demonstrated that emotion design has to be set in a wider context of the role of characters in supplementing basic messages. The choice of the facial expression and empathetic message tone, which were informed by the method, were generally well received, although clearly there was room for improvement in agent's facial expression.

One problem with affect-oriented research is that people are rarely completely candid about expressing emotion [17]. Some users were concerned that they only felt emotion in real life and that imagining how they would feel in response to scenarios was not easy. Another problem was negative reaction to the agents; several users (6) preferred to communicate with real people rather than computer images in affective situations. However, motivations and discussion of feelings were productive when assessing responses to the agent designs. The analysis side of the method, eliciting emotional situations which might occur, appears to be more difficult than the synthesis-design side where reaction to specific agent designs is being assessed. Tools for developing prototype agents have proved successful in demonstrating a range of facial expressions and scripted interactions, so exploration of affective user-centred design does seem to be a promising approach. Although the method proposed separate analysis-response and planning pathways, in practice a combination of both was often necessary. For example, analysis of users' fears about access to sensitive e-mails needed to be combined with advice-giving (agent feedback) so that the system's diagnosis of potential problems could be explained by reference to the original content as well as other indicators. While the scenarios and the method were initially focused on UI design issues, in actual use the method stimulated more wide-ranging debate about affect in socio-technical system design. Users' response to different affective tones in feedback messages and means of presenting those messages, e.g. stronger advice and persuasion versus more neutral presentation of the system's analyses, sparked a debate about the overall conception of the system as either a persuasive agent that influenced users to refer themselves for medical attention or as a healthcare self-management system where the decision-making onus was left with the user.

6 Discussion

EUCD provides a systematic approach to exploring human motivations, emotions and attitudes for designing advanced UI technology where agent/character-based interfaces are becoming more common. Motivation and emotion analysis are particularly pertinent to social computing applications where computer-mediated interactions need to be considered. The EUCD method is not intended to supplant conventional HCI design approaches; instead, it augments scenario-based design [8] with person-oriented and social considerations. One further extension is to create a set of "affective claims" for situations so that the advantages and disadvantages of emotional responses and motivational frustrations can be considered. Even though the method is in its early stages of development, it does show some promise in producing insight into personal problems in applications where individual experience and goals are paramount. EUCD may also augment persuasive design methods such as the Fogg Behavior Model (FBM) [19] since it adds a scenario-based analysis approach and a richer taxonomy of emotions and motivation which can be applied to applications where the system's goal is to influence users [14, 39]. In a memory recall study of experience, Hassenzahl et al. [24] used Sheldon's taxonomy of needs, which are related to motivations, to demonstrate that users' needs and emotions positively influence both hedonic and pragmatic ratings of products. Hassenzahl's concept of hedonics [22] expresses users' attitudes to interactive products in terms of motivational goals and value judgements, which could provide a complementary perspective to the classifications in EUCD. While the emphasis of EUCD is on analysis and understanding of the implications of affective design on users, it could also be used for design guidance by directly applying the motivation and affect taxonomies. In this mode the method synthesises more general guidance on affective design [6] with scenario-based design exploration in the planning pathway.

While emotions and motivation are psychological constructs which require in-depth knowledge for analysis of human problems, the EUCD method delivers a digestible sub-set of psychology, which could be used by non-experts. Experience to date has involved medical personnel who are conversant with the psychology of emotion from their training, so testing the method with non-experts is part of the future research agenda. To deliver the method's advice more effectively we will create a hypertext website so users can explore the links between motivation, emotions, obstacles and possible mitigations. Although the scenario and storyboard analysis has demonstrated that affective issues can be explored with users who are not experts, EUCD is not appropriate for creative use of emotions in entertainment and games applications where fear, anxiety and negative emotions might be manipulated for dramatic effect. Callele et al. [7] do address emotional design in games, although no heuristics linking types of emotional responses to design guidance are given. Desmet's emotional design methods and guidelines [14, 20] are closely related to EUCD, although they are based on a slightly different taxonomy of 25 emotions synthesised from several theories [13]. However, Desmet's design advice focuses on interactive products at the device level, similar to Hassenzahl's hedonics [23] (e.g. mobile phones), whereas EUCD has a narrower focus on applications and episodes within an interactive sequence.

Current sensory technology enables body posture and facial expression to be automatically analysed to detect emotional responses such as disappointment, enabling computer interfaces to portray appropriate emotional response [29]. Furthermore, the OCC model has been formalised [1] so there is the prospect of creating emotional analysis tools based on EUCD for agent-based specifications. In conclusion, EUCD extends HCI design methodology which has focused on human feelings and values [11, 21], as well as analysing the socio-technical implications of affective reactions to inappropriate features, tacit knowledge and managerial changes.

Ideally a validation study comparing design of an affective application with and without the EUCD method could have strengthened claims for the method's effectiveness. Unfortunately such method validation studies are expensive and very difficult to design since matching the context of application, users, and designers is hard to achieve. Although this study has several limitations, such as the preliminary evaluation of the method with a few users, it has produced interesting lessons and insight into how emotion might be employed in UI design in a wider context than persuasive technology. While the EUCD guidelines helped to stimulate design ideas, the method also had indirect effects such as initiating debate about the more general emotional impact of the system, as an empathetic friend or persuasive agent. The value of a detailed method such as EUCD may therefore be realised at different levels, although the trade-off between detailed advice and more general heuristic use of the method awaits further in-depth investigation of use in different applications.

Acknowledgments. The work described in this paper is funded by EPSRC project ref. EP/K015796/1 Software Architecture for Mental Health Self Management (SAMS).

References

1. Adam, C., Herzig, A., Longin, D.: A logical formalization of the OCC theory of emotions. Synthese **168**, 201–248 (2009)

2. Artificial Intelligence Foundation. ALICE chatterbots. www.alice.pandorabots.com. Accessed 2 Feb 2011
3. Bandura, A.: Social Cognitive Theory of Mass Communication. Lawrence Erlbaum Associates, Mahwah (2001)
4. Benford, S., Giannachi, G., Koleva, B., Rodden, T.: From interaction to trajectories: designing coherent journeys through user experiences. In: Proceedings: CHI 2009, 27th International Conference on Human Factors in Computing Systems, pp. 709–718. ACM Press, New York (2009)
5. Bickmore, T., Cassell, J.: Social dialogue with embodied conversational agents. In: van Kuppevelt, J., Dybkjaer, L., Bernsen, N.O. (eds.) Natural, Intelligent and Effective Interaction with Multimodal Dialogue Systems. Kluwer Academic, New York (2004)
6. Brave, S., Nass, C.: Emotion in human-computer interaction. In: Jacko, J., Sears, A. (eds.) Handbook of Human-Computer Interaction, Chap. 26. Lawrence Erlbaum Associates, Mahwah (2003)
7. Callele, D., Neufeld, E., Schneider, K.: Augmenting emotional requirements with emotion markers and emotion prototypes. In: Proceedings, RE 2009, pp. 373–374. IEEE Computer Society Press, Los Alamitos (2009)
8. Carroll, J.M.: Making Use: Scenario-Based Design of Human-Computer Interactions. MIT Press, Cambridge (2000)
9. Cassell, J.: Embodied conversational interface agents. Commun. ACM **43**, 70–80 (2000)
10. Chidambaram, V., Chiang, Y.-H., Mutlu, B.: Designing persuasive robots: how robots might persuade people using vocal and nonverbal cues. In: Proceedings of the 4th ACM/IEEE International Conference on Human Robot Interaction, pp. 293–300. ACM Press, New York (2012)
11. Cockton, G., Kujala, S., Nurkka, P., Hölttä, T.: Supporting worth mapping with sentence completion. In: Gross, T., Gulliksen, J., Kotzé, P., Oestreicher, L., Palanque, P., Prates, R.O., Winckler, M. (eds.) INTERACT 2009. LNCS, vol. 5727, pp. 566–581. Springer, Heidelberg (2009). doi:10.1007/978-3-642-03658-3_61
12. Cooper, A., Reimann, R., Cronin, D.: About Face 3: The Essentials of Interaction Design. Wiley, Indianapolis (2007)
13. Desmet, P.M.: Faces of product pleasure: 25 positive emotions in human-product interactions. Int. J. Des. **6**(2) (2012)
14. Desmet, P.M., Fokkinga, S.F., Ozkaramanli, D., Yoon, J.: Emotion-driven product design. In: Emotion Measurement, p. 405 (2016)
15. Djajadiningrat, J.P., Gaver, W.W., Frens, J.W.: Interaction relabelling and extreme characters: methods for exploring aesthetic interactions. In: Conference Proceedings, DIS-2000 Designing Interactive Systems: Processes, Practices Methods and Techniques, pp. 66–71. ACM Press, New York (2000)
16. Ekman, P.: Basic emotions. In: Dalgleish, T., Power, M. (eds.) Handbook of Cognition and Emotion. Wiley, Chichester (1999)
17. Fineman, S.: Understanding Emotion at Work. Sage Publications, Thousand Oaks (2004)
18. Fogg, B.J.: Persuasive Technology: Using Computers to Change What We Think and Do. Morgan Kaufmann, San Francisco (2003)
19. Fogg, B.J.: A behaviour model for persausive design. In: Persuasive, P. (ed.) 4th International Conference on Persuasive Technology. ACM Press, New York (2009)
20. Fokkinga, S.F., Desmet, P.M.: Ten ways to design for disgust, sadness, and other enjoyments: a design approach to enrich product experiences with negative emotions. Int. J. Des. **7**(1) (2013)
21. Friedman, B.: Value sensitive design. In: Schular, D. (ed.) Liberating Voices: A Pattern Language for Communication Revolution, pp. 366–368. MIT Press, Cambridge (2008)

22. Hassenzahl, M.: The interplay of beauty, goodness, and usability in interactive products. Hum.-Comput.-Interact. **19**(4), 319–349 (2004)

23. Hassenzahl, M., Monk, A.: The inference of perceived usability from beauty. Hum.-Comput. Interact. **25**(3), 235–260 (2010)

24. Hassenzahl, M., Diefenbach, S., Göritz, A.S.: Needs, affect, and interactive products: facets of user experience. Interact. Comput. **22**(5), 353–362 (2010)

25. Hassenzahl, M., Schöbel, M., Trautmann, T.: How motivational orientation influences the evaluation and choice of hedonic and pragmatic interactive products: the role of regulatory focus. Interact. Comput. **20**, 473–479 (2008)

26. Johnson, D., Wiles, J.: Effective affective user interface design in games. Ergonomics **46**, 1332–1345 (2003)

27. Klein, J., Moon, Y., Picard, R.W.: This computer responds to user frustration: theory, design and results. Interact. Comput. **14**, 140–199 (2002)

28. Maslow, A.H., Frager, R., McReynolds, C., Cox, R., Fadiman, J.: Motivation and Personality. Addison Wesley-Longman, New York (1987)

29. McDuff, D., Karlson, A., Kapoor, A., Roseway, A., Czerwinski, M.: AffectAura: an intelligent system for emotional memory. In: Proceedings CHI-2012, pp 848–858. ACM Press, New York (2012)

30. Norman, D.A.: The Design of Everyday Things. Basic Books, New York (1999)

31. Norman, D.A.: Emotional Design: Why We Love (or Hate) Everyday Things. Basic Books, New York (2004)

32. Ortony, A., Clore, G.L., Collins, A.: The Cognitive Structure of Emotions. Cambridge University Press, Cambridge (1988)

33. Partalaa, T., Veikko, S.: The effects of affective interventions in human-computer interaction. Interact. Comput. **16**, 295–309 (2004)

34. Pelachaud, C., Carofiglio, V., De Carolis, B., De Rosis, F.: Embodied virtual agent in information delivering application. In: Proceedings, First International Joint Conference on Autonomous Agents and Multi-Agent Systems. ACM Press, New York (2002)

35. Picard, R.W.: Affective Computing. MIT Press, Cambridge (1997)

36. Picard, R.W.: Affective computing: challenges. Int. J. Hum.-Comput. Stud. **59**, 55–64 (2003)

37. Preece, J., Maloney-Krichmar, D.: Online communities. In: Jacko, J., Sears, A. (eds.) Handbook of Human-Computer Interaction, pp. 596–620. Lawrence Erlbaum Associates, Mahwah (2003)

38. Reeves, B., Nass, C.: The Media Equation: How People Treat Computers, Television and New Media Like Real People and Places. CLSI/Cambridge University Press, Stanford/Cambridge (1996)

39. Torning, K., Olinas-Kukkonen, H.: Persuasive design methods: state of the art review. In: Persuasive, P. (ed.) 4th International Conference on Persuasive Technology. ACM Press, New York (2009)

*i*KnowU – Exploring the Potential of Multimodal AR Smart Glasses for the Decoding and Rehabilitation of Face Processing in Clinical Populations

Simon Ruffieux[1(✉)], Nicolas Ruffieux[2], Roberto Caldara[2], and Denis Lalanne[3]

[1] HumanTech, University of Applied Sciences and Arts, Fribourg, Switzerland
simon.ruffieux@hes-so.ch
[2] iBMLab, University of Fribourg, Fribourg, Switzerland
{nicolas.ruffieux,roberto.caldara}@unifr.ch
[3] Human-IST, University of Fribourg, Fribourg, Switzerland
denis.lalanne@unifr.ch

Abstract. This article presents an explorative study with a smart glasses application developed to help visually impaired individuals to identify faces and facial expressions of emotion. The paper discusses three experiments in which different patients, suffering from distinct pathologies impairing vision, tested our application. These preliminary studies demonstrate the feasibility and usefulness of visual prostheses for face and emotion identification, and offer novel and interesting directions for future wearable see-through devices.

Keywords: Wearable · Smart glasses · Face identification · Emotion recognition · Prosthesis · Rehabilitation · User-study

1 Introduction

Our ability to effectively perceive and identify faces, to decode their emotions and social signals is crucial for everyday life social interactions. This specific aptitude can be impaired in a wide range of clinical conditions, such as low vision, dementia or autism, only to name a few. Such an impairment leads to suboptimal social interactions and can lead to potentially dramatic consequences on psychological well-being of the visually impaired. Worldwide, approximately 32 million people are blind and 191 million live with moderate to severe visual impairment [1]. In Switzerland alone, about 10'000 individuals are blind and over 300'000 have a severe visual handicap [2]. In this population, one of the most frequent complaint relates to the difficulty to identify faces and decode facial expressions of emotion [3, 4].

While automatic recognition of faces and facial expressions of emotion is already well developed and implemented on different static computing platforms (e.g. websites, cameras, desktop computers, etc.) and through online cloud-based services (Amazon Rekognition, Google Cloud Vision API, Microsoft Face API), its application on wearable devices in the wild is more complex (multiple faces to process simultaneously,

© IFIP International Federation for Information Processing 2017
Published by Springer International Publishing AG 2017. All Rights Reserved
R. Bernhaupt et al. (Eds.): INTERACT 2017, Part III, LNCS 10515, pp. 423–432, 2017.
DOI: 10.1007/978-3-319-67687-6_28

targets in motion, changes in luminosity, limited connectivity, etc.) and requires additional developments. The very recent advances in multimodal processing and wearable technologies provide a novel and unique opportunity to create perceptual and cognitive wearable prosthesis. The aim of our project is to develop always available augmented-reality smart glasses that support patients with face and emotion recognition aids. This can be achieved via multimodal information (e.g. sounds, images, texts, vibrations) provided by the glasses to the person wearing them.

The technology of smart glasses has been evolving rapidly these last years and several well-known companies are now working on eyewear computing devices for augmented reality (Microsoft Hololens, Epson Moverio, Vuzix, Google Magic Leap). Naturally, the emergence of such devices has aroused much hope for people with visual and/or cognitive impairment. Hence, the need to fill the enormous gap between this already partially available technology and the potential benefit for individuals who present with visual and/or cognitive impairment. The potential impact of this project for the population is therefore considerable, knowing the lack of wearable vision-based technologies designed to compensate for such impairments. More specifically, there is a huge potential benefit in the elderly population, as they represent a major proportion of the visually impaired.

We thus aim to use smart glasses to support the decoding and rehabilitation of face identification and facial expressions of emotion, by using multimodal solutions in order to provide tailored feedback depending on the specific disabilities of the user. In this study, we describe the initial explorations with a prototype application implemented on the Epson Moverio BT-200 glasses. This prototype has been tested with three participants suffering from various visual pathologies. These experiments performed in indoor conditions allowed us to gather the impressions from participants and identify their specific needs in terms of tailored multimodal feedback provided by the device according to their respective pathology.

2 State of the Art

In recent years, eyewear computing devices have been catching more attention from research, thanks to the affordable and increased hardware availability. Researchers have outlined the potential of these devices in terms of Human-Computer Interaction, notably in terms of multimodal inputs and outputs. The strong inherent advantage of such device being privacy, usability and hand-free access to the digital information thanks to their location on the head of the subject which are very important features for the target population of this study [5, 6].

The current research on eyewear devices to help visually impaired is predominantly an extension of the existing research based on mobile devices such as smartphones or small embedded systems. In their survey, Terven et al. reviewed eight different portable computer-vision-based travel aids assistive technology systems that have been developed this last decade for mobile devices, highlighting three different types of feedbacks: acoustic, electric stimulation or tactile [7]. The authors notably point out the new opportunities for those types of systems with the increased computing power of mobile devices and wide smartphone availability. They conclude by highlighting the need to gather better knowledge of visually impaired user's needs in order to guide the development from prototypes to products. They mention particularly the problem of the acoustic feedback acceptance, which interferes with the remaining senses of the visually impaired individuals. In their survey, Sujith and Safeeda instead provided an overview of computer-vision based projects for visually impaired persons [8]. They compared the various functionalities of the surveyed projects: door detection, obstacle detection & identification, finding specific objects and path finding. They conclude that most of the studied projects focused on a single task, although visually impaired persons would need a single system encompassing all the different mentioned functionalities. In their studies, Jafri et al. focused mostly on object recognition to help visually impaired individuals [9] and draw attention of the research community on the potential of eyewear devices to help visually impaired [6]. In a recent study, Jafri proposed the use of CUDA-based GPU computing in order to perform real-time people and objects detection and recognition on the "Tango Tablet" device [10].

Recently, several studies investigated face recognition with eyewear and wearable devices to improve social interactions. Mandal et al. proposed a system to assist people during social interactions using a face detection system implemented on Google Glass paired with a smartphone. The algorithmic computations are performed on the smartphone, while the feedback is provided through the transparent display of the Google Glasses [11]. Li et al. extended this project by developing a multi-threaded architecture on the smartphone to better handle the constant stream of images and reduce the time required by the system to recognize faces. They notably established that an acceptable delay for face recognition should be below 2.3 s in order to be accepted by users [12]. Finally, Xu et al. proposed the "SocioGlass" project, which combines the two precedent projects and provides dynamic face recognition and adaptive retrieval of personal information in an Android application [13]. Importantly, they proposed to adapt the information provided to the user depending on work or personal context. The use of augmented-reality smart glasses to directly enhance vision of visually impaired has also been investigated in several studies. The idea is to provide a simplified or modified vision of the real world using the transparent display of the glasses in order to compensate for the visual impairment. Hu et al. proposed to enhance night vision for individuals suffering nyctalopia [14]. Hwang and Peli investigated the possibility to use edge enhancement techniques on Google Glasses to enhance the vision of visually impaired [15].

On the commercial side, the company ORCAM developed a pair of smart glasses with a mounted-camera in order to acoustically translate text in real-time for the visually impaired. They use bone conduction to transmit the information to the users, thus reducing the interferences with the auditory sense of the users. The new version of their product also provides face recognition and identification of a wide range of consumer products. Hicks et al. have developed a hardware AR see-through device specifically designed for visually impaired individuals. This device is based on a Moverio BT-200 modified with a depth-based camera [16]. They recently created the Oxsight company to promote and develop new software for their device [17].

Importantly, only limited literature exists on research conducted on the usability, acceptance and real needs of clinical populations for those types of systems, notably with see-through smart glasses. Based on a study on a cohort of 364 individuals suffering from age-related macular degeneration, Cimarolli et al. report that more than half of the patients mentioned the inability to recognize people as the most disabling difficulty for social interactions [4]. Krishna et al. investigated the needs of blind and visually impaired in the context of social interactions [18]. Their work highlighted specific needs such as knowing the facial expression of their interlocutor, identifying the names of the surrounding persons and the direction of their attention, their appearance and if their look had changed since the last meeting. More recently, Sandnes et al. conducted open interviews with visually impaired individuals to better identify their needs, specifically focusing on eyewear computing devices [3]. The authors highlighted the reluctance of visually impaired individuals for highly recognizable and stigmatizing devices visible to all. The interviewed individuals clearly expressed that face recognition and text reading would be the most important feature for a system based on smart glasses. Importantly, to the best of our knowledge, while many devices have been developing in recent years, none has been validated among clinical populations yet.

3   *i*KnowU

The current study takes place in the context of the multi-disciplinary "iKnowU" project that originates from a collaboration between the Human-IST institute and the *i*BMLab (Eye and Brain Mapping Laboratory), both from the University of Fribourg. The intended goal is to create a solution on see-through smart glasses to aid visually impaired individuals to compensate for their difficulties during social interactions. Using collected information about the user's relatives, friends and colleagues, the system should be able to automatically recognize the presence of these persons in the visual field of the camera, their identity and emotion, and report this information in the most adapted way to the user.

This article describes the first explorative step of the project, in which we developed a prototype application and evaluated it with several patients in order to better understand and differentiate their needs and interests depending on their specific disabilities. As illustrated on Fig. 1, difficulties in face and/or emotion processing can result from damages to peripheral visual organs (e.g. age-related macular degeneration), from brain lesions (e.g., prosopagnosia, visual agnosia, dementia) or from psychopathological conditions (e.g. autism, schizophrenia). Whereas most research in this field is performed with specific tools for each population and each deficit, our project intends to use of a unique solution with multimodal augmented reality feedback (visual, auditory, tactile) tailored to maximize the user's residual visual and cognitive abilities for face and emotion processing. Several studies have shown limited adoption of those types of devices, mainly due to false positive/negative and improper handling of the feedback [3]. Therefore understanding the need of each patient and tailoring the feedback is crucial towards a better adoption. Similarly, better 'error handling' strategies can be used to avoid providing unrequested information to the user or to convey algorithms' confidence information directly to the user through the feedback mechanisms.

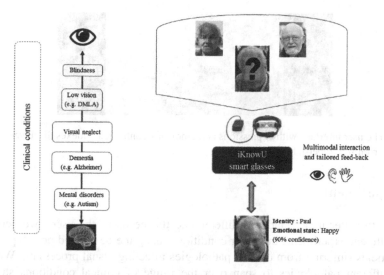

Fig. 1. Left: Clinical conditions with potential difficulties in face and emotion processing. Right: Smart glasses for multimodal interaction and tailored feedback.

As an explorative step and proof of concept for the project, we implemented a prototype of face and emotion recognition application on the BT-200 Epson Moverio smart glasses. Face detection and recognition are based on the standard FaceRecognizer algorithm provided by the OpenCV library [19]. With these algorithms, the system was able to distinguish quite accurately up to five persons in laboratory conditions. The target persons' faces were inserted in the database by using the interface of the developed application. Before each experiment, twenty pictures of each target persons' face were taken from different angles by a member of the team. Emotion recognition has been implemented using the AFFDEX SDK developed by Affectiva [20]. The implemented system is able to recognize five different facial expressions (anger, joy, fear, sadness and surprise) and joint attention. Note that exact accuracies of the implemented algorithms have not been quantified since the goal of the study was to gather first impressions and feedbacks from a clinical population.

The system offers various options to feed information back to the user; in this experiment we used different text and vocal feedbacks. These options could be enabled and disabled according to the capacities and desires of each patient. For face recognition, the user interface highlights detected faces with a green rectangle and recognized persons with a red rectangle around their eyes (potentially flashing to attract user attention) and their name textually presented above their head as shown in Fig. 3. When a new person is recognized, its name is also uttered vocally by the system. For emotions, the interface displays the recognized expressions and emotions with their confidence index textually on the left side of the screen, as shown in Fig. 2. When a new emotion is detected, the system vocally informs the user with a volume that varies according to the confidence index of the algorithm.

Fig. 2. The user interface with expressions and emotions confidence indexes displayed textually to the user on the upper-left of the display.

4   Experiments

In order to better understand and differentiate the needs of the users, we performed three different experiments in indoor conditions using the developed prototype system with patients suffering from distinct pathologies affecting visual processing. We chose those different pathologies to span over the range of clinical conditions shown in Fig. 1. The three patients described below all have in common severe difficulties to identify faces and facial expressions of emotion, which they report as a major handicap for everyday life social interactions. In those experiments, the patients were asked to identify "actors" or relatives (i.e. up to five persons) while wearing the smart glasses in a room with a good lighting level. In addition, the patients were asked to periodically identify the facial expressions of emotion acted by the person facing them. The patient was asked to look at each of the "actors" in turn and utter what he was seeing/hearing through the device. The "actors" were aligned at about 2 m in front of the patient, who was free to move if necessary. At the end of each experiment, we conducted an informal interview with the participant to collect its impressions and feedbacks about the proposed system and the device.

The first experiment was performed with a patient suffering from prosopagnosia (i.e., the inability to recognize faces due to brain damage) consecutive to a severe head injury in 1992. While her general intellectual abilities remained intact, since the accident the patient suffers from major difficulties to visually identify familiar faces, such as her husband or her children [21]. Using our prototype, we observed that this prosthesis improved her ability to identify faces.

In her case, the visual feedbacks (i.e. name of the person shown on the screen) were the most effective, while she found the audio feedbacks to be too intrusive. Furthermore, it has previously been reported that this patient uses a suboptimal strategy to process face identity and expressions, focusing her attention on the mouth instead of the eyes [22, 23]. Whereas automatic visual attention processing is extremely hard to modify through classical rehabilitation techniques, a visual feedback allowed to highlight the eyes (e.g., a flashing red square around the eyes, as shown on Fig. 3) and to train the patient to better focus on this informative part of the face. It can be hypothesized that if the patient is able to integrate such an efficient compensatory technique, she would ultimately be able to better cope without the smart glasses in everyday life situations.

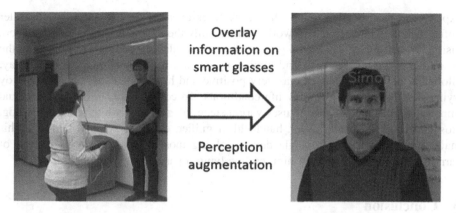

Fig. 3. Overlaying information on the smart glasses and eye focus rehabilitation concept (flashing red square around the eyes). (Color figure online)

The second experiment was conducted with a patient suffering from cortical blindness (i.e. severe loss of vision-despite normal oculomotor behavior- caused by damage to the brain's occipital cortex). This patient is unable to visually identify objects, colors, letters or shapes and is therefore severely incapacitated for everyday life activities [24]. His major complaint concerns his inability to visually identify his relatives.

We performed the experiment at the patient's home, due to the difficulty for him to come to our laboratory. The subject was asked to recognize his wife amongst three people that were sitting on a couch, as the patient had difficulties standing up. Using the smart glasses, he was able to rapidly identify his wife, although the system was not as reliable as usual due to low luminosity conditions. Then we tested the emotion recognition system; his wife sat in front of him and acted different emotions. He successfully detected most emotions relying on the auditory feedback provided by the system. He notably appreciated the fact that the volume of the auditory feedback was modulated according to the confidence indexes inferred by the algorithm; such indexes are visible on the textual feedback shown in Fig. 2.

The patient clearly outlined that, in his case, visual feedbacks were not as useful as the auditory feedback as he was not able to easily process the information shown on the smart glasses display, although he mentioned that some flashing elements on the screen attracted his attention during the experiments (i.e. the red square when a person was recognized). He also mentioned the glasses were quite uncomfortable and that he would probably not wear them during a whole day.

The third experiment was conducted with a 48 years old patient presenting with quasi-blindness due to retinitis pigmentosa. This inherited eye disease causes a progressive degeneration of the rod cells in the retina. Consequently, this patient presents with tubular vision (visual field: 15°), low visual acuity (0.2), defective light-dark adaptation and photophobia. The patient was extremely enthusiastic when he tried the prototype. As the two previous patients, he was able to rapidly identify faces and emotions using the smart glasses. An interesting discovery was made during the experiment because of a trial with a dark filter overlaid on the glasses. This filter obfuscated the view of the real world and left only the view from the glasses' camera visible to the subject. This setup greatly helped him identify people and objects in the room due to the high contrast and luminosity of the live video shown on the display. Globally, the user's feedback was very positive and he reported that he would enjoy trying the prototype in everyday life conditions. To compensate for his severe visual impairment, this patient already uses various technologies (e.g. white cane, guide dog, closed-circuit TV, screen reader, handheld magnifier, etc.). He notably mentioned his major interest in having a single device solving most of his difficulties instead of carrying multiple devices with him, each solving a particular problem.

5   Conclusion

We developed a novel smart glasses application providing assistance for face and facial expressions of emotion and performed an evaluation in indoor conditions with three patients presenting with distinct pathologies impairing their vision.

During the interviews conducted after the trials, the patients' feedback were very positive, as they all reported they would like to use the prototype in everyday life conditions. One patient mentioned that the glasses were a bit uncomfortable and that he would not wear them during a whole day. The experiments and interviews clearly outlined the need to be able to tailor the feedbacks provided by the device to each patient's specific needs. The experiments also highlighted the current limitation of the application and the need to use more advanced algorithms and image processing heuristics to improve the robustness in the wild. In this study, we did not consider online cloud-based detection and recognition solutions, as we aim at providing an independent device that is always functional; indeed, network connectivity is often limited in numerous locations (underground locations, remote areas, etc.). A hybrid approach could however be considered in a future step as cloud-based solutions provide access to powerful algorithms by externalizing computations from the device.

In the future, we plan to further improve the system, notably by developing algorithms that are more robust to light conditions. We also plan on extending output and input feedback mechanisms by adding additional output modalities and by letting users inform the system of misdetections. False positives/negatives handling is indeed crucial for user acceptation of such devices. Such system could also be used for rehabilitation in some cases, as highlighted by the approach used in the first experiment. We will further investigate this axis in the next steps of the project by working in close collaborations with neurologists and clinical populations, assessing the effectiveness of the smart glasses through controlled experiments. In parallel, we are currently conducting a questionnaire survey with clinical populations to further investigate the needs according to the range of patients' disabilities. Our ultimate aim is to develop an effective visual prosthesis for the recognition of face identity and expressions of emotion. While the technology is still young and developing, we believe that in the long term smart glasses could have a similar game-changing effect on the visually impaired population, as the auditory prosthesis did since the 1970's.

References

1. Stevens, G.A., White, R.A., Flaxman, S.R., Price, H., Jonas, J.B., Keeffe, J., Leasher, J., Naidoo, K., Pesudovs, K., Resnikoff, S., Taylor, H., Bourne, R.R.A.: Global prevalence of vision impairment and blindness: magnitude and temporal trends, 1990-2010. Ophthalmology **120**, 2377–2384 (2013)
2. Spring, S.: Handicap visuel et cécité : évolution en suisse, pp. 5–22 (2012)
3. Sandnes, F.E.: What do low-vision users really want from smart glasses? Faces, text and perhaps no glasses at all. In: Miesenberger, K., Bühler, C., Penaz, P. (eds.) ICCHP 2016. LNCS, vol. 9758, pp. 187–194. Springer, Cham (2016). doi:10.1007/978-3-319-41264-1_25
4. Cimarolli, V.R., Boerner, K., Brennan-Ing, M., Reinhardt, J.P., Horowitz, A.: Challenges faced by older adults with vision loss: a qualitative study with implications for rehabilitation. Clin. Rehabil. **26**, 748–757 (2012)
5. Bulling, A., Kunze, K.: Eyewear computers for human-computer interaction. Interactions **23**, 70–73 (2016)
6. Jafri, R., Ali, S.A.: Exploring the potential of eyewear-based wearable display devices for use by the visually impaired. In: Proceedings - 2014 3rd International Conference User Science Engineering Experience Engineer Engage, i-USEr 2014, pp. 119–124 (2015)
7. Terven, J.R., Salas, J., Raducanu, B.: New opportunities for computer vision-based assistive technology systems for the visually impaired. Comput. (Long. Beach. Calif) **47**, 52–58 (2014)
8. Sujith, B., Safeeda, V.: Computer vision-based aid for the visually impaired persons - a survey and proposing. Int. J. Innov. Res. Comput. Commun. Eng. 365–370 (2014)
9. Jafri, R., Ali, S.A., Arabnia, H.R., Fatima, S.: Computer vision-based object recognition for the visually impaired in an indoors environment: a survey. Vis. Comput. **30**, 1197–1222 (2014)
10. Jafri, R.: A GPU-accelerated real-time contextual awareness application for the visually impaired on Google's project Tango device. J. Supercomput. **73**, 887–899 (2017)
11. Mandal, B., Chia, S.-C., Li, L., Chandrasekhar, V., Tan, C., Lim, J.-H.: A wearable face recognition system on Google glass for assisting social interactions. In: Jawahar, C.V., Shan, S. (eds.) ACCV 2014. LNCS, vol. 9010, pp. 419–433. Springer, Cham (2015). doi:10.1007/978-3-319-16634-6_31
12. Chia, S., Mandal, B., Xu, Q., Li, L., Lim, J.: Enhancing social interaction with seamless face recognition on Google glass. In: Proceedings of the 17th International Conference on Human-Computer Interaction with Mobile Devices and Services Adjunct - MobileHCI 2015, pp. 750–757. ACM Press, New York (2015)
13. Xu, Q., Chia, S.C., Mandal, B., Li, L., Lim, J.-H., Mukawa, M.A., Tan, C.: SocioGlass: social interaction assistance with face recognition on Google glass. Sci. Phone Apps Mob. Devices **2**, 7 (2016)
14. Hu, C., Zhai, G., Li, D.: An augmented-reality night vision enhancement application for see-through glasses. In: 2015 IEEE International Conference Multimedia Expo Work, ICMEW 2015 (2015)
15. Hwang, A.D., Peli, E.: An augmented-reality edge enhancement application for Google glass. Optom. Vis. Sci. **91**, 1021–1030 (2014)
16. Hicks, S.L., Wilson, I., Muhammed, L., Worsfold, J., Downes, S.M., Kennard, C.: A depth-based head-mounted visual display to aid navigation in partially sighted individuals. PLoS One **8**, e67695 (2013)
17. Oxsight: Oxsight company. http://smartspecs.co/

18. Krishna, S., Colbry, D., Black, J., Balasubramanian, V., Panchanathan, S.: A systematic requirements analysis and development of an assistive device to enhance the social interaction of people who are blind or visually impaired. In: Work Computer Vision Applications for Visually Impaired (2008)
19. Wagner, P.: Face recognition with opencv. OpenCV 2.4. 9.0 Doc (2012)
20. Mcduff, D.: AFFDEX SDK : a cross-platform real - time multi-face expression recognition toolkit. In: CHI Conference Extended Abstracts on Human Factors in Computing Systems, pp. 3723–3726 (2016)
21. Rossion, B.: A network of occipito-temporal face-sensitive areas besides the right middle fusiform gyrus is necessary for normal face processing. Brain **126**, 2381–2395 (2003)
22. Caldara, R., Schyns, P., Mayer, E., Smith, M.L., Gosselin, F., Rossion, B.: Does prosopagnosia take the eyes out of face representations? Evidence for a defect in representing diagnostic facial information following brain damage. J. Cogn. Neurosci. **17**, 1652–1666 (2005)
23. Fiset, D., Blais, C., Royer, J., Richoz, A.-R., Dugas, G., Caldara, R.: Mapping the impairment in decoding static facial expressions of emotion in prosopagnosia. Soc. Cogn. Affect. Neurosci. (2017). (in press)
24. Ruffieux, N., Ramon, M., Lao, J., Colombo, F., Stacchi, L., Borruat, F.-X., Accolla, E., Annoni, J.-M., Caldara, R.: Residual perception of biological motion in cortical blindness. Neuropsychologia **93**, 301–311 (2016)

Personalized Persuasion in Online Advertisements: A Case Study of a Micro-Funding Website

Suleman Shahid[1,2](✉), Nicole Heise[2], and Sundas Zaman[3]

[1] Department of Computer Science, SBA School of Science and Engineering,
Lahore University of Management Sciences, Lahore, Pakistan
suleman.shahid@lums.edu.pk
[2] Department of Communication and Information Sciences,
Tilburg Center for Cognition and Communication,
Tilburg University, Tilburg, The Netherlands
s.shahid@uvt.nl, nicole.heise@live.com
[3] Department of Computing,
Heriot Watt University, Dubai, United Arab Emirates
sz35@hw.ac.uk

Abstract. This study evaluates the effect of different persuasive communication principles in (online) communication on the attitude and purchasing behaviour of (prospective) customers. It also explores how (prospective) customers' personality effect the way they react to different implementations of persuasive principles. The research was conducted using an online questionnaire, and a non-profit micro funding website was used as a case study. Our results reveal that persuasive communication is more effective than the neutral communication, and it positively influences the behaviour of customers (prospective donators). Furthermore, we found a couple of personality traits that interact with several implementations of the persuasive principles.

Keywords: Online personalization · Persuasion · Web design · Micro funding · Advertisement · Online marketing

1 Introduction

Online personalization is a new phenomenon, applied to websites of organizations that want to offer tailored content and services to their (prospective) customers, based on the data gathered from their customers' interactions with different services [10]. The design of an interactive system, such as a website, should be based upon an understanding of the cognitive abilities of the website users [4]. In case of a typical ecommerce website, these users are actually the (prospective) customers of an organization and it is important to design an optimized user experience. For designing a satisfying online experience, it is not only important to pay attention to visual details and information architecture [7] but also to the relevancy of contents [5].

Recent research has shown that theory-driven and personality-targeted user interface design can be more effective than design applied to the whole population [9].

© IFIP International Federation for Information Processing 2017
Published by Springer International Publishing AG 2017. All Rights Reserved

R. Bernhaupt et al. (Eds.): INTERACT 2017, Part III, LNCS 10515, pp. 433–441, 2017.
DOI: 10.1007/978-3-319-67687-6_29

Moreover, it has been shown that personalized contents are more useful, make (prospective) customers more willing to explore the online contents further, reduce their information overload, and actually assist them in making decisions [11]. Recent studies on crowdfunding has also shown that language used in the crowdfunding project has surprising predictive power (accounting for 58.56% of the variance) around successful funding [8]. Organizations also use this form of personalized communication to achieve specific persuasive goals (e.g. using different customization strategies to satisfy information needs or increase attention). This personalized online communication intends to bring cognitive change in (prospective) customers [9], changing the mental state of a customer who learns something about the organization, its goals, its offers, and forms a particular attitude towards the organization. Mostly, these personalized (persuasive) communication messages are designed to produce a desirable impact on the customers' behaviour i.e. change their attitude and purchasing behaviour. The online communication (and use of persuasive messages) of an organization towards the (prospective) customer can be personalized based on what each one might be interested in, or is more sensitive to, in terms of promotion of products, services, and argumentation.

In this research, we evaluate the extent to which the personalized and persuasive communication is preferred over the neutral communication by (prospective) customers. We also explore how different implementations of the persuasive communication principles, as proposed by Cialdini [2], have a different effect on these customers. Cialdini found six persuasive communication principles for influencing and persuading that assist in decision-making: *reciprocity* (principle that assumes that people are inclined to return the favour to other people, even if unrequested, and compensate to equal proportions), *social proof* (principle that assumes that that people like to do or think like other people that are similar to them, especially when being uncertain), *commitment and consistency* (principle that assumes that people want to live in accordance with their words, attitudes and actions, especially in the eyes of other people, and will therefore do what they say they will do to avoid inconsistencies), and *sympathy* (principle that assumes that people will do things for other people that they like and think of as sympathetic). In this study, the principles *authority* and *scarcity* were not used since they did not seem to apply to the concept non-profit organizations and micro funding projects.

As suggested by many other researchers [5], persuasive principles can be implemented in various ways. This study attempts to compare different implementations of persuasive principles for finding out the effective and ineffective ones, in the context of a non-profit micro funding website. It is important to realize that all persuasive principles might not be suitable for all customers. As previously suggested by Ajzen [1], the individual differences of (prospective) customers such as personality traits influence their attitude and purchasing behaviour. Therefore, it is highly likely that different customers would appreciate different persuasive principles. This research evaluates whether the personality traits, based on the Big Five personality set [3], of (prospective) customers, influence the effectiveness of certain persuasive communication principles in terms of (purchasing) behaviour.

Unlike a number of previous studies where researchers focused on a typical ecommerce website, in this study, we focus on the website of a non-profit micro

funding organization named Kiva Microfunds. Kiva Microfunds is a non-profit organization that lends small amounts of money to different entrepreneurs all around the
world and practices mainly a neutral communication style. Micro funding websites for
a social cause are growing rapidly, and it is important to know how the visitors of such
non-profit websites react to persuasive communication.

2   Methodology

This research, as shown in Table 1, utilizes a subject design with five conditions. The
independent variables were (1) the 5 personality traits *extraversion, agreeableness,
conscientiousness, neuroticism* and *intellect/imagination* on which the respondent
scores low or high, (2) the 5 persuasive principles *reciprocity, social proof, commitment & consistency, sympathy*, and *neutral*, that might or might not influence the
respondent, and (3) the *attitude* and *behaviour* of the respondents towards the topic of
the online advertisement. The independent variables were (1) the type of project in the
online advertisement that is shown to the respondent and (2) the kind of implementation of the persuasive principle that is shown to the respondent.

Table 1. The design of the 5 groups and 25 online advertisements with different implementations of each persuasive principle.

Persuasive principles	Project 1 Cameroon	Project 2 Philippines	Project 3 Indonesia	Project 4 Pakistan	Project 5 Peru
Reciprocity	Ad 1	Ad 6	Ad 11	Ad 16	Ad 21
Social proof	Ad 2	Ad 7	Ad 12	Ad 17	Ad 22
Commitment & consistency	Ad 3	Ad 8	Ad 13	Ad 18	Ad 23
Sympathy	Ad 4	Ad 9	Ad 14	Ad 19	Ad 24
Neutral	Ad 5	Ad 10	Ad 15	Ad 20	Ad 25

To be able to investigate whether different implementations of the same persuasive
communication principles have an effect on the *attitude* and/or *purchasing behaviour*
of (prospective) customers, 5 different groups were created (for randomization) as
shown in Table 1. Respondents saw the same online advertisements of 5 different
micro funding projects, and each persuasive principle integrated in the online advertisements (including one neutral advertisement) in a randomized order. However, each
respondent saw different implementations of each persuasive principle.

2.1   Stimuli - Creating Online Advertisements

25 online advertisements were developed by a professional web designer, based on the
current template of the micro funding projects of Kiva Microfunds. Existing projects
(individual projects with clear description and goals) from 5 different countries and 5
different work fields were carefully selected. The layout and the content of the online

advertisement developed for this research remained very consistent and similar to the original online advertisements of Kiva Microfunds. Adaptations were made in order to exclude unnecessary influencing and persuading communication elements, other than the manipulated persuasive profiles (the confounding factors).

Persuasive principles were implemented in four different parts of the online advertisements, marked red in Fig. 1. Five implementations for each persuasive principle were designed, and after the manipulation check in a pilot, the best implementations were used in the final stimuli.

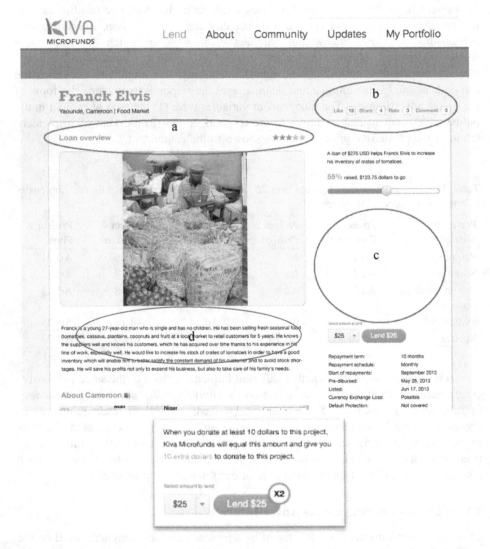

Fig. 1. Left to right, top to bottom. Top part of the online advertisement of a project from Kiva Microfunds (highlighting three areas where persuasive principles were added – areas a, b, d), bottom part of the advertisement, one of the most effective implementation (persuasive principle reciprocity) implemented in the area c. (Color figure online)

The implementations of the *reciprocity* advertisements contain persuasive communication where the respondent is receiving something back from the organization Kiva Microfunds e.g. a message like this "when you donate at least 10 dollars to this project, Kiva will equalize this amount and will give you 10 extra dollars to donate to this project" (Fig. 1 – area c), receive a gadget for free, get an incentive like a free gift card that can be used to get familiar with contributing.

The implementations of the *social proof* advertisements contain content that comes from contributors who rated or reviewed the project displayed in the advertisement e.g. Other evaluator/contributor has rated this project as 5 (Fig. 1 – area a), your Facebook friend has recommended a particular project (Fig. 1 – area b), this project is a popular one and has been viewed by other visitors many times.

The implementations of the *sympathy* advertisements contain contents that directly connect contributor with the person in the advertisement and the contributor feels that they both have something in common e.g. a very personal text aimed at the reader – instead of using the third person form i.e. Fredrick is from Cameron, use of the first person form i.e. I am Oranci, 32 years old women from Indonesia and I need your support in opening a grocery store (Fig. 1 – area d – implemented as a project description), seeing that a relative or good friend has already appreciated and contributed to the project or recommendation from other similar (to your profile) contributors.

The implementations of the *commitment & consistency* advertisements contain content where the visitor is shown a certain commitment that he/she has made to Kiva Microfunds e.g. showing a message that in past you have rated with project very high and shared it with 5 friends (Fig. 1 – area b), you have liked the project, placing a comment with a positive statement about the project and intention to contribute. The neutral advertisements contained information about the project according to the normal standards for an advertisement of Kiva Microfunds without integrated stimuli.

2.2 Procedure

An online questionnaire was conducted and it consisted of 4 different blocks:

(1) Questions about charity/donation habits of participants
(2) Introduction and personality questions (Big 5 personality traits)
(3) Random distribution to 1 of the 5 groups containing 5 online advertisements, where attitude and behaviour (the distribution of 100 dollars to minimum 2 micro funding projects) was measured, and
(4) Demographic and other information.

The questionnaire had a duration time of 10 to 20 min. Each of the 5 groups (created for the sake of randomization) saw the advertisements in a different order, based on the persuasive principle that was implemented. A respondent in group 1 saw advertisements 1, 7, 13, 19, and 25, a respondent in group 2 saw advertisements 6, 12, 18, 24, and 5, a respondent in group 3 saw advertisements 11, 17, 23, 4, and 10, a respondent in group 4 saw advertisements 16, 22, 3, 9, and 15, and a respondent in group 5 saw advertisements 21, 2, 8, 14, and 20. In total, 139 respondents (M = 65,

F = 74), recruited via the university pool, were used for analysis. We ignored all others participants who did not complete the survey.

Furthermore, only those participants who donated to a charity in past or were willing to do so in the near future were allowed to participate. Those who didn't meet this criteria (around 200 respondents) were immediately directed to the 'thank you' page. The respondents were randomly distributed and equally divided among these 5 groups, with 28 respondents in group 1, 29 respondents in group 2, 28 respondents in group 3, 27 respondents in group 4, and 27 respondents in group 5. A chi-square analysis showed that the demographics were equally divided between these groups (gender $(\chi^2(4) = 8.72$, p = .07), age $(\chi^2(20) = 22.98$, p=.29) and education $(\chi^2(16) = 18.13$, p = .32)).

3   Results

Firstly, we analysed the behaviour data (the distribution of the 100 dollars among the micro funding projects, for which we created variables per project and per persuasive principle). Then, we analysed personality data. Each respondent answered 4 questions per personality trait, indicating the extent to which they relate themselves to the statement on a 7-point Likert scale (1 meaning that they cannot relate, 7 meaning that they can relate). The mean scores of respondents on the personality traits were divided in low (lowest until 4.25) or high (4.26 through highest) categories. In this paper we will only report the results of the behaviour and personality analysis, the attitude results will be presented in another avenue.

In paired-samples, t-test with Bonferroni correction (adjusted alpha levels), the neutral online advertisements were found to have received significantly less contributions from the respondents as opposed to the advertisements that contained persuasive communication elements (*reciprocity* (t(138) = −4.40, p < .00), *social proof* (t (138) = 2.68,   p < .01),   *commitment and consistency*   (t(138) = −3.47,   p < .001), *sympathy* (t(138) = −2.88, p < .005)), as shown in Fig. 2 (the mean contributed amount of money, between 0–100 dollars, and the standard deviation). A two-way ANOVA with repeated measures was used to measure the 5 different persuasive principles for each of the groups to which respondents were assigned.

The persuasive principle *reciprocity* was overall found to be the most effective persuasive principle because it received the highest amount of contributed money. The integrated implementations for reciprocity that were found to be working most effectively (based on the amount of money received for particular advertisement) were both related to money: when respondents were said to 'receive a free gift card of 10 dollars' (M = 36.82, SD = 15.58) and when respondents were said to 'receive double amount of dollars for free to spend on the project' (M = 35.52, SD = 30.98).

The persuasive principle *commitment & consistency* was found to be the second most effective principle. The integrated implementations for *commitment & consistency* that were found to be working most effectively were: when respondents were shown that they (and a few others) have 'placed a comment' (M = 34.46, SD = 29.45) and 'liked a project' (M = 29.07, SD = 29.78). The persuasive principle *social proof* was found to be the third most effective principle. The implementation, 'positive evaluations

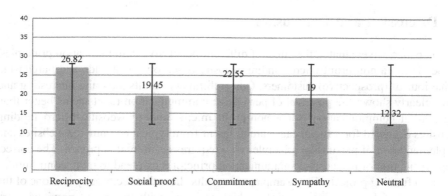

Fig. 2. Behaviour (M) of respondents from 0–100 dollars displayed per persuasive profile.

(comments)' and 'ratings (stars) by friends' was found to be the most effective integrated implementation (M = 28.62, SD = 29.46). The persuasive principle sympathy was the least effective one (still much better than the neutral). The most effective implementation was 'a good friend contributed to the project' (M = 23.93, SD = 21.49).

Additionally, a two-way ANOVA with repeated measures was conducted to measure the effect of personality traits on behaviour. We found two interesting results here. First, for the personality trait *conscientiousness*, the Levene's test showed a significant effect for the respondents who contributed to advertisements that contained the persuasive communication principle *reciprocity* (F(1,137) = 7.67, p < .01), as shown in Fig. 3a and second, for the personality trait *agreeableness*, the Levene's test showed a significant effect for the respondents who contributed to advertisements that contained the persuasive communication *social proof* (F(1,137) = 5.59, p < .05), as shown in Fig. 3b.

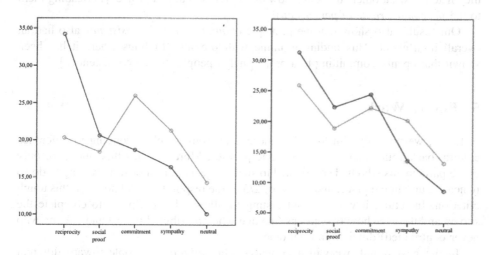

Fig. 3. a. (left) results of the personality trait conscientiousness (blue = low score, green = high score), effect per persuasive principle – b. (right) results of the personality trait agreeableness (blue = low score, green = high score), effect per persuasive principle (Color figure online)

4 Discussion and Conclusion

In this paper, we evaluated the effect of different persuasive communication principles, embedded in a non-profit micro funding website based on the attitude and purchasing behaviour of (prospective) customers. Our preliminary results are quite interesting and have clearly shown the potential of persuasive communication (as it seems better than the neutral communication) for a non-profit micro funding website. Micro funding websites designed for a social cause are different from typical ecommerce websites and implementation of persuasive principles also requires a different approach. The correct implementation of persuasive communication principles can lead to more contributions in micro funding projects. For example, our results show that reciprocity was one of the most successful persuasive principle, which is inline with the recent previous work where it has been shown that principle of Reciprocity is one of the top predictors of successful funding [8]. Our results also show an interesting interplay between personality traits and different persuasive principles. For example, the interaction between the personality trait *conscientiousness* and the persuasive principle *reciprocity* shows that customers with a high need for cognitive processing will go through the central route of persuasion [10], meaning that they will carefully look at the argumentation within the online advertisements and consider the best options on merit (as seen in Fig. 3) [2, 6].

In the case of reciprocity, either the receiver was getting extra benefits, or the contributor was getting something in return. We also found that people pay attention to different evidences that help them in establishing the merit of the project (whether the project is worth a contribution or not). They are mainly able do this by looking at evaluations and ratings given by other contributors, especially by the ones they know (*social proof*). This principle correlates with the personality trait *agreeableness*. This is understandable because people with this trait are sympathetic and good-natured and they listen to what others think and how others feel towards a project [1] (leading them to the *peripheral route of persuasion*).

Our results also show that the principle *commitment and consistency* also had an overall high effect. This finding is inline with previous findings where it has been shown that openly committing to a project helps people to stay consistent [2].

5 Future Work

In future, we not only aim to collect more data from people belonging to difference cultural backgrounds and socio-economic profiles. Moreover, for this study, we only chose participants who had contributed to such projects in past or were willing to do so in near future. In the first round of survey 2/3 of the respondents did not fulfil this tough criterion. In future, it would be interesting to allow all participants to complete the survey and then see how two groups (the one who contributed in past and the one who never contributed) differ from each other.

In the next round, we will also analyse the *attitude* of people toward different persuasive principles and projects. We will also examine the effectiveness of specific implementations of persuasive principles in detail. For example, in this study, mainly one implementation of *Sympathy principle* worked and the one that worked looked similar to the implementation of *social proof.*

References

1. Ajzen, I.: Attitudes, Personality, and Behavior. McGraw-Hill International, New York City (2005)
2. Cialdini, R.B.: Influence, 5th edn. Pearson, Boston (2009)
3. Donnellan, M.B., Oswald, F.L., Baird, B.M., Lucas, R.E.: The mini-IPIP scales: tiny-yet-effective measures of the big five factors of personality. Psychol. Assess. **18**, 192–203 (2006)
4. Esgate, A., Groome, D.: An Introduction to Applied Cognitive Psychology. Psychology Press, New York (2005)
5. Garrett, J.J.: Elements of User Experience, The: User-Centered Design for the Web and Beyond. Pearson Education, London (2010)
6. Kaptein, M., Eckles, D.: Selecting effective means to any end: futures and ethics of persuasion profiling. In: Ploug, T., Hasle, P., Oinas-Kukkonen, H. (eds.) PERSUASIVE 2010. LNCS, vol. 6137, pp. 82–93. Springer, Heidelberg (2010). doi:10.1007/978-3-642-13226-1_10
7. Kramer, J., Noronha, S., Vergo, J.: A user-centered design approach to personalization. Commun. ACM **43**(8), 44–48 (2000)
8. Mitra, T., Gilbert, E.: The language that gets people to give: phrases that predict success on kickstarter. In: The ACM Conference on Computer Supported Cooperative Work (CSCW) (2014)
9. Nov, O., Arazy, O., López, C., Brusilovsky, P.: Exploring personality-targeted UI design in online social participation systems. In: The ACM Conference on Human Factors in Computing Systems (CHI) (2013)
10. Pappas, I.O., Giannakos, M.N., Kourouthanassis, P.E., Chrissikopoulos, V.: Assessing emotions related to privacy and trust in personalized services. In: Douligeris, C., Polemi, N., Karantjias, A., Lamersdorf, W. (eds.) I3E 2013. IAICT, vol. 399, pp. 38–49. Springer, Heidelberg (2013). doi:10.1007/978-3-642-37437-1_4
11. Tam, K.Y., Ho, S.Y.: Web personalization as a persuasion strategy: an elaboration likelihood model perspective. Inf. Syst. Res. **16**(3), 271–291 (2005)

FIT Decision Aid: Matching the Needs of People with Dementia and Caregivers with Products and Services

Nazli Cila[1(✉)], Hester van Zuthem[2], Fleur Thomése[3], Wilma Otten[4], Franka Meiland[5], and Ben Kröse[1]

[1] Digital Life Centre, Amsterdam University of Applied Sciences, Amsterdam, The Netherlands
{n.cila,b.j.a.krose}@hva.nl
[2] Creative Care Lab, Waag Society, Amsterdam, The Netherlands
hester@waag.org
[3] Department of Sociology, Free University, Amsterdam, The Netherlands
gcf.thomese@vu.nl
[4] Expertise Group Child Health, TNO, Leiden, The Netherlands
wilma.otten@tno.nl
[5] Department of Psychiatry, VU University Medical Center, Amsterdam, The Netherlands
fj.meiland@vumc.nl

Abstract. Although there exist various product and services to support people with dementia in their everyday activities and challenges, people with dementia and their informal caregivers experience many unmet needs. In this paper, we present the ongoing development process of a decision aid that aims to reveal these unmet needs and match them with relevant support and care solutions. This entails investigating the needs of people with dementia and caregivers, making an inventory of the product and service solutions, co-creating the question articulation to be used in the decision aid and developing and testing three design concepts. We aim that the insights we gained from the tests will inspire interaction designers and researchers that investigate person-centered dementia care.

Keywords: Dementia · Decision aid · Designing for dementia · Care and wellbeing services · User testing

1 Introduction

Dementia is a syndrome with a set of symptoms linked to neuron death and vascular damage of white matter in the brain, which causes a progressive loss of cognitive functioning, memory, and ability to learn, reason and communicate [20]. Dementia, for which there currently exists no cure, gradually limits everyday activities and imposes a heavy physical, emotional and social burden for people living with dementia and their informal caregivers. Adequate and timely post-diagnostic support is important to care for people with dementia, prevent overburden of caregivers and premature admission of people with dementia to nursing homes, as this is very costly [16].

© IFIP International Federation for Information Processing 2017
Published by Springer International Publishing AG 2017. All Rights Reserved
R. Bernhaupt et al. (Eds.): INTERACT 2017, Part III, LNCS 10515, pp. 442–452, 2017.
DOI: 10.1007/978-3-319-67687-6_30

This post-diagnostic support increasingly exists of assistive technologies, which may enable more personalized support, attuned to the heterogeneous and changing needs of people with dementia and their caregivers, more comfort in use and also more efficient, time and money saving support [17]. Such technologies support coping with the symptoms of dementia, maintaining autonomy and independence, reducing care burden and risk of harm, and improving quality of life [3, 10, 15, 22]. A wide range of devices enters this description, from simple low-tech products such as pill dispensers to high-tech products such as care robots and autonomous fall detection systems. Yet, research and practice show that not all the needs of people with dementia are met despite the solutions in the market and care services offered [1, 18, 19]. People with dementia and their caregivers frequently report that they receive insufficient support in memory, eyesight and hearing problems, finances, transport, information about dementia and available care, finding social company and daytime activities, coping with distress, and preventing accidental self-harm [27, 28]. However, a lack of services or technologies to assist them in these needs may not be the main problem. A gap analysis in the Netherlands, for example, showed that for these unmet needs various types of services are available [7], but people with dementia and their caregivers seem to have difficulty in accessing products and services that can support them. Reasons are that they are not aware of the availability of the relevant services [6, 27], do not know where to go for help [4], or think that taking up the service would not be helpful [32]. Furthermore, the uptake of the support solutions is also low because the information provided about the support is unclear [27] and services are insufficiently attuned to individual needs or situations [14, 15, 17, 27, 28].

There is a clear need for a means that can help people with dementia and caregivers to find out the available relevant support. In the project FIT, we develop a digital decision aid that helps clarifying the specific personal and contextual needs of people with dementia and their caregivers, and offers flexible and personalized advice about available assistive technologies and care services that can alleviate unmet needs. FIT is collaboration between two design research institutes, three research institutes in healthcare, three care organizations, and an SME in the Netherlands, and has three living labs where the decision aid is being tested. We envision that the FIT decision aid (from now on FIT) will support the independent living of people with dementia and increase their and their carers' quality of life with the well-fitting solutions offered.

Decision aids in the health domain are interventions designed to help people make well-informed and deliberative choices among options by providing information about the options and outcomes relevant to a person's health status [23]. Similar online tools were developed for dementia care, such as DEM-DISC [26, 29] or the Decide Guide [21, 22], however more research is needed to create a tool that offers a better clarification of individual demands [26], reveals needs that could be latent or not well-articulated, and is pleasant to use and interact with by people with dementia, caregivers, and care professionals. This is what we aim in FIT.

In this paper, we briefly present the concept development of FIT and insights we gained from the pilot tests conducted with users. We identified some tips to be taken into consideration when developing a decision aid for dementia, and hope our approach will add onto the knowledge on designing for person-centered healthcare in the HCI field.

2 Developing the FIT Decision Aid

The primary users of FIT are the informal caregivers and care professionals, such as general practitioners, case managers or social care providers. Informal caregivers can use FIT together with the person with dementia as a communication tool to investigate needs, or use it by themselves as a tool to find solutions for problematic situations they encounter. People with dementia and caregivers are most likely to learn about possible solutions from their GP's or case managers [15]. In order to inform their clients well, care professionals should be up-to-date about the current developments in assistive technologies and services. FIT can help care professionals to get informed and transfer this knowledge to their clients.

When it comes to people with dementia, we considered them to be the secondary users of FIT. If they are in the early stage of the disease and still cognitively able to use FIT, they may not associate the tool with themselves since it is common to deny having dementia or acknowledging the need of help in early stages [24]. If they acknowledge having dementia and needing help, they may not be able to use FIT anymore. For these reasons, people with dementia were not targeted as autonomous users of FIT. However, we aimed to design FIT to be accessible and inviting for them so that caregivers and care professionals can use it together with them.

The needs and motivations of people with dementia and their caregivers change continuously with the progress of the disease and contextual circumstances. Therefore, we envisioned FIT to be used frequently in the course of the disease. We also aimed for a mobile website that could work in a tablet as well as on a computer so that the care professionals can bring it easily to their home visits.

The development of FIT involved four main overlapping activities: (1) investigating the needs, (2) co-creating the conceptual structure and content of the decision aid, (3) making a comprehensive inventory of the product and service solutions, and (4) generating prototypes. For the first activity, we conducted interviews in the homes with eight people with dementia and their caregivers and two focus groups with 4 people with dementia and 4 informal caregivers separately. These studies helped us extract 10 main need categories that people with dementia and their caregivers experience—daily activities, mental wellbeing, physical health, pleasurable activities, social contact, care relations, information, finances, household, and safety—and gave insight into the attitudes of our user group toward looking for help and support regarding their needs [30]. We distinguished three user groups: (1) people who are not aware that they experience a problem or have unmet needs, (2) people who are aware of their unmet needs but never realized that there are solutions to alleviate these, and (3) people who are aware of their unmet needs and heard of a potential solution, but they do not know which specific solution they want and how to access to it.

We created a conceptual structure intended to accommodate all these user groups in FIT (2nd activity). The structure starts from a higher "need" level, proceeds by asking questions to specify a "goal" to fulfil that need, and ends by finding the "product category" that can realize that goal (Fig. 1). Needs are implicitly felt states of deprivation [27], for example the need of social contact. A goal is a concrete way to fulfill a need, for example "I would like to have someone to talk to" or "I would like to find

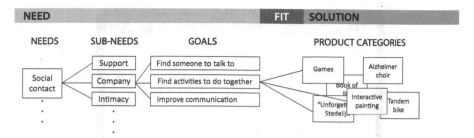

Fig. 1. Conceptual structure of FIT with the social contact need as an example

some activities to do with my loved one". Product category is the type of care and support solutions that can realize those goals, for example playing games (e.g., puzzles, memory games, ball games special for people with dementia) or going to the Alzheimer choir together.

If the users are not aware of their needs, they can start exploring from the need level. This is done by showing our 10 need categories that enable users to select the one they would like to learn more about. Users are then guided via a tree structure of questions to a specific goal they would like to accomplish. This is also the level in which users who are aware of the problems they experience, but not of the solutions, could enter the decision aid. The current understanding of care is not treating illness and its limiting consequences, but on coping with the demands of illness to participate and preserve the good things in life [8]. For this reason, we formulated the goals not in terms of problems, but as "topics of improvement" and "aspects of wellbeing".

The list of goals per need was compiled via multiple co-creation sessions. Four sessions were conducted among the authors of this paper in order to create an initial long-list based on the dementia-needs literature and the topics in the intake forms of various care institutions in the Netherlands. Afterwards, two sessions were conducted with two nurses that experience the everyday life of people with dementia at first hand in order to examine which activities and goals are relevant for the dementia context and which activities and goals are missing. For example, the nurses indicated that the eating and drinking sub-need should have sub-categories such as hand-mouth coordination, chewing, and swallowing since people with dementia may have specific needs regarding one of these issues. This list was shared with all the project partners from academy and practice with care research, nursing, and design backgrounds; each partner contributed to finalizing the list by restructuring categories, taking out doubles, filling gaps, and re-labeling terms from their own area of expertise.

After the users select the goal they would like to achieve, FIT gives advice on care and support that may realize this goal. These could be products (e.g., puzzles, tandem bike), care and welfare services (e.g., meeting events, telephone helplines, respite care), and websites or apps (e.g., Dementia app, the Netherlands Alzheimer Association website). FIT provides information about how this solution can help, examples of available products, where to buy/get it from (information on reimbursement by National Health Service packages or healthcare funds, and links to external sellers). The users, who know what they need but do not know which specific product and where to get it, can enter FIT from this level.

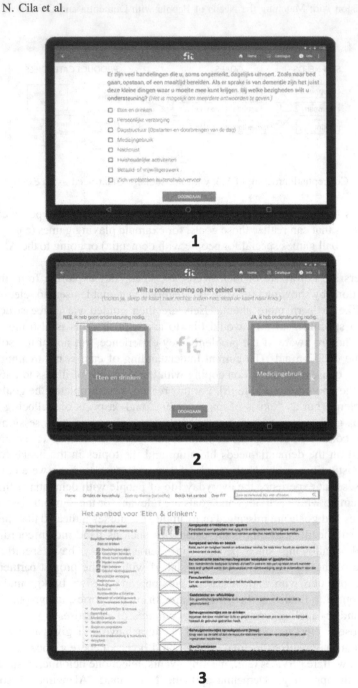

Fig. 2. Creation of three concepts of the decision aid (1: Linear, 2: Card game, 3: Website)

Information about products and services was obtained as the third activity in the development through a comprehensive inventory of current products and care services in the Netherlands [2]. We gathered 1100 unique products and services that are intended for people with dementia or elderly in general. These products and services were matched to specific goals they can realize through two sessions between project partners. In these sessions we included two experts—one owned a web shop that sells products for dementia care and the other created a platform for finding dementia care services in the Amsterdam region—in order to get an in-depth understanding of the benefit and potential of the products and services. For example, we categorized V-shaped or Batwing pillows as products for comfortable sitting, but the web shop owner pointed out that these products are also helpful for the goals of falling asleep, calming down, or increasing the feeling of safety. The majority of the product and service solutions in the decision aid realize multiple goals.

After setting up the conceptual structure of FIT, we created three distinct medium-fidelity concepts (4th activity) to turn the structure into a digital decision aid that users can interact with (Fig. 2). In the creation of these concepts we considered different design aspects regarding navigation, playfulness, and familiarity. The first concept offered a linear way of proceeding through the structure, like an online questionnaire wherein needs, sub-needs, and goals are presented in separate screens and the users choose the options that apply with ticking checkboxes. The second concept was designed as a card game in which the users were asked to drag the cards representing needs, sub-needs and goals into two piles representing "need support" and "don't need support". The last concept had a standard web shop look and feel, in which the solutions could be explored by using the goals as filters at the right side.

3 Testing the FIT Decision Aid

The three concepts were tested with 3 informal caregivers in individual sessions (two daughters and a wife) and 13 care professionals (1 male nurse +8 female nurses +4 female case managers) divided in three focus groups with 4, 6, and 3 participants. Informal caregivers were recruited through the network of the care institutions in the project consortium. Nurses and case managers worked at one of these three partici-pating institutions. The aim of the sessions was gaining insights about the usefulness and usability of the concepts from the potentially varying perspectives of informal caregivers and care professionals. The care professionals also discussed how to inte-grate the decision aid into their standard workload and procedures.

The sessions were conducted at the workplaces of the participants. We started by explaining the project and the aim of the session. Each concept was displayed in a separate tablet and the tablets were given to the participants one-by-one in a random order. All the main functions of the three decision aids were interactive, but we used the actual content for only two need categories in all concepts (i.e., daily activities and care relations) and for the rest we displayed dummy content and image placeholders. The participants were asked to explore each concept and while doing so think-out-loud about plus and minus aspects for each (the care professionals were asked to pair up when exploring the concepts). After the exploration phase, the participants were asked to present their comments and preferences. The discussions were guided with questions regarding the usefulness and usability of each concept and improvements therein.

Starting with the evaluations about the usefulness of the concepts, the participants were very positive about the potential of a decision aid to support fulfilling unmet needs. Especially its "educative dimension", i.e., giving a comprehensive overview of all the possible needs as well as relevant solutions, was appreciated by all of the participants, irrespective of being an informal caregiver or a professional. As one of the nurses stated, "it is also an aid for us, not just for the client"; the decision aid seemed to attain its aim to provide up-to-date information about product and service solutions that are relevant.

Regarding the Linear concept—which is initiated by choosing from 10 main need categories—one of the informal caregivers stated, "It is very good to see all the needs together. There are issues you do not experience right now, but in the future you can encounter them. So you can prepare yourself". Three of the nurses were also specifically positive about this dimension of the Linear concept, as it can be a communication tool to use when talking with the informal caregivers and people with dementia. According to their experience, some of the informal caregivers are unreceptive and unwilling to communicate when it comes to the needs of their loved ones with dementia. This tool would be a means to make problems visible, help focus the conversation, and make the discussion more in depth and to-the-point with the immediate solutions offered. These nurses suggested the decision aid to be a standard part of their intake procedure for home care and also reuse it every 3 to 6 months together with the person with dementia and informal caregiver.

The Card game concept was appreciated for its interactivity and playfulness, but was also considered time consuming. Informal caregivers and care professionals mentioned that they already have enough responsibilities to take care of, so they would prefer the straightforwardness and the overview provided by the other two concepts. However, almost all of the participants considered this concept to be the best fitting option if people with dementia would use the decision aid by themselves. We designed the card game in a way that all the sub-needs and goals are presented as a deck of cards and the users sort the card at the top in one of the two categories without knowing which card will be next. In this way users are forced to think about only one issue at a time and decide if they need support or not for that issue only. Therefore this interaction reduced the memory load of the users, which was also pointed out by all of our participants. However, playing this card game with people with dementia was considered to be burdensome by care professionals and informal caregivers due to their other urgent requirements.

The website concept was mainly appreciated by some of the care professionals, as they could immediately get a long list of product and service solutions and filter among the solutions according to the goals that are relevant. However, this way of interaction was seen as complex by all the informal caregivers and majority of the care professionals.

When it comes to the usability of the concepts, we gained valuable insights regarding the navigation, visual style, and language of the prototypes. We will shortly summarize these below, together with providing some design tips for the design researchers who are investigating similar challenges as ours. Both for informal caregivers and care professionals, the concept Linear was a clear winner in usability. The main reason was that it gave a good overview of all the needs, the hierarchical structure between needs, sub-needs, and goals were clear, and the users would always know where they were in this structure. The ticking checkboxes way of proceeding was also familiar to all of the participants, so they intuitively knew how to use the decision aid. Sorting cards and filtering out from a long list was considered to be burdensome and counterintuitive, respectively *(Tip 1: "Provide the users a clear overview of the content and an indication of where they are in the system at all times")*.

In the design of all the concepts, we allowed the multiple-selection of sub-needs and goals. However, this option caused the users to end up with rather long lists in the follow-up screen. For example, if they selected "eating & drinking", "day structure" and "mobility" as sub-needs under the daily activities main need category; they would end up with a list of 15 goals to choose from. This was considered to be an overwhelming amount of information to process. Also scrolling in this list was considered a problem. Surprisingly, almost all of the participants said they would prefer more screens than having to scroll down in one screen, so that all the information comes in blocks of one screen's worth. Scrolling is considered a usability problem when designing websites for people with dementia [5, 11]. Although our users were not suffering from dementia, they also had similar problems when interacting with the prototypes *(Tip 2: "Minimize choice and complexity, too many options overwhelm the users"* and *Tip 3: "Avoid forcing users to scroll")*.

When designing the visual elements of the prototypes, we paid attention to color use and contrast, and aimed to provide a "calm" look by positioning the items on a white background and having blank spaces around them. All the participants mentioned that they found the appearances of the screens appealing and clean. The participants found the big images we used in the card game concept attractive and suggested us to apply the same approach in the other prototypes as well. Furthermore, some of the older nurses found the 10-font text we used in some screens too small *(Tip 4: "Use high contrast and pay attention to white spaces"* and *Tip 5: "Use big images and large text sizes")*.

Lastly in the language used in the prototypes, we aimed for an empathetic and descriptive tone, e.g., "There are many activities we perform on a daily basis, such as going to bed, getting dressed or preparing food. In the case of dementia, these could be the things to experience difficulties in. With which activities below would you need support?" Although all the participants appreciated the tone of voice, such explanations were sometimes found too wordy. Especially the care professionals stated to prefer short and direct language. Furthermore, some terms such as respite care, mouth-hand coordination, and daily structure were not clear for the informal caregivers *(Tip 6: "Use empathetic and respectful, but short and direct language"* and *Tip 7: "Avoid jargon and technical terms")*.

4 Conclusions

The initial results of this pilot study indicate that the FIT decision aid meets the needs of the informal caregivers and care professionals to get tailored information about products, services and support that can reveal and fulfill unmet needs of people with dementia. The prototypes were perceived as useful and generally user-friendly aids to support them in their caregiving responsibilities. Our findings contribute further to the usability and design requirements that are being developed for people with dementia and their formal and informal caregivers. Our special contribution lies in designing in a flexible way, to accommodate different user groups, and for the decision aid to be usable in different stages of dementia. Underlying these prototypes we also created a comprehensive inventory of needs and goals of people with dementia and informal caregivers, as well as product categories that may meet these needs. We consider this conceptual structure and content of FIT especially applicable for the wider HCI community working in relation to dementia.

The results of this pilot study will be used in the further development of FIT to become a tool to be recommended and used by care professionals in various healthcare institutions in the Netherlands. We are aware that the technological development will constantly add new treatments, tools and systems for supporting dementia. One of the long-term aims of our project is to create a sustainable business model that can keep up with and include such developments in the tool. Further research will focus on (1) building up on the user-friendliness of the Linear concept, (2) implementation of FIT into existing healthcare infrastructures and tackling related issues such as keeping the information on products and services up-to-date, and (3) long-term effect of using FIT on increasing the quality of life of people with dementia and their informal caregivers. In the long run, a decision aid like we developed for dementia care could be developed for people with other chronic diseases such as Parkinson's disease, Multiple Sclerosis, or Rheumatoid Arthritis, since these patients face similar problems in unmet needs and lack of support in the course of their disease.

With the changing description of "health" from the absence of diseases to a capacity to maintain one's integrity, equilibrium and wellbeing [12], the idea of "social health" is gaining importance to help people in the capacity to fulfill potential, managing life with some degree of independence, and participation in social activities [9]. Additionally, the emergence of perspectives on personhood in HCI have invoked recent attempts to consider changes in patient care and involving patients and caregivers in design processes [31]. Dementia care, like any other aspect of care, requires a holistic, person-centered approach that deploys people's strengths rather than focusing on cognitive deficits [13]. This is our long-term aim in FIT as well.

Acknowledgements. We would like to express our deepest gratitude to the nurses, case managers, and informal caregivers who volunteered to take part in this study; and Marieke Janssen, Jacqueline Rempt, Jolanda van Kaam-Winter, and the rest of the FIT consortium for their contribution in making the "fit" between needs and support. This project is funded by the Netherlands Organisation for Health Research and Development (ZonMw) and supported by AUAS program Urban Vitality.

References

1. Alzheimer's Australia: Consumer Engagement in the Aged Care Reform Process (2011). https://fightdementia.org.au/sites/default/files/20120410_ConsumerEngagementAgedCare ReformProcess.REPORT.pdf
2. Bosch, L., Janssen, M., Wildevuur, S.E.: Producten en Diensten ter Ondersteuning van Thuis Wonen met Dementie (2016). https://waag.org/sites/waag/files/public/media/publicaties/fit-producten-diensten.pdf. Accessed 11 Apr 2017
3. Cahill, S., Macijauskiene, J., Nygård, A.-M., Faulkner, J.-P., Hagen, I.: Technology in dementia care. Technol. Disabil. **19**, 55–60 (2007)
4. Coe, M., Neufeld, A.: Male caregivers' use of formal support. West. J. Nurs. Res. **21**, 568–588 (1999)
5. Deep Guide: Creating websites for people with dementia (2013). http://dementiavoices.org. uk/wp-content/uploads/2013/11/DEEP-Guide-Creating-websites.pdf
6. Donath, C., Winkler, A., Graessel, E., Luttenberger, K.: Day care for dementia patients from a family caregiver's point of view: a questionnaire study on expected quality and predictors of utilisation - part II. BMC. Health Serv. Res. **11**, 76 (2011)
7. Dröes, R.M., Meiland, F.J.M., van der Roest, H.G., Maroccini, R., Slagter, R.S., Baida, Z., Haaker, T., Kartseva, V., Hulstijn, J., Schmieman, R., Akkermans, H., Faber, E., Tan, Y.H.: Opportunities for we-centric service bundling in dementia care. Project Freeband/FRUX Health Care Pilot Report, Amsterdam (2005)
8. Dröes, R.M., Boelens-Van Der Knoop, E.C., Bos, J., Meihuizen, L., Ettema, T.P., Gerritsen, D.L., Hoogeveen, F., De Lange, J., SchöLzel-Dorenbos, C.J.: Quality of life in dementia in perspective: an explorative study of variations in opinions among people with dementia and their professional caregivers, and in literature. Dementia **5**(4), 533–558 (2006)
9. Dröes, R.M., Chattat, R., Diaz, A., Gove, D., Graff, M., Murphy, K., Verbeek, H., Vernooij Dassen, M., Clare, L., Johannessen, A., Roes, M.: Social health and dementia: a european consensus on the operationalization of the concept and directions for research and practice. Aging Ment. Health **21**(1), 4–17 (2017)
10. Fleming, R., Sum, S.: Empirical studies on the effectiveness of assistive technology in the care of people with dementia: a systematic review. J. Assist. Tech. **8**(1), 14–34 (2014)
11. Freeman, E.D., Clare, L., Savitch, N., Royan, L., Litherland, R., Lindsay, M.: Improving website accessibility for people with early-stage dementia: a preliminary investigation. Aging Ment. Health **9**(5), 442–448 (2005)
12. Huber, M., Knottnerus, J.A., Green, L., van der Horst, H., Jadad, A.R., Kromhout, D., Leonard, B., Lorig, K., Loureiro, M.I., van der Meer, J.W., Schnabel, P.: How should we define health? BMJ **343** (2011)
13. Kitwood, T.M.: Dementia Reconsidered: The Person Comes First. Oxford University Press, Oxford (1997)
14. Koffman, J., Taylor, S.: The needs of caregivers. Elder Care **9**, 16–19 (1997)
15. Lauriks, S., Reinersmann, A., Van der Roest, H.G., Meiland, F.J.M., Davies, R.J., Moelaert, F., Dröes, R.M.: Review of ICT-based services for identified unmet needs in people with dementia. Ageing Res. Rev. **6**(3), 223–246 (2007)
16. Macdonald, A., Cooper, B.: Long-term care and dementia services: an impending crisis. Age Ageing **36**, 16–22 (2007)
17. Meiland, F.J.M., Innes, A., Mountain, G., et al.: Technologies to support community-dwelling persons with dementia: a position paper on issues regarding development, usability, effectiveness and cost-effectiveness, deployment, and ethics. JMIR Rehabil. Assist. Technol. **4**(1), e1 (2017)

18. Meiland, F.J., Bouman, A.I., Sävenstedt, S., Bentvelzen, S., Davies, R.J., Mulvenna, M.D., Dröes, R.D.: Usability of a new electronic assistive device for community-dwelling persons with mild dementia. Aging Ment. Health **16**(5), 584–591 (2012)

19. Miranda-Castillo, C., Woods, B., Orrell, M.: The needs of people with dementia living at home from user, caregiver and professional perspectives: a cross-sectional survey. BMC Health Serv. Res. **13**, 43 (2013)

20. Prince, M., Bryce, R., Albanese, E., Wimo, A., Ribeiro, W., Ferri, C.P.: The global prevalence of dementia: a systematic review and meta-analysis. Alzheimer's Dement. **9**(1), 63–75 (2013)

21. Span, M., Smits, C., Groen-van de Ven, L.M., Cremers, A., Jukema, J., Vernooij-Dassen, M., Hettinga, M.: Towards an interactive web tool that supports shared decision making in dementia: identifying user requirements. Int. J. Adv. Life Sci. **6**(3&4), 338–349 (2014)

22. Span, M., Smits, C., Groen-van de Ven, L.M., Cremers, A., Jukema, J., Vernooij-Dassen, M., Hettinga, M.: An interactive web tool to facilitate shared decision making in dementia: design issues perceived by caregivers and patients. Int. J. Adv. Life Sci. **6**(3&4), 107–121 (2014)

23. Stacey, D., Légaré, F., Col, N.F., Bennett, C.L., Barry, M.J., Eden, K.B., Holmes-Rovner, M., Llewellyn-Thomas, H., Lyddiatt, A., Thomson, R., Trevena, L., Wu, J.H.C.: Decision aids for people facing health treatment or screening decisions. Cochrane Database Syst. Rev. (1), Article no.: CD001431 (2014)

24. Steeman, E., Casterlé, D., Dierckx, B., Godderis, J., Grypdonck, M.: Living with early-stage dementia: a review of qualitative studies. J. Adv. Nurs. **54**(6), 722–738 (2006)

25. Topo, P.: Technology studies to meet the needs of people with dementia and their caregivers: a literature review. J. Appl. Gerontol. **28**(1), 5–37 (2009)

26. van der Roest, H.G., Meiland, F.J., Jonker, C., Dröes, R.M.: User evaluation of the DEMentia-specific digital interactive social chart (DEM-DISC): a pilot study among informal carers on its impact, user friendliness and usefulness. Aging Ment. Health **14**, 461–470 (2010)

27. van der Roest, H.G., Meiland, F.J.M., Comijs, H.C., Derksen, E., Jansen, A.P.D., van Hout, H.P.J., Dröes, R.M.: What do community-dwelling people with dementia need? A survey of those who are known to care and welfare services. Int. Psychogeriatr. **21**, 949–965 (2009)

28. van der Roest, H.G., Meiland, F.J.M., Maroccini, R., Comijs, H.C., Jonker, C., Dröes, R.M.: Subjective needs of people with dementia: a review of the literature. Int. Psychogeriatr. **19**, 559–592 (2007)

29. van Mierlo, L.D., Meiland, F.J., Van de Ven, P.M., Van Hout, H.P., Dröes, R.M.: Evaluation of DEM-DISC, customized e-advice on health and social support services for informal carers and case managers of people with dementia; a cluster randomized trial. Int. Psychogeriatr. **27** (08), 1365–1378 (2015)

30. van Zuthem, H., Wildevuur, S.E., Bosch, L., Janssen, M., Meiland, F.: De mens zien bij dementie (2016). https://www.waag.org/sites/waag/files/public/media/publicaties/de-mens-zien-dementie-def.pdf. Accessed 11 Jan 2017

31. Wallace, J., Wright, P.C., McCarthy, J., Green, D.P., Thomas, J., Olivier, P.: A design-led inquiry into personhood in dementia. In: Proceedings of the SIGCHI Conference on Human Factors in Computing Systems, pp. 2617–2626 (2013)

32. Winslow, B.W.: Family caregivers' experiences with community services: a qualitative analysis. Public Health Nurs. **20**, 341–348 (2003)

Perswedo: Introducing Persuasive Principles into the Creative Design Process Through a Design Card-Set

Xipei Ren[1(✉)], Yuan Lu[1], Harri Oinas-Kukkonen[2],
and Aarnout Brombacher[1]

[1] Department of Industrial Design, Eindhoven University of Technology,
Eindhoven, The Netherlands
{x.ren,y.lu,a.c.brombacher}@tue.nl
[2] Department of Information Processing Science,
University of Oulu, Oulu, Finland
harri.oinas-kukkonen@oulu.fi

Abstract. In human-computer interaction (HCI), advances of information and communication technology have led to a wealth of Persuasive Technology (PT) researches to support people's behaviors change. Many PT theories have been widely used for design analysis and are supposed to be useful for PT design. However, very limited effort has been taken to bridge the gap between PT theory and design practice. In this paper, we present the formative study of Perswedo, a card-based tool that introduces persuasive principles from Persuasive Systems Design model to support the creative design flow. As an intermediate step to appropriate Perswedo cards to the design activities, we assessed the usefulness and value of Perswedo in the design process as well as the design implications of the cards through three design workshops. Our findings suggest further study to resonate PT theoretical work with design practice.

Keywords: Persuasive principles · Card-based tool · Creative design process

1 Introduction

Persuasive Technology (PT), the study about computing technology designed to change people's attitudes and behaviors [1], has been seen great benefits in many application areas such as health [2] and sustainability [3]. Many PT researches have drawn much attention on theoretical works (e.g. [4, 5]). Amongst those Persuasive Systems Design (PSD) model [6] was developed to support the design of persuasive information systems. In PSD, it highlights the design process with detailed analysis of persuasion context. Furthermore, PSD contains four categories of 28 persuasive principles (seven principles in each category), which by default can inform the design process of persuasive systems [7]. According to Consolvo *et al.* [5], the enclosure of theoretical framework in technology support everyday behavior change.

Given the growing ubiquity of information systems [8] and the complexity of design practice [9], however, the single use of PSD model in the design process has been

© IFIP International Federation for Information Processing 2017
Published by Springer International Publishing AG 2017. All Rights Reserved
R. Bernhaupt et al. (Eds.): INTERACT 2017, Part III, LNCS 10515, pp. 453–462, 2017.
DOI: 10.1007/978-3-319-67687-6_31

criticized for implementing design strategies without the appropriation for the real-life context [10]. Let it alone, the simply use of theoretical knowledge, as Hornecker [11] said, tends to be *tedious* and *overweight* in design process. It is acknowledged that the gap between theoretical framework and design exercise has been a long-existing issue for PT research [12]. To close the gap, according to Stolterman [9], the use of a new theory has to resonate with the existing design practice.

This requirement led to a rich amount of focus on turning design framework into design tools to support the creative design activities, ranging from a screen-based application to specify the placement of interface elements [13] to a card deck to inform design concepts [14]. Here, we particularly observe that as a lightweight tool bringing information into the design flow, card-sets have been complimented to be more affordable in the creative process than other means of tools [11]. Bekker and Antle [15] suggested cards as a tool for designers to use both for accessing knowledge and for supporting the existing way they work in design practice. Therefore, we employed a similar approach to examine **if the transformation of persuasive principles into card-based design tools could be useful and valuable for the creative design process of interactive technology.**

In this paper, we present a formative study of Perswedo, a card-format design tool that derives from PSD model. The paper proceeds as follows. Next section we explain in detail how we designed Perswedo, which is followed by the setup of our evaluation in Sect. 3. This results in the analysis on the usefulness, value, and implications of our current design in Sect. 4. Conclusions are given in the end.

2   Perswedo Cards

2.1   Persuasive Principles from PSD

PT is described as "*any interactive computing system designed to change people's attitudes or behaviors*" [16]. Based on Fogg's work [1], Oinas-Kukkonen and Harjumaa [6] conceptualized the PSD model. The model puts emphasis on detailed and rigorous analysis of the persuasion context from figuring out the intended types of behavior change, to identifying the events of use and users of technologies, to developing the strategies and delivery route to the target users. Moreover, PSD established four categories of persuasive principles (partly derived from Fogg's theory [1]), namely: primary task, system credibility, dialogue and social support. Primary task support typically simplifies or facilitates certain activities; System credibility support aims to influence user through increasing system credibility in various manners. Dialogue support enhances user-computer communications to keep users moving towards target behavior. Social support leverages user's motivation with the help of social factors. In this study, our scope was to introduce PT knowledge into the design of interactive technology. We exclusively selected the categories of dialogue support and social support to develop the card-set, as they are the features that mostly relevant to technology-mediated interaction design [7] and have been widely applied in diverse design topics, such as games [17]. The principles that are addressed by our initial card-set are:

- **Dialogue support:** praise, similarity, reward, liking, reminder, social role, suggestion.
- **Social support:** social facilitation, recognition, social learning, cooperation, competition, social comparison, normative influence.

2.2 Turning Principles into Perswedo Cards

This study aimed to design Perswedo cards as a domain specific carrier [18] bringing PT design principles into design processes. For this purpose, we firstly explored how to convert the knowledge from PSD into the information on the cards. Based on the literature review and the interview with eight design researchers, we designed Perswedo cards (Fig. 1, available from goo.gl/H7JblW) with the following focuses:

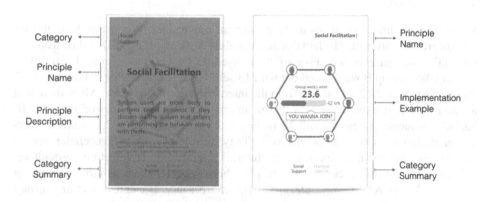

Fig. 1. A Perswedo card from social support category

- **General Contents:** The same as most of the cards [11, 15, 19–21], each Perswedo card includes both text of the principle to provide adequate information [19], and illustration of the example to allow an open interpretation [15];
- **Text:** The description of each principle was displayed directly on the front side of the card, as it clearly explains the principle in one simple sentence [6]. This was also confirmed during our interviews;
- **Illustration:** On the back side of the cards, advised by [15], we designed all the illustrations on the basis of people's everyday technology-mediated physical activity referring to the example requirement from PSD [22]. Two design researchers checked the consistency between example illustrations and principle descriptions on every individual Perswedo card for us.
- **Categorization:** Similar to previous works [11, 15, 19, 20], Perswedo cards were color-coded by different categories. The green color was selected for seven dialogue support cards and yellow color was selected for seven social support cards. Moreover, the name of the current principle and the host category were also placed properly on each card to support designers to distinguish cards without too much effort.

- **Format:** We made each card approximately 3.0" by 4.4" in size to be flexible enough in various design activities. Furthermore, Perswedo cards were printed on PVC, which makes the cards easy to clean and more durable to use.

3 Evaluation

We introduced Perswedo cards in three design workshops to: (I) Examine if current Perswedo Cards are useful in supporting the creative design process; (II) Understand what kind of values can Perswedo cards offer in the design flow; (III) Find design challenges for Perswedo to enlighten next step.

3.1 Participants

We conducted three workshops in three different universities. Workshop A comprised 19 postgraduate students (10 females and 9 males; Age: M = 25.5, SD = 4.0) from the interaction design program. Five of them used to be designers (min: 1year, max: 11year). Workshop B was carried out with 13 senior bachelor students (6 females and 7 males; Age: M = 23.2, SD = 1.3) from the interaction design program. All of them had at least half year experience as a design intern in the industry. In workshop C, 18 bachelor students (8 females and 10 males; Age: M = 21.4, SD = 2.1) studied inter-action design for one year as electives. They were from different bachelor school ranged from electrical engineering, mechanical engineering, architecture, agriculture, finance, and linguistics, etc. Similar to [19], here we refer them as *advanced group* (from workshop A), *intermediate group* (from workshop B), and *elementary group* (from workshop C) with respect to their experience in interaction design.

3.2 Procedures

At the beginning, we allocated students into working groups with size between 5 and 7 persons per group. In all the workshops, participants were asked to design interactive technology for healthy aging. Given the broadness of this topic, students were later dived in several related fields, such as physical activity, food, medication, and healthcare for elderly people. The procedure for three design workshops was very similar: workshop A and C lasted seven consecutive days, while workshop B were split into one day per week in seven weeks. In each workshop, students followed the typical creative design process [23], from analyzing the problem to generating concept, to implementing design (low-fidelity), where we introduced Perswedo after the first stage.

Perswedo cards were introduced with a presentation given by us. We firstly introduced PT, PSD, and persuasive principles to all the participants. We followed by presenting Perswedo cards with a basic instruction to show how to use them in the design process. We also arranged some "warm-up" sessions to facilitate the use of the cards. After then, each group kept one set of Perswedo cards until the end of the workshop.

3.3   Data Collection

We collected data using a combination of survey and observation methods. After the workshops, all the participants were asked to fill in a questionnaire with a 5-point Likert Scale, with 5 being strongly agree, it is consisted of five items adopted from [21] to examine if Perswedo cards were helpful to (i) improve idea; (ii) generate idea; (iii) get the group focus on the topic; (iv) articulate the concept; (v) get the team to consensus on the discussion. Moreover, similar to [19], it asked participants to rate the usefulness of the cards by different elements, including the card format, the principle description, and the design example. In the end, we gave options for participants to leave comments for what values they found about using Perswedo in the design process. Furthermore, they were asked to give suggestions on the current design and usage of Perswedo. We also captured photo and video here to compensate our survey data.

4   Results

From three workshops, we collected 50 responses on the post-questionnaire. 38 among them stated values of the cards in design process, where 21 participants gave additional suggestions to inform our further iteration. In what follows, we present our findings in three folds. To start, we report the quantitative results from the scale to show how our participants assessed the usefulness of Perswedo in the design process. We then cluster the qualitative data based on the logical closeness of different results, where we firstly describe extra values of Perswedo we found from the questionnaire. We end up by presenting the design implications for current cards, which we have to take into account for the further appropriation of Perswedo cards into design practice.

4.1   Usefulness of Perswedo

Our questionnaire data (Fig. 2) indicate that on average the participants rated the usefulness better than neutral. Which implies Perswedo cards were supportive in different design activities for both individual and group. Moreover, it suggests that different elements of the cards positively supported the usage of Perswedo in the design flow. Given the small and uneven group size, it is unwarranted to compare the difference between three groups. However, from the chart we observed that the *advanced*

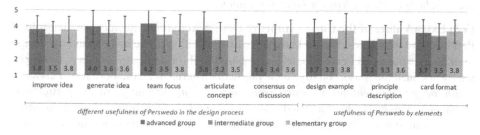

Fig. 2. Participants' average ratings on Perswedo cards from the scale by groups.

group in general gave the most optimistic feedback on the questionnaire, despite they found the descriptions of the persuasive principles were least useful among others. One interpretation of this is perhaps this group of designers were familiar with how cards work in the design process so that they made use of the cards easier in the relatively short time in the workshop. Yet the textual content was less informative for them, as they might already know PT theory beforehand. Furthermore, the *intermediate group* scored the usefulness of Perswedo the lowest among most of the items, which suggest no liner correlation between the design knowledge and the perceived usefulness of the cards.

4.2   Value of Perswedo

(V1) Scope the Design Directions. The results suggest that Perswedo was helpful to *orient the design progress*, as one participant mentioned: *[Perswedo] gives us a basic foundation to start*, as *it's easy to start from the words*. This could be dated back to PSD, in which every principle has been summarized into a keyword [6]. In this way, it helps people to grasp the core meanings of different design guidelines in a nutshell. Moreover, most of the participants appreciated the way how PSD classified design principles. They thought two perspectives, both dialogue support and social support, were *very easy to understand and useful* in guiding design. Participants also stated that color-code clearly differentiated two categories with each other. Also, our explanation in the beginning helped them a more comprehensive understanding of the classification.

(V2) Expand Ways for Concept Development. In addition, 13 participants mentioned that cards were *well designed* and were *clearly easy to use* and consequently helped them to generate new ideas out of the box, as Perswedo *inspired some [persuasive] directions of the design, which sometimes can be forgotten*. Some participants even thought the cards provoked a sort of *challenge*, which stimulated them to *think about a more varied approach of persuasion*. Some others believed that Perswedo led them to *talk about project [more] openness*. Moreover, by acting with multiple cards, it gave external support to expand design rationale, as one student mentioned: *when combining some cards together with each other, it helps to develop more possibilities*. On the flip side, four participants also left comment that *the cards helped the team more focus on the exact topic*. They realized that *when choosing a card, you had a specific purpose for the concept*. Furthermore, information on the cards also helped students to weigh up their existing ideas, as one participant said: *Explanation [on the cards] was a great help to confirm ideas on behavior change*.

(V3) Extra Values of the Cards: Improve Design Activities. Besides the dual-role of Perswedo we found as a domain knowledge carrier [18] to scope and expand the design thinking, we observed Perswedo, as a card-based tool for co-design practice, leveraged teamwork in three ways: Firstly, as a physical material for collaboration, Perswedo *could be good incentives to start group discussion*; Secondly, many participants considered the cards had assisted them to *structure team discussion in a more well-organized way*; Thirdly, since our tool helped students to be more focus on *think,* *draw, and share* during the project, they believed it also provided them an occasion to *identify individual's expertise*, and in return to *learn from each other*.

Moreover, we found that nature of design card-set allowed participants to elaborate their ideas in different sessions by multiple manipulations. For instance: By placing the cards on sketching paper, participants figured out their concept more concretely; By pointing at different cards during discussion, participants communicated their idea more precisely; By linking their work with different principles in the pitch, participants presented their design more clearly; by holding the cards in their hand, participants felt more confident to tell us the story of the concept based on the design guidelines.

4.3   Design Implications for Perswedo

Despite the advantages of using Perswedo, we also learned our participants sometimes encountered difficulties to understand and use the cards as well as the PSD theory properly in the design process. Similar as what have been revealed previously [21], our approach of simplifying and abstracting the theoretical framework could bring danger to hinder or mislead design activities. Therefore, in the following we elaborate on what need to be done further to bring persuasive principles more appropriate to the actual design activities.

(I1) Design Example: Topic Relevance. During workshops, three participants mentioned that the examples we offered on the cards, mostly about to motivate physical activity, were *not always relevant to their design topics*. Therefore, they suggested us to redesign examples to enable broader use of Perswedo. For instance, some students expected to *get the real cases from designers or experts as references*. Some students came to think of depicting *more information on the backside*, such as *offering two examples for two directions on the back*. From what participants suggested, showing multiple examples from various directions instead of single case on the cards would make the cards more inclusive to use in different design activities. In addition, prior studies [24] inform us that enabling the customization of Perswedo could also improve a wider usage in design process. To make the cards customizable, for instance, we can offer a DIY service platform with a database so that the content of the cards can be adapted for different use. Another example will be leaving the editable space on the cards, where designers can add their own interest.

(I2) Persuasive Principles: Generative and Informative. In terms of the principle descriptions, some participants complained: *The descriptions are not easy to understand when I first read them.* Hence, their *discussion sometimes focuses on the cards instead of on the idea for design project.* From the feedback, we also learned that some design principles in PSD *were very similar* for our participants and somehow *might confuse* them during the usage. If we look back to PSD model itself, even though some principles look similar to each other from the descriptions, the principles are actually distinct to each other from the psychological perspective. For example, the meaning of *reminder* and *suggestion* are quite close. However, *reminder* is suggested to use for people who have a goal in their mind, while *suggestion* is more likely to introduce certain behavior to people who have no goal so far. Therefore, it is necessary to introduce more comprehensive story of the theory to our audience. To do so, supplementary tools, such as booklets, articles, and websites, that explain the story in detail should be added into the ecology surrounds our cards. Moreover, the foldable cards with space for more information could be another interesting direction to explore. Additionally, we also have interest to explore layman terms for persuasive principles so that more people with different background can use it without much confusion. Provocative content on the cards, such as transforming the guidelines into colloquial questions [11, 21], is also effective to facilitate the creative process.

(I3) Language Variations. Since our participants were not all from English speaking countries, their fluencies in English were quite different. Therefore, the participants, who were not used of English as working language, had hard time to understand the meaning of Perswedo, as they stated: *For the tester whose mother tone isn't English, it's needed some times to understand the text on the card.* Some of them also noted that they could *only refer to the graphics* while using the cards. We have to admit that we overlooked the language issue when developing Perswedo. However, our participants considered that there should be a way for Perswedo *to cross the culture and language.* Despite the ordinary way to translate PSD principles into different versions, some students suggested *more icons or info-graphics [on the cards] will [help designers] to understand [the concept] more clearly and instantly.* Which means there is a chance to use visual elements to optimize the interaction between users and Perswedo.

5 Conclusions

In this paper, Perswedo cards are developed to support flexible access to the persuasive principles from PSD in the creative design process. As a work to close the gap between PT theory and design practice, we reflect on what we learned here to discuss on the role of card-based PSD and the challenges of using PSD in the creative design.

Although PT theories have been critiqued for prescribing behavioral change strategies [10] and unreflective in defining behavior changes [25], similar to [12], our study reveals the proper inclusion of PT knowledge can inform the design process. As the participants assessed the cards and the individual element were useful in different activities, and in turn indicated the potential usefulness of PSD framework in the design practice. This was achieved by the card-formal presentation of PSD supported the participants to *scope the design directions* and to *expand the concept development.*

Yet, we have to admit the current design and usage of Perswedo cards still lack considerations to appropriate PSD more into the design flow. As mentioned earlier, this study implies the further improvement of Perswedo by focusing on *topic relevance* in design examples, *informative and generative* in principle descriptions, and *language variations.* More importantly, according to [11], the design cards alone are not a method itself. The specific mechanisms and design methods would support generative use of theoretical framework [20]. Similarly, our participants suggested us to *integrate cards into toolkit or structured design approach* to instruct the use of persuasive principles. Therefore, this study reveals the challenge that designers need to remain openness to any supportive design methods while using card-based PSD principles in the design process.

In the future, we firstly plan to improve the card design of Perswedo based on the design implications from this study. We then plan to further associate Perswedo cards with other cards-sets, such as context information [24] and design methods [14], to improve the use of PT theories in the co-design practice. The new version of Perswedo will be evaluated in professional design projects, which will have more thorough process to follow. Moreover, we will also bring the cards into several workshops to see how PSD knowledge will influence users and stakeholders to design PT in the participatory design [12].

Acknowledgment. The first author of this paper is being sponsored by China Scholarship Council. We thank all participants who volunteered to take part in the studies. A special thanks to Vincent Visser for your help to organize the workshops.

References

1. Fogg, B.: Persuasive Technology: Using Computers to Change What We Think and Do. Morgan Kaufmann Publishers, Burlington (2003)
2. Lin, J.J., Mamykina, L., Lindtner, S., Delajoux, G., Strub, H.B.: Fish'n'Steps: encouraging physical activity with an interactive computer game. In: Dourish, P., Friday, A. (eds.) UbiComp 2006. LNCS, vol. 4206, pp. 261–278. Springer, Heidelberg (2006). doi:10.1007/11853565_16
3. He, H., Greenberg, S., Huang, E.: One size does not fit all: applying the transtheoretical model to energy feedback technology design. In: 28th International Conference, pp. 927–936 (2010)
4. Hekler, E.B., Klasnja, P., Froehlich, J.E., Buman, M.P.: Mind the theoretical gap: interpreting, using, and developing behavioral theory in HCI research. In: Proceedings of CHI 2013, pp. 3307–3316 (2013)
5. Consolvo, S., McDonald, D.W., Landay, J.A.: Theory-driven design strategies for technologies that support behavior change in everyday life. In: Proceedings of the 27th International Conference on Human Factors in Computing Systems - CHI 2009, pp. 405–414 (2009)
6. Oinas-Kukkonen, H., Harjumaa, M.: Persuasive systems design: key issues, process model, and system features. Commun. Assoc. Inf. Syst. **24**, 485–500 (2009)
7. Torning, K., Oinas-Kukkonen, H.: Persuasive system design: state of the art and future directions. In: Proceedings of the 4th International Conference on Persuasive Technology, p. 1 (2009)
8. Oinas-Kukkonen, H.: A foundation for the study of behavior change support systems. Pers. Ubiquit. Comput. **17**, 1223–1235 (2012)
9. Stolterman, E.: The nature of design practice and implications for interaction design research. Int. J. Des. **2**, 55–65 (2008)
10. Purpura, S., Schwanda, V., Williams, K., Stubler, W., Sengers, P.: Fit4life: the design of a persuasive technology promoting healthy behavior and ideal weight. In: Proceedings of the 2011 Annual Conference on Human Factors in Computing Systems - CHI 2011, p. 423 (2011)
11. Hornecker, E.: Creative idea exploration within the structure of a guiding framework: the card brainstorming game. In: Proceedings of the Fourth International Conference on Tangible Embedded Embodied Interaction, vol. 10, pp. 101–108 (2010)

12. Davis, J.: Early experiences with participation in persuasive technology design. In: Proceedings of the 12th Participatory Design Conference: Research Papers, vol. 1, pp. 119–128 (2012)
13. Li, Y., Landay, J.A.: Activity-based prototyping of ubicomp applications for long-lived, everyday human activities. In: Proceedings of ACM CHI 2008 Conference on Human Factors in Computing System, vol. 1, pp. 1303–1312 (2008)
14. Guterman, J.: IDEO Method Cards (2010). http://www.redi-bw.de/db/ebsco.php/search. ebscohost.com/login.aspx%3Fdirect%3Dtrue%26db%3Dbth%26AN%3D51605598%26site %3Dehost-live
15. Bekker, M.M., Antle, A.N.: Developmentally situated design (DSD): making theoretical knowledge accessible to designers of children's technology. In: Proceedings of the CHI 2011 Conference, pp. 2531–2540 (2011)
16. Fogg, B.: Persuasive computers: perspectives and research directions. In: SIGCHI Conference on Human Factors in Computing Systems, pp. 98, 225–232 (1998)
17. Alahäivälä, T., Oinas-Kukkonen, H.: Understanding persuasion contexts in health gamification: a systematic analysis of gamified health behavior change support systems literature (2015)
18. Wölfel, C., Merritt, T.: Method card design dimensions: a survey of card-based design tools. In: Kotzé, P., Marsden, G., Lindgaard, G., Wesson, J., Winckler, M. (eds.) INTERACT 2013 Part I. LNCS, vol. 8117, pp. 479–486. Springer, Heidelberg (2013). doi:10.1007/978-3-642-40483-2_34
19. Deng, Y., Antle, A.N., Neustaedter, C.: Tango cards: a card-based design tool for informing the design of tangible learning games (2014)
20. Lucero, A., Arrasvuori, J.: PLEX cards: a source of inspiration when designing for playfulness. In: Proceedings of the Fun and Games, vol. 15, pp. 28–37 (2010)
21. Mueller, F.F., Gibbs, M.R., Vetere, F., Edge, D.: Supporting the creative game design process with exertion cards, pp. 2211–2220 (2014)
22. Matthews, J., Win, K.T., Oinas-Kukkonen, H., Freeman, M.: Persuasive technology in mobile applications promoting physical activity a systematic review. J. Med. Syst. **40**, 72 (2016)
23. Warr, A., O'Neill, E.: Understanding design as a social creative process. Proceedings of the 5th Conference on Creativity and Cognition, pp. 118–127 (2005)
24. Halskov, K., Dalsgård, P.: Inspiration card workshops. In: Proceedings of the 6th Conference on Designing Interactive Systems, pp. 2–11 (2006)
25. Brynjarsdottir, H., Håkansson, M., Pierce, J., Baumer, E., DiSalvo, C., Sengers, P.: Sustainably unpersuaded: how persuasion narrows our vision of sustainability. In: Proceedings of the 2012 ACM Annual Conference on Human Factors in Computing Systems - CHI 2012, pp. 947 (2012)

Towards the Applicability of NAO Robot for Children with Autism in Pakistan

Muneeb Imtiaz Ahmad[1]([⊠]), Suleman Shahid[2], and Anam Tahir[2]

[1] Human Machine Interaction Group, MARCS Institute,
Western Sydney University, Sydney, Australia
muneeb.ahmad@uws.edu.au
[2] Department of Computer Science, Lahore University of Management Sciences,
Lahore, Pakistan

Abstract. In this paper, we present a HRI study that reports on the potential of NAO as a socially assistive robot in Pakistan. Our findings generated through interviewing 2 parents and 5 teachers on the plausibility of using NAO robot as an interaction partner show that both groups welcomed the use of NAO at schools. They, however, were sceptical due to missing NAO's facial expressions and certain body parts such as nose and lips. They also emphasised the importance of creating natural text to speech interface for the Urdu Language. Our findings taken from 7 autistic children to measure their level of social interaction during HRI revealed that children positively engaged with the NAO robot and showed a significant number of both verbal and non-verbal behaviours.

Keywords: Autism spectrum disorder · Children-robot interaction · Socially Assistive Robots

1 Introduction

Autism Spectrum Disorder (ASD) is a pervasive, behavioural development disorder that typically manifests in the first three years of life [7]. Children with Autism show signs of social, emotion, communication impairment. Based on the level of their impairment, children are regarded as suffering from Low- or High-Functioning ASD. The prevalence of ASD is growing all over the world. However, most of this research on ASD, both at understanding the causes of Autism and developing digital solutions to support children with Autism, is witnessed in the western world [1] and a lack of research has been found in countries from the eastern world such as Pakistan. It is estimated that 350,000 children in Pakistan suffer from autism and this number is increasing day by day [12].

The integration of technology-based interventions including use of mobile tablets [21], robots [18], computer-based interventions [10] to help children with ASD can be witnessed widely in the western world. Socially Assistive Robots (SARs), as introduced by [18], is a commonly used term that encompasses all

© IFIP International Federation for Information Processing 2017
Published by Springer International Publishing AG 2017. All Rights Reserved
R. Bernhaupt et al. (Eds.): INTERACT 2017, Part III, LNCS 10515, pp. 463–472, 2017.
DOI: 10.1007/978-3-319-67687-6_32

types of robots that can be used to assist people with special needs. These SARs are being used to support individuals suffering from autism, elderly with Alzheimer's and dementia and several other impairments [13].

SARs have been successfully utilised in helping children with autism develop communication and social skills [16]. However, the potential impact of such robots has been under-studied in the countries that are part of the eastern world such as Pakistan. To the best of our knowledge, SARs have never been used in the Pakistani context to support Autistic children or other children with special needs but we do find a handful of studies conducted at schools in Pakistan where technology-based interventions were fruitful in improving the social and emotional skills of children with Autism [5,6]. We understand that due to socio-cultural differences, findings from studies where SARs were used with these children in the western world cannot be generalised to the Pakistani context [1]. Therefore, before designing and conducting interaction studies with SARs in Pakistan, different factors are needed to be taken into consideration. These factors include technology acceptance, understanding parents and teachers views on the use of SARs in schools or at homes.

We find numerous studies conducted with parents and teachers on their views on the acceptance of SARs in the western world [14,16]. However, one of the issues with these studies is that the effect of parents' or teachers' hypothetical knowledge about robots has an effect on their opinions about future robotic design. Different studies have addressed this aspect and showed its impact on the quality of results [3]. Therefore, our research focuses on collecting observations from teachers and parents who first interacted with the NAO robot before providing feedback on their applicability and informing on their future designs and capabilities.

Another important aspect is to study the initial response of autistic children to a social robot, based on the level of their autism. Studies have been conducted where social engagement of children with autism has been measured in an interaction with the NAO robot [19]. However, we don't find any study that focuses on child's level of autism while investigating their interaction with social robots. We, therefore, conducted a HRI study with autistic children to measure the difference between their levels of social interaction and engagement during their interaction with the NAO robot depending on the level of autism.

Keeping these aforementioned aspects, we, in this paper, report an initial HRI study conducted with parents, teachers to inform their views on acceptance towards using a NAO robot and its future design interaction with their children. In addition, we also report a study conducted with autistic children to measure the effect of NAO robot's interaction on children's social interactions and overall engagement. To the best of our knowledge, this is the first study with a SAR in this context that has been conducted in Pakistan.

2   Method

In our present study, we have followed the procedure as described by [17] in which children were exposed to a NAO robot to evaluate their initial responses.

However, we conducted our study with parents, teachers to get their views on the potential of NAO robot as a helping assistant for children with autism. In addition, we also measured social interaction of autistic children during their interaction with the NAO robot.

2.1 Interaction Scenario

We programmed NAO robot to autonomously display behaviours during the interaction, however, speech recognition was controlled via Wizard of Oz (WoZ). NAO was capable of autonomously showing three emotions (Happiness, boredom and sadness) through displaying gesture as reported by [9].

NAO robot began the one-to-one interaction with the participant through asking introductory questions: (Hello, I am NAO, What is your name, "How are you today", "Have you interacted with a robot before", "Do you like me" and "Let me show you my emotions". After the dialogue, NAO displayed sad emotion through playing a sound with a gesture and uttering "I am feeling sad, Can you smile for me". Another gesture displaying boredom was played with saying "I am feeling bored, can you smile a bit more". Lastly, a gesture displaying happiness was played while saying "I am happy to see you smiling". At the end, NAO said "Good Bye! I had fun interacting with you." and waved goodbye gesture.

2.2 Participants

We conducted our study with two parents (1-male, 1-female), five teachers (2-males and 3-females) and seven children with autism spectrum disorder (6-males, 1-female) at a school for special children in Lahore, Pakistan. The ages of the parents, teachers were between 25 35 respectively whereas the children aged between 10–12 years. None of the participants had ever interacted with a robot.

Although we were informed that all participating children were diagnosed with high functioning ASD, we, however, conducted a Gilliam Autism Rating Scale-Second Edition (GARS-2) test to identify the level of autism [8]. The test informs about the participant's Autism Index (AI). In case, if AI is 85 or above, the person is very likely to be an autistic, and if it is 70–84, the person is possibly autistic. 3 out of 7 participants were found to be likely autistic while others belonged to the possibly autistic group.

2.3 Procedure

Our study was conducted in two phases. In the first phase, NAO interacted with parents that lasted for 3 min followed by a 5-min interview. NAO began with an introductory dialogue followed by an interaction showing three different emotions (happiness, sadness and boredom) through displaying gestures simultaneously with LED lights. Lastly, the robot thanked the parents for participation and displayed the bye gesture along with a dialogue. An interview followed the interaction where we inquired about the potential of NAO robot as a helping agent for autistic children.

In the second phase, NAO interacted with autistic children in the presence of teachers. The teachers monitored the sessions and played a calming role for the autistic children. The interaction also lasted for 3 min following the same procedure as for the parents. After the interaction, one of the researchers interviewed the teacher about the potential of NAO as an assistive robot.

2.4   Setup and Materials

The set up of the study required using two portions. The first portion was for children and parents to engage with the NAO. We conducted our study in a quiet room, and as shown on the left side of Fig. 1 below. The room was divided into two portions. On one side, the child and the parent independently interacted with NAO that had been placed on a table in front of the participant. On the other side, one of the researchers was controlling the speech recognition capabilities of NAO through a Wizard of Oz (WoZ) setup.

Fig. 1. Setup: a parent (left) and a child (right) interacting with NAO robot.

We used NAO robot designed and developed by Aldebaran robotics. It is a humanoid robot measuring 58 cm in height. It provides researchers with a platform to design various applications driven by their creativity and requirements.

The interview questions were designed to discuss the potential of NAO as a tool to provide edutainment. In addition, we inquired about the activities where NAO can provide assistance. Moreover, what in their opinion are the missing capabilities of NAO and in what ways, these gaps can be covered. Lastly, we also asked them about the applicability of the NAO robot at homes and overall acceptance of such a robot in general.

3   Results

In this section, we present both quantitative and qualitative results. Our quantitative findings are based on measuring social interaction and the initial reaction of children with different level of autism during the HRI. Our qualitative findings are a reflection of both teachers and parents views on the potential of NAO as an assistive agent for their children.

3.1   Quantitative Results

Our goal of the study was to measure the amount of Social Interaction (SI) and Engagement (E) during our interaction sessions of both most likely and possibly autistic children. We predict that there will be a significant effect of autism level of the child on the SI or E. In order to measure SI or E, we analysed videos for all the sessions.

Video Analysis. In order to measure the amount of SI or E, we coded both verbal and non-verbal behaviours during the sessions. We followed the coding scheme as reported by [4, 11] respectively. We measured the frequencies and durations of eye gazes, verbal responses, and facial expressions of all the participants during the sessions. Eye-gaze referred to an event when the child gaze was facing towards the robot. Verbal response referred to the number of times the child spoke with the robot or answered robot query. Facial expression referred to the number of time a child smiled back at the robot.

We conducted an independent-samples t-test to compare the frequencies and durations of eye gazes, verbal responses and facial expressions in most likely and possibly autistic children determined through conducting the GARS-2 test [8]. We found a significant difference for the number eye gazes of most likely (M = 13, SD = 118) and possibly (M = 26.67, SD = 24.67) autistic children $t(-3.34) = 0.01$, $p < 0.02$. We also found a significant difference for the frequency of facial expressions of most likely (M = 1.75, SD = 12.75) and possibly (M = 8.33, SD = 34.67) autistic children $t(-2.79) = 0.01$, $p < 0.02$. Our results witnessed a higher number of eye gaze and facial expressions for the possibly autistic children. In case of durations, we found a significant difference for eye gazes of most likely (M = 7.18, SD = 4.13) and possibly (M = 4.13, SD = 5.11) autistic children $t(2.46) = 0.03$, $p < 0.04$. We also witnessed significant difference for the durations of facial expressions of most likely (M = 0.9, SD = 3.36) and possibly (M = 2.75, SD = 0.38) autistic children $t(-2.79388) = 0.01$, $p < 0.02$. The durations of both eye gaze and facial expressions were also found to be higher for possibly autism children as compared to more likely autistic children.

On the other hand, we didn't find significant difference for the number of verbal responses of most likely (M = 9.5, SD = 59) and possibly (M = 10.67, SD = 162.67) autistic children $t(-0.22) = 0.41$, $p = 0.41$. We also didn't find significant difference for the durations of verbal responses of most likely (M = 0.81, SD = 0.92) and possibly (M = 1.39, SD = 0.47) autistic children $t(-1.43) = 0.10$, $p = 0.10$. We only witnessed a minor difference for the frequencies and durations of verbal response among two groups as shown in the mean value plot of eye-gaze, verbal response and facial expressions in Fig. 2.

Discussion: Our results confirmed our prediction and showed that children with the different level of autism showed different level of social interaction and engagement during HRI. However, we only found the number of non-verbal interactions to be significant among two groups of autistic individuals with varying

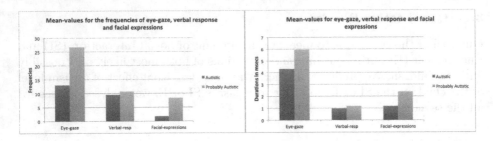

Fig. 2. Mean values for the frequencies (left) and durations (right) of eye-gaze, facial expressions and verbal response.

autism based on the GARS-2 test results. We didn't find differences in the verbal interaction. We conjecture that the reason for this difference may be due to the social skills of each individual. As literature shows that high-functioning autistic children may also have varying social skills among each other [15]. We, however, also believe that more research studies with higher number of participants are required to consolidate these findings. In general, results showed that all children showed a certain level of interaction and engagement with the robot. This confirms the potential of NAO as a SAR in Pakistan and also directs for more research in the future.

3.2 Qualitative Results

In order to analyse data taken from the interviews, we performed content analysis on the transcriptions generated from audio recordings. We present the main themes resulting from the qualitative analysis performed on the interview data with parents and teachers. To keep the identities anonymous, the parents are labelled as P1 and P2, while teachers are listed as T1, T2, T3, T4, and T5 respectively.

Anthropomorphism. Our findings show that both parents and teachers were comfortable with the use of NAO to help their children and students. However, both teachers and parents emphasised on the need of facial expressions for NAO. One of the parents mentioned: "Facial expressions are missing. For example, if one teacher is wearing a veil and the other one has her face uncovered children will connect better with the second one (P1)". Teachers mentioned as "the body parts and facial expressions are missing. If NAO uses voice or gestures to explain emotions, it'll be necessary that a teacher is present to translate those emotions to the child (T3)."

On the positive side, both teachers and parents welcomed the inclusion of LED lights to display different emotions as an alternative solution. However, they considered it a short-term solution. They reported: "Yes, it will but will be short term. (P2)".

NAO for Edutainment: In general, the response of parents and children towards using NAO for edutainment was very positive. One father mentioned that his child will be attracted towards NAO, however, it depends on the type of autism of the child. One parent mentioned: "It varies on the autism level. My elder daughter is high functioning she will be attracted because of the fact that it talks. Younger one is destructive she won't accept it (P1)." Teachers, on the other hand, focused on the importance of the level of exposure a child may have with the NAO robot. They believed that in the case of more exposure, children will get comfortable and in a long-term interaction, this will result in a positive way. One teacher mentioned: "It can but for that, we need to give children exposure. If they interact with it twice or thrice a week they will get comfortable with it (T1)."

Teachers were of the view that it may take 6 to 7 interactions on average to get familiar with the NAO robot. They commented: "It may take up to 6–7 days on a regular basis. If they interact with it daily for a week, he will start responding to its commands next week. (T1)" Another mentioned that it may take them less time as compared to the humans to familiarise. They commented: "The child will get comfortable with the robots faster as compared to humans as interaction with toys is usually better (T2)." Others also mentioned that the familiarisation time may depend on the type of autism. They commented: "It also depend on the autism level. Children with mild to moderate autism level might get comfortable with it within a month others might take longer (T5)."

We witnessed that both parents and teachers speculated that NAO can help children develop speech, vocabulary and basic cognition. One parent said: "NAO can assist my child to develop Language, vocabulary, and speech (P2)." Teachers reported as "It can help develop basic cognition, object recognition such as fruit names (T1)." One of the teachers also pointed that NAO can help autistic children with fears about human body and expressions learn about non-verbal communications, however, they were sceptical due to missing facial expressions of NAO. One teacher reported: "Some children have fear of human body and expressions so this might work with these children. But, the absence of facial expression is an opposing element (T3)."

NAO for Collaborative Learning: We found that both parents and teachers welcomed the application of NAO in a collaborative task. They were presented with a situation and were also asked about their opinions. The situation involved three children working in a group and NAO asks the first one to touch its head and in response to that it stands up. Later, NAO asks the second one to touch its feet and it sits down and Lastly NAO asks the third one to touch its hand and it waves.

All of them were positive towards the utilisation of NAO in this manner however, they focused on the need of the presence of a teacher to monitor the activity. They reported: "It will be good because when it responds to their action children will enjoy it and it will fascinate them. (T4)" and "It will work but will require a teacher to monitor the scenario (T5)."

Applicability of NAO at Homes: In general, both parents and teachers wanted to utilise NAO at schools before it may be used at homes. One parent said: "Starting from school first (P1)."

Future Possibilities with NAO: Teachers emphasised on the need of adopting the voice of NAO though changing its tone in combination with facial expressions. One teacher mentioned: "Facial expressions and voice tone variation are important. Children not making an eye contact with the robot because they don't find anything attractive. If I ask him to smile and with that, I am smiling and my tone is varying the child will respond accordingly (T2)."

Teachers mentioned that the robotic voice of NAO may not be suitable for autistic children. They emphasised on the need of a regional voice for NAO that should be in the Urdu language. In addition, the text to speech conversion needs to be slow as children may not understand the speech.

Discussion: The key lessons we learned about conducting research in future with NAO robot in Pakistan with children suffering from autism are as follow:

The Need for the Natural Text-to-Speech Feature for Social Robots. In literature, the challenge of an unnatural and too paced voice of a robot has been reported [2]. Our results also indicated that teachers wanted a robot to speak in the Urdu language in a naturalistic way. It, therefore, directs researchers towards creating text-to-speech interfaces in the Urdu language that are currently nonexistent.

Design and Evaluate the User's Perception of Existing Facial Expressions for Social Robots in Pakistan. Most recently, an exploratory study was performed with SAR in Pakistan [20] where autistic children participated in a collaborated play. It resulted in positive findings towards improving social interaction. Otherwise, we don't find interaction studies where robots have been used to help autistic children understand a certain emotion through a gesture. Therefore, we believe research is needed to evaluate the perception of children with autism in Pakistan on existing gestures used to display emotions. In addition, based on these result, future interaction on helping autistic children understand emotions can be designed.

Long-Term Interaction with a Social Robot. Our results showed that children with autism may require time to get familiar with the robot. However, the familiarisation time may vary depending on the different factors such as type and level of autism. Therefore, we need to find empirical evidence on the time it may require by a child with varying degree of autism to get familiar with a robot.

Acceptance of Socially Assistive Robots. We need to conduct more studies in Pakistan to assess the acceptance of robot in Pakistan. Our results, however, showed that robots were accepted but we need to interview more parents and teachers to consolidate our findings.

4 Conclusion, Limitations and Future Work

In this paper, we presented our results on parent's and teacher's opinion on the potential of NAO as a SARs in Pakistan. Teachers and parents reacted positively towards using robots as a tool for edutainment, helping them understand basic human emotions, and develop speech and basic cognition. In addition, teachers pointed towards the missing facial expressions in NAO and focused on designing robots with expressions in the future. Our results of our interaction study with autistic individuals also showed that robot technology has a positive effect towards developing social skills in both children suffering from different levels of autism. Children were able to display both verbal and non-verbal skills during HRI. In general, results generated from parents, teachers and children showed the potential of NAO robot as a therapist agent in Pakistan.

One of the argued limitations can be a relatively smaller group of participants but, our study was conducted in a school and it is a common group size for studies conducted with autistic children at schools [1,19]. We tried to control the effect of hypothetical knowledge of our participants through an interaction with NAO, however, some results can still be based on their previous knowledge of robots.

References

1. Ahmad, M.: Design and evaluation of a mobile learning application for autistic children in a developing country. Ph.D. thesis, University Paderborn (2013)
2. Ahmad, M.I., Mubin, O., Orlando, J.: Children views' on social robot's adaptations in education. In: Proceedings of the 28th Australian Conference on Computer-Human Interaction, pp. 145–149. ACM (2016)
3. Ahmad, M.I., Mubin, O., Orlando, J.: Understanding behaviours and roles for social and adaptive robots in education: teacher's perspective. In: Proceedings of the Fourth International Conference on Human Agent Interaction, pp. 297–304. ACM (2016)
4. Ahmad, M.I., Mubin, O., Orlando, J.: Adaptive social robot for sustaining social engagement during long-term children-robot interaction. Int. J. Hum.-Comput. Interact. (2017, just-accepted)
5. Ahmad, M.I., Shahid, S.: Design and evaluation of mobile learning applications for autistic children in Pakistan. In: Abascal, J., Barbosa, S., Fetter, M., Gross, T., Palanque, P., Winckler, M. (eds.) INTERACT 2015 Part I. LNCS, vol. 9296, pp. 436–444. Springer, Cham (2015). doi:10.1007/978-3-319-22701-6_32
6. Ahmad, M.I., Shahid, S., Maganheim, J.S.: A game-based intervention for improving the communication skills of autistic children in Pakistan. In: Miesenberger, K., Fels, D., Archambault, D., Peňáz, P., Zagler, W. (eds.) ICCHP 2014 Part I. LNCS, vol. 8547, pp. 513–516. Springer, Cham (2014). doi:10.1007/978-3-319-08596-8_80

7. Frith, U., Happé, F.: Autism spectrum disorder. Curr. Biol. **15**(19), R786–R790 (2005)
8. Gilliam, J.E.: GARS-2: Gilliam Autism Rating Scale. Pro-Ed, Austin (2006)
9. Häring, M., Bee, N., André, E.: Creation and evaluation of emotion expression with body movement, sound and eye color for humanoid robots. In: 2011 RO-MAN, pp. 204–209. IEEE (2011)
10. Hetzroni, O.E., Tannous, J.: Effects of a computer-based intervention program on the communicative functions of children with autism. J. Autism Dev. Disord. **34**(2), 95–113 (2004)
11. Hourcade, J.P., Williams, S.R., Miller, E.A., Huebner, K.E., Liang, L.J.: Evaluation of tablet apps to encourage social interaction in children with autism spectrum disorders. In: Proceedings of the SIGCHI Conference on Human Factors in Computing Systems, pp. 3197–3206. ACM (2013)
12. Haider, I., Maroof Qureshi, M., Azeem, Q.F.: The autism puzzle (2015). https://www.dawn.com/news/1173610. Accessed 12 April 2017
13. Leite, I., Martinho, C., Paiva, A.: Social robots for long-term interaction: a survey. Int. J. Soc. Robot. **5**(2), 291–308 (2013)
14. Mundy, P.,: Development of socially assistive robots for children with autism spectrum disorders (2009). Institute10, M.I.N.D
15. Rao, P.A., Beidel, D.C., Murray, M.J.: Social skills interventions for children with asperger's syndrome or high-functioning autism: a review and recommendations. J. Autism Dev. Disord. **38**(2), 353–361 (2008)
16. Scassellati, B., Admoni, H., Matarić, M.: Robots for use in autism research. Annu. Rev. Biomed. Eng. **14**, 275–294 (2012)
17. Shamsuddin, S., Yussof, H., Ismail, L.I., Mohamed, S., Hanapiah, F.A., Zahari, N.I.: Initial response in HRI-a case study on evaluation of child with autism spectrum disorders interacting with a humanoid robot NAO. Procedia Eng. **41**, 1448–1455 (2012)
18. Tapus, A., Mataric, M.J., Scassellati, B.: Socially assistive robotics. IEEE Robot. Autom. Mag. **14**(1), 35 (2007)
19. Tapus, A., Peca, A., Aly, A., Pop, C., Jisa, L., Pintea, S., Rusu, A.S., David, D.O.: Children with autism social engagement in interaction with NAO, an imitative robot: a series of single case experiments. Interact. Stud. **13**(3), 315–347 (2012)
20. Tariq, S., Baber, S., Ashfaq, A., Ayaz, Y., Naveed, M., Mohsin, S.: Interactive therapy approach through collaborative physical play between a socially assistive humanoid robot and children with autism spectrum disorder. In: Agah, A., Cabibihan, J.-J., Howard, A.M., Salichs, M.A., He, H. (eds.) ICSR 2016. LNCS, vol. 9979, pp. 561–570. Springer, Cham (2016). doi:10.1007/978-3-319-47437-3_55
21. Venkatesh, S., Phung, D., Duong, T., Greenhill, S., Adams, B.: TOBY: early intervention in autism through technology. In: Proceedings of the SIGCHI Conference on Human Factors in Computing Systems, pp. 3187–3196. ACM (2013)

Pointing and Target Selection

Dynamics of Pointing with Pointer Acceleration

Jörg Müller$^{(\boxtimes)}$

Department of Computer Science, Aarhus University, Aarhus, Denmark
joerg.mueller@acm.org

Abstract. In this paper we investigate the dynamics (including velocities and accelerations) of mouse pointing when Pointer Acceleration (PA)
functions are used. We also propose a simple model for these dynamics
from a control theoretic perspective. The model allows us to simulate the
effect of PA functions on pointing dynamics. In particular, it reproduces
and explains many important phenomena we observe in pointing dynamics with PA functions. These include: (1) Pointer position, velocity, and
acceleration over time, (2) Different accelerations when moving in different directions, and the resulting mouse drift when using PA functions, (3)
Discontinuous jumps in phase space and associated acceleration peaks in
Hooke plots when using Step PA functions. We identify parameters of
the model using a reciprocal pointing task with the mouse controlling a
pointer on a computer screen using sigmoid and step PA functions and
constant gain. Our model explains the human-computer system including the PA function as a closed-loop dynamical system. In particular,
we use a second-order model resembling a spring-mass-damper system
(second order lag). Our model explains and allows to simulate the role
of PA functions in pointing, including the phenomena described above.

1   Introduction

The contribution of this paper is an investigation of pointing dynamics using
Pointer Acceleration (PA) functions. PA functions adjust the mouse gain depending on mouse velocity. PA functions are implemented in all major operating systems and are used by millions of users on a daily basis. Given their ubiquity
and importance, it is very surprising how little we know about them. Consider
the simple case of pointing with the Trackpoint under Windows. The Trackpoint
microcontroller applies a force-to-motion function to the applied force that has
been optimized for pointing at text targets [26]. Windows treats the Trackpoint
as a mouse and applies to the output of this function a PA function that has
presumably been optimized for mouse movements. We do not know how these
transfer functions interact to produce the final pointer movement. Similarly,
Windows ignores the resolution of mice when applying PA functions, forcing
users to reduce the resolution on the mouse microcontroller to obtain usable
mouse gains. We can reverse engineer the PA functions implemented in major
operating systems [6], but do not know anything about their design rationale.
Transfer functions are crucial not only for Desktop settings, but also for mid-air
gestures and Virtual and Augmented Reality interaction [10,13,14,17,25].

© IFIP International Federation for Information Processing 2017
Published by Springer International Publishing AG 2017. All Rights Reserved
R. Bernhaupt et al. (Eds.): INTERACT 2017, Part III, LNCS 10515, pp. 475–495, 2017.
DOI: 10.1007/978-3-319-67687-6_33

In addition to analyzing pointing dynamics, we also provide a simple model of pointing dynamics with PA functions. While our model is certainly not at the point where it can actually be used for the optimization of transfer functions, it aims to be a first step in that direction. At the current point, the model can quantitatively predict pointer position and velocity over time with some accuracy. More importantly, it reproduces and explains many important phenomena we observe in pointing dynamics with PA functions qualitatively. These include: (1) Shape of pointer position, velocity, and acceleration over time and space (2) Different accelerations when moving in different directions, and the resulting mouse drift when using PA functions (3) Discontinuous jumps in phase space and associated acceleration peaks in Hooke plots when using Step PA functions.

2   Related Work

2.1   Traditional Understanding of Pointing in HCI

Pointing is often understood as a discrete event in HCI. A pointer is moved from a start position to a target of a certain width W at a distance D. When the target is reached, a delimiter, such as a mouse click, terminates the movement. Of interest is usually only the overall movement time MT and error rate. The dynamics of the movement itself, such as the position, velocity, and acceleration over time, of both pointer and pointing device, are often not investigated. The model for movement time most often used in HCI is Fitts' law [11,12]. It allows to predict movement time as $MT = a + b \log_2(\frac{D}{W} + 1)$ in the Shannon formulation [20]. The constants a and b are specific for a certain user and input device, but independent from distance to and width of the target. They can be obtained from pointing data of a user by linear regression. Fitts' derived the relationship from the Shannon-Hartley theorem [28]. This theorem gives the channel capacity of a continuous channel with Gaussian noise. Conclusions from the channel capacity to the actual movement that takes place are not straightforward. Crossman and Goodeve [9] proposed an alternative derivation of Fitts' law based on assumptions about the actual pointer movement. They assume that pointing consists of a series of sub-movements of equal duration and error, until the target is reached. Meyer et al. [21] developed an extension of the Crossman Goodeve model that assumes that humans optimize the durations of sub-movements to minimize the overall movement time under noise.

2.2   Current Understanding of Transfer Functions in HCI

Transfer functions map data from an input device (e.g., mouse) to the interface (e.g., pointer movement). As such they are an essential component of systems that enable interaction of humans with computers. Design of transfer functions has a long history in HCI [2,13,14,17,23,25,26]. One important case of transfer functions are pointer acceleration (PA) functions. PA functions increase the mouse gain with increasing mouse velocity. Jellinek and Card [16] performed three experiments investigating PA functions. The tested PA functions did not result in different performance. They concluded that PA functions do not improve performance, and would "violate Fitts' law" if they would. They also concluded that PA functions are preferred by some users because they "lower the device footprint" and require less clutching (repositioning of the mouse).

Nancel et al. [23] analyze transfer functions for mid-air pointing on display walls. They present a theoretical analysis of dual-precision pointing techniques based on Fitts' law. Further, they present detailed tuning guidelines for the parametrization of sigmoid pointer acceleration functions.

The most thorough investigations of transfer functions in HCI are by Casiez et al. In [7], they compare movement times in reciprocal pointing for static gains (1,2,4,6,8,12) and six levels for the PA function implemented in Windows XP/Vista. They find that PA results in 3.3% faster pointing, and 5.6% for small targets. They also propose a theoretical explanation based on Meyer et al.'s stochastically optimized sub-movement model.

2.3 Dynamical Systems Perspective

In contrast to modeling pointing as a discrete movement or series of sub-movements, it has also been modeled as a dynamical system. Dynamical systems can be modeled as differential equations, which have as a solution a prediction of pointer position over time [24,29]. The dynamical systems perspective on human-computer interaction and pointing is developed in detail in [22]. In [22], four models from manual control theory are compared regarding their ability to model pointing with a mouse. One of the compared models is the second order lag, which also serves as the basis for the model in this paper. As earlier examples, Jagacinsky and Flach [15] show how human pointing can be modeled as a simple first order lag or second order lag (2OL). They also show how Fitts' law can be derived from either of these models. The VITE model [5] is a neural network model of pointing. The model is governed by the differential equations $\frac{dV}{dt} = \alpha(-V + T - P)$ and $\frac{dP}{dt} = G[V]^+$. $T(t)$ is the target position, $V(t)$ "the activity of the agonist's DV population", or in other words, related to the velocity of the end-effector, $P(t)$ is "the activity of the agonist's PPC population", or in other words, related to the position of the end-effector. $G(t)$ is the "GO signal", which can be used to modulate the mapping from V to P. The model can be used to predict end-effector position, velocity, and acceleration over time given a start and target position. Beamish et al. [3] have extended the model with a delay term and have proven that Fitts' law follows from this model. Recently, the VITE model has been extended to include Pointer Acceleration functions [30]. It was shown that the resulting model is stable under any PA function, and theoretical performance bounds of the model have been derived. [1] propose an extension of the VITE model with Bang-bang control. When the error is large, Bang-bang control is used, and VITE is used for corrections close to the target. This model is related to Costello's Surge model of manual control [8].

In contrast to [1,3,30], our work is of more empirical nature. We present a dataset of pointing with PA functions, an empirical analysis of pointing dynamics

with pointer acceleration, a model of pointing with PA functions that can replicate phenomena we observe in that dataset, a system identification process that
can learn parameters of the model from the dataset, and an analysis of model
behavior in comparison to user behavior.

3   Mouse Noise and PA Functions

The analysis of pointing dynamics and transfer functions is complicated by sensor
noise. Mouse data is very noisy. Furthermore, different mouse models exhibit
widely different noise characteristics. Raw mouse data (phase space plot: velocity
plotted over position) for four commercial mice is shown in Fig. 2. While the
Logitech G502 exhibits a relatively clean and high-resolution velocity profile,
velocity spikes appear at changing regular rates. The Razer DeathAdder has a
similarly high resolution sensor, but exhibits more high frequency noise. The
velocity bump at the beginning of the movement remains inexplicable. More
conventional mice like the Logitech UAS144 or Dell mouse have much lower
resolution. Also, the UAS144 mouse seems to loose tracking accuracy at high
velocities. For everyday pointing, this noise is usually not noticeable, because
the integration of pointer velocity to position smoothes noise out. However, for
the analysis of pointing dynamics, this noise is critical. Furthermore, the noise
gets increased considerably when using PA functions, because velocity spikes get
multiplied with a higher gain factor. When using Step PA functions, the gain can
even oscillate between low and high gain with the noise frequency. To address
this issue, in this paper we apply a median filter and a second order IIR low-
pass filter to the mouse velocity *before* applying the PA function. In practice,
this is not done because it makes the selection of individual pixels more difficult.

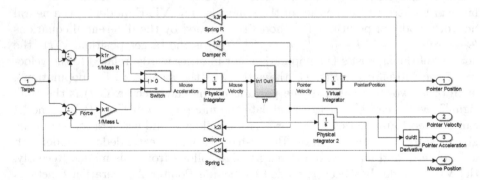

Fig. 1. Our control theoretical model of pointing with a pointer acceleration function.
The model predicts pointer position, velocity and acceleration as well as mouse position
over time given a target position. The model can loosely be interpreted as switching
between two spring-mass-damper systems depending on the movement direction of the
pointer. Further, the velocity of the system gets modified by a nonlinearity within
the loop, the pointer acceleration function, breaking the strict spring-mass-damper
interpretation.

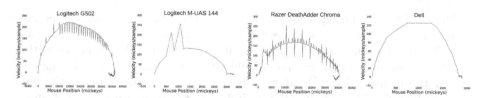

Fig. 2. Noise for different mice. Logitech G502, Logitech UAS144, Razer DeathAdder, and a Dell mouse, respectively. The noise gets amplified by PA functions. The Dell mouse seems to exhibit less noise but provides much lower temporal and spatial resolution.

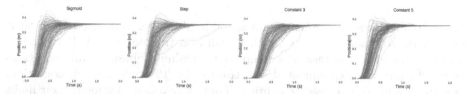

Fig. 3. Overview of time series of pointer position for all participants using the different transfer functions.

In particular, very small corrective movements of the mouse get filtered out. For our analysis of pointing dynamics, especially using PA functions, this step is however necessary. Otherwise, the noise of the mouse obscures pointing dynamics and influences of PA functions.

4 Dataset

We captured data using the *serial pointing task* [11], where a user clicks alternatingly at two one-dimensional targets. The Dataset and model are available at http://joergmueller.info/PAdynamics/.

4.1 Method

Participants. 12 unpaid participants (3 female, mean age 30.6 years (SD 8.1), all normal or corrected to normal eyesight, all expert computer users) participated in the study. They had on average 16.4 years (SD 6.5) of experience of mouse use, and currently used a mouse on average for 37.6 hours (SD 31.6) per week. While one participant was left-handed, all preferred to use the mouse with the right hand and used the right hand in the experiment.

Task and Materials. Two one-dimensional targets were displayed. The task was to click on the targets serially. A new trial started as soon as the user clicked on the previous target. Missed trials were not repeated, but annotated in the dataset.

The *condition* of the experiment is pointer acceleration function. The pointer acceleration function is varied between blocks, but kept constant within each block. We cover 4 different pointer acceleration functions. The *sigmoid* function provides a gain of 3 when the mouse velocity is below 10 cm/s, and a gain of 5 when the mouse velocity is above 30 cm/s. Between these points, the gain increases linearly. The *step* function switches instantly between gains 3 and 5 at 20 cm/s. In addition, *constant gain* of *3* and *5* was tested. We chose the parameters to be consistent between the different functions and be usable for pointing in an iterative tuning process. Each condition is repeated for 50 trials. The order of conditions was counterbalanced using a Latin square.

Procedure. Users were asked to adjust table, display and mouse pad to their preferences. All users were resting their palm on the mouse pad. Participants were introduced to the task and completed a training phase for all conditions before starting the experiment. Users trained for 10 trials in each condition. Users took a break after each condition. They were asked to stretch their limbs and relax briefly. Users were asked to adjust mouse position in the first trial of each condition and to avoid clutching during the experiment. To enable this, we used a very large mouse pad (900×450 mm). Users were asked to click on the targets as quickly as possible while maintaining an error rate of below 5%. Targets were shown at a distance of 35.98 cm (1300 px) with a target width of 1.38 mm (5 px), leading to an index of difficulty (ID) of $log_2(\frac{D}{W} + 1) = 8.028$.

Apparatus. Data was captured on a Dell Precision 7810 PC with an AOC G2460PQU monitor ($24''$, 1920×1080 px resolution, 140 Hz, no Vsync). The Logitech G502 mouse was used with no additional weights. The software used libpointing.org [6] for accessing the raw mouse data, instead of using the mouse data that is provided preprocessed by the operating system. The raw mouse data was filtered with a median filter with window size 3 to filter outlier samples (visible for Logitech G502 in Fig. 2). The resulting signal was filtered with a low-pass IIR filter with a critical frequency of 15 Hz and a quality factor of 1. Meaningful frequencies in human movement are below this frequency [27], so that they were preserved in the signal. Filtering was performed to remove high-frequency noise components in the mouse, which would otherwise hinder the investigation of the impact of pointer acceleration functions on pointing dynamics. OpenGL (glfw3) was used for low-latency graphics generation. The program was running at approximately 2000 Hz, such that the frequency of the overall apparatus was limited by the 140 Hz of the monitor. Mouse events were logged as they were delivered to the program by libpointing. Data was captured under Microsoft Windows 10. Latency was measured with a Sony DSC-RX10M2 camera at 1000 FPS. The mouse was hit with a hard object at high speeds, and the number of frames from impact to pointer motion on the display was counted. The latency was 25 ms. The x-dimension of the mouse was used to move a white crosshair pointer (1 px wide) that only moved horizontally.

4.2   Preprocessing

In order to facilitate further analysis, data was preprocessed. We dropped the
first 20 trials from each condition. This was done to remove trials where substantial learning of the new PA function was taking place. Naive calculation
of derivatives (pointer acceleration) from mouse movement data would greatly
increase any remaining noise in the signal. Therefore, we filter the pointer velocity using a Savitzky-Golay filter with a 4th degree polynomial and a window size
of 21 samples (20 ms) to calculate pointer acceleration as the 1st derivative of
pointer velocity. We used the same filter to calculate mouse acceleration from
mouse velocity as filtered in the apparatus.

5   Summary Statistics

Figures 3, 4, and 5 provide an overview of the dataset. Figure 3 shows the pointer
position over time for all participants and all trials separated by PA function.
In this visualization it is very difficult to detect differences between the functions. The only visible difference is that with constant gain 3 there seems to
be less overshooting of the target. Figure 4 shows the pointer velocity plotted
over pointer position (left column) as well as mouse velocity plotted over mouse
position (right column). Because position and velocity determine the state of
an inertial (second order) system, this visualization is called a phase space plot
for such systems. The differences between the PA functions become much more
obvious in this visualization. In particular, the phase space plot for the Step PA
function is very different from the others. Whenever the velocity crosses the step,
there is a sudden jump in pointer velocity. The center parts of the individual
curves seem simply to be "lifted" up from their normal elliptical shape.

Figure 5 shows the pointer acceleration plotted over pointer position (left
column) as well as mouse acceleration over mouse position (right column). This
type of visualization is called a Hooke plot. The individual acceleration and
deceleration spikes when using the Step PA function are clearly visible. Although
the acceleration when crossing the step happens instantaneously, it is smoothed
in this plot. This is because the acceleration is calculated from a polynomial
approximation of velocity to manage noise. Also the Sigmoid PA function creates
acceleration and deceleration spikes (although smoother) that can be seen when
following individual trajectories. The isolated spike in the plot for constant gain
5 is the only clutching event in the data.

Figure 6 (left) shows the maximum pointer velocities achieved in the experiment, separated by PA function and whether the movement is to the left or
to the right. Figure 6 (right) shows the maximum pointer accelerations achieved
in the experiment, separated by PA function and whether the movement is to
the left or to the right. It can be seen that the PA functions achieve higher
accelerations than constant gain. Maximum acceleration of the Step PA function is infinite and therefore not shown. The surge movement denotes the initial
(often ballistic) movement towards the target. We calculate the surge movement
from mouse acceleration as follows. The point where the deceleration is larger

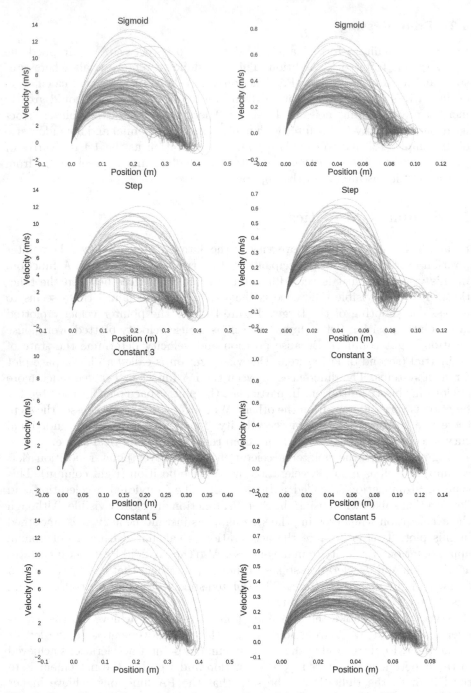

Fig. 4. Overview of phase space plots for all participants using the different transfer functions. Left column shows pointer velocity over pointer position, right column shows corresponding mouse velocity over mouse position. Note how the pointer profiles for the Step TF are "lifted up". Also, the endpoints of mouse profiles with PA functions have more variance.

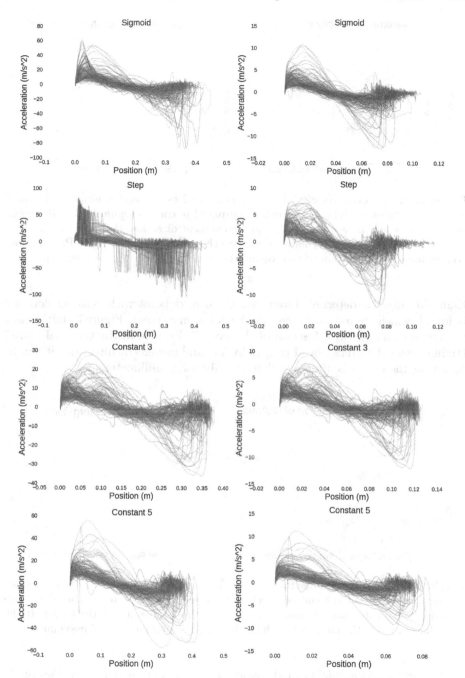

Fig. 5. Overview of Hooke plots for all participants using the different transfer functions. Left column shows pointer acceleration over pointer position, right column shows corresponding mouse acceleration over mouse position. The Step PA function creates infinite acceleration when the velocity crosses the Step (peaks smoothed here due to filtering). These peaks are still visible in the Sigmoid TF, but smoother.

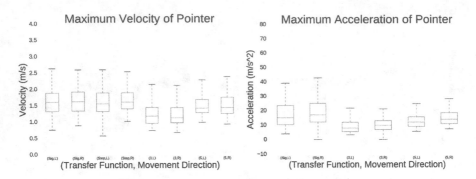

Fig. 6. Left: Maximum velocity of pointer separated by TF and movement direction. The PA functions reach higher velocities compared to constant gain. Right: Maximum pointer accelerations separated by TF and movement direction. Pointing with the Sigmoid PA function reaches higher accelerations than static gain. The Step PA functions creates infinite acceleration when crossing the step and is therefore not shown.

than $-0.5 \, \text{m/s}^2$ is detected. From there, the next point with zero acceleration is found, which we use as the end of the surge movement. Figure 7 (left) shows the surge endpoints as a fraction of the overall distance to the target. Figure 7 (right) shows the overshoot of targets by TF and movement direction. It can be seen that the target is often overshot by only a few millimeters.

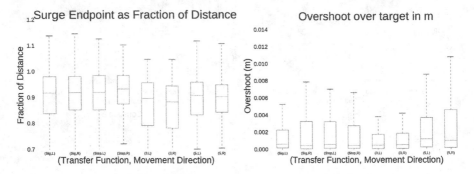

Fig. 7. Left: The surge denotes the initial ballistic pointer movement with a N-shaped acceleration profile at the end of which the acceleration drops to 0. The plot shows the endpoints of this ballistic movement as a fraction of distance to the target. Right: Overshoot denotes the amount by which the target is overshot at the maximum.

We performed a number of statistical tests comparing characteristics of the individual trials by TF. A Friedman test revealed a significant effect of TF on maximum velocity ($\chi^2(3) = 404.04$, $p < 0.01$). A post-hoc test using Wilcoxon tests with Bonferroni correction showed the significant differences between all pairs of TFs except Step PA and Sigmoid PA ($p < 0.01$). A Friedman test revealed a significant effect of TF on maximum acceleration ($\chi^2(3) = 760.21$, p < 0.01). A post-hoc test using Wilcoxon tests with Bonferroni correction showed the significant differences between all pairs of TFs. A Friedman test revealed a significant effect of TF on overshoot ($\chi^2(3) = 17.998$, p < 0.01). A post-hoc test using Wilcoxon tests with Bonferroni correction showed the significant differences between constant gain 3 and 5 (p < 0.01). A Friedman test revealed a significant effect of TF on surge endpoint ($\chi^2(3) - 44.387$, p < 0.01). A post-hoc test using Wilcoxon tests with Bonferroni correction showed the significant differences between all pairs of TFs except Step PA and Sigmoid PA and Sigmoid PA and constant gain 5 (p < 0.05). We did not find an effect of PA function on trial time (Friedman, $\chi^2(3) = 6.137$, p > 0.05).

6 Control Theoretical Model of Transfer Functions

6.1 Modelling Process

We developed the model in an iterative process. In each iteration, the experimental design and apparatus were updated, data collected, data analyzed, the model designed, the model simulated, and model behavior analyzed. We iterated individual phases as well as the whole cycle. Key aspects of iteration were: selection of conditions and parameterization of PA functions, filtering of mouse data to detect phenomena caused by PA functions, detection and presentation of phenomena, and model design. The key tradeoff in the model design is between predictive accuracy and model complexity. For this paper, we decided to present the simplest possible model that can replicate the phenomena we are interested in to a satisfactory degree.

6.2 The Model

Our model of pointing dynamics with PA functions (Fig. 1) is a switching controller, switching between two second order lag (2OL) controllers based on movement direction. Additionally, between the two integrators (at the mapping from mouse velocity to pointer velocity), a non-linear pointer acceleration function is introduced. This PA function changes the gain based on mouse velocity. The PA function is implemented as a lookup table, which linearly interpolates between table points.

The model can loosely be interpreted from a physical perspective. In this perspective, the pointer is interpreted as consisting of a mass, a spring, and a damper. The spring exerts a force on the user's arm that is proportional to the distance between pointer and target. The motion of the pointer is damped, similar to friction which exerts a force on the arm that is proportional to the velocity of the pointer and opposes the direction of movement. These forces are added and translate into acceleration of the arm according to Newton's second law $F = ma$. The arm/mouse acceleration is then integrated to yield mouse velocity. Mouse velocity is then fed into the transfer function. The transfer function translates mouse velocity to pointer velocity by applying a speed dependent

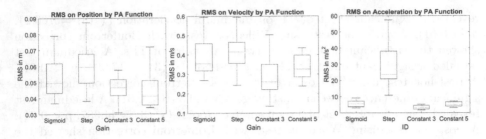

Fig. 8. RMSE of position (top left), velocity (top right) and acceleration (bottom) between model and user behavior for the Sigmoid PA function, Step PA function, constant gain 3 and constant gain 5.

gain. This pointer velocity then gets multiplied with the damping parameter k_2 and exerts a proportional negative force on the arm. The pointer velocity also gets integrated to yield pointer position. The pointer position gets multiplied with the spring parameter k_3 and exerts a proportional force in the direction of the error. The parameters k_1, k_2 and k_3 are different depending on movement direction. The model discretely switches between the parameter sets depending on the velocity being above 0 (movement to the right) or below (movement to the left).

The model corresponds to the equilibrium point hypothesis of motor control [27]. In this hypothesis, it is assumed that the brain only sets the target position ("equilibrium point") of the system. The feedback loops and parameters are thought of describing the mechanical properties of the biomechanical system and reflex loops. Alternatively, it can be interpreted as the brain computing the error and controlling the force exerted on the muscles directly. In any case, the model describes the overall system of brain, biomechanical system, reflex loops and computer, and the boundaries between these modules can be drawn in the model in many different ways.

6.3   Model Implementation

We implement the model in Simulink as a block diagram. Simulink is a Matlab extension that allows simulation of linear and non-linear systems. Because the transfer function introduces a nonlinearity inside the feedback loop, simulation of the system is not as straightforward as with linear systems, such as a pure 2OL. The discontinuous nature of the switching control and the transfer function influence the choice of solver for the model. We chose a fixed-step solver (ode5, Dormand-Prince) with a step width of 1 ms to simulate the model.

6.4   System Identification Process

The 2OL model has three free parameters for each direction (mass $1/k_1$, spring k_3, damping k_2). These parameters need to be adjusted to fit the experimental

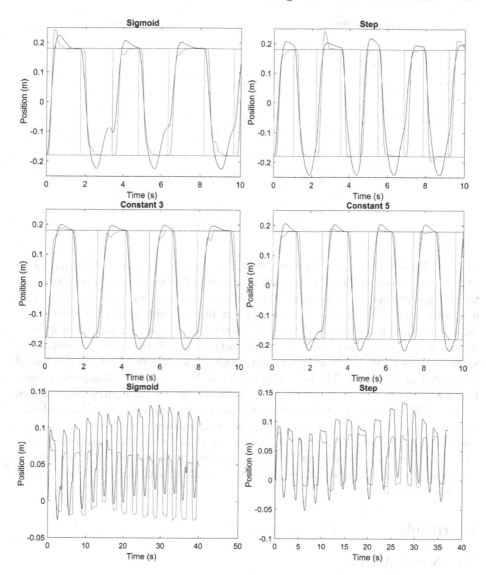

Fig. 9. Top: Time Series of pointer position predicted by the model (blue), as well as the actual pointer position (red) for one user. The target position is shown for orientation (yellow). Bounds of the targets are shown as horizontal colored lines (ID 8). The model can predict the position over time of the pointer rather well. However, no apparent differences in the dynamic behavior with the four transfer functions are visible in the time series. Bottom: Time Series of mouse position predicted by the four models (blue), as well as the actual mouse position (red) for one user. It can be seen that the mouse of the user (red) is drifting considerably when using a PA function, but less so with a constant gain. The reason for this is that users reach different velocities when moving left vs. right. Because the PA function increases the gain as a function of velocity, the mouse is drifting into the direction where higher velocities are reached. This effect is stronger for the sigmoid PA function than for the step PA function. (Color figure online)

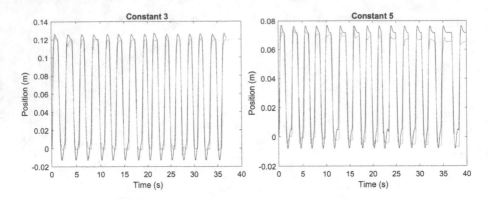

Fig. 9. (*continued*)

data. This process is called *System Identification*. There exists a comprehensive literature on System Identification with a wealth of methods specialized for identifying specific classes of systems [19]. Because the transfer functions introduce a nonlinearity in the model, the parameters are difficult to identify using classical system identification techniques. Therefore, we resorted to a very general technique based on simulation and optimization. In this technique, an optimizer aims to identify the parameter set that minimizes the error between the model and experimental data. The objective function determines which aspects of user behavior the model is fit to. As objective function we use the sum of sum squared errors (SSE) between actual pointer position, velocity and acceleration, and simulated pointer position, velocity, and acceleration, over time. As optimizer, we used the Simplex search method as implemented in the Matlab fminsearch function. We split the experimental data into a training and a test set. For each PA function, we use the first half of trials for training, and the remaining half of trials for evaluation.

7   Results

7.1   Model Accuracy

Figure 9 (top) shows the actual and predicted pointer position over time. It is clear that regardless of the PA function used, our models are able to predict the pointer position over time rather well. However, in order to detect differences in the dynamic behavior between different PA functions, pointer velocity and acceleration must be investigated. Figure 8 shows the root mean square error (RMSE) between pointer position, velocity, and acceleration over time as predicted by the model and observed from the participants. The models do not predict acceleration using the Step PA function well. This might be an artifact of our evaluation procedure. For the user, acceleration is calculated from a polynomial approximation of pointer velocity, smoothing out discontinuous acceleration spikes. For the model, pointer acceleration is calculated directly.

7.2   Model Parameters

Table 1 shows the model parameters identified from the pointing data through the optimization process. When interpreting the model as a spring-mass damper system, the parameter k_1 can be interpreted as the inverse of the mass (e.g., of the arm) $1/m$. Similarly, parameter k_2 can be interpreted as the damping, and k_3 as the spring pulling the arm to the target. The damping does not seem to be changed between left and right movements. The lower constant gain 3 is counterbalanced with lower mass ($m = 1/k_1$) compared to gain 5. This can be interpreted as the model adjusting to the PA function and changing its parameters accordingly. Similarly, we can expect users to change their behavior as we change the PA function.

Table 1. Identified model parameters. Given are mean (min, max) for each PA Function.

PA function	Sigmoid	Step	Constant 3	Constant 5
k1l	2.59 (0.33, 5.93)	2.77 (0.33, 5.86)	3.26 (0.39, 9.64)	2.71 (0.48, 6.12)
k1r	5.78 (2.78, 14.06)	5.49 (3.49, 13.17)	5.42 (3.37, 11.33)	5.14 (2.55, 8.91)
k2l	0.28 (0.11, 0.43)	0.26 (0.11, 0.41)	0.29 (0.13, 0.44)	0.28 (0.13, 0.39)
k2r	0.29 (0.15, 0.47)	0.28 (0.17, 0.45)	0.36 (0.22, 0.47)	0.32 (0.20, 0.43)
k3l	1.90 (0.97, 4.18)	1.91 (0.95, 4.30)	1.92 (0.89, 5.45)	2.20 (0.88, 5.23)
k3r	1.04 (0.76, 1.42)	1.10 (0.76, 1.46)	0.99 (0.80, 1.61)	0.92 (0.77, 1.12)

7.3   Mouse Drift

Movements in different directions achieve different velocities. This creates problems when PA functions are used. Movement in the faster direction gets amplified by higher gains, which results in less distance covered by the physical mouse. When the user is moving the pointer back to the original position at lower speed, the mouse needs to cover more space because of the lower gain of the PA function. Over time, the mouse is thus drifting, creating the need to clutch because of the limited workspace. This behavior gets replicated by the model. Figure 9 (bottom) shows the actual mouse position (red), as integrated from mouse displacements, and the mouse position predicted by the model (blue) over time. It can be seen that with static gain, neither actual nor predicted mouse positions drift. With both PA functions, both actual and predicted mouse position drift considerably. The drift is larger for the Sigmoid function, because differences in gain are integrated over more different velocities, and therefore more time. It should be noted that the model is not trained on the mouse movements, but only on the resulting pointer movements. Thus, mouse drift is an emergent property of the model and does not exactly replicate user mouse drift.

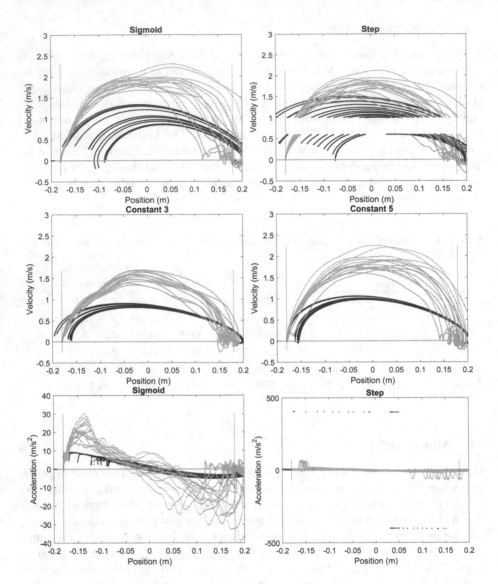

Fig. 10. Top: Phase space plot of pointer velocity predicted by the models (blue), as well as phase space plot of the actual pointer (red) for one user. For the Step TF, there is a jump in velocity when the velocity crosses the step both during acceleration and deceleration. This phenomenon is replicated by the model (blue). Bottom: Hooke plots of pointer acceleration predicted by the model (blue), as well as the actual pointer acceleration (red). The reached acceleration is higher than for constant gain. The Step TF results in steep acceleration and deceleration spikes when the velocity crosses the step. This behavior is replicated by the model. For constant gain 3, this user shows two acceleration spikes per movement. One hypothesis might be that this user starts to accelerate the mouse, but only overcomes the static friction of the arm on the table slightly later, resulting in a second acceleration spike. (Color figure online)

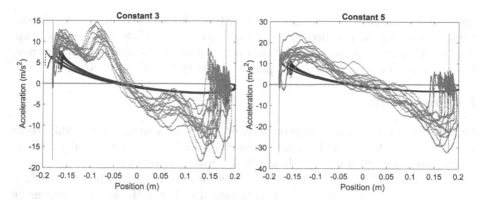

Fig. 10. (*continued*)

7.4   Phase Space Behavior

Figure 10 (top) shows the phase space plots for the two PA functions and two constant gains. In these plots, pointer velocity is plotted over pointer position. For constant gain, a symmetric phase space plots (e.g., almost half-circle) indicates an open-loop movement, in which acceleration and deceleration are equally steep. During open-loop movements, visual feedback does not influence the motion. Closed-loop movement, in which the user adapts the deceleration phase according to visual feedback, is often characterized by asymmetric phase space plots (e.g., half-egg shaped). The acceleration is steeper, while the deceleration more gradually homes in on the target. The control model presented in this paper represents closed-loop control. In the above plots it becomes clear that PA functions introduce distortions in phase space plots that do not appear in physical (constant gain) behavior. In particular the step PA function contains discontinuities that do not appear otherwise. The center section of the plot is practically "lifted up" where the velocity crosses the threshold. This effect is also replicated by the model.

7.5   Hooke Plots

Figure 10 (bottom) shows the Hooke portraits of all transfer functions. In these plots, pointer acceleration is plotted over pointer position. It can be seen that the user Hooke portraits are approximately N shaped, which is indicative of the high ID used in the task [4]. With low ID, one could expect a more backslash (\) shaped Hooke plot, indicating oscillatory behavior. While the user Hooke plot is relatively symmetric N shaped, the model deviates from the user by a more asymmetric shape. The momentary increase in acceleration is indicative of the second order of the model (two chained integrators), where the model can switch acceleration (but not velocity or position) instantaneously, e.g., when the target switches. The acceleration then falls gradually as the pointer approaches the target. The most obvious impact the Step PA function has are the discontinuous acceleration and deceleration spikes when the velocity crosses the step. The model replicates these spikes, however in different positions than the user, because the model underestimates pointer velocity (see Fig. 10 (bottom)).

8 Discussion

Our model can predict pointer position over time with some accuracy, while there are systematic deviations from user behavior in velocity and especially acceleration. More importantly, it qualitatively reproduces phenomena that appear in human pointing behavior with pointer acceleration functions. These include the discontinuous phase space plot and acceleration spikes in Hooke plot when using Step PA functions. Also the mouse drift when using PA functions is explained and predicted qualitatively, although not quantitatively (the quantity of mouse drift differs between model and user). Note that mouse drift due to PA functions is only one of multiple causes of mouse drift. Another one is the fact that the coordinate system of the mouse rotates with the mouse, and is not fixed in space, as explained by [18].

There exist numerous opportunities for improving the model. In particular, the systematic deviations from user behavior regarding velocity and acceleration behavior warrant further investigation. Perhaps most importantly for the case of simulation of PA functions, the model systematically underestimates user velocities. This will result in the application of PA gain at different moments compared to the user. For example, in Fig. 10, we see that the Step PA function switches gain at different moments from the actual data. This and other issues should be addressed in future work.

More generally, modeling and simulation of pointing dynamics is important for HCI for a variety of reasons. First, the phenomena of pointing dynamics are very fast (in the order of milliseconds), so that they are less accessible to human intuition than slower phenomena in interaction. This might also explain why pointing dynamics has not received very much attention in HCI to date. Second, many inputs and outputs of the human-computer system are not be easily accessible, or the phenomena of interest are obscured by noise. For example, due to the noisy mouse sensor, mouse and pointer acceleration are difficult to investigate, because phenomena are obscured by noise in mouse motion data. Third, there is considerable variability in human pointing dynamics. In order to detect patterns and phenomena in dynamics, many trials are necessary, increasing the cost of experiments. Simulations of pointing dynamics can be used in an exploratory way to predict phenomena that can then be validated or refuted by experiments.

Computational modeling of PA functions and their simulation might ultimately lead to the ability to computationally optimize PA functions and other transfer functions. This might ultimately lead the field of HCI to conducting more simulations of interaction. However, given the model developed in this paper, we are still quite far from that vision, and it can be seen merely as a first step towards this long-term direction.

At the current step, the model can be seen as more of a tool for thought and inspiration. It shows that we can computationally understand and simulate the effect of PA functions on pointing. In particular, it provides researchers, practitioners and students a concise way of thinking about PA functions. This might help to understand the way PA functions influence the pointing process more deeply. It provides a common vocabulary and conceptual framework for discussing and integrating knowledge about phenomena related to PA functions. It can help in the generation of research questions and hypotheses, and conceptually guide the design of PA functions. We hope that control theoretical modeling of human-computer interaction will become an important research direction for HCI in the future.

9   Conclusion

We have investigated the dynamics (including velocities and accelerations) of mouse pointing when Pointer Acceleration (PA) functions are used. To model these dynamics, we have proposed a simple control theoretical model of pointing dynamics using PA functions. The model demonstrates phenomena including pointer position, velocity, and acceleration over time, different accelerations when moving in different directions, and the resulting mouse drift when using PA functions, and discontinuous jumps in phase space and associated acceleration peaks in Hooke plots when using Step PA functions. We believe that the analysis and control theoretic modelling of interaction dynamics, including Pointer Acceleration functions, provides a promising direction of future research in human-computer interaction.

References

1. Aranovskiy, S., Ushirobira, R., Efimov, D., Casiez, G.: Modeling pointing tasks in mouse-based human-computer interactions. In: 2016 IEEE 55th Conference on Decision and Control (CDC), pp. 6595–6600. IEEE (2016)
2. Barrett, R.C., Selker, E.J., Rutledge, J.D., Olyha, R.S.: Negative inertia: a dynamic pointing function. In: Conference Companion on Human Factors in Computing Systems, CHI 1995, pp. 316–317. ACM, New York (1995). http://doi.acm.org/10.1145/223355.223692
3. Beamish, D., Bhatti, S.A., MacKenzie, I.S., Wu, J.: Fifty years later: a neurodynamic explanation of fitts' law. J. R. Soc. Interface 3(10), 649–654 (2006). http://rsif.royalsocietypublishing.org/content/3/10/649
4. Bootsma, R.J., Fernandez, L., Mottet, D.: Behind fitts law: kinematic patterns in goal-directed movements. Int. J. Hum. Comput. Stud. 61(6), 811–821 (2004)
5. Bullock, D., Grossberg, S.: Neural dynamics of planned arm movements: emergent invariants and speed-accuracy properties during trajectory formation. Psychol. Rev. 95(1), 49 (1988)
6. Casiez, G., Roussel, N.: No more bricolage!: methods and tools to characterize, replicate and compare pointing transfer functions. In: Proceedings of the 24th Annual ACM Symposium on User Interface Software and Technology, UIST 2011, pp. 603–614. ACM, New York (2011). http://doi.acm.org/10.1145/2047196.2047276

7. Casiez, G., Vogel, D., Balakrishnan, R., Cockburn, A.: The impact of control-display gain on user performance in pointing tasks. Hum. Comput. Inter. **23**(3), 215–250 (2008)
8. Costello, R.G.: The surge model of the well-trained human operator in simple manual control. IEEE Trans. Man–Mach. Syst. **9**(1), 2–9 (1968)
9. Crossman, E.R.F.W., Goodeve, P.J.: Feedback control of hand-movement and fitts' law. Quart. J. Exp. Psychol. **35**(2), 251–278 (1983)
10. Feuchtner, T., Müller, J.: Extending the body for interaction with reality. In: Proceedings of the 2017 CHI Conference on Human Factors in Computing Systems, CHI 2017, pp. 5145–5157. ACM, New York (2017). http://doi.acm.org/10.1145/3025453.3025689
11. Fitts, P.M.: The information capacity of the human motor system in controlling the amplitude of movement. J. Exp. Psychol. **47**(6), 381–391 (1954)
12. Fitts, P.M., Peterson, J.R.: Information capacity of discrete motor responses. J. Exp. Psychol. **67**(2), 103 (1964)
13. Frees, S., Kessler, G.D., Kay, E.: Prism interaction for enhancing control in immersive virtual environments. ACM Trans. Comput. Hum. Inter. (TOCHI) **14**(1), 2 (2007)
14. Gallo, L., Minutolo, A.: Design and comparative evaluation of smoothed pointing: a velocity-oriented remote pointing enhancement technique. Int. J. Hum. Comput. Stud. **70**(4), 287–300 (2012)
15. Jagacinski, R.J., Flach, J.M.: Control Theory for Humans: Quantitative Approaches to Modeling Performance. Lawrence Erlbaum, Mahwah (2003)
16. Jellinek, H.D., Card, S.K.: Powermice and user performance. In: Proceedings of the SIGCHI Conference on Human Factors in Computing Systems, CHI 1990, pp. 213–220. ACM, New York (1990). http://doi.acm.org/10.1145/97243.97276
17. König, W.A., Gerken, J., Dierdorf, S., Reiterer, H.: Adaptive pointing–design and evaluation of a precision enhancing technique for absolute pointing devices. In: Gross, T., Gulliksen, J., Kotzé, P., Oestreicher, L., Palanque, P., Prates, R.O., Winckler, M. (eds.) INTERACT 2009. LNCS, vol. 5726, pp. 658–671. Springer, Heidelberg (2009). doi:10.1007/978-3-642-03655-2_73
18. Lee, B., Bang, H.: A mouse with two optical sensors that eliminates coordinate disturbance during skilled strokes. Hum.-Comput. Inter. **30**(2), 122–155 (2015). http://dx.doi.org/10.1080/07370024.2014.894888
19. Ljung, L.: System Identification—Theory for the User. Prentice Hall, Englewood Cliffs (1987)
20. MacKenzie, I.S.: Fitts' law as a research and design tool in human-computer interaction. Hum. Comput. Inter. **7**(1), 91–139 (1992)
21. Meyer, D.E., Smith, J.E.K., Kornblum, S., Abrams, R.A., Wright, C.E.: Speed-accuracy trade-offs in aimed movements: toward a theory of rapid voluntary action. In: Jeannerod, M. (ed.) Attention and Performance XIII, pp. 173–226 (1990)
22. Müller, J., Oulasvirta, A., Murray-Smith, R.: Control theoretic models of pointing. ACM Trans. Comput. Hum. Inter. **24**(4) (2017)
23. Nancel, M., Pietriga, E., Chapuis, O., Beaudouin-Lafon, M.: Mid-air pointing on ultra-walls. ACM Trans. Comput. Hum. Inter. (TOCHI) **22**(5), 21 (2015)
24. Poulton, E.C.: Tracking Skill and Manual Control. Academic Press, New York (1974)
25. Poupyrev, I., Billinghurst, M., Weghorst, S., Ichikawa, T.: The go-go interaction technique: non-linear mapping for direct manipulation in VR. In: Proceedings of the 9th Annual ACM Symposium on User Interface Software and Technology, pp. 79–80. ACM (1996)

26. Rutledge, J.D., Selker, E.J.: Force-to-motion functions for pointing. In: Proceedings of the IFIP TC13 3rd International Conference on Human-Computer Interaction, pp. 701–706. North-Holland Publishing Co. (1990)

27. Schmidt, R.A., Lee, T.: Motor Control and Learning. Human Kinetics, Champaign (1988)

28. Shannon, C.E., Weaver, W.: The Mathematical Theory of Communication. University of Illinois Press, Champaign (2015)

29. Sheridan, T.B., Ferrell, W.R.: Man-Machine Systems: Information, Control, and Decision Models of Human Performance. MIT Press, Cambridge (1974)

30. Varnell, J.P., Zhang, F.: Characteristics of human pointing motions with acceleration. In: Proceedings of IEEE 54th Annual Conference on Decision and Control (CDC2015), Osaka, Japan, pp. 5364–5369 (2015)

How Can Adding a Movement Improve Target Acquisition Efficacy?

Alexander R. Payne[1(✉)], Beryl Plimmer[1], Andrew McDaid[1],
Andrew Luxton-Reilly[1], and T. Claire Davies[2]

[1] University of Auckland, Auckland, New Zealand
apay876@aucklanduni.ac.nz, {b.plimmer,andrew.mcdaid,
a.luxton-reilly}@auckland.ac.nz
[2] Queen's University, Kingston, Canada
claire.davies@queensu.ca

Abstract. People with motor impairments, such as cerebral palsy (CP), have difficulty acquiring small targets with a mouse. To improve upon this many assistive technologies enlarge targets, generally by introducing an extra movement. Often this improves accuracy however there appears to be a time penalty of performing all aspects of a movement twice. We investigate if it is possible for an extra movement to improve efficacy, and if this time penalty can be counterbalanced by a reduction of errors and corrective movements.

We measure overall interaction efficacy in a controlled 1D experiment. Participants acquire targets under three conditions: a single movement, a double movement, and using an example assistive tool. We anticipate that a double movement may only increase efficacy when the single movement target is so small that corrective movements are disproportionately time consuming. Therefore we investigated the effects of task scale, and of motor control. The results show that it is possible for two movements to be more efficient than one. However, this appears to be an edge case that only occurs at a very small scale. We suggest that tool designers must focus on how and why their tool is going to be attractive to users, since in real world situations it is unlikely to improve pointing efficacy. Users may choose to use a tool because it improves accuracy, or requires less effort, but they are unlikely to use it because it is faster.

Keywords: Cerebral palsy · Motor impairment · Breadth · Depth · Fitts's law · Mouse pointing · Target size

1 Introduction

Motor impairments make acquiring small targets with a mouse more difficult. For all users, with or without motor impairments, acquiring targets that are too small for their motor ability is slower than Fitts's Law predicts due to motor and visual difficulty [1].

Electronic supplementary material The online version of this chapter (doi:10.1007/978-3-319-67687-6_34) contains supplementary material, which is available to authorized users.

© IFIP International Federation for Information Processing 2017
Published by Springer International Publishing AG 2017. All Rights Reserved
R. Bernhaupt et al. (Eds.): INTERACT 2017, Part III, LNCS 10515, pp. 496–514, 2017.
DOI: 10.1007/978-3-319-67687-6_34

So, motor impairments such as cerebral palsy (CP), or those resulting from aging, can result in slow target acquisition that is not well modelled by Fitts's Law [2–4].

Accessibility tools often make target acquisition easier by replacing a single input movement with two or more inputs. For example: Motor-Magnifier, Visual-Motor-Magnifier, Click-and-Cross, Cross-and-Cross, Ballistic Square, Scanning Area Cursor (all [5]), Expansion Cursor [6], Adaptive Click-and-Cross [7], and Pointing Magnifier [8]. In all these tools, the purpose of the extra movement is to allow for increased target sizes thus avoiding the requirement for fine pointing. The difference between these tools and simply making all targets larger is they do not rely on unused screen space being available. The cost of these tools is that the user has to make extra inputs.

Despite generally improving accuracy, these tools often result in slower interaction. This paper asks what is the potential for two movements to be more efficient than one when a fair comparison is made? When or how can more movements be faster, and is there potential to improve throughput based on improved accuracy?

The benefit of two movements is the reduced pointing difficulty for each movement, so we investigate the potential improvements from a purely pointing perspective. Therefore, our experiment (Fig. 1) aims to avoid other effects such as interaction techniques, aesthetics, and navigation.

Fig. 1. Task Equipment. The task focuses on pointing and not other aspects of a realistic interface, such as aesthetics and navigation.

As a side note, previous work has suggested that menu navigation is slower with increased depth of menus [9–11]. So, even if it is possible for pointing to be faster with an assistive technology that adds a movement, navigation is a further design obstacle that must be considered.

Our experiment aims to uncover the fundamental potential of assistive pointing techniques that replace a single movement with two or more. Hence one and two movements are compared in as fair a scenario as possible. This does not aim to be realistic (Fig. 2 shows screen shots of the task), but focuses on *if* and *how* pointing can be more efficient with additional movements. As an example assistive technique, an Expansion Cursor will be compared to single and double movements (Fig. 3).

Of the example assistive tools mentioned, only two resulted in faster interaction and that was for a very specific situation. Both the Visual-Motor-Magnifier and the Click-and-Cross [5] were quicker than a standard cursor for people with motor

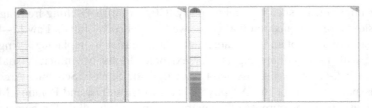

Fig. 2. Screen layout for our 1D clicking task. Left shows *Larger* scale artificial screen, right shows *Smaller* scale artificial screen. This is the *Single* movement task.

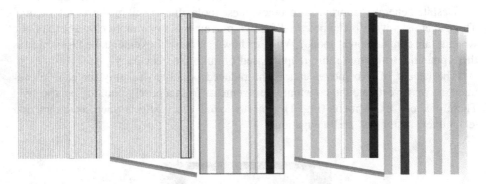

Fig. 3. Left: *Single* movement trials. Centre: *Expansion* trials where columns inside the purple box are expanded when the mouse button is held down. Right: *Double* movement trials. For all trials the black column is the target and the semi-transparent column is the starts zone. In *Double* trials the purple column is the second target. The pink highlight shows cursor location.

impairments pointing at 4 pixel targets. For 16 pixel targets they were both slower, and for people without motor impairments they were slower for all target sizes.

We hypothesize that adding a movement has the most potential to improve efficacy when corrective movements are problematic. In the case where Visual-Motor-Magnifier and Click-and-Cross [5] were faster than standard pointing, participants made significantly fewer sub-movements using the tools despite an addition input movement being required. Previous work also suggests small and difficult targets take disproportionately long to acquire according to Fitts's Law [1]. Adding a movement may avoid the problem of corrective movements since the targets can be larger.

We examine the effects of reduced motor ability and small scale movements since they are likely to result in increased time spent making corrective movements.

To investigate motor ability the experiment involved participants with and without CP. We hypothesize that increasing target size via an extra movement will be more useful to participants with CP since CP has been shown to result in increased number of sub-movements [12–14]. It seems reasonable that the increased time spent making corrective movements should diminish for larger targets.

Considering task scale is a useful way of highlighting the issue of small targets and corrective movements. According to Fitts's Law, scale should not affect acquisition times, therefore any changes observed are precisely due to the nature of the target.

Since it is not clear if participants with CP would adhere to Fitts's Law anyway, we only investigate the scale effect for participants without CP. We hypothesize that adding a movement may be more beneficial for smaller scale trials.

2 Background Theory and Task Rationale

We explore the potential of two movements to communicate more efficiently than one movement from a pointing perspective. This should highlight the potential of assistive tools to improve interaction efficacy. As a third condition, we also included an assistive tool that makes use of adding a movement. For this we used a modified version of the Expansion Cursor [6] (Fig. 3 shows trial types).

Our experiment aims to *fairly* compare the three trial types (*Single, Expansion, Double*). We measure the time it takes to communicate a set amount of information, using a set amount of screen space. Also in the interests of fairness, we aim to generalize for all possible target locations, and all possible cursor start locations. The fairness of our experiment set-up is based on two key theories: information theory [15], and Fitts's Law [16].

2.1 Information Theory and Fitts's Law

Information theory suggests the amount of information being communicated, H, is dependent on the number of possible outcomes, n, and the probability of each outcome occurring, p_i. This is defined by the Shannon-Weiner [15] measure of information (Eq. 1). Information is maximized if the probability of each outcome occurring is equal [15], and the equation reduces to Eq. 2.

$$H = \sum_{i=1}^{n} p_i \log_2 \left(\frac{1}{p_i} \right)$$
(1)

$$H = \log_2(n)$$
(2)

Hence, the number of possible alternatives directly informs the amount of information being communicated. In terms of the experiment task, the number of possible outcomes is the number of potential targets. To calculate the efficacy a screen layout, we must know the amount of information being communicated. Therefore the probability of selecting each target location should be equal.

Fitts's Law [16] relates movement time, MT, to movement amplitude, A, and target width, W. The key implication is that smaller movements to larger targets should be the fastest. A current iteration of this equation is Eq. 3 [17]. The MT also depends on the participant via constants a and b.

$$MT = a + b \times \log_2 \left(\frac{A}{W} + 1 \right)$$
(3)

Fitts's original experiment was based on a tapping task between 1D targets, and has been widely applied to HCI and 2D targets [18]. Similar to Chapuis & Dragicevic's experiment [1], our experiment reflects Fitts's task [16] by using 1D targets. For reasons further explained in Sect. 2.3, this reduces the complexity of controlling for possible cursor start locations and maintaining equal probability for each outcome.

Our experiment is concerned with communication rate; the time required (Fitts's Law) to communicate a set amount of information (information theory). The task screen layout (Figs. 1, 2 and 3) is intended to be as efficient as possible for a set screen size. It is based on the assumption that communication rate is maximized for a screen full of targets (number of possible outcomes is maximized and target width is maximized) that are equally likely to be selected (so all target positions are tested).

2.2   Scale, Motor Skills, and Magnification Level

These theories also informed our experiment set-up in terms of expected factors (scale, motor skills, and magnification level) and making fair comparisons.

Scale relates to the size of the screen and the targets. If the screen is larger, targets will become larger as well as the distance between them. Fitts's law suggests scale is not important as long as the amplitude to width ratio remains constant. However, this does not necessarily apply when small targets are involved. There is a small target effect where acquiring smaller targets takes longer than larger targets for the same A/W ratio [1]. We expect this effect to be important since single movements to smaller targets may encounter it, whereas double movements potentially avoid it.

A person's motor skills may also affect the potential benefits of adding a movement. The small target effect is due to motor effects and the visibility of targets [1]. Therefore, a person's motor skills are likely to interact with this effect. We investigate this by comparing participants with and without CP. Cerebral palsy is a common physical disability resulting from damage to the brain at, or around, birth [19]. (See [20] for a modern definition). We expect adding a movement to be more beneficial for people with motor impairments since fine pointing can be avoided.

Aside from scale and motor skills, magnification level may affect the potential of adding a movement. We define magnification level as the ratio of target sizes between *Double* and *Single* conditions. If target width is important for speed, it seems plausible that increasing the magnification level could further benefit an additional movement. Previous research of accessibility tools used magnification levels of 3 [6] and 4 [5, 7, 21]. For this experiment we chose a fixed magnification level that was as high as practically possible, at a value of 10. The rationale being that a higher magnification level should allow the best chance of larger targets (for *Double* trials) to avoid the small target effect, whilst the smaller targets (for *Single* trials) may still suffer from it.

2.3   Controlling for Target Locations and Cursor Start Position

To generalize the efficacy of a screen layout, we must assume that each target could be selected, and that the cursor could start from any position. Practically it is not possible to perform trials to every possible target location for every possible cursor location. Hence, we must control for target position and cursor start location.

The easiest way to control for target location is to perform trials to every target, but this requires performing too many trials. For a 1D target layout, position can be defined by distance from the center of the screen. Thus, we can halve the number of trials by performing trials to every second target. This also maintains equal probability of each target position being selected so we can calculate the amount of information being communicated.

We aim to generalize the results for the cursor starting from any location on the screen. Since this affects the movement amplitude, it must be controlled for. Therefore, each target location requires an actual cursor start location that can account for all possible start locations. For each target position we calculate an expected average movement time and then infer a representative movement amplitude. These calculations can be found in the supplementary material. Note that these calculations do not depend on a and b values, and are greatly simplified by making the task 1D instead of 2D. For 2D targets, direction would have an effect on target width [22].

3 Methodology

The experiment involved 2 participant groups (W/o CP, CP), 2 scales (*Larger*, *Smaller*), and 3 trial types (*Single*, *Expansion*, *Double*). Our key measure reflecting communication rate was time per information (Time/Info). Other performance measures were task completion time, accuracy, reaction time, traversal time, corrective time, and click time. We also considered subjective measures of user preference and workload to examine how user perceptions relate to the primary performance measures.

3.1 Participants

There were 15 participants; 10 without cerebral palsy (group name W/o CP) and 5 with CP (group name CP). Ethical approval was granted by our university and all participants (and parents for the two participants under 16) signed a consent form. These populations were recruited to establish whether motor skills interact with the potential benefits of adding a movement. Previous work suggests the latter group should take longer to complete pointing movements [2], whilst still being regular mouse users. All participants had normal or corrected to normal vision. The entire group W/o CP (37.1 years ±11.2) used their preferred right hand.

Part of the definition of CP is that it causes activity limitation [20]. The manual ability classification system (MACS) is a validated method of qualifying the effects of CP on people's hand activities [23]. We sought participants who regularly use a computer mouse, and were therefore from levels I & II. Further (self-reported) demographics of the group with CP can be seen in Table 1.

3.2 Test Conditions

Participants sat at a desk and performed a target acquisition task. A Dell S2240T 21.5" Monitor (resolution 1920 × 1080) plugged into a Lenovo T520 laptop computer

Table 1. Participant information for participants with CP. MACS: Manual ability classification system [23].

Participant	Hand used	Age	MACS level
1	Right	34	II
2	Left	64	I
3	Right	13	I
4	Right	15	I
5	Left	38	I

(Windows 7 Professional SP1) was used with a Dell optical mouse (Fig. 1). The pointer speed was the second fastest option, enhance pointer precision was enabled.

All tasks involved acquiring 1D targets. The screen layout (Fig. 2) had an artificial screen containing all the target columns, and a progress bar showing how many trials had been completed. The artificial screen width was 500 or 200 pixels depending on the scale being tested (*Larger* or *Smaller*). Both participant groups performed the *Larger* scale trials. Only the group W/o CP performed the *Smaller* scale trials because the two pixel targets are too small for participants with CP to reliably acquire. In fact they were chosen to be small for people W/o CP to engender the small target effect between *Single* and *Double* trials.

The artificial screen area differed from an actual screen since the cursor could leave the area during trials; edges did not constrain movement. The corresponding target widths are shown in Table 2. The scales were also chosen since the Expansion Cursor [6] study suggested most participants with CP will prefer the *Double* movement compared to 5 pixel targets (*Larger* scale), and most participants W/o CP will prefer an extra movement for 2 pixel targets (*Smaller* scale).

Table 2. Target widths (pixels) for different conditions. For *Expansion* trials, users could enlarge targets from the *Single* width (5 or 2) to the *Double* width (50 or 20) with a zoom.

Scale	Single	Expansion	Double	Groups
Larger	5	5 => 50	50	W/o CP, CP
Smaller	2	2 => 20	20	W/o CP

The initial movement of every trial was from a semi-transparent start zone (30 pixels wide) to a target column. The location of the start zone varied depending on the target location and the desired movement amplitude. For each target, the center-to-center amplitude of the movement was determined based on the target width and location. Using Fitts's Law, a theoretical average movement time to a specific target was calculated for the cursor starting from all possible locations (within the artificial screen). This average time was used to calculate a representative movement amplitude which was then used in the actual experiment. See supplementary material for the maths used. As mentioned, this does not depend on a and b values from Fitts's Law.

This experiment was intended to test communication via motor input, and visual acuity was not supposed to be a limiting factor. Target columns did not have a border, but were alternating colors in order to make them visually distinguishable. Furthermore, a semi-transparent pink highlight was applied to the column of the current cursor location. This ensured a high contrast change occurred when the pink highlight was over the black target column. It was easy to see if the cursor was over the target.

For all trial types, targets were acquired by releasing the mouse button over them. Videos of trials being performed can be viewed in the supplementary material.

Single

For *Single* movement trials, the artificial screen was divided into 100 target columns (Fig. 3, left). As such, the target width was either 5 or 2 pixels depending on the scale (see Table 2). The current target column was black.

Double

For *Double* movement trials, the artificial screen was divided into 10 target columns so the target width was either 50 or 20 pixels (Fig. 3, right). The initial target column was black. Once it was acquired, it would return to its original color and a second target column would appear purple. These columns had to be distinguishable since in some instances, the second target column would be the same column as the initial target. Once the second target was acquired, the trial would finish.

Expansion

For the *Expansion* trials, there were 100 target columns, the same as for *Single* trials. However, when the mouse button was depressed the columns near the cursor would expand to be 10 times larger (Fig. 3, center). The expanded targets were the size of the *Double* movement targets. As with the other trials, the target was acquired via releasing the mouse button. This meant that participants could choose to zoom in on the target and correct their movement to make sure they were acquiring the right target. Depression of the mouse button initiated the zoom with a focal point on the column in which the mouse was positioned. Participants could also choose to ignore the zoom, and just perform *Expansion* trials in exactly the same way as *Single* trials.

To make it clearer which target columns would be expanded, a purple box followed the cursor (Fig. 3, center). All the columns inside the purple box were expanded once the zoom was activated. When the zoom was active, the zoom area could not be moved. If the target was not inside the purple box after zooming, it could not be selected and the trial counted as a miss.

3.3 Procedure

In a test session, participants performed blocks of 25 trials twice for the three trial types at one scale. Therefore each test session involved 150 trials (25 × 2 × 3). The order of trial types was counterbalanced within a test session in the order ABCCBA. Ordering of trial types was also counterbalanced between participants. This should reduce confounding effects of learning. Also, at the start of each block of 25 trials participants had the opportunity to practice that trial type until ready to start.

For each trial type, 50 of the 100 possible target location/combinations were used across a test session. For the *Single* and *Expansion* trials, every second target location was used so targets appeared at every possible distance from the screen center. For

Double trials, equivalent target combinations were used (i.e. every initial target position, and every second final target position). The direction of movements was also controlled: there were equal numbers of left and right movements. To discourage anticipatory movements, the movement direction appeared random to participants.

Each test session was conducted at a fixed scale. The test sessions for the group with CP only examined the *Larger* (500 pixel) scale. The group W/o CP performed the two scales, each one in a separate test session. Between the participants W/o CP, ordering of test session scales was counterbalanced.

Participants initiated individual trials by clicking the start zone (30 pixels wide). After a randomized wait period (1–2 s at 0.1 s intervals) the target column turned black. Experimental design ensured that the timing and location of the target column being designated was not predictable. To prevent anticipation and to control movement amplitudes, the target would not appear if the cursor was outside the start zone. If the cursor left the start zone for an extended period (0.5 s) the trial was aborted and the participant had to reinitiate the trial by clicking the start zone again. Participants were instructed to "select the target as quickly and accurately as you can."

Once the target was acquired, participants would receive speed and accuracy feedback. After a successful trial, the target column and a box surrounding the artificial screen would turn green. This would be recorded in the progress bar (see Fig. 2). If the trial was inaccurate, the feedback was red. After a trial, the participant's time was also displayed. This allowed a sense of speed without being judgmental. Also, participants were unaware of the performance of other participants.

Once a trial type was completed, participants reported workload measures via a NASA TLX based survey [24]. The six Likert scale questions asked about three task properties (Mental Demand, Physical Demand, Time Demand) and three personal experience properties (Your Performance, Effort, Frustration). As per NASA TLX methodology, participants gave a score out of 20. Once a test session was completed, participants were also asked for their most and least preferred trial types.

3.4 Data Processing

The data of the 3,750 trials was recorded in Excel workbooks. Trials were discarded when the participant was distracted (29), confused about the task (10), activated the zoom near the start zone (20), or when they did not notice the second target in the *Double* task (10). The distracted and confused trials were, for example, when the participant was looking away from the screen, or when they did not know where the target was. These were discarded since they did not reflect the user's pointing performance. Trials were discarded based on observation during experimentation in conjunction with viewing the recorded data in Excel.

For each of accuracy, time per information, preference, and workload, one value was calculated for each trial type of a test session (i.e. one value for 50 trials). Accuracy was defined as the percentage of successful trials.

For time per information values, time is the total time of all trials, successful or not (but excluding discarded trials). Information was defined as the total number of successful trials multiplied by inherent information, $\log_2(100)$, in a single trial. For *Expansion* trials, zooming in on the wrong location pushed the target out of the screen unexpectedly. In this case, the time recorded was not an accurate reflection of time spent pointing. In calculating time per information, the recorded time for any 'push out' trial was replaced with an average time for that test block. However, if the push out occurred because of clicking near the start zone (i.e. not near target at all), then the trial was discarded. Also, if the push out click was quick (i.e. within the normal range of durations of *Single* trial clicks) and the zoom was not used, the time was not replaced since it did reflect time spent pointing.

Trial types were assigned a preference rank from first (1) to third (3) based on participants' responses to their most preferred and least preferred interactions.

The time measures (completion times, reaction times, traversal times, correction times, and click times) were calculated for each individual trial. Completion times were the time from when the target appeared to when the trial was completed. The four other times were components of the completion time. The reaction time was from when the target appeared to when the cursor had moved 10% of the direct distance to its final location. The traversal time was from when the cursor had moved 10% of the distance to 90% of the distance. The correction times were from 90% of the distance to when the mouse button was depressed. Lastly, the click time was from when the button was depressed to when it was released and the target was selected. For *Double* trials, these component times were the cumulative values of the two movements. For the *Expansion* trials, the component times could not be calculated since the distinction between correction time and click time is blurred.

3.5   Statistical Analysis

Statistical analysis was performed using IBM's SPSS Statistics 22. The only independent variable directly analyzed was *Trial Type*.

For accuracy, time per information, preference, and workload measures, non-parametric Friedman tests were used to test for overall significance. For pairwise comparisons, Wilcoxon signed-rank tests were used along with Bonferroni correction. Since there were 3 comparison pairings, significance was set at $p < 0.017$. Reported p-values are unadjusted.

A repeated measures mixed model was used for time values. *Trial Type* and *Trial#* were used as repeated variables. *Trial Type* was the only fixed factor, whilst *Participant* was a random variable. The data set were natural log transformed to improve kurtosis and skewness except for the traversal times. Outliers that were 3.29 standard deviations outside the mean were deleted.

4   Results

The following sections discuss the results. Mean completion times and standard error values are shown in Table 3 and Fig. 4, along with medians and quartiles for Time/Info and accuracy. Figure 5 shows means and standard error values of times for the different components of the task. Note that in the terms *Smaller* and *Larger* refer to test sessions by the group W/o CP. The group with CP only used larger targets.

Table 3. Median values (with quartiles) for Time/Info and accuracy, and mean completion times (with standard error) across different groups and trial types. * denotes that *Trial Type* was a significant main effect of the relevant measure for that participant group and scale.

	Single	Expansion	Double
W/o CP – Larger			
Time/Info (ms/bit)*	269 (234, 298)	308 (257, 330)	268 (257, 313)
Completion time (ms)*	1649 (56)	1845 (63)	1833 (62)
Accuracy (%)	96.0 (93.5, 98.5)	97.0 (92.2, 100)	100 (96.9, 100)
W/o CP – Smaller			
Time/Info (ms/bit)*	422 (393, 500)	346 (317, 425)	292 (269, 333)
Completion time (ms)*	2448 (94)	2164 (83)	1911 (74)
Accuracy (%)*	93.9 (87.9, 94.0)	96.0 (87.7, 98.5)	98.0 (96.0, 100)
CP			
Time/Info (ms/bit)	420 (356, 667)	448 (338, 935)	364 (313, 545)
Completion time (ms)*	2283 (429)	2656 (499)	2453 (461)
Accuracy (%)*	77.6 (69.5, 89.9)	83.3 (82.6, 92.9)	100 (86.0, 100)

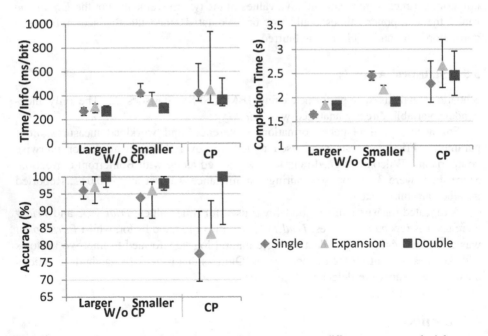

Fig. 4. Time/Info, task completion times, and accuracy across different groups and trial types. Mean completion times are shown with error bars for standard error (since this is based on analysis of variance). Other measures show medians with error bars for the 25th and 75th percentiles (since analysis was based on non-parametric Friedman tests).

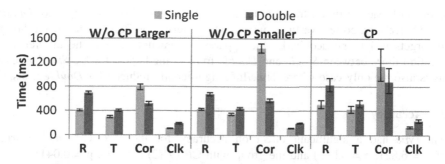

Fig. 5. Graphs of mean component times (ms) with standard error bars of *Single* and *Double* trials. R: Reaction time, T: Traversal time, Cor: Correction time, Clk: Click time.

4.1 Time Per Information (Time/Info)

Trial Type had a significant effect on Time/Info for the group W/o CP for both *Larger* ($\chi^2(2) = 9.600$, p = 0.008) and *Smaller* scales ($\chi^2(2) = 16.800$, p < 0.001), but it did not reach significance for the group with CP ($\chi^2(2) = 5.200$, p = 0.074).

In pairwise comparisons for *Larger* scale trials (the group W/o CP), the difference between *Single* and *Expansion* trials was closest to significance (Z = −2.191, p = 0.028). For 9 of the 10 participants, *Single* trials elicited a lower Time/Info value. The difference between *Single* and *Double* trials did not reach significance (Z = −1.886, p = 0.059). The medians were almost identical, although for 9 of the 10 participants *Single* trials elicited a lower Time/Info value than *Double* trials.

For *Smaller* scale, *Double* trials had significantly less Time/Info than both *Single* (Z = −2.803, p = 0.005) and *Expansion* (Z = −2.803, p = 0.005). In both cases for all 10 participants, the *Double* trials elicited lower Time/Info. *Single* trials did not result in significantly less efficacy compared to *Expansion* trials (Z = −2.191, p = 0.028).

4.2 Completion Times and Components

For all groups, *Trial Type* significantly affected completion times (W/o CP *Larger*: F (2,978.261) = 54.782, p < 0.001; W/o CP *Smaller*: F(2,982.607) = 91.763, p < 0.001; CP: (F(2,481.980) = 18.311, p < 0.001). For W/o CP *Larger*, *Single* trials were performed significantly faster than both the *Double* trials (p < 0.001) and the *Expansion* trials (p < 0.001). Contrary to the *Larger* scale results, for the *Smaller* scale the *Single* trials were performed significantly slower than both the *Double* trials (p < 0.001) and the *Expansion* trials (p < 0.001). *Double* trials were also significantly faster than *Expansion* trials (p < 0.001) for this scale.

For the group with CP, the *Single* trials were performed significantly faster than both the *Double* trials (p = 0.012) and the *Expansion* trials (p < 0.001). This is similar to the *Larger* scale results for the group W/o CP. However, *Double* trials were significantly faster than *Expansion* trials (p = 0.005), akin to the *Smaller* scale results.

For each test session type (W/o CP *Larger*, W/o CP *Smaller*, CP) all component times were significantly different (all p < 0.001) between *Single* and *Double* trials. The durations of reaction times, traversal times, and click times were all larger for *Double* trials. Conversely, corrective times were always shorter for *Double* trials even though two targets had to be acquired. One apparent interaction is that the difference in correction times between *Single* and *Double* trials is the largest for the *Smaller* scale. This is also the only case where Time/Info significantly reduced for *Double* trials.

4.3   Accuracy

Trial Type had a significant effect on accuracy for the W/o CP *Smaller* trials ($\chi^2(2) = 6.821$, p = 0.033) and the group with CP ($\chi^2(2) = 6.400$, p = 0.041).

For W/o CP *Smaller*, there was a significant difference between *Double* and *Single* trials (Z = −2.550, p = 0.011). During *Double* trials 9 of the 10 participants were more accurate than during *Single* trials.

For the group with CP, the difference between *Double* and *Single* trials was closest to significance (Z = −2.023, p = 0.043). Despite not reaching significance, all 5 participants were more accurate for *Double* trials than *Single* trials.

4.4   Preferences

For W/o CP *Smaller* scale, *Trial Type* had a significant effect on preference ranking, ($\chi^2(2) = 6.200$, $p = 0.045$). *Double* trials were significantly preferred over *Single* ones (Z = −2.495, $p = 0.013$). *Double* was ranked higher than *Single* by 9 participants, and lower by the other 1. The actual preference responses can be seen in Table 4.

Table 4. Votes for most preferred and least preferred trial types. * denotes that *Trial Type* was a significant main effect that participant group and scale.

	Preferred (+Most/−Least)		
	Single	Expansion	Double
W/o CP − larger	+4/−4	+1/−5	+5/−1
W/o CP − smaller*	+1/−7	+4/−3	+5/−0
CP	+1/−2	+2/−1	+2/−2

As an observation for both *Larger* and *Smaller* scale trials, half the participants W/o CP preferred *Double* trials the most and almost none disliked it. When the scale got smaller, it seems votes went from *Single* towards *Expansion*. The data of participants with CP does not reveal any preferences in particular.

4.5   Workload Measures (NASA TLX)

None of the task properties (Mental Demand, Physical Demand, Time Demand) varied significantly with *Trial Type* for any test session. The main workload measure that varied with *Trial Type* was Frustration (Fig. 6). This was significant for the group W/o CP at both *Larger* ($\chi^2(2) = 7.784$, $p = 0.020$) and *Smaller* scales ($\chi^2(2) = 9.556$, $p = 0.008$), but not for the group with CP ($\chi^2(2) = 5.333$, $p = 0.069$).

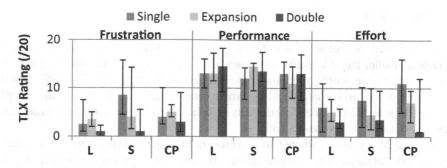

Fig. 6. Median TLX workload measures for Frustration, Performance and Effort. Error bars show the 25th and 75th percentiles. L: W/o CP *Larger*, S: W/o CP *Smaller*, CP: CP.

For the *Larger* scale trials, there was a significant difference between *Double* and *Expansion* trials (Z = −2.699, p = 0.007). For 9 of the 10 participants, *Double* trials were less frustrating than *Expansion* trials. For the other participant, they were tied. The median ratings were 1.0 and 3.5 respectively.

For *Smaller* scale trials, *Double* trials were significantly less frustrating than *Single* trials (Z = −2.524, p = 0.012), but not significantly less than the *Expansion* trials (Z = −2.243, p = 0.025). For *Expansion* trials, 7 participants rated frustration as higher, two as equal, and one as lower than *Double* trials. For *Single* trials, 8 participants rated frustration as higher and two as equal to *Double* trials. The median values for *Single*, *Expansion*, and *Double* trials were 8.5, 4.0 and 1.0 respectively.

Further examination of the group with CP revealed Frustration was most likely to be different between *Double* and *Single* trials (Z = −2.121, p = 0.034). This seems counterintuitive since the medians suggest there should be a greater difference between *Double* and *Expansion* trials. Yet for all 5 participants, *Double* trials were less frustrating than *Single* trials. Regardless, the Friedman test suggested there was no main effect of *Trial Type* (recall, p = 0.069).

Performance ratings for the group W/o CP changed significantly with *Trial Type* for *Smaller* scale trials ($\chi^2(2) = 6.324$, p = 0.042). No pairwise comparisons were significant, but in general participants rated their performance as being worse for the *Single* trials compared to both the *Expansion* trials (Z = −2.222, p = 0.026) and the *Double* trials (Z = −2.200, p = 0.028). In both cases, 8 of the 10 participants rated their performance as worse for *Single* trials. The median value for *Single* was 12.0, whereas the median for *Expansion* was 14.5 and the median for *Double* was 13.5.

Also for *Smaller* scale, changes in Effort were close to significance ($\chi^2(2) = 5.852$, p = 0.054). If we permit ourselves to perform pairwise comparisons on the Effort data, participants came closest to rating *Single* trials as requiring more effort than *Double* trials (Z = −2.207, p = 0.027), and to a lesser extent *Expansion* trials (Z = −1.897, p = 0.058). Compared to *Double* trials, 6 of the 10 participants rated effort as being higher for *Single* trials, the other 4 participants rated it as being equal. Compared to *Expansion* trials, 5 participants rated effort higher for *Single* trials, 4 rated them equal, and 1 rated the *Single* trials as requiring less effort. The medians were 7.5 for *Single* trials, 4.5 for *Expansion* trials, and 3.5 for *Double* trials.

5 Discussion

We investigated the potential of improving pointing efficacy by replacing one movement to a smaller target with two movements to larger targets. Since pointing was the primary interest we sought to minimize the role navigational and cognitive effects such as searching for targets and deciding which one to acquire. However, the sample assistive tool tested did alter functionality and involved decision making since there was access to an elective zoom lens.

We sought conditions where two movements to larger targets decreases the time it takes to communicate a set amount of information. We expected this would only be possible when corrective movements were problematic. So we expected scale (i.e. the small target effect) and motor skills to influence the likelihood of an extra movement increasing efficacy.

5.1 Scale

Scale was investigated for participants W/o CP and had a clear effect on the potential of adding a movement. For the *Larger* scale, adding the extra movement resulted in significantly slower completion times, and potentially less effective communication. In stark contrast, adding the extra movement resulted in significantly faster and more effective communication for *Smaller* scale trials. This importance of scale is likely due to the small target effect [1], whereby reducing the scale results in reduced conformity to Fitts's Law for smaller *Single* targets, but not for larger *Double* targets.

This is also reflected in the component times. When the scale is reduced there is a large increase in the correction times of *Single* trials. By contrast, all of the other component times do not appear to vary greatly across the different scales. Furthermore, correction times are the only component where *Double* trials are faster than *Single* trials. All of this suggests that corrective movements are a problem for the *Smaller* scale *Single* trials, and as a result the *Double* trials increase efficacy.

5.2 Motor Impairment

The effects of users' motor skills were more difficult to interpret. The results of both the *Smaller* scale trials and the group with CP's trials suggested they were subjectively more difficult than the *Larger* scale trials since they were generally slower. However, the results of the group with CP did not replicate the results of the *Smaller* scale trials.

In contrast to the *Smaller* scale trials, it is difficult to determine if the small target effect is present in the *Single* versus *Double* results for the group with CP. For that group, there was a significant difference in accuracy (and almost frustration) between the two trial types. These differences suggest the *Single* targets were sufficiently small to be 'too small', whilst the *Double* targets were not. Despite this, the *Single* trials were still significantly faster than the *Double* ones.

If we compare the component times for the group with CP, it is clear that the difference in correction times between *Single* and *Double* trials bears more similarity to the *Larger* scale trials than the *Smaller* scale ones. We hypothesized that motor impairments would increase the benefit of an additional movement since motor impairments tend to result in an increased number of sub-movements [12–14]. Whilst *Single* trials did on average involve over a second of correction time for the group with CP, the significant reduction in correction time for *Double* trials was not enough to make them faster. This pattern is similar to the *Larger* scale trials even though the completion times suggest the difficulty is more like the *Smaller* scale trials.

Another clear distinction is that there is much greater variability in the results of participants with CP. Whilst this trend is common in pointing tasks [2, 25–27], it also suggests a larger sample size would benefit future research.

5.3   Expansion Cursor

Since single movements are likely to be faster than double movements for most target sizes larger than 5 pixels, it seems any assistive tool should only add a movement when the user finds the target to be very small. The Expansion Cursor accommodates this with a discretionary zoom. However, there appears to be a cost to this functionality. In every performance measure the Expansion Cursor was never the best. It seems that depending on the situation, a single movement or a double movement may be optimal, but not the Expansion Cursor. The point is that any assistive tool that aims to switch between one or two movements based on context will not be 100% efficient. In the case of the Expansion Cursor there is probably a time cost associated with the decision to use it or not. Likewise there is an added dexterity requirement compared to *Double* trials: the user must hold the mouse button down whilst they make corrective movements. This possibly has an effect on accuracy.

These issues may appear specific to the Expansion Cursor. However any assistive tool that adds a movement implicitly has to have some mechanism to determine when to add that movement. That decision, whether performed automatically by the computer or the user, will not be correct 100% of the time. Hence there will be a cost relative to the optimal scenario of a single or double movement.

It should be noted that most tools in the literature do not involve a mechanism for users to make a single movement when the target is easy to acquire (e.g. all of the enhanced area cursors in [5]). Avoiding this mechanism does not solve the problem of costs associated with it since the assistive tool is likely to become a hindrance for larger targets. If the tool is still useful for larger targets, it suggests the user would benefit from targets being universally bigger in motor space. This universal enlargement can always happen by reducing the mouse speed (i.e. the C-D gain), hence a tool that improves acquisition of larger targets appears to be redundant.

5.4   User Experience

So far, this discussion has neglected to mention what the participants thought about the experiment. From a user-perspective, there seems to be a larger risk to making targets too small, than there is to introducing an extra movement layer.

When comparing the smallest targets (*Smaller* scale *Single* trials, 2 pixels) to larger ones (*Smaller* scale *Double* trials, 20 pixels), participants reported increased frustration and effort that resulted in worse performances. This was reflected in participants' comments. For *Single* trials, participants mentioned that you "find yourself going over and back trying to get it (the target)", you had to be more precise, it was a matter of getting it right, and that it was frustrating trying to make such a small adjustment when you were 1 pixel off the target.

By contrast, half of the participants preferred the *Double* movement for *Larger* scale trials, even though it was significantly slower than *Single* trials. They mentioned that it was easier, the targets were bigger and less stressful, and that you didn't have to think too much about it. Only one participant rated *Double* as their least preferred for *Larger* trials. Furthermore, all 5 of the participants in the group with CP rated *Double* trials as less frustrating than *Single* trials. Again, this is despite *Double* trials being significantly slower.

5.5   Summary of Potential to Improve Efficacy

There are two components to the potential for a double movement to improve efficacy (Time/Info). The first is accuracy. *Double* trials seemed likely to improve accuracy although that was only significant for *Smaller* scale trials. Improved accuracy effectively increases the amount of information communicated per target acquired.

The second aspect of improving efficacy is time. *Double* trials inherently increased reaction time, traversal time, and click time, presumably since they all had to be performed twice. However an additional input that enlarges targets can potentially reduce correction times enough to reduce completion times overall.

Both accuracy and speed gains appear to relate to the difficulty of acquiring very small targets. *Double* movements can avoid this difficulty since the targets can be larger. However, the benefit of larger targets seems to diminish when the *Single* movement target is already large enough. This is apparent in the different results between 2 and 5 pixel wide *Single* targets. If the *Single* targets were a more reasonable size (i.e. even bigger than 5 pixels), the potential for an extra movement to benefit target acquisition efficacy presumably disappears.

How motor skills interact with all of this is less clear. Previous work has demonstrated that CP can result in an increased number of sub-movements for pointing tasks [12–14]. The results agree with this since the group with CP appear to spend more time making corrections than the group W/o CP for the same task scale. However, this increase in corrections does not seem to result in added potential for two movements to be faster than one. *Double* movements were significantly slower than *Single* movements for both participant groups when performing the same task scale.

5.6   Limitations

The limitations of this experiment relate to it being a controlled lab experiment. First, it did not aim to accurately represent real-life interaction. The targets were 1D instead of 2D, and we aimed to minimize the interactions of navigation and other practicalities. Likewise, the participants were only aiming to click a black target column; they had no other intrinsic task goal informing their experience. This test scenario avoided confounds and allowed pointing to be explicitly investigated. Also, if this trade-off is to be more thoroughly understood, future work should consider a broader range of magnification levels and scales.

6 Conclusion

In this experiment we have demonstrated that it is possible for two movements to result in more effective pointing than one movement. However, it seems that this is dependent on the single movement being to a target that is frustratingly small and requires a disproportionate amount of time spent making corrective movements. In this experiment, even a 5-pixel wide target was not sufficiently small for an extra movement to improve efficacy for people with and without motor impairments. Only a 2-pixel wide target was small enough. Outside of correction time, *Double* movements resulted in significant increases in all other time components. This presumably stems from all aspects of target acquisition having to be performed twice. Regardless of speed, *Double* movements tended to improve accuracy for all of the conditions tested. Again, it appears this potential improvement depends on the *Single* trial target being small enough to impair accuracy.

These results help define the potential of assistive tools that replace one movement to a small target with two movements to larger targets. Efficacy benefits are possible for very small targets, but practically unlikely. The design of tools that add a movement should focus on the ways they can potentially improve user experience, such as improving accuracy, reducing frustration and attentional demands. Improving speed and efficacy is unlikely to be a potential benefit. Furthermore, assistive tools need a mechanism of aiding small target acquisition, but not interfering with larger target acquisition.

The Expansion Cursor takes this distinction into account and allows users to choose when they wish to use a zoom lens. However, the results demonstrated that there is a cost to this mechanism. We propose that any mechanism that makes a distinction between easy and difficult targets is likely to entail performance costs relative to the ideal scenario of either a single or double movement. This is design issue common to assistive tools. Regardless, the main accessibility benefit of such assistive tools is making accurate target acquisition easier, but not faster.

References

1. Chapuis, O., Dragicevic, P.: Effects of motor scale, visual scale, and quantization on small target acquisition difficulty. ACM Trans. Comput.-Hum. Interact. **18**, 13 (2011)
2. Davies, T.C., AlManji, A., Stott, N.S.: A cross-sectional study examining computer task completion by adolescents with cerebral palsy across the manual ability classification system levels. Dev. Med. Child Neurol. **56**, 1180–1186 (2014)
3. Almanji, A., Payne, A., Amor, R., Davies, C.: A nonlinear model for mouse pointing task movement time analysis based on both system and human effects. IEEE Trans. Neural Syst. Rehabil. Eng. **23**(6), 1003–1011 (2014)
4. Bakaev M.: Fitts' law for older adults: considering a factor of age, pp. 260–263 (2008)
5. Findlater, L., Jansen, A., Shinohara, K., Dixon, M., Kamb, P., Rakita, J., Wobbrock, J.O.: Enhanced area cursors: reducing fine pointing demands for people with motor impairments, pp. 153–162 (2010)
6. Payne, A.R., Plimmer, B., McDaid, A., Luxton-Reilly, A., Davies, T.C.: Expansion cursor: a zoom lens that can be voluntarily activated by the user at every individual click, pp. 81–90 (2016)

7. Li, L., Gajos, K.Z.: Adaptive click-and-cross: adapting to both abilities and task improves performance of users with impaired dexterity, pp. 299–304 (2014)
8. Jansen, A., Findlater, L., Wobbrock, J.O.: From the lab to the world: lessons from extending a pointing technique for real-world use, pp. 1867–1872 (2011)
9. Kiger, J.I.: The depth/breadth trade-off in the design of menu-driven user interfaces. Int. J. Man-Mach. Stud. **20**, 201–213 (1984)
10. Landauer, T.K., Nachbar, D.: Selection from alphabetic and numeric menu trees using a touch screen: breadth, depth, and width. ACM SIGCHI Bull. **16**, 73–78 (1985)
11. Zaphiris, P., Shneiderman, B., Norman, K.L.: Expandable indexes vs. sequential menus for searching hierarchies on the world wide web. Behav. Inf. Technol. **21**, 201–207 (2002)
12. Hwang, F., Keates, S., Langdon, P., Clarkson, J.: Mouse movements of motion-impaired users: a submovement analysis, pp. 102–109 (2004)
13. Hwang, F., Keates, S., Langdon, P., Clarkson, J.: A submovement analysis of cursor trajectories. Behav. Inf. Technol. **24**, 205–217 (2005)
14. Saavedra, S., Joshi, A., Woollacott, M., Van Donkelaar, P.: Eye hand coordination in children with cerebral palsy. Exp. Brain Res. **192**, 155–165 (2009)
15. Seow, S.C.: Information theoretic models of HCI: a comparison of the hick-hyman law and fitts' law. Hum.-Comput. Interact. **20**, 315–352 (2005)
16. Fitts, P.M.: The information capacity of the human motor system in controlling the amplitude of movement. J. Exp. Psychol. **47**, 381 (1954)
17. MacKenzie, I.S.: Fitts' law as a research and design tool in human-computer interaction. Hum.-Comput. Interact. **7**, 91–139 (1992)
18. Card, S.K., English, W.K., Burr, B.J.: Evaluation of mouse, rate-controlled isometric joystick, step keys, and text keys for text selection on a CRT. Ergonomics **21**, 601–613 (1978)
19. Bax, M.C.: Terminology and classification of cerebral palsy. Dev. Med. Child Neurol. **6**, 295–297 (1964)
20. Rosenbaum, P., Paneth, N., Leviton, A., Goldstein, M., Bax, M., Damiano, D., Dan, B., Jacobsson, B.: A report: the definition and classification of cerebral palsy april 2006. Dev. Med. Child Neurol. Suppl. **109**, 8–14 (2007)
21. Ramos, G., Cockburn, A., Balakrishnan, R., Beaudouin-Lafon, M.: Pointing lenses: facilitating stylus input through visual-and motor-space magnification, pp. 757–766 (2007)
22. Zhang, X., Zha, H., Feng, W.: Extending Fitts' law to account for the effects of movement direction on 2D pointing, pp. 3185–3194 (2012)
23. Eliasson, A., Krumlinde-Sundholm, L., Rösblad, B., Beckung, E., Arner, M., Öhrvall, A., Rosenbaum, P.: The manual ability classification system (MACS) for children with cerebral palsy: scale development and evidence of validity and reliability. Dev. Med. Child neurol. **48**, 549–554 (2006)
24. NASA: NASA TLX: Task load index (2016). http://humansystems.arc.nasa.gov/groups/TLX/. Accessed July 2016
25. Smits-Engelsman, B.C.M., Rameckers, E.A.A., Duysens, J.: Children with congenital spastic hemiplegia obey Fitts' law in a visually guided tapping task. Exp. Brain Res. **177**, 431–439 (2007)
26. Payne, A.R., Plimmer, B., Davies, T.C.: Repeatability of eye-hand movement onset asynchrony measurements and cerebral palsy: a case study, pp. 31–38 (2015)
27. Al Manji, A., Davies, C., Amor, R.: Examining dynamic control-display gain adjustments to assist mouse-based pointing for youths with cerebral palsy. J. Virtual Worlds Hum. Comput. Interact. **3**, 1–9 (2015)

Information-Theoretic Analysis of Human Performance for Command Selection

Wanyu Liu[1,2(✉)], Olivier Rioul[1], Michel Beaudouin-Lafon[2], and Yves Guiard[1,2]

[1] LTCI, Telecom ParisTech, Université Paris-Saclay, 75013 Paris, France
{wanyu.liu,olivier.rioul,yves.guiard}@telecom-paristech.fr
[2] LRI, Univ. Paris-Sud, CNRS, Inria, Université Paris-Saclay, 91400 Orsay, France
mbl@lri.fr

Abstract. Selecting commands is ubiquitous in current GUIs. While a number of studies have focused on improving rapid command selection through novel interaction techniques, new interface design and innovative devices, user performance in this context has received little attention. Inspired by a recent study which formulated information-theoretic hypotheses to support experimental results on command selection, we aim at explaining user performance from an information-theoretic perspective. We design an ad-hoc command selection experiment for information-theoretic analysis, and explain theoretically why the transmitted information from the user to the computer levels off as difficulty increases. Our reasoning is based on basic information-theoretic concepts such as entropy, mutual information and Fano's inequality. This implies a bell-shaped behavior of the throughput and therefore an optimal level of difficulty for a given input technique.

Keywords: Human performance · Command selection · Information theory · Mutual information · Entropy · Throughput · Fano's inequality

1 Introduction

Selecting commands remains one of the most common interactions in graphical user interfaces. Many previous studies have strived to improve rapid command selection, e.g., marking menus [10] and flower menus [1], to propose novel command selection techniques, e.g., FastTap on tablets [7], and to design command selection on innovative devices, e.g., smartwatches [11]. When an application has a large number of commands, designers often use a hierarchical navigation structure to partition the components or come up with new designs such as finger identification [5], particularly when interaction is constrained by scarcity of screen real estate.

However, apart from some menu models [2,3] that are mostly applicable to linear menus, few researchers have systematically investigated user performance

© IFIP International Federation for Information Processing 2017
Published by Springer International Publishing AG 2017. All Rights Reserved
R. Bernhaupt et al. (Eds.): INTERACT 2017, Part III, LNCS 10515, pp. 515–524, 2017.
DOI: 10.1007/978-3-319-67687-6_35

in command selection. We are inspired by a recent study where Roy et al. [17] analyzed command selection data in information-theoretic terms such as transmitted information and successfully transmitted information rate, also known as throughput (TP), from the user to the computer. In the communication channel considered in [17], a user serves as the source of information with her hand as the information emitter, and transmits information to the system with the touch screen as the receiver of the coded message. The code shared by the source (the user) and the destination (the system) is the mapping of a set of touch events to a set of commands. Roy et al. hypothesized that the transmitted information levels off, as in absolute judgment tasks [13], and that TP as a function of the command's entropy is bell-shaped. As they were focused on comparing two input techniques, the authors used these measurements to illustrate the differences between two techniques. In this paper, we provide instead a theoretical analysis of these phenomena.

Information theory, first introduced by Shannon in 1948 [19], has been used in various domains including psychology [12,14,15]. In HCI, there are two major design principles that are derived from information theory: Fitts' law [6] and the Hick-Hyman law [8,9] starting from the early 1980s [16]. Fitts' [6] work was an empirical determination of the information capacity of the human motor system. Likewise, Hick's [8] and Hyman's [9] experiments assessed the cognitive information capacity in choice-reaction experiments. Fitts' law and the Hick-Hyman law are the only two surviving information-theoretic concepts used in HCI [18], despite the fact that we humans constantly send information to and receive information from computers, and vice versa.

Intrigued by the observations in [17], we aim to provide an information-theoretic analysis of user performance in command selection tasks. We thus replicated Roy et al.'s experiment [17], tailored for an information-theoretic analysis. Using basic concepts including entropy, mutual information and Fano's inequality, we provide an information-theoretic explanation for why transmitted information (mutual information between the user and the computer) should level off as the command's entropy increases, and why the rate of successfully transmitted information is a bell-shaped curve. Grounded in the fundamental principles of information theory, these formulations provide a general tool to evaluate human performance in command selection tasks.

2   Data Collection

The goal was to achieve a better undertanding of human performance in a command selection task from the information-theoretic perspective and to provide theoretical formulations for it. Similar to Roy et al.'s study [17], we consider users as information sources, who emit information with an interaction instrument, and transmit it to the system. In order to avoid the fat finger problem [20] and to collect a wider range of data, we choose to use a mouse as interaction instrument instead of the user's hand. We also assume equally probable commands, thus the input entropy (the task difficulty) is the $\log_2$ of the number of possible commands.

2.1   Participants and Apparatus

Twelve volunteers (1 female), age 23 to 31 (mean $= 26.6$, $\sigma = 1.9$), were recruited from our institution. All of them were right-handed and interacted with WIMP interfaces regularly.

The experiment was conducted on a Macbook Pro with a 2.7 GHz processor, 8 GB RAM and resolution at 227 pixels per inch. The software was implemented in Java and the experiment window was 600×400 pixels. The targets representing the commands were displayed at the top of the window as a row of adjacent rectangles. The total area covered by the targets was 256 pixels wide and 30 pixels high. The width of the targets depended on the experimental condition. A circle positioned 150 pixels down below the target area was used to reset the cursor position of each trial. A standard mouse was used with the same sensitivity for all participants.

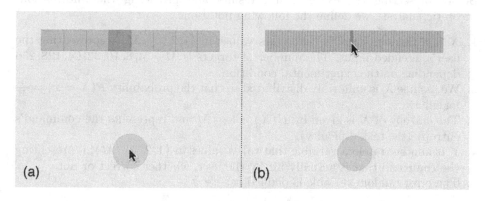

Fig. 1. (a) The cursor gets reset at the center of the circle when the trial starts in condition 8; (b) correctly selected target command turns green in condition 64. (Color figure online)

2.2   Task, Stimulus and Design

In response to a visual stimulus, participants were instructed to click on the highlighted target command (Fig. 1(a)) as fast and accurately as they could. If they correctly hit the target command, it turned green (Fig. 1(b)). Clicking on a non-target command would turn it red. In both cases the trial was complete after a single selection. The cursor was then reset automatically in the same position at the start of each trial.

Based on a pilot study, we used 4, 8, 16, 32, 64, 128 and 256 commands in the experiment, corresponding to 2 to 8 bits of information. Note that more than 7 bits of information is relatively high for normal users to process, but we wanted to push the limits of the participants. The size of the target representing each command was inversely proportional to the number of commands in the set, so that the set of target commands always occupied the same overall space.

We used a within-participant design and counter-balanced the order of the number of commands across participants with a Latin square. There were 3 replications for each block. A block consisted of presenting all targets in random order. Since we assumed a uniform distribution, each command should appear the same number of times. However, this would result in a very long and tiring selection in condition 128 and 256. In order to keep the duration of the experiment manageable, each participant had to select only 64 targets in conditions 128 and 256, but the full range was covered across all participants.

The total duration of the experiment was around 20 min per participant. In summary, the design was: 12 Participants $\times$ (4 + 8 + 16 + 32 + 64 + 64 + 64 Commands) $\times$ 3 Replications = 9,072 trials.

3   Information-Theoretic Concepts and Notations

Before presenting the experimental results and providing the information-theoretic analysis, we define the following notations.

1. X is a random variable that takes values in $\{1, 2, \ldots, M\}$, representing the user's intended input. The number of targets is $M = 4, 8, 16, 32, 64, 128, 256$ depending on the experimental condition.
2. We assume X is uniformly distributed so that the probability $P(X = x) = \frac{1}{M}$ for all x.
3. The entropy of X is given by $H(X) = \log_2 M$ and represents the command's entropy (the task difficulty).
4. Y is another random variable that takes values in $\{1, 2, \ldots, M\}$, representing the command that is actually hit by the user, whether correct or not.
5. The error random variable is defined as:

$$E = \begin{cases} 0 & \text{if } X = Y; \\ 1 & \text{if } X \neq Y. \end{cases} \tag{1}$$

6. The probability of error $P_e = P(X \neq Y)$ representing the error rate, has binary entropy:

$$H(E) = -P_e \log_2 P_e - (1 - P_e) \log_2 (1 - P_e). \tag{2}$$

7. The transmitted information in bits conveyed from the user to the computer is defined by Shannon's mutual information:

$$I(X;Y) = \sum_x \sum_y P(X = x, Y = y) \log_2 \frac{P(X = x, Y = y)}{P(X = x)P(Y = y)}$$

Shannon's capacity is defined as the maximum possible transmitted information.

8. Throughput (TP) or information rate, in bits per second, is defined as the ratio of the transmitted information to movement time (MT), i.e., the average time to select the command for a given number of commands: $TP = I(X;Y)/MT$.

4   Experimental Results

In this section, we present findings on reaction time (RT), movement time (MT), error rate P_e, transmitted information $I(X;Y)$, and throughput TP as a function of the command's entropy (task difficulty).

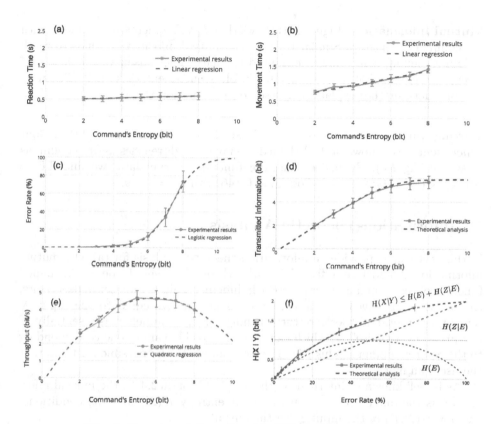

Fig. 2. Experimental results with 95% confidence intervals.

Task Completion Time. Figure 2(a) and (b) indicate that both reaction time RT and the movement time MT required to select a command are linear functions of the command's entropy. This is in line with the Hick-Hyman Law and Fitts' Law since time is proportional to task difficulty, which is logarithmic in the number of choices. We run linear regressions and find that $RT = 0.473 + 0.017 \times \log_2 M$ with $r^2 = 0.959$ and $MT = 0.540 + 0.104 \times \log_2 M$ with $r^2 = 0.968$. Task completion time is dominated by movement time MT.

Error Rate. Figure 2(c) demonstrates that when the command's entropy is small and the task is easy, users do not tend to make mistakes, hence P_e is very small. When the command's entropy increases, users make more and more errors, up to 73.5% when entropy equals 8 bits. It is obvious that when the command's entropy gets very high, the error rate would level off at 100%, as shown in Fig. 2(c). Fitting a logistic curve to the data, we obtain $P_e = 1/(1 + e^{-1.4 \times (\log_2 M - 7.4)})$ with $r^2 = 0.992$.

Mutual Information. Figure 2(d) shows that $I(X;Y)$ increases gradually with the command's entropy. Similar to [17], transmitted information tends to reach an upper bound, confirming the limited capacity. The reason why it levels off given in [17] was that it is similar to absolute judgment tasks [13]. The next section offers another explanation based on information theory.

Throughput. Similar to Roy et al.'s study [17], throughput (TP) in our experiment also shows a bell-shaped behavior and reaches a maximum as shown in Fig. 2(e). Fitting a quadratic function to the data, we find TP = $-0.341 \times (\log_2 M)^2 + 1.710 \times \log_2 M - 0.146$ with $r^2 = 0.979$.

5   Information-Theoretic Analysis

In this section, we provide an information-theoretic analysis for (a) why mutual information should level off; and (b) why throughput should be a bell-shaped function of the command's entropy (task difficulty). Since the user makes errors, the output Y received by the computer is not always equal to the input X sent by the user, and therefore there is noise in the channel: Y is essentially X perturbed by a "noise" Z, which can take M possible values: one corresponding to the correct command plus $M - 1$ corresponding to the possible mistakes that the user can make.

As is well known in information theory [4, Theorem 2.4.1], the mutual information is the difference between the input entropy $H(X)$ and the conditional entropy $H(X|Y)$ of the input given the output:

$$I(X;Y) = H(X) - H(X|Y) \tag{3}$$

The conditional entropy is a measure of the uncertainty about X knowing Y; but if we know Y, the uncertainty on the noise Z is the same as that on X, so we can rewrite Eq. (3) as:

$$I(X;Y) = H(X) - H(Z|Y) \tag{4}$$

Here $H(X) = \log_2 M$ represents the task difficulty. We now would like to bound the penalty term—also known as *equivocation*—$H(Z|Y)$ in the transmitted information. Since the knowledge of the output Y reduces the uncertainty on the noise Z (conditioning reduces entropy [4, Theorem 2.6.5]), we have:

$$H(Z|Y) \leq H(Z) \tag{5}$$

In words, the equivocation does not exceed the entropy of the noise. Thus it is the noise's entropy that penalizes the transmitted information.

In our experiment, users make errors as defined in Eq. (1), and we can use the chain rule [4, Theorem 2.2.1]: $H(Z) = H(Z, E) = H(E) + H(Z|E)$ where [4, Theorem 2.2.1]

$$H(Z|E) = P_e \times H(Z|E = 1) + (1 - P_e) \times H(Z|E = 0) = P_e \times H(Z|E = 1) \quad (6)$$

since there remains no uncertainty on the noise Z if there is no error ($E = 0$). Combining the above, we have that the equivocation is bounded by:

$$H(X|Y) \leq H(E) + P_e \times H(Z|E = 1) \quad (7)$$

This is known in information theory as *Fano's inequality* [4, Theorem 2.10.1].

Here $H(E)$ is given by Eq. (2) and is at most one bit (when $P_e = 0.5$). Hence making errors penalizes the amount of transmitted information by at most one bit. However, considering the second term of Eq. (7), the uncertainty on "wrong selections" $H(Z|E = 1)$ incurs an additional penalty on the amount of transmitted information: How users make errors, not just the fact that they make errors, affects the amount of transmitted information. In our case, errors are clustered near the actual target, hence the entropy of the noise is lower than if they were evenly distributed.

The relationship between error rate P_e and $H(X|Y)$ observed from empirical data matches exactly the above illustration as shown in Fig. 2(f).

We can now reason as follows:

For small M: users do not tend to make errors, $H(E) \approx 0$ and $P_e \approx 0$, therefore $H(X|Y)$ is close to zero or remains very small when the error rate is low. So $I(X; Y)$ increases with $H(X) = \log_2 M$;

For large M: we tend to have $P_e = 1$, $H(E) = 0$, users cannot make a correct selection, but the errors are clustered around the target as in pointing tasks [22]. Doubling the number of commands from M to $2M$ adds 1 bit to the command's entropy, but since the error area around the correct target is approximately the same physical size, the number of possible errors is also doubled. Hence the equivocation is also increased by 1 bit. In our data, the possible errors in condition 128 are 1–3 around the target while in condition 256 they are 1–5 around the target, which corresponds approximately to the same physical area. As a result, the amount of transmitted information $I(X; Y) = H(X) - H(Z|Y)$ is not increasing any more and levels off as illustrated in Fig. 2(d).

We can now turn to the theoretical analysis of the throughput TP. As seen above, movement time MT is a linear function of $\log_2 M$.

For small M: $\log_2 M$ is also small, and MT is dominated by the intercept, hence can be considered as approximately constant. TP increases slowly with difficulty $\log_2 M$;

For large M: MT grows linearly with $\log_2 M$, and transmitted information $I(X;Y)$ levels off. Hence TP gradually decreases as demonstrated in Fig. 2(e).

However, we should distinguish the ceiling effect of transmitted information in our case from that in absolute judgment tasks [13]. Roy et al. claimed that they have the same characteristics but in our case, the errors made by users are around the target since they can see where it is, and therefore $H(Z)$ is only a few bits. In absolute judgment tasks, although the key message is that human short-term memory has a limited capacity, we would expect that when the number of randomly ordered stimuli increases, $H(Z)$ gets close to $\log_2(M - 1)$ as Y can take any value in $\{1, 2, \ldots, M\}$. If this were the case, mutual information $I(X;Y)$ should go down, instead of leveling off as $I(X;Y) \approx \log_2 M - \log_2(M-1)$ at first order when M is very large. Since the stimuli's entropy never gets very large in this type of tasks, the phenomenon is thus never observed. This would require further investigation in the context of absolute judgment tasks.

In summary, in command selection tasks, the amount of transmitted information gradually increases with the command's entropy until it reaches its capacity, and then levels off. Correspondingly, TP demonstrates a bell-shaped behavior, increasing to reach a maximum and then decreasing. This maximum (corresponding to an entropy of 6 bits, i.e. 64 commands in our experiment) provides the optimal vocabulary size for the given selection technique.

6   Conclusion and Future Work

In this paper, we provide an information-theoretic analysis of user performance in command selection tasks. The maximum in mutual information from the user to the computer indicates the channel capacity while the maximum in throughput illustrates that there is an optimal level of the command's entropy, or task difficulty, to maximize human performance for any given interaction technique.

Following Soukoreff and MacKenzie [21] who argue that people are imperfect information processors, we demonstrate that when the command's entropy increases, users tend to make more errors. Obviously, a very high command entropy is not realistic nor desirable since no interface designer nor HCI researcher would want users to make 100% errors: the design would be useless. But it is necessary and even vital to consider such cases to understand the phenomenon correctly. Armed with a theoretically justified model, one can now use it to evaluate any command selection task.

Interestingly, whether there is a time constraint also affects the amount of transmitted information. In our experiment and most other HCI experiments, participants are instructed to move as fast or as accurately as they can, sometimes both. We can imagine that if they could take their time to complete the task, the error rate would be always low, therefore the mutual information $I(X;Y)$ would always increase with $H(X)$. The theoretical formulations have shown that *how* users make errors affects the transmitted information, which is tightly related to both the experimental design and the instructions to the users. We plan to investigate this more thoroughly in future work.

Acknowledgments. This research was partially funded by Labex DigiCosme (ANR-11-LABEX-0045-DIGICOSME), operated by the French Agence Nationale de la Recherche (ANR) as part of the program "Investissement d'Avenir" Idex Paris-Saclay (ANR-11-IDEX-0003-02), and by European Research Council (ERC) grant n° 695464 ONE: Unified Principles of Interaction.

References

1. Bailly, G., Lecolinet, E., Nigay, L.: Flower menus: a new type of marking menu with large menu breadth, within groups and efficient expert mode memorization. In: Proceedings of the Working Conference on Advanced Visual Interfaces, pp. 15–22. ACM (2008)
2. Bailly, G., Oulasvirta, A., Brumby, D.P., Howes, A.: Model of visual search and selection time in linear menus. In: Proceedings of the 32nd Annual ACM Conference on Human Factors in Computing Systems, pp. 3865–3874. ACM (2014)
3. Cockburn, A., Gutwin, C., Greenberg, S.: A predictive model of menu performance. In: Proceedings of the SIGCHI Conference on Human Factors in Computing Systems, pp. 627–636. ACM (2007)
4. Cover, T.M., Thomas, J.A.: Elements of Information Theory. Wiley, Hoboken (2012)
5. Ewerling, P., Kulik, A., Froehlich, B.: Finger and hand detection for multi-touch interfaces based on maximally stable extremal regions. In: Proceedings of the 2012 ACM International Conference on Interactive Tabletops and Surfaces, pp. 173–182. ACM (2012)
6. Fitts, P.M.: The information capacity of the human motor system in controlling the amplitude of movement. J. Exp. Psychol. **47**, 381–391 (1954)
7. Gutwin, C., Cockburn, A., Scarr, J., Malacria, S., Olson, S.C.: Faster command selection on tablets with FastTap. In: Proceedings of the SIGCHI Conference on Human Factors in Computing Systems, pp. 2617–2626. ACM (2014)
8. Hick, W.E.: On the rate of gain of information. Q. J. Exp. Psychol. **4**, 11–26 (1952)
9. Hyman, R.: Stimulus information as a determinant of reaction time. J. Exp. Psychol. **45**, 188–196 (1953)
10. Kurtenbach, G., Buxton, W.: User learning and performance with marking menus. In: Proceedings of the SIGCHI Conference on Human Factors in Computing Systems, pp. 258–264. ACM (1994)
11. Lafreniere, B., Gutwin, C., Cockburn, A., Grossman, T.: Faster command selection on touchscreen watches. In: Proceedings of the 2016 CHI Conference on Human Factors in Computing Systems, pp. 4663–4674. ACM (2016)
12. McGill, W.: Multivariate information transmission. Trans. IRE Prof. Group Inf. Theory **4**(4), 93–111 (1954)
13. Miller, G.A.: The magical number seven, plus or minus two: some limits on our capacity for processing information. Psychol. Rev. **63**, 81–97 (1956)
14. Miller, G.A.: What is information measurement? Am. Psychol. **8**(1), 3 (1953)
15. Miller, G.A., Frick, F.C.: Statistical behavioristics and sequences of responses. Psychol. Rev. **56**(6), 311–324 (1949)
16. Newell, A., Card, S.K.: The prospects for psychological science in human-computer interaction. Hum.-Comput. Interact. **1**, 209–242 (1985)

17. Roy, Q., Guiard, Y., Bailly, G., Lecolinet, É., Rioul, O.: Glass+skin: an empirical evaluation of the added value of finger identification to basic single-touch interaction on touch screens. In: Abascal, J., Barbosa, S., Fetter, M., Gross, T., Palanque, P., Winckler, M. (eds.) INTERACT 2015. LNCS, vol. 9299, pp. 55–71. Springer, Cham (2015). doi:10.1007/978-3-319-22723-8_5

18. Seow, S.C.: Information theoretic models of HCI: a comparison of the Hick-Hyman law and Fitts' law. Hum.-Comput. Interact. **20**(3), 315–352 (2005)

19. Shannon, C.E.: A mathematical theory of communication. Bell Syst. Tech. J. **27**, 379–423, 623–656 (1948)

20. Siek, K.A., Rogers, Y., Connelly, K.H.: Fat finger worries: how older and younger users physically interact with PDAs. In: Costabile, M.F., Paternò, F. (eds.) INTERACT 2005. LNCS, vol. 3585, pp. 267–280. Springer, Heidelberg (2005). doi:10.1007/11555261_24

21. Soukoreff, R.W., MacKenzie, I.S.: An informatic rationale for the speed-accuracy trade-off. In: 2009 IEEE International Conference on Systems, Man and Cybernetics, SMC 2009, pp. 2890–2896. IEEE (2009)

22. Wobbrock, J.O., Cutrell, E., Harada, S., MacKenzie, I.S.: An error model for pointing based on Fitts' law. In: Proceedings of the SIGCHI Conference on Human Factors in Computing Systems, pp. 1613–1622. ACM (2008)

One Fitts' Law, Two Metrics

Julien Gori[1]([✉]), Olivier Rioul[1], Yves Guiard[1,2], and Michel Beaudouin-Lafon[2]

[1] LTCI, Telecom ParisTech, Université Paris-Saclay, 75013 Paris, France
{julien.gori,olivier.rioul,yves.guiard}@telecom-paristech.fr
[2] LRI, Univ. Paris-Sud, CNRS, Inria, Université Paris-Saclay, 91400 Orsay, France
mbl@lri.fr

Abstract. Movement time in Fitts' law is usually considered through the ambiguous notion of the average of minimum movement times. In this paper, we argue that using two distinct metrics, one relating to minimum time and the other relating to average time can be advantageous. Both metrics have a lot of support from theoretical and empirical perspectives. We also give two examples, one in a controlled experiment and the other in a field study of pointing, where making the minimum versus average distinction is fruitful.

1 Introduction

In Human Computer Interaction (HCI), Fitts' law is recognized as "the law of pointing", and is regularly used for, e.g., device evaluation or interface design. It relates the time MT to reach a target to target size W and target distance D. The law is described by the following equation:

$$MT = a + b \cdot ID, \tag{1}$$

where MT represents movement time and ID represents a function of D and W. Most of the efforts of researchers, since Fitts' seminal paper [5], have been directed towards the study of ID; initially Fitts [5] proposed ID $= \log_2 \frac{2D}{W}$, but today the most common formulation in HCI is the so-called Shannon formulation, due to MacKenzie [11], ID $= \log_2\left(1 + \frac{D}{W}\right)$. Perhaps surprisingly, the interpretation of MT has rarely been discussed, yet there is room for doubt: is the measure under consideration a minimum, an average, or an average minimum?

1.1 Time Metrics

Fitts' formal hypothesis in 1954 [5] was that: *"If the amplitude and tolerance limits of a task are controlled by E [the experimenter], and S [the participant] is instructed to work at his maximum rate, then the average time per response will be directly proportional to the minimum amount of information per response demanded by the particular conditions of amplitude and tolerance"* [5, p. 2].

© IFIP International Federation for Information Processing 2017
Published by Springer International Publishing AG 2017. All Rights Reserved
R. Bernhaupt et al. (Eds.): INTERACT 2017, Part III, LNCS 10515, pp. 525–533, 2017.
DOI: 10.1007/978-3-319-67687-6_36

Note that the expression *minimum amount of information* is used by Fitts to denote ID, which is not the matter here (see, e.g., [13] for an analysis of ID). For movement time Fitts gave the formula MT $= \frac{\text{ID}}{C}$, where C is the capacity of the human motor channel, representing the participant's *maximum rate*. If C is a maximum, the movement times should correspond to minimum movement times. Yet, we should, according to Fitts, consider the average of those minima over all time measures. Fitts' MT metric is thus an average of the minimum movement times. This raises three issues:

- Evidently, the oxymoron "average-minimum" described by Fitts is confusing. Several authors use, instead, different wordings, which suggest other interpretations of MT. A few examples are given by Soukoreff et al. [13] who consider "movement time performance for rapid aimed movements", Hoffman [8] "movement time", and Drewes [3] "mean time".
- Fitts needs the participant (S) to work at his or her maximum rate, so that the resulting movement times reflect S's full commitment to the pointing task. Yet, it is well documented that subjects are rarely fully committed to boring, repetitive tasks such as those composing Fitts' pointing experiments. The use of the average of MT's is thus based on a false premise, resulting from a shortcoming of the experimental design. It is unreasonable to take it for granted that the participants routinely perform to their fullest capabilities during the course of an experiment, even if they were instructed to do so.
- Fitts' average-minimum metric cannot be defined in a field study, because the participant are never instructed to operate at their maximum rate.

In this paper, we argue that there is a lot to be gained if one separates the average-minimum metric into two distinct metrics instead: a *minimum time metric* that relates to *extreme* performance, and an *average time metric* that relates to *mean* performance; each metric bringing its own valuable information. We show that there is enough evidence in Fitts' law literature that both follow Fitts' law, albeit with different slopes and intercepts, therefore providing essentially two Fitts' laws for the price of one.

2   Fitts' Law Is About Extreme Performance

We have two reasons to assert that Fitts' law should be interpreted as a law of extreme performance: First, a theoretical argument that exploits and precisely interprets the information theoretic analogy that was first used by Fitts, and subsequently successfully considered by, e.g., MacKenzie [9,11] and Zhai et al. [15]; Second, a pragmatic argument related to the recent unification of Schmidt's and Fitts' laws, due to Guiard and Rioul [7].

2.1   Shannon's Channel Capacity Theorem

Fitts derived his law by analogy with Shannon's channel capacity for the Gaussian additive channel. In information theory, the capacity of a channel of input X and output Y is defined by $C = \max_{p(x)} I(X;Y)$, where $I(X;Y)$ is the mutual information between X and Y and the maximum is taken over all input probability distributions. The channel coding theorem [2] states that C is the *maximum allowable bit rate* for which reliable transmission is possible over the considered channel. The capacity is reached at the limit of a (perfectly) optimal coding scheme. Anything less will give lower transmitted information.

2.2 Unified Pointing Paradigms

Recently, Guiard and Rioul [7] have shown that the time minimisation paradigm introduced by Fitts [5], the spread minimisation paradigm of Schmidt et al. [12] and the dual minimisation paradigm of Guiard [6] can receive a unified account provided that the participants are assumed to invest less than 100 percent of their resource in their performance. Accordingly, only the best performing samples should be expected to describe the speed-accuracy trade off. The less-than-total resource investment assumption thus matches common sense, as well as the information theoretic concept of capacity. Based on this idea, Guiard and Rioul were able to merge the linear law of Schmidt and the logarithmic description of Fitts law, describing them as different regions of the same speed-accuracy trade-off function.

Thus, Fitts' law should estimate an extremum, rather than an average. In other words:

- for a set of movements that have the same duration, only the movements with the highest ID are susceptible of achieving the capacity, or equivalently,
- for a set of movements of fixed ID, only the movements of shortest duration are susceptible of achieving the capacity.

This is in line with the idea that Fitts' law can only be seen as an extreme performance in a constrained condition of speed. This rationale makes sense: We cannot expect a model to account for the perturbations induced by a badly designed experiment, fatigue, or lassitude.

3 Two Metrics

3.1 The Average Time Metric

The average time metric is defined through the following relation:

$$\mu(\mathrm{MT}) = a + b \cdot \mu(\mathrm{ID}),\tag{2}$$

where $\mu(X)$ is the mean of X per block. In controlled experiments with speeding instructions, $\mu(\mathrm{ID}) = \mathrm{ID}$. Controlled Fitts' law studies exclusively handle the average metric (see, e.g., [13], which is used as a reference by many researchers). There is thus an abundance of results showing that this linear relation between mean MT and mean ID holds well and provides for good fits. Field studies such as Chapuis et al. [1] have shown that this relationship would hold as well, with r^2

coefficients for mean movement times regularly close to 1 (min 0.740, max 0.988, mean 0.941, std. dev. 0.044 for 24 different participants). The usual method to fit the average law is to perform linear regression on the data averaged per block (e.g. [13]).

3.2 The Minimum Time Metric

The minimum time metric for Fitts' law is defined as:

$$\min(\text{MT}) = a + b \cdot \text{ID}, \tag{3}$$

in line with the theoretical arguments of the previous section. We will now call this relationship Fitts' *min* metric. We next give an illustration of the min metric from data acquired in the field.

3.3 A Field Study Example

Figure 1 illustrate Fitts' min and average metrics, using a field study by Chapuis et al. [1]. For several months, Chapuis et al. unobtrusively logged cursor motion from several participants using their own hardware. They were able to identify offline the start and end of movements as well as the target information for several hundreds of thousands of click-terminated movements. With this information, one can then represent the movements in a MT versus ID graph, as normally done in a controlled Fitts law experiment.

Chapuis and his colleagues kindly allowed us to access their raw data. To compute task difficulty in the 2D space of computer screens we followed the suggestion given by Mackenzie and Buxton [10] and chose $\text{ID} = \log_2\left(1 + \frac{D}{\min(H,W)}\right)$, where H and W are the height and width of the target, respectively. Whenever an item was clicked, it was considered the target, hence target misses were not considered as errors in [1].

Figure 1 shows the data from one representative participant (P3) of Chapuis et al.'s field study. The I_D axis is truncated at 6 bits because beyond that level of difficulty the density of data points dropped dramatically.

Obviously, the data obtained with no speeding instructions (and no experimenter to recall them) exhibits a huge amount of stochastic variability along both dimensions of the plot. While in the X dimension, most I_D values fell in the range from 0.5 to 6 bits (presumably a reflection of the geometric layout of the graphical user interface), the variability along the Y dimension is extreme.

Linear regression performed on the whole data set of Fig. 1 shows that in the field experiment of Chapuis et al. movement time varied totally independently of the index of difficulty. With an r-square coefficient close to 0 ($r^2 = 0.03$), this data seems to totally fail to corroborate Fitts' law. This impression, however, is quite false.

In the right panel of Fig. 1, which ignores all MT data above 2 s and thus zooms-in on the Y-axis towards the bottom of the plot, one can distinctly see that the bottom edge of the cloud of data points does not touch the X axis.

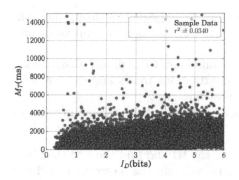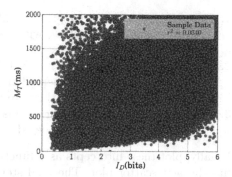

Fig. 1. Movement time as a function of task difficulty in one representative participant of [1]. Shown are over 90,000 individual movement measures. *Left*: MT up to 15 s. *Right*: MT up to 2 s. (lower part of the graph on the left)

Rather, in the downward direction, the density drops sharply: no matter the ID region considered, the distribution of performance measures has an unending tail above and what we call a *front* below, which in comparison is very steep (see [1] for the histogram of movement times). The unending tail is understandable as "it is always possible to do worse" [7]. In contrast, the movement time cannot be reduced below a certain critical value which accurately defines the front.

A closer look at the right panel of Fig. 1 reveals that the bottom edge of the scatter plot is approximately *linear*: this linear edge is what justifies Fitts' law. In other words, the empirical regularity in Fitts' law is, in essence, a *front of performance*, a lower bound that cannot be passed by human performance. Figure 1 also reveals a number of presumable fast outliers. Many reasons may explain why a small proportion of data cross the frontier. Some data points may correspond to lucky movements, failures in the analysis software, etc.

A front of performance is observable in data from the field study of Chapuis et al. because unsupervised everyday pointing does offer, albeit in a minority of cases, opportunities to perform with high levels of speed and accuracy. The difference between a field study and a controlled experiment is thus one of degree, not of nature. Experimenters have recourse to pressurizing speed/accuracy instructions simply to get rid of endless, uninformative, tails in their distributions of MT measures.

3.4   Estimating the Parameters of Fitts' Law Min

Estimates of parameters a and b of Eq. 3 cannot be obtained through conventional linear regression, which leverages all movement-time measures. We tentatively designed a new technique that estimates a and b for Fitts' min metric. First, slice the MT vs. ID scatter plot into vertical slices (i.e. split the range of ID into contiguous intervals). Then, for each slice (i.e. for all MT measures that fall inside each ID interval):

1. Draw the frequency histogram of MT for the interval (the histogram will exhibit strong positive skew, with its mode close to its minimum value and with an extended tail);
2. Fit the portion between the mode and the minimum value of each distribution with a linear curve (we observed that distributions fronts are not just very steep, more often than not they are almost linear);
3. Find the intercept of this curve: this is an estimate of the minimum value of MT for the ID interval considered.

Finally, plot these intercepts as a function of the ID and find the line that best fits the new scatter plot. The final step is to estimate the intercept a and the slope b of Eq. 3.

The technique has the following characteristics:

1. It specifies the parameters of a straight line, and this is Fitts' min in its law form;
2. It takes into account only the points corresponding to the best performance, through the exclusive consideration of the fronts of the performance distributions. The technique does not just discard "slow" outliers—i.e. movements of unusually long duration—it ignores all data points, but the very best.
3. It also eliminates "fast" outliers, i.e. movements of abnormally short duration.

Figure 2(a) displays the min law obtained for one participant pointing at a pager button[1]. Intercepts and slopes have been computed using both linear regression and best-performance fit; the parameters are respectively $a = 804$ ms and $\frac{1}{b} = 9.34$ bit/s and $a = 79$ ms and $\frac{1}{b} = 8.20$ bit/s. The slopes are similar

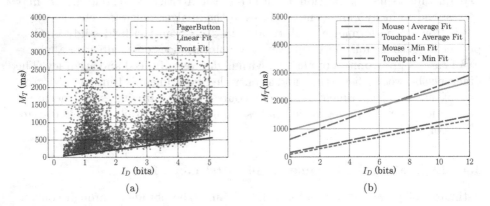

(a)   (b)

Fig. 2. (a) Fitting Fitts' law to the pager button data-set for a single participant. Red line: linear regression; blue line: front of performance. (b) Comparison between Fitts' min law versus Fitts' average law, for one participant using mouse and touch-pad. (Color figure online)

---

[1] A button such as "Next Page" and "Previous Page" in a paginated control.

but the intercepts are strikingly different. While the best-performance fit, corresponding to the min law, yields intercepts close to those met in controlled experiments, linear regression, corresponding to the average law, produces very high intercepts, comparable to those reported by Evans and Wobbrock [4].

4   Using the Two Metrics

Having two metrics instead of one can only add precision in the analysis of movements, and allows to observe phenomena that were not possible before. We give two examples, one for controlled experiments and a second for field studies, to illustrate the potential benefits.

4.1   A Possible Scenario for Controlled Experiments

As already emphasized, a Fitts task requires participants to work at their maximum rate. The quality of the measures depends on the experimenter's success at motivating participants. With participants that performed extremely well, indeed the min law and the average law would be extremely close to each other. An easy way to measure that is simply to quantify the difference between the two fits. The closer they are, the better the experiment. The distance between the two fits is thus in this particular case a measure of the quality of the experiment, and could prove well suited as a quantifier of experimental noise.

4.2   An Example from a Field Study

Field studies of pointing are very useful in the sense that they give us information about the natural behavior of users in the real world. The variability of movement times will be much higher than in a controlled experiments. The min and the average variants of Fitts' laws thus provide two very different types of information, the former giving the parameters of the law for best performance, and the latter giving average performance. The min law is expected to remain unchanged across systems (e.g., which operating system), environmental conditions (e.g., in a noisy crowded room or on the contrary alone in a well isolated office), human conditions (e.g., tired and bored or time-pressured), whereas the average law is expected to reflect all these changes. Importantly, the min law is expected to give similar results for both controlled experiments or field studies, whereas the average law is a reflection of all the differences that can occur between a controlled experiment and a field study.

As an example, we provide a comparison between mouse and touch-pad from Chapuis et al.'s dataset. We compared the behavior of one participant who happened to regularly alternate between the mouse and the touch-pad. The results of the fits for each device are displayed in Fig. 2(b), and the parameters are reported in Table 1.

With linear regression, the touch-pad has a higher intercept than the mouse, but the mouse has a steeper slope, hence the lines cross at about ID = 7.

Table 1. Intercept (a) and inverse of slope $(\frac{1}{b})$ of the min and average law for the mouse and touch-pad for participant 3 from Chapuis et al.'s experiment [1].

	Intercept (ms)		$\frac{1}{b}$ (bit per s)	
	Average	Min	Average	Min
Mouse	647	114	5.46	10.81
Touch-pad	968	178	7.15	10.23

This would suggest that the touch-pad is slower than the mouse for most tasks, but is faster for high-difficulty tasks. This observation is untypical and needs investigation: is it that the effort required to handle the touch-pad is less than for the mouse, or is the average law victim of some artefact, such as irregular distribution of ID or unusually long movement times for low ID, which tilts the linear regression fit? By contrast, our performance fit tends to show that the mouse is always a bit faster than the touch-pad. This result is consistent with those found in the literature for controlled experiments, e.g., Yun and Lee [14].

5   Conclusion

There are good reasons to use two metrics for Fitts' law. On the one hand, the min metric has a solid theoretical background, supported by Shannon's channel coding theorem and Guiard & Rioul's study of the speed-accuracy tradeoff. On the other hand, the average law can claim more than 60 years of empirical validation. We expect the min metric to give robust and consistent results. It relates to the human motor capacity, and hence is a useful reference for HCI experimenters. The average metric is expected to reflect everything that is not related to the human motor system, e.g. environment or device.

We have given two examples where the min metric provides useful information when compared to the average metric. In the case of the field study of mouse versus touchpad, the min law gives results that are consistent for both field study and controlled experiment. We expect this to be a general property. For the average law, the touchpad apparently outperforms the mouse for high ID's. This is probably worth investigating. This dual characterization certainly opens new perspectives for Fitts' law in HCI research, in both field studies and controlled experiments, and may lead to finer results.

References

1. Chapuis, O., Blanch, R., Beaudouin-Lafon, M.: Fitts' law in the wild: a field study of aimed movements (2007)
2. Cover, T.M., Thomas, J.A.: Elements of Information Theory. Wiley, New Jersey (2012)
3. Drewes, H.: Only one Fitts' law formula please! In: Extended Abstracts on Human Factors in Computing Systems, CHI 2010, pp. 2813–2822. ACM (2010)

4. Evans, A., Wobbrock, J.: Taming wild behavior: the input observer for obtaining text entry and mouse pointing measures from everyday computer use. In: Proceedings of the SIGCHI Conference on Human Factors in Computing Systems, CHI 2012, NY, USA, pp. 1947–1956 (2012). http://doi.acm.org/10.1145/2207676. 2208338

5. Fitts, P.M.: The information capacity of the human motor system in controlling the amplitude of movement. J. Exp. Psychol. **47**(6), 381 (1954)

6. Guiard, Y., Olafsdottir, H.B., Perrault, S.T.: Fitt's law as an explicit time/error trade-off. In: Proceedings of the SIGCHI Conference on Human Factors in Computing Systems, pp. 1619–1628. ACM (2011)

7. Guiard, Y., Rioul, O.: A mathematical description of the speed/accuracy trade-off of aimed movement. In: Proceedings of the 2015 British HCI Conference, pp. 91–100. ACM (2015)

8. Hoffmann, E.R.: Which version/variation of Fitts law? A critique of information-theory models. J. Mot. Behav. **45**(3), 205–215 (2013)

9. Mackenzie, I.S.: Fitts' law as a performance model in human-computer interaction. Ph.D. thesis, University of Toronto (1992)

10. MacKenzie, I.S., Buxton, W.: Extending Fitts' law to two-dimensional tasks. In: Proceedings of the SIGCHI Conference on Human Factors in Computing Systems, pp. 219–226. ACM, New York (1992)

11. MacKenzie, I.S.: A note on the information-theoretic basis for Fitts law. J. Mot. Behav. **21**(3), 323–330 (1989)

12. Schmidt, R.A., Zelaznik, H., Hawkins, B., Frank, J.S., Quinn Jr., J.T.: Motor-output variability: a theory for the accuracy of rapid motor acts. Psychol. Rev. **86**(5), 415 (1979)

13. Soukoreff, R.W., MacKenzie, I.S.: Towards a standard for pointing device evaluation, perspectives on 27 years of Fitts law research in HCI. Int. J. Hum.-Comput. Stud. **61**(6), 751–789 (2004)

14. Yun, S., Lee, G.: Design and comparison of acceleration methods for touchpad. In: Extended Abstracts on Human Factors in Computing Systems, CHI 2007, CHI EA 2007, pp. 2801–2812. ACM, New York (2007). http://doi.acm.org/10.1145/1240866.1241082

15. Zhai, S., Kristensson, P.O., Appert, C., Andersen, T.H., Cao, X.: Foundational issues in touch-screen stroke gesture design-an integrative review. Found. Trends Hum.-Comput. Interact. **5**(2), 97–205 (2012)

Towards Pupil-Assisted Target Selection in Natural Settings: Introducing an On-Screen Keyboard

Christoph Strauch[✉], Lukas Greiter, and Anke Huckauf

Department of General Psychology, Ulm University, Ulm, Germany
{christoph.strauch, lukas.greiter,
anke.huckauf}@uni-ulm.de

Abstract. Preliminary reports have shown the possibility to assist input commands in HCI via pupil dilation. Applicability of these findings is however subject to further investigations, since the specificity of changes in diameter is low, e.g. through variations in brightness. Investigating employability and shape of pupil size dynamics outside a strictly controllcced laboratory, we implemented the emulation of selection via an integrated mechanism of pupil dilation and constriction that could speed up a dwell time of 1.5 s. During the operation of an on-screen keyboard, 21 subjects were able to type via this mechanism, needing 1 s on average per keystroke and producing only slightly more than 1% false positive selections. Hereby, pupil dynamics were assessed. More than 90% of keystrokes could be accelerated under assistance of pupil variations. As suggested from basic research, pupil dilated when fixating later selected keys and constricted shortly afterwards. This finding was consistent between all subjects, however, pupil dynamics were shifted in regard to temporal occurrence and amplitude of diameter changes. Pupil-Assisted Target Selection shows potential in non-strictly controlled environments for computer input and may be further improved on the basis of this data. This might culminate in an integrated gaze-based object selection mechanism that could go beyond the benchmarking dwell time performance.

Keywords: Eye typing · Gaze-based interaction · Physiological computing

1 Introduction

Brightness-independent pupil size changes are a variable that could assist object selection in computer input [1–3]. Hereby, especially implicit pupil size changes in response to selection, which might reveal user intention, are promising. Pupil size changes are associated with comparably short latencies, which enables high-resolution information retrieval. Moreover, changes require no cognitive effort of the user and are trackable remotely even with low-cost trackers [4]. A first interface evaluating the idea of employing pupil size changes as a mean to select in eyes only interaction, shows a promising performance, although a dwell time approach can't be outperformed. The authors report a specific dilation and a subsequent constriction that accompanies selections [1]. However, it is not yet clear whether the crucial signal components that

© IFIP International Federation for Information Processing 2017
Published by Springer International Publishing AG 2017. All Rights Reserved
R. Bernhaupt et al. (Eds.): INTERACT 2017, Part III, LNCS 10515, pp. 534–543, 2017.
DOI: 10.1007/978-3-319-67687-6_37

have been identified in basic-research paradigms, can be reproduced if brightness is not strictly controlled, baselines thus differ, and when users interact repeatedly with interfaces in natural environments. With this paper, we are – to our knowledge – the first to present an emulated selection in a standard interface that was operated under assistance of pupil size changes, in this case implicit changes in size as a mean to operate an on-screen keyboard. We evaluate the keyboard next to a window and test whether pupil size dynamics, similar to these reported in basic-research, can be obtained during eye-typing.

2 Related Work

Regulated by two antagonistic muscle systems, the pupil determines the influx of light onto the retina analogously to the aperture of a camera onto the sensor. Similarly to the aperture, also the visual acuity is influenced by these changes. Variations in pupil size, however, are not only limited to visual adjustments of the eye, but can also indicate psychological processes. In comparison to other peripheral-physiological indicators, these changes occur fast and are sensitive to even small changes in activity. Pupil size changes indicate a broad variety of psychological processes, ranging from cognitive effort [5], to emotional activation [6], visual search [7], or attentional processes [8, 9]. This variety is boon and bane to researchers simultaneously: on the one hand, it enables the investigation of many factors in controlled experiments, on the other hand, the low specificity leads to a convoluted signal that makes it hard to conclude from. This low specificity hinders the application of pupil size changes in HCI up to now.

However, among these factors, some may lead to a pupillary response that could be specific, and also highly relevant to HCI. In addition to changes in arousal, e.g. elicited by emotional activation [6], pupil size can indicate activity of locus cocruleus and the norepinephrine system in almost perfect temporal synchrony. This nucleus is linked to, among others, attentional processes [10]. Einhäuser and colleagues [8] report that pupil size changes can indicate a selected number from a set of numbers and therefore may reveal decisions. de Gee et al. [11] describe larger pupil dilations, when subjects think that they have identified a signal for which they have to look out. Also, spotting the correct target in a visual search task is associated with increased pupil diameter [7, 12]. Fixations not on target cause no considerable increase in pupil diameter, while fixations on targets cause an increase of about 0.06 mm on average [13]. However, in another publication, Bednarik et al. [14] use a machine learning approach to investigate multiple object selection accompanying eye-based variables, including pupil size changes and state that they cannot replicate the endings of [13], still pupil size helps to predict object selection above chance [14]. A possible reason is seen in the applied character of the investigation that is in contrast to the basic research scenario reported by [13]. Unfortunately, no signal dynamics are given in [14]. When provided, signal courses are largely comparable among studies and show a fast dilation in response to the process that is taking place around the fixation of intended objects. Given the high similarity of signal courses, it seems that pupil size variations emerge as specific in paradigms that are comparable to the aforementioned and could therefore be identified easily. Moreover, constrictions that directly follow the dilation after selections are reported to carry information, that is, bigger constrictions are associated with correct foregoing selections, compared to smaller constrictions associated with uncertain selections and erroneous selections [15].

As of today, three different pupil-based mechanisms are introduced that can reportedly be employed to select. Voluntarily, pupil size can be modulated by means of cognitive strategies, which leads to the idea to use pupil size expansion as an input mechanism to HCI [16]. Stoll et al. [17] demonstrate that voluntary changes in diameter could serve as a binary communication channel that enables severely disabled patients to say either yes or no via a computer. Ehlers et al. [3] build on this approach and show a live implementation of this idea, here, even a search and select task can be performed, although selection times are long. Another method builds on the phenomenon that pupil size oscillations can reveal covert attention to differentially flickering objects on a screen, hereby subjects can select between a limited number of letters [2]. Given the comparable long selection times and limited possibilities for application in standard interfaces, we focus on the implicit diameter changes described in the preceding paragraph. The identification of relevant objects and the decision for yes in comparison to no seems to lead to a pupil dilation. It could thus be assumed that the intention to select is reflected in pupil diameter. In a first interface building on this idea [1], users select from a set of nine circularly arranged objects in a visual search task. Objects are either selected via a dwell time, a specific increase in pupil size following a short dwell time, or either an increase in pupil size or a certain dwell time, whichever of both selects first. Similarly to the aforementioned studies on implicit changes, this investigation produced a pupil dilation of about 0.05 mm shortly after the later selected targets were fixated. It is concluded, that pupil size changes may assist gaze-based interaction and may be especially beneficial in combination with dwell times [1].

Eye-typing is a standard procedure to assess the eligibility of an input technique in eyes only interaction for evaluating the usability of computer operation [18]. However, there are application scenarios that are not covered by this method, such as the operation of public displays or mobile devices. A variety of methods have been proposed in order to increase the probability of predicting the user's intention correctly in eyes only interaction, in order to differentiate fixations with the intention to select from visual scanning to avoid the Midas-touch problem [19]. Those vary from eye-gestures [18], or smooth pursuits to moving objects [20], to dwell times, systematically prolonged fixation durations that are necessary to select [18, 19]. Key performance indicators for eye-typing comprise words typed per minute (wpm), with a word defined as five characters including space and punctuation, selection time, error rates, and keystrokes per character (KSPC). The best possible value for KSPC is 1, which results, if no character had to be corrected [21].

In order to investigate whether pupil size variations during object selections are comparable to these reported by e.g. [1, 13], whether they can be found even when selecting repeatedly in short time as in computer input, and to check for applicability of these changes in a natural environment, therefore, we implemented an on-screen keyboard that can be operated via a new combination of pupil size variations and dwell time. We are also the first to include the post-decisional constriction into an implicit pupil-based selection and to report a pupil-assisted on-screen keyboard in a regular layout. Pupil size changes for every selected key are presented and the on-screen keyboard is evaluated next to a window in a user study.

3 Methods

3.1 System

Pupil size and gaze were tracked using a SMI iView X RED 120 eye-tracker (SensoMotoric Instruments GmbH, Teltow) mounted to the screen (DELL P2210 1650 * 1050 Pixels, 55 Hz). The eye tracker was automatically set to a sampling rate of 55 Hz. For both, implementation of the on-screen keyboard and data collection, PsychoPy version 1.84.02 was used [22]. Participants were seated 40 cm from the screen.

The implemented on-screen keyboard is illustrated in Fig. 1. Keys except *space* and *backspace* had an on-screen size of 11.76 cm^2. The layout corresponded to the German QWERTZ-keyboard and contained keys for *dot, comma, space*, and *backspace* in addition to the letters of the alphabet, and thus contained 33 selectable keys. Written text and cursor were displayed centered above the keyboard. Line breaks shaped text legible also for longer input. Keys were highlighted in light blue, when entered by gaze. Successful selection was indicated by a dark blue frame around the key for 0.2 s and the specific command being applied to the text field. For this study a non-commercial keyboard was chosen since it allowed to have full access on every code component. Words per minute, selection times, error rates, and keystrokes per character (KSPC) were assessed in conjunction with the system-usability (SUS) scale, a

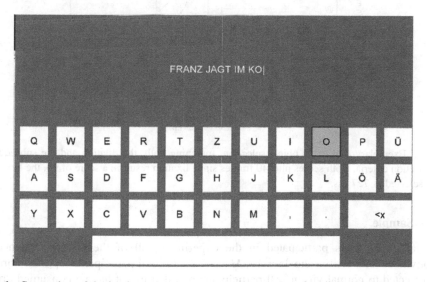

Fig. 1. Screenshot of the implemented on-screen keyboard. Gaze highlighted keys in light blue while a combination of pupil deviation criteria and fixation duration selected (highlighted by a dark blue frame) (Color figure online).

common unipolar usability scale, ranging from zero to 100, where 100 marks the best possible evaluation [23]. Moreover, a binary variable tracked whether keystrokes were accelerated via the pupil criteria.

Characters were selected on the basis of a score, which integrated dwell time and pupil size changes. Pupil deviation criteria were determined based on a preliminary study and on data from previous empirical results [1]. An exemplary pupil size dynamic of a keystroke during the preliminary study is depicted in Fig. 2. in conjunction with the dilation and the constriction criteria. The score was computed as follows: A dwell timer, starting at zero at fixation, increased by one each frame. If a pupil dilation over 0.04 mm in a moving window of 0.36 s (equals 20 frames) was detected, the score was once increased by 25. A detected subsequent pupil constriction of more than 0.07 mm in a second moving window of 0.36 s increased the score again once by 25. A character was selected when the score exceeded 82, which implies that all characters could be selected within a range of a maximum 1.5 s (only dwell) and a minimal selection time of 0.73 s (dwell in addition to both pupil criteria). 1.5 s is higher than regular dwell times, which go up to 1 s for novice users [18], thus, for this study this long dwell time serves as a hedge that prevents from being unable to select. After each selection and whenever looking away from the current key, the score was set to zero.

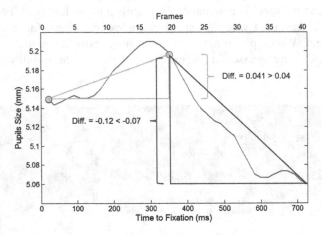

Fig. 2. Exemplary trial of an object selection, matching both, the dilation and the subsequent constriction criteria. Both scores plus 40 frames since fixation result in a score of 90, the key was thus selected at 727 ms.

3.2   Sample

A total of 21 users participated in the experiment, all of them were students at Anonymous University (female = 13, M_{Age} = 22.76). All participants reported normal or corrected to normal vision. All participants reported to not having consumed drugs prior to the experiment, neuronal diseases or traumatic brain injuries. Users signed an informed consent and took part in the study on a voluntary basis. They were partially rewarded with course credits. Of 21 users, 15 were novices to gaze-based interaction. Six users took part in a previous study on gaze-based interaction but had no further experience.

3.3   Procedure

The study was carried out in a silent area next to a window. Brightness ranged from 45 lx to 3500 lx. After signing an informed consent, users were instructed about the on-screen keyboard and the task using a printed screenshot. If subjects remarked errors, they were asked to only correct those errors that are not more than two characters before the current letter, in order to ensure comparable numbers of characters and time typed among subjects. Then participants were asked to sit down in front of the eye tracker and where calibrated using the automatic nine-point calibration and validation by SMI. The task consisted of three sequential conditions. The pangram, a sentence containing every letter of the alphabet, *Franz jagt im komplett verwahrlosten Taxi quer durch Bayern* (Franz chases in the completely neglected taxi across Bavaria), the negatively connoted words *Selbstmord* (suicide) and *Albtraum* (nightmare), and the positively connoted words *Liebe* (love) and *Erfolg* (success) had to be typed succes-sively using the on-screen keyboard. Emotional words were chosen to estimate whether these lead to differential signal dynamics, given the susceptibility of pupil diameter to emotionally elicited arousal e.g. [24]. Participants were not aware of the underlying selection criteria, but were instructed to select a focused character by merely intending to select. After writing all words, users were handed out a system-usability scale (SUS).

4   Results

On average, 91.6 letters, including space, were typed. After calibration, users needed $M = 241.46$ s on average to type the required text ($SD = 74.60$ s). $M = 4.55$ words were typed per minute ($SD = 1.24$). On average, users needed $M = 1.04$ s ($SD = 0.05$ s) from fixation of a key until its selection. False positive selections of keys accounted for $M = 1.10\%$ of all key selections, clear spelling mistakes were not considered to be false positive. KSPC was $M = 1.02$ ($SD = 0.03$). User satisfaction, as assessed with the SUS, revealed an average satisfaction of $M = 77.64$ ($SD = 11.71$). Pupil size changes lowered the selection score in $M = 93.19\%$ ($SD = 4.52\%$) of selections.

This finding suggests that pupil changes that fulfill at least the dilation criterion must have been present at more than 90% of all keys selected. However, this does not allow precise conclusions on the underlying signal. Signal dynamics can reveal, whether a common course can be found, a feature that is crucial for developing future selection criteria. Pupil dynamics accompanying all keystrokes were analyzed post-hoc with regard to the preceding and the following development. For the further analysis, the average of 700 ms to 600 ms prior to fixation of later selected keys was subtracted from every following data point as a local baseline. Signal shapes for emotional words and the neutral sentence showed no remarkable difference, all keystrokes were thus analyzed together. As illustrated in Fig. 3, every user showed a consistent double peaked signal with the first local maximum in a window between 300 ms prior to key

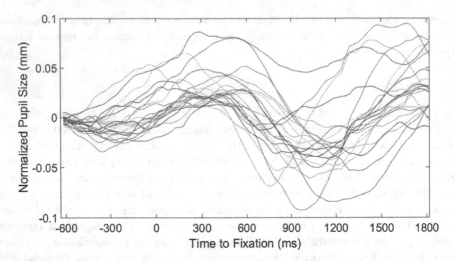

Fig. 3. Individually averaged user signal dynamics around the point of fixation of the later selected key (21 averages consisting of n = 1814 signal courses). Baseline corrected with a local, directly preceding baseline of 100 ms

fixation until 700 ms post key fixation. Also, within participants the same signal dynamics can be found temporarily shifted. Signal dynamics thus vary in regard to both, amplitude and temporal occurrence. This could be explained by cognitive processes, such as the intention to select, which should only on average be linked to the onset of fixations.

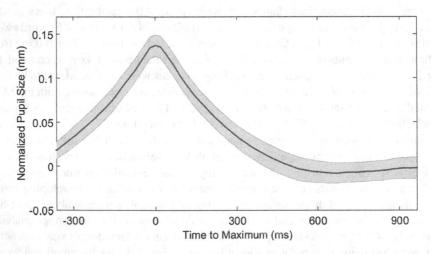

Fig. 4. Averaged signal dynamics of all participant means oriented at the local maximum of a window between 300 ms before until 700 ms after fixation. Only trials in which the maximum was not the first data point of the window were considered (21 averages, consisting of n = 1301 signal courses). Shaded bars mark functional 95% confidence intervals for every data point.

Klingner [13] argues to reorient signal dynamics in order to be able to identify underlying signal patterns. This is crucial in order to be able to determine an estimate for the effect size of dilations and constrictions. All signal dynamics were consequently oriented at the local maximum between 300 ms prior to until 700 ms post fixation, a feature that could be observed in every subject (Fig. 4). Functional confidence intervals in accordance to [6] reveal that the averaged pupil size between subjects differs significantly from baseline mean until 500 ms post to the local maximum. Dilations go up 0.13 mm on average ($SD = 0.03$ mm).

5   Discussion and Conclusion

Pupil size variations can be used as a mean to support dwell time based on-screen-keystrokes during computer input. We implemented a system that led to a user performance that is almost competitive to the performance of dwell time on-screen keyboards, operated by novices (employing slow dwell times of 1 s), in regard to selection times and error rates [18]. However, words per minute are still slightly below the average scores of novices writing with dwell time based interfaces [25]. KSPC were slightly better than for users typing with a novice dwell time of 876 ms [26]. User satisfaction, assessed with SUS can be described as usable [27]. However, for the previous findings, it has to be pointed out, that the comparability between studies on gaze-based interaction may be limited by between study factors such as accuracy of tracking or the sample of users [28]. Thus, in order to give a more stable estimation of the performance of this selection mechanism, a comparative dwell-time baseline condition is needed and should be addressed as a next step. For a comparison, a shorter dwell time adjusted to the time window of occurrences of the signal maxima might be applied. For over 90% of keystrokes, pupil size changes lowered the dwell time. Thus, for now, pupil assisted eye-typing cannot outperform dwell time, but there is further potential for improvements. Keystrokes were highly consistently reflected in pupil size changes between every of the 21 users. Still, temporal phase and pupil dilation differed between subjects. Further analyses may reveal whether this variance effects system performance. The obtained signal dynamics correspond to signal dynamics reported in [1, 11, 13] and therefore replicate these findings outside the laboratory, in a much applied scenario, and with another eyetracker. When orienting the signals at the local maximum that is apparent between 300 ms prior to and 700 ms post to fixation, it becomes evident that effect sizes are substantially larger than in the averaged key-fixation aligned data

The combination of pupil size variations and dwell as a mean to operate an on-screen keyboard was implemented on a self-developed keyboard. In a future investigation, this method could also be evaluated on existing commercial on-screen keyboards that have an optimal layout or on other interfaces, such as public displays to estimate the performance and usability compared to already existing input mechanisms. Since this approach may especially be beneficial to severely disabled users, it has to be evaluated to which extent these can use this setup, if neuronal diseases or brain injuries are present. It has to be stated that the integration of pupil diameter variation and fixation was chosen as a best estimation and is therefore subject to further improvements. The reported effect sizes may serve as an orientation for future pupil supported interfaces. Given the comparably large average effect size, it should be possible to find criteria that are robust to non-selection related variations in pupil diameter. Also, future interfaces should tailor criteria to the individual user, given the variance in maximum dilations between users. Bednarik et al. [14] only found a moderate prediction rate for pupil size changes during interaction. This might be explained by the controlled setting of the investigation or an effect that can only be found on average but not on single trial basis. Still, user performance and signal dynamics that were comparable for every participant seem promising. The shifted occurrence of the same signal pattern both between and within users, may be an indicator for cognitive processes, such as decisions, which differ in timing. However, from this experiment, signal dynamics in response to not intended objects cannot be derived. Orienting response [29] could partially explain the observed signal dynamics, still the keyboard was present permanently which should limit this effect. A small dilation in combination with a subsequent stronger constriction is also linked to fixations [30], however this finding might partially be explained with the orienting response [29] and/or visual search [7] and does not match the finding of [13].

This investigation collected data on pupil size variations during key selection. We are the first to describe an on-screen keyboard that could be operated using pupil size variations. Implementation and evaluation reveal a very high precision and selection times that are almost comparable to novice dwell times. Further room for adjustments might even allow to improve pupil assisted selection mechanisms beyond this level. Signal dynamics correspond to those obtained in controlled laboratory studies and were clearly found for every user, effect sizes in dilation are promising when aligning these dynamics.

References

1. Strauch, C., Ehlers, J., Huckauf, A.: Pupil-assisted target selection (PATS). In: Bernhaupt, R., et al. (eds.) INTERACT 2017, Part III. LNCS, vol. 10515, pp. 297–312. Springer, Cham (2017)
2. Mathôt, S., Melmi, J.-B., van der Linden, L., van der Stigchel, S.: The mind-writing pupil: a human-computer interface based on decoding of covert attention through pupillometry. PLoS ONE 11(2), e0148805 (2016)
3. Ehlers, J., Strauch, C., Huckauf, A.: A view to a click: pupil size changes as input command in eyes-only human-computer interaction. Int. J. Hum.-Comput. Stud. (submitted)
4. Dalmaijer, E.: Is the low-cost eyetribe eye tracker any good for research? PeerJ PrePrints, January 2014
5. Hess, E.H., Polt, J.M.: Pupil size in relation to mental activity during simple problem-solving. Science 143(3611), 1190–1192 (1964)
6. Ehlers, J., Strauch, C., Georgi, J., Huckauf, A.: Pupil size changes as an active information channel for biofeedback applications. Appl. Psychophysiol. Biofeedback 42, 1–9 (2016)
7. Privitera, C.M., Renninger, L.W., Carney, T., Klein, S., Aguilar, M.: Pupil dilation during visual target detection. J. Vis. 10(10), 3 (2010)
8. Einhäuser, W., Koch, C., Carter, O.: Pupil dilation betrays the timing of decisions. Front. Hum. Neurosci. 4, 18 (2010)
9. Wierda, S.M., van Rijn, H., Taatgen, N.A., Martens, S.: Pupil dilation deconvolution reveals the dynamics of attention at high temporal resolution. Proc. Nat. Acad. Sci. 109(22), 8456–8460 (2012)

10. Gilzenrat, M.S., Nieuwenhuis, S., Jepma, M., Cohen, J.D.: Pupil diameter tracks changes in control state predicted by the adaptive gain theory of locus coeruleus function. Cogn. Affect. Behav. Neurosci. **10**(2), 252–269 (2010)
11. de Gee, J.W., Knapen, T., Donner, T.H.: Decision-related pupil dilation reflects upcoming choice and individual bias. Proc. Nat. Acad. Sci. **111**(5), E618–E625 (2014)
12. Low, T., Bubalo, N., Gossen, T., Kotzyba, M., Brechmann, A., Huckauf, A., Nürnberger, A.: Towards identifying user intentions in exploratory search using gaze and pupil tracking. In: Proceedings of the 2017 Conference on Human Information Interaction and Retrieva. ACM (2017)
13. Klingner, J.: Fixation-aligned pupillary response averaging. In: Proceedings of the 2010 Symposium on Eye-Tracking Research & Applications, pp. 275–282. ACM (2010)
14. Bednarik, R., Vrzakova, H., Hradis, M.: What do you want to do next: a novel approach for intent prediction in gaze-based interaction. In: Proceedings of the Symposium on Eye Tracking Research and Applications, pp. 83–90. ACM (2012)
15. Urai, A.E., Braun, A., Donner, T.H.: Pupil-linked arousal is driven by decision uncertainty and alters serial choice bias. Nat. Commun. **8** (2017)
16. Ekman, I., Poikola, A.W., Mäkäräinen, M.K.: Invisible eni: using gaze and pupil size to control a game. In: Proceedings of the 2008 CHI Conference on Human Factors in Computing Systems. ACM (2008)
17. Stoll, J., et al.: Pupil responses allow communication in locked-in syndrome patients. Curr. Biol. **23**(15), R647–R648 (2013)
18. Majaranta, P.: Text Entry by Eye Gaze. Tampereen yliopisto, Tampere (2009)
19. Jacob, R.J.K.: The use of eye movements in human-computer interaction techniques: what you look at is what you get. ACM Trans. Inf. Syst. (TOIS) **9**(2), 152–169 (1991)
20. Vidal, M., Bulling, A., Gellersen, H.: Pursuits: spontaneous interaction with displays based on smooth pursuit eye movement and moving targets. In: Proceedings of the 2013 ACM International Joint Conference on Pervasive and Ubiquitous Computing. ACM (2013)
21. Soukoreff, R.W., MacKenzie, I.S.: Metrics for text entry research: an evaluation of MSD and KSPC, and a new unified error metric. In: Proceedings of the 2003 CHI Conference on Human Factors in Computing Systems (2003)
22. Peirce, J.W.: PsychoPy—psychophysics software in Python. J. Neurosci. Methods **162**(1), 8–13 (2007)
23. Brooke, J.: SUS-A quick and dirty usability scale. Usability Eval. Ind. **189**(194), 4–7 (1996)
24. Partala, T., Surakka, V.: Pupil size variation as an indication of affective processing. Int. J. Hum.-Comput. Stud. **59**(1), 185–198 (2003)
25. Majaranta, P., Räihä, K.-J.: Text entry by gaze: utilizing eye-tracking. In: Text Entry Systems: Mobility, Accessibility, Universality, pp. 175–187 (2007)
26. Majaranta, P., Ahola, U.K., Spakov, O.: Fast eye-typing with an adjustable dwell time. In: Proceedings of the 2009 CHI Conference on Human Factors in Computing Systems. ACM (2009)
27. Lewis, J.R., Sauro, J.: The factor structure of the system usability scale. In: Kurosu, M. (ed.) HCD 2009. LNCS, vol. 5619, pp. 94–103. Springer, Heidelberg (2009). doi:10.1007/978-3-642-02806-9_12
28. Räihä, K.-J.: Life in the fast lane: effect of language and calibration accuracy on the speed of text entry by gaze. In: Abascal, J., Barbosa, S., Fetter, M., Gross, T., Palanque, P., Winckler, M. (eds.) INTERACT 2015. LNCS, vol. 9296, pp. 402–417. Springer, Cham (2015). doi:10.1007/978-3-319-22701-6_30
29. Wang, C., Munoz, D.P.: Modulation of stimulus contrast on the human pupil orienting response. Eur. J. Neurosci. **40**(5), 2822–2832 (2014)
30. Mathôt, S., Melmi, J.-B., Castet, E.: Intrasaccadic perception triggers pupillary constriction. PeerJ **3**, e1150 (2015)

Author Index

Printed in the United States
by Bookmasters

Printed in the United States
By Bookmasters